Brief Contents

Focus on Writing
Paragraphs and Essays

Focus on Writing

Paragraphs and Essays

Third Edition

Laurie G. Kirszner
University of the Sciences, Emeritus

Stephen R. Mandell
Drexel University

Bedford/St. Martin's
Boston ◆ New York

For Bedford/St. Martin's

Publisher for College Success and Developmental Studies: Edwin Hill
Executive Editor for Developmental Studies: Alexis Walker
Developmental Editor: Karrin M. Varucene
Senior Production Editor: Jessica Gould
Senior Production Supervisor: Jennifer Peterson
Senior Marketing Manager: Christina Shea
Copy Editor: Wendy Annibell
Indexer: Melanie Belkin
Photo Researcher: Naomi Kornhauser
Art Director: Lucy Krikorian
Text Design: Jerilyn Bockorick
Cover Design: Marine Bouvier Miller
Cover Photo: Rain droplets on acer leaf (sugar maple) reflections, South Ontario © David Q.
    Cavagnaro/Getty Images.
Composition: Cenveo Publisher Services
Printing and Binding: RR Donnelley and Sons

President, Bedford/St. Martin's: Denise B. Wydra
Editorial Director for English and Music: Karen S. Henry
Director of Development: Erica T. Appel
Director of Marketing: Karen R. Soeltz
Production Director: Susan W. Brown
Director of Rights and Permissions: Hilary Newman

Manufactured in the United States of America.

8 7 6 5 4 3
f e d c b a

For information, write: Bedford/St. Martin's, 75 Arlington Street, Boston, MA 02116
(617-399-4000)

ISBN 978-1-4576-3327-0 (Student Edition)
ISBN 978-1-4576-3347-8 (Instructor's Annotated Edition)
ISBN 978-1-4576-4821-2 (Loose-leaf Edition)

Acknowledgments

Acknowledgments and copyrights are continued at the back of the book on pages 777–778, which constitute an extension of the copyright page. It is a violation of the law to reproduce these selections by any means whatsoever without the written permission of the copyright holder.

Preface

Our goal with the first edition of *Focus on Writing: Paragraphs and Essays* was to create an appealing text that motivates students to improve their writing and gives them the tools to do so. We developed the popular **TEST** tool specifically for this purpose. The letters that spell **TEST** stand for **T**opic sentence or **T**hesis statement, **E**vidence, **S**ummary statement, and **T**ransitions; this acronym helps students understand how paragraphs and essays are constructed and teaches them how to revise their own writing by checking for unity, support, and coherence.

In addition to retaining this important and successful feature, the third edition of *Focus on Writing* continues to reflect two of our central beliefs: that in college, writing comes first; and that students learn writing and grammar skills best in the context of their own writing. Accordingly, the text's activities not only get students writing immediately but also encourage them to return to their own writing to apply the new skills they are learning and—with the help of **TEST**—to create a polished draft. Similarly, Grammar in Context boxes introduce fundamental concepts where they are most relevant to the student's writing.

In this third edition, we have used engaging images and a contemporary design to appeal to today's visual learners. The text explanations and instructions are streamlined throughout to make them as useful as possible. In addition, to meet student needs expressed by many instructors, we have expanded on our step-by-step guidance for developing paragraphs, and we now offer more coverage of critical reading and thinking, college success, and research as well as models that reflect realistic student work.

It is our hope that this new edition of *Focus on Writing* will continue to motivate and empower students to become confident writers and capable editors of their own writing.

Organization

Focus on Writing has a flexible organization that permits instructors to teach various topics in the order that works best for them and their students. The book is divided into three sections, which are color-coded to help students and instructors more easily navigate the book:

- **Writing Paragraphs and Essays**, Chapters 2–17, is a comprehensive discussion of the writing process.
- **Revising and Editing Your Writing**, Chapters 18–36, is a thorough review of sentence skills, grammar, punctuation, and mechanics.
- **Becoming a Critical Reader**, Chapters 37 and 38, introduces students to critical reading skills and includes nineteen professional essays, each illustrating a particular pattern of development.

Features

If you TEST the following paragraph, you will see that it contains all four elements of an effective paragraph.

> Although most people do not know it, the modern roller coaster got its start in Coney Island in Brooklyn, New York. First, in 1888, the Flip Flap Railway, which featured a circular loop, was built. The coaster was the first to go upside down, but it frequently injured riders' necks. Next, in 1901, the Loop-the-Loop, which was safer than the Flip Flap Railway, was built. Then, from 1884 through the 1930s, over thirty roller coasters were constructed in Coney Island. Finally, in 1927, the most famous roller coaster in history, the Cyclone, was built at a cost of over $100,000. Although it began operating over eighty years ago, it is still the standard by which all roller coasters are measured. It has steep drops, a lot of speed, and only lap belts to hold riders in their seats. Still in operation, the Cyclone is the most successful ride in Coney Island history. It is the last survivor of the wooden roller coasters that once drew crowds to Coney Island. With their many innovations, Coney Island's roller coasters paved the way for the high-tech roller coasters in amusement parks today.

TEST
- ☐ Topic Sentence
- ☐ Evidence
- ☐ Summary Statement
- ☐ Transitions

Central to this text is our philosophy that students learn to write best by working with their own writing. This philosophy is supported by innovative features designed to make students' writing practice meaningful, productive, and enjoyable.

TEST helps students write and revise. This easy-to-remember tool, introduced in Chapter 2, helps students check their paragraphs and essays for unity, support, and coherence. By applying TEST to their writing, students can quickly see where their drafts need more work.

"Focus on Writing" activities engage and motivate students. These activities ask students to begin writing immediately by responding to a chapter-opening visual and prompt. An end-of-chapter prompt sends students back to their initial writing to apply the new skills they have learned and to work toward a final draft.

Students get the writing help they need—in a clear, step-by-step format. Eleven chapters on paragraph writing and four on essay writing cover the writing process and nine patterns of development. Each chapter includes a student-focused case study and an abundance of clear examples and engaging exercises.

Instruction and activities emphasize critical reading and thinking skills. With a full chapter on reading critically and a set of critical reading/thinking questions for each professional reading at the back of the book, *Focus on Writing* helps students build essential critical thinking and reading skills.

Grammar coverage is thorough yet accessible. Nineteen grammar chapters clearly and concisely convey the rules of English grammar.

New to This Edition

Access to 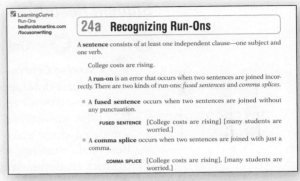 **LearningCurve.** Each new copy of *Focus on Writing* comes with access to LearningCurve, innovative adaptive online quizzes that let students learn at their own pace, with a gamelike interface that keeps them engaged. Quizzes are keyed to grammar instruction in the book, so what is taught in class gets reinforced at home. Instructors can also check in on each student's activity in a gradebook.

The LearningCurve icon appears throughout *Focus on Writing*, in Grammar in Context boxes and in the margins of the grammar chapters.

A student access code is printed in every new student copy. Students who do not purchase a new print book can purchase access by going to **bedfordstmartins.com/focusonwriting.** Instructors can also get access at this site.

LearningCurve
Run-Ons
bedfordstmartins.com
/focusonwriting

24a   Recognizing Run-Ons

A **sentence** consists of at least one independent clause—one subject and one verb.

College costs are rising.

A **run-on** is an error that occurs when two sentences are joined incorrectly. There are two kinds of run-ons: *fused sentences* and *comma splices.*

- A **fused sentence** occurs when two sentences are joined without any punctuation.

    FUSED SENTENCE   [College costs are rising] [many students are worried.]

- A **comma splice** occurs when two sentences are joined with just a comma.

    COMMA SPLICE   [College costs are rising], [many students are worried.]

Expanded coverage and guidance for developing paragraphs. New explanations and exercises help students understand how to use evidence to support a paragraph's topic sentence. Streamlined case studies of student writers not only teach by example but also guide students step by step through the writing process.

Even more emphasis on critical reading and thinking. A new section in the chapter on reading critically—Reading in the Classroom, in the Community, and in the Workplace—includes visual examples and strategies for reading textbooks, news articles, and workplace communications.

A new opening chapter—"Writing and College Success." This new chapter gives students practical advice on how to succeed in college, with an emphasis on academic issues such as the difference between formal and informal writing and how to perform well on writing tests.

A new chapter—"Writing a Research Paper." This chapter guides students through the process of writing a research paper, from choosing a topic to documenting sources. Special attention is given to evaluating sources and avoiding plagiarism—particularly challenging issues for today's students.

New FYI (For Your Information) boxes. Offering students useful writing tips and technology-related advice, these boxes appear throughout the book.

FYI

What to Avoid in Introductions

When writing an introduction, avoid the following:

- Beginning your essay by announcing what you plan to write about.

    PHRASES TO AVOID
    This essay is about . . .
    In my essay, I will discuss . . .

- Apologizing for your ideas.

    PHRASES TO AVOID
    Although I don't know much about this subject . . .
    I might not be an expert, but . . .

Support for Instructors and Students

Focus on Writing is accompanied by comprehensive teaching and learning support.

Student Resources

📖 = Print   🖥 = Online   💿 = CD-ROM

🖥 **Exercise Central 3.0**, at **bedfordstmartins.com/exercisecentral**, is the largest database of editing exercises on the Internet. This comprehensive resource contains more than nine thousand exercises that offer immediate feedback; the program also recommends personalized study plans and provides tutorials for common problems. Best of all, students' work reports to a gradebook, allowing instructors to track students' progress quickly and easily.

🖥 **The free companion Web site for *Focus on Writing*, at bedfordstmartins.com/focusonwriting**, provides students with grammar tutorials; advice on avoiding plagiarism, doing research, and succeeding in college; additional writing exercises; annotated model essays; and much more.

Free with the Print Text

💿 ***Exercise Central to Go: Writing and Grammar Practices for Basic Writers* CD-ROM** provides hundreds of practice items to help students build their writing and editing skills. No Internet connection is necessary. **Free** when packaged with the print text. Package ISBN: 978-1-4576-6806-7

📖 ***The Bedford/St. Martin's ESL Workbook*, Second Edition**, includes a broad range of exercises covering grammatical issues for multilingual students of varying language skills and backgrounds. Answers are at the back. **Free** when packaged with the print text. Package ISBN: 978-1-4576-6802-9

💿 **The *Make-a-Paragraph Kit* is a fun, interactive CD-ROM that teaches students about paragraph development. It also contains exercises to help students build their own paragraphs, audiovisual tutorials on four of the most common errors for basic writers, and the content from *Exercise Central to Go: Writing and Grammar Practices for Basic Writers*. **Free** when packaged with the print text. Package ISBN: 978-1-4576-6801-2

📖 **The *Bedford/St. Martin's Planner* includes everything that students need to plan and use their time effectively, with advice on preparing schedules and to-do lists plus blank schedules and calendars (monthly and weekly). The planner fits easily into a backpack or purse, so students can take it everywhere. **Free** when packaged with the print text. Package ISBN: 978-1-4576-6803-6

Journal Writing: A Beginning is designed to give students an opportunity to use writing as a way to explore their thoughts and feelings. This writing journal includes a generous supply of inspirational quotations placed throughout the pages, tips for journaling, and suggested journal topics. **Free** when packaged with the print text. Package ISBN: 978-1-4576-6804-3

From Practice to Mastery (study guide for the Florida Basic Skills Exit Tests) gives students all the resources they need to practice for—and pass—the Florida tests in reading and writing. It includes pre- and post-tests, abundant practices, many examples, and clear instruction in all the skills covered on the exams. **Free** when packaged with the print text. Package ISBN: 978-1-4576-6805-0

Premium

WritingClass provides students with a dynamic, interactive online course space preloaded with LearningCurve quizzes, exercises, diagnostics, video tutorials, writing and commenting tools, and more. *WritingClass* helps students stay focused and lets instructors see how students are progressing. It is available at a significant discount when packaged with the print text. To learn more about *WritingClass*, visit **yourwritingclass.com**. For access card, use ISBN 978-0-312-57385-0.

SkillsClass offers all that *WritingClass* offers, plus guidance and practice in reading and study skills. It is available at a significant discount when packaged with the print text. To learn more about *SkillsClass*, visit **yourskillsclass.com**. For access card, use ISBN 978-1-4576-2346-2.

Re:Writing Plus, **now with VideoCentral**, gathers all of our premium digital content for the writing class into one online collection. This impressive resource includes innovative and interactive help with writing a paragraph; tutorials and practices that show how writing works in a student's real-world experience; VideoCentral, with more than 140 brief videos for the writing classroom; the first-ever peer review game, *Peer Factor*; *i-cite: visualizing sources*; plus hundreds of models of writing and hundreds of readings. *Re:Writing Plus* can be purchased separately or it may be packaged with *Focus on Writing* at a significant discount. ISBN: 978-0-312-48849-9

Free Instructor Resources

The Instructor's Annotated Edition of Focus on Writing contains answers to all practice exercises, in addition to numerous teaching ideas, reminders, and cross-references useful to teachers at all levels of experience. ISBN: 978-1-4576-3347-8

Classroom Resources and Instructor's Guide for Focus on Writing, **Third Edition**, offers advice for teaching developmental writing as well as chapter-by-chapter pointers for using *Focus on Writing* in the classroom. It contains answers to all of the book's practice exercises, sample syllabi, additional teaching materials, and full chapters on collaborative learning. To download, see **bedfordstmartins.com/focusonwriting/catalog**.

Diagnostic and Mastery Tests for Focus on Writing, **Third Edition**, offers tests that complement the topics covered in *Focus on Writing*. To download, see **bedfordstmartins.com/focusonwriting/catalog**.

Testing Tool Kit: Writing and Grammar Test Bank **CD-ROM** allows instructors to create secure, customized tests and quizzes from a pool of nearly two thousand questions covering 47 topics. It also includes ten prebuilt diagnostic tests. ISBN: 978-0-312-43032-0

Supplemental Exercises for Focus on Writing, **Third Edition**, offers additional practice with essential skills. To download, see **bedfordstmartins.com/focusonwriting/catalog**.

TeachingCentral at **bedfordstmartins.com/teachingcentral** offers the entire list of Bedford/St. Martin's print and online professional resources in one place. You will find landmark reference works, sourcebooks on pedagogical issues, award-winning collections, and practical advice for the classroom.

Answers to all grammar exercises in *Focus on Writing*, Third Edition, are now available for download to instructors at **bedfordstmartins.com/focusonwriting**.

e-Book Options

The e-Book for *Focus on Writing*, value priced, can be purchased in formats for use with computers, tablets, and e-readers. For more information, visit **bedfordstmartins.com/focusonwriting/formats**.

Ordering Information

To order any of the ancillaries for *Focus on Writing*, Third Edition, contact your local Bedford/St. Martin's sales representative, email **sales_support@bfwpub.com**, or visit our Web site at **bedfordstmartins.com**.

Acknowledgments

In our work on *Focus on Writing*, we have benefited from the help of a great many people.

We are grateful to Linda Crawford of McLennan Community College, who lent her expertise and a fresh eye to existing ESL teaching tips and also wrote new tips. We are grateful to Timothy Jones of Oklahoma City Community College, who used his tech savvy to contribute advice for instructors and students on using technology both inside and outside the classroom. Additionally, we thank Jessica Carroll, who made important contributions to the exercises and writing activities in the text.

Instructors throughout the country have contributed suggestions and encouragement at various stages of the book's development. For their collegial support, we thank Sandra Albers, Leeward Community College; Monique Blake, Broward College; Reed Breneman, Wake Technical Community College; Robyn Browder, Tidewater Community College; Susan Buchler, Montgomery County Community College; Joanna Christopher, John A. Logan College; Shari Clevenger, Northeastern State University; Karin Deol, Imperial Valley College; Jennifer Ferguson, Cazenovia College; Katherine Firkins, California State University, Northridge; David Freeman, Valencia College; Joyce Gatta, Middlesex Community College; Kendra Haggard, Northeastern State University; Curt Hutchison, Leeward Community College; Patrice Johnson, Eastfield College; Ken Kouba, Prairie State College; Kevin Lamkins, Capital Community College; Jonathan Lowndes, Broward College; Angelina Misaghi, California State University, Northridge; Ela Newman, University of Texas at Brownsville; Thomas Nicholas, Prairie State College; Donna Obrzut, Henry Ford Community College; Charles Porter, Wor-Wic Community College; Patricia Pullenza, Mesa Community College; Margaret Quinn, Montgomery County Community College; Minati Roychoudhuri, Capital Community College; Robin Smith, Towson University; Selena Stewart-Alexander, Eastfield College; Qiana Towns, Davenport University; and Brenda Tuberville, Rogers State University.

At Bedford/St. Martin's, we thank founder and former president Charles Christensen, former president Joan Feinberg, and former editor in chief Nancy Perry, who believed in this project and gave us support and encouragement from the outset. We thank president Denise Wydra, editorial director for English and music Karen Henry, executive editor for developmental studies Alexis Walker, and director of development Erica Appel for overseeing this edition. We are also grateful to Shuli Traub, managing editor; Jennifer Peterson, senior production supervisor; and Jessica Gould, senior project editor, for guiding the book ably through production, and to Lucy Krikorian, art director, for once again overseeing the book's design. Thanks also go to Christina Shea, senior marketing manager, and to our outstanding copy editor

Wendy Annibell. And finally, we thank our talented editor, Karrin Varucene, whose patience, hard work, and dedication kept the project moving along.

It almost goes without saying that *Focus on Writing* could not exist without our students, whose words appear on almost every page of the book in sample sentences, paragraphs, and essays. We thank all of them, past and present, who allowed us to use their work.

Finally, we are grateful for the survival and growth of the writing partnership we entered into when we were graduate students. We had no idea then of the wonderful places our collaborative efforts would take us. Now, we know.

Laurie G. Kirszner
Stephen R. Mandell

A Note to Students

As teachers—and as former students—we know how demanding college can be and how hard it is to juggle academic assignments with work and family responsibilities. We also know that you don't want to waste your time. That's why in *Focus on Writing* we make information easy to find and use and include many different features to help you become a better writer.

Boxes

Preview boxes. Each chapter starts with a list of key concepts that will be discussed in the chapter. Looking at these boxes before you begin the chapter will give you an overview of what's to come.

Writing prompt boxes. Most chapters start with a Focus on Writing activity, accompanied by a visual, that asks you to begin writing about a topic. Later in the chapter, a TEST-Revise-Edit prompt guides you to fine-tune your writing.

FYI boxes. Throughout the book, purple-outlined boxes with the letters FYI (For Your Information) highlight useful information, explain key concepts, and offer tips for using technology.

Grammar in Context boxes. Throughout the writing chapters, boxes identify key grammar issues. These boxes will help you understand how particular grammatical concepts are relevant to your writing.

---

grammar in context

Exemplification

When you write an exemplification paragraph, always use a comma after the introductory transitional word or phrase that introduces an example.

For example, Burma became Myanmar in 1989.

For instance, the Gold Coast changed its name to Ghana in 1957.

Finally, Zimbabwe gave up its British name after winning independence.

For information on using commas with introductory transitional words and phrases, see 34b.

✓ LearningCurve For more practice with comma usage, complete the Commas activity at **bedfordstmartins.com/focusonwriting**.

Word Power boxes. In the margins, Word Power boxes define unfamiliar words that appear in the text's explanations and reading selections.

Checklists

Self-Assessment Checklists. Chapters 2 and 13 include Self-Assessment Checklists that enable you to measure your understanding of basic paragraph and essay structure.

Review Checklists. All grammar chapters and some of the writing chapters end with a summary of the most important information in the chapter. Use these checklists to review material for quizzes or to remind yourself of key points.

TEST Checklists. All paragraph development chapters and each section of the essay development chapter end with a checklist that helps you check your writing for the **TEST** elements.

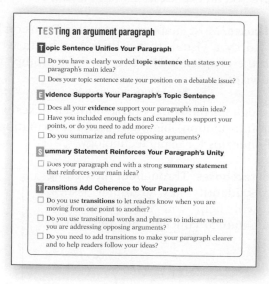

TESTing an argument paragraph

Topic Sentence Unifies Your Paragraph

- ☐ Do you have a clearly worded **topic sentence** that states your paragraph's main idea?
- ☐ Does your topic sentence state your position on a debatable issue?

Evidence Supports Your Paragraph's Topic Sentence

- ☐ Does all your **evidence** support your paragraph's main idea?
- ☐ Have you included enough facts and examples to support your points, or do you need to add more?
- ☐ Do you summarize and refute opposing arguments?

Summary Statement Reinforces Your Paragraph's Unity

- ☐ Does your paragraph end with a strong **summary statement** that reinforces your main idea?

Transitions Add Coherence to Your Paragraph

- ☐ Do you use **transitions** to let readers know when you are moving from one point to another?
- ☐ Do you use transitional words and phrases to indicate when you are addressing opposing arguments?
- ☐ Do you need to add transitions to make your paragraph clearer and to help readers follow your ideas?

Contents

16 Patterns of Essay Development 253

Unit 4 Research 323

17 Writing a Research Paper 325

REVISING AND EDITING YOUR WRITING

Unit 5 Writing Effective Sentences

18 Writing Simple Sentences

☑ **LearningCurve** activity is available for this topic. Visit **bedfordstmartins.com/focusonwriting**.

☑ LearningCurve activity is available for this topic. Visit **bedfordstmartins.com/focusonwriting**.

☑ **LearningCurve** activity is available for this topic. Visit **bedfordstmartins.com/focusonwriting**.

☑ LearningCurve activity is available for this topic. Visit **bedfordstmartins.com/focusonwriting**.

Unit 7 Understanding Basic Grammar   533

29 Verbs: Past Tense ☑ 535

30 Verbs: Past Participles ☑ 546

31 Nouns and Pronouns ☑ 560

☑ LearningCurve activity is available for this topic. Visit **bedfordstmartins.com/focusonwriting**.

✓ LearningCurve activity is available for this topic. Visit **bedfordstmartins.com/focusonwriting**.

Unit 8 Understanding Punctuation and Mechanics

34 Using Commas ☑

☑ LearningCurve activity is available for this topic. Visit **bedfordstmartins.com/focusonwriting**.

✓ LearningCurve activity is available for this topic. Visit **bedfordstmartins.com/focusonwriting**.

Thematic Table of Contents

History and Politics

Language

Media and Society

Race and Culture

1 Writing and College Success

focus on writing

Most of us write every day. Look through some of your own recent emails, Facebook posts, and texts. To whom are you writing? What reasons do you have for writing? What different styles of writing do you use? Write for a few minutes about your personal writing habits.

How Writing Can Help You Succeed

Writing is not just something you do in school; writing is a life skill. If you can write clearly, you can express your ideas convincingly to others—in school, on the job, and in your community.

Writing takes many different forms. In college, you might write a single paragraph, an essay exam, a short paper, or a long research paper. At work, you might write a memo, a proposal, or a report. In your daily life as a citizen of your community, you might write a letter or an email asking for information or explaining a problem that needs to be solved.

Writing is important. If you can write, you can communicate; if you can communicate effectively, you can succeed in school and beyond.

Most people agree that the best way to learn to write is by writing. In a sense, then, you are already something of an expert when it comes to writing; after all, you have been writing for years—not just for your classes but also in your everyday life. For example, on your Facebook page, you update your profile, post and respond to comments, and send messages; you probably text every day. In these situations, you write fluently, confidently, and concisely, without self-consciousness, because you know your audience and you know what you want to say.

Of course, this informal, casual writing has its limitations. As you probably already know, college writing is different from informal writing; "textspeak," abbreviations, and shorthand are not acceptable in college writing assignments, and spontaneous bursts of words are acceptable only in the very roughest of first drafts or in activities like brainstorming and freewriting. The trick is to use the experience you have with informal writing and to make it work for you in an academic context.

College writing requires you to pull your thoughts together so you can develop (and support) ideas and opinions and express them clearly for a variety of audiences. When you write informally to someone you know well, there is no need to explain, give examples, or support claims; you assume your reader will understand what you mean (and often agree with you). When your audience is a college instructor or your classmates, however, you can't always count on your readers' knowing exactly what you mean or understanding the context for your writing.

Academic writing also needs to be grammatically correct. You can't assume that your readers will be willing to tolerate (or ignore) errors you might make in grammar, sentence structure, punctuation, or mechanics. In addition, your writing has to follow certain formal conventions and formats, so you can't produce shapeless, slang-filled, punctuation-free documents and expect your readers to figure out what you mean.

Much of the writing you do every day—texts, Facebook updates, blog posts, emails, and so on—use first person (*I*) and informal style, including contractions and slang. For example, if you are planning to see your academic adviser, you might text a friend about your appointment.

An email to your adviser, however, should not use abbreviations or shorthand, and it should not omit words or punctuation to save time or space. For example, if you have concerns about a course, you might send the following email to your instructor.

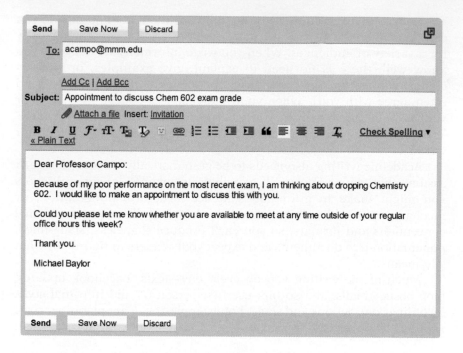

As you go through this book, you will learn skills and strategies for writing well. In the rest of this chapter, you will learn some practical strategies for making the most of your college education.

Strategies for College Success

1a   Orientation Strategies

Some strategies come in handy even before school begins, as you orient yourself to life as a college student. In fact, you may already have discovered some of them.

1. *Make sure you have everything you need:* a college catalog, a photo ID, a student handbook, a parking permit, and any other items that entering students at your school are expected to have.

2. *Read your school's orientation materials* (posted on the school Web site or distributed as handouts) carefully. These materials will help you to familiarize yourself with campus buildings and offices, course offerings, faculty members, extracurricular activities, and so on.

3. ***Be sure you know your academic adviser's name*** (and how to spell it), email address, office location, and office hours. Enter this information into your personal address book.

4. ***Read your library's orientation materials.*** This information (available online or distributed during a tour) will tell you about the library's hours and services and explain procedures such as how to use the online catalog.

5. ***Be sure you know where things are***—not just how to find the library and the parking lot but also where you can do photocopying or buy a newspaper.

1b First-Week Strategies

College can seem like a confusing place at first, but from your first day as a college student, there are steps you can take to help you get your bearings.

1. ***Make yourself at home.*** Find places on campus where you can get something to eat or drink, and find a good place to study or relax before or between classes. As you explore the campus, try to locate all the things you need to feel comfortable—for example, ATMs, rest rooms, and vending machines.

2. ***Know where you are going and when you need to be there.*** Check the building and room number for each of your classes and the days and hours the class meets. Copy this information onto the front cover of the appropriate notebook. Pay particular attention to classes with irregular schedules (for example, a class that meets from 9 a.m. to 10 a.m. on Tuesdays but from 11 a.m. to noon on Thursdays).

3. ***Get to know your fellow students.*** Networking with other students is an important part of the college experience. Get the name, phone number, and email address of at least one student in each of your classes. If you are absent from class, you will need to get in touch with someone to find out what material you missed.

4. ***Familiarize yourself with each course's syllabus.*** At the first meeting of every course, your instructor will hand out a **syllabus**, an outline or summary of course requirements, policies, and procedures. (The syllabus may also be posted on the course's Web page.) A syllabus gives you three kinds of useful information:

   ▪ Practical information, such as the instructor's office location and email address and what books and supplies to buy

   ▪ Information that can help you plan a study schedule—for example, when assignments are due and when exams are scheduled

WORD POWER

networking
interacting with others
to share information

■ Information about the instructor's policies on absences, grading, class participation, and so on

Read each syllabus carefully, ask questions about anything you do not understand, and refer to all your course syllabi regularly.

5. ***Buy books and supplies.*** When you buy your books and supplies, be sure to keep the receipts, and do not write your name in your books until you are certain that you are not going to drop a course. (If you write in a book, you will not be able to return it for a full refund.) If your schedule of courses is not definite, wait a few days to buy your texts. You should, however, buy a separate notebook for each course you are taking before the first day of class. In addition to the books and other items required for a particular course (for example, a lab notebook, a programmable calculator, art supplies), you may want to buy pens and pencils in different colors, paper clips or a stapler, self-stick notes, highlighters, and so on.

6. ***Set up your notebooks.*** For each of your classes, write your instructor's name, email address, phone number, and office hours and location on the inside front cover of a notebook; write your own name, address, and phone number on the outside, along with the class location and meeting times. (Notebooks with pocket folders can help you keep all your course papers and notes in one place.)

1c Day-to-Day Strategies

As you get busier and busier, you may find that it is hard to keep everything under control. Here are some strategies to help you as you move through the semester.

1. ***Find a place to study.*** As a college student, you will need your own private place to work and study. If possible, this space should be a quiet place with good lighting, a comfortable chair, a clean work surface, storage for supplies, and so on.

2. ***Set up a bookshelf.*** Keep your textbooks, calculator, supplies, and everything else you use regularly for your coursework in one place—ideally, in your own workspace. That way, when you need something, you will know exactly where it is.

3. ***Set up a study schedule.*** Try to identify thirty- to forty-five-minute blocks of free time before, between, and after classes. Set this time aside for review. Remember, studying should be part of your regular routine, not something you do only the night before an exam.

FYI

Checking Your Computer Skills

Don't wait until you have an assignment due to discover that your computer skills need improvement. Be sure your basic computer skills are at the level you need for your work and that you understand how to access course sites and to use the online materials you need for your classes. If you need help, get it right away. Your school's computer lab, writing center, and library are good places to turn for help.

4. *Establish priorities.* It is very important to understand what your priorities are. Before you can establish priorities, however, you have to know which assignments are due first, which ones can be done in steps, and which tasks or steps will be most time consuming. Then, you need to decide which tasks are most pressing. For example, studying for a test to be given the next day is more pressing than reviewing notes for a test scheduled for the following week. Finally, you have to decide which tasks are more important than others. For example, studying for a midterm is more important than studying for a quiz, and the midterm for a course you are in danger of failing is more important than the midterm for a course in which you are doing well. Remember, you cannot do everything at once; you need to know what must be done immediately and what can wait.

5. *Check your email.* Check your school email account regularly—if possible, several times a day. If you miss a message, you may miss important information about changes in assignments, canceled classes, or rescheduled quizzes. (If your classes have course Web pages, check those as well.)

6. *Schedule conferences.* Try to meet with each of your instructors during the semester even if you are not required to do so. You might schedule one conference during the second or third week of the semester and another a week or two before a major exam or paper is due. Your instructors will appreciate and respect your initiative.

7. *Become familiar with the student services available on your campus.* There is nothing wrong with getting help from your school's writing center or tutoring center or from the center for disabled students (which serves students with learning disabilities as well as physical challenges), the office of international students, or the counseling center, as well as from your adviser or course instructors. You should take advantage of all the available services you need.

WORD POWER

priorities things considered more important than others

FYI

Asking for Help

Despite all your careful planning, you may still run into trouble. For example, you may miss an exam and have to make it up; you may miss several classes in a row and fall behind in your work; you may have trouble understanding the material in one of your courses; or a family member may get sick. Do not wait until you are overwhelmed to ask for help. If you have an ongoing personal problem or a family emergency, let your instructors and the dean of students know immediately.

1d Time-Management Strategies

Learning to manage your time is very important for success in college. Here are some strategies you can adopt to make this task easier.

1. *Use an organizer.* New electronic tools are constantly being developed to help you stay organized. For example, Schoolbinder, a free online organizer, can help you manage your time and create a study schedule. If you have trouble blocking out distractions when you are studying, a site like StudyRails can be helpful. For a small monthly fee, this site will help you plan a study schedule and alert you to when it's time to focus on schoolwork. It can also be programmed to block your go-to recreational sites during hours when you should be studying.

   You can use the calendar function on your smartphone to keep track of deadlines and appointments (see the example on page 9). At the beginning of the semester, enter key pieces of information from each course syllabus—for example, the date of every quiz and exam and the due date of every paper. As the semester progresses, continue to add assignments and deadlines. In addition, enter information such as days when a class will be canceled or will meet in the computer lab or in the library, reminders to bring a particular book or piece of equipment to class, and appointments with instructors or other college personnel. (If you like, you can also note reminders and schedule appointments that are not related to school—for example, changes in your work hours, a dental appointment, or lunch with a friend.) Some students also like to keep a separate month-by-month "to do" list. Deleting completed items can give you a feeling of accomplishment—and make the road ahead look shorter.

Note: If you are most comfortable with paper and pencil, purchase a "week-on-two-pages" academic year organizer—one that begins in September, not January; this format gives you more writing room for Monday through Friday than for the weekend, and it also lets you view an entire week at once.

2. *Use a calendar.* Buy a large wall calendar, and post it where you will see it every morning—on your desk, on the refrigerator, or wherever you keep your phone, your keys, and your ID. At the beginning of the semester, fill in important dates such as school holidays, work commitments, exam dates, and due dates for papers and projects. When you return from classes each day, update the calendar with any new information you have entered into your organizer.

3. *Plan ahead.* If you think you will need help from a writing center tutor to revise a paper that is due in two weeks, don't wait until day thirteen to make an appointment; all the tutoring slots may be filled by then. To be safe, make an appointment about a week in advance.

4. *Learn to enjoy downtime.* When you have a free minute, take time for yourself—and don't feel guilty about it.

1e   Note-Taking Strategies

Learning to take notes in a college class takes practice, but taking good notes is essential for success in college. Here are some basic guidelines that will help you develop and improve your note-taking skills.

During Class

1. *Come to class.* If you miss class, you miss notes—so come to class, and come on time. Sit where you can see the board or screen and hear the instructor. Do not feel you have to keep sitting in the same place in each class every day; change your seat until you find a spot that is comfortable for you.

2. *Develop a system of shorthand to make note taking faster and more efficient.* You can use texting abbreviations and even symbols in your notes, but remember not to use such abbreviations in your college writing.

3. *Date your notes.* Begin each class by writing the date at the top of the page. Instructors frequently identify material that will be on a test by dates. If you do not date your notes, you may not know exactly what to study.

4. *Know what to write down.* You cannot possibly write down everything an instructor says. If you try, you will miss a lot of important information. Listen carefully *before* you write, and listen for cues to what is important. For example, sometimes the instructor will tell you that something is important or that a particular piece of information will be on a test. If the instructor emphasizes an idea or underlines it on the board, you should do the same in your notes.

5. *Include examples.* Try to include an example for each important concept introduced in class—something that will help you remember what the instructor was talking about. (If you do not have time to include examples as you take notes during class, add them when you review your notes.) For instance, if your world history instructor is explaining *nationalism*, you should write down not only a definition but also an example, such as "Germany in 1848."

6. *If you take notes by hand, write legibly and use helpful signals.* Use blue or black ink for your note taking, but keep a red or green pen handy to highlight important information, jot down announcements (such as a change in a test date), note gaps in your notes, or question confusing points. Do not take notes in pencil, which is hard to read and not as permanent as ink.

7. *Ask questions.* If you do not hear (or do not understand) something your instructor said, or if you need an example to help you understand something, *ask!* Do not, however, immediately turn to another

student for clarification. Instead, wait to see if the instructor explains further or if he or she pauses to ask if anyone has a question. If you are not comfortable asking a question during class, make a note of the question and ask the instructor—or send an email—after class.

After Class

1. *Review your notes.* After every class, try to spend ten or fifteen minutes rereading your notes, filling in gaps and examples while the material is still fresh in your mind. You might also recopy or retype important information from your notes to reinforce what you have learned.
2. *Copy announcements* (such as quiz dates) onto your calendar.
3. *Enter reminders* (for example, a note to schedule a conference before your next paper is due) into your organizer.
4. *Write questions* you want to ask the instructor at the top of the next blank page in your class notebook.

Before the Next Class

1. *Reread your notes.* Leave time to skim the previous class's notes just before each class. This strategy will get you oriented for the next class and will remind you of anything that needs clarification or further explanation. (You might want to give each day's notes a title so you can remember the topic of each class. This strategy can help you find information when you study.)
2. *Ask for help.* Call or email a classmate if you need to fill in missing information; if you still need help, see the instructor during his or her office hours, or come to class early to ask your question before class begins.

1f   Homework Strategies

Doing homework is an important part of your education. Homework gives you a chance to practice your skills and measure your progress. If you are having trouble with the homework, chances are you are having trouble with the course. Ask the instructor or teaching assistant for help *now*; do not wait until the day before the exam. Here are some tips for getting the most out of your homework.

1. *Write down the assignment.* Do not expect to remember your assignment. If you are not exactly sure what you are supposed to do, check with your instructor or with another student.
2. *Do your homework, and do it on time.* Teachers assign homework to reinforce classwork, and they expect homework to be done on a

regular basis. It is easy to fall behind in college, but trying to do three— or five—nights' worth of homework in one night is not a good idea.

3. *Be an active reader.* Get into the habit of highlighting and annotating your textbooks and other material as you read. (See Chapter 37 for information on active reading.)

4. *Join study groups.* A study group of three or four students can be a valuable support system for homework as well as for exams. If your schedule permits, review homework assignments or class notes with other students regularly. In addition to learning information, you will learn different strategies for doing assignments.

1g   Taking Exams

Preparation for an exam should begin well before the exam is announced. In a sense, you begin this preparation on the first day of class.

Before the Exam

1. *Attend every class.* Regular attendance in class—where you can listen, ask questions, and take notes—is the best possible preparation for exams. If you do have to miss a class, arrange to copy—and read—another student's notes *before the next class* so you will be able to follow the discussion.

2. *Keep up with the reading.* Read every assignment, and read it before the class in which it will be discussed. If you do not, you may have trouble understanding what is going on in class.

3. *Take careful notes.* Take careful, thorough notes, but be selective. If you can, compare your notes on a regular basis with those of other students in the class; working together, you can fill in gaps or correct errors. Establishing a buddy system will also force you to review your notes regularly instead of just on the night before the exam.

4. *Study on your own.* When an exam is announced, adjust your study schedule—and your priorities—so you have time to review everything. (This is especially important if you have more than one exam in a short period of time.) Over a period of several days, review all your material (class notes, readings, and so on), and then review it again. Make a note of anything you do not understand, and keep track of topics you need to review. Try to predict the most likely questions, and—if you have time—practice answering them.

5. *Study with a group.* If you can, set up a study group. Studying with others can help you understand the material better. However, do not come to group sessions unprepared and expect to get all the information you need from the other students. You must first study on your own.

6. ***Make an appointment with your instructor.*** Make a conference appointment with the course instructor or teaching assistant a few days before the exam. Bring to this meeting any specific questions you have about course content and about the format of the upcoming exam. (Be sure to review all your study material before the conference.)

7. ***Review the material one last time.*** The night before the exam is not the time to begin your studying; it is the time to review. When you have finished your review, get a good night's sleep.

During the Exam

By the time you walk into the exam room, you will already have done all you could to get ready for the test. Your goal now is to keep the momentum going and not do anything to undermine all your hard work.

> **FYI**
>
> **Taking Essay Exams**
>
> If an exam question asks you to write an essay, remember that what you are really being asked to do is write a **thesis-and-support essay**. Chapter 13 tells you how to do this.

1. ***Read through the entire exam.*** Be sure you understand how much time you have, how many points each question is worth, and exactly what each question is asking you to do. Many exam questions call for just a short answer—*yes* or *no*, *true* or *false*. Others ask you to fill in a blank with a few words, and still others require you to select the best answer from among several choices. If you are not absolutely certain what kind of answer a particular question calls for, ask the instructor or the proctor *before* you begin to write.

2. ***Budget your time.*** Once you understand how much each section of the exam and each question are worth, plan your time and set your priorities, devoting the most time to the most important questions. If you know you tend to rush through exams, or if you find you often run out of time before you get to the end of a test, you might try checking your progress when about one-third of the allotted time has passed (for a one-hour exam, check after twenty minutes) to make sure you are pacing yourself appropriately.

3. ***Reread each question.*** Carefully reread each question *before* you start to answer it. Underline the **key words**—the words that give specific information about how to approach the question and how to phrase your answer. (These key words are listed in the FYI box on page 14.)

Remember, even if everything you write is correct, your response is not acceptable if you do not answer the question. If a question asks you to *compare* two novels, writing a *summary* of one of them will not be acceptable.

4. ***Brainstorm to help yourself recall the material.*** If you are writing a paragraph or an essay, look frequently at the question as you brainstorm. Quickly write down all the relevant points you can think of—what the textbook had to say, your instructor's comments, and so on. The more information you can think of now, the more you will have to choose from when you write your answer.

5. ***Write down the main idea.*** Looking closely at the way the question is worded and at your brainstorming notes, write a sentence that states the main idea of your answer. If you are writing a paragraph, this sentence will be your **topic sentence**; if you are writing an essay, it will be your **thesis statement**.

6. ***List your key supporting points.*** You do not want to waste your limited (and valuable) time making a detailed outline, but an informal outline that lists just your key points is worth the little time it takes. An informal outline will help you plan a clear direction for your paragraph or essay.

7. ***Draft your answer.*** You will spend most of your time actually writing the answers to the questions on the exam. Follow your outline, keep track of time, and consult your brainstorming notes when you need to—but stay focused on your writing.

8. ***Reread, revise, and edit.*** When you have finished drafting your answer, reread it carefully to make sure it says everything you want it to say—and that it answers the question.

FYI

Key Words

Here are some words that can help you decide how to approach an exam question that calls for a paragraph or an essay.

analyze	give examples	illustrate
argue	identify	recount
compare	identify or explain	summarize
contrast	causes, origins,	support
define	contributing	take a stand
demonstrate	factors	trace
describe	identify or explain	
evaluate	results, effects,	
explain	outcomes	

Model Essay Exam

The following essay exam was written by a student in an introductory psychology class in response to the following question:

> Define and explain one of the following concepts related to memory: retrieval, flashbulb memories, déjà vu, false memories. *Be sure to give examples from the text, class discussion, or your own experiences to support the points you make.*

Déjà Vu

Memory is a group of mental processes that allow people to form, store, and retrieve information. Memory concepts include retrieval, the process of recovering stored information; flashbulb memories, very specific remembered images or details of a vivid, rare, or important personal event; and false memories, recollections that are distorted or that recall things that never happened. Perhaps the most interesting memory concept is déjà vu. Déjà vu is a French phrase meaning "already seen." Déjà vu is a feeling that one has experienced something before but is unable to remember when or where.

INTRODUCTION

Definition of term

When people experience déjà vu, they find it impossible to explain the feeling of familiarity, so people often think it must somehow be related to the paranormal. However, déjà vu can actually be explained scientifically, through concepts related to memory.

Thesis statement

Researchers and scientists have discovered several characteristics of déjà vu. It seems to occur most commonly in young adults ages twenty to twenty-four, and the older we get, the less often we tend to have feelings of déjà vu. Researchers have also found that feelings of déjà vu most commonly occur later in the day, when a person is tired or under emotional stress, and when a person is around other people. Most often a feeling of déjà vu is triggered by something that is seen—for example, a coffee mug in a specific place on a desk with an open book next to it. Something about the placement of the items and the specific pages of the open book seem very familiar, but the observer cannot explain why. Sometimes déjà vu can also be triggered by something a person smells, hears, or touches. For example, a case recorded by two researchers focuses on a blind man who experienced déjà vu when he zipped up his jacket while listening to a certain song.

Characteristics of déjà vu

When a feeling of déjà vu is triggered, a person is often confused by it. Something seems so familiar, but the person is unable to explain why. Because it is difficult and even impossible to give a logical explanation for the feeling of familiarity, people sometimes think the feeling must be related to the paranormal. For example, a person may think something seems

Misperceptions about déjà vu

2. *Know what's being asked.* When you take the test, read through each essay question and all of the directions. Make sure you understand them before continuing. Some standardized tests require you to write multiple essays in a limited amount of time; find out in advance if that is the case with your test.

3. *Tackle easy questions first.* Read all the questions, and begin with the one that seems the easiest. Starting strong will help ease your anxiety and give you momentum. In addition, you will score higher if you finish your best work before time runs out.

4. *Make an informal outline.* Quickly jot down your initial essay ideas. Then, develop a thesis, and make a rough outline of your essay. The few minutes you spend planning will improve your essay's organization and keep you on track as you work.

5. *Get down to business.* On standardized essay tests, keep your writing lean and efficient. Avoid long, complicated introductions. Instead, begin your first paragraph with a sentence that directly answers the essay question and states your thesis. After you've stated your thesis, keep it in mind for the rest of your essay. Look back at the question as you write, and make sure your essay is actually answering it.

6. *Manage your time.* If you run out of time before you finish writing, quickly jot down a list of your remaining ideas. If you have time, check your essay, looking for a clear thesis, effective support, appropriate transitions, and a strong summary statement. Finally, quickly proofread your work and correct any grammatical or mechanical errors.

1i   Strategies for Maintaining Academic Honesty

Academic honesty—the standard for truth and fairness in work and behavior—is very important in college. Understanding academic honesty goes beyond simply knowing that it is dishonest to cheat on a test. To be sure you are conforming to the rules of academic honesty, follow these guidelines:

- Don't reuse papers you wrote in high school. The written work you are assigned in college is designed to help you learn, and your instructors expect you to do the work for the course when it is assigned.

- Don't copy information from a book or article or paste material from a Web site directly into your papers. Using someone else's words or ideas without proper acknowledgment constitutes **plagiarism**, a very serious offense.

- Don't ask another student (or a friend or family member) to help you write or revise a paper. If you need help, ask your instructor or a writing center tutor.
- Don't allow another student to copy your work on a test.
- Don't allow another student to turn in a paper you wrote (or one you helped him or her write).
- Don't work with other students on a take-home exam unless your instructor gives you permission to work collaboratively.
- Never buy a paper from a Web site. Even if you edit it, it is still not your own work.

1j   Strategies for Staying Safe on Campus

Colleges are very concerned about student safety. You should be, too. To stay safe on campus, keep the following guidelines in mind.

- If you drive to school, be sure to lock your car, and always park in a well-lit space.
- If you live on campus, never give your room key or dorm access card to anyone else.
- Be aware of your surroundings at all times, and report strangers loitering on school property to campus police. Also report any suspicious or dangerous behavior—even by fellow students.
- If you live in a building that has buzzer access, don't buzz people in unless you know them. Get in the habit of keeping doors and windows locked.
- Don't wear valuable jewelry or bring large sums of money to class. Keep money, credit cards, and other valuables in a safe place, and don't flash them around.
- Don't walk alone at night. If you need to be out at night—to go to the library, to your dorm room, to a public transportation stop, or to leave a party, for example—call your school's van or escort service (even if it means having to wait).
- Get in the habit of checking your school newspaper or Web site for crime statistics. If you know what kinds of crimes are most common on your campus and where they generally occur, you will be able to protect yourself.
- Be sure you know where the emergency call stations are located on your campus—and don't hesitate to call campus police for help if you feel threatened.

- If you are in a situation where trouble arises, leave, and then call to report the situation. Don't get involved or try to calm things down.

- Finally, be sure you know how college officials will contact students (for example, by text message) in case of a campuswide weather or crime emergency.

think about your writing

Look back at your response to the Focus on Writing prompt on page 1. Now that you have read this chapter, what have you learned about the kinds of writing you will be doing in various situations in college? Add this information to your response.

review checklist

Writing and College Success

- [ ] Some strategies come in handy even before school begins. (See 1a.)

- [ ] From your first day as a college student, there are steps you can take to help you succeed. (See 1b.)

- [ ] Day-to-day strategies can help you adjust to college life. (See 1c.)

- [ ] Learning to manage your time is a key part of college success. (See 1d.)

- [ ] Learning to take good notes is essential for success in your college courses. (See 1e.)

- [ ] Doing homework gives you a chance to practice your skills and assess your academic progress. (See 1f.)

- [ ] Preparation for an exam should begin well before the exam is announced. (See 1g.)

- [ ] Learning how to approach standardized tests can help you succeed. (See 1h.)

- [ ] Understanding academic honesty is a key part of a college education. (See 1i.)

- [ ] As a college student, you need to be concerned about your safety on campus. (See 1j.)

unit

1 Focus on Paragraphs

2 Understanding the Writing Process

focus on writing

Today's college students may find themselves in either a traditional classroom or a career-oriented setting. What do you think is the primary purpose of college—to give students a general education or to prepare them for specific careers? Think about this question as you read the pages that follow.

In this chapter, you will learn to

- focus on your assignment, purpose, and audience (2a)
- find ideas to write about (2b)
- identify your main idea and write a topic sentence (2c)
- choose supporting points (2d)
- develop supporting points (2e)
- make an outline (2f)
- draft, TEST, revise, and edit your paragraph (2g–2j)

Because paragraphs are central to almost every kind of writing, learning how to write one is an important step in becoming a competent writer. (Although a paragraph can be a complete piece of writing in itself—as it is in a short classroom exercise or an exam answer—most of the time, a paragraph is part of a longer piece of writing.)

A **paragraph** is a group of sentences that is unified by a single main idea. The **topic sentence** states the main idea, and the rest of the sentences in the paragraph provide **evidence** (examples and details) to support the main idea. The sentences in a paragraph are linked by **transitions**, words and phrases (such as *also* and *for example*) that show how ideas are related. At the end of the paragraph, a **summary statement** reinforces the main idea.

Paragraph Structure

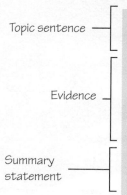

Topic sentence —

      In every paragraph you write, you need to include a main idea, supporting evidence, transitions, and a summary statement. First, state the main idea of the paragraph in a topic sentence. This idea will unify your paragraph. Then, add sentences to provide support for

Evidence —

your topic sentence. In these sentences, you present and develop the evidence that will help readers understand your main idea. Next, check to make sure you have linked these sentences with transitions. Finally, write a summary

Summary statement —

statement, a sentence that reinforces your paragraph's main idea. If you follow this general structure, you are on your way to writing an effective paragraph.

Transitions (boxed)

The first letters of these four elements—**T**opic sentence, **E**vidence, **S**ummary statement, and **T**ransitions—spell TEST. Whenever you write a paragraph, you should TEST it to make sure it is complete.

FYI

The first sentence of a paragraph is **indented**, starting about half an inch from the left-hand margin. Every sentence begins with a capital letter and, in most cases, ends with a period. (Sometimes a sentence ends with a question mark or an exclamation point.)

PRACTICE

2-1   Bring two paragraphs to class—one from a newspaper or magazine article and one from a textbook. Compare your paragraphs with those brought in by other students. What features do all your paragraphs share? How do the paragraphs differ from one another?

The Writing Process

Writing is a **process**, a series of steps that begins in your college classes when you get an assignment.

Step 1: Planning

You start by thinking about what you want to say and finding ideas to write about. Then, you identify the main idea you want to get across.

Step 2: Organizing

Once you have material to write about, you arrange the points that support your main idea in an order that makes sense to you.

Step 3: Drafting

When you have decided how to arrange your ideas, you write a draft.

Step 4: TESTing

When you finish your draft, you TEST it to make sure it includes all the elements of an effective paragraph.

Step 5: Revising and Editing

Finally, you revise and edit your draft until you are satisfied with it.

The five steps in the writing process are explained and illustrated in the pages that follow.

Step 1: Planning

2a Focusing on Your Assignment, Purpose, and Audience

In college, a writing task usually begins with an assignment that gives you a topic to write about. Instead of jumping in headfirst and starting to write, take time to consider some questions about your **assignment** (*what* you are expected to write about), your **purpose** (*why* you are writing), and your **audience** (*for whom* you are writing). Answering these questions at this point will save you time in the long run.

Questions about Assignment, Purpose, and Audience

Assignment

- What is your assignment? Is it included on your course syllabus or posted on the class Web page?
- Do you have a word or page limit?
- When is your assignment due?
- Will you be expected to work on your assignment only at home, or will you be doing some work in class?
- Will you be expected to work on your own or with others?
- Will you be allowed to revise before you hand in your assignment?
- Will you be allowed to revise after your assignment is graded?
- Does your instructor require a particular **format**?

Purpose

- Are you expected to express your personal reactions—for example, to tell how you feel about a piece of music or a news event?
- Are you expected to present information—for example, to answer an exam question, describe a process in a lab report, or summarize a story or essay you have read?
- Are you expected to argue for or against a position on a controversial issue?

WORD POWER

format specified arrangement of elements in a document—for example, where to type your name, the date, and the course number

Audience

- Who will read your paper—just your instructor or other students as well?
- How much will your readers know about your topic?
- Will your readers expect you to use **formal** or **informal** language?

PRACTICE

2-2   Each of the following writing tasks has a different audience and purpose. Think about how you would approach each task. (Use the Questions about Assignment, Purpose, and Audience listed above to help you decide on the best strategy.) Be prepared to discuss your ideas with your class or in a small group.

1. For the other students in your writing class, a description of your best or worst educational experience

2. For the instructor of an education course, a discussion of your first day of kindergarten

3. An email to your community's school board in which you try to convince members to make two or three changes that you believe would improve the schools you attended (or those your children might attend)

4. A thank-you note to a work supervisor—either past or current—telling what you appreciate about his or her guidance and how it has helped you develop and grow as an employee

5. A letter to a restaurant where you received poor service and were served terrible food, describing your experience and suggesting ways the service and food could be improved

2b   Finding Ideas to Write About

Once you know what, why, and for whom you are writing, you can begin the process of finding material to write about. This process is different for every writer.

In this chapter, you will be following the writing process of Stella Drew, a student in an introductory writing course, who was given the following assignment:

WORD POWER

curriculum all the courses required by a school

Should community service—unpaid work in the community—be a required part of the college curriculum? Write a paragraph in which you answer this question.

Before she drafted her paragraph, Stella used a variety of strategies to find ideas to write about. The pages that follow illustrate the four strategies her instructor asked the class to try:

- freewriting,
- brainstorming,
- clustering,
- journal writing.

FYI

Keep in mind that you do not have to use all four of the strategies listed above every time you write a paragraph. Try out the various strategies, and see which ones work best for you.

Freewriting

When you **freewrite**, you write for a set period of time—perhaps five minutes—without stopping, and you keep writing even if what you are writing doesn't seem to have a point or a direction. Your goal is to relax and let ideas flow without worrying about whether or not they are related—or even make sense. (If you have trouble thinking of something to say, keep repeating the last word of your freewriting until something else comes to mind.) Sometimes you can freewrite without a topic in mind, but at other times you will focus your attention on a particular topic. This strategy is called **focused freewriting**.

When you finish freewriting, read what you have written. Then, underline any ideas you think you might be able to use. If you find an idea you want to explore further, freewrite again, using that idea as a starting point.

Stella's focused freewriting on the topic of whether or not community service should be a required part of the college curriculum appears on the following page.

Community service. Community service. Sounds like what you do instead of going to jail. Service to the community—service in the community. Community center. College community—community college. Community service—I guess it's a good idea to do it—but when? In my spare time—spare time—that's pretty funny. So after school and work and all the reading and studying I also have to do <u>service</u>? Right. And what could I do anyway? Work with kids. Or homeless people. Old people? Sick people? Or not people—maybe animals. Or work for a political candidate. Does that count? But when would I do it? Maybe other people have time, but I don't. OK idea, could work—but not for me.

Stella's freewriting

PRACTICE

2-3   Reread Stella's freewriting on the topic of community service for college students (above). If you were advising her, which of her ideas would you suggest she explore further? Underline these ideas in her freewriting, and be prepared to discuss your suggestions with the class or in a small group.

freewrite

Write (or type) for at least five minutes on the following topic: What is the primary purpose of college—to give students a general education or to prepare them for careers?

When you are finished, reread your freewriting, and underline any ideas you think you might be able to use in your paragraph.

(continued from previous page)

handled problems on the job. Reading over these entries can help you understand your strengths and weaknesses and become a more effective employee.

■ *Your ideas about current events*   Expressing your opinions in your journal can be a good way to explore your reactions to social or political issues. Your journal entries may encourage you to write to your local or school newspaper or to public officials—and even to become involved in community projects or political activities.

■ *Your impressions of what you see*   Many writers carry their journals with them everywhere so they can record any interesting or unusual things they observe. You can later incorporate these observations into essays or other pieces of writing.

■ *Aspects of your personal life*   Although you may not want to record the intimate details of your life if your instructor plans to collect your journal, writing about relationships with family and friends, personal problems, hopes and dreams, and so on can help you develop a better understanding of yourself and others.

Here is Stella's journal entry on the topic of community service for college students.

> I'm not really sure what I think about community service. I guess I think it sounds like a good idea, but I still don't see why we should have to do it. I can't fit anything else into my life. I guess it would be possible if it was just an hour or two a week. And maybe we could get credit and a grade for it, like a course. Or maybe it should just be for people who have the time and want to do it. But if it's not required, will anyone do it?

Stella's journal entry

write a journal entry

For your first journal entry, write down your thoughts about the topic you have been working on in this chapter: the purpose of college.

2c Identifying Your Main Idea and Writing a Topic Sentence

When you think you have enough material to write about, it is time to identify your **main idea**—the idea you will develop in your paragraph.

To find a main idea for your paragraph, begin by looking over what you have already written. As you read through your freewriting, brainstorming, clustering, or journal entries, look for the main idea that your material seems to support. The sentence that states this main idea and gives your writing its focus will be your paragraph's **topic sentence**.

The topic sentence is usually the first sentence of your paragraph, and it is important because it tells both you and your readers what the focus of your paragraph will be. An effective topic sentence has three characteristics.

1. *A topic sentence is a complete sentence.* There is a difference between a *topic* and a *topic sentence*. The **topic** is what the paragraph is about. A **topic sentence**, however, is a complete sentence that includes a subject and a verb and expresses a complete thought. This sentence includes both a topic and the writer's idea about the topic.

   TOPIC Community service for college students

   TOPIC SENTENCE Community service should be required for all students at our school.

2. *A topic sentence is more than just an announcement of what you plan to write about.* A topic sentence makes a point about the topic the paragraph discusses.

   ANNOUNCEMENT In this paragraph, I will explain my ideas about community service.

   TOPIC SENTENCE My ideas about community service changed after I started to volunteer at a soup kitchen for homeless people.

3. *A topic sentence presents an idea that can be discussed in a single paragraph.* If your topic sentence is too broad, you will not be able to discuss it in just one paragraph. If your topic sentence is too narrow, you will not be able to say much about it.

   TOPIC SENTENCE TOO BROAD Students all over the country participate in community service, making important contributions to their communities.

TOPIC SENTENCE TOO NARROW	Our school has a community service require-ment for graduation.
EFFECTIVE TOPIC SENTENCE	Our school's community service requirement has had three positive results.

When Stella Drew reviewed her notes, she saw that they included two different kinds of ideas: ideas about the value of doing community service and ideas about the problems it presents. The material on the value of community service seemed more convincing, so she decided that her paragraph should support a community service requirement. She stated her main idea in a topic sentence.

Community service is so important that college students should be required to do it.

When Stella thought about how to express her topic sentence, she knew it had to be a complete sentence, not just a topic, and that it would have to make a point, not just announce what she planned to write about. When she reread the topic sentence she had written, she felt confident that it did these things. Her topic sentence was neither too broad nor too narrow, and it made a statement she could support in a paragraph.

PRACTICE

2-7   Read the following items. Put a check mark next to each one that has all three characteristics of an effective topic sentence. Be prepared to explain why some items are effective topic sentences while others are not.

Examples

Speaking two languages, an advantage in today's workplace

_____

Our school should not abandon the foreign language requirement.

_____✓_____

1. The new farmers' market makes it easier for people in the neighborhood to buy fresh produce. _____

2. Eating a balanced diet with plenty of proteins and carbohydrates

_____

3. In this paragraph, I will look at the disadvantages of a large high school. ————————

4. The best size for high schools: not too large, not too small. ————————

5. Participation in sports is important for children because it teaches them how to compete. ————————

6. The history of sports goes back to before the earliest civilizations. ————————

7. Spending a quiet evening at home can have several advantages. ——————— —

8. Television, the most popular leisure activity in the United States ————————

PRACTICE

2-8   Decide whether each of the following statements could be an effective topic sentence for a paragraph. If a sentence is too broad, write *too broad* in the blank following the sentence. If the sentence is too narrow, write *too narrow* in the blank. If the sentence is an effective topic sentence, write *OK* in the blank.

Example: Unfortunately, many countries in today's world are involved in conflicts. ——*too broad*——

1. Deciding what to do in life is a difficult task for many young people. ————————

2. A college career counselor can help students decide what kind of work they would like to do. ————————

3. The college career counseling office has three full-time employees and two part-time employees. ————————

4. Safe driving reduces the number of accidents and saves lives. ————————

5. Different countries, and even different states, have different rules of the road. _____

6. Texting while driving greatly increases the chance of an accident. _____

7. Some students are much happier with their college experience than other students. _____

8. Joining a study group is a good way for students who commute to get to know other students. _____

9. Flu shots are especially important for people in certain high-risk groups. _____

10. Flu shots occasionally result in soreness in the area where the shot was given. _____

identify your main idea, and write a topic sentence

Look over the work you have done so far, and try to identify the main idea your material seems to support. Do you think college should give students a general education or prepare them for careers? Write a topic sentence that expresses your main idea on the lines below.

Topic sentence: _____

_____

Step 2: Organizing

2d   Choosing Supporting Points

After you have stated your paragraph's main idea in a topic sentence, you will need to provide specific **evidence** (examples and details) to **support** your main idea.

When you choose points to support your topic sentence, make sure they are *relevant*, *distinct*, and *specific*.

1. **Relevant** points are directly related to your main idea.

   TOPIC SENTENCE   College is necessary because it teaches students important skills for their future careers.

   SUPPORTING POINTS

   - Students learn to write in college, and knowing how to write well is important for any job.

   - Students learn to think critically in college, and knowing how to think critically is necessary for almost any career.

   - ~~Choosing a career path is difficult.~~

   The third supporting point above is not relevant because it does not support the topic sentence. (It does not provide an example of how skills learned in college will help students in their future careers.)

2. **Distinct** points are different from other points you plan to use.

   TOPIC SENTENCE   College is necessary because it teaches students important skills for their future careers.

   SUPPORTING POINTS

   - Students learn to write in college, and knowing how to write well is important for any job.

   - Students learn to think critically in college, and knowing how to think critically is necessary for almost any career.

   - ~~College writing courses will prepare students to write on the job.~~

   The third point above is not distinct because it is saying the same thing as the first point.

3. **Specific** points communicate exactly what you want to say; they are not general or vague.

   - Students learn *to write in college, and knowing how to write well is important* ~~things in college that will help them~~ in any job.

   The original point above is not specific because it does not tell what "things" students learn. The revision clarifies the point the writer is using to support the topic sentence.

As she continued to work on her paragraph, Stella listed several points from her notes that she thought she could write about. After she read through her list of points, she crossed out those that did not support her topic sentence or that overlapped with other points. She decided that the remaining two points would give her enough material to write about in her paragraph.

TOPIC SENTENCE   Community service is so important that college students should be required to do it.

- ~~Community service helps people.~~
- ~~Some community service activities could be boring.~~
- ~~Community service can help the world.~~
- Community service helps the community.
- ~~College students are busy.~~
- ~~Community service takes a lot of time.~~
- ~~Community service might not relate to students' majors.~~
- ~~Community service can be upsetting or depressing.~~
- Community service can be part of a student's education.

PRACTICE

2-9   In each of the following two cases, the topic sentence and a tentative list of supporting points have been provided. Read each list of points carefully, and consider whether the points support the topic sentence. Cross out any points that are not relevant, distinct, and specific.

1. *Topic Sentence:* Even though some fans may object, professional sports teams should abandon their Indian logos and nicknames.

   - Indian logos and nicknames are offensive to many people.

   - Indian logos and nicknames misrepresent Indians and perpetuate troubling stereotypes.

   - Some Indian tribes have given teams official permission to use tribal names or symbols.

   - Many high school and college teams have already abandoned their Indian names and logos.

WORD POWER

perpetuate to cause to last for a long time

- Some sports teams change their names when they move to a different city.

- Tradition is not a strong enough reason to keep racist names and logos.

- Change is difficult, but fans will get used to new names and logos.

- Many people dislike teams' Indian nicknames and logos.

- Changing a name or a logo is not a big deal.

- Team names and logos that are disrespectful of other races and cultures are unacceptable.

2. *Topic Sentence:* The government should ban unpaid internships because they are unfair.

- Internships can be hard to find.

- Employers benefit financially from interns' free labor.

- Many unpaid interns do boring, menial work and gain few valuable job skills.

- Some students are just looking to boost their résumés and do not mind working for free.

- The government has a responsibility to protect workers from being exploited.

- Without government involvement, few employers will offer to pay their interns.

- Employers are taking advantage of their interns' unpaid work.

- A lot of unpaid interns do not benefit much from their internship experiences.

- Low-income interns cannot afford to work without pay as wealthier students can.

- Nobody wants to work for free.

- Interns do not have enough power to negotiate with employers for paid positions.

choose supporting points

Review your freewriting, brainstorming, clustering, and journal writing to find the points that can best support your topic sentence. Write your topic sentence on the lines below; then, list your supporting points.

Topic sentence: _____

_____

Supporting points:

- _____

- _____

- _____

Check carefully to make sure each point on your list supports your topic sentence. Cross out any points that are not relevant, distinct, and specific.

2e Developing Supporting Points

Now that you have identified points that support your main idea, you need to **develop** them, explaining them more fully and making clear how they relate to your topic sentence. One way to develop your points is to provide examples. To come up with examples, ask yourself *how? why?* or *what?* for each point.

After Stella chose the two points she was going to use to support her main idea, she went back and added examples to develop each point.

SUPPORTING POINT	EXAMPLES
Community service helps the community. (How? In what specific ways?)	— Volunteers can help feed the homeless. — They can work with the elderly. — They can tutor in schools.
Community service can be part of a student's education. (How?)	— Students can learn about themselves and others. — Students can learn about their community and the world. — Students can discover what they want to do for a career.

develop your supporting points

Review your list of supporting points, and then list examples you can use to develop each point. If you like, you can make a chart like the one on page 44 to help you arrange your supporting points.

2f   Making an Outline

After you have decided which points to use to support your topic sentence and chosen examples to develop each point, your next step is to make an informal **outline**. You do this by arranging your supporting points in the order in which you plan to discuss them in your paragraph.

When Stella thought she had listed enough examples to develop the two points she would discuss in her paragraph, she made the following informal outline.

Outline

Topic sentence: Community service is so important that college students should be required to do it.

- Community service helps the community.
  — Volunteers can help feed the homeless.
  — Volunteers can help the elderly.
  — Volunteers can tutor students.

- Community service can be part of a student's education.
  — Students can learn about themselves.
  — Students can learn about others.
  — Students can learn about their community.
  — Students can learn about the world.
  — Students can discover what they want to do for a career.

Stella's informal outline

make an outline

Look over your supporting points, and decide which ones you want to include in your paragraph. Then, make an informal outline that arranges your supporting points in the order in which you plan to write about them.

Step 3: Drafting

2g Drafting Your Paragraph

Once you have written a topic sentence for your paragraph, selected the points you will discuss, and arranged them in the order in which you plan to write about them, you are ready to write a first draft.

In a **first draft**, your goal is to get your ideas down on paper. Begin your paragraph with a topic sentence that states the paragraph's main idea. Then, following your informal outline, write or type without worrying about correct wording, spelling, or punctuation. If a new idea occurs to you, write it down. Don't worry about whether it fits with the other ideas. Your goal is not to produce a perfect piece of writing but simply to create a working draft. Later on, when you revise, you will have a chance to rethink ideas and rework sentences.

Because you will be making changes to this first draft, you should leave wide margins, skip lines, and leave extra blank lines in places where you might need to add material. (If you write by hand, feel free to be messy and to cross out; remember, the only person who will see this draft is you.)

When you have finished your first draft, don't make any changes right away. Take a break (overnight if possible), and think about something—anything—else. Then, return to your draft, and read it with a fresh eye.

Here is the first draft of Stella's paragraph on the topic of community service for college students. Note that she included a brief working title to help her focus on her topic.

Community Service

Community service is so important that college students should be required to do it. When college students do community service, they spend their time doing good for someone or for the community.

Working in a homeless shelter, doing chores for senior citizens, and tutoring children are all examples of community service. Community service activities like these are good for the community, and they can be more fulfilling for students than playing sports or participating in school activities. Community service can be an important part of a college education. Students can learn a lot about themselves and others and can discover what they want to do with their lives. Community service can also make the world a better place.

Stella's first draft

PRACTICE

2-10   Reread the first draft of Stella's paragraph. Working in a group of three or four students, make a list of changes that you think Stella should make. For example, what should she add? What should she cross out? Have one member of your group write down all your suggestions, and be prepared to exchange ideas with the class.

draft your paragraph

Write a first draft of your paragraph about the purpose of a college education. Be sure you state your main idea in the topic sentence and support the topic sentence with specific evidence. If you handwrite your draft, leave wide margins and skip lines; if you type your draft, leave extra space between lines. (This will make it much easier to revise and edit.) Finally, add a working title.

Step 4: TESTing

2h   TESTing Your Paragraph

When you have finished your draft, the first thing you should do is "test" what you have written to make sure it includes all the elements of an effective paragraph. You do this by asking the following four **TEST** questions.

T ■ **Topic sentence**—Does your paragraph have a topic sentence that states its main idea?

E ■ **Evidence**—Does your paragraph include specific points that support your topic sentence? Are these points developed with evidence (examples and details)?

Why Should Be Required
Community Service
∧ ∧
Community service is so important that college students should be

required to do it. When college students do community service, they spend
helping a person or organization in their communities. For example, they can work
their time doing good for someone or for the community. Working in
∧   s   do   or tutor or mentor at-risk   ∧
homeless shelter, doing chores for senior citizens, and tutoring children. are
∧   ∧
all examples of community service. Community service activities like these
are also good for the students who give their time. This work
are good for the community, and they can be more fulfilling for students than
∧   also
playing sports or participating in school activities. Community service can be
∧
an important part of a college education. Students can learn a lot about
, about their communities, about different kinds of people, and about their world. They
themselves and others and can discover what they want to do with their lives.
∧   ∧ even
Community service can also make the world a better place. For example,
working in a school can lead a student to a career as a teacher. For all
these reasons, community service should be a required part of the college
curriculum.

Stella's revised draft with handwritten revisions

When she revised, Stella did not worry about being neat. She crossed out words, added material, and changed sentences and words. When she felt her revision was complete, she was ready to move on to edit her paragraph.

2j Editing Your Paragraph

When you **edit**, you check for correct grammar, punctuation, mechanics, and spelling. Then, you go on to **proofread** carefully for typographical errors that your spell checker may not identify, checking to make sure that you have indented the first sentence of your paragraph and that every sentence begins with a capital letter and ends with a period. Finally, you check your essay's **format** to make sure it satisfies your instructor's requirements.

Remember, editing is a vital step in the writing process. Many readers will not take your ideas seriously if your paragraph contains grammatical or mechanical errors. You can use the following checklist to guide your editing.

self-assessment checklist

Editing Your Paragraph

☐ Are all your sentences complete and grammatically correct?

☐ Do all your subjects and verbs agree?

☐ Have you used the correct verb tenses?

☐ Are commas used where they are required?

☐ Have you used apostrophes correctly?

☐ Have you used other punctuation marks correctly?

☐ Have you used capital letters where they are required?

☐ Are all words spelled correctly?

For help with grammar, punctuation, mechanics, and spelling, see Units 5–8 of this text.

When Stella edited her paragraph, she began by printing out her revised draft. Then, she checked grammar, punctuation, mechanics, and spelling and proofread for typos. The final version of her paragraph appears below.

Why Community Service Should Be Required

Topic sentence — Community service is so important that college students should be required to do it. When college students do community service, they spend their time helping a person or organization in their communities. For example, they can work in homeless shelters, do chores for senior citizens, or tutor or mentor at-risk children. Community service activities like these are good for the community, and they are also good for the students who give their time. This work can be more fulfilling than playing sports or participating in school activities. Community service can also be an important part of a college education. Students can learn a lot about themselves, about their communities, about different kinds of people, and about their world. They can even discover what they want to do with their lives. For example, working in a school can lead a student to a career as a teacher. For all these reasons, community service should be a required part of the college curriculum.

Evidence

Summary statement

T E S T

■ Topic Sentence
□ Evidence
□ Summary Statement
□ Transitions

PRACTICE

2-11   Reread the final draft of Stella's paragraph about community service for college students (p. 51), and compare it with her first draft (pp. 46–47). Then, working in a group of three or four students, answer the following questions about her revision. (Be prepared to discuss your responses to these questions with the class.)

1. Why do you think Stella did not revise her paragraph's topic sentence? Do you agree with her decision?

2. What new supporting material did Stella add to her paragraph? Can you think of any new material she *should* have added?

3. What did Stella cross out? Why do you think she deleted this material? Do you think she should cross out any additional material?

4. Why do you think Stella added "For example" and "also" to her final draft?

5. In her revision, Stella added a sentence at the end of the paragraph. Do you think this sentence is necessary? Why or why not?

self-assess

Use the Self-Assessment Checklist on page 49 to help you revise your draft. Can you add any material to support your points more fully? Should any material be crossed out because it does not support your main idea? Can anything be stated more clearly? In preparation for revising and editing your paragraph, list some of the changes you might make in your draft.

revise and edit your paragraph

Revise your draft. Cross out unnecessary material and material you want to rewrite, and add new and rewritten material between the lines and in the margins. After you finish your revision, edit your paragraph, checking grammar, punctuation, mechanics, and spelling—and proofread carefully for typos. When you are satisfied with your paragraph, print it out.

review checklist

Understanding the Writing Process

- [ ] Before you start to write, consider your assignment, purpose, and audience. (See 2a.)

- [ ] Use freewriting, brainstorming, clustering, and journal writing to help you find ideas. (See 2b.)

- [ ] Identify your main idea, and write a topic sentence. (See 2c.)

- [ ] Choose points to support your main idea. (See 2d.)

- [ ] Develop your supporting points with evidence. (See 2e.)

- [ ] Make an informal outline by arranging your points in the order in which you plan to discuss them. (See 2f.)

- [ ] Write a first draft of your paragraph. (See 2g.)

- [ ] TEST your paragraph. (See 2h.)

- [ ] Revise your paragraph. (See 2i.)

- [ ] Edit your paragraph. (See 2j.)

3 TESTing Your Paragraphs

focus on writing

These pictures show a student's closet before (left) and after (right) she organized it. How do you organize your own closet (or your desk, furniture, or other items in your room)? Does everything have its place, or do you arrange items more randomly? Write a paragraph about how you organize a space of your own.

In this chapter, you will learn how to **TEST** your paragraphs.

As you learned in Chapter 2, you should **TEST** every paragraph after you finish drafting. **TEST**ing will tell you whether or not your paragraph includes all the elements of an effective paragraph.

T opic sentence
E vidence
S ummary statement
T ransitions

If you **TEST** the following paragraph, you will see that it contains all four elements of an effective paragraph.

> Although most people do not know it, the modern roller coaster got its start in Coney Island in Brooklyn, New York. First, in 1888, the Flip Flap Railway, which featured a circular loop, was built. The coaster was the first to go upside down, but it frequently injured riders' necks. Next, in 1901, the Loop-the-Loop, which was safer than the Flip Flap Railway, was built. Then, from 1884 through the 1930s, over thirty roller coasters were constructed in Coney Island. Finally, in 1927, the most famous roller coaster in history, the Cyclone, was built at a cost of over $100,000. Although it began operating over eighty years ago, it is still the standard by which all roller coasters are measured. It has steep drops, a lot of speed, and only lap belts to hold riders in their seats. Still in operation, the Cyclone is the most successful ride in Coney Island history. It is the last survivor of the wooden roller coasters that once drew crowds to Coney Island. With their many innovations, Coney Island's roller coasters paved the way for the high-tech roller coasters in amusement parks today.

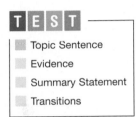

T E S T

- Topic Sentence
- Evidence
- Summary Statement
- Transitions

WORD POWER

innovation something newly invented; a new way of doing something

3a TESTing for a Topic Sentence

The first thing you do when you **TEST** a paragraph is look for a **topic sentence (T)**. An effective paragraph focuses on a single main idea, and it includes a topic sentence that states this main idea.

A paragraph is **unified** when all its sentences support the main idea stated in the topic sentence. When you revise, you can make your paragraphs unified by crossing out sentences that do not support your topic sentence and, if necessary, adding sentences that do.

The following paragraph is not unified because it contains sentences that do not support the paragraph's topic sentence. (These sentences have been crossed out.)

The weak economy has led many people to move away from the rural Ohio community where I was raised. Over the years, farmland has become more and more expensive. Years ago, a family could buy each of its children twenty-five acres on which they could start farming. Today, the price of land is so high that the average farmer cannot afford to buy this amount of land, and those who choose not to farm have few alternatives. ~~After I graduate, I intend to return to my town and get a job there. Even though many factories have moved out of the area, I think I will be able to get a job. My uncle owns a hardware store, and he told me that after I graduate, he will teach me the business. I think I can contribute something to both the business and the community.~~ Young people just cannot get good jobs anymore. Factories have moved out of the area and taken with them the jobs that many young people used to get after high school. As a result, many eighteen-year-olds have no choice but to move away to find employment.

The following revised paragraph is unified. It discusses only the idea that is stated in the topic sentence.

The weak economy has led many people to move away from the rural Ohio community where I was raised. Over the years, farmland has become more and more expensive. Years ago, a family could buy each of its children twenty-five acres on which they could start farming. Today, the price of land is so high that the average farmer cannot afford to buy this amount of land, and those who choose not to farm have few alternatives. Young people just cannot get good jobs anymore. Factories have moved out of the area and taken with them the jobs that many young people used to get after high school. As a result, many eighteen-year-olds have no choice but to move away to find employment.

T E S T

- Topic Sentence
- Evidence
- Summary Statement
- Transitions

PRACTICE

3-1   The following paragraphs are not unified because some sentences do not support the topic sentence. First, underline the topic sentence in each paragraph. Then, cross out any sentences that do not support the topic sentence.

1. Although many people still get down on one knee to propose, others have found more creative ways to pop the question. Using Jumbotrons, computer games, or even zero-gravity chambers, some people are making the moment truly memorable. Last year, one English graffiti artist asked his girlfriend to marry him by spray-painting his proposal on the side of a building. In 2011, a man used the Sunday crossword puzzle in the

Washington Post to propose to his girlfriend. As she completed the puzzle, she saw that the answers to several of the clues spelled out her name and a question. Weddings are also becoming more unusual. Some couples are choosing to get married while skydiving or riding bicycles. One couple recently got married in a shark tank. Several brave people have also proposed on television. By buying ad space and recording a brief video clip, they appear on the screen during a favorite show. People are clearly using their imaginations to ask this age-old question in unexpected ways.

2. When new technologies appear, we often create retronyms to describe the old or original form of those technologies. *Snail mail, manual transmission,* and *landline* are all examples of retronyms. Before email, snail mail was the only kind of mail. The retronym came about because we needed a way to distinguish between the new, instant electronic mail and the old-fashioned, hand-delivered kind. Snail mail takes a frustratingly long time these days. Some people even worry that the Postal Service is becoming obsolete. Likewise, we created the retronym *manual transmission* when many vehicles began being equipped with automatic transmissions. The word *landline* works in a similar way, helping us differentiate between our home phones and our cell phones. As long as technology continues to develop, we will continue to need retronyms to clarify meaning. Many other tools can help us communicate clearly as well, like learning a foreign language.

3. Hoping to inspire others to follow their lead, Kevin Salwen and his daughter Hannah wrote *The Power of Half,* describing their family's rewarding choice to give more and live with less. The book tells how the family sold their luxurious home, gave half the money to charity, and used the other half to buy a smaller house. Smaller houses are becoming more popular these days, as people look for more energy-efficient ways to live. By making this decision, the Salwens were able to help people in need and become a closer and happier family. Kevin and Hannah hope that readers of their book will also feel encouraged to give more. The Salwens believe that most Americans have more than they need and that if everyone gave away half of their possessions, the world would be a better place. Some people criticized the Salwens' choice of charity, the Hunger Project, because it helps needy people in Ghana rather than in the United States.

PRACTICE

3-2 The following paragraph has no topic sentence. Read it carefully, and then choose the most appropriate topic sentence from the list that follows the paragraph.

While continuing to make its famous interlocking plastic bricks, Lego has created a number of popular video games, such as *Lego*

Racer and *Lego Star Wars*. The company also shares ownership of four Legoland amusement parks and owns dozens of retail stores in Europe and North America. Lego spokespeople say they hope to make a feature film in the near future. Meanwhile, the company makes products using licensed characters from other movies, such as *Harry Potter* and *Lord of the Rings*, and has its own television series on the Cartoon Network. The Lego Group also offers special programs to accompany its products. For example, the Lego Group has developed an educational branch, Lego Education, which sponsors competitions for students and provides lesson plans and professional development for educators. With such wide-ranging programs and merchandise, the company will likely continue to thrive.

Put a check mark next to the topic sentence that best expresses the main idea of the paragraph above.

1. The Lego Group has been very successful in the video game market.

   _____

2. Because of a decline in sales, the Lego Group is now pursuing the education market. _____

3. Today, the Lego Group is much more than just a manufacturer of children's construction toys. _____

4. The founder of the Lego Group, a Danish man named Ole Kirk Christiansen, had a passion for making children's toys. _____

5. By diversifying its products and services, the Lego Group has spread itself too thin. _____

PRACTICE

3-3 The following paragraphs do not have topic sentences. Think of a topic sentence that expresses each paragraph's main idea, and write it on the lines above the paragraphs.

Example: *Possible answer: Rock and roll originated in African-American music but was reinterpreted by white performers.*

Early 1950s African American musicians included performers such as Johnny Ace, Big Joe Turner, and Ruth Brown. Groups like the Drifters and the Clovers were also popular. By the mid-1950s, white performers such as Bill Haley and the Comets, Jerry Lee Lewis, and Elvis Presley were imitating African American music. Their songs had a beat and lyrics that appealed to a white audience. Eventually, this combination of black and white musical styles became known as rock and roll.

1. _____

_____

The Japanese word *manga* was first used in the 1700s to describe illustrated books. Early manga comics first started appearing in the late 1800s, when artists working in Europe began to influence those working in Japan. These early manga were similar to French and British political cartoons of the day. Modern-style manga, which were first produced in Japan during the U.S. occupation in the late 1940s, looked like American comic books. The first post–World War II manga focused on stereotypically male topics, such as space travel and sports. Today, there are many types of manga, including romance, horror, mystery, and comedy, and they appeal to both adults and children around the world.

2. _____

_____

First, you have to find a suitable job to apply for. Once you decide to apply, you have to put together your résumé and send it to your potential employer. Then, when you are invited in for an interview, you need to decide what you are going to wear. At the interview, you need to speak slowly and clearly and answer all questions directly and honestly. After the interview, you need to send a note to the person who interviewed you, thanking him or her. Finally, if everything goes well, you will get an email or a phone call offering you the job.

3. _____

_____

There are no written records left by the Native Americans themselves. Most of the early European settlers in North America were more interested in staying alive than in writing about the Native Americans. In addition, as the westward expansion took place, the Europeans encountered the Native Americans in stages, not all at once. Also, the Native Americans spoke at least fifty-eight different languages, which made it difficult for the Europeans to speak with them. Most important, by the time scholars decided to study Native American culture, many of the tribes no longer existed. Disease and war had wiped them out.

PRACTICE

3-4   Choose one of the following topic sentences. Then, write a paragraph that develops the main idea that is stated in the topic sentence. After you finish, check to make sure that all the sentences in your paragraph support your topic sentence.

1. Online education has a number of advantages over traditional classroom instruction.

2. People who use smartphones tend to do three annoying things.

3. My campus is (or is not) accessible to students with physical disabilities.

3b   TESTing for Evidence

The next thing you do when you **TEST** a paragraph is to make sure you have enough **evidence (E)**—details and examples—to support the main idea stated in your topic sentence.

A paragraph is **well developed** when it includes enough evidence to explain and support its main idea. The following paragraph does not include enough evidence to support its main idea.

> Although pit bulls have a bad reputation, they actually make good pets. Part of their problem is that they can look frightening. Actually, though, pit bulls are no worse than other breeds of dogs. Even so, the bad publicity they get has given them a bad reputation. Pit bulls really do not deserve their bad reputation, though. Contrary to popular opinion, pit bulls can (and do) make friendly, affectionate, and loyal pets.

The following revised paragraph now includes enough evidence to support the main idea stated in the topic sentence.

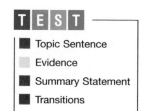

T E S T
■ Topic Sentence
▢ Evidence
■ Summary Statement
■ Transitions

Evidence added

> Although pit bulls have a bad reputation, they actually make good pets. Part of their problem is that they can look frightening. Their wide, powerful jaws, short muscular legs, and large teeth are ideally suited for fighting, and they were bred for this purpose. In addition, some pit bulls—especially males—can be very aggressive toward both people and other dogs. Actually, though, pit bulls are no worse than

other breeds of dogs. As several recent newspaper articles have
pointed out, the number of reported bites by pit bulls is no greater
than the number of bites by other breeds. In fact, some breeds, such
as cocker spaniels, bite more frequently than pit bulls. Even so, the
bad publicity they get has given them a bad reputation. The problem
is that whenever a pit bull attacks someone, the incident is reported
on the evening news. Contrary to popular opinion, pit bulls can (and
do) make friendly, affectionate, and loyal pets.

Evidence added

Evidence added

Note: Length alone is no guarantee that a paragraph includes enough
supporting evidence for your main idea. A long paragraph that consists
of one generalization after another will still not include enough support
for the topic sentence.

PRACTICE
3-5
Underline the specific supporting evidence in each of the
following paragraphs.

1. Hearing people have some mistaken ideas about the deaf community. First, some hearing adults think that all deaf people consider
themselves disabled and would trade anything not to be "handicapped."
Hearing people do not realize that many deaf people do not consider
themselves handicapped and are proud to be part of the deaf community, which has its own language, customs, and culture. Second, many
hearing people think that all deaf people read lips, so there is no need to
learn sign language to communicate with them. However, lip reading—
or speech reading, as deaf people call the practice—is difficult. Not all
hearing people say the same words in the same way, and facial expressions can also change the meaning of the words. If hearing people make
more of an attempt to understand the deaf culture, communication
between them will improve.

2. In 1996, the National Basketball Association (NBA) approved a
women's professional basketball league. Within fifteen months, eight
teams had been formed, four in the Eastern Conference and four in
the Western Conference. Next, the teams began to draft players for
these teams and to select a logo and uniforms. The final logo selected,
a red, white, and blue shield, showed the silhouette of a woman player
dribbling the ball, with the letters "WNBA" above her. The uniforms
consisted of shorts and jerseys in the colors of the different teams.
That first season, games were played in the summer when the television sports schedule was lighter so they could be televised during
prime time. At the end of that season, the Houston Comets became

the first WNBA champions. Today, the WNBA consists of ten teams that each play thirty-four regular-season games televised to audiences worldwide.

3. One of the largest celebrations of the passage of young girls into womanhood occurs in Latin American and Hispanic cultures. This event is called La Quinceañera, or the fifteenth year. It acknowledges that a young woman is now of marriageable age. The day usually begins with a Mass of Thanksgiving. The young woman wears a full-length white or pastel-colored dress and is attended by fourteen friends and relatives who serve as maids of honor and escorts. Her parents and godparents surround her at the foot of the altar. When the Mass ends, other young relatives give small gifts to those who attended, while the young woman places a bouquet of flowers on the altar of the Virgin. Following the Mass is an elaborate party, with dancing, cake, and toasts. Finally, to end the evening, the young woman dances a waltz with her favorite escort. For young Hispanic women, the Quinceañera is an important milestone.

PRACTICE
3-6   Provide two or three specific pieces of evidence (examples or details) to support each of the following topic sentences.

1. When it comes to feeding a family, there are several alternatives to fast food.

   - _____
   - _____
   - _____

2. A romantic relationship with a coworker can create serious problems.

   - _____
   - _____
   - _____

3. When scheduling classes, you need to keep several things in mind.

   - _____
   - _____
   - _____

4. Consumers should take the following steps to protect themselves from identity theft.

   • _____

   • _____

   • _____

5. Choosing the right career is harder than I thought it would be.

   • _____

   • _____

   • _____

PRACTICE

3-7   The two paragraphs that follow do not include enough supporting evidence. Suggest some examples and details that might help each writer develop his or her topic sentence more fully.

1. Young adults who move back in with their parents after college face many challenges. Feeling dependent on one's parents after living away from home can be frustrating. Living at home can restrict a person's freedom. Also, some parents can be overbearing and treat the young graduate as if he or she is a child. Of course, the success of the living situation depends on how well the college graduate and his or her parents communicate. Despite these drawbacks, living at home for a while after college can make sense.

2. Audiences are noticing more and more female action heroes in today's big-budget Hollywood movies. Brave, independent, and highly skilled, these heroines battle the forces of evil and win. Sometimes well-known stars play these characters. In other cases, lesser-known actresses play these parts. As long as action films with female leads continue to do well at the box office, Hollywood will continue to make them.

3c TESTing for a Summary Statement

The third thing you do when you TEST a paragraph is to make sure it ends with a **summary statement (S)**—a sentence that reinforces your paragraph's main idea. By reminding readers what your paragraph is about, a summary statement helps to further **unify** your paragraph.

The following paragraph has no summary statement.

> Overpopulation is one of the biggest concerns for scientists. In 1900, there were 1.6 billion people on Earth, a quarter of today's population. At that time, life expectancy was also much shorter than it is now. By 2000, the world's population had grown to over 6 billion, and today, the average life expectancy worldwide is almost sixty-five years. The low death rate, combined with a high birth rate, is adding the equivalent of one new Germany to the world's population each year. According to a United Nations study, if present trends continue, by 2050 the world's population will be between 7.3 and 10.5 billion— so large that much of the world may be either malnourished or starving.

The summary statement in the following revised paragraph reinforces the paragraph's main idea and brings the paragraph to a close.

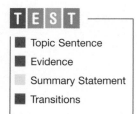

T E S T
- ▪ Topic Sentence
- ▪ Evidence
- ▪ Summary Statement
- ▪ Transitions

> Overpopulation is one of the biggest concerns for scientists. In 1900, there were 1.6 billion people on Earth, a quarter of today's population. At that time, life expectancy was also much shorter than it is now. By 2000, the world's population had grown to over 6 billion, and today, the average life expectancy worldwide is almost sixty-five years. The low death rate, combined with a high birth rate, is adding the equivalent of one new Germany to the world's population each year. According to a United Nations study, if present trends continue, by 2050 the world's population will be between 7.3 and 10.5 billion—so large that much of the world may be either malnourished or starving. Given these increases, it is no wonder that scientists who study population are worried.

PRACTICE

3-8   Read the following two paragraphs, which do not include summary statements. Then, on the lines below each paragraph, write a summary statement that adds unity to the paragraph by reinforcing the main idea stated in the topic sentence. Be careful not to use the same wording as in the topic sentence.

1. Founded more than fifty years ago, NASCAR has become one of the most successful spectator sports in the world. In December 1947, Bill France formed the National Association for Stock Car Auto Racing (NASCAR). The first NASCAR race was held at Daytona Beach's auto racecourse in 1948. From this modest start, France turned NASCAR into a highly successful business. Attendance grew 8.2 percent during 1997, and 2,102,000 fans attended the thirty-one NASCAR events in 1998. This was the first time that NASCAR attendance topped the two

million mark. Then, in 2007, NASCAR negotiated a new multimillion-dollar television deal with Fox Sports/Speed, TNT, and ABC/ESPN. As a result, these networks now televise NASCAR's most popular events.

_____

_____

2. The creators of the new languages Esperanto and Loglan worked hard to achieve their goals. L. L. Zamenhof's goal in inventing Esperanto was to bring about world peace and understanding. To accomplish this objective, Zamenhof dedicated years to constructing Esperanto's complex and politically neutral grammar and vocabulary. He hoped that one day Esperanto could act as a universal second language for international communication. James Cooke Brown invented Loglan for different, but equally ambitious, reasons. Essentially, Brown wanted to show that language limits the way people think. His theory was that a clear and unbiased language could produce clearer, less biased thinking in its users. For that reason, Brown worked hard to make Loglan as logical, neutral, and regular as possible.

_____

_____

3d   TESTing for Transitions

The final thing you do when you **TEST** a paragraph is make sure the paragraph includes **transitions (T)** that connect ideas in a clear, logical order.

Transitional words and phrases create **coherence** by indicating how ideas are connected in a paragraph—for example, in *time order*, *spatial order*, or *logical order*. By signaling the order of ideas in a paragraph, these words and phrases make it easier for readers to follow your discussion.

- You use **time** signals to show readers the order in which events occurred.

    In 1883, my great-grandfather came to this country from Russia.

- You use **spatial** signals to show readers how people, places, and things stand in relation to one another. For example, you can move from top to bottom, from near to far, from right to left, and so on.

    Next to my bed is a bookcase that also serves as a room divider.

▪ You use **logical** signals to show readers how ideas are connected. For example, you can move from the least important idea to the most important idea or from the least familiar idea to the most familiar idea.

Certain strategies can help you do well in college. First, you should learn to manage your time effectively.

Because transitional words and phrases create coherence, a paragraph without them can be difficult to understand. You can avoid this problem by checking to make sure you have included all the words and phrases that you need to link the ideas in your paragraph.

Frequently Used Transitional Words and Phrases

SOME WORDS AND PHRASES THAT SIGNAL TIME ORDER

after	finally	phrases that
afterward	later	include dates
at first	next	(for example,
before	now	"In June,"
during	soon	"In 1904")
earlier	then	
eventually	today	

SOME WORDS AND PHRASES THAT SIGNAL SPATIAL ORDER

above	in front	on the left
behind	inside	on the right
below	in the center	on top
beside	near	over
in back	next to	under
in between	on the bottom	

SOME WORDS AND PHRASES THAT SIGNAL LOGICAL ORDER

also	in fact
although	last
as a result	moreover
consequently	next
even though	not only . . . but also
first . . . second . . . third	one . . . another
for example	similarly
for instance	the least important
furthermore	the most important
however	therefore
in addition	

The paragraph below has no transitional words and phrases to link ideas.

> During his lifetime, Jim Thorpe faced many obstacles. Thorpe was born in 1888, the son of an Irish father and a Native American mother. He was sent to the Carlisle Indian School in Pennsylvania. "Pop" Warner, the legendary coach at Carlisle, discovered Thorpe. Thorpe left Carlisle to play baseball for two seasons in the newly formed East Carolina minor league. He returned to Carlisle, played football, and was named to the All-American team. Thorpe went to the Olympic Games in Stockholm, where he won two gold medals. Thorpe's career took a dramatic turn for the worse when a sportswriter who had seen him play baseball in North Carolina exposed him as a professional. The Amateur Athletic Union stripped him of his records and medals. Thorpe died in 1953. The International Olympic Committee returned Thorpe's Olympic medals to his family in 1982. Ironically, only in death was Thorpe able to overcome the difficulties that had frustrated him while he was alive.

The following revised paragraph is coherent because it includes transitional words and phrases that connect its ideas.

> During his lifetime, Jim Thorpe faced many obstacles. Thorpe was born in 1888, the son of an Irish father and a Native American mother. In 1904, he was sent to the Carlisle Indian School in Pennsylvania. The next year, "Pop" Warner, the legendary coach at Carlisle, discovered Thorpe. Thorpe left Carlisle in 1909 to play baseball for two seasons in the newly formed East Carolina minor league. In 1912, he returned to Carlisle, played football, and was named to the All-American team. Thorpe then went to the Olympic Games in Stockholm, where he won two gold medals. The next year, however, Thorpe's career took a dramatic turn for the worse when a sportswriter who had seen him play baseball in North Carolina exposed him as a professional. As a result, the Amateur Athletic Union stripped him of his records and medals. Thorpe died in 1953. After years of appeals, the International Olympic Committee returned Thorpe's Olympic medals to his family in 1982. Ironically, only in death was Thorpe able to overcome the difficulties that had frustrated him while he was alive.

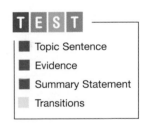

T E S T

■ Topic Sentence
■ Evidence
■ Summary Statement
▢ Transitions

PRACTICE

3-9   Read the following paragraph carefully. Then, select transitional words and phrases from the accompanying alphabetized list, and write them in the appropriate blanks. When you have finished, reread your paragraph to make sure that it is coherent.

TRANSITIONS

after	for centuries
at first	however
before	in fact
by 1904	in 1897

The history of Jell-O is full of surprising setbacks. _____ Jello became "America's Most Famous Dessert," gelatin struggled for attention. _____, people experimented with the substance, but no one could make it appealing. By adding flavored syrup _____, Pearle B. Wait was the first to make gelatin taste good. Wait's wife, May, named the product Jell-O. _____, Wait could not market his new creation and ended up selling the company for $450 in 1899. _____, the next owner, Orator Francis Woodward, had the same problem. _____, he had supposedly tried to sell the company for even less money. _____ failing to find a buyer, Woodward started a major marketing campaign. He advertised in magazines and gave out free Jell-O cookbooks. _____, Jell-O was finally on its way to becoming the country's best-known dessert.

PRACTICE

3-10 The following paragraph includes no transitions. Read the paragraph carefully. Then, after consulting the list of transitional words and phrases on page 66, add appropriate transitional words and phrases to connect the paragraph's ideas in **time order**.

In 1856, my great-great-great-grandparents, Anne and Charles McGinley, faced many hardships to come to the United States. _____ they left Ireland, their landlords, who lived in England, had raised the rent on their land so much that my ancestors could not afford to pay it. _____ it took them three years to save the money for passage. _____ they had saved the money, they had to look for a ship that was willing to take them. _____, my great-great-great-grandparents were able to leave. They and their ten children spent four long months on a small ship. Storms, strong tides, and damaged sails made the trip longer than it should have been. _____, in November 1856, they saw land, and two days later they sailed into New York Harbor. _____ they took a train to Baltimore, Maryland, where their cousins lived and where we live today. At that time, they couldn't have known how thankful their descendants would be for their courage and sacrifice.

PRACTICE

3-11 The following paragraph includes no transitions. Read the paragraph carefully. Then, after consulting the list of transitional words and phrases on page 66, add appropriate transitional words and phrases to connect the paragraph's ideas in **spatial order**.

> **WORD POWER**
> **lure** to attract, entice, or tempt; something that tempts

    Casinos are designed to lure players into gambling. As soon as people walk in the door, they are steered toward the gaming room. _____ are the slot machines, blinking and making lots of noise. _____ of the slot machines are the table games—blackjack, roulette, and craps. _____ the gambling area, the ceiling is painted a dull, neutral color. _____ the floor is a carpet that has a complicated pattern that is hard to look at. Both the ceiling and the carpet are designed to make sure that gamblers look just at the games they are playing. _____ of the casino are the bathrooms, and players have to walk through the entire slot machine area if they want to use one. The casino designers are betting that gamblers will not be able to resist stopping to play. It is clear, then, that the design of the casinos makes it difficult for the average person to resist the lure of gambling.

PRACTICE

3-12   The following paragraph includes no transitions. Read the paragraph carefully. Then, after consulting the list of transitional words and phrases on page 66, add appropriate transitional words and phrases to connect the paragraph's ideas in **logical order**.

My high school had three silly rules. The _____ silly rule was that only seniors could go outside the school building for lunch. In spite of this rule, many students went outside to eat because the cafeteria was not big enough to hold everyone. Understanding the problem, the teachers just looked the other way as long as we came back to school on time. The _____ silly rule was that we had to attend 95 percent of all the classes for each course. If we did not, we were supposed to fail. Of course, that rule was never enforced, because if it were, almost every student in the school would have failed everything. The _____ silly rule was that students were not supposed to throw their hats into the air at graduation. At one point in the past, a parent—no one can remember who—complained that a falling hat could poke someone in the eye. _____, graduating classes were told that under no circumstances could they throw their hats into the air. _____, on graduation day, we did what every graduating class has always done—ignored the silly rule and threw our hats into the air.

TEST · Revise · Edit

Review the paragraph you drafted in response to the Focus on Writing prompt on page 54. Next, **TEST** your paragraph to make sure it includes a topic sentence, evidence, a summary statement, and transitions. Then, prepare a final revised and edited draft of your paragraph.

EDITING PRACTICE

TEST each of the following paragraphs to make sure it is **unified**, **well developed**, and **coherent**. Begin by underlining the topic sentence. Then, cross out any sentences that do not support the topic sentence. If necessary, add evidence (details and examples) to support the topic sentence. Next, decide whether you need to make any changes to the paragraph's summary statement. (If the paragraph includes no summary statement, write one.) Finally, add transitional words and phrases where they are needed.

1.   In 1979, a series of mechanical and human errors in Unit 2 of the nuclear generating plant at Three Mile Island, near Harrisburg, Pennsylvania, caused an accident that changed the nuclear power industry. A combination of stuck valves, human error, and poor decisions caused a partial meltdown of the reactor core. Large amounts of radioactive gases were released into the atmosphere. The governor of Pennsylvania evacuated pregnant women from the area. Other residents then panicked and left their homes. The nuclear regulatory agency claimed that the situation was not really dangerous and that the released gases were not a health threat. Activists and local residents disagreed with this. The reactor itself remained unusable for more than ten years. Large demonstrations followed the accident, including a rally of more than 200,000 people in New York City. Some people came just because the day was nice. By the mid-1980s, as a result of the accident at Three Mile Island, new construction of nuclear power plants in the United States had stopped.

2.   A survey of the history of cigarette advertisements shows how tobacco companies have consistently encouraged people to smoke. One of the earliest television ads showed two boxes of cigarettes

dancing to an advertising jingle. Many people liked these ads. Other advertisements were more subtle. Some were aimed at specific audiences. Marlboro commercials, with the rugged Marlboro man, targeted men. Virginia Slims made an obvious pitch to women by saying, "You've come a long way, baby!" Salem, a mentholated cigarette, showed rural scenes and targeted people who liked the freshness of the outdoors. Kent, with its "micronite filter," appealed to those who were health conscious by claiming that Kent contained less tar and nicotine than any other brand. This claim was not entirely true. Other brands had less tar and nicotine. Merit and other high-tar and high-nicotine cigarettes began to use advertisements that were aimed at minorities. Cigarette companies responded to the national decline in smoking by directing advertising at young people. Camel introduced the cartoon character Joe Camel, which was aimed at teenagers and young adults.

3.   Cities created police forces for a number of reasons. The first reason was status: after the Civil War, it became a status symbol for cities to have a uniformed police force. A police force provided jobs. This meant that politicians were able to reward people who had worked to support them. Police forces made people feel safe. Police officers helped visitors find their way. They took in lost children and sometimes fed the homeless. They directed traffic, enforced health regulations, and provided other services. Police officers kept order. Without a police force, criminals would have made life in nineteenth-century cities unbearable.

COLLABORATIVE ACTIVITY

In a newspaper or magazine, find an illustration or photograph that includes a lot of details. Then, write a paragraph describing what you see. (Include enough details so that readers will be able to "see" it almost as clearly as you can.) Decide on a specific spatial order—from top to bottom or from left to right, for example—that makes sense to you, and follow this order as you organize the details in your paragraph. Finally, trade paragraphs with another student, and offer suggestions that could improve his or her paragraph.

review checklist

TESTing Your Paragraphs

☐ A topic sentence states a paragraph's main idea. (See 3a.)

☐ A paragraph should include enough evidence—examples and details—to support its main idea. (See 3b.)

☐ A paragraph should end with a summary statement that reinforces its main idea and helps to unify the paragraph. (See 3c.)

☐ A paragraph should include transitional words and phrases that indicate how ideas are connected. (See 3d.)

unit

2 Patterns of Paragraph Development

4 Exemplification

focus on writing

Most colleges have a student services center, where students can get information and advice on making the most of the programs and support the school provides. Brainstorm to develop a list of the programs and services your school offers (or should offer) to help students adjust to college. You will return to this topic and review your brainstorming later in the chapter when you write your exemplification paragraph.

In Chapters 2 and 3, you learned how to write effective paragraphs. In Chapters 4 through 12, you will learn different ways of organizing your ideas within paragraphs. Understanding these patterns of paragraph development can help you organize ideas and become a more effective, more confident writer.

4a   Exemplification Paragraphs

What do we mean when we tell a friend that an instructor is *good* or that a football team is *bad*? What do we mean when we say that a movie is *boring* or that a particular war was *wrong*? To clarify general statements like these, we use **exemplification**—that is, we give **examples** to illustrate a general idea. In daily conversation and in school, you use specific examples to help explain your ideas.

GENERAL STATEMENT	SPECIFIC EXAMPLES
Today is going to be a hard day.	Today is going to be a hard day because I have a math test in the morning, a lab quiz in the afternoon, and work in the evening.

GENERAL STATEMENT	SPECIFIC EXAMPLES
My car is giving me problems.	My car is burning oil and won't start on cold mornings. In addition, it needs a new set of tires.

An **exemplification paragraph** uses specific examples to explain or clarify a general idea. Personal experiences, class discussions, observations, conversations, and readings can all be good sources of examples.

When you TEST an exemplification paragraph, make sure it follows these guidelines:

T ■ An exemplification paragraph should begin with a **topic sentence** that states the paragraph's main idea.

E ■ An exemplification paragraph should present **evidence**—in the form of examples—that supports and clarifies the general statement made in the topic sentence. Examples should be arranged in **logical order**—for example, from least to most important or from general to specific. The number of examples you need depends on your topic sentence. A broad statement will probably require more examples than a relatively narrow one.

S ■ An exemplification paragraph should end with a **summary statement** that reinforces the paragraph's main idea.

T ■ An exemplification paragraph should include **transitions** that introduce the examples and connect them to one another and to the topic sentence.

Paragraph Map: Exemplification

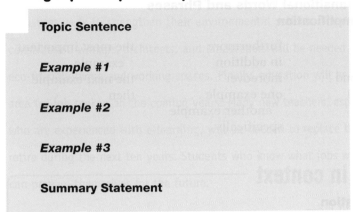

Topic Sentence

Example #1

Example #2

Example #3

Summary Statement

Model Paragraph: Exemplification

The following paragraph uses several examples to support the idea that some countries change their names for political reasons.

New Government, New Name

When countries change their names, it is often for political reasons. Sometimes a new government decides to change the country's name to separate itself from an earlier government. For example, Burma became Myanmar when a military government took over in 1989. Cambodia has had several name changes as well. After a coup in 1970, it was called the Khmer Republic. Then, in 1975, under communist rule, it became Kampuchea. Gaining independence from another nation is another reason for a country to change its name. For instance, in 1957, after gaining independence from Great Britain, the Gold Coast became Ghana. Another name change occurred when the French Sudan became Mali. After gaining independence from France in 1960, it decided to reject its colonial past. Finally, Zimbabwe gave up its former British name, Rhodesia, several years after winning independence. These name changes can be confusing, but they reveal the changing political climate of the countries in which they occur.

—Kim Seng (student)

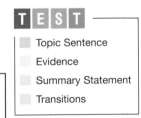

TE**S**T

☐ Topic Sentence
☐ Evidence
☐ Summary Statement
☐ Transitions

Examples presented in logical order

were often impolite and demanding. The tips were bad. It was hard to be pleasant when you knew that the people you were waiting on were probably going to leave you a bad tip. Finally, the owner of the restaurant did not show us any respect. He often yelled at us, saying that if we didn't work harder, he would fire us. He never did, but his constant threats didn't do much to help our morale.

draft your paragraph

Using your informal outline as a guide, draft your exemplification paragraph.

When she finished her draft, Sarah scheduled a conference with her instructor, who suggested that her paragraph would be stronger if she made some of her examples more specific. For example, what experience did she have that made her want to quit? Exactly how were customers rude? Her instructor also reminded her that she needed to TEST her paragraph. As she TESTed her paragraph, Sarah assessed her draft.

- She checked her **topic sentence** and decided that it was effective.

- When she evaluated her **evidence**, she realized she needed to add more examples and details and delete irrelevant materials.

- She noticed that she did not have a **summary statement**, so she planned to add one at the end of her paragraph.

- She decided she needed to add more **transitions** to make it easier for readers to follow her discussion.

After TESTing her paragraph, Sarah went on to revise and edit her draft. The final draft below includes all the elements that she looked for when she applied the TEST strategy.

TEST

- Topic Sentence
- Evidence
- Summary Statement
- Transitions

My Worst Job

Waiting tables at the Jersey shore was the worst job I ever had. First, I had never worked in a restaurant before, so I made a lot of mistakes. Once, I forgot to bring salads to a table I waited on. A person at the table complained so loudly that the owner had to calm him down. I was so frustrated and upset that I almost quit. Second, the customers at the restaurant were often rude. All they wanted was to get their food as fast as possible so they could get back to the beach or the boardwalk. They were on vacation, and they wanted to be treated well. As a result, they were frequently very demanding. No one ever said, "excuse me," "please," or "thank you," no matter what I did for them. Third, the tips were usually bad. It was hard to be pleasant when you knew that the people you were waiting on were probably going to leave you a bad tip. Finally, the owner of the restaurant never showed his workers any respect. He would yell at us, saying that if we didn't work harder, he would fire us. He never did, but his constant threats didn't do much to help our morale. Even though I survived the summer, I promised myself that I would never wait tables again.

TEST · Revise · Edit

Look back at the draft of your exemplification paragraph. Using the TEST checklist on page 86, evaluate your paragraph to make sure it includes a topic sentence, evidence, a summary statement, and transitions. Then, prepare a revised and edited draft of your paragraph.

PRACTICE

4-3   For additional practice in writing an exemplification paragraph, choose one of the topics below.

Effective (or ineffective) teachers
Qualities that make a great athlete
Successful movies
Challenges that older students face
Traditions your family follows
Unattractive clothing styles
Peer pressure
Benefits of a vegan diet

Things you can't do without
Terrible dates
Extreme sports
Role models
Rude cell-phone behavior
Advantages of recycling
Acts of courage
Credit-card debt

Then, follow the process outlined in 4b to create your exemplification paragraph.

TESTing an exemplification paragraph

T opic Sentence Unifies Your Paragraph

☐ Do you have a clearly worded **topic sentence** that states your paragraph's main idea?

☐ Does your topic sentence state an idea that can be supported by examples?

E vidence Supports Your Paragraph's Topic Sentence

☐ Does all your **evidence**—the examples you present—support your paragraph's main idea?

☐ Do you need to add more examples?

S ummary Statement Reinforces Your Paragraph's Unity

☐ Does your paragraph end with a **summary statement** that reinforces your main idea?

T ransitions Add Coherence to Your Paragraph

☐ Do you use **transitions** to introduce each example your paragraph discusses?

☐ Do you need to add transitions to make your paragraph clearer and to help readers follow your ideas?

4c Writing about Visuals

Look at the public service advertisement on page 87 and think about the following questions:

- What are the key elements of the ad? How do the image and the text work together?
- What do you think the ad's primary purpose is?
- What audience do you think the ad hopes to reach?
- Do you think the ad is effective—that is, does it achieve its purpose? Does it speak in a convincing way to the audience it wants to reach?

Write an **exemplification** paragraph in which you explain why you find the ad effective or ineffective. In your paragraph, be sure to support your topic sentence with specific examples of what the ad does (or doesn't) do.

5 Narration

focus on writing

These four panels are from Lynda Barry's book *One! Hundred! Demons!,* a graphic story about the author's childhood. Look at the panels, and then brainstorm to identify some experiences that you could discuss in a paragraph about a difficult period in your own childhood. You will return to this topic and review your brainstorming later in the chapter when you write your narrative paragraph.

In this chapter, you will learn to write a narrative paragraph.

PREVIEW

5a Narrative Paragraphs

Narration is writing that tells a story. For example, a narrative paragraph could tell how an experience you had as a child changed you, how the life of Martin Luther King Jr. is inspiring, or how the Battle of Gettysburg was the turning point in the Civil War.

When you TEST a **narrative paragraph**, make sure it follows these guidelines:

T ▪ A narrative paragraph should begin with a **topic sentence** that states its main idea, letting readers know why you are telling a particular story.

E ▪ A narrative paragraph should present **evidence**—events and details—in **time order**, usually in the order in which the events actually occurred. Effective narrative paragraphs include only those events that tell the story and avoid irrelevant information that could distract or confuse readers.

S ▪ A narrative paragraph should end with a **summary statement** that reinforces the paragraph's main idea.

T ▪ A narrative paragraph should include **transitions** that connect events to one another and to the topic sentence.

Paragraph Map: Narration

Topic Sentence

Event #1

Event #2

Event #3

Summary Statement

Model Paragraph: Narration

T E S T

☐ Topic Sentence
☐ Evidence
☐ Summary Statement
☐ Transitions

The student writer of the following paragraph presents a series of events to support the idea that the fashion designer Chloe Dao had a difficult life.

Overnight Success

Events arranged in time order

Chloe Dao had to overcome a lot of difficulties to become a successful fashion designer. When Dao was a baby, her parents decided to leave her native country, Laos, and come to the United States. Unfortunately, the Viet Cong captured her and her family as they tried to cross the border. They were sent to a refugee camp, where they stayed for four years. In 1979, when she was eight, Dao and her family were allowed to come to the United States. Once they arrived, they had to earn enough money to live on. Dao's mother worked three jobs. On the weekends, the entire family ran the snack bar at a flea market. Finally, they saved enough money to open a dry cleaning business. When she was twenty, Dao moved to New York to attend school. After she graduated, she got a job as production manager for designer Melinda Eng. Eventually, she opened a boutique, where she featured clothes that she designed. Her big break came in 2006 when she was chosen as a finalist on the reality show *Project Runway*. Although Chloe Dao may appear to be an "overnight success," she had to struggle to get where she is today.

—Christine Clark (student)

Transitions in Narrative Paragraphs

As you arrange your ideas in a narrative paragraph, be sure to use clear transitional words and phrases. These signals help readers follow your narrative by indicating the order of the events you discuss.

Some Transitional Words and Phrases for Narration

after	first . . . second . . . third	specific dates
as	immediately	(for example, "In 2006")
as soon as	later	suddenly
before	later on	then
by the time	meanwhile	two hours (days, months,
earlier	next	years) later
eventually	now	until
finally	soon	when

grammar in context

Narration

When you write a narrative paragraph, you tell a story. As you become involved in your story, you might begin to string events together without proper punctuation. If you do, you will create a **run-on**.

INCORRECT (RUN-ON)	Dao's mother worked three jobs on the weekends, the entire family ran a snack bar at a flea market.
CORRECT	Dao's mother worked three jobs. On the weekends, the entire family ran the snack bar at a flea market.

For information on how to identify and correct run-ons, see Chapter 24.

☑ **LearningCurve** For more practice with run-ons, complete the Run-Ons activity at bedfordstmartins.com/focusonwriting.

Analyzing a Narrative Paragraph

Read this narrative paragraph; then, follow the instructions in Practice 5-1.

Two men who risked their lives in the 1904 Harwick mine disaster were the inspiration for the Hero Fund, a charity that awards money to heroes and their families. The Harwick mine disaster began with a small explosion near the entry to the Harwick mine in Pennsylvania. Within seconds, this small explosion caused a chain reaction in which more and more coal dust was stirred up and ignited. Then, a strong blast sent materials and even a mule flying out of the mine shaft. Ten hours later, a rescue party led by Selwyn Taylor went down into the mine. The rescue party found only one survivor, but Taylor believed more men might still be alive deep within the mine. As he advanced, however, Taylor was overcome by fumes. The following day, another rescue worker, Daniel Lyle, was also overcome by fumes while searching for survivors. Neither Taylor nor Lyle found any survivors, and both men died as a result of their efforts. Three months after the mine disaster, Pittsburgh steelmaker Andrew Carnegie founded the Hero Fund to provide financial assistance to the families of those injured or killed while performing heroic acts. The Hero Fund continues to honor people like Selwyn Taylor and Daniel Lyle, ordinary people who take extraordinary risks to save others' lives.

—Kevin Smiley (student)

PRACTICE

5-1

1. Underline the topic sentence of the paragraph on page 91.

2. List the major events discussed in the paragraph. The first event has been listed for you.

A small explosion occurred near the entry to the mine.

_____

_____

_____

_____

_____

_____

3. Circle the transitional words and phrases that the writer uses to link events in time.

4. Underline the paragraph's summary statement.

PRACTICE

5-2　Following are four possible topic sentences for narrative paragraphs. List three or four events that could support each topic sentence. For example, if you were recalling a barbecue that turned into a disaster, you could tell about burning the hamburgers, spilling the soda, and forgetting to buy paper plates.

1. One experience made me realize that I was no longer as young as I thought.

2. The first time I _____, I got more than I bargained for.

3. I didn't think I had the courage to _____, but when I did, I felt proud of myself.

4. I remember my reactions to one particular event very clearly.

5b Case Study: A Student Writes a Narrative Paragraph

Here is how one student, Todd Kinzer, wrote a narrative paragraph. When Todd's instructor asked the class to write a paragraph about an experience that had a great impact on them, Todd tried to narrow this assignment to a topic for his paragraph. He began by listing some experiences that he could write about.

> Accident at camp—Realized I wasn't as strong as I thought I was
>
> Breaking up with Lindsay—That was painful
>
> Shooting the winning basket in my last high school game—Sweet
>
> The last Thanksgiving at my grandparents' house—Happy and sad

As Todd looked over the experiences on his list, he realized that he could write about all of them. He decided, however, to focus on the last Thanksgiving he spent at his grandparents' house. This occasion was especially meaningful to him because his grandfather had died shortly after the holiday.

Todd began by freewriting on his topic. He typed whatever came into his mind about the dinner, without worrying about spelling, punctuation, or grammar. Here is Todd's freewriting paragraph.

> Thanksgiving. Who knew? I remember the smells when I woke up. I can see Granddad at the stove. We were all happy. He told us stories about when he was a kid. I'd heard some of them before, but so what? I loved to hear them. We ate so much I could hardly move. They say turkey has something in it that puts you to sleep. We watched football all afternoon and evening. I still can't believe Granddad is dead. I guess I have the topic for my paragraph.

freewrite

Look back at the brainstorming you did in response to the Focus on Writing prompt on page 88. Choose one experience from your notes, and then freewrite about that experience. Be sure to write nonstop, without worrying about spelling, punctuation, or grammar.

After he finished freewriting, Todd arranged the main events he planned to write about in an informal outline that reflected the order in which they occurred.

Grandfather cooking

Grandfather told stories

Sat down for Thanksgiving dinner

Watched football on TV

make an outline

Create an informal outline for your paragraph by arranging the events you remember from your childhood experience in the order in which they occurred. (Keep in mind that you will add details to develop these events when you draft your paragraph.)

Using his informal outline as a guide, Todd drafted the following paragraph.

Last Thanksgiving, my grandparents were up early. My grandfather stuffed the turkey, and my grandmother started cooking the other dishes. When I got up, I could smell the turkey in the oven. The table was already set for dinner, so we ate breakfast in the kitchen. My grandfather told us about the Thanksgivings he remembered from when he was a boy. When we sat down for dinner, a fire was burning in the fireplace. My grandmother said grace. My grandfather carved the turkey, and we all passed around dishes of food. For dessert, we had pecan pie and ice cream. After dinner, we watched football on TV. When I went to bed, I felt happy. This was my grandfather's last Thanksgiving.

draft your paragraph

Using your informal outline as a guide, draft your narrative paragraph.

Todd knew his draft needed a lot of work. Before he wrote the next draft, he tried to recall what other things had happened that Thanksgiving. He also tried to decide which idea was the most important and what additional supporting information could make his paragraph stronger. Todd sent his draft to his instructor as an email attachment, and his instructor returned the draft along with her comments. After considering his instructor's suggestions and TESTing his paragraph, Todd decided to make the following changes.

- He decided that he needed to add a **topic sentence** that stated his paragraph's main idea.
- He decided that he needed to add some more details and examples and to delete irrelevant sentences so that all his **evidence** would support his main idea.
- He decided to write a stronger **summary statement**.
- He decided that he needed to add **transitions** to indicate the time order of the events in his paragraph.

After TESTing his paragraph, Todd made some additional revisions; then, he edited his paragraph, checking grammar, punctuation, mechanics, and spelling and looking carefully for typos. The final draft below includes all the elements Todd looked for when he TESTed his paragraph.

Thanksgiving Memories

This past Thanksgiving was happy and sad because it was the last one I would spend with both my grandparents. The holiday began early. At five o'clock in the morning, my grandfather woke up and began to stuff the turkey. About an hour later, my grandmother began cooking corn pie and pineapple casserole. At eight o'clock, when I got up, I could smell the turkey cooking. While we ate breakfast, my grandfather told us about Thanksgivings he remembered when he was a boy. Later, my grandfather made a fire in the fireplace, and we sat down for dinner. After my grandmother said grace, my grandfather carved and served the turkey. The rest of us passed around dishes of sweet potatoes, mashed potatoes, green beans, asparagus, cucumber salad, relish, cranberry sauce, apple butter, cabbage salad, stuffing, and, of course, corn pie and pineapple casserole. For dessert, my grandmother served pecan pie with scoops of ice cream. After dinner, we turned on the TV and the whole family watched football all evening. That night, I remember thinking that life couldn't get much better. Four months later, my grandfather died in his sleep. For my family and me, Thanksgiving would never be the same.

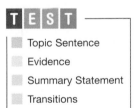

T E S T
- Topic Sentence
- Evidence
- Summary Statement
- Transitions

TEST · Revise · Edit

Look back at the draft of your narrative paragraph. Using the **TEST** checklist on pages 96–97, evaluate your paragraph to make sure it includes a topic sentence, evidence, a summary statement, and transitions. Then, prepare a revised and edited draft of your paragraph.

PRACTICE

5-3 For additional practice in writing a narrative paragraph, choose one of the topics below.

A difficult choice	An embarrassing situation
A historic event	A disastrous day
A time of self-doubt	A sudden understanding or insight
A success	Something funny a friend did
A dangerous experience	Unexpected good luck
A lesson you learned	A conflict with authority
A happy moment	An event that changed your life
An instance of injustice	A misunderstanding

Then, follow the process outlined in 5b to create your narrative paragraph.

TESTing a narrative paragraph

T opic Sentence Unifies Your Paragraph

☐ Do you have a clearly worded **topic sentence** that states your paragraph's main idea?

☐ Does your topic sentence give readers an idea of why you are telling the story?

E vidence Supports Your Paragraph's Topic Sentence

☐ Do you include enough information about the events you discuss?

☐ Does all your **evidence**—events and details—support your paragraph's main idea?

☐ Do you need to include more events or details in your narrative?

Summary Statement Reinforces Your Paragraph's Unity

☐ Does your paragraph end with a **summary statement** that reinforces your main idea?

Transitions Add Coherence to Your Paragraph

☐ Do your **transitions** indicate the time order of events in your paragraph?

☐ Do you need to add transitions to make your paragraph clearer and to help readers follow your ideas?

5c Writing about Visuals

The picture below shows a bride and groom at a Las Vegas wedding chapel. Study the picture carefully, and then write a **narrative** paragraph that tells the story behind it. (If you prefer, you can write a paragraph about a wedding that you attended.)

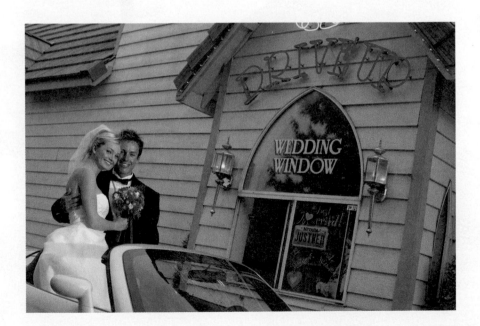

6 Description

focus on writing

Brainstorm to develop a list of people you encounter every day—for example, a bus driver, a street vendor, and a worker in your school cafeteria. You will return to this topic and review your brainstorming later in the chapter when you write your descriptive paragraph.

In this chapter, you will learn to write a descriptive paragraph.

PREVIEW

6a Descriptive Paragraphs

In a personal email, you may describe a new boyfriend or girlfriend. In a biology lab manual, you may describe the structure of a cell. In a report for a nursing class, you may describe a patient you treated.

When you write a **description**, you use words to paint a picture for your readers. With description, you use language that creates a vivid impression of what you have seen, heard, smelled, tasted, or touched. The more details you include, the better your description will be.

The following description is flat because it includes very few descriptive details.

> **FLAT** Today, I saw a beautiful sunrise.

In contrast, the passage below is full of descriptive details that convey the writer's impression of the scene. This revised description relies on sight (*glowed red; turned slowly to pink, to aqua, and finally to blue*), touch (*the soft sandy beach; felt the cold water*), and sound (*heard the waves hit the shore*) to create a vivid picture.

> **VIVID** Early this morning as I walked along the soft sandy beach, I saw the sun rise slowly out of the ocean. At first, the ocean glowed red. Then, it turned slowly to pink, to aqua, and finally to blue. As I stood watching the sun, I heard the waves hit the shore, and I felt the cold water swirl around my toes. For a moment, even the small grey and white birds that hurried along the shore seemed to stop and watch the dazzling sight.

When you **TEST** a **descriptive paragraph**, make sure it follows these guidelines:

T ■ A descriptive paragraph should begin with a topic sentence that conveys the main idea or general impression you want to communicate in your paragraph—for example, "The woods behind my house may seem ordinary, but to me, they are beautiful" or "The old wooden roller coaster is a work of art."

E ■ A descriptive paragraph should present **evidence**—descriptive details—that supports the topic sentence. Details should be presented in a clear **spatial order** that reflects the order in which you observed the person, place, or thing you are describing. For example, you can move from near to far or from top to bottom.

99

S ■ A descriptive paragraph should end with a **summary statement** that reinforces the paragraph's main idea.

T ■ A descriptive paragraph should include **transitions** that connect details to one another and to the topic sentence.

Paragraph Map: Description

Topic Sentence

Detail #1

Detail #2

Detail #3

Summary Statement

Model Paragraph: Description

TEST

■ Topic Sentence
■ Evidence
■ Summary Statement
■ Transitions

The student writer of the following paragraph uses descriptive details to support the idea that the Lincoln Memorial is a monument to American democracy.

The Lincoln Memorial

Descriptive details arranged in spatial order

The Lincoln Memorial was built to celebrate American democracy. In front of the monument is a long marble staircase that leads from a reflecting pool to the memorial's entrance. Thirty-six columns—which symbolize the thirty-six states reunited after the Civil War—surround the building. Inside the building are three rooms. The first room contains the nineteen-foot statue of Lincoln. Seated in a chair, Lincoln looks exhausted after the long Civil War. One of Lincoln's hands is a fist, showing his strength, and the other is open, showing his kindness. On either side of the first room are the two other rooms. Carved on the wall of the second room is the Gettysburg Address. On the wall of the third room is the Second Inaugural Address. Above the Gettysburg Address is a mural showing an angel freeing the slaves. Above the Second Inaugural Address is another mural, which depicts the people of the North and the South coming back together. As its design shows, the Lincoln Memorial was built to celebrate both the sixteenth president and the nation's struggle for democracy.

—Nicole Lentz (student)

Transitions in Descriptive Paragraphs

As you arrange your ideas in a descriptive paragraph, be sure to use appropriate transitional words and phrases to lead readers from one detail to another.

Some Transitional Words and Phrases for Description

above	in	outside
at the edge	in back of	over
at the entrance	in front of	spreading out
behind	inside	the first . . . the second
below	nearby	the least important . . .
between	next to	the most important
beyond	on	the next
down	on one side . . . on the	under
farther	other side	

---

grammar in context

Description

When you write a descriptive paragraph, you sometimes use **modifiers**—words and phrases that describe other words in the sentence. A modifier should be placed as close as possible to the word it is supposed to modify. If you place a modifying word or phrase too far from the word it modifies, you create a **misplaced modifier** that will confuse readers.

CONFUSING (MISPLACED MODIFIER)	Seated in a chair, the long Civil War has clearly exhausted Lincoln. (Was the Civil War seated in a chair?)
CLEAR	Seated in a chair, Lincoln looks exhausted after the long Civil War.

For information on how to identify and correct misplaced modifiers, see Chapter 28.

Analyzing a Descriptive Paragraph

Read this descriptive paragraph; then, follow the instructions in Practice 6-1.

Gen's Lunches

My friend Gen's lunches are as original as they are delicious. Nearly every day, Gen prepares a bento box, or traditional Japanese lunch. Today, she has brought an oval baby blue bento box. In the center of the box are three flattened rice balls that Gen calls onigiri. Using strips and dots of nori seaweed, she has given her onigiri adorable eyes and smiles. Using molded deli meat, she has even added pink circles to the cheeks. Surrounding the rice balls are small portions of tasty foods. For example, above the rice to the left are three breaded and fried zucchini strips that shine with golden oil. Directly above the rice sit two peeled hardboiled eggs; I can just imagine their yummy crumbly yellow yolks. A deli-meat flower perches on each egg, and a cherry tomato snuggles nearby. Above the rice to the right nestle three wedges of sweet winter squash. The contrast between their bright orange flesh and their striped green rinds is very pleasing. Gen's bento boxes always make me hungry, but it's hard to watch her eat her lovely creations—especially the sweet onigiri with their smiling faces.

PRACTICE

6-1

1. Underline the topic sentence of the paragraph above.

2. In a few words, summarize the main idea of the paragraph.

_____

3. What are some of the details the writer uses to describe Gen's bento box lunch? The first detail has been listed for you.

 oval baby blue box _____

_____

_____

_____

_____

_____

4. Circle the transitional words and phrases that the writer uses to lead readers from one detail to another.

5. Underline the paragraph's summary statement.

PRACTICE
6-2   Each of the five topic sentences below states a possible main idea for a descriptive paragraph. For each, list three details that could help convey the main idea. For example, to support the idea that sitting in front of a fireplace is relaxing, you could describe the crackling of the fire, the pine scent of the smoke, and the changing colors of the flames.

1. The most valuable possession I own is _____.

2. The most beautiful place I ever visited is _____.

3. One look at my instructor told me that this was going to be an interesting semester.

4. One of my favorite stores to shop at is _____.

5. My neighborhood is full of distinctive sounds and smells.

6b   Case Study: A Student Writes a Descriptive Paragraph

Here is how one student, Jared Lopez, wrote a descriptive paragraph. When Jared was asked to write a descriptive paragraph about someone he admired, he decided to write about his uncle Manuel, who had been a father figure to him.

Because he was very familiar with his paragraph's subject, Jared did not have to brainstorm or freewrite to find material to write about. Instead, he immediately started to list the features of his uncle that he considered the most memorable.

Looks friendly

Hands

Dark eyes

Distinguished looking

Tall

list details

Choose a person from the brainstorming you did in response to the Focus on Writing prompt on page 98, and then list the details that best describe that person.

_____

_____

_____

After reviewing the list of features he planned to discuss, Jared arranged the features in an informal outline in the order in which he planned to discuss them.

Tall

Looks friendly

Dark eyes

Distinguished looking

Hands

make an outline

Create an informal outline for your paragraph by arranging the details you listed in the order in which you plan to discuss them. You might arrange them in the order in which you observe them— for example, from near to far or from top to bottom—or, as Jared did, in order of importance.

Jared decided to begin his paragraph with a general description of his uncle Manuel and then move on to concentrate on his uncle's most distinctive feature: his hands. Here is the first draft of Jared's paragraph.

My uncle's name is Manuel, but his friends call him Manny. He is over six feet tall. Uncle Manny's eyes are dark brown, almost black. They make him look very serious. When he laughs, however, he looks friendly. His nose is long and straight, and it makes Uncle Manny look very distinguished. Most interesting to me are Uncle Manny's hands. Even though he hasn't worked as a stonemason since he opened his own construction company ten years ago, his hands are still rough and scarred. They are large and strong, but they can be gentle too.

draft your paragraph

Using your informal outline as a guide, draft your descriptive paragraph.

After a conference with his instructor, Jared **TEST**ed his paragraph.

- He decided that he needed to add a **topic sentence** that stated the main idea of his description.
- He decided that he needed to add more descriptive details to give readers more **evidence** of his uncle's strength and gentleness.
- He decided that he needed to add a stronger **summary statement** to unify his paragraph.
- He decided to include more **transitions** to move readers from one part of his description to the next.

Next, Jared revised and edited his draft. The final draft that follows includes all the elements Jared looked for when he **TEST**ed it.

My Uncle Manny

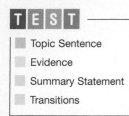
My uncle Manuel is a strong but gentle person who took care of my mother and me when my father died. Manuel, or "Manny" as his friends and family call him, is over six feet tall. This is unusual for a Mexican of his generation. The first thing most people notice about my uncle Manny is his eyes. They are large and dark brown, almost black. They make him look very serious. When he laughs, however, the sides of his eyes crinkle up and he looks warm and friendly. Another thing that stands out is his nose, which is long and straight. My mother says it makes Uncle Manny look strong and distinguished. The most striking thing about Uncle Manny is his hands. Even though he hasn't worked as a stonemason since he opened his own construction company ten years ago, his hands are still rough and scarred from carrying stones. No matter how much he tries, he can't get rid of the dirt under the skin of his fingers. Uncle Manny's hands are big and rough, but they are also gentle and comforting. To me, they show what he really is: a strong and gentle man.

TEST · **Revise** · **Edit**

Look back at the draft of your descriptive paragraph. Using the **TEST** checklist on page 107, evaluate your paragraph to make sure it includes a topic sentence, evidence, a summary statement, and transitions. Then, prepare a revised and edited draft of your paragraph.

PRACTICE

6-3   For additional practice in writing a descriptive paragraph, chose one of the topics below.

A favorite place	A favorite article of clothing
A place you felt trapped in	A useful object
A comfortable spot on campus	A pet
An unusual person	A building you think is ugly
Your dream house	Your car or truck
A family member or friend	The car you would like to have
A work of art	A statue or monument
A valued possession	Someone you admire
Your workplace	A cooking disaster

Then, follow the process outlined in 6b to create your descriptive paragraph.

TESTing a descriptive paragraph

Topic Sentence Unifies Your Paragraph

☐ Do you have a clearly worded **topic sentence** that states your paragraph's main idea—the general impression you want to convey?

☐ Does your topic sentence identify the person, place, or thing you will describe in your paragraph?

Evidence Supports Your Paragraph's Topic Sentence

☐ Does all your **evidence**—descriptive details—support your paragraph's main idea?

☐ Do you have enough descriptive details, or do you need to include more?

Summary Statement Reinforces Your Paragraph's Unity

☐ Does your paragraph end with a **summary statement** that reinforces your main idea?

Transitions Add Coherence to Your Paragraph

☐ Do your **transitions** lead readers from one detail to the next?

☐ Do you need to add transitions to make your paragraph clearer and to help readers follow your ideas?

6c Writing about Visuals

The picture on page 108 shows a house surrounded by lush landscaping. Write a paragraph describing the house for a real estate brochure. Use your imagination to invent details that describe its setting, exterior, and interior. Your goal in this **descriptive** paragraph is to persuade a prospective buyer to purchase the house.

7 Process

focus on writing

This picture shows the board game Mancala, which archaeologists believe has existed in one form or another for at least 1,300 years. Brainstorm to develop a list of games you know well and could explain to others. You will return to this topic and review your brainstorming later in the chapter when you write your process paragraph.

In this chapter, you will learn to write a process paragraph.

7a Process Paragraphs

When you describe a **process**, you tell readers how something works or how to do something. For example, you could explain how the optical scanner at the checkout counter of a food store works, how to hem a pair of pants, or how to set up an email account on a smartphone. A **process paragraph** tells readers how to complete a process by listing steps in time order.

When you **TEST** a process paragraph, make sure it follows these guidelines:

T ▪ A process paragraph should begin with a **topic sentence** that identifies the process you are explaining and the point you want to make about it (for example, "Parallel parking is easy once you know the secret" or "By following a few simple steps, you can design a résumé that will get noticed").

E ▪ A process paragraph should discuss all the steps in the process, one at a time. These steps should be presented in strict **time order**—the order in which they occur. A process paragraph should present enough **evidence**—examples and details—to explain the steps and make the process clear to readers.

S ▪ A process paragraph should end with a **summary statement** that reinforces the paragraph's main idea.

T ▪ A process paragraph should include **transitions** that connect the steps in the process to one another and to the topic sentence.

Paragraph Map: Process

Topic Sentence

Step #1

Step #2

Step #3

Summary Statement

110

There are two types of process paragraphs: *process explanations* and *instructions*.

Model Paragraph: Process Explanations

In a **process explanation**, your purpose is to help readers understand how something works or how something happens—for example, how a hurricane forms or how to do a database search. With a process explanation, you do not expect readers to perform the process.

In the following process explanation paragraph from a psychology exam, the writer explains the four stages children go through when they acquire language.

> Children go through four distinct stages when they learn language. The first stage begins as soon as infants are born. By crying, they let people know when they need something or if they are in pain. The second stage begins when children are about a year old and are able to communicate with single words. For example, a child will use the word *food* to mean anything from "I'm hungry" to "feed the dog." The third stage begins at about twenty months. During this stage, children begin to use two-word sentences, such as "dada car" (for "This is dada's car"). Finally, at about thirty months, children begin to learn the rules that govern language. They learn how to form simple sentences, plurals, and the past tense of verbs. No matter what language they speak, all children follow the same process when they learn language.
>
> —Jennifer Gulla (student)

TEST
- Topic Sentence
- Evidence
- Summary Statement
- Transitions

Steps presented in time order

Model Paragraph: Instructions

When you write **instructions**, your purpose is to give readers the information they need to perform a task or activity—for example, to fill out an application, to operate a piece of machinery, or to help someone who is choking. Because you expect readers to follow your instructions, you address them directly, using **commands** to tell them what to do (*check the gauge . . . pull the valve*).

In the following paragraph, the writer gives a humorous set of instructions on how to get food out of a defective vending machine.

Man vs. Machine

> There is a foolproof method of outsmarting a vending machine that refuses to give up its food. First, approach the vending machine coolly. Make sure that you don't seem frightened or angry. The machine will sense these emotions and steal your money. Second, be polite.

TEST
- Topic Sentence
- Evidence
- Summary Statement
- Transitions

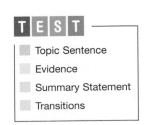

Step-by-step instructions presented in time order

Step-by-step
instructions presented
in time order

Say hello, compliment the machine on its selection of goodies, and smile. Be careful. If the machine thinks you are trying to take advantage of it, it will steal your money. Third, if the machine steals your money, remain calm. Ask nicely to get the food you paid for. Finally, it is time to get serious. Hit the side of the vending machine with your fist. If this doesn't work, lower your shoulder and throw yourself at the machine. (A good kick or two might also help.) When the machine has had enough, it will drop your snack, and you can grab it. If you follow these few simple steps, you should have no trouble walking away from vending machines with the food you paid for.

—Adam Cooper (student)

Transitions in Process Paragraphs

Transitions are very important in process paragraphs like the two you have just read. They enable readers to clearly identify each step—for example, *first*, *second*, *third*, and so on. In addition, they establish a sequence that lets readers move easily through the process you are describing.

Some Transitional Words and Phrases for Process

after that, after this	first	subsequently
as	immediately	the first (second, third) step
as soon as	later	the next step
at the same time	meanwhile	the last step
at this point	next	then
during	now	when
finally	once	while
	soon	

grammar in context

Process

When you write a process paragraph, you may find yourself making **illogical shifts** in tense, person, and voice. If you shift from one tense, person, or voice to another without good reason, you may confuse readers.

CONFUSING (ILLOGICAL SHIFT) First, the vending machine should be approached coolly. Make sure that you don't seem frightened or angry. (illogical shift from passive to active voice)

> CLEAR   First, approach the vending machine coolly. Make
> sure that you don't seem frightened or angry.
> (consistent use of active voice)
>
> *For information on how to avoid illogical shifts in tense, person, and
> voice, see Chapter 27.*
>
> ✔ **LearningCurve** For more practice with shifts in tense and voice, complete the Verbs and
> Active and Passive Voice activities at **bedfordstmartins.com/focusonwriting.**

Analyzing a Process Paragraph

Read this process paragraph; then, follow the instructions in Practice 7-1.

An Order of Fries

I never realized how much work goes into making French fries until I worked at a potato processing plant in Hermiston, Oregon. The process begins with freshly dug potatoes being shoveled from trucks onto conveyor belts leading into the plant. During this stage, workers pick out any rocks that may have been dug up with the potatoes because these could damage the automated peelers. After the potatoes have gone through the peelers, they travel on a conveyor belt through the "trim line." Here, workers cut out any bad spots, being careful not to waste potatoes by trimming too much. Next, the potatoes are sliced by automated cutters and then deep-fried for about a minute. After this, they continue along a conveyor belt to the "wet line." Here, workers again look for bad spots, and they throw away any rotten pieces. At this point, the potatoes go to a second set of fryers for three minutes before being moved to subzero freezers for ten minutes. Then, it's on to the "frozen line" for a final inspection. The inspected fries are weighed by machines and then sealed into five-pound plastic packages, which are weighed again by workers who also check that the packages are properly sealed. Finally, the bags are packed into boxes and made ready for shipment to various restaurants across the western United States. This process goes on twenty-four hours a day to bring consumers the French fries they enjoy so much.

—Cheri Rodriguez (student)

PRACTICE

7-1

1. Underline the topic sentence of the paragraph on page 113.

2. Is this a process explanation or instructions?

_____

How do you know? _____

3. List the steps in the process. The first step has been listed for you.

The potatoes are unloaded, and the rocks are sorted out. _____

_____

_____

_____

_____

_____

_____

4. Circle the transitional words and phrases that the writer uses to move readers from one step to the next.

5. Underline the paragraph's summary statement.

PRACTICE

7-2

Following are four possible topic sentences for process paragraphs. List three or four steps that explain the process each topic sentence identifies. For example, if you were explaining the process of getting a job, you could list preparing a résumé, looking at ads in newspapers or online, writing a job application letter, and going on an interview. Make sure each step follows logically from the one that precedes it.

1. Getting the lowest prices when you shop is not a simple process.

2. Getting the most out of a student-teacher conference requires some preparation.

3. Cage-training a puppy can be a tricky process.

4. Choosing the perfect outfit for a job interview can be challenging.

7b Case Study: A Student Writes a Process Paragraph

Here is how one student, Manasvi Bari, wrote a process paragraph. When Manasvi was assigned to write a paragraph in which she explained a process she performed every day, she decided to write about how to get a seat on a crowded subway car. To make sure she had enough to write about, she made the following list of possible steps she could include.

Don't pay attention to heat

Get into the train

Get the first seat

Look as if you need help

Get to a pole

Don't travel during rush hour

Choose your time

Be alert

Squeeze in

After looking over her list, Manasvi crossed out steps that she didn't think were essential to the process she wanted to describe.

~~Don't pay attention to heat~~

Get into the train

Get the first seat

Look as if you need help

~~Get to a pole~~

~~Don't travel during rush hour~~

~~Choose your time~~

Be alert

Squeeze in

list the steps in the process

Choose one game from the brainstorming you did in response to the Focus on Writing prompt on page 109, and then list the steps you need to discuss in order to explain how to play the game. (Assume that your readers know nothing about the game you are describing.)

_____

_____

_____

_____

_____

Now, cross out any steps that you don't think readers will need in order to understand how to play the game.

Once she had decided on her list of steps, Manasvi made an informal outline, arranging the steps in the order in which they should be performed.

Get into the train

Be alert

Get the first seat

Squeeze in

Look as if you need help

make an outline

Create an informal outline for your paragraph by arranging the steps for playing your game in the order in which they should be performed.

At this point, Manasvi thought that she was ready to begin writing her paragraph. Here is her draft.

> When the train arrives, get into the car as fast as possible. Be alert. If you see an empty seat, grab it and sit down immediately. If there is no seat, ask people to move down, or squeeze into a space that seems too small. If none of this works, you'll have to use some imagination. Look helpless. Drop your books, and look as if the day can't get any worse. Sometimes a person will get up and give you a seat. If this strategy doesn't work, stand near someone who looks as if he or she is going to get up. When the person gets up, jump into the seat as fast as you can. Don't let the people who are getting on the train get the seat before you do.

draft your paragraph

Using your informal outline as a guide, draft your process paragraph.

Manasvi showed the draft of her paragraph to a writing center tutor. Together, they **TEST**ed her paragraph and made the following decisions.

- They decided that she needed to add a **topic sentence** that identified the process and stated the point she wanted to make about it.
- They decided that her **evidence**—the examples and details that described the steps in her process—was clear and complete.
- They decided that she needed to add a **summary statement** that reinforced the point of the process.
- They decided that she needed to add **transitions** that helped readers follow the steps in the process.

At this point, Manasvi revised and edited her paragraph. The final draft below includes all the elements Manasvi looked for when she **TEST**ed her paragraph.

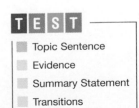

T E S T
- Topic Sentence
- Evidence
- Summary Statement
- Transitions

Surviving Rush Hour

Anyone who takes the subway to school in the morning knows how hard it is to find a seat, but by following a few simple steps, you should be able to get a seat almost every day. First, when the train arrives, get into the car as fast as possible. Be alert. As soon as you see an empty seat, grab it and sit down immediately. Meanwhile, if there is no seat, ask people to move down, or try to squeeze into a space that seems too small. If none of this works, the next step is to use some imagination. Look helpless. Drop your books, and look as if the day can't get any worse. Sometimes a person will get up and give you a seat. Don't be shy. Take it, and remember to say thank you. Finally, if this strategy doesn't work, stand near someone who looks as if he or she is going to get up. When the person gets up, jump into the seat as fast as you can. By following these steps, you should be able to get a seat on the subway and arrive at school rested and relaxed.

TEST · Revise · Edit

Look back at the draft of your process paragraph. Using the **TEST** checklist on page 119, evaluate your paragraph to make sure it includes a topic sentence, evidence, a summary statement, and transitions. Then, prepare a revised and edited draft of your paragraph.

PRACTICE

7-3   For additional practice in writing a process paragraph, choose one of the topics below.

Studying for exams
Strategies for winning arguments
How to arrange a tailgate party
How to be a good friend
How to discourage telemarketers
Your morning routine
How to deep-fry a turkey
How to perform a particular
  household repair
How to quit smoking
How to save money

How to drive in snow
How to apply for
  financial aid
A process involved in a
  hobby of yours
How to build something
How to make your
  favorite dish
How to prepare for a storm
How to operate a piece of
  machinery

Then, follow the process outlined in 7b to create your process paragraph.

TESTing a process paragraph

Topic Sentence Unifies Your Paragraph

☐ Do you have a clearly worded **topic sentence** that states your paragraph's main idea?

☐ Does your topic sentence identify the process you will discuss?

☐ Does your topic sentence indicate whether you will be explaining a process or giving instructions?

Evidence Supports Your Paragraph's Topic Sentence

☐ Have you included all the steps in the process?

☐ Have you included enough **evidence**—examples and details—to explain the steps and make the process clear to readers?

☐ If your paragraph is a set of instructions, have you included all the information readers need to perform the process?

Summary Statement Reinforces Your Paragraph's Unity

☐ Does your paragraph end with a **summary statement** that reinforces your main idea?

Transitions Add Coherence to Your Paragraph

☐ Do your **transitions** move readers from one step in the process to the next?

☐ Do you need to add transitions to make your paragraph clearer and to help readers follow your ideas?

7c Writing about Visuals

The picture on page 120 shows John Belushi as John "Bluto" Blutarski in the infamous toga scene from the 1978 film *Animal House*. Study the picture carefully, and then list the steps that would be involved in planning a party like this one. Use this list to help you write a **process** paragraph that presents step-by-step instructions in the order in which they need to be done. Be sure to include any necessary cautions and reminders—for example, "Don't forget to invite your neighbors"—to help your readers avoid potential problems.

8 Cause and Effect

focus on writing

This picture shows a variety of electronic devices. Freewrite about the electronic devices that have had an impact, positive or negative, on you and your family. You will return to this topic and review your freewriting later in the chapter when you write your cause-and-effect paragraph.

8a Cause-and-Effect Paragraphs

Why is the cost of college so high in the United States? How does smoking affect a person's health? What would happen if the city increased its sales tax? How dangerous is the flu? All these questions have one thing in common: they try to determine the causes or effects of an action, event, or situation.

A **cause** is something or someone that makes something happen. An **effect** is something brought about by a particular cause.

CAUSE		EFFECT
Increased airport security	⟶	Long lines at airports
Weight gain	⟶	Health problems
Seat belt laws passed	⟶	Traffic deaths reduced

A **cause-and-effect paragraph** examines or analyzes reasons and results. It helps readers understand why something happened or is happening or shows how one thing affects another.

When you **TEST** a cause-and-effect paragraph, make sure it follows these guidelines:

T ▪ A cause-and-effect paragraph should begin with a **topic sentence** that tells readers whether the paragraph is focusing on causes or on effects—for example, "There are several reasons why the cost of gas is so high" (causes) or "Going to the writing center has given me confidence as well as skill as a writer" (effects).

E ▪ A cause-and-effect paragraph should present **evidence**—examples and details—to support the topic sentence and explain each cause and effect. Causes or effects should be arranged in **logical order**—for example, from least to most important.

S ▪ A cause-and-effect paragraph should end with a **summary statement** that reinforces the paragraph's main idea.

T ▪ A cause-and-effect paragraph should include **transitions** that connect causes or effects to one another and to the topic sentence.

Paragraph Map: Cause and Effect

> **Topic Sentence**
>
> *Cause (or effect) #1*
>
> *Cause (or effect) #2*
>
> *Cause (or effect) #3*
>
> **Summary Statement**

Model Paragraph: Causes

The following paragraph focuses on **causes**.

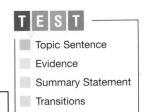

Why Young People Don't Vote

    There are several reasons why young adults do not often vote in national elections. The first reason is that many young people are just not interested in politics. They are busy getting an education or working, and they do not take the time to think about politics or which candidate to vote for. Another reason is that they do not think that their vote is important. They think that because millions of people are voting, their vote will not have an effect on the outcome of an election. A third reason is that many young people do not think that the candidates are speaking to them. They do not think that national issues such as capital gains taxes, Social Security, and Medicare have much to do with them. Finally, many young people are turned off by politics and politicians. As far as they are concerned, politicians just want to get elected and will say anything to get votes. Until these issues are addressed, many young people will continue to stay away from the polls.

—Moniquetta Hall (student)

Causes arranged in logical order

Model Paragraph: Effects

The following paragraph focuses on **effects**.

The Negative Effects of Climate Change

Effects arranged in logical order

Climate change caused by global warming would have several negative effects. One effect would be an increase in the number of intense storms. Large hurricanes and other types of storms would damage property and kill many people. Another effect would be a rise in sea level. As the earth warms, the polar ice would melt and raise the level of the earth's oceans. Coastal cities and low-lying areas would probably be flooded. Still another effect would be the spread of certain kinds of diseases. Many diseases, now found only in warm areas, would spread to areas that were once cool but then became warm. Malaria and yellow fever, for example, could become as common in the United States as they are in Africa and Southeast Asia. Finally, climate change associated with global warming would affect agriculture. Farming areas, such as the Midwest, where American farmers grow corn and wheat, would become dry. As a result, there would be food shortages, and many people could go hungry. No one knows for certain what will happen, but if global warming continues, our lives will certainly be affected.

—Jackie Hue (student)

Transitions in Cause-and-Effect Paragraphs

Transitions in cause-and-effect paragraphs, as illustrated in the two paragraphs above, introduce individual causes or effects. They may also show the connections between a cause and its effects or between an effect and its causes. In addition, they may indicate which cause or effect is more important than another.

Some Transitional Words and Phrases for Cause and Effect

accordingly	moreover	the first (second, third)
another cause	since	reason
another effect	so	the most important cause
as a result	the first (second,	the most important effect
because	third, final) cause	therefore
consequently	the first (second,	
for	third, final) effect	
for this reason		

grammar in context

Cause and Effect

When you write a cause-and-effect paragraph, you should be careful not to confuse the words *affect* and *effect*. *Affect* is a verb meaning "to influence." *Effect* is a noun meaning "result."

> *effect*
> One ~~affect~~ would be an increase in the number of storms.

(*effect* is a noun)

> No one knows for certain what will happen, but if global warming continues, our lives will certainly be ~~effected~~.
> *affected*

(*affect* is a verb)

For more information on effect *and* affect, *see 23g.*

Analyzing a Cause-and-Effect Paragraph

Read this cause-and-effect paragraph; then, follow the instructions in Practice 8-1.

The Decline of Orphanages in the United States

There are several reasons for the decline of U.S. orphanages after World War II. First, people discovered that children who are not hugged and snuggled fail to thrive. As a result, "child rescue" groups were formed to bring the warmth of families to children. Second, although the U.S. government supported many orphanages, religious groups ran many others. Some politicians distrusted this relationship between religious groups and orphans; after all, the United States has a tradition of separation of church and state. Finally, the government saw that it was less expensive to give financial assistance to poor parents than to maintain large orphanages. Consequently, a program called Aid to Dependent Children, which was part of the 1935 Social Security Act, was established to support children in their own homes. In 1960, the program was expanded to include children in foster care. For these reasons, orphanages are seldom seen in the United States today.

PRACTICE

8-1

1. Underline the topic sentence of the paragraph on page 125.

2. List the words that tell you the writer is moving from one cause to another in the paragraph. The first answer has been listed for you.

First _____

_____

_____

3. List the causes the writer describes. The first cause has been listed for you.

"Child rescue" movements were formed to bring the warmth of families to children.

_____

_____

_____

4. Circle the transitional words and phrases that the writer uses to identify causes.

5. Underline the paragraph's summary statement.

PRACTICE

8-2

Following are four possible topic sentences for cause-and-effect paragraphs. For each topic sentence, list the effects that could result from the cause identified in the topic sentence. For example, if you were writing a paragraph about the effects of excessive drinking on campus, you could list low grades, health problems, and vandalism.

1. Having a baby can change your life.

2. Being bilingual has many advantages.

3. College has made me a different person.

4. Impulse buying can have negative effects on a person's finances.

PRACTICE

8-3   List three causes that could support each of the following topic sentences.

1. The causes of teenage obesity are easy to identify.

2. Chronic unemployment can have many causes.

3. The high cost of college tuition is not easy to explain.

4. There are several reasons why professional athletes' salaries are so high.

8b   Case Study: A Student Writes a Cause-and-Effect Paragraph

Here is how one student, Sean Jin, wrote a cause-and-effect paragraph. When Sean was asked to write a cause-and-effect essay for his composition class, he had no trouble thinking of a topic because of a debate that was going on in his hometown about building a Walmart Superstore there. He decided to write a paragraph that discussed the effects that such a store would have on the local economy.

Sean's instructor told the class the main problem to watch for in planning a cause-and-effect essay is making sure that a **causal relationship** exists—that one event actually causes another. In other words, just because one event follows another closely in time, students should not assume that the second event was caused by the first.

With this advice in mind, Sean brainstormed to develop a list of possible effects a Walmart would have on his small town. Here is Sean's list of effects.

Provide new jobs

Offer low-cost items

Pay low wages

Push out small businesses

list effects

Choose one electronic device from the freewriting you did in response to the Focus on Writing prompt on page 121. Then, brainstorm to develop a list of the effects that device has had on you and your family.

_____

_____

_____

_____

_____

_____

After reviewing his list of effects, Sean drafted a topic sentence that introduced his topic and communicated the point he wanted to make about it. Here is Sean's topic sentence.

Walmart can have good and bad effects on a small town.

write a topic sentence

Review your list of effects, and then draft a topic sentence for your cause-and-effect paragraph.

_____

_____

Next, Sean made an informal outline that arranged the effects on his list in a logical order. This outline helped him check to make sure he had included enough examples to explain each effect and to support his topic sentence. Here is Sean's outline.

Good effects

Provides new jobs

 —Store needs many employees
 —Many people out of work in rural town and need jobs

Offers low-cost items
—Families on a budget can buy things they usually can't afford
—Walmart prices lower than most other stores' prices

Bad effects

Pays low wages
—Walmart pays less than other stores

Pushes out small businesses
—Forces many small businesses to close
—Local businesses can't match low prices or wide selection

make an outline

Create an informal outline for your paragraph by arranging your list of effects in a logical order—for example, from least to most important.

After completing his outline, Sean wrote the following draft of his paragraph.

> Walmart can have good and bad effects on a small town. It provides jobs. A large store needs a lot of employees. So, many people from the area will be able to find work. Walmart's prices are low. Families that don't have much money may be able to buy things they can't afford to buy at other stores. Not all of Walmart's effects are positive. Walmart pays employees less than other stores. Walmart provides jobs, but those jobs don't pay very much. When Walmart comes into an area, many small businesses are forced to close. They just can't match Walmart's prices or stock as much merchandise as Walmart can.

draft your paragraph

Using your informal outline as a guide, draft your cause-and-effect paragraph.

When he finished his draft, Sean went to the writing center and met with a tutor. After going over his draft with the tutor and TESTing his paragraph, Sean made the following decisions.

- He decided that he needed to sharpen his **topic sentence** to tie his discussion of Walmart to the small town in which he lived.
- He decided to provide more **evidence** to support his topic sentence— for example, what exactly does Walmart pay its salespeople?
- He realized that he needed to add a **summary statement** to reinforce his main idea.
- He decided to add **transitions** to identify positive and negative effects.

Now Sean was ready to revise and edit his paragraph. The final draft below includes all the elements Sean looked for when he TESTed his paragraph.

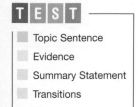

T E S T

- ☐ Topic Sentence
- ☐ Evidence
- ☐ Summary Statement
- ☐ Transitions

Walmart Comes to Town

When Walmart comes to a small town like mine, it can have good and bad effects. The first and most positive effect is that it provides jobs. A large Walmart Superstore needs a lot of employees, so many people will be able to find work. In my rural town, over 15 percent of the people are out of work. Walmart could give these people a chance to improve their lives. Another positive effect that Walmart can have is to keep prices low so families on tight budgets will be able to buy things they cannot afford to buy at other stores. My own observations show that many items at a local Walmart are cheaper than those at other stores. Not all of Walmart's effects are positive, however. One negative effect Walmart can have is that it can actually lower wages in an area. My aunt, a longtime employee, says that Walmart pays beginning workers between $8 and $10 an hour. This is less than they would get in stores that pay union wages. Another negative effect Walmart can have is to drive other, smaller businesses out. When Walmart comes into an area, many small businesses are forced to close. They just cannot match Walmart's prices or selection of merchandise. It is clear that although Walmart can have a number of positive effects, it can also have some negative ones.

TEST · **Revise · Edit**

Look back at the draft of your cause-and-effect paragraph. Using the TEST checklist on pages 131–132, evaluate your paragraph to make sure it includes a topic sentence, evidence, a summary statement, and transitions. Then, prepare a revised and edited draft of your paragraph.

PRACTICE

8-4   For additional practice in writing a cause-and-effect paragraph, choose one of the topics below.

Why a particular video went viral

Some causes (or effects) of stress

The negative health effects of junk food

Why some college students engage in binge drinking

The reasons you decided to attend college

The effects of a particular government policy

How becoming a vegetarian might change (or has changed) your life

The benefits of home cooking

Why a particular sport is (or is not) popular

How an important event in your life influenced you

The possible effects of violent song lyrics on teenagers

The problems of social-networking sites

Why some people find writing difficult

Why students drop out of high school or college

How managers can get the best (or the worst) from their employees

Then, follow the process outlined in 8b to create your cause-and-effect paragraph.

TESTing a cause-and-effect paragraph

T opic Sentence Unifies Your Paragraph

☐ Do you have a clearly worded **topic sentence** that states your paragraph's main idea?

☐ Does your topic sentence identify the cause or effect on which your paragraph will focus?

E vidence Supports Your Paragraph's Topic Sentence

☐ Do you need to add any important causes or effects?

☐ Do you need to explain your causes or effects more fully?

(continued)

(continued from previous page)

☐ Does all your **evidence**—examples and details—support your paragraph's main idea?

Summary Statement Reinforces Your Paragraph's Unity

☐ Does your paragraph end with a **summary statement** that reinforces your main idea?

Transitions Add Coherence to Your Paragraph

☐ Do your **transitions** show how your ideas are related?

☐ Do your transitions clearly introduce each cause or effect?

☐ Do you need to add transitions to make your paragraph clearer and to help readers follow your ideas?

8c Writing about Visuals

The picture below shows a homeless man with a winning lottery ticket. Write a **cause-and-effect** paragraph in which you discuss the ways in which this man's life might change now that he has won the lottery. Try to consider negative as well as positive effects.

9 Comparison and Contrast

focus on writing

These two pictures are from *Red Carpet Fashion Awards*, a Web site that tracks the latest in celebrity fashion trends. Look at the two pictures, and then brainstorm to identify the differences that can best help you write a paragraph that answers the question, "Who wore it better?" You will return to this topic and review your brainstorming later in the chapter when you write your comparison-and-contrast paragraph.

In this chapter, you will learn to write a comparison-and-contrast paragraph.

9a Comparison-and-Contrast Paragraphs

When you buy something—for example, a hair dryer, a smartphone, a computer, or a car—you often comparison-shop, looking at various models to determine how they are alike and how they are different. In other words, you *compare and contrast*. When you **compare**, you consider how things are similar. When you **contrast**, you consider how they are different. A **comparison-and-contrast paragraph** can examine just similarities, just differences, or both similarities and differences.

When you **TEST** a comparison-and-contrast paragraph, make sure it follows these guidelines:

T ■ A comparison-and-contrast paragraph should begin with a **topic sentence** that tells readers whether the paragraph is going to discuss similarities, differences, or both. The topic sentence should also make clear the main point of the comparison—why you are comparing or contrasting the two subjects (for example, "The writers Toni Morrison and Maya Angelou have similar ideas about race and society" or "My parents and I have different ideas about success").

E ■ A comparison-and-contrast paragraph should include enough **evidence**—examples and details—to make the similarities and differences clear to readers. A comparison-and-contrast paragraph should discuss the same or similar points for both subjects, one by one. Points should be arranged in **logical order**—for example, from least to most important.

S ■ A comparison-and-contrast paragraph should end with a **summary statement** that reinforces the paragraph's main idea.

T ■ A comparison-and-contrast paragraph should include **transitions** that connect the two subjects being compared and link the points you make about each subject.

There are two kinds of comparison-and-contrast paragraphs: *subject-by-subject comparisons* and *point-by-point comparisons*.

Subject-by-Subject Comparisons

In a **subject-by-subject comparison**, you divide your comparison into two parts and discuss one subject at a time. In the first part of the paragraph, you discuss all your points about one subject. Then, in the second part, you discuss the same (or similar) points about the other subject. (In each part of the paragraph, you discuss the points in the same order.)

A subject-by-subject comparison is best for paragraphs in which you do not discuss too many points. In this situation, readers will have little difficulty remembering the points you discuss for the first subject when you move on to discuss the second subject.

Paragraph Map: Subject-by-Subject Comparison

Topic Sentence

Subject A
> Point #1

> Point #2

> Point #3

Subject B
> Point #1

> Point #2

> Point #3

Summary Statement

Model Paragraph: Subject-by-Subject Comparison

The writer of the following paragraph uses a subject-by-subject comparison to compare two places to eat on campus.

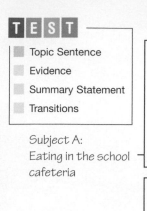

T E S T

- [ ] Topic Sentence
- [ ] Evidence
- [ ] Summary Statement
- [ ] Transitions

*Subject A:
Eating in the school
cafeteria*

*Subject B:
Eating at the food
trucks*

Food trucks are a good alternative to the campus cafeteria. Eating in the cafeteria takes a lot of time. Students have to go into a building, wait in line, walk down some stairs, and find a table. In addition, the cafeteria usually has a limited variety of food, with only two or three different hot meals and some prepackaged sandwiches. The food is cooked in advance, and after sitting on a steam tray for a few hours, it is dry and lukewarm. Finally, food in the cafeteria costs a lot. Students who are not on a food plan can easily spend seven or eight dollars for dinner. In contrast, the food trucks are much quicker than the cafeteria. Most food trucks serve a meal in less than five minutes. If the weather is nice, students can sit anywhere on campus and eat. In addition, the food trucks offer a lot of choices. Some of the trucks, such as the ones that sell Chinese food, even sell platters. In addition, the food from the trucks is fresh and hot most of the time. Finally, meals from a food truck usually cost less than five dollars. This is a big savings, especially if a student is on a tight budget. For this reason, the food trucks are often a better choice than the cafeteria.

—Dan Lindt (student)

Point-by-Point Comparisons

When you write a **point-by-point comparison**, you discuss a point about one subject and then discuss the same point for the second subject. You use this alternating pattern throughout the paragraph.

A point-by-point comparison is a better strategy for long paragraphs in which you discuss many points. It is also a better choice if the points you are discussing are technical or complicated. Because you compare the two subjects one point at a time, readers will be able to see one point of comparison before moving on to the next point.

Paragraph Map: Point-by-Point Comparison

Topic Sentence

Point #1

    Subject A

    Subject B

Point #2

    Subject A

    Subject B

Point #3

    Subject A

    Subject B

Summary Statement

Model Paragraph: Point-by-Point Comparison

In the following paragraph, the writer uses a point-by-point-comparison to compare two characters in a short story.

T E S T

▨ Topic Sentence
▨ Evidence
▨ Summary Statement
▨ Transitions

Two Sisters

Although they grew up together, Maggie and Dee, the two sisters in Alice Walker's short story "Everyday Use," are very different. Maggie, who was burned in a fire, is shy and has low self-esteem. When she walks, she shuffles her feet and looks down at the ground. Her sister Dee, however, is confident and outgoing. She looks people in the eye when she talks to them and is very opinionated. —Point 1: Different personalities

Maggie and Dee also have different attitudes toward life. Maggie never complains or asks for anything more than she has. She has remained at home with her mother in rural Georgia. In contrast, Dee has always wanted nicer things. She has gone away to school and hardly ever visits her mother and Maggie. —Point 2: Different attitudes toward life

The biggest difference between Maggie and Dee is their attitude toward tradition. Although Maggie values her family's rural American traditions, Dee values her African heritage. Maggie cherishes her family's handmade quilts and furniture, hoping to use them with her own family. In contrast, Dee sees the handmade objects as things to be displayed and shown off, not used every day. The many differences between Maggie and Dee add conflict and tension to the story. —Point 3: Different attitudes toward tradition

—Margaret Caracappa (student)

Transitions in Comparison-and-Contrast Paragraphs

Transitions are important in a comparison-and-contrast paragraph. Transitions tell readers when you are changing from one point (or one subject) to another. Transitions also make your paragraph more coherent by showing readers whether you are focusing on similarities (for example, *likewise* or *similarly*) or differences (for example, *although* or *in contrast*).

Some Transitional Words and Phrases for Comparison and Contrast

although	one difference . . . another difference
but	one similarity . . . another similarity
even though	on the contrary
however	on the one hand . . . on the other hand
in comparison	similarly
in contrast	though
like	unlike
likewise	whereas
nevertheless	

grammar in context

Comparison and Contrast

When you write a comparison-and-contrast paragraph, you should express the points you are comparing in **parallel** terms to highlight their similarities or differences.

NOT PARALLEL   Although Maggie values her family's traditions, the African heritage of her family is the thing that Dee values.

PARALLEL   Although Maggie <u>values</u> her family's <u>traditions</u>, Dee <u>values</u> her African <u>heritage</u>.

For more information on revising to make ideas parallel, see Chapter 22.

☑ LearningCurve For more practice with parallelism, complete the Parallelism activity at **bedfordstmartins.com/focusonwriting.**

Analyzing a Comparison-and-Contrast Paragraph

Read this comparison-and-contrast paragraph; then, follow the instructions in Practice 9-1.

Virtual and Traditional Classrooms

Taking a course online is very different from taking a course in a traditional classroom. One difference is that students in an online course have more flexibility than students in a traditional course. They can do their schoolwork at any time, scheduling it around other commitments, such as jobs and childcare. Students in a traditional course, however, must go to class at a specific time and place. Another difference is that students in an online course can feel isolated from the teacher and other students because they never actually come into physical contact with them. Students in a traditional classroom, however, are able to connect with the teacher and their classmates because they interact with them in person. A final difference is that in an online course, students use email or a discussion board to discuss course material. A student who is a slow typist or whose Internet connection is unreliable is clearly at a disadvantage. In a traditional course, most of the discussion takes place in the classroom, so technology is not an issue. Because online and traditional courses are so different, students must think carefully about which type of course best fits their needs.

—William Hernandez (student)

PRACTICE

1. Underline the topic sentence of the paragraph above.

2. Does this paragraph deal mainly with similarities or differences?

_____ How do you know? _____

_____

3. Is this paragraph a subject-by-subject or point-by-point comparison?

_____ How do you know? _____

_____

4. List some of the contrasts the writer describes. The first contrast has been listed for you.

When it comes to their schedules, students in an online course have more flexibility

than students in a traditional course do.

_____

_____

_____

_____

_____

5. Circle the transitional words and phrases the writer uses to move from one point of comparison to the next.

6. Underline the paragraph's summary statement.

PRACTICE

9-2   Following are three topic sentences. For each topic sentence, list three or four similarities or differences between the two subjects. For example, if you were writing a paragraph comparing health care provided by a local clinic with health care provided by a private doctor, you could discuss the cost, the length of waiting time, the quality of care, and the frequency of follow-up visits.

1. My mother (or father) and I are very different (or alike).

2. My friends and I have different views on _____.

3. Two of my college instructors have very different teaching styles.

9b   Case Study: A Student Writes a Comparison-and-Contrast Paragraph

Here is how one student, Jermond Love, wrote a comparison-and-contrast paragraph. When Jermond was given this assignment for his composition class, he began by brainstorming to find a topic. When he reviewed his brainstorming notes, he decided that the following topics looked most promising.

Football and soccer

American and Caribbean cooking

The differences between my brother and me

Life in Saint Croix versus life in New York City

After considering each of these topics, Jermond decided to write about the differences between life in Saint Croix, the Caribbean island where he was raised, and life in New York City. He listed various points that he thought he could compare and contrast. Then, he crossed out the ones he didn't want to write about.

Size

~~Economy~~

~~Businesses~~

Lifestyle

~~Politics~~

~~Education~~

~~Music~~

~~Agriculture~~

~~Sports~~

~~Living conditions~~

~~Industry~~

~~Traditions~~

After thinking about the relative sizes of Saint Croix and New York City as well as their respective lifestyles, Jermond brainstormed again to identify some specific differences that he could discuss in his paragraph.

Population: 60,000 versus over 8 million

Hurried versus laid-back lifestyle

Five boroughs versus Christiansted and Frederiksted

Friendly versus not friendly

list differences

Look over the brainstorming you did in response to the Focus on Writing prompt on page 133, and then cross out the differences that you do not want to discuss in your paragraph. On the lines below, list the differences you do plan to discuss.

_____

_____

_____

_____

After reviewing his list of differences, Jermond drafted the following topic sentence. This sentence told readers that he was going to focus on differences, and it also identified the main point he was going to make in his comparison-and-contrast paragraph.

TOPIC SENTENCE   Life in Saint Croix is very different from life in New York City.

write a topic sentence

Review your list of differences, and then draft a topic sentence for your comparison-and-contrast paragraph. Be sure your topic sentence makes clear "who wore it better."

_____

_____

At this point, Jermond created the following informal outline, presenting his ideas in the order in which he was going to discuss them in his paragraph.

Size
    Saint Croix
        Small size
        Small population
        Christiansted and Frederiksted
    New York City
        Large size
        Large population
        Five boroughs

Lifestyle
    Saint Croix
        Laid-back
        Friendly

    New York City
        In a hurry
        Not always friendly

Jermond thought that a point-by-point organization would be easier for his readers to follow than a subject-by-subject organization. With this organization, readers would be able to keep track of his comparison as he discussed each of his points, one at a time.

make an outline

Decide whether you will write a subject-by-subject or point-by-point comparison. Then, use the appropriate format (see the paragraph maps on pages 135 and 136–137) to help you create an outline for your comparison-and-contrast paragraph. Before you begin, decide on the order in which you will present your points—for example, from least to most important. (For a subject-by-subject comparison, begin by deciding which subject you will discuss first.)

Using his informal outline as a guide, Jermond drafted his paragraph. Here is his draft.

Iwo Jima memorial statue near Arlington National Cemetery

Vietnam Veterans Memorial in Washington, D.C.

10 Classification

focus on writing

This picture shows fans at a football game. Look at the picture, and then brainstorm to identify the categories of fans you often see at a particular sporting event. You will return to this topic and review your brainstorming later in the chapter when you write your classification paragraph.

10a   Classification Paragraphs

When you **classify**, you sort items (people, things, ideas) into categories or groups. You classify when you organize bills into those you have to pay now and those you can pay later, or when you sort the clothes in a dresser drawer into piles of socks, T-shirts, and underwear.

In a **classification paragraph**, you tell readers how items can be sorted into categories or groups. Each category must be **distinct**. In other words, none of the items in one category should also fit into another category. For example, you would not classify novels into mysteries, romances, and e-books, because both mystery novels and romance novels could also be e-books.

When you **TEST** a classification paragraph, make sure it follows these guidelines:

T ▪ A classification paragraph should begin with a **topic sentence** that introduces the subject of the paragraph. It may also identify the categories you will discuss (for example, "Before you go camping, you should sort the items you are thinking of packing into three categories: absolutely necessary, potentially helpful, and not really necessary").

E ▪ A classification paragraph should discuss one category at a time and should include enough **evidence**—examples and details—to explain each category and show how it is distinct from the other categories. The categories should be arranged in **logical order**—for example, from least to most important or from smallest to largest.

S ▪ A classification paragraph should end with a **summary statement** that reinforces the paragraph's main idea.

T ▪ A classification paragraph should include **transitions** to introduce the categories you discuss and connect them to one another and to the topic sentence.

Paragraph Map: Classification

Topic Sentence

Category #1

Category #2

Category #3

Summary Statement

Model Paragraph: Classification

The writer of the following paragraph classifies bosses into three distinct groups.

T E S T

- Topic Sentence
- Evidence
- Summary Statement
- Transitions

Types of Bosses

I've had three kinds of bosses in my life: the uninterested boss, the supervisor, and the micromanager. The first type is an uninterested boss. This boss doesn't care what workers do as long as they do the job. When I was a counselor at summer camp, my boss fell into this category. As long as no campers (or worse yet, parents) complained, he left you alone. He never cared if you followed the activity plan for the day or gave the kids an extra snack to keep them quiet. — *First type of boss*

The second type of boss is the supervisor. This kind of boss will check you once in a while and give you helpful advice. You'll have a certain amount of freedom but not too much. When I was a salesperson at the Gap, my boss fell into this category. She helped me through the first few weeks of the job and encouraged me to do my best. At the end of the summer, I had learned a lot about retail business and had good feelings about the job. — *Second type of boss*

The last, and worst, type of boss is the micromanager. This kind of boss gets involved in everything. My boss at Taco Bell was this kind of person. No one could do anything right. There was always a better way to do anything you tried to do. If you rolled a burrito one way, he would tell you to do it another way. If you did it the other way, he would tell you to do it the first way. This boss never seemed to understand that people need praise every once in a while. — *Last type of boss*

Even though the supervisor expects a lot and makes you work, it is clear to me that this boss is better than the other types.

—Melissa Burrell (student)

Transitions in Classification Paragraphs

Transitions are important in a classification paragraph. They tell readers when you are moving from one category to another (for example, *the first type, the second type*). They can also indicate which categories you think are more important than others (for example, *the most important, the least important*).

Some Transitional Words and Phrases for Classification

one kind . . . another kind	the first group . . . the last group
one way . . . another way	the first type . . . the second type
the first (second, third) category	the most (or least) important group
	the next part

---

grammar in context

Classification

When you write a classification paragraph, you may list the categories you are going to discuss. If you use a **colon** to introduce your list, make sure that a complete sentence comes before the colon.

> **INCORRECT**   Basically, bosses can be divided into: the uninterested boss, the supervisor, and the micromanager.

> **CORRECT**   Basically, I've had three kinds of bosses in my life: the uninterested boss, the supervisor, and the micromanager.

For more information on how to use a colon to introduce a list, see 36g.

Analyzing a Classification Paragraph

Read this classification paragraph; then, follow the instructions in Practice 10-1.

Unusual Smartphone Applications

Generally, there are three kinds of unusual smartphone applications: those that are harmlessly entertaining, those that are surprisingly useful, and those that are deadly serious. The first kind is harmlessly entertaining. The purpose of the odd apps in this category is to be amusing, silly, or fun. People enjoy using them to do unimportant things, such as "pop" bubble wrap, blow out birthday candles, or add steam to their photos. Goofy apps like iMilk, which creates a virtual glass of milk that tilts when you pretend to drink it, fall into this first category. The second kind of unusual app is also odd but surprisingly useful, helping people accomplish various tasks. For example, Guitar Toolkit helps users tune their guitars and find chords, and Cubecheater helps users find the fastest solution to a Rubik's Cube puzzle. Also in this category is iStutter, an app that trains stutterers to speak with more fluency. The third kind of unusual app is the deadly serious kind, which can actually help save lives. Often, this kind of app is available only to select groups, not to the general public. For example, trained minesweepers use the PETAL app for the iPhone to help them determine the size and shape of landmines. Another example is the U.S. Army's specialized app for training soldiers how to launch missiles. Although they are certainly not equally important, each of these three kinds of apps has its uses.

—Emily Bentz (student)

PRACTICE

1. Underline the topic sentence of the paragraph.

2. What is the subject of the paragraph? _____

3. What three categories does the writer describe?

   _____

   _____

   _____

4. Circle the transitional phrases the writer uses to introduce the three categories.

5. Underline the paragraph's summary statement.

PRACTICE

10-2 List items in each of the following groups; then, sort the items into three or four categories.

1. All the items on your desk

2. Buildings on your college campus

3. Web sites you visit

4. The various parts of a piece of equipment you use for a course or on the job

10b Case Study: A Student Writes a Classification Paragraph

Here is how one student, Corey Levin, wrote a classification paragraph. For a college composition course, Corey participated in a service-learning project at a local Ronald McDonald House, a charity that houses families of seriously ill children receiving treatment at nearby hospitals. He met several professional athletes there and was surprised to learn that many of them regularly donate time and money to charity.

When Corey was asked by his composition instructor to write a paragraph about what he had learned from his experience, he decided to write a paragraph that classified the ways in which professional athletes give back to their communities. Based on his experience, he was able to come up with the following three categories.

Starting charitable foundations

Guidance

Responding to emergencies

list categories

Look back at the brainstorming you did in response to the Focus on Writing prompt on page 149, and cross out any categories that you do not plan to discuss. List the remaining categories—the ones that you will discuss in your classification paragraph—on the lines below.

_____

_____

_____

Corey then made an informal outline, listing examples to develop each of the three categories.

Foundations
    Michael Jordan
    Troy Aikman

Guidance
    Shaquille O'Neal
    The Philadelphia 76ers

Responding to emergencies
    Ike Reese
    Vince Carter

make an outline

Create an informal outline for your paragraph by arranging the categories of sports fans in the order in which you will discuss them and listing examples to develop each of your categories.

After completing his informal outline, Cory drafted the following topic sentence for his paragraph.

High-profile athletes find many ways to give back to their communities.

write a topic sentence

Review your list of categories, and then draft a topic sentence for your classification paragraph.

_____

_____

Then, using his informal outline as a guide, Cory wrote the following draft of his paragraph.

High-profile athletes find many ways to give back to their communities. Many athletes as well as teams do a lot to help people. I met some of them when I volunteered at the Ronald McDonald House. For example, Michael Jordan and the Chicago Bulls built a Boys and Girls Club on Chicago's West Side. Troy Aikman set up a foundation that builds playgrounds for children's hospitals. Shaquille O'Neal's Shaq's Paq provides guidance for inner-city children. The Philadelphia 76ers visit schools and have donated over five thousand books to local libraries. Ike Reese, formerly with the Atlanta Falcons, collects clothing and food for families that need help. Vince Carter of the Orlando Magic founded the Embassy of Hope Foundation. It distributes food to needy families at Thanksgiving and hosts a Christmas party for disadvantaged families.

draft your paragraph

Using your informal outline as a guide, draft your classification paragraph.

Following his instructor's suggestion, Corey emailed his draft to a classmate for feedback. In her email reply to Corey, she **TEST**ed his paragraph and made the following suggestions.

- Keep the **topic sentence** the way it is. "Many ways" shows you're writing a classification paragraph.
- Add more specific **evidence**. Give examples of each category of "giving back" to support the topic sentence. You also need to explain the athletes' contributions in more detail.
- Add a **summary statement** to sum up the paragraph's main idea.
- Add **transitions** to introduce the three specific categories you're discussing.

With these comments in mind, Corey revised and edited his paragraph. The final draft below includes all the elements Corey looked for when he **TEST**ed his paragraph.

Giving Back

T E S T

☐ Topic Sentence
☐ Evidence
☐ Summary Statement
☐ Transitions

High-profile athletes find many ways to give back to their communities. One way to give back is to start a charitable foundation to help young fans. For example, Michael Jordan and the Chicago Bulls built a Boys & Girls Club on Chicago's West Side. In addition, Troy Aikman set up a foundation that builds playgrounds for children's hospitals. Another way athletes give back to their communities is by mentoring, or giving guidance to young people. Many athletes work to encourage young people to stay in school. Shaquille O'Neal's Shaq's Paq, for example, provides guidance for inner-city children. The Philadelphia 76ers visit schools and have donated over five thousand books to local libraries. One more way athletes can contribute to their communities is to respond to emergencies. Football player Ike Reese, formerly with the Atlanta Falcons, collects clothing and food for families that need help. Basketball player Vince Carter founded the Embassy of Hope Foundation. It distributes food to needy families at Thanksgiving and hosts a Christmas party for disadvantaged families. These are just some of the ways that high-profile athletes give back to their communities.

TEST · **Revise** · **Edit**

Look back at the draft of your classification paragraph. Using the **TEST** checklist on page 158, evaluate your paragraph to make sure it includes a topic sentence, evidence, a summary statement, and transitions. Then, prepare a revised and edited draft of your paragraph.

PRACTICE

10-3   For additional practice in writing a classification paragraph, choose one of the topics below.

Your friends	Popular music
Drivers	Fitness routines
Public transportation commuters	Roommates
Television shows	Part-time jobs
Parents or children	Teachers
Types of success	Student housing
Radio stations	T-shirt slogans

Then, follow the process outlined in 10b to create your classification paragraph.

11 Definition

Vegan (vē'gən) n.

A vegan is someone who tries to live without exploiting animals, for the benefit of animals, people and the planet.

Vegans eat a plant-based diet, with nothing coming from animals; no meat, fish, milk, eggs or honey.

Vegan lifestyle avoids leather, wool, silk & other animal products for clothing or any other purpose as much as possible.

focus on writing

Read the definition of the word *vegan* printed on the shopping bag pictured above, and consider how this definition could be developed further. Then, brainstorm to identify some words you have encountered in your college courses for which you could write one-paragraph definitions. You will return to this topic and review your brainstorming later in the chapter when you write your definition paragraph.

In this chapter, you will learn to write a definition paragraph.

PREVIEW

11a Definition Paragraphs

During a conversation, you might say that a friend is stubborn, that a stream is polluted, or that a neighborhood is dangerous. In order to make yourself clear, you have to define what you mean by *stubborn*, *polluted*, or *dangerous*. Like conversations, academic assignments also may involve definition. In a history paper, for example, you might have to define *imperialism*; on a biology exam, you might be asked to define *mitosis*.

A **definition** tells what a word means. When you want your readers to know exactly how you are using a specific term, you define it.

When most people think of definitions, they think of the **formal definitions** they see in a dictionary. Formal definitions have a three-part structure.

- The term to be defined
- The general class to which the term belongs
- The things that make the term different from all other items in the general class to which the term belongs

TERM	CLASS	DIFFERENTIATION
Ice hockey	is a game	played on ice by two teams on skates who use curved sticks to try to hit a puck into the opponent's goal.
Spaghetti	is a pasta	made in the shape of long, thin strands.

A single-sentence formal definition is often not enough to define a specialized term (*point of view* or *premeditation*, for example), an abstract concept (*happiness* or *success*, for example), or a complicated subject (*stem-cell research*, for example). In these cases, you may need to expand the basic formal definition by writing a definition paragraph. In fact, a **definition paragraph** is an expanded formal definition.

When you TEST a definition paragraph, make sure it follows these guidelines:

T ▪ A definition paragraph should begin with a formal definition in the **topic sentence**.

E ▪ A definition paragraph does not follow any one pattern of development; in fact, it may define a term by using any of the patterns discussed in this text. For example, a definition paragraph may explain a concept by *comparing* it to something else or by giving *examples*. For this reason, your discussion of each category should include **evidence**—examples and details—that is appropriate for the pattern of development that you use.

S ▪ A definition paragraph should end with a **summary statement** that reinforces the paragraph's main idea.

T ▪ A definition paragraph should include **transitions** that are appropriate for the pattern or patterns of organization you use.

Here is one possible structure for a definition paragraph. Notice that this paragraph uses a combination of **narration** and **exemplification**.

Paragraph Map: Definition

Topic Sentence

Point #1
  Narrative

Point #2
  Example

  Example

Point #3
  Example

  Example

Summary Statement

Model Paragraph: Definition

The writer of the following paragraph uses narration and exemplification to define the term *business casual*.

Business Casual

Business casual is a dress code that is followed in many professional workplaces. Until recently, men and women dressed formally for work. For example, men wore dark suits and plain ties while women wore dark jackets and skirts. In the 1990s, however, the rise of technology companies in Silicon Valley made popular a new style of work attire, called *business casual*. Today, business casual is the accepted form of dress in many businesses. For men, this usually means wearing a collared shirt with no tie and khaki pants, sometimes with a sports jacket and loafers. For women, it means wearing a skirt or pants with a blouse or collared shirt. Women can wear low heels or flats. High-tech companies can be even more informal. They may even allow employees to wear jeans and T-shirts to work. While business casual may be the new norm, every company has its own standards for what is acceptable.

—Chase Durbin (student)

Narrative

Examples of men's business casual

Examples of women's business casual

Transitions in Definition Paragraphs

Transitions are important for definition paragraphs. In the paragraph above, the transitional words and phrases *until recently*, *in the 1990s*, and *today* tell readers when they are moving from one narrative event to another. The transitional phrases *for men* and *for women* introduce examples.

The following box lists some of the transitional words and phrases that are frequently used in definition paragraphs. You can also use the transitional words and phrases associated with the specific pattern (or patterns) that you use to develop your paragraph.

> **Some Transitional Words and Phrases for Definition**
>
> | | |
> |---|---|
> | also | often |
> | for example | one characteristic . . . another |
> | for men (for women) | characteristic |
> | however | one way . . . another way |
> | in addition | sometimes |
> | in particular | specifically |
> | in the 1990s (or another time) | the first kind . . . the second kind |
> | like | until recently |

grammar in context

Definition

A definition paragraph often includes a formal definition of the term or concept you are going to discuss. When you write your formal definition, be careful not to use the phrases *is where* or *is when*.

Business casual is ~~when employees wear informal attire~~ *a dress code that is followed in many professional workplaces.*
~~to work.~~

Analyzing a Definition Paragraph

Read this definition paragraph; then, follow the instructions in Practice 11-1.

Loans That Change Lives

Microloans are small loans given to people who live in extreme poverty. The idea for such loans originated in 1974, when a Bangladeshi economist loaned $27 to a group of local women. The women used the loan to purchase bamboo to make furniture. After they sold the furniture, they repaid the loan and kept a small profit for themselves. As a result of this experience, the economist created a bank for microloans. Similar microcredit banks now exist throughout the world. For example, microcredit banks can be found in Bosnia, Peru, Ethiopia, and Russia. Microloans are different from ordinary loans because they are not awarded on the basis of credit history or financial means; instead, they are based on trust. A microcredit bank trusts a borrower to make money even if he or she has no or little income at the time of the loan. Some people see microloans as a wonderful opportunity for poor businesspeople; others criticize microloans because they can encourage governments to reduce their support for the poor. Even so, microloans have helped countless people all over the world to lift themselves out of poverty.

**PRACTICE
11-1**

1. Underline the topic sentence of the paragraph on page 164.

2. What is the subject of this definition? _____

3. What is the writer's one-sentence definition of the subject?

_____

4. List some of the specific information the writer uses to define his subject. The first piece of information has been listed for you.

Microloans originated in Bangladesh in 1974. _____

_____

_____

_____

5. Circle the transitional words and phrases the writer uses.

6. What patterns of development does the writer use in his definition? List them here.

_____

_____

_____

7. Underline the paragraph's summary statement.

**PRACTICE
11-2**

Following are four possible topic sentences for definition paragraphs. Each topic sentence includes an underlined word. In the space provided, list two possible patterns of development that you could use to develop a definition of the underlined word. For example, you could define the word *discrimination* by giving examples (exemplification) and by telling a story (narration).

1. During the interview, the job candidate made a sexist comment.

Possible strategy: _____

Possible strategy: _____

2. <u>Loyalty</u> is one of the chief characteristics of golden retrievers.

   Possible strategy: _____

   Possible strategy: _____

3. More than forty years after President Johnson's Great Society initiative, we have yet to eliminate <u>poverty</u> in the United States.

   Possible strategy: _____

   Possible strategy: _____

4. The problem with movies today is that they are just too <u>violent</u>.

   Possible strategy: _____

   Possible strategy: _____

11b Case Study: A Student Writes a Definition Paragraph

Here is how one student, Lorraine Scipio, wrote a definition paragraph. On a history exam, Lorraine was asked to write a one-paragraph definition of the term *imperialism*. Lorraine had studied for the exam, so she knew what imperialism was. Because she wanted to make sure that she did not leave anything out of her definition (and because she had a time limit), she quickly listed some supporting examples and details on the inside front cover of her exam book. Then, she crossed out two items that did not seem relevant.

A policy of control

Military

~~Lenin~~

Establish empires

Cultural superiority

Raw materials and cheap labor

Africa, etc.

~~Cultural imperialism~~

Nineteenth-century term

list examples and details

Review the brainstorming you did in response to the Focus on Writing prompt on page 160, and choose a word to define. Then, list the examples and details that can best help you develop a definition of that word.

_____

_____

_____

_____

Now, cross out the items on your list that do not seem relevant to your definition.

After reviewing her list of examples and details, Lorraine drafted the topic sentence that appears below.

The goal of imperialism is to establish an empire.

write a topic sentence

Review your list of examples and details, and then draft a topic sentence for your definition paragraph. Include a formal definition of the term you are defining.

_____

_____

Next, Lorraine made an informal outline, quickly arranging her supporting examples and details in the order in which she planned to write about them.

Establish empires

Nineteenth-century term

Cultural superiority

Africa, etc.

Raw materials and cheap labor

A policy of control

Military

make an outline

Create an informal outline for your paragraph by arranging your examples and details in the order in which you plan to discuss them.

Referring to the material on her list, Lorraine wrote the following draft of her definition paragraph. Notice that she uses several different patterns to develop her definition.

> The goal of imperialism is to establish an empire. The imperialist country thinks that it is superior to the country it takes over. It justifies its actions by saying that it is helping the other country. But it isn't. Countries such as Germany, Belgium, Spain, and England have been imperialist in the past. The point of imperialism is to take as much out of the occupied countries as possible. Often, imperialist countries sent troops to occupy other countries and to keep order. As a result, imperialism kept the people in occupied countries in poverty and often broke down local governments and local traditions.

draft your paragraph

Using your informal outline as a guide, draft your definition paragraph. Remember, you can use any of the patterns of development discussed in Unit 2 of this text to help you define your term. Begin by identifying the term. Then, you can describe it, give examples, tell how it works, explain its purpose, consider its history or future, or compare it with other similar terms.

After she finished her draft, Lorraine reread it quickly, **TEST**ing her paragraph to help her make sure it answered the exam question. Then, she made the following changes.

- Because the exam question asked for a definition, she rewrote her **topic sentence** as a formal definition.
- She strengthened her **evidence**, explaining her supporting examples and details more fully. She also deleted some vague statements that did not support her topic sentence.

- She added **transitional words and phrases** to make the connections between her ideas clearer.
- She added a **summary statement** to reinforce the negative effects of imperialism.

Lorraine made her changes directly on the draft she had written, crossing out unnecessary information and adding missing information. She also edited her paragraph for grammar, punctuation, and mechanical errors. Then, because she had some extra time, she neatly rewrote her paragraph.

Lorraine's revised and edited paragraph appears below. (Because this is an exam answer, she does not include a title.) Notice that the final draft includes all the elements Lorraine looked for when she **TEST**ed her paragraph.

Imperialism is the policy by which one country takes over the land or the government of another country. In the nineteenth century, the object of imperialism was to establish an empire. The imperialist country thought that it was superior to the country it took over. It justified its actions by saying that it was helping the other country. For instance, countries such as Germany, Belgium, Spain, and England followed their imperialist ambitions in Africa when they claimed large areas of land. The point of imperialism was to take as much out of the occupied countries as possible. For example, in South America and Mexico, Spain removed tons of gold from the areas it occupied. It made the natives slaves and forced them to work in mines. In order to protect their interests, imperialist countries sent troops to occupy the country and to keep order. As a result, imperialism kept the people in occupied countries in poverty and often broke down local governments and local traditions. Although European imperialism occasionally had benefits, at its worst it brought slavery, disease, and death.

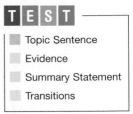

T E S T
- Topic Sentence
- Evidence
- Summary Statement
- Transitions

FYI

Writing Paragraph Answers on Exams

When you write paragraph answers on exams, you do not have much time to work, so you need to be well prepared. Know your subject well, and memorize important definitions. You may have time to write an outline, a rough draft, and a final draft, but you will have to work quickly. Your final draft should include all the elements of a good paragraph: a topic sentence, supporting details, transitions, and a summary statement.

TEST · Revise · Edit

Look back at the draft of your definition paragraph. Using the
TEST checklist on page 171, evaluate your paragraph to make
sure it includes a topic sentence, evidence, a summary statement,
and transitions. Then, prepare a revised and edited draft of your
paragraph.

PRACTICE

11-3   For additional practice in writing a definition paragraph,
choose one of the topics below.

A negative quality, such as envy, dishonesty, or jealousy

An ideal friend or neighbor

A type of person, such as a worrier or show-off

A social concept, such as equality, opportunity, or discrimination

An important play or strategy in a particular sport or game

A hobby you pursue or an activity associated with that hobby

A technical term or specific piece of equipment that you use in
your job

An object (such as an article of clothing) that is important to your
culture or religion

A particular style of music or dancing

A controversial term, the definition of which not all people agree on,
such as *affirmative action*, *right to life*, or *gun control*

A goal in life, such as success or happiness

Then, follow the process outlined in 11b to create your definition
paragraph.

TESTing a definition paragraph

Topic Sentence Unifies Your Paragraph

- ☐ Do you have a clearly worded **topic sentence** that states your paragraph's main idea?
- ☐ Does your topic sentence identify the term you are defining?

Evidence Supports Your Paragraph's Topic Sentence

- ☐ Does all your **evidence**—examples and details—support your paragraph's main idea?
- ☐ Do you need to add more examples or details to help you define your term?

Summary Statement Reinforces Your Paragraph's Unity

- ☐ Does your paragraph end with a **summary statement** that reinforces your main idea?

Transitions Add Coherence to Your Paragraph

- ☐ Are your **transitions** appropriate for the pattern (or patterns) of development you use?
- ☐ Do you need to add transitions to make your paragraph clearer and to help readers follow your ideas?

11c Writing about Visuals

The pictures on page 172 show various kinds of families. Look at the pictures, and then write a **definition** paragraph in which you define *family*. How do the groups below fit (or not fit) your definition?

An empty-nest couple

A mixed-race family

A two-father family

A single-parent family

12 Argument

Politics has been [too] concerned with right or left instead of right or wrong.

focus on writing

Many people, like those seen in this photo, expressed their political points of view at the Rally to Restore Sanity and/or Fear, which took place in Washington, D.C., in October 2010. Brainstorm to develop a list of political issues that interest you. Review your brainstorming, choose one issue, and then write a journal entry exploring your thoughts on this issue. You will return to this journal entry later in the chapter when you write your argument paragraph.

In this chapter, you will learn to write an argument paragraph.

12a Argument Paragraphs

When most people hear the word *argument*, they think of heated exchanges on television interview programs. These discussions, however, are more like shouting matches than arguments. True **argument** involves taking a well-thought-out position on a **debatable topic**—a topic about which reasonable people may disagree (for example, "Should teenagers who commit felonies be tried as adults?").

In an **argument paragraph**, you take a position on an issue, and your purpose is to persuade readers that your position has merit. You attempt to convince people of the strength of your ideas by presenting **evidence**— in this case, facts and examples. In the process, you address opposing ideas, and if they are strong, you acknowledge their strengths. If your evidence is solid and your logic is sound, you will present a convincing argument.

FYI

Evidence

You can use two kinds of **evidence** in your argument paragraphs: *facts* and *examples*.

1. A **fact** is a piece of information (such as "Alaska officially became a state in 1959") that can be verified. If you make a statement, you should be prepared to support it with facts—using statistics, observations, or statements that are generally accepted as true.

2. An **example** is a specific illustration of a general statement. To be convincing, an example should clearly relate to the point you are making.

When you **TEST** an argument paragraph, make sure it follows these guidelines:

T ■ An argument paragraph should begin with a **topic sentence** that clearly states your position. Using words like *should*, *should not*, or *ought to* in your topic sentence will make your position clear to your readers.

The federal government <u>should</u> lower taxes on gasoline.

The city <u>ought to</u> spend 20 percent of its budget on helping businesses convert to sustainable energy sources.

E ■ An argument paragraph should present points that support the topic sentence in **logical order.** For example, if your purpose is to argue in favor of placing warning labels on unhealthy snack foods, you should give reasons—arranging them from least to most important—why this policy should be instituted. Each of these points should then be supported with **evidence**—facts and examples.

An argument paragraph should also address and **refute** (argue against) opposing arguments. By showing that an opponent's arguments are weak, inaccurate, or misguided, you strengthen your own position. If an opposing argument is particularly strong, you may want to **concede** (accept) its strengths and then point out its weaknesses or shortcomings.

S ■ An argument paragraph should end with a **summary statement** that reinforces the paragraph's main idea—the position you take on the issue.

T ■ An argument paragraph should include **transitions** to connect the points you are making to one another and to the topic sentence.

Paragraph Map: Argument

Topic Sentence

Point #1

Point #2

Point #3

Opposing Argument #1
(plus refutation)

Opposing Argument #2
(plus refutation)

Summary Statement

Model Paragraph: Argument

The following paragraph argues in favor of an emergency notification system for college students.

TEST

- Topic Sentence
- Evidence
- Summary Statement
- Transitions

Point 1 and support

Point 2 and support

Opposing argument 1 (plus refutation)

Opposing argument 2 (plus refutation)

Why Our School Should Set Up an Emergency Notification System

Our school should set up an emergency notification system that would deliver an instant message to students' cell phones in a campus crisis. The first reason why we should set up an emergency notification system is that it is needed. Currently, it takes an hour or two to inform the whole campus of something—for example, that school is closing because of bad weather or that a school event has been canceled. Another reason why we should set up an emergency notification system is that it will make our campus safer by warning students if a crime takes place on campus. For example, when a shooting took place in 2007 on the campus of Virginia Tech, the school was unable to warn students to evacuate the campus. The result was that more than thirty people were killed. An emergency notification system might have saved the lives of many of these people. One objection to an instant-messaging emergency notification system is that email notification works just as well. However, although many students check their email just once or twice a day, most students carry cell phones and read instant messages whenever they get them. Another objection is that some students do not have cell phones. The same system that delivers instant messages to students, however, could also deliver messages to digital message boards around campus. Because communicating with students in a crisis situation can save lives, our school should set up an emergency notification system.

—Ashley Phillips (student)

Transitions in Argument Paragraphs

Transitions are important in argument paragraphs. In the paragraph above, the transitional words and phrases *the first reason* and *another reason* tell readers they are moving from one point to another. In addition, the transitional phrases *one objection* and *another objection* indicate that the writer is addressing two opposing arguments.

> ## Some Transitional Words and Phrases for Argument
>
> | | | |
> |---|---|---|
> | accordingly | finally | nonetheless |
> | admittedly | first . . . second . . . | of course |
> | after all | for this reason | one . . . another |
> | although | however | on the one hand . . . on the |
> | because | in addition | other hand |
> | but | in conclusion | since |
> | certainly | in fact | the first reason |
> | consequently | in summary | therefore |
> | despite | meanwhile | thus |
> | even so | moreover | to be sure |
> | even though | nevertheless | truly |

grammar in context

Argument

When you write an argument paragraph, you should use both **compound sentences** and **complex sentences**. By doing this, you not only show the relationship between ideas but also eliminate choppy sentences.

COMPOUND SENTENCE An emergency notification system will help all of us communicate better. ~~It~~ *, and it* will ensure our school's safety.

COMPLEX SENTENCE *Because communicating* ~~Communicating~~ with students in a crisis situation can save lives. ~~Our~~ *, our* school should set up an emergency notification system.

For more information on how to create compound sentences, see Chapter 19. For more information on how to create complex sentences, see Chapter 20.

Analyzing an Argument Paragraph

Read this argument paragraph; then, follow the instructions in Practice 12-1.

Why We Need Full-Body Scanners

Because of their advantages, airport full-body scanners are a necessary tool in the fight against terrorism. One reason why airport scanners are necessary is that the federal government needs a quick and effective way of screening passengers. Because of their ease of operation, whole-body scanners accomplish this goal. Well over a million people fly throughout the United States each day. A single airport scanner is capable of screening thousands of people a day and is much faster than other methods of screening. Another reason why airport scanners are necessary is that they provide an additional layer of security. For example, scanners are able to detect both metallic and nonmetallic items that are taped to the body. In other words, scanners will detect both weapons and bomb materials that metal detectors might miss. People who oppose scanners say that they are unsafe. However, the literature that the government distributes at airports makes it clear that airport scanners expose passengers to less radiation than they experience when they fly at high altitudes. Opponents also point out that scanners violate the Constitution's guarantee of privacy because they show a three-dimensional image of a person's naked body. To deal with this objection, the Transportation Security Administration has made sure that the TSA officer who operates a scanner never sees the images of the person being scanned. He or she sees only a screen that indicates whether the person has successfully cleared the screening. In addition, the images themselves are deleted immediately after a person has left the screening area. Given the recent attempts that terrorists have made to attack the United States, airport scanners are a useful and effective way of keeping people safe when they fly.

—Carl Manni (student)

PRACTICE

12-1

1. Underline the topic sentence of the paragraph on page 178.

2. What issue is the subject of the paragraph?

_____

3. What is the writer's position?

_____

4. What specific points does the writer use to support his topic sentence?

_____

_____

5. List some evidence (facts and examples) that the writer uses to support his points. The first piece of evidence has been listed for you.

A single full-body scanner is capable of screening thousands of people a day.

_____

_____

_____

6. What other evidence could the writer have used?

_____

_____

_____

7. What opposing arguments does he mention?

_____

_____

8. How does he refute these arguments?

_____

_____

9. Circle the transitional words and phrases the writer uses to move readers through his argument.

10. Underline the paragraph's summary statement.

PRACTICE
12-2 Following are four topic sentences for argument paragraphs. List two or three points that could support each topic sentence. For example, if you were arguing in support of laws requiring motorcycle riders to wear safety helmets, you could say helmets cut down on medical costs and save lives.

1. High school graduates should perform a year of public service before going to college.

2. All student athletes should be paid a salary by their college or university.

3. College students caught cheating should be expelled.

4. The U.S. government should forgive all federal student loans.

PRACTICE
12-3 Choose one of the topic sentences from Practice 12-2. Then, list two types of evidence that could support each point you listed. For example, if you said that wearing safety helmets saves lives, you could list "accident statistics" and "statements by emergency room physicians."

_____

_____

PRACTICE
12-4 List opposing arguments for the topic sentence you selected for Practice 12-3. Then, list the weaknesses of each of these arguments.

Opposing argument #1: _____

Weaknesses: _____

Opposing argument #2: _____

Weaknesses: _____

12b   Case Study: A Student Writes an Argument Paragraph

Here is how one student, Phillip Zhu, wrote an argument paragraph. Phillip, a computer science major, was asked to write an argument paragraph on an issue that interested him. Because he was taking a course in computer ethics, he decided to write about an issue that had been discussed in class: the way many employers now search social-networking sites, such as Facebook, to find information about job applicants.

Phillip had already formed an opinion about the issue, so he was ready to write the following topic sentence that expressed his position.

> Employers should not use social-networking sites to find information about job applicants.

write your topic sentence

Look back at the journal entry you wrote in response to the Focus on Writing prompt on page 173. Determine your position on the political issue you chose to write about, and then draft a topic sentence that clearly states the position you will take in your argument paragraph.

_____

_____

Phillip then listed the following points that he could use to support his topic sentence.

Social-networking sites should be private

People exaggerate on social-networking sites

Stuff meant to be funny

No one warns applicant

Need email address to register

Expect limited audience

Employers can misinterpret what they find

Employers going where they don't belong

Not an accurate picture

Not fair

Not meant to be seen by job recruiters

list your supporting points

Review your topic sentence, and list as many points as you can in support of your position on the issue. Then, look back at your journal entry to find evidence to support your points.

_____

_____

_____

_____

After identifying his three most important supporting points, Phillip arranged them into an informal outline.

Social-networking sites should be private
    Need email address to register
    Expect limited audience
    Employers going where they don't belong

People exaggerate on social-networking sites
    Stuff meant to be funny
    Not meant to be seen by job recruiters
    No one warns applicant

Employers can misinterpret what they find
    Not an accurate picture
    Not fair

make an outline

Create an informal outline for your paragraph by arranging the points that support your position in the order that you think will be most convincing to your readers—for example, from the least important point to the most important point. Under each point, list the evidence (facts and examples) that you will use as support.

Once Phillip finished his informal outline, he tried to think of possible arguments against his position because he knew he would have to consider and refute these opposing arguments in his paragraph. He came up with two possible arguments against his position.

1. Employers should be able to find out as much as they can.

2. Applicants have only themselves to blame.

list opposing arguments

Review your informal outline, and then list one or more possible arguments against your position on the lines below.

_____

_____

_____

Now, try to think of ways in which these opposing arguments are weak or inaccurate.

Phillip then wrote the following draft of his paragraph.

Employers should not use social-networking sites to find information about job applicants. For one thing, social-networking sites should be private. By visiting these sites, employers are going where they do not belong. People also exaggerate on social-networking sites. They say things that are not true, and they put things on the sites they would not want job recruiters to see. No one ever tells applicants that recruiters search these sites, so they feel safe posting all kinds of material. Employers can misinterpret what they read. Employers and recruiters need to get as much information as they can. They should not use unfair ways to get this information. Applicants have only themselves to blame for their problems. They need to be more careful about what they put up online. This is true, but most applicants don't know that employers will search social-networking sites.

draft your paragraph

Guided by your informal outline and your list of opposing arguments, draft your argument paragraph. Begin your paragraph with a topic sentence that clearly states the position you are taking on the issue.

After finishing his draft, Phillip scheduled a conference with his instructor. Together, they went over his paragraph and **TEST**ed his paragraph. They agreed that Phillip needed to make the following changes.

- They decided he needed to make his **topic sentence** more specific and more forceful.

- They decided he should add more **evidence** (facts and examples) to his discussion. For example, what social-networking sites is he talking about? Which are restricted? How do employers gain access to these sites?

- They decided he needed to delete irrelevant discussion blaming job applicants for their problems.

- They decided he should add **transitional words and phrases** to clearly identify the points he is making in support of his argument and also to identify the two opposing arguments he discusses.

- They decided he needed to add a strong **summary statement** to reinforce his position.

After **TEST**ing his paragraph, Phillip revised and edited it. The final draft below includes all the elements Phillip looked for when he **TEST**ed his paragraph.

Unfair Searching

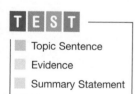

Employers should not use social-networking sites, such as MySpace and Facebook, to find information about job applicants. First, social-networking sites should be private. People who use these sites do not expect employers to access them. However, some employers routinely search social-networking sites to find information about job applicants. Doing this is not right, and it is not fair. By visiting these sites, employers are going where they do not belong. Another reason employers should not use information from social-networking sites is that people frequently exaggerate on them or say things that are not true. They may also put statements and pictures on the sites that they would not want job recruiters to see. Because no one ever tells applicants that recruiters search these sites, they feel safe posting embarrassing pictures or making exaggerated claims about drinking or sex. Finally, employers can misinterpret the material they see. As a result, they may reject a good applicant because they take seriously what is meant to be a joke. Of course, employers need to get as much information about a candidate as they can. They should not, however, use unfair tactics to get this information.

In addition, prospective employers should realize that the profile they see on a social-networking site does not accurately represent the job applicant. For these reasons, employers should not use social-networking sites to do background checks.

TEST · Revise · Edit

Look back at the draft of your argument paragraph. Using the **TEST** checklist on page 186, evaluate your paragraph to make sure it includes a topic sentence, evidence, a summary statement, and transitions. Then, prepare a revised and edited draft of your paragraph.

PRACTICE

12-5   For additional practice in writing an argument paragraph, choose one of the topics below.

AN ISSUE RELATED TO YOUR SCHOOL

Grading policies
Required courses
Attendance policies
Campus security
Cell phones in class

Financial aid
All-male or all-female classes
Childcare facilities
Sexual harassment policies
The physical condition
    of classrooms

AN ISSUE RELATED TO YOUR COMMUNITY

The need for a traffic signal, a youth center, or something else you think would benefit your community

An action you think local officials should take, such as changing school hours, cleaning up a public space, or improving services for the elderly

A new law you would like to see enacted

A current law you would like to see changed

A controversy you have been following in the news

Then, follow the process outlined in 12b to create your argument paragraph.

TESTing an argument paragraph

Topic Sentence Unifies Your Paragraph

☐ Do you have a clearly worded **topic sentence** that states your paragraph's main idea?

☐ Does your topic sentence state your position on a debatable issue?

Evidence Supports Your Paragraph's Topic Sentence

☐ Does all your **evidence** support your paragraph's main idea?

☐ Have you included enough facts and examples to support your points, or do you need to add more?

☐ Do you summarize and refute opposing arguments?

Summary Statement Reinforces Your Paragraph's Unity

☐ Does your paragraph end with a strong **summary statement** that reinforces your main idea?

Transitions Add Coherence to Your Paragraph

☐ Do you use **transitions** to let readers know when you are moving from one point to another?

☐ Do you use transitional words and phrases to indicate when you are addressing opposing arguments?

☐ Do you need to add transitions to make your paragraph clearer and to help readers follow your ideas?

12c Writing about Visuals

Reprinted on page 187 is a public service advertisement about the dangers of texting while driving. Many states are considering (and some have already enacted) laws that ban cell-phone use by drivers in moving vehicles. Look at the ad, and then write an **argument** paragraph in which you take one of two positions: either that such a ban is a good idea or that texting is no more dangerous than other activities that drivers routinely engage in.

```
                    @"===,                                        ,_____cctI
                    "?TEXTINGAAAAAAAAA,,,,,,,,,,,,,,,,,,,,,,;LLLLLLLLLL
          ~",,,     1"""""""""""""""###WHILEOOOOOOOOOOOOOOOOOOOOOOOOOOOOOO
         '"EEEEE, !'"***"~~~~~~"OOOIIIIIIIIIIIIIIIIIIIIIIIIIIIIIIIIIIII
          ,EEEEE)>"'''???????"WWW!MMMMMMMMMMMMMMMMMMMMMMMMMMMMMMMMMMMMMM
           "E.,)+="WWW~~~~~~#"OOO1OOOOOOOOOOOOOOOOOOOOOOOOOOOOOOOOOOOOO
          ,~:#")LLL!"+++???????"$$$1===========##/
          &LLLLLLLLL;;;;;;;;;;;;;;,,,/
          1#LLLLLDRIVINGLLLLLLLLLL!
         ,!###LLLLLL"'EEEE,'"KILLS!
         !#####LLL"  "EEE"  "LLLL"
         !########L!  "EEJ. "LL!
        1!#########1   "JJ*,1"
        !##########"!      ,1"
        1#########"   1"~~,~~"
        !#########"
       !#########!
       !#########1
       !##########!
       1###########
      !"###########"
      !############!
      1#########"'
      1####"'
      """"
```

U.S. Department of Transportation
National Highway Traffic Safety Administration

13 Writing an Essay

focus on writing

Most people would agree that a window washer, like the one pictured here, has a challenging job. Think about the most difficult job you've ever had. This is the topic you will be writing about as you go through this chapter. (If you have never had a job, you may write about a specific task that you disliked or about a difficult job that a friend or relative has had.)

Much of the writing you do in school will be more than just one paragraph. Often, you will be asked to write an **essay**—a group of paragraphs on a single subject. When you write an essay, you follow the same process you follow when you write a paragraph: you begin by planning and then move on to organizing your ideas, drafting, TESTing, and revising and editing.

In this chapter, you will see how the strategies you learned for writing paragraphs can help you write essays.

Step 1: Planning

13a Understanding Essay Structure

Understanding the structure of a paragraph can help you understand the structure of an essay. In a paragraph, the main idea is stated in a **topic sentence**, and the rest of the paragraph supports this main idea with **evidence** (details and examples). **Transitional words and phrases** help readers follow the discussion. The paragraph ends with a **summary statement** that reinforces the main idea.

Paragraph

> The **topic sentence** states the main idea of the paragraph.
> **Evidence** supports the main idea.
> **Transitional words and phrases** show the connections between ideas.
> A **summary statement** reinforces the main idea of the paragraph.

The structure of an essay is similar to the structure of a paragraph:

- The essay's first paragraph—the *introduction*—begins with opening remarks that create interest and closes with a **thesis statement**. This thesis statement, like a paragraph's topic sentence, presents the main idea. (For more on introductions, see 15a.)
- The *body* of the essay contains several paragraphs that support the thesis statement. Each body paragraph begins with a topic sentence that states the main idea of the paragraph. The other sentences in the paragraph support the topic sentence with **evidence** (details and examples).
- **Transitional words and phrases** lead readers from sentence to sentence and from paragraph to paragraph.
- The last paragraph—the *conclusion*—ends the essay. The conclusion includes a **summary statement** that reinforces the thesis. It ends with concluding remarks. (For more on conclusions, see 15b.)

The first letters of these four key elements—thesis statement, evidence, summary statement, and transitions—spell **TEST**. Just as you did with paragraphs, you can **TEST** your essays to see whether they include all the elements of an effective essay.

Many of the essays you will write in college will have a **thesis-and-support** structure.

Essay

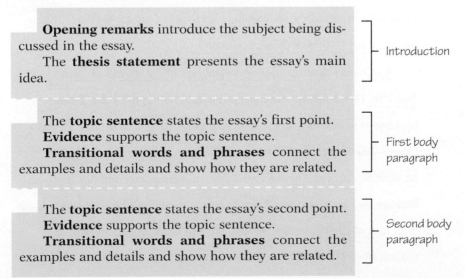

Opening remarks introduce the subject being discussed in the essay.
The **thesis statement** presents the essay's main idea.

— Introduction

The **topic sentence** states the essay's first point.
Evidence supports the topic sentence.
Transitional words and phrases connect the examples and details and show how they are related.

— First body paragraph

The **topic sentence** states the essay's second point.
Evidence supports the topic sentence.
Transitional words and phrases connect the examples and details and show how they are related.

— Second body paragraph

> The **topic sentence** states the essay's third point.
> **Evidence** supports the topic sentence.
> **Transitional words and phrases** connect the examples and details and show how they are related.
>
> — Third body paragraph

> The **summary statement** reinforces the thesis, summarizing the essay's main idea.
> **Concluding remarks** present the writer's final thoughts on the subject.
>
> — Conclusion

The following essay by Jennifer Chu illustrates the structure of an essay. (Note that transitional words and phrases are shaded.)

Becoming Chinese American

Introduction

Although I was born in Hong Kong, I have spent most of my life in the United States. However, my parents have always made sure that I did not forget my roots. They always tell stories of what it was like to live in Hong Kong. To make sure my brothers and sisters and I know what is happening in China, my parents subscribe to Chinese cable TV. When we were growing up, we would watch the celebration of the Chinese New Year, the news from Asia, and Chinese movies and music videos. As a result, even though I am an American, I value many parts of traditional Chinese culture.

Thesis statement

Topic sentence (states essay's first point)

First body paragraph

Evidence (supports topic sentence)

The Chinese language is an important part of my life as a Chinese American. Unlike some of my Chinese friends, I do not think the Chinese language is unimportant or embarrassing. First, I feel that it is my duty as a Chinese American to learn Chinese so that I can pass it on to my children. In addition, knowing Chinese enables me to communicate with my relatives. Because my parents and grandparents do not speak English well, Chinese is our main form of communication. Finally, Chinese helps me identify with my culture. When I speak Chinese, I feel connected to a culture that is over five thousand years old. Without the Chinese language, I would not be who I am.

Chinese food is another important part of my life as a Chinese American. One reason for this is that everything we Chinese people eat has a history and a meaning. At a birthday meal, for example, we serve long noodles and buns in the shape of peaches. This is because we believe that long noodles represent long life and that peaches are served in heaven. Another reason is that to Chinese people, food is a way of reinforcing ties between family and friends. For instance, during a traditional Chinese wedding ceremony, the bride and the groom eat nine of everything. This is because the number nine stands for the Chinese words "together forever." By taking part in this ritual, the bride and groom start their marriage by making Chinese customs a part of their life together.

Topic sentence (states essay's second point)

Second body paragraph

Evidence (supports topic sentence)

Religion is the most important part of my life as a Chinese American. At various times during the year, Chinese religious festivals bring together the people I care about the most. During Chinese New Year, my whole family goes to the temple, where we say prayers and welcome others with traditional New Year's greetings. After leaving the temple, we all go to Chinatown and eat dim sum until the lion dance starts. As the colorful lion dances its way down the street, people beat drums and throw firecrackers to drive off any evil spirits that may be around. Later that night, parents give children gifts of money in red envelopes that symbolize joy and happiness in the coming year.

Topic sentence (states essay's third point)

Third body paragraph

Evidence (supports topic sentence)

My family has taught me how important it is to hold on to my Chinese culture. When I was six, my parents sent me to a Chinese American grade school. My teachers thrilled me with stories of Fa Mulan, the Shang Dynasty, and the Moon God. I will never forget how happy I was when I realized how special it is to be Chinese. This is how I want my own children to feel. I want them to be proud of who they are and to pass their language, history, and culture on to the next generation.

Summary statement (reinforces essay's thesis)

Conclusion

PRACTICE

13-1 Following is an essay organized according to the diagram on pages 193–194. Read the essay, and then answer the questions that follow it.

Enhanced Water

Flavored or "enhanced" water has grown in popularity since it was introduced in the late 1990s. Most enhanced waters are owned by soft drink companies like Coca-Cola and Pepsi. These companies have spent millions of dollars trying to convince consumers that enhanced water is better than ordinary water. However, this is not the case.

There is no question that our bodies need fluid to stay hydrated. In fact, most experts say that people should drink about 64 ounces (eight cups) of water per day. Only athletes and people who are involved in strenuous activities, such as hiking, need to drink significantly more water. These individuals may benefit from the salt and carbohydrates found in sports drinks like Gatorade, but they are the exception. People who exercise at a normal rate, for about an hour a day, usually need only a few additional cups of plain water to restore lost fluids.

Despite marketing claims, it is not clear that enhanced water is more healthful than regular water. The labels on most enhanced water drinks, such as VitaminWater and SoBe Lifewater, make health claims that have not been scientifically proven. For instance, the label on VitaminWater's drink "Defense" implies that its vitamins and minerals will prevent a person from getting sick. Scientists generally agree, however, that there is no magic formula for preventing illness. Another example of a misleading claim appears on the label on SoBe's strawberry-kiwi-flavored "Calm-o-mile" drink, which lists herbs that are supposed to relieve stress. However, the amount of herbs found in this drink is too small to provide any health benefits. Moreover, many enhanced water drinks actually contain ingredients that the body does not need—for example, caffeine, artificial flavors and colors, and sugar or artificial sweeteners.

In addition to making questionable marketing claims, manufacturers of enhanced waters present nutritional information in a confusing way. For example, just a quick glance at the label for a SoBe Lifewater drink would lead someone to believe that a serving has 40 calories, 16 grams of carbohydrates, and 10 grams of sugar. These amounts may sound reasonable, but a closer look at the label reveals that each 20-ounce bottle actually contains two and a half servings. In other words, a person who drinks the whole bottle is actually consuming 100 calories, 40 grams of carbohydrates, and 25 grams of sugar—more carbohydrates and sugar than in a glazed doughnut.

In most cases, regular tap water is all people need to stay healthy and hydrated. The drink manufacturers ignore this fact, saying that enhanced water is lower in calories and sugar than non-diet soft drinks. They also say that, although the herbs and vitamins in their drinks may not have proven health benefits, at least they are not harmful. Finally, the drink manufacturers claim that their products get people to drink more fluids. Although all these claims are partially true, consumers do not need the ingredients in enhanced water or its extra cost.

1. Underline the essay's thesis statement.

2. Underline the topic sentence of each body paragraph.

3. What point does the first body paragraph make? What evidence supports this point?

_____

_____

_____

_____

_____

4. What point does the second paragraph make? What evidence supports this point?

_____

_____

_____

_____

5. What point does the third body paragraph make? What evidence supports this point?

_____

_____

6. What transitions does the essay include? How do they connect the essay's ideas?

_____

_____

_____

_____

7. Where in the conclusion does the writer restate the essay's thesis? Underline this statement.

13b Moving from Assignment to Topic

Many essays you write in college begin as **assignments** given to you by your instructors. Before you focus on any assignment, however, you should take time to think about your **purpose** (what you want to accomplish by writing your essay) and your **audience** (the people who will read your essay). Once you have considered these issues, you are ready to move on to thinking about the specifics of your assignment.

The following assignments are typical of those you might be given in a composition class.

- Discuss some things you would change about your school.
- What can college students do to improve the environment?
- Discuss an important decision you made during the past three years.

Because these assignments are so general, you need to narrow them before you can start to write. What specific things would you change? Exactly what could you do to improve the environment? Answering these questions will help you narrow these assignments into **topics** that you can write about.

ASSIGNMENT	TOPIC
Discuss some things you would change about your school.	Three things I would change to improve the quality of life at Jackson County Community College
What can college students do to improve the environment?	The campus recycling project

Jared White, a student in a first-year composition course, was given the following assignment.

ASSIGNMENT

Discuss an important decision you made during the past few years.

Jared narrowed this assignment to the following topic:

TOPIC

Deciding to go back to school

In the rest of this chapter, you will be following Jared's writing process.

PRACTICE

13-2 Decide whether the following topics are narrow enough for an essay of four or five paragraphs. If a topic is suitable, write *OK* in the blank. If it is not, write in the blank a revised version of the same topic that is narrow enough for a brief essay.

Examples

Successful strategies for quitting smoking ___*OK*___

Horror movies ___*1950s Japanese monster movies*___

1. Violence in American public schools _____

_____

2. Ways to improve your study skills _____

_____

3. Using pets as therapy for nursing-home patients _____

_____

4. Teachers _____

_____

5. Safe ways to lose weight _____

_____

decide on a topic

Look back at the Focus on Writing prompt on page 191. To narrow this assignment to a topic you can write about, you need to decide which difficult job to focus on. Begin by listing several jobs you could discuss.

FYI

Visit the Study Guides and Strategies Web site (studygs.net /writing/prewriting.htm) to learn how to use one of the graphic organizers or to find other information about the writing process.

13c   Finding Ideas to Write About

Before you start writing about a topic, you need to find out what you have to say about it. Sometimes ideas may come to you easily. More often, you will have to use specific strategies, such as *freewriting* or *brainstorming*, to help you come up with ideas.

Freewriting

When you **freewrite**, you write for a fixed period of time without stopping. When you do **focused freewriting**, you write with a topic in mind. Then, you read what you have written and choose ideas you think you can use.

The following focused freewriting was written by Jared White on the topic "Deciding to go back to school."

Deciding to go back to school. When I graduated high school, I swore I'd never go back to school. Hated it. Couldn't wait to get out. What was I thinking? How was I supposed to support myself? My dad's friend needed help. He taught me how to paint houses. I made good money, but it was boring. I couldn't picture myself doing it forever. Even though I knew I was going to have to go back to school, I kept putting off the decision. Maybe I was lazy. Maybe I was scared—probably both. I had this fear of being turned down. How could someone who had bad grades all through high school go to college? Also, I'd been out of school for six years. And even if I did get in (a miracle!), how would I pay for it? How would I live? Well, here I am—the first one in my family to go to college.

Jared's freewriting

**PRACTICE
13-3**   Reread Jared White's freewriting. If you were advising Jared, which ideas would you tell him to explore further? Why?

freewrite

Choose two of the difficult jobs you listed, and freewrite about each of them. Then, choose one of the jobs to write about. Circle the ideas about this job that you would like to explore further in an essay.

Brainstorming

When you **brainstorm** (either individually or with others in a group), you write down (or type) all the ideas you can think of about a particular topic. After you have recorded as much material as you can, you look over your notes and decide which ideas are useful and which ones are not.

Here are Jared's brainstorming notes about his decision to go back to school.

Deciding to Go Back to School
Money a problem
Other students a lot younger
Paying tuition—how?
No one in family went to college
Friends not in college
Couldn't see myself in college
Considered going to trade school
Computer programmer?
Grades bad in high school
Time for me to grow up
Wondered if I would get in
Found out about community college
Admission requirements not bad
Afraid—too old, failing out, looking silly
Took time to get used to routine
Found other students like me
Liked studying

Jared's brainstorming

PRACTICE

13-4   Reread Jared's brainstorming notes. Which ideas would you advise him to explore further? Why?

brainstorm

Review your freewriting. Then, brainstorm about the job for which you have found the most interesting ideas. What ideas about this job did you get from brainstorming that you did not get from freewriting?

Keeping a Journal

When you keep a **journal**, you keep an informal record of your thoughts and ideas. As you learned in Chapter 2, your journal can be a notebook (or section of a notebook) or a computer file. In your journal, you record your thoughts about your assignments, identify ideas that you want to explore further, and keep notes about things you read or see. After rereading your journal entries, you can decide to explore an idea further in another journal entry or to use material from a specific entry in an essay.

Following is an entry in Jared's journal that he eventually used in his essay about returning to school.

When I was working as a house painter, I had a conversation that helped convince me to go to college. One day, I started talking to the guy whose house I was painting. I told him that I was painting houses until I figured out what I was going to do with the rest of my life. He asked me if I had considered going to college. I told him that I hadn't done well in high school, so I didn't think college was for me. He told me that I could probably get into the local community college. That night I looked at the community college's Web site to see if going to college might be a good idea.

Jared's journal entry

write journal entries

Write at least two journal entries for the topic you have been exploring for this chapter: the hardest job you ever had. Which of your entries do you want to explore further? Which could you use in your essay?

13d   Stating Your Thesis

After you have gathered information about your topic, you need to decide on a thesis for your essay. You do this by reviewing the ideas from your brainstorming, freewriting, and journal entries and then asking, "What is the main point I want to make about my topic?" The answer to this question is the **thesis** of your essay. You express this point in a **thesis statement**: a single sentence that clearly expresses the main idea that you will discuss in the rest of your essay.

Keep in mind that each essay has just *one* thesis statement. The details and examples in the body of the essay all support (add to, discuss, or explain) this thesis statement.

TOPIC	THESIS STATEMENT
Three things I would change about Jackson County Community College	If I could change three things to improve Jackson County Community College, I would expand the food choices, decrease class size in first-year courses, and ship some of my classmates to the North Pole.
The campus recycling project	The recycling project recently begun on our campus should be promoted more actively.

Like a topic sentence in a paragraph, a thesis statement in an essay tells readers what to expect. An effective thesis statement has two important characteristics.

1. *An effective thesis statement makes a point about a topic, expressing the writer's opinion or unique view of the topic. For this reason, it must do more than state a fact or announce what you plan to write about.*

STATEMENT OF FACT   Many older students are returning to school.

ANNOUNCEMENT   In this essay, I will discuss older students going back to school.

A statement of fact is not an effective thesis statement because it gives you nothing to develop in your essay. After all, how much can you say about the *fact* that many older students are returning to school? Likewise, an announcement of what you plan to discuss gives readers no indication of the position you will take on your topic. Remember, an effective thesis statement makes a point.

2. *An effective thesis statement is clearly worded and specific.*

VAGUE THESIS STATEMENT   Returning to school is difficult for older students.

The vague thesis statement above gives readers no sense of the ideas the essay will discuss. It does not say, for example, *why* returning to school is difficult for older students. Remember, an effective thesis statement is specific.

FYI

Evaluating Your Thesis Statement

Once you have a thesis statement, you need to evaluate it to determine if it is effective. Asking the following questions will help you decide:

- Is your thesis statement a complete sentence?

- Does your thesis statement clearly express the main idea you will discuss in your essay?

- Is your thesis statement specific and focused? Does it make a point that you can cover within your time and page limits?

- Does your thesis statement make a point about your topic—not just state a fact or announce what you plan to write about?

- Does your thesis statement avoid vague language?

- Does your thesis statement avoid statements like "I think" or "In my opinion"?

After freewriting, brainstorming, and reviewing his journal entries, Jared decided on a topic and wrote the following effective thesis statement for his essay.

EFFECTIVE THESIS
STATEMENT

Although I realized it would be difficult in some ways, I decided that if I really wanted to attend college full-time, I could.

Jared knew that his thesis statement had to be a complete sentence that made a point about his topic and that it should be both clearly worded and specific. When he reviewed his thesis statement, he felt sure that it satisfied these criteria and expressed an idea he could develop in his essay.

PRACTICE

13-5   In the space provided, indicate whether each of the following items is a statement of fact (*F*), an announcement (*A*), a vague statement (*VS*), or an effective thesis (*ET*).

Examples

My drive to school takes more than an hour. ____*F*____

I hate my commute between home and school. ____*VS*____

1. Students who must commute a long distance to school are at a disadvantage compared to students who live close by. _____

2. In this paper, I will discuss cheating. _____

3. Schools should establish specific policies to discourage students from cheating. _____

4. Cheating is a problem. _____

5. Television commercials are designed to sell products. _____

6. I would like to explain why some television commercials are funny. _____

7. Single parents have a rough time. _____

8. Young people are starting to abuse alcohol and drugs at earlier ages than in the past. _____

9. Alcohol and drug abuse are both major problems in our society. _____

10. Families can do several things to help children avoid alcohol and drugs. _____

PRACTICE

13-6   Label each of the following thesis statements *F* if it is a statement of fact, *A* if it is an announcement, *VS* if it is a vague statement, or *ET* if it is an effective thesis. Revise those that are not effective thesis statements.

Examples

The World Health Organization has warned that people can get sick from drinking unclean water. _____*F*_____

Possible rewrite: The World Health Organization should make access to clean water its first priority in disease prevention.

A few simple changes could make the dining halls safer for students with food allergies. _____*ET*_____

1. The TV show *Heroes* was on the air for four seasons before being canceled in 2010. _____

2. To survive in Los Angeles, a new restaurant needs a good location and a unique menu. _____

3. My essay will show that Johnny Depp is a better actor than Brad Pitt. _____

4. Highway speed limits are ineffective. _____

5. In this essay, I will discuss the pros and cons of choosing tap water over bottled water. _____

6. Studying abroad enables college students to gain independence and self-confidence. _____

7. The National Weather Service predicts this will be an average year for hurricanes. _____

8. By teaching me critical problem-solving skills, the Army prepared me well for a career in engineering. _____

9. Sugary soda is high in calories and low in nutritional value. _____

10. People have their own definitions of justice. _____

PRACTICE

13-7 Rewrite the following vague thesis statements to make them effective.

Example

My relatives are funny.

Rewrite: _My relatives think they are funny, but sometimes their humor_

can be offensive.

1. Online courses have advantages.

2. Airport security is more trouble than it is worth.

3. Athletes are paid too much.

4. Many people get their identities from their cars.

5. Cheating in college is out of control.

PRACTICE

13-8 A list of broad topics for essays follows. Select five of these topics, narrow them, and generate a thesis statement for each.

1. Careers
2. Reality television
3. U.S. immigration policies
4. Music
5. Texting in class

6. Required courses
7. Computer games
8. Disciplining children
9. Street sense
10. The cost of gasoline

PRACTICE

13-9 Read the following groups of statements. Then, write a thesis statement that could express the main point of each group.

1. Thesis statement _____

_____

■ *Gap year* is a term that refers to a year that students take off before they go to college.

■ Many college students spend most of their time studying and socializing with their peers.

- Studies show that high school students who take a year off before they go to college get better grades.
- Many students take community-service jobs in order to broaden their interests and to increase their social awareness.

2. Thesis statement _____

_____

- Some people post too much personal information on social-networking sites such as Facebook.
- Child predators frequently use social-networking sites to find their victims.
- Some experts believe that people can become addicted to social-networking sites.
- Employers have fired employees because of information they have seen on their employees' social-networking sites.

3. Thesis statement _____

_____

- A student at Indiana University at Bloomington was able to create her own major in environmental ethics.
- Drexel University has begun recruiting students who would design their own majors.
- Some students get bored with traditional majors that force them to choose from a rigid list of courses.
- Many employers are impressed with students who design their own majors.

4. Thesis statement _____

_____

- One way to pay for college is to get a job.
- The majority of students supplement their college tuition with loans or grants.
- According to the College Board, only 22 percent of all federal aid for college tuition goes to scholarships.
- Some students enlist in the armed forces and become eligible for tuition assistance programs.

5. Thesis statement _____

_____

- You can save time in the kitchen by washing and putting away items as you cook.
- Keep your kitchen well stocked so that you will not have to run to the store to get an ingredient.
- Keep your countertops free of clutter so you don't have to put things away before you cook.
- Shred things like cheese in advance and store them in plastic bags.

---

state your thesis

Review your freewriting, brainstorming, and journal entries. Then, write a thesis statement for your essay.

Step 2: Organizing

13e Choosing Supporting Points

Once you have decided on a thesis statement, look over your freewriting, brainstorming, and journal entries again. Identify **evidence** (details and examples) that best supports your thesis.

Jared made the following list of possible supporting points about his decision to go back to school. When he reviewed his list, he crossed out several points that he thought would not support his thesis.

Deciding to Go Back to School: Pros and Cons

Money a problem

Other students a lot younger

Paying tuition—how?

No one in family went to college

Friends not in college

(continued)

(continued from previous page)

Couldn't see myself in college

~~Considered going to trade school~~

~~Computer programmer?~~

Grades bad in high school

Wondered if I would get in

Found out about community college

Admission requirements not bad

Afraid—too old, failing out, looking dumb

~~Took time to get used to routine~~

Found other students like me

Liked studying

Jared's list of supporting points

PRACTICE

13-10 Review Jared's list of supporting points above. Do you see any points he crossed out that you think he should have kept? Do you see any other points he should have crossed out?

13f Making an Outline

After you have selected the points you think will best support your thesis, make an informal outline. Begin by arranging your supporting points into groups. Then, arrange them in the order in which you will discuss them (for example, from general to specific, or from least to most important). Arrange the supporting points for each group in the same way. This informal outline can guide you as you write.

When Jared looked over his list of supporting points, he saw that they fell into three groups of excuses for not going back to school: not being able to pay tuition, not being a good student in high school, and not being able to picture himself in college. He arranged his points under these three headings to create the following informal outline.

Excuse 1: Not being able to pay tuition

    Needed to work to live

    Didn't have much saved

    Found out about community college (low tuition)

    Found out about grants, loans

Excuse 2: Not being a good student in high school

    Got bad grades in high school: wasn't motivated and didn't work

    Looked into admission requirements at community college—doable!

    Made a commitment to improve study habits

Excuse 3: Not being able to picture myself in college

    No college graduates in family

    No friends in college

    Afraid of being too old, looking dumb

    Found other students like me

    Found out I liked studying

Jared's informal outline

PRACTICE

13-11 Look over Jared's informal outline above. Do you think his arrangement is effective? Can you suggest any other ways he might have arranged his points?

FYI

Preparing a Formal Outline

An informal outline like the one that appears above is usually all you need to plan a short essay. However, some writers—especially when they are planning a longer, more detailed essay—prefer to use formal outlines.

Formal outlines use a combination of numbered and lettered headings to show the relationships among ideas. For example, the most important (and most general) ideas are assigned a Roman numeral; the next most important ideas are assigned capital letters. Each level develops the idea above it, and each new level is indented.

Here is a formal outline of the points that Jared planned to discuss in his essay.

(continued)

(continued from previous page)

Thesis statement: Although I realized it would be difficult in some ways, I decided that if I really wanted to attend college full-time, I could.

I. Difficulty: Money
    A. Needed to work to live
    B. Didn't have much money saved
    C. Found out about community college (low tuition)
    D. Found out about grants/loans
II. Difficulty: Academic record
    A. Got bad grades in high school
        1. Didn't care
        2. Didn't work
    B. Found out about reasonable admissions requirements at community college
    C. Committed to improving study habits
III. Difficulty: Imagining myself as a student
    A. Had no college graduates in family
    B. Had no friends in school
    C. Felt anxious
        1. Too old
        2. Out of practice at school
    D. Found other students like me
    E. Discovered I like studying

make an outline

Review the freewriting, brainstorming, and journal entries you wrote. Then, list the points you plan to use to support your thesis statement. Cross out any points that do not support your thesis statement. Finally, group the remaining points into an informal outline that will guide you as you write.

Step 3: Drafting

13g Drafting Your Essay

After you have decided on a thesis for your essay and have arranged your supporting points in the order in which you will discuss them, you are ready to draft your essay.

At this stage of the writing process, you should not worry about spelling or grammar or about composing a perfect introduction or conclusion. Your main goal is to get your ideas down so you can react to them. Remember that the draft you are writing will be revised, so leave extra space between lines as you type. Follow your outline, but don't hesitate to depart from it if you think of new points.

As you draft your essay, be sure that it has a **thesis-and-support** structure—that it states a thesis and supports it with evidence. Include a **working title**, a temporary title that you will revise later so that it accurately reflects the content of your completed essay. This working title will help you focus your ideas.

Following is the first draft of Jared's essay.

Going Back to School

I was out of school for six years after I graduated from high school. The decision to return to school was one I had a lot of difficulty making. I had been around enough to know that without more education, I'd never get anywhere in life, but I always found reasons for not taking the plunge. However, after a lot of thinking, I realized that my reasons for not going to college were just excuses. Although I realized it would be difficult in some ways, I decided that if I really wanted to attend college full-time, I could.

My first excuse for not going to college was that I couldn't afford to go to school full-time. I had worked since I finished high school, but I hadn't put much money away. I kept wondering how I would pay for books and tuition. I needed to support myself and pay for rent, food, and car expenses. I was working as a house painter, and a house I was painting belonged to a college instructor. Painting wasn't hard work, but it was boring. I'd start in the morning and work without a break until lunch. We began talking. When I told him about my situation, he told me I should look at our local community college. He also told me about some loans and grants I'd probably be able to apply for. I went online and looked at the college's Web site. I found out that tuition was one hundred dollars a credit, less than I thought it would be. If I got just one of the grants he mentioned, I might be able to make it.

Now that I had taken care of my first excuse, I had to deal with my second—that I hadn't been a good student in high school. When I was a teenager, I didn't care much about school. School bored me to death. Probably as a result, I got bad grades. Now that I was considering going back to school, though, I wondered what price I would have to pay for

(continued)

(continued from previous page)

my laziness and immaturity. The answer to this question was not as bad as I thought it would be. According to the community college's Web site, all I needed to be admitted was a high school diploma and county residence. I would have to take some placement tests, but I would be judged on my ability, not my high school grades. I knew I could do better if I made a real effort to study harder and smarter. The Web site was easy to navigate, and I had no problem finding information.

I had a hard time picturing myself in college. No one in my family had ever gone to college. My friends were just like me; they all went to work right after high school. I had no role model or mentor who could give me advice. I thought I was just too old for college. After all, I was probably at least six years older than most of the students. How would I be able to keep up with the younger students in the class? I hadn't opened a textbook for years, and I'd never really learned how to study. Most of my fears disappeared during my first few weeks of classes. I saw a lot of students who were as old as I was, and some were even older. Studying didn't seem to be a problem either. I actually enjoyed learning. History, which had put me to sleep in high school, suddenly became interesting. So did math and English. It soon became clear to me that I was going to like being in college.

Going to college as a full-time student has changed my life, both personally and financially. I am no longer the same person I was in high school. I allowed laziness and insecurity to hold me back. Now, I have options that I didn't have before. When I graduate from community college, I plan to transfer to the state university and get a four-year degree.

Jared's first draft

PRACTICE

13-12 Reread Jared's first draft. What changes would you suggest? What might he have added? What might he have deleted? Which of his supporting details and examples do you find most effective?

draft your essay

Draft an essay about your most difficult job. When you finish your draft, give your essay a working title.

Step 4: TESTing

13h   TESTing Your Essay

Before you begin to revise the first draft of your essay, you should **TEST** it to make sure it contains the four elements that make it clear and effective.

T ▪ **Thesis Statement**—Does your essay include a thesis statement that states your main idea?

E ▪ **Evidence**—Does your essay include evidence—examples and details—that supports your thesis statement?

S ▪ **Summary Statement**—Does your essay's conclusion include a summary statement that reinforces your thesis and sums up your main idea?

T ▪ **Transitions**—Does your essay include transitional words and phrases that show readers how your ideas are related?

As you reread your essay, use the **TEST** strategy to identify the four elements of an effective essay. If your essay includes them, you can move on to revise and edit it. If not, you should supply whatever is missing.

When Jared reread the draft of his essay, he used the **TEST** strategy to help him quickly survey his essay.

▪ He decided that his **thesis statement** clearly stated his main idea.

▪ He thought he could add some more **evidence** in his body paragraphs and delete some irrelevant details.

▪ He thought his **summary statement** summed up the idea expressed in his thesis statement.

▪ He realized he needed to add more **transitions** to connect ideas.

TEST your essay

TEST your draft to make sure it includes all the elements of an effective essay. If any elements are missing, add them.

Step 5: Revising and Editing

13i Revising Your Essay

When you **revise** your essay, you do not simply correct errors; instead, you resee, rethink, reevaluate, and rewrite your work. Some of the changes you make—such as adding, deleting, or rearranging sentences or even whole paragraphs—will be major. Others will be small—for example, adding or deleting words or phrases.

It is a good idea to revise on hard copy and not on the computer screen. On hard copy, you are able to see a full page—or even two or three pages next to each other—as you revise. When you have finished, you can type your changes into your document. (Do not delete sentences or paragraphs until you are certain you do not need them. Instead, move unwanted material to the end of your draft—or save multiple, dated drafts.)

Before you begin revising, put your essay aside for a while. This "cooling-off" period allows you to see your draft more objectively when you return to it. (Keep in mind that revision is usually not a neat process. When you revise, you write directly on your draft: draw arrows, underline, cross out, and write above lines and in the margins.)

There are a number of strategies you can use to help you revise: you can schedule a conference with your instructor, make an appointment at the writing center, participate in a peer-review session with your classmates, communicate with your instructor electronically, or use a revision checklist, such as the one on page 218. Sometimes you may decide to use just one of these strategies (for example, when you are writing a short paper), but at other times you may employ several of them (for example, when you are writing a research paper). The following chart shows you the advantages of each revision strategy.

STRATEGIES FOR REVISING	
STRATEGY	**ADVANTAGES**
FACE-TO-FACE CONFERENCE WITH INSTRUCTOR	▪ Provides one-to-one feedback that can't be obtained in the classroom ▪ Builds a student-teacher relationship ▪ Enables students to collaborate with their instructors ▪ Allows students to ask questions that they might not ask in a classroom setting

WRITING CENTER	■ Offers students a less formal, less stressful environment than an instructor conference ■ Enables students to get help from trained tutors (both students and professionals) ■ Provides a perspective other than the instructor's ■ Offers specialized help to students whose first language is not English
PEER REVIEW	■ Enables students working on the same assignment to share insights with one another ■ Gives students the experience of writing for a real audience ■ Gives students several different readers' reactions to their work ■ Enables students to benefit from the ideas of their class-mates
ELECTRONIC COMMUNICATION WITH INSTRUCTOR	■ Enables students to submit email questions before a draft is due ■ Gives students quick answers to their questions ■ Enables instructors to give feedback by annotating drafts electronically ■ Enables students to react to their instructor's responses when they have time ■ Eliminates time spent traveling to instructor's office
REVISION CHECKLIST	■ Gives students a tool that enables them to revise in an orderly way ■ Enables students to learn to revise independently ■ Enables students to focus on specific aspects of their writing

FYI

You can watch a helpful YouTube video created by the Texas A&M Writing Center on how to give useful peer responses. At YouTube .com, type "A Peer Response Demonstration" in the search box. Find the video uploaded by tamuwritingcenter.

self-assessment checklist

Revising Your Essay

☐ Does your essay have an introduction, a body, and a conclusion?

☐ Does your introduction include a clearly worded thesis statement that states your essay's main idea?

☐ Does each body paragraph have a topic sentence?

☐ Does each topic sentence introduce a point that supports the thesis?

☐ Does each body paragraph include enough examples and details to support the topic sentence?

☐ Are the body paragraphs unified, well developed, and coherent?

☐ Does your conclusion include a concluding statement that restates your thesis or sums up your main idea?

13j   Editing Your Essay

When you **edit** your essay, you check grammar and sentence structure. Then, you look at punctuation, mechanics, and spelling. As you edit, think carefully about the questions in the Self-Assessment Checklist below.

self-assessment checklist

Editing Your Essay

EDITING FOR COMMON SENTENCE PROBLEMS

☐ Have you avoided run-ons? (See Chapter 24.)

☐ Have you avoided sentence fragments? (See Chapter 25.)

☐ Do your subjects and verbs agree? (See Chapter 26.)

- [ ] Have you avoided illogical shifts? (See Chapter 27.)
- [ ] Have you avoided dangling and misplaced modifiers? (See Chapter 28.)

EDITING FOR GRAMMAR

- [ ] Are your verb forms and verb tenses correct? (See Chapters 29 and 30.)
- [ ] Have you used nouns and pronouns correctly? (See Chapter 31.)
- [ ] Have you used adjectives and adverbs correctly? (See Chapter 32.)

EDITING FOR PUNCTUATION, MECHANICS, AND SPELLING

- [ ] Have you used commas correctly? (See Chapter 34.)
- [ ] Have you used apostrophes correctly? (See Chapter 35.)
- [ ] Have you used capital letters where they are required? (See 36a.)
- [ ] Have you used quotation marks correctly where they are needed? (See 36b.)

When Jared typed the first draft of his essay about deciding to return to college, he left extra space so he could write more easily between the lines. Before revising this draft, he met with his instructor to discuss it. Then, he used the Self-Assessment Checklist above to help him revise his essay.

Jared's first draft, with his handwritten revisions and edits along with the transitions he added after he finished **TEST**ing his essay, appears on the following pages.

<del>Going Back to School</del> Starting Over

I was out of school for six years after I graduated from high school. The decision to return to school was one I had a lot of difficulty making. I had been around enough to know that without more education, I'd never get anywhere in life, but I always found reasons for not taking the plunge. However, after a lot of thinking, I realized that my reasons for not going to college were just excuses. Although I realized it would be difficult in some ways, I decided that if I really wanted to attend college full-time, I could.

The other day, my sociology instructor mentioned that half the students enrolled in college programs across the country are twenty-five or older. His remark caught my attention because I am one of those students.

My first excuse for not going to college was that I couldn't afford to go to school full-time. I had worked since I finished high school, but I hadn't put much money away. I kept wondering how I would pay for books and tuition. I also needed to support myself and pay for rent, food, and car expenses. ~~The solution to my problem came unexpectedly.~~ I was working as a house painter, and a house I was painting belonged to a college instructor. ~~Painting wasn't hard work, but it was boring. I'd start in the morning and work without a break until lunch.~~ During my lunch break, we ~~We~~ began talking. When I told him about my situation, he told me I should look at our local community college. He also told me about some loans and grants I'd probably be able to apply for. Later, I went online and looked at the college's Web site. I found out that tuition was one hundred dollars a credit, less than I thought it would be. If I got just one of the grants he mentioned, I might be able to make it.

The money I'd saved, along with what I could make painting houses on the weekends, could get me through.

Now that I had taken care of my first excuse, I had to deal with my second—that I hadn't been a good student in high school. When I was a teenager, I didn't care much about school. In fact, school ~~School~~ bored me ~~to death~~. Probably as a result, I got bad grades. Now that I was considering going back to school, though, I wondered what price I would have to pay for my laziness and immaturity. The answer to this question was not as bad as I thought it would be. According to the community college's Web site, all I needed to be admitted was a high school diploma and county residence. I would have to take some placement tests, but I would be judged on my ability, not my high school grades. I knew I could do better if I made a real effort to study harder and smarter. ~~The Web site was easy to navigate, and I had no problem finding information.~~

In class, I would stare out the window or watch the second hand on the clock move slowly around. I never bothered with homework. School just didn't interest me.

My biggest problem still bothered me: I had a hard time picturing myself in college. No one in my family had ever gone to college. My friends were just like me; they all went to work right after high school. I had no role model or mentor who could give me advice. Besides, I thought I was just too old for college. After all, I was probably at least six years older than most of the students. How would I be able to keep up with the younger students in the class? I hadn't opened a textbook for years, and I'd never really learned how to study. ~~Most~~ ^However, most^ of my fears disappeared during my first few weeks of classes. I saw a lot of students who were as old as I was, and some were even older. Studying didn't seem to be a problem either. I actually enjoyed learning. History, which had put me to sleep in high school, suddenly became interesting. So did math and English. It soon became clear to me that I was going to like being in college.

　　Going to college as a full-time student has changed my life, both personally and financially. I am no longer the same person I was in high school. ^In the past,^ I allowed laziness and insecurity to hold me back. Now, I have options that I didn't have before. When I graduate from community college, I plan to transfer to the state university and get a four-year degree. The other day, one of my instructors asked me if I had ever considered becoming a teacher. The truth is, I never had, but now I might. I'd like to be able to give kids like me the tough, realistic advice I wish someone had given me.

PRACTICE
13-13　Working in a group of three or four students, answer the following questions:

- What kind of material did Jared add to his draft?
- What did he delete?
- Why do you think he made these changes?
- Do you agree with the changes he made?

Be prepared to discuss your reactions to these changes with the class.

　　When his revisions and edits were complete, Jared proofread his essay to make sure he had not missed any errors. The final revised and edited version of his essay appears on pages 222–223. (Marginal annotations have been added to highlight key features of his paper.) Note that the final draft includes all the elements Jared looked for when he **TEST**ed his essay.

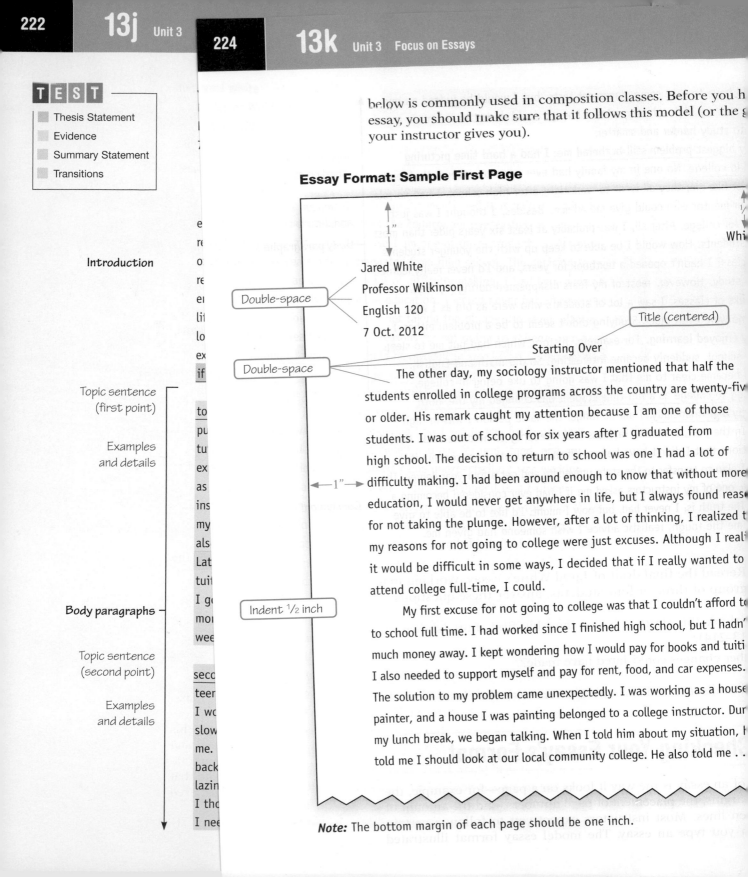

T E S T

- Thesis Statement
- Evidence
- Summary Statement
- Transitions

Introduction

Topic sentence
(first point)

Examples
and details

Body paragraphs

Topic sentence
(second point)

Examples
and details

below is commonly used in composition classes. Before you h
essay, you should make sure that it follows this model (or the g
your instructor gives you).

Essay Format: Sample First Page

1"

Whi

Double-space

Jared White
Professor Wilkinson
English 120
7 Oct. 2012

Title (centered)

Starting Over

Double-space

1"

The other day, my sociology instructor mentioned that half the
students enrolled in college programs across the country are twenty-fiv
or older. His remark caught my attention because I am one of those
students. I was out of school for six years after I graduated from
high school. The decision to return to school was one I had a lot of
difficulty making. I had been around enough to know that without more
education, I would never get anywhere in life, but I always found reas
for not taking the plunge. However, after a lot of thinking, I realized t
my reasons for not going to college were just excuses. Although I real
it would be difficult in some ways, I decided that if I really wanted to
attend college full-time, I could.

Indent ½ inch

My first excuse for not going to college was that I couldn't afford t
to school full time. I had worked since I finished high school, but I hadn'
much money away. I kept wondering how I would pay for books and tuiti
I also needed to support myself and pay for rent, food, and car expenses.
The solution to my problem came unexpectedly. I was working as a house
painter, and a house I was painting belonged to a college instructor. Dur
my lunch break, we began talking. When I told him about my situation, h
told me I should look at our local community college. He also told me . . .

Note: The bottom margin of each page should be one inch.

revise and edit your essay

Revise your draft, using the Self-Assessment Checklist on page 218 to guide you. (If your instructor gives you permission, you may use one of the other revision strategies listed in the chart on pages 216–217.) When you have finished revising, edit your draft, using the Self-Assessment Checklist on pages 218–219 as a guide. Then, prepare a final revised and edited draft of your essay. Finally, make sure that your essay's format follows your instructor's guidelines.

EDITING PRACTICE

1. The following student essay is missing its thesis statement and topic sentences and has no summary statement. First, write an appropriate thesis statement on the lines provided. (Make sure your thesis statement clearly communicates the essay's main idea.) Then, fill in the topic sentences for the second, third, and fourth paragraphs. Finally, add a summary statement in the conclusion.

Preparing for a Job Interview

A lot of books and many Web sites give advice on how to do well on a job interview. Some recommend practicing your handshake, and others suggest making eye contact. This advice is useful, but not many books tell how to get mentally prepared for an interview. [Thesis statement:] _____

_____

_____

_____

[Topic sentence for the second paragraph:] _____

_____

_____

_____

Feeling good about how you look is important, so you should probably wear a dress or skirt (or, for males, a jacket and tie) to an interview. Even if you will not be dressing this formally on the job, try to make a good first impression. For this reason, you should never come to an interview dressed in jeans or shorts. Still, you should be careful not to overdress. For example, wearing a suit or a dressy dress to an interview at a fast-food restaurant might make you feel good, but it could also make you look as if you do not really want to work there.

[Topic sentence for the third paragraph:] _____

_____

_____

Going on an interview is a little like getting ready to compete in a sporting event. You have to go in with the right attitude. If you think you are not going to be successful, chances are that you will not be. So, before you go on any interview, spend some time building your confidence. Tell yourself that you can do the job and that you will do well in the interview. By the time you get to the interview, you will have convinced yourself that you are the right person for the job.

[Topic sentence for the fourth paragraph:] _____ —

_____

_____

Most people go to an interview knowing little or nothing about the job. They expect the interviewer to tell them what they will have to do. Most interviewers, however, are impressed by someone who has taken the time to do his or her homework. For this reason, you should always do some research before you go on an interview—even for a part-time job. Most of the time, your research can be nothing more than a quick look at the company's Web site, but this kind of research really pays off. Being able to talk about the job can give you a real advantage over other candidates. Sometimes the interviewer will be so impressed that he or she will offer you a job on the spot.

[Summary statement:] _____

_____

_____

Of course, following these suggestions will not guarantee that you get a job. You still have to do well at the interview itself. Even so, getting mentally prepared for the interview will give you an advantage over people who do almost nothing before they walk in the door.

2. Now, using the topic sentence below, write another body paragraph that you could add to the essay above. (This new paragraph will go right before the essay's conclusion.)

Another way to prepare yourself mentally is to anticipate and answer some typical questions interviewers ask.

_____

_____

_____

_____

COLLABORATIVE ACTIVITY

Working in a group, come up with thesis statements suitable for essays on three of the following topics.

Living on a budget	Gun safety
Social-networking sites	Drawbacks of online dating
Safe driving	Patriotism
Sustainable energy	Community service
Honesty	Preparing for a test

Then, exchange your group's three thesis statements with those of another group. Choose the best one of the other group's thesis statements. A member of each group can then read the thesis statement to the class and explain why the group chose the thesis statement it did.

review checklist

Writing an Essay

- ☐ Most essays have a thesis-and-support structure. The thesis statement presents the main idea, and the body paragraphs support the thesis. (See 13a.)

- ☐ Begin by focusing on your assignment, purpose, and audience to help you find a topic. (See 13b.)

- ☐ Find ideas to write about. (See 13c.)

- ☐ Identify your main idea, and develop an effective thesis statement. (See 13d.)

- ☐ List the points that best support your thesis, and arrange them in the order in which you plan to discuss them, creating an informal outline of your essay. (See 13e and 13f.)

- ☐ Write your first draft, making sure your essay has a thesis-and-support structure. (See 13g.)

- ☐ **TEST** your essay. (Sec 13h.)

- ☐ Revise your essay. (See 13i.)

- ☐ Edit your essay. (See 13j.)

- ☐ Make sure your essay's format is correct. (See 13k.)

14 TESTing Your Essays

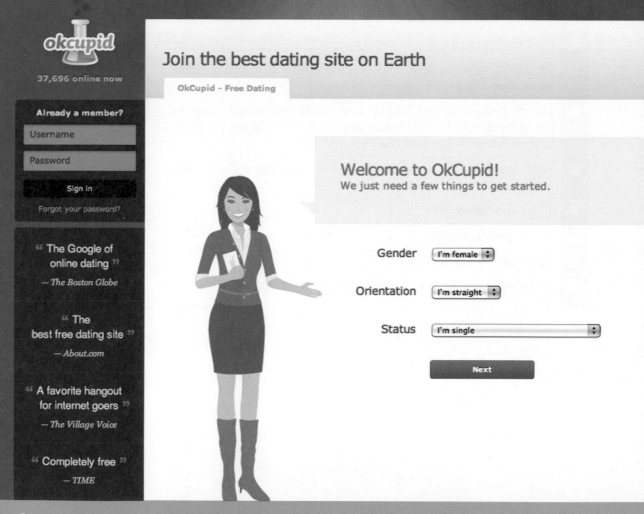

focus on writing

Thousands of people have used sites like OkCupid to meet people. Assume that you are writing an article about online dating for your school newspaper. What tips would you give students who were thinking about using an online dating site? What are the advantages and disadvantages of meeting people this way? Make sure your article is written in the form of a thesis-and-support essay.

In this chapter, you will learn how to **TEST** your essays.

Just as you **TEST** your paragraphs, you should also **TEST** your essays. **TEST**ing will tell you whether your essay includes the basic elements it needs to be effective. Once you finish **TEST**ing your essay, you will go on to revise and edit it.

T hesis Statement
E vidence
S ummary Statement
T ransitions

14a TESTing for a Thesis

The first thing you do when you **TEST** your essay is to make sure it has a clear **thesis statement (T)** that identifies the essay's main idea. By stating the main idea, your thesis statement helps to unify your essay.

The following introduction is from an essay written by a student, Amber Ransom, on the dangers of social networking. Notice that Amber states her thesis in the last sentence of her introduction, where readers expect to see it.

INTRODUCTION

Social-networking sites have many advantages. These sites, such as Facebook and MySpace, enable people to create profiles and to personalize them with pictures. "Friends" can browse these profiles and post comments that can then be viewed by anyone who has access to the profile. Many people meet online and then go on to form close friendships in real life. Some schools even set up social-networking sites for students so they can keep in touch, get advice, ask questions about schoolwork, and get feedback on assignments. Despite their many benefits, however, social-networking sites can create serious problems that people should be aware of.

T **E** **S** **T**
☐ Thesis Statement
■ Evidence
■ Summary Statement
■ Transitions

14b TESTing for Evidence

The next thing you do when you **TEST** your essay is to check your **evidence (E)** to make sure that the body of your essay includes enough examples and details to support your thesis. Remember that without evidence, your essay is really only a series of unsupported general statements. A well-developed essay includes enough evidence to explain, illustrate, and clarify the points you are making.

At this stage of your college career, most of your evidence will come from your personal experience and observations or from class lectures or discussions. (Later, when you do research, you will be able to supplement this material with information from print and electronic sources.)

The following body paragraphs are from Amber's essay on the dangers of social networking. Notice that Amber's body paragraphs present the evidence she needs to develop and support the points she makes in her essay. In addition, the topic sentence of each body paragraph connects the paragraph to the essay's thesis.

BODY PARAGRAPHS

TEST
- Thesis Statement
- Evidence
- Summary Statement
- Transitions

One problem with social-networking sites is the amount of time people devote to them. Some users spend hours every day just checking in with their "friends." This can be an especially serious problem for some students, who can become more interested in socializing online than in learning. Because they can access social-networking sites with their smartphones and laptops, students often spend more time in class communicating with their friends than listening to their instructors. These problems are not limited to students. In fact, some people have been fired from their jobs because of their excessive involvement with social-networking sites. For example, a waitress was fired because she couldn't resist posting pictures of herself at the beach on a day when she was supposed to be at home sick, and a medical technician was fired because of negative comments he made online about his supervisor.

Another problem with social-networking sites is that they can reveal a lot of personal information. Some people include so much personal information in their profiles that they risk identity theft, identity fraud, or even worse. Even though sites like Facebook have privacy settings, users often ignore them and post personal information such as birthdays, schools they attended, dates of graduation, email addresses, job titles, and even phone numbers. Dishonest people can access this information, allowing them to establish false identities, get credit cards, and gain access to checking accounts. An even more serious problem occurs with sexual predators, who routinely surf social-networking sites to search for victims. Children are especially vulnerable to these predators because they are often unaware of the danger.

One of the most serious problems with social-networking sites is that they make cyberbullying—the use of computers (as well as cell phones and other devices) to embarrass, annoy, or even threaten others—easier. Cyberbullies spread vicious rumors in online social spaces. Sometimes they set up false profiles on networking sites, using people's real names, pictures, and email addresses. As a result, victims are flooded with anonymous email messages that harass and threaten them. In one famous case, Megan Meier, a fourteen-year-old girl, committed suicide after being cyberbullied by the jealous mother of a former friend. The mother set up a false MySpace account and pretended to be a boy, taunting Megan so much that she eventually committed suicide.

14c   TESTing for a Summary Statement

The third thing you do when you **TEST** your essay is to look at your conclusion and make sure that it includes a **summary statement (S)**. Most often, your conclusion will begin with this statement, which reinforces your essay's thesis. By reinforcing your thesis, this summary statement helps to unify your essay.

The following conclusion is from Amber's essay on the dangers of social networking. Notice that it begins with a summary statement and ends with some general concluding remarks.

CONCLUSION

Despite their benefits, social-networking sites have created many problems. The amount of time that people spend on these sites, the lack of privacy, and the use of sites by cyberbullies are a concern for everyone. Unfortunately, many people underestimate the potential danger of social-networking sites. As a result, they post personal information and make it easy for someone to target them. Once users know the risks, however, they can take steps to keep themselves and their families safe. The basic rule for everyone who uses these sites is not to post information about yourself that you do not want everyone to know.

T E S T
- Thesis Statement
- Evidence
- Summary Statement
- Transitions

14d   TESTing for Transitions

The last thing you do when you **TEST** your essay is to make sure that it includes **transitions (T)**—words and phrases that connect your ideas. Make sure you have included all the transitions you need to tell readers how one sentence (or paragraph) is connected to another. Including transitions makes your essay coherent, with its sentences arranged in a clear, logical sequence that helps readers understand your ideas.

By linking sentences and paragraphs, transitions emphasize the relationship between ideas and help readers understand your essay's logic. By reminding readers of what has come before, transitions prepare readers for new information and help them understand how it fits into the discussion. In this sense, transitions are the glue that holds the ideas in your essay together.

Transitions are categorized according to their function. For example, they may indicate **time order** (*first, second, now, next, finally,* and so on), **spatial order** (*above, behind, near, next to, over,* and so on), or **logical order** (*also, although, therefore, in fact,* and so on). (For a full list of transitions, see 3d.)

Here are the thesis statement and the body paragraphs from Amber's essay on the dangers of social networking. Notice how the highlighted transitions link the sentences and the paragraphs of the essay.

THESIS + BODY PARAGRAPHS

- Thesis Statement
- Evidence
- Summary Statement
- Transitions

Despite their many benefits, however, social-networking sites can create serious problems that people should be aware of.

One problem with social-networking sites is the amount of time people devote to them. Some users spend hours every day just checking in with their "friends." This can be an especially serious problem for some students, who can become more interested in socializing online than in learning. Because they can access social-networking sites with their smartphones and laptops, students often spend more time in class communicating with their friends than listening to their instructors. These problems are not limited to students. In fact, some people have been fired from their jobs because of their excessive involvement with social-networking sites. For example, a waitress was fired because she couldn't resist posting pictures of herself at the beach on a day when she was supposed to be at home sick, and a medical technician was fired because of negative comments he made online about his supervisor.

Another problem with social-networking sites is that they can reveal a lot of personal information. Some people include so much personal information in their profiles that they risk identity theft, identity fraud, or even worse. Even though sites like Facebook have privacy settings, users often ignore them and post personal information such as birthdays, schools they attended, dates of graduation, email addresses, job titles, and even phone numbers. Dishonest people can access this information, allowing them to establish false identities, get credit cards, and gain access to checking accounts. An even more serious problem occurs with sexual predators, who routinely surf social-networking sites to search for victims. Children are especially vulnerable to these predators because they are often unaware of the danger.

One of the most serious problems with social-networking sites is that they make cyberbullying—the use of computers (as well as cell phones and other devices) to embarrass, annoy, and even threaten others—easier. Cyberbullies spread vicious rumors in online social spaces. Sometimes they set up false profiles on networking sites, using people's real names, pictures, and email addresses. As a result, victims are flooded with anonymous email messages that harass and threaten them. In one famous case, Megan Meier, a fourteen-year-old girl, committed suicide after being cyberbullied by the jealous mother of a former friend. The mother set up a false MySpace account and pretended to be a boy, taunting Megan so much that she eventually committed suicide.

14e Putting It Together

Here is Amber's completed essay, which includes a title and the heading required by her instructor.

Amber Ransom
Professor Fallows
Composition 101
5 Nov. 2011

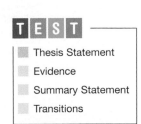

T E S T
  Thesis Statement
  Evidence
  Summary Statement
  Transitions

The Dangers of Social Networking

Social-networking sites have many advantages. These sites, such as Facebook and MySpace, enable people to create profiles and to personalize them with pictures. "Friends" can browse these profiles and post comments that can then be viewed by anyone who has access to the profile. Many people meet online and then go on to form close friendships in real life. Some schools even set up social-networking sites for students so they can keep in touch, get advice, ask questions about schoolwork, and get feedback on assignments. Despite their many benefits, however, social-networking sites can create serious problems that people should be aware of.

Introduction

Topic sentence (states first point)

    <u>One problem</u> with social-networking sites is the amount of time people <u>devote to them.</u> Some users spend hours every day just checking in with their "friends." This can be an especially serious problem for some students, who can become more interested in socializing online than in learning. Because they can access social-networking sites with their smartphones and laptops, students often spend more time in class communicating with their friends than listening to their instructors. These problems are not limited to students.

Examples and details

In fact, some people have been fired from their jobs because of their excessive involvement with social-networking sites. For example, a waitress was fired because she couldn't resist posting pictures of herself at the beach on a day when she was supposed to be at home sick, and a medical technician was fired because of negative comments he made online about his supervisor.

Topic sentence (states second point)

    <u>Another problem</u> with social-networking sites is that they can reveal a lot <u>of personal information.</u> Some people include so much personal information in their profiles that they risk identity theft, identity fraud, or even worse. Even though sites like Facebook have privacy settings, users often ignore them and post personal information such as birthdays, schools they attended, dates of graduation, email addresses, job titles, and even phone numbers.

Body paragraphs

Examples and details

Dishonest people can access this information, allowing them to establish false identities, get credit cards, and gain access to checking accounts. An even more serious problem occurs with sexual predators, who routinely surf social-networking sites to search for victims. Children are especially vulnerable to these predators because they are often unaware of the danger.

Topic sentence (states third point)

    <u>One of the most serious problems</u> with social-networking sites is that they <u>make cyberbullying—the use of computers (as well as cell phones and other</u> <u>devices) to embarrass, annoy, or even threaten others—easier.</u> Cyberbullies spread vicious rumors in online social spaces. Sometimes they set up false profiles on networking sites, using people's real names, pictures, and email addresses. As a result, victims are flooded with anonymous email messages

Examples and details

that harass and threaten them. In one famous case, Megan Meier, a fourteen-year-old girl, committed suicide after being cyberbullied by the jealous mother of a former friend. The mother set up a false MySpace account and pretended to be a boy, taunting Megan so much that she eventually committed suicide.

    <u>Despite their benefits, social-networking sites have created many</u> <u>problems.</u> The amount of time that people spend on these sites, the lack of privacy, and the use of sites by cyberbullies are concerns for everyone. Unfortunately, many people underestimate the potential danger of

social-networking sites. As a result, they post personal information and make it easy for someone to target them. Once users know the risks, however, they can take steps to keep themselves and their families safe. The basic rule for everyone who uses these sites is not to post information about yourself that you do not want everyone to know.

Conclusion

PRACTICE

14-1   Read the final draft of Amber's essay. What changes would you make to her essay? For example, do you think her thesis is appropriate? What additional evidence could she have included? Does her summary statement help to unify her essay? Does she include enough transitions?

TEST · Revise · Edit

Look back at your response to the Focus on Writing prompt on page 230. Then, **TEST** your essay to make sure that it includes a thesis statement, evidence, a summary statement, and transitions. Finally, prepare a revised and edited draft of your essay.

EDITING PRACTICE

A first-year student wrote the following essay for her composition class. Read the essay, TEST it, and then answer the questions on pages 239–240.

"Green" Is Good for Women

For a job to be considered "green," it must provide services that help preserve the environment or conserve natural resources. In the United States, as in other places around the world, green job growth is booming as people become more interested in clean energy and sustainable living. The new green economy is providing valuable opportunities for all American workers, but particularly for women. New jobs in green industries are offering women better access to equal, high-paying employment.

Traditionally, women in the workforce have not had equal access to secure, high-paying jobs. New green jobs give women the chance to break into lucrative fields and break away from the old limitations. Unlike many traditionally female jobs, many of the new green jobs offer high wages as well as benefits and job security. For example, recycling coordinators, weatherization installers, and energy engineers all have high starting salaries and promotion potential. Because of the rapid growth in green industries, employers are eager to recruit and train new workers, many of whom will be women.

Because of the shortage of skilled workers, women may find it easier to get started in a good green job. Green jobs exist in a variety of fields, including science, engineering, technology, business, manufacturing, management, and consulting. In addition, today's green jobs are available to people with a range of skill levels and educational backgrounds. Women reentering the workforce after a gap or looking to change careers can get started without years of schooling. Many entry-level green jobs require only a training program or certificate.

For example, to become a solar panel installer or technical salesperson, people can earn certification through a professional organization. Some employers even offer apprenticeship programs. Energy auditors, organic gardeners, and electricians, for example, often complete such on-the-job training programs to gain necessary skills and experience. In addition, several organizations, including the Department of Labor, are offering resources and support for women looking to get started in green jobs.

Finally, the green economy offers women the opportunity to earn equal pay and to gain leadership positions. Because many green careers did not exist ten years ago, these new jobs do not have a history of unequal wages or male dominance. American women have struggled for years to earn the same amount as men do for the same work, but the pay gap still exists. Women have also struggled to reach the highest levels of leadership and management. The green economy offers employers and employees the chance to start fresh. For example, creative, business-minded women are taking advantage of the green economy to start their own green companies. Some women now own their own energy consulting and accounting businesses, run their own environmental remediation businesses, and make and sell their own green products. Because of the demand for these consumer goods and services, women have unprecedented opportunities to jump in and become leaders in their fields.

Over the next few decades, careers that support the environment will certainly continue to gain strength. As clean energy and environmentally friendly practices become more and more the norm, green jobs will eventually just be regular jobs. Women who get started in green jobs now will find themselves well positioned for success in the future job market.

PRACTICE

14-2

1. Underline the essay's thesis statement. Does the thesis statement clearly and accurately express the essay's main idea?

If necessary, revise the thesis on the lines below.

_____

_____

2. What evidence does the writer provide to support the topic sentence of the first body paragraph? What additional evidence could the writer have provided?

3. What evidence does the writer provide to support the topic sentence of the second body paragraph? What additional evidence could the writer have provided?

4. What evidence does the writer provide to support the topic sentence of the third body paragraph? What additional evidence could the writer have provided?

5. Does the essay's conclusion include a summary statement? If not, write one on the lines below.

_____

_____

6. Does the writer provide enough transitions? If necessary, add transitions to the essay.

COLLABORATIVE ACTIVITY

Bring in an op-ed column that appears in a newspaper (either print or online) or an essay that you have written. Working in a group of three or four students, TEST the op-ed article or essay, and decide what changes you would make to improve it.

review checklist

TESTing Your Essays

☐ An essay should include a thesis statement that identifies its main idea. (See 14a.)

☐ An essay should include evidence—examples and details—to support its thesis. (See 14b.)

☐ An essay's conclusion should include a summary statement that reinforces the thesis and helps unify the essay. (See 14c.)

☐ An essay should include transitions that indicate how ideas are connected. (See 14d.)

15 Introductions and Conclusions

focus on writing

This picture shows the actor Charlie Chaplin caught in a factory machine in the film *Modern Times* (1936). Think about the title of the film and what the scene here seems to suggest, and then print out a copy of the essay about your most difficult job that you wrote for Chapter 13. At the end of this chapter, you will work on revising the introduction and conclusion of this essay.

In this chapter, you will learn to
- write an introduction (15a)
- choose a title (15a)
- write a conclusion (15b)

When you draft an essay, you usually spend the most time on the **body** because it is the section in which you develop your ideas. A well-constructed essay, however, is more than a series of body paragraphs. It also includes an **introduction** and a **conclusion**, both of which contribute to the essay's overall effectiveness.

15a Introductions

An **introduction** is the first thing people see when they read your essay. If your introduction is interesting, it will make readers want to read further. If it is not, readers may get bored and stop reading.

Your introduction should be a full paragraph that moves from general to specific ideas. It should begin with some general **opening remarks** that will draw readers into your essay. The **thesis statement**, a specific sentence that presents the main idea of your essay, usually comes at the end of the introduction. The following diagram illustrates the shape of an introduction.

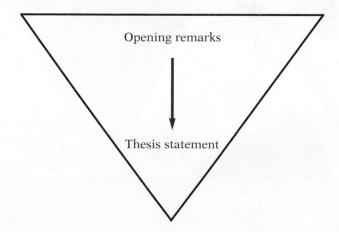

Opening remarks

Thesis statement

Here are some options you can experiment with when you write your introductions. (In each of the sample introductory paragraphs that follow, the thesis statement is underlined and labeled.)

Beginning with a Narrative

You can begin an essay with a narrative drawn from your own experience or from a current news event.

> On the first day my sister and I attended school in America, our parents walked us directly to the entrance of our new classroom. Even though she barely spoke any English, Mom tried earnestly to teach us how to ask for permission to use the bathroom: "Can I go to the bathroom?" Like parrots, she had us repeat this question over and over. At the time, neither of us realized that the proper way of asking for permission is "May I go to the bathroom?" This grammar slip did not matter, though, because we forgot the question as soon as our parents left. Reluctantly, we entered the classroom, more timid than two mice trying not to awaken a sleeping cat. We didn't know yet that going to school where English was the only language spoken would prove to be very difficult.
>
> —Hilda Alvarado (student)

Thesis statement

Beginning with a Question (or a Series of Questions)

Asking one or more questions at the beginning of your essay is an effective strategy. Because readers expect you to answer the questions, they will want to read further.

> Is it worth giving up a chance to go to college to make a respectable salary today? "For me it was," says Mario Sarno, general manager of Arby's store #219. At nineteen years of age, Mario looks like a salesman. He is of medium height and build and has an outgoing personality that makes him stand out. As general manager, Mario's major tasks are to maintain the fast-food environment and to ensure that customers are happy. At the age of seventeen, Mario was noticed by an Arby's corporate supervisor and was promoted to manager. Mario's positive experience suggests that students should consider the advantages of going directly into the job market.
>
> —Lucus J. Anemone (student)

Thesis statement

Beginning with a Definition

A definition at the beginning of your essay can give readers important information. As the following introduction shows, a definition can help explain a complicated idea or a confusing concept.

"Getting inked" is how many people refer to the act of getting a tattoo. Although some people may see it as a form of torture, tattooing is an art form that dates back over hundreds of years. The craft has been more formally defined as the practice of permanently marking the skin through punctures or incisions, which receive various dyes or pigments. Although Polynesian in origin, tattooing has a rich history in the United States.

Thesis statement

—Kristen L. McCormack (student)

Beginning with a Quotation

An appropriate saying or some interesting dialogue can draw readers into your essay.

According to the comedian Jerry Seinfeld, "When you're single, you are the dictator of your own life. . . . When you're married, you are part of a vast decision-making body." In other words, before you can do anything when you are married, you have to talk it over with someone else. These words kept going through my mind as I thought about asking my girlfriend to marry me. The more I thought about Seinfeld's words, the more I put off asking. I never thought about the huge price that I would pay for this delay.

Thesis statement

—Dan Brody (student)

Beginning with a Surprising Statement

You can begin your essay with a surprising or unexpected statement. Because your statement takes readers by surprise, it catches their attention.

Some of the smartest people I know never went to college. In fact, some of them never finished high school. They still know how to save 20 percent on the price of a dinner, fix their own faucets when they leak, get discounted prescriptions, get free rides on a bus to Atlantic City, use public transportation to get anywhere in the city, and live on about twenty-two dollars a day. Some people would call them old and poor, but I would call them survivors who have learned to make it through life on nothing but a Social Security check. These survivors are my grandparents' friends, and they have taught me many things I cannot learn in school.

Thesis statement

—Sean Ragas (student)

FYI

What to Avoid in Introductions

When writing an introduction, avoid the following:

- Beginning your essay by announcing what you plan to write about.

  PHRASES TO AVOID

  This essay is about . . .
  In my essay, I will discuss . . .

- Apologizing for your ideas.

  PHRASES TO AVOID

  Although I don't know much about this subject . . .
  I might not be an expert, but . . .

FYI

Choosing a Title

Every essay should have a **title** that suggests the subject of the essay and makes people want to read it. Here are a few tips for properly formatting your title.

- Capitalize all words except for articles (*a, an, the*), prepositions (*at, to, of, around,* and so on), and coordinating conjunctions (*and, but,* and so on), unless they are the first or last word of the title.
- Do not underline or italicize your title or enclose it in quotation marks. Do not type your title in all capital letters.
- Center the title at the top of the first page. Double-space between the title and the first line of your essay.

As you consider a title for your paper, think about the following options.

- *A title can highlight a key word or term that appears in the essay.*
  In Praise of the F Word
  Fish Cheeks
- *A title can be a straightforward announcement.*
  Dnt Txt N Drv
  The Case for Short Words

(continued)

(continued from previous page)

- *A title can establish a personal connection with readers.*
  The Men We Carry in Our Minds
  How Facebook Is Making Friending Obsolete

- *A title can be a familiar saying or a quotation from your essay itself.*
  Men Are from Mars, Women Are from Venus
  I Want a Wife

PRACTICE
15-1   Look through the student essays in Chapter 16, and find one introduction you think is particularly effective. Be prepared to explain the strengths of the introduction you chose.

PRACTICE
15-2   Using the different options for creating titles discussed in the FYI box above, write two titles for each of the essays described below.

1. A student writes an essay about three people who disappeared mysteriously: Amelia Earhart, aviator; Ambrose Bierce, writer; and Jimmy Hoffa, union leader. In the body paragraphs, the student describes the circumstances surrounding their disappearances.

   _____

   _____

2. A student writes an essay arguing against doctors' letting people select the gender of their babies. In the body paragraphs, she presents reasons why she thinks it is unethical.

   _____

   _____

3. A student writes an essay explaining why America should elect a woman president. In the body paragraphs, he gives his reasons.

   _____

   _____

4. A student writes an essay describing the harmful effects of steroids on student athletes. In the body paragraphs, he shows the effects on the heart, brain, and other organs.

_____

_____

5. A student writes an essay explaining why she joined the Navy Reserve. In the body paragraphs, she discusses her need to earn money for college tuition, her wish to learn a trade, and her desire to see the world.

_____

_____

15b Conclusions

Because your conclusion is the last thing readers see, they often judge your entire essay by its effectiveness. For this reason, conclusions should be planned, drafted, and revised carefully.

Like an introduction, a **conclusion** should be a full paragraph. It should begin with a **summary statement** that reinforces the essay's main idea, and it should end with some general **concluding remarks.** The following diagram illustrates the general shape of a conclusion.

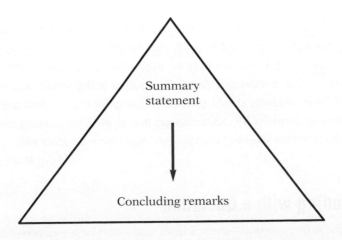

Here are some options you can experiment with when you write your conclusions. (In each of the sample concluding paragraphs that follow, the summary statement is underlined and labeled.)

Concluding with a Narrative

A narrative conclusion can bring an event discussed in the essay to a logical, satisfying close.

Summary statement

I went to Philadelphia with my boys to share the thing my father and I had shared—a love for history. Unfortunately, they were more interested in horse-and-buggy rides, overpriced knickknacks, the tall buildings, and parades. As we walked into Independence Hall, though, I noticed that the boys became quiet. They felt it. They felt the thick historical air around us. I watched them look around as the guide painted a vivid picture of the times and spoke of the marches down Broad Street and the clashing of ideas as our forefathers debated and even fought for freedom. I felt my husband behind me and took my eyes off of my boys to turn to the left; I could almost see my father. I almost whispered out loud to him, "We were here."

—Shannon Lewis (student)

Concluding with a Recommendation

Once you think you have convinced readers that a problem exists, you can make recommendations in your conclusion about how the problem should be solved.

Summary statement

Solutions for the binge-drinking problem on college campuses are not easy, but both schools and students need to acknowledge the problem and to try to solve it. Schools that have an alcohol-free policy should aggressively enforce it, and schools that do not have such a policy should implement one. In addition, students should take responsibility for their actions and resolve to drink responsibly. No one should get hurt or die from drinking too much, but if something does not change soon, many more students will.

—April Moen (student)

Concluding with a Quotation

A well-chosen quotation—even a brief one—can be an effective concluding strategy. In the following paragraph, the quotation reinforces the main idea of the essay.

I'll never forget the day I caught the ball on a penalty kick, winning the game for my team. My opponent's foot made contact with the ball, and everything around me fell silent. The ball came at me, hurtling over my head toward the top right of the goal. As I dived to catch it, I closed my eyes. The ball smacked into my hands so hard I thought it must have split my gloves. When I opened my eyes, I realized that I had caught the ball and saved the game for our team. The crowd cheered wildly, and my team surrounded me as I got to my feet. As the celebration died down, my coach walked up to me and, as I handed him the game-winning ball, he said, "To the playoffs we go!"

—Jacob Kinley (student)

Summary statement

Concluding with a Prediction

This type of conclusion not only sums up the thesis but also looks to the future.

Whether people like it or not, texting is not going to go away anytime soon. This generation and future generations are going to use "text speak" and become even more comfortable with communicating via text messages. Texting has already had a large impact on today's world. In fact, texting has helped put the written word back into our lives, making people more comfortable with the skill of writing. & it's a fast, EZ way 2 communic8.

—Courtney Anttila (student)

Summary statement

FYI

What to Avoid in Conclusions

When writing a conclusion, avoid the following:

- Introducing new ideas. Your conclusion should sum up the ideas you discuss in your essay, not open up new lines of thought.
- Apologizing for your opinions, ideas, or conclusions. Apologies will undercut your readers' confidence in you.

PHRASES TO AVOID

At least that is my opinion . . .
I could be wrong, but . . .

- Using unnecessary phrases to announce your essay is coming to a close.

PHRASES TO AVOID

In summary, . . .
In conclusion, . . .

PRACTICE

15-3 Look at the student essays in Chapter 16, and locate one conclusion you think is particularly effective. Be prepared to explain the strengths of the conclusion you chose.

TEST · Revise · Edit

Look back at the essay you wrote in response to the Focus on Writing prompt on page 191 (Chapter 13). TEST what you have written one more time. Then, revise and edit your introduction and conclusion. Make sure your introduction creates interest, prepares readers for the essay to follow, and includes a clear thesis statement. Also, make sure your conclusion contains a summary statement and includes general concluding remarks. Finally, make sure your essay has an appropriate title.

EDITING PRACTICE

The following student essay has an undeveloped introduction and conclusion. Decide what introductory and concluding strategies would be best for the essay. Then, rewrite both the introduction and the conclusion. Finally, suggest an interesting title for the essay.

This essay is about three of the most dangerous jobs. They are piloting small planes, logging, and fishing.

Flying a small plane can be dangerous. For example, pilots who fly tiny planes that spray pesticides on farmers' fields do not have to comply with the safety rules for large airplanes. They also have to fly very low in order to spray the right fields. This leaves little room for error. Also, pilots of air-taxis and small commuter planes die in much greater numbers than airline pilots do. In some places, like parts of Alaska, there are long distances and few roads, so many small planes are needed. Their pilots are four times more likely to die than other pilots because of bad weather and poor visibility. In general, flying a small plane can be very risky.

Another dangerous job is logging. Loggers always are at risk of having parts of trees or heavy machinery fall on them. Tree trunks often have odd shapes, so they are hard to control while they are being transported. As a result, they often break loose from equipment that is supposed to move them. In addition, weather conditions, like snow or rain, can cause dangers. Icy or wet conditions increase the risk to loggers, who can fall from trees or slip when they are sawing a tree. Because loggers often work in remote places, it is very hard to get prompt medical aid. For this reason, a wound that could easily be treated in a hospital may be fatal to a logger.

Perhaps the most dangerous occupation is working in the fishing industry. Like loggers, professional fishermen work in unsafe conditions. They use heavy machinery to pull up nets and to move large amounts of fish. The combination of icy or slippery boat decks and large nets and cages makes the job unsafe. The weather is often very bad, so fishermen are at risk of falling overboard during a storm and drowning. In fact, drowning is the most common cause of death in this industry. Also, like logging, fishing is done far from medical help, so even minor injuries can be very serious.

In conclusion, piloting, logging, and fishing are three of the most dangerous occupations.

COLLABORATIVE ACTIVITY

Find a magazine or newspaper article that interests you. Cut off the introduction and conclusion, and bring the body of the article to class. Ask your group to decide on the best strategies for introducing and concluding the article. Then, collaborate on writing new opening and closing paragraphs and an interesting title.

review checklist

Introductions and Conclusions

☐ The introduction of your essay should include opening remarks and a thesis statement. (See 15a.) You can begin an essay with any of the following options.

A narrative   A quotation
A question   A surprising statement
A definition

☐ Your title should suggest the subject of your essay and make people want to read further. (See 15a.)

☐ The conclusion of your essay should include a summary statement and some general concluding remarks. (See 15b.) You can conclude an essay with any of the following options.

A narrative   A quotation
A recommendation   A prediction

16 Patterns of Essay Development

In this chapter, you will learn to organize your essays according to different patterns of development:

- exemplification (16a)
- narration (16b)
- description (16c)
- process (16d)
- cause and effect (16e)
- comparison and contrast (16f)
- classification (16g)
- definition (16h)
- argument (16i)

As you learned in Chapters 4 through 12, writers have a variety of options for developing ideas within a paragraph. These options include *exemplification, narration, description, process, cause and effect, comparison and contrast, classification, definition*, and *argument*. When you write an essay, you can use these same patterns of development to help you organize your material.

In your college courses, different assignments and writing situations call for different patterns of essay development.

- If an essay exam question asked you to compare two systems of government, you would use *comparison and contrast*.

- If an English composition assignment asked you to tell about a childhood experience, you would use *narration*.

- If a section of a research paper on environmental pollution called for examples of dangerous waste-disposal practices, you would use *exemplification*.

The skills you learned for writing paragraphs can also be applied to writing essays.

16a Exemplification Essays

Exemplification illustrates a general statement with one or more specific examples. An **exemplification essay** uses specific examples to support a thesis.

When you **TEST** an **exemplification** essay, make sure it includes all these elements:

T ■ **Thesis Statement**—The introduction of an exemplification essay should include a clear **thesis statement** that identifies the essay's main idea—the idea the examples will support.

E ■ **Evidence**—The body paragraphs should present **evidence**, fully developed examples that support the thesis. Each body paragraph should be introduced by a topic sentence that identifies the example or group of related examples that the paragraph will discuss.

S ■ **Summary Statement**—The conclusion of an exemplification essay should include a summary statement that reinforces the essay's thesis.

T ■ **Transitions**—An exemplification essay should use appropriate **transitional words and phrases** to connect examples within paragraphs and between one paragraph and another.

Moving from Assignment to Thesis

The wording of your assignment may suggest that you write an exemplification essay. For example, you may be asked to *illustrate* or to *give examples*. Once you decide that your assignment calls for exemplification, you need to develop a thesis that reflects this purpose.

ASSIGNMENT	THESIS STATEMENT
Education Should children be taught only in their native languages or in English as well? Support your answer with examples of specific students' experiences.	The success of students in a bilingual third-grade class suggests the value of teaching elementary school students in English as well as in their native languages.
Literature Does William Shakespeare's *Othello* have to end tragically? Illustrate your position with references to specific characters.	Each of the three major characters in *Othello* contributes to the play's tragic ending.
Composition Discuss the worst job you ever had, including plenty of specific examples to support your thesis.	My summer job at a fast-food restaurant was my worst job because of the endless stream of rude customers, the many boring tasks I had to perform, and my manager's insensitivity.

Organizing an Exemplification Essay

In an exemplification essay, each body paragraph can develop a single example or discuss several related examples. The topic sentence should introduce the example (or group of related examples) that the paragraph will discuss. Each example you select should clearly support your thesis.

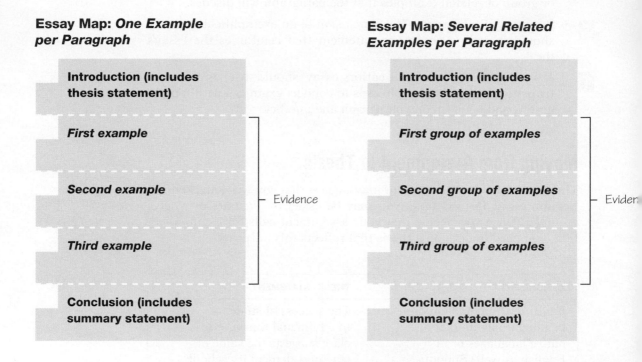

Essay Map: *One Example per Paragraph*

Introduction (includes thesis statement)

First example

Second example   — Evidence

Third example

Conclusion (includes summary statement)

Essay Map: *Several Related Examples per Paragraph*

Introduction (includes thesis statement)

First group of examples

Second group of examples   — Evider

Third group of examples

Conclusion (includes summary statement)

Transitions in Exemplification Essays

Transitional words and phrases should introduce your examples and indicate how one example is related to another.

> **Some Transitional Words and Phrases for Exemplification**
>
> | | | |
> |---|---|---|
> | also | furthermore | the most important |
> | besides | in addition | example |
> | finally | moreover | the next example |
> | first | one example . . . | |
> | for example | another example | |
> | for instance | specifically | |

Case Study: A Student Writes an Exemplification Essay

When Kyle Sims, a student in a first-year writing course, was asked to write an essay about a popular hobby or interest, his instructor encouraged him to use his own experience as a source of ideas. Kyle imagined that most of his classmates would write about topics like video games or sports, and while he knew a lot about sports, his knowledge came from being a spectator, not a participant. He decided to use this knowledge by writing about extreme sports.

Once he had settled on a topic, Kyle did some **freewriting** on his laptop. When he read over his freewriting, he saw that he had come up with three kinds of information: ideas about the dangers of extreme sports, about the challenges they present, and about the equipment they require. He then wrote a **thesis statement**—"Extreme sports are different from more familiar sports because they are dangerous, they are physically challenging, and they require specialized equipment"—that identified the three points he wanted to make. After **brainstorming** about each of these points, he had enough material for a first draft.

As he wrote his **first draft**, Kyle devoted one paragraph to each point, using examples to develop his body paragraphs. When he finished his draft, he **TEST**ed it to make sure it included a thesis statement, supporting evidence, a summary statement, and transitional words and phrases. He was satisfied with his thesis, which told readers what points he was going to make about extreme sports and also conveyed the idea that they were not like ordinary sports. His summary statement seemed logical and appropriate. However, realizing that his readers might not know much about extreme sports, Kyle added more examples to illustrate a range of different kinds of extreme sports and more transitions to lead readers from one example to the next.

When Kyle **revised** his draft, he rewrote his topic sentences so they clearly identified the three points he wanted to make about extreme sports. After he finished his revision, he **edited** and **proofread** carefully and made sure his essay met his instructor's **format** requirements.

The following final draft includes all the elements Kyle looked for when he **TEST**ed his essay.

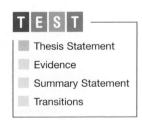

T | E | S | T
- Thesis Statement
- Evidence
- Summary Statement
- Transitions

Model Exemplification Essay

Read Kyle's finished essay, and answer the questions in Practice 16-1.

Going to Extremes

1   For years, sports like football, baseball, and basketball have been popular in cities, suburbs, and small rural towns. For some young people, however, these sports no longer seem exciting, especially when compared to "extreme sports," such as snowboarding and BMX racing. Extreme sports

Introduction

are different from more familiar sports because they are dangerous, they are physically challenging, and they require specialized equipment.

Topic sentence (introduces first point)

First, extreme sports are dangerous. For example, snowboarders take chances with snowy hills and unpredictable bumps. They zoom down mountains at high speeds, which is typical of extreme sports. In addition, snowboarders and skateboarders risk painful falls as they do their tricks.

Examples

Also, many extreme sports, like rock climbing, bungee jumping, and skydiving, are performed at very high altitudes. Moreover, the bungee jumper has to jump from a very high place, and there is always a danger of getting tangled with the bungee cord. People who participate in extreme sports accept—and even enjoy—these dangers.

Topic sentence (introduces second point)

In addition, extreme sports are very difficult. For instance, surfers have to learn to balance surfboards while dealing with wind and waves. Bungee jumpers may have to learn how to do difficult stunts while jumping off a high bridge or a dam. Another example of the physical challenge of extreme sports can be found in BMX racing. BMX racers have to learn to steer a lightweight bike on a dirt track that has jumps and banked corners. These extreme sports require skills that most people do not naturally have. These special skills have to be learned, and participants in extreme sports enjoy this challenge.

Examples

Body paragraphs

Topic sentence (introduces third point)

Finally, almost all extreme sports require specialized equipment. For example, surfers need surfboards that are light but strong. They can choose epoxy boards, which are stronger, or fiberglass boards, which are lighter. They can choose shortboards, which are shorter than seven feet and are easier to maneuver, or they can use longboards, which are harder and slower to turn in the water but are easier to learn on. Also, surfers have to get special wax for their boards to keep from slipping as they are paddling out into the water. For surfing in cold water, they need wetsuits that trap their own body heat. Other extreme sports require different kinds of specialized equipment, but those who participate in them are willing to buy whatever they need.

Examples

Conclusion

Clearly, extreme sports are very different from other sports. Maybe it is because they are so different that they have become so popular in recent years. Already, snowboarding, BMX racing, and other extreme sports are featured in the Olympics. The Summer and Winter X Games are televised on ESPN and ABC, and sports like BMX racing, snowboarding, surfing, and snowmobiling get national attention on these programs. With all this publicity, extreme sports are likely to become even more popular—despite their challenges.

2

3

4

5

PRACTICE

16-1

1. Restate Kyle's thesis in your own words.

2. What three points about extreme sports does Kyle make in the topic sentences of his body paragraphs?

3. What examples of extreme sports does Kyle give in paragraph 1? What examples of dangers does he give in paragraph 2? In paragraph 4, Kyle discusses surfing, giving examples of the equipment surfers need. List this equipment.

4. Is Kyle's introduction effective? How else might he have opened his essay?

5. Paraphrase Kyle's summary statement.

6. What is this essay's greatest strength? What is its greatest weakness?

grammar in context

Exemplification

When you write an exemplification essay, you may introduce your examples with transitional words and phrases like *First* or *In addition.* If you do, be sure to use a comma.

First, extreme sports are dangerous.

In addition, extreme sports are very difficult.

Finally, almost all extreme sports require specialized equipment.

For information on using commas with introductory and transitional words and phrases, see 34b.

✔ LearningCurve For more practice with comma usage, complete the Commas activity at bedfordstmartins.com/focusonwriting.

Step-by-Step Guide: Writing an Exemplification Essay

Now, you are ready to write an exemplification essay on one of the topics listed below (or a topic of your choice).

TOPICS

Reasons to start (or not to start) college right after high school
The three best products ever invented
What kinds of people or images should appear on U.S. postage stamps? Why?

Advantages (or disadvantages) of being a young parent
Athletes who really are role models
Four items students need to survive in college
What messages do rap or hip-hop artists send to listeners?
Study strategies that work
Traits of a good employee
Three or four recent national or world news events that gave you hope

As you write your essay, follow these steps:

1. Planning
   - Make sure your topic calls for exemplification.
   - Find ideas to write about.
   - Identify your main idea, and write a thesis statement.

2. Organizing
   - Choose and develop examples to support your thesis.
   - Arrange your supporting examples in a logical order, making an outline if necessary.

3. Drafting
   - Draft your essay.

4. TESTing
   - TEST your essay, referring to the TESTing an Exemplification Essay checklist below.

5. Revising and Editing
   - Revise and edit your essay, referring to the two Self-Assessment checklists in Chapter 13.

TESTing an exemplification essay

Thesis Statement Unifies Your Essay

☐ Does your introduction include a **thesis statement** that clearly states your essay's main idea?

Evidence Supports Your Essay's Thesis Statement

☐ Do you have enough **evidence**—fully developed examples—to support your thesis?

☐ Do all your examples support your thesis, or should some be deleted?

Summary Statement Reinforces Your Essay's Main Idea

☐ Does your conclusion include a **summary statement** that reinforces your essay's thesis?

Transitions

☐ Do you include **transitions** that move readers from one example to the next?

16b   Narrative Essays

Narration tells a story, usually presenting a series of events in chronological (time) order, moving from beginning to end. A **narrative essay** can tell a personal story, or it can recount a recent or historical event or a fictional story.

When you **TEST** a **narrative** essay, make sure it includes all these elements:

T ▪ **Thesis Statement**—The introduction of a narrative essay should include a **thesis statement** that communicates the main idea—the point the story is making.

E ▪ **Evidence**—The body paragraphs should tell the story, one event at a time, with each event providing **evidence**—examples and details—to support the thesis. Events are usually presented in chronological (time) order.

S ▪ **Summary Statement**—The conclusion of a narrative essay should include a **summary statement** that reinforces the essay's main idea.

T ▪ **Transitions**—Throughout a narrative essay, **transitional words and phrases** should connect events in time, showing how one event leads to the next.

Moving from Assignment to Thesis

The wording of your assignment may suggest that you write a narrative essay. For example, you may be asked to *tell, trace, summarize events,* or *recount.* Once you decide that your assignment calls for narration, you need to develop a thesis statement that reflects this purpose.

ASSIGNMENT	THESIS STATEMENT
Composition Tell about a time when you had to show courage even though you were afraid.	In extraordinary circumstances, a person can exhibit great courage and overcome fear.
American history Summarize the events that occurred during President Franklin Delano Roosevelt's first one hundred days in office.	Although many thought they were extreme, the measures enacted by Roosevelt during his first one hundred days in office were necessary to fight the economic depression.
Political science Trace the development of the Mississippi Freedom Democratic Party.	As the Mississippi Freedom Democratic Party developed, it found a voice that spoke for equality and justice.

Organizing a Narrative Essay

When you write a narrative essay, you can discuss one event or several in each paragraph of your essay.

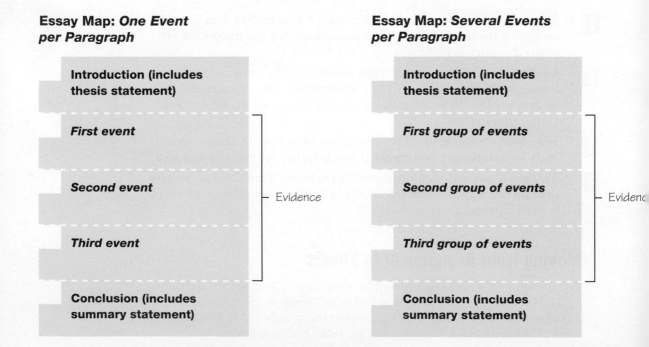

Essay Map: *One Event per Paragraph*

Introduction (includes thesis statement)

First event

Second event

— Evidence

Third event

Conclusion (includes summary statement)

Essay Map: *Several Events per Paragraph*

Introduction (includes thesis statement)

First group of events

Second group of events

— Evidenc

Third group of events

Conclusion (includes summary statement)

Transitions in Narrative Essays

Sometimes, to add interest to your narrative, you may decide not to use exact chronological order. For example, you might begin with the end of your story and then move back to the beginning to trace the events that led to this outcome. However you arrange the events, carefully worded topic sentences and clear transitional words and phrases will help readers follow your narrative.

Some Transitional Words and Phrases for Narration

after	eventually	next
as	finally	now
as soon as	first . . . second . . .	soon
at first	third	then
at the same time	immediately	two hours (days,
before	later	months, years)
by this time	later on	later
earlier	meanwhile	when

Case Study: A Student Writes a Narrative Essay

Elaina Corrato, a returning student who was older than most of her class-mates, wasn't sure how to proceed when her writing instructor gave the class an assignment to write about a milestone in their lives. The first topic that came to mind was her recent thirtieth birthday, but she was reluctant to reveal her age to her classmates. However, when she learned that no one except her instructor would read her essay, she decided to write about this topic.

Elaina began by rereading entries she had made in her **writing journal** in the days before and after her birthday as well as on the day itself. These entries gave her all the material she needed for her first draft, which she decided would focus on the "big day" itself. Even before she began to write, she saw that her essay would be a narrative that traced her reactions to the events she experienced on that day.

As she **drafted** her essay, Elaina was careful to discuss events in the order in which they occurred and to include transitional words and phrases to move her discussion smoothly from one event to the next. Because she knew what she wanted to say, she found it easy to write a well-developed first draft that included plenty of information. When she **TEST**ed her essay, however, Elaina saw at once that she had not stated a thesis or included a summary statement to reinforce her main idea.

At this point, Elaina emailed her draft to her instructor and asked him for suggestions. (Her instructor offered this option to students whose

> **WORD POWER**
>
> **milestone** an important event; a turning point

off-campus work commitments made it difficult for them to schedule face-to-face conferences.) He explained that her thesis should not be just a general overview of the day's events ("My thirtieth birthday was an event-filled day"); instead, it should make a point about how those events affected her. With this advice, Elaina found it was not difficult to write a thesis that expressed how she felt about turning thirty. Once she had a **thesis statement**, she was able to add a summary statement that reinforced her main idea, ending her essay on an optimistic note. With all the required elements in place, she went on to **revise**, **edit**, and **proofread** her essay.

The final draft that follows includes all the elements Elaina looked for when she **TEST**ed her essay.

Model Narrative Essay

Read Elaina's finished essay, and answer the questions in Practice 16-2.

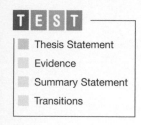

T E S T
- Thesis Statement
- Evidence
- Summary Statement
- Transitions

Reflections

Introduction

Turning thirty did not bother me at all. My list of "Things to Do before I Die" was far from complete, but I knew I had plenty of time to do them. In fact, turning thirty seemed like no big deal to me. If anything, it was a milestone I was happy to be approaching. Unfortunately, other people had different ideas about this milestone, and eventually their ideas made me rethink my own.   1

Topic sentence (introduces first group of events)

As the big day approached, my family kept teasing me about it. My sister kept asking me if I felt any different. She couldn't believe I wasn't upset, but I didn't pay any attention to her. I was looking forward to a new chapter in my life. I liked my job, I was making good progress toward my college degree, and I was healthy and happy. Why should turning thirty be a problem? So, I made no special plans for my birthday, and I decided to treat it as just another day.   2

Events and details

Topic sentence (introduces second group of events)

My birthday fell on a Saturday, and I enjoyed the chance to sleep in. After I got up and had breakfast, I did my laundry and then set out for the supermarket. I rarely put on makeup or fixed my hair on Saturdays. After all, I didn't have to go to work or to school. I was only running errands in the neighborhood. Later on, though, as I waited in line at the deli counter, I caught sight of my reflection in the mirrored meat case. At first, I thought it wasn't really me. The woman staring back at me looked so old! She had bags under her eyes, and she even had a few gray hairs. I was so upset by my reflection that on my way home I stopped and bought a mud mask— guaranteed to make me look younger.   3

Body paragraphs

Events and details

4   As I walked up the street toward my house, I saw something attached to the front railing. When I got closer, I realized that it was a bunch of black balloons. There was also a big sign that said "Over the Hill" in big black letters. I'd been trying to think about my birthday in positive terms, but my family seemed to have other ideas. Obviously, it was time for the mud mask.

Topic sentence (introduces third group of events)

Events and details

5   After quickly unloading my groceries, I ran upstairs to apply the mask. The box promised a "rejuvenating look," and that was exactly what I wanted. I spread the sticky brown mixture on my face, and it hardened instantly. As I sat on my bed, waiting for the mask to work its magic, I heard the doorbell ring. Then, I heard familiar voices and my husband calling me to come down, saying that I had company. I couldn't answer him. I couldn't talk (or even smile) without cracking the mask. At this point, I retreated to the bathroom to make myself presentable for my friends and family. This task was not easy.

Topic sentence (introduces fourth group of events)

Body paragraphs

Events and details

6   When I managed to scrub off the mud mask, my face was covered with little red pimples. Apparently, my sensitive skin couldn't take the harsh chemicals. At first, I didn't think the promise of "rejuvenated" skin was what I got. I had to admit, though, that my skin did look a lot younger. In fact, when I finally went downstairs to celebrate my birthday, I looked as young as a teenager—a teenager with acne.

Topic sentence (introduces fifth group of events)

Events and details

7   Despite other people's grim warnings, I discovered that although turning thirty was a milestone, it wasn't a game-changer. I learned a lot that day, and I learned even more in the days that followed. What I finally realized was that I couldn't ignore turning thirty, but having a thirtieth birthday didn't have to mean that my life was over.

Conclusion

PRACTICE
16-2

1. Restate the thesis statement of "Reflections" in your own words.

2. What specific events and details support Elaina's thesis? List as many as you can.

3. Do you think paragraph 2 is necessary? How would Elaina's essay be different without it?

4. Paraphrase Elaina's summary statement. Do you think her summary statement effectively reinforces her essay's main idea?

5. What is this essay's greatest strength? What is its greatest weakness?

grammar in context

Narration

When you write a narrative essay, you tell a story. When you get caught up in your story, you might sometimes find yourself stringing a list of incidents together without proper punctuation, creating a **run-on**.

> **INCORRECT** As the big day approached, my family kept teasing me about it, my sister kept asking me if I felt any different.

> **CORRECT** As the big day approached, my family kept teasing me about it. My sister kept asking me if I felt any different.

For information on how to identify and correct run-ons, see Chapter 24.

✔**LearningCurve** For more practice with run-ons, complete the Run-Ons activity at **bedfordstmartins.com/focusonwriting**.

Step-by-Step Guide: Writing a Narrative Essay

Now, you are ready to write a narrative essay on one of the topics listed below (or a topic of your choice).

TOPICS

The story of your education
Your idea of a perfect day
The plot summary of a terrible book or movie
A time when you had to make a split-second decision
Your first confrontation with authority
An important historical event
A day on which everything went wrong
A story from your family's history
Your employment history, from first to most recent job
A biography of your pet

As you write your essay, follow these steps:

1. Planning
   - Make sure your topic calls for narration.
   - Find ideas to write about.
   - Identify your main idea, and write a thesis statement.

2. Organizing

- Choose events and details to support your thesis.
- Arrange events in chronological order, making an outline if necessary.

3. Drafting

- Draft your essay.

4. **TEST**ing

- **TEST** your essay, referring to the **TEST**ing a Narrative Essay checklist below.

5. Revising and Editing

- Revise and edit your essay, referring to the two Self-Assessment checklists in Chapter 13.

TESTing a narrative essay

Thesis Statement Unifies Your Essay

☐ Does your introduction include a **thesis statement** that clearly states your essay's main idea?

Evidence Supports Your Essay's Thesis Statement

☐ Does all your **evidence**—events and details—support your thesis, or should some be deleted?

☐ Do you include enough specific details to make your narrative interesting?

☐ Are the events you discuss arranged in clear chronological (time) order?

Summary Statement Reinforces Your Essay's Main Idea

☐ Does your conclusion include a **summary statement** that reinforces your essay's thesis?

Transitions

☐ Do you include enough **transitions** to make the sequence of events clear to your reader?

16c Descriptive Essays

Description tells what something looks, sounds, smells, tastes, or feels like. A **descriptive essay** uses details to give readers a clear, vivid picture of a person, place, or object.

When you describe a person, place, object, or scene, you can use **objective description**, reporting only what your senses of sight, sound, smell, taste, and touch tell you ("The columns were two feet tall and made of white marble"). You can also use **subjective description**, conveying your attitude or your feelings about what you observe ("The columns were tall and powerful looking, and their marble surface seemed as smooth as ice"). Many essays combine these two kinds of description.

FYI

Figures of Speech

Descriptive writing, particularly subjective description, is frequently enriched by **figures of speech**—language that creates special or unusual effects.

- A **simile** uses *like* or *as* to compare two unlike things.

  Her smile was like sunshine.

- A **metaphor** compares two unlike things without using *like* or *as*.

  Her smile was a light that lit up the room.

- **Personification** suggests a comparison between a nonliving thing and a person by giving the nonliving thing human traits.

  The sun smiled down on the crowd.

When you **TEST** a **descriptive** essay, make sure it includes all these elements:

T - **Thesis Statement**—A descriptive essay should include a **thesis statement** that expresses the essay's main idea.

E - **Evidence**—The body paragraphs should include **evidence**, descriptive details that support the thesis. Details should be arranged in spatial order—for example, from far to near or from top to bottom.

S ■ **Summary Statement**—The conclusion of a descriptive essay should include a **summary statement** that reinforces the essay's thesis.

T ■ **Transitions**—A descriptive essay should include **transitional words and phrases** that connect details and show how they are related.

Moving from Assignment to Thesis

The wording of your assignment may suggest that you write a descriptive essay. For example, it may ask you to *describe* or to *tell what an object looks like*. Once you decide that your assignment calls for description, you need to develop a thesis statement that reflects this purpose.

ASSIGNMENT	THESIS STATEMENT
Composition Describe a room that was important to you when you were a child.	Pink-and-white striped wallpaper, tall shelves of cuddly stuffed animals, and the smell of Oreos dominated the bedroom I shared with my sister.
Scientific writing Describe a piece of scientific equipment.	The mass spectrometer is a complex instrument, but every part is ideally suited to its function.
Art history Choose one modern painting and describe its visual elements.	The disturbing images crowded together in Pablo Picasso's *Guernica* suggest the brutality of war.

Organizing a Descriptive Essay

When you plan a descriptive essay, you focus on selecting details that help your readers see what you see, feel what you feel, and experience what you experience. Your goal is to create a single **dominant impression**, a central theme or idea to which all the details relate—for example, the liveliness of a street scene or the quiet of a summer night. This dominant impression unifies the description and gives readers an overall sense of what the person, place, object, or scene looks like (and perhaps what it sounds, smells, tastes, or feels like).

You can arrange details in a descriptive essay in many different ways. For example, you can move from least to most important details, from top to bottom (or from bottom to top or side to side), or from far to near (or near to far). Each of your essay's body paragraphs may focus on one key characteristic of the subject you are describing or on several related descriptive details.

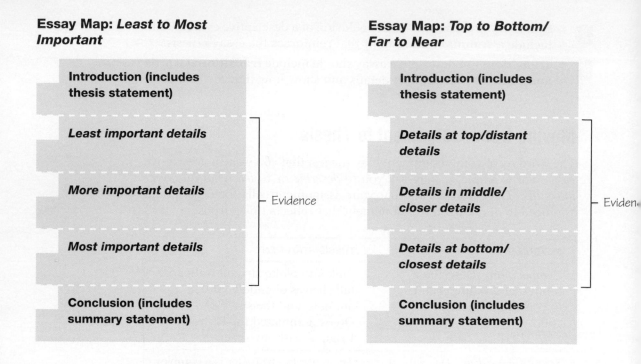

Essay Map: *Least to Most Important*

- Introduction (includes thesis statement)
- Least important details
- More important details — Evidence
- Most important details
- Conclusion (includes summary statement)

Essay Map: *Top to Bottom/ Far to Near*

- Introduction (includes thesis statement)
- Details at top/distant details
- Details in middle/ closer details — Eviden
- Details at bottom/ closest details
- Conclusion (includes summary statement)

Transitions in Descriptive Essays

As you write, use transitional words and expressions to connect details and show how they work together to create a full picture for readers. (Many of these useful transitions indicate location or distance.)

Some Transitional Words and Phrases for Description

above	in front of	outside
behind	inside	over
below	nearby	the least important
between	next to	the most important
beyond	on	under
in	on one side . . . on	
in back of	the other side	

Case Study: A Student Writes a Descriptive Essay

All the students in James Greggs's first-year composition course were also enrolled in sociology, psychology, or education courses with service-learning requirements that reinforced course content. For this reason,

James's composition instructor asked that the students' descriptive essays focus on a person, setting, or item related to their service-learning experiences.

Although James was enjoying his service-learning project—building a deck for elderly residents of a trailer home—he had trouble deciding which aspect of this project to write about. At first, he thought he might describe his team supervisor or one of the other students he worked with, but when he **brainstormed** to find details to include in his essay, he found he had a hard time being objective about his coworkers. Although he was required to keep a **journal** for the service-learning component of his sociology class, he realized that these entries focused on his own reactions and included few objective details. He finally settled on writing a description of the deck his team built for the trailer home.

Consulting photos he had taken of the building site and diagrams he had prepared of the trailer, James wrote a **first draft**, arranging his material from far (the field in which the trailer sat) to near (the trailer itself and the deck he helped to build).

When James **TEST**ed his draft, he saw that his essay had no thesis statement—no sentence that tied all the details together to indicate the main idea he wanted his description to convey. At this point, he emailed his instructor for help, but she reminded him that he had missed her deadline for scheduling appointments, and she recommended that he make an appointment with a tutor in the writing center.

James's writing center tutor suggested that his essay would be more interesting and convincing if his thesis tied the objective details of the project to his conclusions about its value. What did his class contribute? What did they learn? Was the project worth the trouble? She also reviewed his draft with him, suggesting places where he could expand or clarify his description. Because his assignment called for a descriptive essay, not a process essay, she recommended that he delete material that summarized the steps his group took as they built the deck. Finally, she reminded him that he would need to write a summary statement to reinforce his thesis.

When James **revised** his draft, he incorporated his tutor's suggestions and added both a thesis statement and a summary statement. He also added transitional words and phrases to move readers through his description, added more detail, and deleted irrelevant material. Then, he **edited** and **proofread** his essay.

The following final draft includes all the elements James looked for when he **TEST**ed his essay.

Model Descriptive Essay

Read James's finished essay, and answer the questions in Practice 16-3.

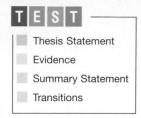

T E S T

- Thesis Statement
- Evidence
- Summary Statement
- Transitions

Introduction

Topic sentence
(introduces first
group of details)

Descriptive details

Topic sentence
(introduces second
group of details)

Body paragraphs

Descriptive details

Topic sentence
(introduces third
group of details)

Descriptive details

Building and Learning

Throughout the United States, houses reflect not only the lives of the people who live in them but also the diversity of the American population. Some are large and elaborate, others are modest but well maintained, and still others are in need of repair. Unfortunately, most college students know little about homes other than those in their own neighborhood. I too was fairly sheltered until I participated in a service-learning project for my sociology class. For this project, I, along with some classmates, added a deck to a trailer that was the home of three elderly sisters living on Social Security and disability. It was hard work, but my experience convinced me that all college students should be required to do some kind of service-learning project.

The trailer we worked on was located at the end of a small dirt road about thirty minutes from campus. Patches of green and brown grass dotted the land around the trailer, and in the far right-hand corner of the property stood three tall poplar trees. Although the bushes in front of the trailer were trimmed, the woods behind the trailer were beginning to overrun the property. (We were told that members of a local church came once a month to trim the hedges and cut back the trees.) Dominating the right front corner of the lawn, a circular concrete basin looked like a large birdbath. The basin housed a white well pipe with a rusted blue cap. About thirty feet to the left of the concrete basin stood a telephone pole and a bright red metal mailbox.

Like the property on which it stood, the trailer was well maintained. It was approximately thirty-five feet long and seven feet high; it rested on cinderblocks, which raised it about three feet off the ground. Under the trailer was an overturned white plastic chair. The trailer itself was covered with sheets of white vinyl siding that ran horizontally, except for the bottom panels on the right side, which ran vertically. The vinyl panels closest to the roof were slightly discolored by dirt and green moss.

At the left end of the trailer was a small window—about two feet wide and one foot high. Next to the window was a dark red aluminum door that was outlined in green trim. It had one window at eye level divided by metal strips into four small sections. The number "24" in white plastic letters was glued to the door below this window. To the right of the door was a lightbulb in a black ceramic socket. Next to the light was a large window that was actually two vertical rows of three windows—each the same size as the small window on the left. Further to the right were two smaller windows. Each of these small windows tilted upward and was

1

2

3

4

framed with silver metal strips. On either side of each of these windows was a pair of green metal shutters.

5   The deck we built replaced three wooden steps that had led up to the trailer. A white metal handrail stood on the right side of these steps. It had been newly painted and was connected to the body of the trailer by a heart-shaped piece of metal. In front of the steps, two worn gray wooden boards led to the road.

Topic sentence (introduces fourth group of details)

Descriptive details

6   Building the deck was hard work, but the finished deck provided a much better entranceway than the steps did and also gave the trailer a new look. The deck was not very large—ten feet by eight feet—but it extended from the doorway to the area underneath the windows immediately to the right of the door. We built the deck out of pressure-treated lumber so that it wouldn't rot or need painting. We also built three steps that led from the deck to the lawn, and we surrounded the deck with a wooden railing that ran down the right side of the steps. After we finished, we bought two white plastic chairs at a local thrift store and put them on the deck.

Topic sentence (introduces fifth group of details)

Descriptive details

7   Now that I look back at the project, I believe that activities like this should be part of every student's college education. Both the residents of the trailer and our class benefited from the service-learning project. The residents of the trailer were happy with the deck because it gave them a place to sit when the weather was nice. They also liked their trailer's new look. Those of us who worked on the project learned that a few days' work could make a real difference in other people's lives.

Conclusion

**PRACTICE
16-3**

1. Paraphrase James's thesis statement.

2. What determines the order in which James arranges the elements of his description?

3. What details does James provide to describe the property, the trailer, and the deck?

4. What kinds of signals do James's transitions give readers? Do you think he includes enough transitions? Where could he add more?

5. This essay is primarily an objective description. Does it include any subjective details?

6. What is this essay's greatest strength? What is its greatest weakness?

grammar in context

Description

When you write a descriptive essay, you may use **modifiers**—words and phrases that describe other words in the sentence—to create a picture of your subject. If you place a modifying word or phrase too far from the word it is supposed to describe, you create a potentially confusing **misplaced modifier**.

CONFUSING   Next to the window outlined in green trim was a dark red aluminum door. (Was the window outlined in green trim?)

CLEAR   Next to the window was a dark red aluminum door outlined in green trim.

For information on how to identify and correct misplaced modifiers, see Chapter 28.

Step-by-Step Guide: Writing a Descriptive Essay

Now, you are ready to write a descriptive essay on one of the topics listed below (or a topic of your choice).

TOPICS

An abandoned building
A person or fictional character
   who makes you laugh (or
   frightens you)
Your room (or your closet
   or desk)
A family photograph

A historical site or monument
An advertisement
An object you cherish
Someone whom everyone notices
Someone whom no one notices
The home page of a Web site you
   visit often

As you write your essay, follow these steps:

1. Planning
   - Make sure your topic calls for description.
   - Find ideas to write about.
   - Decide what dominant impression you want to convey.
   - Write a thesis statement that identifies your main idea.

2. Organizing
 - Choose details that help to convey your dominant impression.
 - Arrange your details in an effective order, making an outline if necessary.

3. Drafting
 - Draft your essay.

4. **TEST**ing
 - **TEST** your essay, referring to the **TEST**ing a Descriptive Essay checklist below.

5. Revising and Editing
 - Revise and edit your essay, referring to the two Self-Assessment checklists in Chapter 13.

TESTing a descriptive essay

Thesis Statement Unifies Your Essay

☐ Does your introduction include a **thesis statement** that communicates your essay's main idea?

☐ Does your introduction identify the subject of your description?

Evidence Supports Your Essay's Thesis Statement

☐ Does all your **evidence**—descriptive details—support the dominant impression communicated by your thesis, or should some details be deleted?

☐ Do you describe your subject in enough detail, or do you need to add details to create a more vivid picture?

☐ Are your supporting details arranged in an effective order within your essay and within paragraphs?

Summary Statement Reinforces Your Essay's Main Idea

☐ Does your conclusion include a **summary statement** that reinforces your essay's thesis?

Transitions

☐ Do you include **transitions** that introduce your details and move readers smoothly from one aspect of your subject to another?

16d   Process Essays

A **process** is a series of chronological steps that produces a particular result. **Process essays** explain the steps in a procedure, telling how something is (or was) done. A process essay can be organized as either a *process explanation* or a set of *instructions*.

When you **TEST** a **process** essay, make sure it includes all these elements:

T ■ **Thesis Statement**—A process essay should include a **thesis statement** that expresses the essay's main idea, identifying the process you will explain and telling why it is important or why you are explaining it.

E ■ **Evidence**—The body paragraphs should provide **evidence**—examples and details—that explains all the steps in the process and supports the essay's thesis. Each paragraph's topic sentence should identify the step (or group of related steps) that the paragraph will explain. Steps should be presented in strict chronological (time) order.

S ■ **Summary Statement**—The conclusion of a process essay should include a **summary statement** that reinforces the essay's thesis.

T ■ **Transitions**—A process essay should include **transitional words and phrases** that link the steps in the process and show how they are related.

Moving from Assignment to Thesis

The wording of your assignment may suggest that you write a process essay. For example, you may be asked to *explain a process*, *give instructions*, *give directions*, or *give a step-by-step account*. Once you decide that your assignment calls for process, you need to develop a thesis statement that reflects this purpose.

ASSIGNMENT	THESIS STATEMENT
American government Explain the process by which a bill becomes a law.	The process by which a bill becomes a law is long and complex, involving numerous revisions and a great deal of compromise.
Pharmacy practice Summarize the procedure for conducting a clinical trial of a new drug.	To ensure that drugs are safe and effective, scientists follow strict procedural guidelines for testing and evaluating the drugs.

Technical writing Write a set of instructions for applying for a student internship in a government agency.	If you want to apply for a government internship, you need to follow several important steps.

If your purpose is simply to help readers understand a process, not actually perform it, you will write a process explanation. **Process explanations**, like the first two examples above, often use present tense verbs ("Once a bill *is* introduced in Congress" or "A scientist first *submits* a funding application") to explain how a procedure is generally carried out. However, when a process explanation describes a specific procedure that was completed in the past, it uses past tense verbs ("The next thing I *did*").

If your purpose is to enable readers to actually perform the steps in a process, you will write instructions. **Instructions**, like the technical writing example above, always use present tense verbs in the form of commands to tell readers what to do ("First, *meet* with your adviser").

Organizing a Process Essay

Whether your essay is a process explanation or a set of instructions, you can either devote a full paragraph to each step of the process or group a series of minor steps together in a single paragraph.

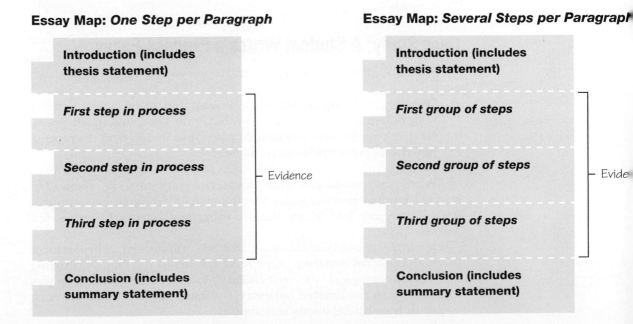

Essay Map: *One Step per Paragraph*

- Introduction (includes thesis statement)
- *First step in process*
- *Second step in process* — Evidence
- *Third step in process*
- Conclusion (includes summary statement)

Essay Map: *Several Steps per Paragraph*

- Introduction (includes thesis statement)
- *First group of steps*
- *Second group of steps* — Evide
- *Third group of steps*
- Conclusion (includes summary statement)

As you write your process essay, discuss each step in the order in which it is performed, making sure your topic sentences clearly identify each step or group of steps. (If you are writing instructions, you may also include reminders or warnings that readers might need to know when performing the process.)

Transitions in Process Essays

Transitions are extremely important in process essays because they enable readers to follow the sequence of steps in the process and, in the case of instructions, to perform the process themselves.

Some Transitional Words and Phrases for Process

after that	immediately	the final step
as	later	the first (second,
as soon as	meanwhile	third) step
at the end	next	then
at the same time	now	the next step
before	once	when
finally	soon	while
first	subsequently	

Case Study: A Student Writes a Process Essay

Jen Rossi, a student in a first-year writing course, was given this assignment:

> Write a set of instructions for a process that you are very familiar with but that your classmates probably do not know much about. Be sure your readers will be able not just to understand the process but also to perform the steps themselves.

When she considered what she might want to write about, Jen rejected familiar process topics like following a recipe or performing a household repair. Instead, she decided to explain how to sell items at flea markets.

Jen knew a lot about this topic, but she still needed to **brainstorm** to get all the steps down on paper. Next, she **listed the steps**, arranging them in chronological order and checking to make sure that no step was missing. When she **drafted** her essay, she made sure she identified each step with transitional words and phrases.

Jen's biggest challenge was developing a **thesis statement**. Before she wrote her draft, she came up with a tentative thesis—"Selling at a flea market is a process that requires a number of steps"—but she knew this sentence was only a placeholder. Her thesis statement told readers what she planned to write about, but it didn't tell them why she was explaining this process or how she felt about it.

When she TESTed her draft, she saw that while she had a tentative thesis and plenty of support, she had not included a summary statement. She quickly jotted down a placeholder sentence—"These are the steps in selling at a flea market"—that she could revise when she revised her thesis statement.

With the help of classmates in her **peer-review** group, Jen revised her thesis statement and summary statement so they both communicated her essay's main idea: that following a process can establish a routine to make flea market selling easier. She also added a few more examples (for instance, examples of heavy and small items in paragraph 5 and examples of small and large items in paragraph 7) in response to suggestions from her classmates. Once she made these revisions, she went on to **edit** and **proofread** her essay.

The final draft that follows includes all the elements Jen looked for when she TESTed her essay.

T E S T

- Thesis Statement
- Evidence
- Summary Statement
- Transitions

Model Process Essay

Read Jen's finished essay, and answer the questions in Practice 16-4.

For Fun and Profit

1　　Selling items at a flea market can be both fun and profitable. In fact, it can lead to a hobby that will be a continuing source of extra income. Your first flea market can take a lot of work, but establishing a routine will make each experience easier and more rewarding than the last one.

Introduction

2　　The first step in the process is to call to reserve a spot at the flea market. If possible, try to get a spot near the entrance, where there is a lot of foot traffic. Once you have your spot, recruit a helper—for example, one of your roommates—and get to work.

Topic sentence (identifies first step)

Examples and details

3　　The next step is sorting through all the items you've managed to accumulate. Your helper will come in handy here, encouraging you to sell ugly or useless things that you may want to hold on to. Make three piles—keep, sell, and trash—and, one by one, place each item in a pile. (Before you decide to sell or discard an item, check with roommates and family members to make sure you aren't accidentally throwing out one of their prized possessions.)

Topic sentence (identifies second step)

Body paragraphs

Examples and details

Topic sentence
(identifies third step)

Next, price the items for sale. This can actually be the hardest step in the process. It's always difficult to accept the fact that you might have to set a low price for something that has sentimental value for you (a giant-sized stuffed animal, for example). It can be just as hard to set a high price on the ugly lamp or old record album that might turn out to be someone's treasure. In all likelihood, you will return from your first flea market with a lot of unsold items. You will also probably realize, too late, that you sold some items too cheaply. (Don't worry; you won't make these mistakes again.)

Examples and details

Topic sentence
(identifies fourth step)

The next step is packing up items to be sold. You may want to borrow a friend's truck or van for the heavy, bulky items (boxes of books or dishes, for example). The small items (knickknacks, silk flowers, stray teaspoons) can be transported by car.

Examples and details

Topic sentence
(identifies fifth step)

Body paragraphs

The final steps in your preparation take place on the day before the event. Borrow a couple of card tables. Then, go to the bank and get lots of dollar bills and quarters, and collect piles of newspaper and grocery bags. Now, your planning is complete, and you are ready for the big day.

Examples and details

Topic sentence
(identifies sixth step)

On the day of the flea market, get up early, and (with your trusty helper's assistance) load your vehicle. When you arrive at the site where the event is to be held, have your helper unload the car. Meanwhile, set things up, placing small items (such as plates or DVDs) on the card tables and large items (such as your parents' old lawnmower) on the ground near the tables.

Examples and details

Topic sentence
(identifies seventh step)

Now, the actual selling begins. Before you can even set up your tables, people will start picking through your items, offering you cash for picture frames, pots and pans, and old video games. Don't panic! Try to develop a system: one of you can persuade buyers that that old meat grinder or vase is just what they've been looking for; the other person can negotiate the price with prospective buyers. Then, while one of you wraps small items in the newspapers or bags you brought, the other person can take the money and make change.

Examples and details

Conclusion

Finally, at the end of the day, the process will come to an end. Now, count your money. (Don't forget to give a share to your helper.) Then, load all the unsold items into your vehicle, and bring them back home. The process ends when you store the unsold items in the back of your closet, ready to pack them all up again and follow the same routine for the next flea market.

4

5

6

7

8

9

PRACTICE
16-4

1. Restate Jen's thesis statement in your own words.

2. What identifies Jen's essay as a set of instructions rather than a process explanation?

3. Review the transitional words and phrases that link the steps in the process. Are any other transitions needed? If so, where?

4. List the major steps in the process of selling at a flea market. Does Jen present these steps in strict chronological order?

5. Paraphrase Jen's summary statement. Do you think she needs to revise this sentence so it more clearly reinforces her thesis statement?

6. What is the essay's greatest strength? What is its greatest weakness?

grammar in context

Process

When you write a process essay, you may have problems keeping tense, person, and voice consistent throughout. If you shift from one tense, person, or voice to another without good reason, you will confuse your readers.

CONFUSING Make three piles—keep, sell, and trash—and, one by one, every item should be placed in a pile. (shift from active to passive voice and from present to past tense)

CLEAR Make three piles—keep, sell, and trash—and, one by one, place every item in a pile. (consistent voice and tense)

For information on how to avoid illogical shifts in tense, person, and voice, see Chapter 27.

☑ **LearningCurve** For more practice with shift in tense and voice, complete the Verbs and Active and Passive Voice activities at **bedfordstmartins.com/focusonwriting.**

Step-by-Step Guide: Writing a Process Essay

Now, you are ready to write a process essay on one of the topics listed below (or a topic of your choice).

TOPICS

An unusual recipe
Finding an apartment
Applying for a job
Getting dressed for a typical Saturday night
A religious ritual or cultural ceremony
A task you often do at work
A do-it-yourself project that didn't get done
Your own writing process
A self-improvement program (past, present, or future)
Applying for financial aid

As you write your essay, follow these steps:

1. Planning

   ■ Make sure your topic calls for process.

   ■ Decide whether you want to explain a process or write instructions.

   ■ Find ideas to write about.

   ■ Identify your main idea, and write a thesis statement.

2. Organizing

   ■ Identify the most important steps in the process.

   ■ List the steps in chronological order, making an outline if necessary.

3. Drafting

   ■ Draft your essay.

4. **TES**Ting

   ■ **TEST** your essay, referring to the **TES**Ting a Process Essay checklist on page 283.

5. Revising and Editing

   ■ Revise and edit your essay, referring to the two Self-Assessment checklists in Chapter 13.

TESTing a process essay

Thesis Statement Unifies Your Essay

☐ Does your introduction include a **thesis statement** that expresses your essay's main idea, identifying the process you will explain and indicating why you are writing about it?

Evidence Supports Your Essay's Thesis Statement

☐ Does all your **evidence**—examples and details—support your thesis, or should some be deleted?

☐ Do you identify and explain every step that readers will need to understand (or perform) the process? Should any steps in the process be deleted?

☐ Are the steps in the process given in strict chronological order?

☐ If you are writing instructions, have you included all necessary warnings or reminders?

Summary Statement Reinforces Your Essay's Main Idea

☐ Does your conclusion include a **summary statement** that reinforces your essay's thesis?

Transitions

☐ Do you include **transitions** that introduce your steps and clearly show how the steps in the process are related?

16e   Cause-and-Effect Essays

A **cause** makes something happen; an **effect** is a result of a particular cause or event. **Cause-and-effect essays** identify causes or predict effects; sometimes, they do both.

When you **TEST** a **cause-and-effect** essay, make sure it includes all these elements:

T ■ **Thesis Statement**—The introduction of a cause-and-effect essay should include a **thesis statement** that communicates the essay's main idea and indicates whether it will focus on causes or on effects.

E ■ **Evidence**—The body paragraphs should include **evidence**—examples and details—to illustrate and explain the causes or effects you examine. The topic sentence of each paragraph should identify the causes or effects the paragraph will discuss.

S ■ **Summary Statement**—The conclusion of a cause-and-effect essay should include a **summary statement** that reinforces the essay's thesis.

T ■ **Transitions**—A cause-and-effect essay should include **transitional words and phrases** that make clear which causes lead to which effects.

Moving from Assignment to Thesis

The wording of your assignment may suggest that you write a cause-and-effect essay. For example, the assignment may ask you to *explain why, predict the outcome, list contributing factors, discuss the consequences*, or tell what *caused* something else or how something is *affected* by something else. Once you decide that your assignment calls for cause and effect, you need to develop a thesis statement that reflects this purpose.

ASSIGNMENT	THESIS STATEMENT
Women's studies What factors contributed to the rise of the women's movement in the 1970s?	The women's movement of the 1970s had its origins in the peace and civil rights movements of the 1960s.
Public health Discuss the possible long-term effects of smoking.	In addition to its well-known negative effects on smokers themselves, smoking also causes significant problems for those exposed to secondhand smoke.
Media and society How has the Internet affected the lives of those who have grown up with it?	The Internet has created a generation of people who learn differently from those in previous generations.

A cause-and-effect essay can focus on causes or on effects. When you write about causes, be sure to examine *all* relevant causes. You should emphasize the cause you consider the most important, but do not forget to consider other causes that may be significant. Similarly, when you write about effects, consider *all* significant effects of a particular cause, not just the first few that you think of.

If your focus is on finding causes, as it is in the first assignment on page 284, your introductory paragraph should identify the effect (the women's movement). If your focus is on predicting effects, as it is in the second and third assignments, you should begin by identifying the cause (smoking, the Internet).

Organizing a Cause-and-Effect Essay

In the body of your essay, you will probably devote a full paragraph to each cause (or effect). You can also group several related causes (or effects) together in each paragraph.

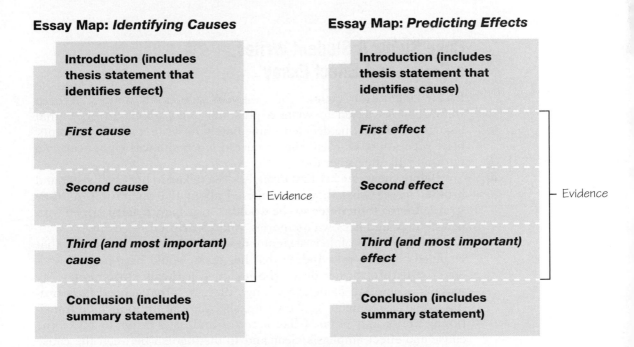

Essay Map: *Identifying Causes*

- **Introduction (includes thesis statement that identifies effect)**
- **First cause**
- **Second cause** — Evidence
- **Third (and most important) cause**
- **Conclusion (includes summary statement)**

Essay Map: *Predicting Effects*

- **Introduction (includes thesis statement that identifies cause)**
- **First effect**
- **Second effect** — Evidence
- **Third (and most important) effect**
- **Conclusion (includes summary statement)**

Transitions in Cause-and-Effect Essays

Transitions are important in cause-and-effect essays because they establish causal connections, telling readers that A caused B and not the other way around. They also make it clear that events have a *causal* relationship (A *caused* B) and not just a *sequential* relationship (A *came before* B). Remember, when one event follows another, the second is not necessarily the result of the first. For example, an earthquake may occur the day before you fail an exam, but that doesn't mean the earthquake caused you to fail.

> ### Some Transitional Words and Phrases for Cause and Effect
>
> | | | |
> |---|---|---|
> | accordingly | for this reason | the most important |
> | another cause | since | cause |
> | another effect | so | the most important |
> | as a result | the first (second, | effect |
> | because | third) cause | therefore |
> | consequently | the first (second, | |
> | for | third) effect | |

Case Study: A Student Writes a Cause-and-Effect Essay

In an orientation course for first-year education majors, Andrea DeMarco was asked to write a personal essay about an event that changed her life. She decided immediately to write about her parents' brief separation, an event that occurred when she was eight years old but that still affects her today.

Before she wrote her first draft, Andrea talked to her older sister and brother to see what they remembered about the separation. As they spoke, Andrea **took notes** so she wouldn't forget any details. Armed with her siblings' and her own memories, Andrea **drafted** her essay.

The wording of her assignment—to write about an event that changed her life—told Andrea that her essay would have a cause-and-effect structure. In her draft, she included a **thesis statement**—"My parents' separation made everything different"—that echoed the wording of the assignment. As she wrote, she was careful to include transitional words and phrases like *because* and *as a result* to make the cause-and-effect emphasis clear and to distinguish between the cause (the separation) and its effects. Her summary statement also reinforced the cause-and-effect emphasis of her essay.

When Andrea TESTed her draft, she saw that it included all the required elements—thesis statement, evidence, summary statement, and transitions—so she moved on to **revise** her draft. When she finished her revisions, she **edited** and **proofread** her essay.

The final draft that follows includes all the elements Andrea looked for when she TESTed her essay.

Model Cause-and-Effect Essay

Read Andrea's finished essay, and answer the questions in Practice 16-5.

How My Parents' Separation Changed My Life

1   Until I was eight, I lived the perfect all-American life with my perfect all-American family. I lived in a suburb of Albany, New York, with my parents, my sister and brother, and our dog, Daisy. We had a Ping-Pong table in the basement, a barbecue in the backyard, and two cars in the garage. My dad and mom were high school teachers, and every summer we took a family vacation. Then, it all changed. My parents' separation made everything different.

2   One day, just before Halloween, when my sister was twelve and my brother was fourteen (Daisy was seven), our parents called us into the kitchen for a family conference. We didn't think anything was wrong at first; they were always calling these annoying meetings. We figured it was time for us to plan a vacation, talk about household chores, or be nagged to clean our rooms. As soon as we sat down, though, we knew this was different. We could tell Mom had been crying, and Dad's voice cracked when he told us the news. They were separating—they called it a "trial separation"—and Dad was moving out of our house.

3   After that day, everything seemed to change. Every Halloween we always had a big jack-o'-lantern on our front porch. Dad used to spend hours at the kitchen table cutting out the eyes, nose, and mouth and hollowing out the insides. That Halloween, because he didn't live with us, things were different. Mom bought a pumpkin, and I guess she was planning to carve it up. But she never did, and we never mentioned it. It sat on the kitchen counter for a couple of weeks, getting soft and wrinkled, and then it just disappeared.

4   Other holidays were also different because Mom and Dad were not living together. Our first Thanksgiving without Dad was pathetic. Christmas was different, too. We spent Christmas Eve with Dad and our relatives on his side and Christmas Day with Mom and her family. Of course, we got twice as many presents as usual. I realize now that both our parents were trying to make up for the pain of the separation. The worst part came when I opened my big present from Mom: Barbie's Dream House. This was something I had always wanted. Even at eight, I knew how hard it must have been for Mom to afford it. The trouble was, I had gotten the same thing from Dad the night before.

5   The separation affected each of us in different ways. The worst effect of my parents' separation was not the big events but the disruption in our everyday lives. Dinner used to be a family time, a chance to talk about our day and make plans. But after Dad left, Mom seemed to stop eating. Sometimes she would just have coffee while we ate, and sometimes she

TEST
- Thesis Statement
- Evidence
- Summary Statement
- Transitions

Introduction

Topic sentence
(identifies first effect)

Examples and details

Topic sentence
(identifies
second effect)

Examples and details

Body paragraphs

Topic sentence
(identifies third effect)

Examples and details

Topic sentence
(identifies
fourth effect)

Examples and details

Body paragraphs

wouldn't eat at all. She would microwave some frozen thing for us or heat up soup or cook some hot dogs. We didn't care—after all, now she let us watch TV while we ate—but we did notice.

Topic sentence
(identifies fifth effect)

    Other parts of our routine changed, too. Because Dad didn't live with us 6 anymore, we had to spend every Saturday and every Wednesday night at his apartment, no matter what else we had planned. Usually, he would take us to dinner at McDonald's on Wednesdays, and then we would go back to his place and do our homework or watch TV. That wasn't too bad. Saturdays

Examples and details

were a lot worse. We really wanted to be home, hanging out with our friends in our own rooms in our own house. Instead, we had to do some planned activity with Dad, like go to a movie or a hockey game.

    As a result of what happened in my own family, it is hard for me to 7 believe any relationship is forever. By the end of the school year, my parents had somehow worked things out, and Dad was back home again. That June, at a family conference around the kitchen table, we made our summer

Conclusion

vacation plans. We decided on Williamsburg, Virginia, the all-American vacation destination. So, things were back to normal, but I wasn't, and I'm still not. Now, ten years later, my mother and father are all right, but I still worry they'll split up again. And I worry about my own future husband and how I will ever be sure he's the one I'll stay married to.

PRACTICE
16-5

1. Restate Andrea's thesis statement in your own words. Does this statement identify a cause or an effect?

2. List the specific effects of her parents' separation that Andrea identifies.

3. Review the transitional words and phrases Andrea uses to make causal connections clear to her readers. Do you think she needs more of these transitions? If so, where?

4. Is Andrea's relatively long concluding paragraph effective? Why or why not? Do you think it should be shortened or divided into two paragraphs?

5. Is Andrea's straightforward title effective, or should she have used a more creative or eye-catching title? Can you suggest an alternative?

6. What is this essay's greatest strength? What is its greatest weakness?

grammar in context

Cause and Effect

When you write a cause-and-effect essay, you may have trouble remembering the difference between *affect* and *effect*.

> *effect*
> The worst ~~affect~~ of my parents' separation was not the big
>
> events but the disruption in our everyday lives. (*effect* is a noun)

> *affected*
> The separation ~~effected~~ each of us in different ways.
>
> (*affect* is a verb)

For information on affect *and* effect, *see Chapter 23.*

Step-by-Step Guide: Writing a Cause-and-Effect Essay

Now, you are ready to write a cause-and-effect essay on one of the topics listed below (or a topic of your choice).

TOPICS

A teacher's positive (or negative) effect on you
Why you voted a certain way in a recent election (or why you did not vote)
How your life would be different if you dropped out of school (or quit your job)
How a particular invention has changed your life
Why texting is so popular
A movie or book that changed the way you look at life
How a particular season (or day of the week) affects your mood
How having a child would change (or has changed) your life
How a particular event made you grow up

As you write your essay, follow these steps:

1. Planning
   - Make sure your topic calls for cause and effect.
   - Decide whether your essay will focus on causes, effects, or both.
   - Find ideas to write about.
   - Identify your main idea, and write a thesis statement.

2. Organizing
   - Choose causes or effects to support your thesis
   - Arrange causes and effects in an effective order, making an outline if necessary.

3. Drafting
   - Draft your essay.

4. TESTing
   - **TEST** your essay, referring to the **TEST**ing a Cause-and-Effect Essay checklist below.

5. Revising and Editing
   - Revise and edit your essay, referring to the two Self-Assessment checklists in Chapter 13.

TESTing a cause-and-effect essay

Thesis Statement Unifies Your Essay

- ☐ Does your introduction include a **thesis statement** that indicates your main idea and makes clear whether your essay will focus on causes or effects?

Evidence Supports Your Essay's Thesis Statement

- ☐ Does all your **evidence**—examples and details—support your thesis, or should some be deleted?
- ☐ Do you identify and explain all causes or effects relevant to your topic, or do you need to add any?
- ☐ Do you arrange causes and effects to indicate which are more important than others?
- ☐ Does each body paragraph identify and explain one particular cause or effect (or several closely related causes or effects)?

Summary Statement Reinforces Your Essay's Main Idea

- ☐ Does your conclusion include a **summary statement** that reinforces your essay's thesis?

Transitions

- ☐ Do you include **transitions** that introduce each of your causes or effects and make your essay's cause-and-effect connections clear?

16f   Comparison-and-Contrast Essays

Comparison identifies similarities, and **contrast** identifies differences. **Comparison-and-contrast essays** explain how two things are alike or how they are different; sometimes, they discuss both similarities and differences.

When you TEST a **comparison-and-contrast** essay, make sure it includes all these elements:

- **T** ▪ **Thesis Statement**—The introduction of a comparison-and-contrast essay should include a **thesis statement** that communicates the essay's main idea, telling readers what two items you are going to compare or contrast and whether you are going to emphasize similarities or differences.

- **E** ▪ **Evidence**—The body paragraphs should include **evidence**—examples and details—that supports the thesis statement. The topic sentence of each paragraph should identify the similarity or difference the paragraph will examine, and the examples and details should explain the similarity or difference.

- **S** ▪ **Summary Statement**—The conclusion of a comparison-and-contrast essay should include a **summary statement** that reinforces the essay's thesis.

- **T** ▪ **Transitions**—A comparison-and-contrast essay should include **transitional words and phrases** to help readers move from point to point and from subject to subject.

Moving from Assignment to Thesis

The wording of your assignment may suggest that you write a comparison-and-contrast essay—for example, by asking you to *compare*, *contrast*, *discuss similarities*, or *identify differences*. Once you decide that your assignment calls for comparison and contrast, you need to develop a thesis statement that reflects this purpose.

ASSIGNMENT	THESIS STATEMENT
Philosophy What basic similarities do you find in the beliefs of Henry David Thoreau and Martin Luther King Jr.?	Although King was more politically active, both he and Thoreau strongly supported the idea of civil disobedience.
Nutrition How do the diets of native Japanese and Japanese Americans differ?	As they become more and more assimilated, Japanese Americans consume more fats than native Japanese do.

(continued)

(*continued from previous page*)

Literature Contrast the two sisters in Alice Walker's short story "Everyday Use."	Unlike Maggie, Dee—her more successful, better-educated sister—has rejected her family's heritage.

Organizing a Comparison-and-Contrast Essay

When you organize a comparison-and-contrast essay, you can choose either a *point-by-point* or a *subject-by-subject* arrangement. A **point-by-point** comparison alternates between the two subjects you are comparing or contrasting, moving back and forth from one subject to the other. A **subject-by-subject** comparison treats its two subjects separately, first fully discussing one subject and then moving on to consider the other subject. In both kinds of comparison-and-contrast essays, the same points are discussed in the same order for both subjects.

Essay Map: *Point-by-Point Comparison*   **Essay Map:** *Subject-by-Subject Comparison*

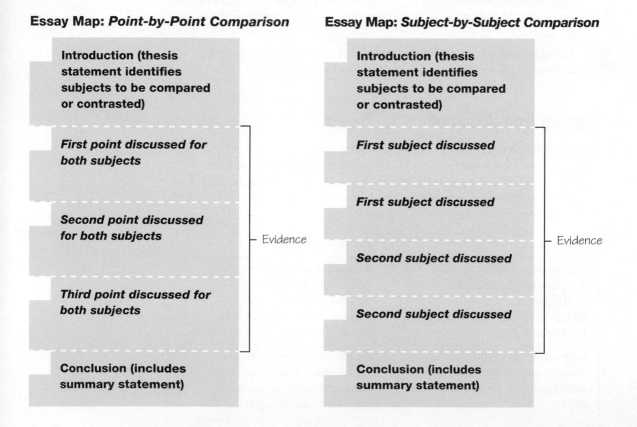

Introduction (thesis statement identifies subjects to be compared or contrasted)

First point discussed for both subjects

Second point discussed for both subjects   — Evidence

Third point discussed for both subjects

Conclusion (includes summary statement)

Introduction (thesis statement identifies subjects to be compared or contrasted)

First subject discussed

First subject discussed

Second subject discussed   — Evidence

Second subject discussed

Conclusion (includes summary statement)

Transitions in Comparison-and-Contrast Essays

The transitional words and phrases you use in a comparison-and-contrast essay tell readers whether you are focusing on similarities or on differences. Transitions also help move readers through your essay from one subject to the other and from one point of comparison or contrast to the next.

> ### Some Transitional Words and Phrases for Comparison and Contrast
>
> | | |
> |---|---|
> | although | likewise |
> | but | nevertheless |
> | even though | on the contrary |
> | however | on the one hand . . . on the other hand |
> | in comparison | similarly |
> | in contrast | unlike |
> | instead | whereas |
> | like | |

Case Study: A Student Writes a Comparison-and-Contrast Essay

Nisha Jani, a student in a first-year writing course, was given the following assignment:

> Some people claim that males and females are so different that at times they seem to belong to two different species. Do you agree, or do you think males and females are more alike than different? Write an essay that supports your position.

When Nisha read this assignment, the key words *different* and *alike* told her that the assignment called for a comparison-and-contrast essay. After **brainstorming**, she decided to write about the differences between boys and girls—specifically, middle school boys and girls. She didn't want to write a serious essay, and she thought she could use humor if she wrote about the habits of two typical seventh-graders. Based on her own experiences and those of her younger brother and sister, Nisha thought that the differences between seventh-grade boys and girls would be more interesting (and more obvious) than the similarities. So, when she drafted a **thesis statement** for her essay, she made sure that it focused on differences: "The typical boy and girl lead very different lives."

Once she had a thesis statement, she **listed** some of the most obvious differences between male and female seventh-graders, including the way girls and boys get ready for school, how they behave in class and during lunch, and what they do after school. When she reviewed the ideas on her list, she decided to follow her two subjects (Johnny and Jane) through a typical school day, and this decision led her to structure her essay as a point-by-point comparison that would contrast boys' and girls' behavior at different points of their day.

When Nisha thought she had enough material to write about, she **wrote a draft** of her essay. Then, she TESTed her draft to see if it included a thesis statement, supporting evidence, a summary statement, and transitional words and phrases. Although her TEST showed her that she had included all the required elements, she thought she still needed to **revise** to strengthen her draft. After a **conference** with her instructor, she revised her thesis statement to make it a bit more specific, added more examples and details, sharpened her summary statement so it reinforced her essay's main idea, and added more transitions to make the contrast between her two subjects clearer. After she finished these revisions, she **edited** her essay.

The final draft that follows includes all the elements Nisha looked for when she TESTed her essay.

Model Comparison-and-Contrast Essay

Read Nisha's finished essay, and answer the questions in Practice 16-6.

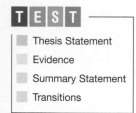

TEST
- Thesis Statement
- Evidence
- Summary Statement
- Transitions

Another Ordinary Day   1

Introduction

"Boys are from Jupiter and get stupider / Girls are from Mars and become movie stars / Boys take a bath and smell like trash / Girls take a shower and smell like a flower." As simple playground songs like this one suggest, the two sexes are very different. As adults, men and women have similar goals, values, and occupations, but as children and teenagers, boys and girls often seem to belong to two different species. In fact, from the first moment of the day to the last, the typical boy and girl live very different lives.

Topic sentence (identifies first difference)

Body paragraphs

The sun rises, and the alarm clock signals the beginning of another day   2
for Johnny and Jane, two seventh-grade classmates. Johnny, an average thirteen-year-old boy, wakes up late and has to hurry. He throws on his favorite jeans, a baggy T-shirt, and a baseball cap. Then, he has a hearty high-cholesterol breakfast and runs out of the house to school, usually forgetting some vital book or homework assignment. Jane, unlike Johnny, wakes up early and takes her time. She takes a long shower and then blow-dries her hair. For Jane, getting dressed can be a very difficult process,

one that often includes taking everything out of her closet and calling friends for advice. After she makes her decision, she helps herself to some food (probably low- or no-fat) and goes off to school, making sure she has with her everything she needs.

3   School is a totally different experience for Johnny and Jane. Johnny will probably sit in the back of the classroom with a couple of other guys, throwing paper airplanes and spitballs. These will be directed at the males they do not like and the females they think are kind of cute. (However, if their male friends ever ask the boys about these girls, they will say girls are just losers and deny that they like any of them.) On the opposite side of the classroom, however, Jane is focused on a very different kind of activity. At first, it looks as if she is carefully copying the algebra notes that the teacher is putting on the board, but her notes have absolutely nothing to do with algebra. Instead, she is writing about boys, clothes, and other topics that are much more important to her than the square root of one hundred twenty-one. She proceeds to fold the note into a box or other creative shape, which can often put origami to shame. As soon as the teacher turns her back, the note is passed and the process begins all over again.

4   Lunch, a vital part of the school day, is also very different for Johnny and Jane. On the one hand, for Johnny and his friends, it is a time to compare baseball cards, exchange sports facts, and of course tell jokes about every bodily function imaginable. In front of them on the table, their trays are filled with pizza, soda, fries, and chips, and this food is their main focus. For Jane, on the other hand, lunch is not about eating; it is a chance to exchange the latest gossip about who is going out with whom. The girls look around to see what people are wearing, what they should do with their hair, and so on. Jane's meal is quite a bit smaller than Johnny's: it consists of a small low-fat yogurt and half a bagel (if she feels like splurging, she will spread some cream cheese on the bagel).

5   After school, Johnny and Jane head in different directions. Johnny rushes home to get his bike and meets up with his friends to run around and play typical "guy games," like pick-up basketball or touch football. Johnny and his friends play with every boy who shows up, whether they know him or not. They may get into physical fights and arguments, but they always plan to meet up again the next day. In contrast to the boys, Jane and her friends are very selective. Their circle is a small one, and they do everything together. Some days, they go to the mall (they will not necessarily buy anything there, but they will consider the outing productive anyway because they will have spent time together). Most days, though, they just

Examples and details

Topic sentence (identifies second difference)

Examples and details

Body paragraphs

WORD POWER

origami the Japanese art of folding paper into shapes representing flowers or animals

Topic sentence (identifies third difference)

Examples and details

Topic sentence (identifies fourth difference)

Examples and details

Body paragraphs

talk, with the discussion ranging from school to guys to lipstick colors. When Jane gets home, she will most likely run to the phone and talk for hours to the same three or four girls.

At the age of twelve or thirteen, boys and girls do not seem to have very much in common. Given this situation, it is amazing that boys and girls grow up to become men and women who interact as neighbors, friends, and coworkers. What is even more amazing is that so many grow up to share lives and raise families together, treating each other with love and respect.

Conclusion

6

PRACTICE
16-6

1. Restate Nisha's thesis statement in your own words.

2. Does Nisha's opening paragraph identify the subjects she will discuss? Does it tell whether she will focus on similarities or on differences?

3. Nisha's essay is a point-by-point comparison. What four points does she discuss for each of her two subjects?

4. Review the topic sentences in Nisha's body paragraphs. What part of the day does each topic sentence identify?

5. Review the transitional words and phrases Nisha uses to move readers from one subject (Johnny) to the other (Jane). Do you think these transitions are effective, or should they be revised to make the contrast clearer?

6. What is this essay's greatest strength? What is its greatest weakness?

grammar in context

Comparison and Contrast

When you write a comparison-and-contrast essay, be sure to present the points you are comparing or contrasting in **parallel** terms to highlight their similarities or differences.

┌─PARALLEL─┐
Johnny, an average thirteen-year-old boy, wakes up late and has

to hurry.

┌─PARALLEL─┐
Jane, unlike Johnny, wakes up early and takes her time.

For information on revising to make ideas parallel, see Chapter 22.

☑ **LearningCurve** For more practice with parallelism, complete the Parallelism activity at **bedfordstmartins.com/focusonwriting.**

Step-by-Step Guide: Writing a Comparison-and-Contrast Essay

Now, you are ready to write a comparison-and-contrast essay on one of the topics listed below (or a topic of your choice).

TOPICS

Two coworkers
Two movie heroes
How you expect your life to be different from the lives of your parents
Men's and women's ideas about their body images
Two ways of studying for an exam
Risk-takers and people who play it safe
Country and city living (or, compare suburban living with either)
Two popular magazines (features, ads, target audiences, pictures)
Leaders and followers
Designer products and counterfeit products
Optimists and pessimists

As you write your essay, follow these steps:

1. Planning
   - Make sure your topic calls for comparison and contrast.
   - Find ideas to write about.
   - Decide whether you want to discuss similarities, differences, or both.
   - Identify your main idea, and write a thesis statement.

2. Organizing
   - Identify specific points of comparison or contrast to support your thesis.
   - Decide whether to structure your essay as a point-by-point or subject-by-subject comparison.
   - Arrange your points in a logical order, making an outline if necessary.

3. Drafting
   - Draft your essay.

4. TESTing
   - TEST your essay, referring to the TESTing a Comparison-and-Contrast Essay checklist on page 298.

5. Revising and Editing
   - Revise and edit your essay, referring to the two Self-Assessment checklists in Chapter 13.

TESTing a comparison-and-contrast essay

T hesis Statement Unifies Your Essay

☐ Does your introduction include a **thesis statement** that expresses your main idea, identifying the two subjects you will compare and indicating whether your essay will examine similarities or differences?

E vidence Supports Your Essay's Thesis Statement

☐ Do you discuss all significant points of comparison or contrast that apply to your two subjects, explaining each similarity or difference using specific examples and details?

☐ Does all your **evidence**—examples and details—support your thesis, or should some be deleted?

☐ Have you treated similar points for both of your subjects?

☐ Is your essay's organization consistent with either a point-by-point comparison or a subject-by-subject comparison?

S ummary Statement Reinforces Your Essay's Main Idea

☐ Does your conclusion include a **summary statement** that reinforces your essay's thesis, reminding readers what your two subjects are and how they are alike or different?

T ransitions

☐ Do you include **transitions** that introduce each of your points of comparison or contrast and move readers from one subject or point to another?

16g Classification Essays

Classification is the act of sorting items into appropriate categories. **Classification essays** divide a whole (your subject) into parts and sort various items into categories.

When you **TEST** a **classification** essay, make sure it includes all these elements:

T ■ **Thesis Statement**—The introduction of a classification essay should include a **thesis statement** that communicates the essay's main idea and indicates what the essay will classify.

E ▪ **Evidence**—The body paragraphs should provide **evidence**—examples and details—to support the thesis statement. The topic sentence of each paragraph should identify the category it will discuss, and the examples and details should explain the category and differentiate it from other categories.

S ▪ **Summary Statement**—The conclusion of a classification essay should include a **summary statement** that reinforces the essay's thesis.

T ▪ **Transitions**—A classification essay should include **transitional words and phrases** to show how categories are related to one another and to the thesis.

Moving from Assignment to Thesis

The wording of your assignment may suggest that you write a classification essay. For example, you may be asked to consider *kinds*, *types*, *categories*, *components*, *segments*, or *parts of a whole*. Once you decide that your assignment calls for classification, you need to develop a thesis statement that reflects this purpose.

ASSIGNMENT	THESIS STATEMENT
Business What kinds of courses are most useful for students planning to run their own businesses?	Courses dealing with accounting, management, and computer science offer the most useful skills for future business owners.
Biology List the components of blood and explain the function of each.	Red blood cells, white blood cells, platelets, and plasma have distinct functions.
Education Classify elementary school children according to their academic needs.	The elementary school population includes special-needs students, students with reading and math skills at or near grade level, and academically gifted students.

Organizing a Classification Essay

As a rule, each paragraph of a classification essay examines a separate category—a different part of the whole. For example, a paragraph could focus on one kind of course in the college curriculum, one component of the blood, or one type of child. Within each paragraph, you discuss the individual items that you have put into a particular category—for example, accounting courses, red blood cells, or gifted students. If you consider some categories less important than others, you may decide to discuss those minor categories together in a single paragraph, devoting full paragraphs only to the most significant categories.

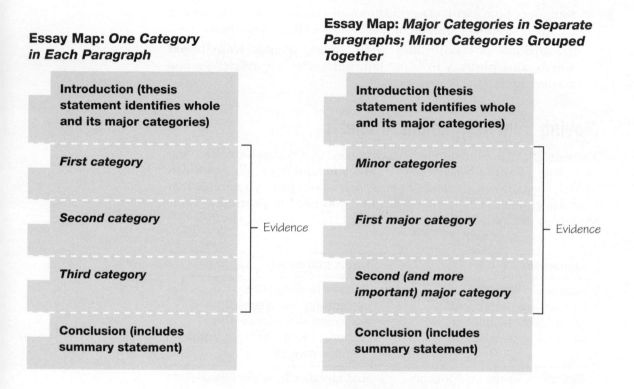

Essay Map: *One Category in Each Paragraph*

Introduction (thesis statement identifies whole and its major categories)

First category

Second category

Third category

Conclusion (includes summary statement)

— Evidence

Essay Map: *Major Categories in Separate Paragraphs; Minor Categories Grouped Together*

Introduction (thesis statement identifies whole and its major categories)

Minor categories

First major category

Second (and more important) major category

Conclusion (includes summary statement)

— Evidence

Transitions in Classification Essays

In a classification essay, topic sentences identify the category or categories discussed in each paragraph. Transitional words and phrases signal movement from one category to the next and may also tell readers which categories you consider more (or less) important.

Some Transitional Words and Phrases for Classification

one kind . . . another kind the final type	the first (second, third) category the last group	the most important component the next part

Case Study: A Student Writes a Classification Essay

Rob O'Neal, a student in a first-year writing course, was given the following assignment.

> Write a classification essay focusing on a type of consumer product—for example, cell phones, jeans, mountain bikes, or hair gels. Discuss three or four categories of the product you select, examining the same features for each category.

At first, Rob was overwhelmed by the possibilities; after all, he was a consumer, and there were many products to choose from. Stuck in traffic on his way home from school, he started noticing the names of the different cars around him and thinking about all the different models he had learned to identify when he was younger and fascinated by everything related to cars. At this point, he realized that he could write his essay about cars, classifying them on the basis of the kinds of names they had.

When Rob got home, he **brainstormed**, listing all the car names he could think of. Then, he made a **cluster diagram** to help him sort all the names into categories. When he looked over his diagram, he saw that he could organize the car names he had listed into three categories—those that suggest exciting destinations, those that suggest toughness, and those that suggest exploration and discovery. Identifying these three categories led him to a **thesis statement** for his essay: "The names auto manufacturers choose for their cars appeal to Americans' deepest desires."

When he **drafted** his essay, Rob developed each branch of his cluster diagram into one of his body paragraphs and wrote topic sentences that clearly identified and defined each category. When he TESTed his essay, he saw that it included all the required elements, but he still wasn't completely satisfied with his draft. To help him plan his revision, he made a **writing center appointment** and went over his draft with a tutor. She advised him to add more examples of each kind of car name as well as more transitional words and phrases—such as *for example* and *also*—to help readers move smoothly through his essay. When he finished making the revisions suggested by his writing center tutor (as well as some he decided on himself), he went on to **edit** and **proofread** his essay.

The final draft that follows includes all the elements Rob looked for when he TESTed his essay.

Model Classification Essay

Read Rob's finished essay, and answer the questions in Practice 16-7.

T E S T

■ Thesis Statement
■ Evidence
■ Summary Statement
■ Transitions

Selling a Dream

Introduction

The earliest automobiles were often named after the men who manufactured 1
them—Ford, Studebaker, Nash, Olds, Chrysler, Dodge, Chevrolet, and so on. Over
the years, however, American car makers began competing to see what kinds
of names would sell the most cars. Many car names seem to have been chosen
simply for how they sound: Alero, Corvette, Neon, Probe, Caprice. Many others,
however, are designed to sell specific dreams to consumers. Americans always
seem to want to be, do, and become something different. They want to be tough
and brave, to explore new places, to take risks. The names auto manufacturers
choose for their cars appeal to Americans' deepest desires.

Topic sentence
(identifies first
category)

Some American cars are named for places people dream of traveling to. 2
Park Avenue, Malibu, Riviera, Seville, Tahoe, Yukon, Aspen, and Durango are
some names that suggest escape—to New York City, California, Europe, the
West. Other place names—Sebring, Daytona, and Bonneville, for example—
are associated with the danger and excitement of car racing. And then there is
the El Dorado, a car named for a fictional paradise: a city of gold.

Examples and details

Topic sentence
(identifies second
category)

Other car names convey rough and tough, even dangerous, images. 3
Animal names fall into this category, with models like Ram, Bronco, and
Mustang suggesting powerful, untamed beasts. The "rough and tough"
category also includes car names that suggest the wildness of the Old West:
Wrangler and Rodeo, for example. Because the American auto industry was
originally centered near Detroit, Michigan, where many cities have Indian
names, cars named for the cities where they are manufactured inherited
these names. Thus, cars called Cadillac, Pontiac, and Cherokee recall the
history of Indian nations, and these too might suggest the excitement of
the untamed West.

Examples and details

Body paragraphs

Topic sentence
(identifies third
category)

The most interesting car names in terms of the dream they sell, however, 4
were selected to suggest exploration and discovery. Years ago, some car names
honored real explorers, like DeSoto and LaSalle. Now, model names only sell an
abstract idea. Still, American car names like Blazer, Explorer, Navigator, Journey,
Mountaineer, Expedition, Caravan, and Voyager (as well as the names of foreign
cars driven by many Americans, such as Nissan's Pathfinder and Quest and
Honda's Passport, Pilot, and Odyssey) have the power to make drivers feel they
are blazing new trails and discovering new worlds—when in fact they may
simply be carpooling their children to a soccer game or commuting to work.

Examples and details

Most people take cars for granted, but manufacturers still try to make 5
consumers believe they are buying more than just transportation. Today, however,
the car is just an ordinary piece of machinery, a necessity for many people.
Sadly, the automobile is no longer seen as the amazing invention it once was.

Conclusion

PRACTICE

16-7

1. Restate Rob's thesis statement in your own words.

2. What three categories of car names does Rob discuss in his essay?

3. Is Rob's treatment of the three categories similar? Does he present the same kind of information for each kind of car name?

4. How do Rob's topic sentences move readers from one category to the next? How do they link the three categories?

5. Do you think Rob should have included additional examples in each category? Should he have included any additional categories?

6. What is this essay's greatest strength? What is its greatest weakness?

grammar in context

Classification

When you write a classification essay, you may want to list the categories you are going to discuss or the examples in each category. If you do, use a **colon** to introduce your list, and make sure that a complete sentence comes before the colon.

> Many car names seem to be chosen simply for how they sound: Alero, Corvette, Neon, Probe, Caprice.

For information on how to use a colon to introduce a list, see 36g.

Step-by-Step Guide: Writing a Classification Essay

Now, you are ready to write a classification essay on one of the topics below (or a topic of your own).

TOPICS

Types of teachers (or bosses)
Ways to lose (or gain) weight
Items hanging on your walls
Kinds of moods
Kinds of stores in a local
    shopping mall
Kinds of learning styles

Traits of oldest children, middle
    children, and youngest children
Kinds of desserts
Kinds of workers you encounter
    in a typical day
College students' clothing choices
Kinds of tattoos

As you write your essay, follow these steps:

1. Planning
   - Make sure your topic calls for classification.
   - Find ideas to write about.
   - Identify your main idea, and write a thesis statement.

2. Organizing
   - Decide what categories you will discuss.
   - Sort examples and details into categories.
   - Arrange your categories in an effective order, making an outline if necessary.

3. Drafting
   - Draft your essay.

4. TESTing
   - **TEST** your essay, referring to the **TEST**ing a Classification Essay checklist below.

5. Revising and Editing
   - Revise and edit your essay, referring to the two Self-Assessment checklists in Chapter 13.

TESTing a classification essay

T hesis Statement Unifies Your Essay

☐ Does your introduction include a **thesis statement** that clearly identifies the subject of your classification and the categories you will discuss?

E vidence Supports Your Essay's Thesis Statement

☐ Does all your **evidence**—examples and details—support your thesis, or should some be deleted?

☐ Do you treat each major category similarly and with equal thoroughness?

S ummary Statement Reinforces Your Essay's Main Idea

☐ Does your conclusion include a **summary statement** that reinforces your essay's thesis?

16h Definition Essays

Definition explains the meaning of a term or concept. A **definition essay** presents an *extended definition*, using various patterns of development to move beyond a simple dictionary definition.

When you **TEST** a **definition** essay, make sure it includes all the following elements:

T ▪ **Thesis Statement**—The introduction of a definition essay should include a **thesis statement** that communicates the essay's main idea and identifies the term you are going to define.

E ▪ **Evidence**—The body paragraphs should include **evidence**—examples and details—that supports the thesis statement and defines your term. Body paragraphs may use different patterns of development.

S ▪ **Summary Statement**—The conclusion of a definition essay should include a **summary statement** that reinforces the essay's thesis.

T ▪ **Transitions**—A definition essay should include **transitional words and phrases** to move readers from one section of the definition to the next.

Moving from Assignment to Thesis

The wording of your assignment may suggest that you write a definition essay. For example, you may be asked to *define* or *explain* or to answer the question *What is x?* or *What does x mean?* Once you decide that your assignment calls for definition, you need to develop a thesis statement that reflects this purpose.

ASSIGNMENT	THESIS STATEMENT
Art Explain the meaning of the term *performance art*.	Unlike more conventional forms of art, *performance art* extends beyond the canvas.
Biology What did Darwin mean by the term *natural selection*?	*Natural selection*, popularly known as "survival of the fittest," is a good deal more complicated than most people think.

(continued)

(continued from previous page)

Psychology What is *attention deficit disorder*?	Attention deficit disorder (ADD), once narrowly defined as a childhood problem, is now known to affect adults as well as children.

Organizing a Definition Essay

As the thesis statements above suggest, definition essays can be developed in various ways. For example, you can define something by telling how it occurred (narration), by describing its appearance (description), by giving a series of examples (exemplification), by telling how it operates (process), by telling how it is similar to or different from something else (comparison and contrast), or by discussing its parts (classification).

Some definition essays use a single pattern of development; others combine several patterns of development, perhaps using a different one in each paragraph.

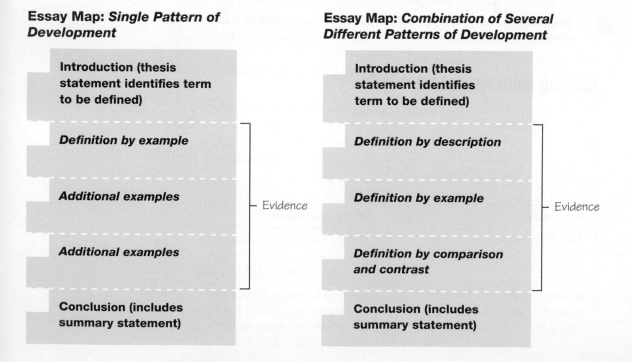

Essay Map: *Single Pattern of Development*

Introduction (thesis statement identifies term to be defined)

Definition by example

Additional examples

Additional examples — Evidence

Conclusion (includes summary statement)

Essay Map: *Combination of Several Different Patterns of Development*

Introduction (thesis statement identifies term to be defined)

Definition by description

Definition by example — Evidence

Definition by comparison and contrast

Conclusion (includes summary statement)

Transitions in Definition Essays

The kinds of transitions used in a definition essay depend on the specific pattern or patterns of development in the essay.

> ### Some Transitional Words and Phrases for Definition
>
> also   like
> for example   one characteristic . . . another characteristic
> in addition   one way . . . another way
> in particular   specifically

Case Study: A Student Writes a Definition Essay

Kristin Whitehead, a student in a first-year writing course, was given the following assignment:

> From the attached list, choose a slang term, an abbreviation or shorthand used in text messages, or a technical term used in one of your classes. Write an essay in which you define this term, developing your definition with any patterns that seem appropriate.

Because her instructor gave the class a list of topics to choose from, Kristin was able to decide on a topic quickly. She chose to define *street smart*, a term with which she was very familiar. She was particularly interested in defining this term because she thought of herself as a street-smart person and was impatient with some of her fellow first-year students, who she felt lacked this important quality.

Kristin had learned from experience how important it was to be street smart, and she **brainstormed** about her experiences to find information to guide her as she drafted her essay. In her **thesis statement**, she indicated why she was defining this term (because she saw it as a "vital survival skill"), and in her body paragraphs she defined her term by giving examples of behavior that she considered to be (and *not* to be) street smart.

When she **TEST**ed her draft, she was satisfied with the wording of her thesis statement and her supporting evidence, but she knew that she still needed to add a summary statement that did more than just repeat the wording of her thesis statement; she also needed to add clearer topic sentences. Since she knew she was going to meet with her **peer-review** group, she decided to ask her classmates for advice about these two issues. With their help, she revised her summary statement and tied her body paragraphs together by adding the same introductory phrase to the topic sentences of paragraphs 2, 3, and 4. When she finished **revising** her essay, Kristin went on to **edit** and **proofread** it.

The final draft that follows includes all the elements Kristin looked for when she **TEST**ed her essay.

TEST

- Thesis Statement
- Evidence
- Summary Statement
- Transitions

Model Definition Essay

Read Kristin's finished essay, and answer the questions in Practice 16-8.

Street Smart

Introduction

I grew up in a big city, so I was practically born street smart. I learned the hard way how to act and what to do, and so did my friends. To us, being *street smart* meant having common sense. We wanted to be cool, but we needed to be safe, too. Now I go to college in a big city, and I realize that not everyone here grew up the way I did. Many students are from suburbs or rural areas, and they are either terrified of the city or totally ignorant of city life. The few suburban or rural students who are willing to venture downtown are

Thesis statement

not street smart—but they should be. Being street smart is a vital survival skill, one that everyone should learn.

Topic sentence (identifies first point)

For me, being street smart means knowing how to protect my possessions. Friends of mine who are not used to city life insist on wearing all their jewelry when they go downtown. I think this is asking for trouble, and I know better. I always tuck my chain under my shirt and leave my gold earrings home. Another thing that surprises me is how some of my friends wave their money around.

Examples and details

They always seem to be standing on the street, trying to count their change or stuff dollars into their wallets. Street-smart people make sure to put their money safely away in their pockets or purses before they leave a store. A street-smart person will also carry a backpack, a purse strapped across the chest, or no purse at all. A person who is not street smart carries a purse loosely over one shoulder or dangles it by its handle. Again, these people are asking for trouble.

Topic sentence (identifies second point)

Being street smart also means protecting myself. It means being aware of my surroundings at all times and looking alert. A lot of times, I have been downtown with people who kept stopping on the street to talk about where

Body paragraphs

they should go next or walking up and down the same street over and over again. A street-smart person would never do this. It is important that I look as if I know where I am going at all times, even if I don't. Whenever possible,

Examples and details

I decide on a destination in advance, and I make sure I know how to get there. Even if I am not completely sure where I am headed, I make sure my body language conveys my confidence in my ability to reach my destination.

Topic sentence (identifies third point)

Finally, being street smart means protecting my life. A street-smart person does not walk alone, especially after dark, in an unfamiliar neighborhood. A street-smart person does not ask random strangers for directions; when lost, he or she asks a shopkeeper for help. A street-smart person takes main streets instead of side streets. When faced with danger or the threat of danger, a

Examples and details

street-smart person knows when to run, when to scream, and when to give up money or possessions to avoid violence.

1

2

3

4

5   ==Being street smart is vitally important—sometimes even a matter of life
and death.== Some people think it is a gift, but I think it is something almost
anyone can learn. Probably the best way to learn how to be street smart is to
hang out with people who know where they are going.   *Conclusion*

PRACTICE

16-8   1. Restate Kristin's thesis statement in your own words.

2. In your own words, define the term *street smart*. Why does
this term require more than a one-sentence definition?

3. Where does Kristin use examples to develop her definition? Where
does she use comparison and contrast?

4. What phrase does Kristin repeat in her topic sentences to tie her
essay's three body paragraphs together?

5. Kristin's conclusion is quite a bit shorter than her other paragraphs. Do
you think she should expand this paragraph? If so, what should she add?

6. What is this essay's greatest strength? What is its greatest weakness?

grammar in context

Definition

When you write a definition essay, you may begin with a one-sentence
definition that you expand in the rest of your essay. When you write
your definition sentence, do not use the phrase *is when* or *is where*.

> *means knowing*
> For me, being street smart ~~is when I know~~ how to protect my
> ⌃
> possessions.

> *means protecting*
> Being street smart **is** also ~~where I protect~~ myself.
> ⌃

*For information on how to structure a definition sentence, see the
Grammar in Context box in 11a.*

Step-by-Step Guide: Writing a Definition Essay

Now, you are ready to write a definition essay on one of the topics listed
below (or a topic of your choice).

TOPICS

Upward mobility	Responsibility	Courage
Peer pressure	Procrastination	Happiness
Success	Security	Home
Loyalty	Ambition	Family

As you write your essay, follow these steps:

1. Planning
   - Make sure your topic calls for definition.
   - Find ideas to write about.
   - Identify your main idea, and write a thesis statement.

2. Organizing
   - Decide what patterns of development to use to support your thesis.
   - Arrange supporting examples and details in an effective order, making an outline if necessary.

3. Drafting
   - Draft your essay.

4. TESTing
   - TEST your essay, referring to the TESTing a Definition Essay checklist below.

5. Revising and Editing
   - Revise and edit your essay, referring to the two Self-Assessment checklists in Chapter 13.

TESTing a definition essay

Thesis Statement Unifies Your Essay

- ☐ Does your introduction include a **thesis statement** that identifies the term your essay will define and provides a brief definition?

Evidence Supports Your Essay's Thesis Statement

- ☐ Is all your **evidence**—examples and details—clearly related to the term you are defining, or should some be deleted?
- ☐ Do you use appropriate patterns of development to support your definition, or should you explore other options?

Summary Statement Reinforces Your Essay's Main Idea

- ☐ Does your conclusion include a **summary statement** that reinforces your essay's thesis?

Transitions

- ☐ Do you include **transitions** that introduce your points and link your ideas?

16i Argument Essays

Argument takes a stand on a debatable issue—that is, an issue that has two sides (and can therefore be debated). An **argument essay** uses different kinds of *evidence*—facts, examples, and sometimes expert opinion—to persuade readers to accept a position.

When you **TEST** an **argument** essay, make sure it includes all these elements:

T ▪ **Thesis Statement**—The introduction of an argument essay should include a **thesis statement** that expresses the essay's main idea: the position you will take on the issue.

E ▪ **Evidence**—The body paragraphs should include **evidence**—facts, examples, and expert opinion—to support the thesis statement convincingly. The topic sentence of each body paragraph should identify one point of support for your thesis.

S ▪ **Summary Statement**—The conclusion of an argument essay should include a strong **summary statement** that reinforces the essay's thesis.

T ▪ **Transitions**—An argument essay should include logical **transitional words and phrases** that show how your points are related and move readers through your argument.

Moving from Assignment to Thesis

The wording of your assignment may suggest that you write an argument essay. For example, you may be asked to *debate, argue, consider, give your opinion, take a position,* or *take a stand*. Once you decide that your assignment calls for argument, you need to develop a thesis statement that takes a position on the topic you will write about in your essay.

ASSIGNMENT	THESIS STATEMENT
Composition Explain your position on a current social issue.	People should be able to invest some of their Social Security contributions in the stock market.
American history Do you believe that General Lee was responsible for the South's defeat at the Battle of Gettysburg? Why or why not?	Because Lee refused to listen to the advice given to him by General Longstreet, he is largely responsible for the South's defeat at the Battle of Gettysburg.

(continued)

(continued from previous page)

Ethics Should physician-assisted suicide be legalized?	Although many people think physician-assisted suicide should remain illegal, it should be legal in certain situations.

Organizing an Argument Essay

An argument essay can be organized *inductively* or *deductively*. An **inductive argument** moves from the specific to the general—that is, from a group of specific observations to a general conclusion based on these observations. An essay on the first topic in the list above, for example, could be an inductive argument. It could begin by presenting facts, examples, and expert opinion about the benefits of investing in the stock market and end with the conclusion that people should be able to invest part of their Social Security contributions in the stock market.

A **deductive argument** moves from the general to the specific. A deductive argument begins with a **major premise** (a general statement that the writer believes his or her audience will accept) and then moves to a **minor premise** (a specific instance of the belief stated in the major premise). It ends with a **conclusion** that follows from the two premises. For example, an essay on the last topic in the list above could be a deductive argument. It could begin with the major premise that all terminally ill patients who are in great pain should be given access to physician-assisted suicide. It could then go on to state and explain the minor premise that a particular patient is both terminally ill and in great pain, offering facts, examples, and the opinions of experts to support this premise. The essay could conclude that this patient should, therefore, be allowed the option of physician-assisted suicide. The deductive argument presented in the essay would have three parts.

MAJOR PREMISE   All terminally ill patients who are in great pain should be allowed to choose physician-assisted suicide.

MINOR PREMISE   John Lacca is a terminally ill patient who is in great pain.

CONCLUSION   Therefore, John Lacca should be allowed to choose physician-assisted suicide.

Before you present your argument, think about whether your readers are likely to be hostile toward, neutral toward, or in agreement with your position. Once you understand your audience, you can decide which points to make in support of your argument. Strive for a balanced, moderate tone, and avoid name-calling or personal attacks.

Begin each paragraph of your argument essay with a topic sentence that clearly introduces a point in support of your thesis. Throughout your essay, include specific examples that will make your arguments persuasive. Keep in mind that arguments that rely just on generalizations are not as convincing as those that include vivid details and specific examples.

In addition to presenting your case, your essay should also briefly summarize arguments *against* your position and **refute** them (that is, argue against them) by identifying factual errors or errors in logic. If an opposing argument is particularly strong, concede its strength—but try to point out some weaknesses as well. If you deal with opposing arguments in this way, your audience will see you as a fair and reasonable person.

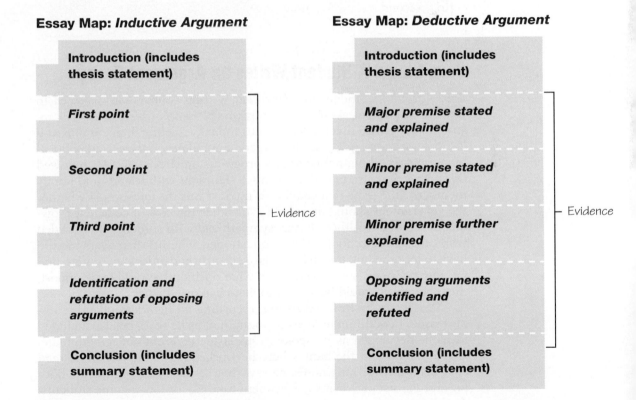

Essay Map: *Inductive Argument*

| Introduction (includes thesis statement) |
| *First point* |
| *Second point* |
| *Third point* |
| *Identification and refutation of opposing arguments* |
| Conclusion (includes summary statement) |

⊢ Evidence

Essay Map: *Deductive Argument*

| Introduction (includes thesis statement) |
| *Major premise stated and explained* |
| *Minor premise stated and explained* |
| *Minor premise further explained* |
| *Opposing arguments identified and refuted* |
| Conclusion (includes summary statement) |

⊢ Evidence

Transitions in Argument Essays

Transitions are extremely important in argument essays because they not only signal the movement from one part of the argument to another but also relate specific points to one another and to the thesis statement.

Some Transitional Words and Phrases for Argument		
accordingly	granted	of course
admittedly	however	on the one
although	in addition	hand . . . on the
because	in conclusion	other hand
but	indeed	since
certainly	in fact	so
consequently	in summary	therefore
despite	meanwhile	thus
even so	moreover	to be sure
even though	nevertheless	truly
finally	nonetheless	
first, second . . .	now	

Case Study: A Student Writes an Argument Essay

Alex Norman, a student in a first-year writing course, was assigned to write an argument essay on a controversial issue of his choice. His instructor suggested that students find a topic by reading their campus and local newspapers, going online to read national news stories and political blogs, and watching public affairs programs on television. Alex followed this advice and also talked about his assignment with friends and family members. One issue that caught his interest was the question of whether the government should do more to subsidize the cost of college for low-income students. Although Alex sympathized with students who needed help paying for school, he also questioned whether taxpayers should have to foot the bill. Because this issue clearly had at least two sides, and because he wasn't sure at the outset what position he could best support, Alex thought it would be a good topic to explore further.

Alex began by **brainstorming**, recording all his ideas on this complex issue. In addition to ideas he thought of as he read, he also included ideas he developed as he spoke to his sister, a recent college graduate, and to his boss at the bank where he worked part-time. When he read over his brainstorming notes, he saw that he had good arguments both for and against increasing government funding for low-income students. At this point, he wasn't sure what position to take in his essay, so he scheduled an appointment for a **conference** with his instructor.

Alex's instructor pointed out that he could make a good case either for or against greater government subsidies; like many controversial issues, this one had no easy answers. She encouraged him to support the position that seemed right to him and to use the information on the opposing side to present (and refute) opposing arguments. She also recommended that Alex email his first draft to her so she could review it.

After he thought about his instructor's comments, Alex decided to argue in favor of increasing government grants to help low-income students pay for college. Before he began to draft his essay, he wrote a **thesis statement** that presented his position on the issue; then, he arranged supporting points from his brainstorming notes into an **outline** that he could follow as he wrote. As he **drafted** his essay, Alex made sure to support his thesis with evidence and to explain his position as clearly and thoroughly as possible. He paid special attention to choosing transitional words and phrases that would indicate how his points were logically connected to one another.

When Alex finished his draft, he **TEST**ed it, taking a quick inventory to make sure he had included all four necessary components of an essay. Then, he emailed the draft to his instructor. Following her suggestions, he **revised** his draft, this time focusing on his topic sentences, his presentation (and refutation) of opposing arguments, and his introductory and concluding paragraphs. When he was satisfied with his revisions, he **edited** and **proofread** his paper.

The final draft that follows includes all the elements Alex looked for when he **TEST**ed his essay.

T E S T

- Thesis Statement
- Evidence
- Summary Statement
- Transitions

Model Argument Essay

Read Alex's finished essay, and answer the questions in Practice 16-9.

Increase Grant Money for Low-Income College Students

1   The price of college tuition has more than doubled over the last two decades. Today, low-income students are finding it especially difficult (and sometimes impossible) to pay for school. Should the government help these students more than it does now? If so, what form should that help take? Rather than reducing aid or asking students to borrow more, the government should give larger grants to subsidize tuition for low-income students.

Introduction

2   If this is a country that is committed to equal opportunity, then college should be affordable for all. To compete in today's high-tech job market, people need a college degree. However, students' access to college is too often determined by their parents' income. This is unfair. Therefore, the government should make it a priority to support students who are being priced out of a college education. Specifically, the government should give larger grants to low-income students. Although some critics see these grants as unnecessary "handouts," such awards are the best way for the government to invest in the future and to maintain our nation's core values. After all, the country's economy benefits when more of its citizens earn college degrees. Even more important, by giving low-income students the same

Topic sentence (introduces first point)

Body paragraphs

Facts, examples, expert opinion

opportunities to succeed as their more affluent peers, the United States
keeps its promise to treat all its citizens fairly.

Some people argue that the best way to help students who are   3
struggling to pay for college is to offer them more loans at a lower
interest rate. However, this solution is inadequate, unfair, and short-sighted.
First of all, lowering the interest rate on student loans only reduces the
average monthly payments by a few dollars. Second, student loans already

unfairly burden low-income students. Why should they have to take on more
debt simply because their parents make less money? The government should
be trying to reduce the amount these students have to borrow, not increase
it. Finally, forcing graduates to start their careers with such a heavy
financial burden is unwise for the country's economy. Although loans might
cost the government less in the short term, in the long term student debt
makes it more difficult for Americans to be successful and competitive.

The federal government does have a program in place to help students   4
who demonstrate need, but Pell Grant funding needs to be expanded. As Joy
Resmovits reports, despite the rising cost of tuition, college students actually
receive proportionally less government grant money than ever before. In fact,
Pell Grants are limited to $5,645 per student per year. At most, Pell grants

cover only a third of average college costs. Meanwhile, the education gap
between rich and poor is growing. As education policy expert Andrew

J. Rotherham observes, while 75 percent of wealthy students earn a
four-year degree by age 24, less than 10 percent of low-income students do.
To help close this gap, the government should offer more funding to those
most in need of financial assistance.

Some would argue, however, that the government should do just the   5
opposite. One of the most common criticisms of government subsidies is
that they are in some way to blame for the rising costs of college. Critics
point out that government grants only make it easier for schools to charge
more. This may be true, but, as Andrew Rotherham points out, the government
could do more to regulate college tuition. For example, the government could

offer incentives to schools that keep their costs down or award more generous
grants to students who attend affordable schools. Ultimately, withdrawing
aid and abandoning students to the free market is irresponsible as well as
counterproductive. Instead, the government should take steps to prevent
people from taking advantage of its generosity.

With the cost of college continuing to rise, now is the time for the   6
government to help the hardest-hit students by offering them more help
to pay for their education. Rather than cutting spending on student aid,
the government should fund more grants to low-income students. However,

it must do so in ways that discourage future increases in tuition. By acting   *Conclusion*
wisely and prudently, the government can improve access to higher
education for all and support the country's economic future.

Works Cited

Resmovits, Joy. "Pell Grants for Poor Students Lose $170 Billion in
     Ryan Budget." *The Huffington Post*. TheHuffingtonPost.com, Inc.,
     27 Mar. 2012. Web. 19 Apr. 2012.

Rotherham, Andrew J. "How to Fix Pell Grants." *Time*. Time, Inc., 24 May
     2012. Web. 19 Apr. 2012.

PRACTICE

16-9   1. In your own words, summarize the position Alex takes in
             his essay.

2. List the facts and examples Alex uses to support his thesis. Where
   does he include expert opinion?

3. Can you list any other supporting evidence that Alex should have
   included but didn't?

4. Review the transitional words and phrases Alex uses. How do they
   move his argument along? Should he add any transitions?

5. Where does Alex address opposing arguments? Can you think of
   other arguments he should have addressed?

6. What is this essay's greatest strength? What is its greatest weakness?

grammar in context

Argument

When you write an argument essay, you need to show the
relationships between your ideas by combining sentences to create
compound sentences and **complex sentences.**

The federal government does have a program in place to help

students who demonstrate need/ *, but* Pell Grant funding needs to be

expanded. (compound sentence)

(continued)

(continued from previous page)

>   *Although some critics*
> ~~Some critics~~ see these grants as unnecessary "handouts,"
> ^*such*
> ~~Such~~ awards are the best way for the government to invest in the
> ^
> future and to maintain our nation's core values. (complex sentence)
>
> *For information on how to create compound sentences, see Chapter 19.*
> *For information on how to create complex sentences, see Chapter 20.*

Step-by-Step Guide: Writing an Argument Essay

Now, you are ready to write an argument essay on one of the topics listed below (or a topic of your choice).

TOPICS

Teenagers who commit serious crimes should (or should not) be tried as adults.

Citizens without criminal records should (or should not) be permitted to carry concealed weapons.

Human beings should (or should not) be used as subjects in medical research experiments.

College financial aid should (or should not) be based solely on merit.

Government funds should (or should not) be used to support the arts.

Public high schools should (or should not) be permitted to distribute condoms to students.

The minimum wage should (or should not) be raised.

College athletes should (or should not) be paid to play.

Convicted felons should (or should not) lose the right to vote.

As you write your essay, follow these steps:

1. Planning
   - Make sure your topic calls for argument.
   - Find ideas to write about.
   - Decide on the position you will support, and write a thesis statement that clearly expresses this position.

2. Organizing
   - List the key points in support of your thesis.
   - Arrange your key supporting points in an effective order.
   - List evidence (facts, examples, and expert opinion) in support of each point.

- List arguments against your position.
- Make an outline that includes key supporting and opposing points.

3. Drafting
   - Draft your essay.

4. **TEST**ing
   - **TEST** your essay, referring to the **TEST**ing an Argument Essay checklist below.

5. Revising and Editing
   - Revise and edit your essay, referring to the two Self-Assessment checklists in Chapter 13.

TESTing an argument essay

T hesis Statement Unifies Your Essay

☐ Does your introduction include a **thesis statement** that clearly expresses the stand you take on the issue you will discuss? Is this issue debatable—that is, does it really have two sides?

E vidence Supports Your Essay's Thesis Statement

☐ Does all your **evidence**—facts, examples, and expert opinion— support your thesis, or should some be deleted?

☐ Do you have enough evidence to support your points?

☐ Have you considered whether readers are likely to be hostile toward, neutral toward, or in agreement with your position— and have you chosen your points accordingly?

☐ Is your evidence presented in a clear inductive or deductive order?

S ummary Statement Reinforces Your Essay's Main Idea

☐ Does your conclusion include a **summary statement** that reinforces your essay's thesis?

T ransitions

☐ Do you include **transitions** that introduce your points?

☐ Do you include enough transitional words and phrases to help readers follow the logic of your argument?

Although this chapter presents student essays that are structured primarily around a single pattern of development—exemplification, narration, description, process, cause and effect, comparison and contrast, classification, definition, or argument—professional writers often combine several patterns in a single essay.

The following short newspaper commentary, "Whatever Happened to Walking to School?" by Lenore Skenazy, combines several of the patterns of development that are explained and illustrated in this chapter. Read the essay carefully, and then answer the Questions for Discussion on pages 321–322.

WHATEVER HAPPENED TO WALKING TO SCHOOL?

Lenore Skenazy

If you think the first week of September means kids skipping off to school, you might want to check your calendar—for the century. The way you got to school isn't the way they do.

Take the bus. Sure, about 40% of kids still ride the cheery yellow chugger, but in many towns it doesn't stop only at the bus stops anymore. It stops at each child's house.

Often, the kids aren't waiting outside to get on. They are waiting in their parents' cars—cars the parents drove from the garage to the sidewalk so their children would be climate-controlled and safe from the predators so prevalent on suburban driveways.

Those of us who remember using our own legs for transit now run the risk of sounding Abe Lincolnesque. Today, only about one in 10 kids walks to school, says Lauren Marchetti, director of the National Center for Safe Routes to School.

The shift is so profound that the language itself has changed. "Arrival" and "dismissal" have become "drop-off and "pick-up" because an adult is almost always involved—even when it doesn't make sense.

"When we first moved to town we found a house three blocks from the school," says Annie Anderson, a mom in Corpus Christi, Texas. "The day before school started a lady knocked on my door and asked if I'd like to join the carpool."

"Carpool to where?" Ms. Anderson asked. "She proceeded to explain that not only would I pick up her kid and others every morning of my assigned week, but I would need to pick up their 'carpool seats' before Monday and pass them to the next parent on Friday." Ms. Anderson declined and allowed her second-grader to walk instead. He beat the car every day.

Driving makes sense if the bus takes forever, or if school is on the way to work. But too often drop-off in the morning means snarls and traffic, and afternoon pick-up has become the evacuation of Saigon. At schools around the country, here's how it works:

First, the "car kids" are herded into the gym. "The guards make sure all children sit still and do not move or speak during the process," reports a dad in Tennessee. Outside, "People get there 45 minutes early to get a spot. And the scary thing is, most of the kids live within biking distance," says Kim Meyer, a mom in Greensboro, N.C.

When the bell finally rings, the first car races into the pick-up spot, whereupon the car-line monitor barks into a walkie-talkie: "Devin's mom is here!"

Devin is grabbed from the gym, escorted to the sidewalk and hustled into the car as if under enemy fire. His mom peels out and the next car pulls up. "Sydney's mom is here!"

Kerry Buss, a curriculum developer in Fairfax County, Va., says her son's school does this, "And this is the same school that took out the bike racks to discourage kids from biking." It's also the school her husband attended as a child. Back then, "he and his sister walked to school like every other kid in the neighborhood. It was unheard of that there'd be a bus, much less a car line."

How did we get to this point? How did we forget that it's just a walk to school?

Simple. We bought the line that good parenting is the same as over-parenting. That the more we could do for our children, the better. We forgot the joy of scuffing down the street when we were young, crunching leaves, picking up seeds, and decided we'd do it all for our kids, independence be damned!

Except independence is good. Children who walk to school are healthier, for obvious reasons. New studies suggest they may do better academically, too. "You can see the difference in the kids who walk or bike," says Jerry Flynn, principal of St. Thomas Aquinas, a Catholic school in Indianapolis that has been encouraging parents to stop driving their kids. "They're bright, chatty, ready to go."

And one day, they might even get to tell their own kids something more than: "When I was your age, I walked 10 feet to the SUV—and it was uphill both ways."

QUESTIONS FOR DISCUSSION

1. What patterns of development are used in this essay? Work with another student to decide where each pattern is used. Then, label the section of the essay where each pattern appears.

2. What is the thesis of this essay? Restate it in your own words. If you were to add this thesis statement to the essay, where would you put it?

3. How does each pattern of development that you identified in Question 1 support the essay's thesis?

4. Look again at the thesis statement you supplied in your answer to Question 2. What pattern of development does it suggest?

5. What do you think is this essay's primary pattern of development? Explain.

review checklist

Patterns of Essay Development

- [ ] **Exemplification** essays use specific examples to support a thesis. (See 16a.)

- [ ] **Narrative** essays tell a story by presenting a series of events in chronological order. (See 16b.)

- [ ] **Descriptive** essays use details to give readers a clear, vivid picture of a person, place, or object. (See 16c.)

- [ ] **Process** essays explain the steps in a procedure, telling how something is (or was) done or how to do something. (See 16d.)

- [ ] **Cause-and-effect** essays identify causes or predict effects. (See 16e.)

- [ ] **Comparison-and-contrast** essays explain how two things are alike or how they are different. (See 16f.)

- [ ] **Classification** essays divide a whole into parts and sort various items into categories. (See 16g.)

- [ ] **Definition** essays use various patterns to develop an extended definition. (See 16h.)

- [ ] **Argument** essays take a stand on a debatable issue, using evidence to persuade readers to accept a position. (See 16i.)

unit
4 Research

17 Writing a Research Paper

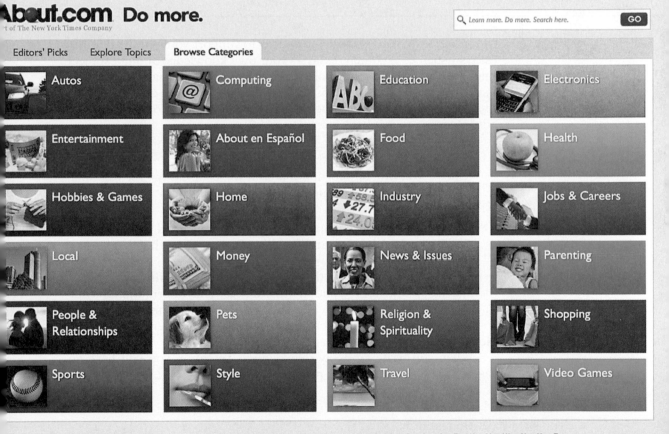

About.com Do more.
t of The New York Times Company

Learn more. Do more. Search here.   GO

Editors' Picks   Explore Topics   **Browse Categories**

Autos	Computing	Education	Electronics
Entertainment	About en Español	Food	Health
Hobbies & Games	Home	Industry	Jobs & Careers
Local	Money	News & Issues	Parenting
People & Relationships	Pets	Religion & Spirituality	Shopping
Sports	Style	Travel	Video Games

Explore Topics: # A B C D E F G H I J K L M N O P Q R S T U V W X Y Z

focus on writing

The About.com directory enables users to search for information by clicking on increasingly specific categories and subcategories. Some students use this tool when they begin their research.

This chapter will guide you through the process of writing a short research paper on a topic of your own choosing. To begin the process, brainstorm to develop a list of topics that you could research and write about.

In this chapter, you will learn to

- choose a topic (17a)
- do research (17b)
- take notes (17c)
- watch out for plagiarism (17d)
- develop a thesis (17e)
- make an outline (17f)
- write your paper (17g)
- document your sources (17h)

In some essays, you use your own ideas to support your thesis. In other essays—such as argument essays—your own knowledge about a subject might not be enough to support your thesis. In these situations, you will have to supplement your ideas with **research**—a careful examination of the ideas and opinions of others. Doing research gives you a number of advantages:

- It exposes you to a cross-section of opinion.

- It helps you find supporting material for your essay—for example, an expert's opinion, a memorable quotation, or a useful fact or statistic.

- It tells readers that you are someone who has gained a fuller understanding of your topic—and for this reason are worth listening to.

When you write an essay that calls for research, you find material on the Internet, in the library, and in other places. This information may be in print or electronic form, and it may be drawn from a variety of sources—for example, journals, magazines, newspapers, pamphlets, blogs, encyclopedias, DVDs, and books.

When you write an essay that requires research, you will have an easier time if you follow this process:

1. Choose a topic.
2. Do research.
3. Take notes.
4. Watch out for plagiarism.
5. Develop a thesis.
6. Make an outline.
7. Write your paper.
8. Document your sources.

17a   Choosing a Topic

The first step in writing an essay that calls for research is finding a topic to write about. Before you choose a topic, ask the following questions.

- What is your page limit?
- When is your paper due?
- How many sources are you expected to use?
- What kinds of sources are you expected to use?

The answers to these questions will help you determine if your topic is too broad or too narrow.

When May Compton, a student in a composition course, was asked to write a three- to four-page essay that was due in five weeks, she decided that she wanted to write about the counterfeit designer goods that seemed to be for sale everywhere. May was used to seeing sidewalk vendors selling brand-name sunglasses and jewelry. Recently, she and her friends had been invited to a "purse party," where they were able to buy expensive handbags at extremely low prices. Even though these handbags were not identified as fakes, she was sure that they were. Because May was a marketing major, she wondered how these copies were marketed and sold. She also wondered if these counterfeits had any negative effects on consumers.

May decided to explore the problem of counterfeit designer merchandise in her paper because she could discuss it in the required number of pages and would be able to finish her paper within the five-week time limit.

choose a topic

Look back at the brainstorming that you did to find a topic for your research paper, and choose a topic to write about. Keep in mind that the topic you choose should be one that you are interested in as well as one that you know something about.

17b   Doing Research

When you do research, you—like most students—probably go straight to the Internet. If you do this, however, you are shortchanging yourself. Your college library gives you access to valuable resources—for example, books, journals, and electronic databases—that are available nowhere else, including on the Internet. For this reason, when you begin your research, you should use your college library as well as the Internet.

Finding Information in the Library

For the best results, you should do your library research systematically. Once you get a sense of your topic, you should consult the library's **online catalog**—a comprehensive information system that gives you access to the resources housed in the library. A search of the online catalog is not as "open" as a search of the Internet, where anything and everything is posted. Library resources have been screened by librarians (as well as instructors) and, in many cases, conform to academic standards of reliability.

You search the online catalog just as you would search the Internet: by carrying out a *keyword search* or a *subject search*. You do a **keyword search** the same way you would search using Google or About.com—by entering your keywords in a search box to retrieve a list of books, periodicals, and other materials that are relevant to your topic. The more specific your keywords are, the more focused your search will be. Thus, the keywords *Facebook privacy* will yield more specific (and useful) results than *social networking*.

You do a **subject search** by entering a subject heading related to your topic. Unlike keywords, subject headings are predetermined and come from a list of subject headings published by the Library of Congress. Many online catalogs provide lists of subject headings that you can use. A subject search is best when you want information about a general topic—for example, *rap music*, *discography*, or *Mark Twain*.

After consulting the online catalog, you should look at the **electronic databases**—such as InfoTrac and ProQuest—that your college library subscribes to. These databases enable you to obtain information from newspapers, magazines, and journals that you cannot freely access by doing a Web search. Most of the library's electronic databases enable you to retrieve the full text of articles. (You can usually search them remotely, from home or from anywhere on campus.)

Most online catalogs list the databases to which the library subscribes along with descriptions of the material the databases contain. For example, a database may contain articles on a wide variety of subjects, or it may focus on a specific subject area. Unlike Web sites, many library databases get information from experts in a particular field. In addition, database sources usually contain full bibliographic information—sometimes in the form of a works-cited entry.

Evaluating Library Sources

All in all, the sources in library databases are usually much more reliable than the sources you access on the Internet. Even so, you should still **evaluate** them—that is, determine their usefulness and reliability—before you use them in your paper. For example, an article in a respected periodical, such as the *New York Times* or the *Wall Street Journal*, is more trustworthy and credible than one in a tabloid, such as the *National Enquirer* or the *Sun*. You should also look at the date of publication to decide if the book or periodical is up-to-date. Finally, consider the author. Is he or she an expert? Does the author have a particular point of view to advance? Your instructor or college librarian can help you select sources that are both appropriate and reliable.

WORD POWER

tabloid a newspaper that emphasizes stories with sensational content

Finding Information on the Internet

The Internet can give you access to a great deal of information that can help you support your ideas and develop your essay. However, you have to be very careful when using the Internet because it is an "open" source; anyone can create a Web site and upload material. Unlike the resources available in your college library, no one is responsible for checking the accuracy of information or the credentials of people who post on the Internet. For this reason, it is your responsibility (and obligation) to determine the trustworthiness of an Internet source and decide whether it is appropriate for your paper.

Once you are online, you need to connect to a **search engine**, which helps you find information by sorting through the millions of documents that are available on the Internet. Among the most popular search engines are Google, Yahoo!, and Bing.

There are two ways to use a search engine to access information:

1. *You can do a keyword search.* All search engines let you do a keyword search. You type a term (or terms) into a box, and the search engine looks for documents that contain the term, listing all the hits that it finds.

2. *You can do a subject search.* Some search engines, such as About .com and Yahoo!, let you do a subject search. First, you choose a broad subject from a list: *Humanities, Arts, Entertainment, Business*, and so on. Each of these general subjects then leads you to more specific subjects, until eventually you get to the subtopic that you want.

Evaluating Internet Sources

Just as you would with library sources, you should determine whether information you find on the Internet is believable and useful. With the Internet, however, you have problems that you generally don't have with the sources available in your college library. Because anyone can publish on the Internet, it is often difficult—if not impossible—to judge the credentials of an author or the accuracy of his or her claims. To make matters worse, sometimes sources have no listed author. Dates can also be missing, so it may be difficult to tell when information was originally posted and when it was updated. Finally, it is often hard to determine if a site has a purpose other than providing information. For example, is the site trying to sell something or advance a political or social agenda? If it is, it may contain information that is biased or incorrect.

You can evaluate Internet sources by asking some basic questions:

- *Who is the author of the site?* Avoid information written by unnamed authors or by authors with questionable credentials.

- *Who is the sponsoring organization?* Be especially careful of using information from Web sites that are sponsored by companies trying to sell something or organizations that have a particular agenda.

- *Can you verify information posted on the site?* Make sure you are able to check the source of the information. For example, you should see if an article on a site includes documentation. Also, cross-check information you find there. Does the same information appear in other sources that are reliable?

- *Does the site contain errors?* In addition to factual errors, look out for mistakes in grammar or spelling. Errors such as these should raise a red flag about the accuracy of the information on the site you are visiting.

- *Do the links on the site work?* Make sure that the links on the site are "live." The presence of "dead" links is a good indication that a site is not being properly maintained.

- *Is the information up-to-date?* Make sure the site's information is current. Avoid sites that contain information that seems old or outdated. A reliable site will usually include the date information was posted and the date it was revised.

When in doubt, the surest strategy for determining whether a Web site is reliable is to check with a reference librarian or with your instructor. Unless you can be certain that a site is reliable, do not use it as a source.

FYI

Using Wikipedia as a Source

Most college students regularly consult Wikipedia, the open-source online encyclopedia. The rationale behind Wikipedia is that if a large number of people review information, errors will eventually be discovered and corrected. Because there are no full-time editors, however, Wikipedia articles can (and do) contain inaccurate as well as biased information. In addition, anyone—not just experts—can write and edit entries. Understandably, some instructors distrust—or at least question—the accuracy of Wikipedia entries. Be sure to check the accuracy of the information you find in Wikipedia by comparing it to the information in other sources you are using. (Keep in mind that many instructors do not consider articles from any encyclopedia— print or electronic—acceptable for college research.)

May Compton began her research by doing a subject search of her college library's online catalog to find books on her topic. Under the general subject of *counterfeits*, she found the headings *counterfeit coins* and *counterfeit money*. She did not, however, find any books on counterfeit designer goods. She thought that her topic might be too recent for any books to have been published on the subject, so she turned to her library's databases.

A quick look at the InfoTrac database showed May that many recent articles had been written about counterfeit designer merchandise. Although some articles just reported police raids on local counterfeiting operations, a few discussed the reasons for counterfeiting and the negative effects of counterfeit goods.

Because May's topic was so current, she found that the Internet was a good source of information. For example, using Google to search for the keywords *counterfeit designer goods*, she found a site maintained by the Resource for Security Executives that gave recent statistics of counterfeit seizures by the Department of Homeland Security. Using the same keywords on Yahoo!, May found an article in the *Arizona Republic* that discussed the purse parties that are often used to sell counterfeit designer handbags.

find information

Review the topic you chose for your research paper. Then, do research in the library and on the Internet to help you find information on this topic. Remember, you will be using this information to support the points you make in your research paper.

17c   Taking Notes

Once you have gathered the source material you will need, read it carefully, recording any information you think you can use in your essay. Record your notes either in computer files that you have created for this purpose or on index cards.

Remember that taking notes involves more than just copying down or downloading information. As you record information, you should put it into a form that you can use when you write your paper. For this reason, you should always *paraphrase, summarize,* or *quote* relevant information from your sources.

FYI

Avoiding Plagiarism

When you transfer information from Web sites into your notes, you may carelessly cut and paste text without recording where the material came from. If you then copy this material into your paper without citing the source, you are committing **plagiarism**—stealing someone else's ideas. Also keep in mind that you must document *all* material that you get from the Internet, just as you document material that you get from print sources. For information on documentation, see 17h. For information on plagiarism, see 17d.

Paraphrasing

When you **paraphrase**, you use your own words to convey a source's key ideas. You paraphrase when you want to include detailed information from the source but not the author's exact words. Paraphrasing is useful when you want to make a difficult discussion easier to understand while still presenting a comprehensive overview of the original.

Writing a Paraphrase

1. Read the passage until you understand it.
2. Note the main idea of the passage, and list key supporting points.
3. Draft your paraphrase, beginning with the source's main idea and then presenting the source's most important supporting points.
4. When you revise, make sure you have used your own words and phrasing, and not the words or sentence structure of the original. Use quotation marks to identify any unique or memorable phrases that you have borrowed from the source.
5. Document your source.

Here is a passage from the article "Hot Fakes," by Joanie Cox, followed by a student's paraphrase.

ORIGINAL

Always pay close attention to the stitching. On a Kate Spade bag, the logo is stitched perfectly straight; it's not a sticker. Most designers stitch a simple label to the inside of their purses. On Chanel bags, however, the interior label is usually stamped and tends to match the color of the exterior. Study the material the bag is made from. A real Chanel Ligne Cambon multipocket bag, for example, is constructed from buttery lambskin leather, not vinyl.

PARAPHRASE

It is often possible to tell a fake designer handbag from a genuine one by looking at the details. For example, items such as logos should not be crooked. You should also look for the distinctive features of a particular brand of handbag. Counterfeiters will not take the time to match colors, and they may use vinyl instead of expensive leather (Cox).

Note that this paraphrase doesn't simply change a word here and there. Instead, the student has taken the time to fully understand the main idea and supporting points of the passage and has restated ideas in her own words.

Summarizing

Unlike a paraphrase, which presents the key points of a source in detail, a **summary** is a general restatement, in your own words, of just the main idea of a passage. For this reason, a summary is always much shorter than the original.

> ### Writing a Summary
>
> 1. Read the passage until you understand it.
> 2. Jot down the main idea of the passage.
> 3. As you write, make sure you use your own words, not those of your source.
> 4. When you revise, make sure your summary contains only the ideas of the source.
> 5. Document your source.

Here is a student's summary of the original passage on page 333.

SUMMARY

Buyers who want to identify fake handbags should check details such as the way the label is sewn and the material the item is made from (Cox).

Quoting

When you **quote**, you use the author's exact words as they appear in the source, including all punctuation and capitalization. Enclose all words from your source in quotation marks—*followed by appropriate documentation*. Because quotations can distract readers, use them only when you think that the author's exact words will add something to your discussion.

> **When to Quote**
>
> 1. Quote when the words of a source are so memorable that to put them into your own words would lessen their impact.
> 2. Quote when the words of a source are so precise that a paraphrase or summary would change the meaning of the original.
> 3. Quote when the words of a source add authority to your discussion. The exact words of a recognized expert can help you make your point convincingly.

Here is how a student writer incorporated a quotation from the original passage on page 333 into her notes.

QUOTATION

Someone who wants to buy an authentic designer handbag should look carefully at the material the purse is made from. For example, there is a big difference between vinyl and Chanel's "buttery lambskin leather" (Cox).

Working Sources into Your Writing

To show readers why you are using a source and to help you blend source material smoothly into your essay, introduce paraphrases, summaries, and quotations with **identifying tags**, phrases that name the source or its author. You can position an identifying tag at various places in a sentence.

As one celebrity fashion columnist points out, "A real Chanel Ligne Cambon multipocket bag, for example, is constructed from buttery lambskin leather, not vinyl" (Cox).

"A real Chanel Ligne Cambon multipocket bag, for example," <u>says one celebrity fashion columnist,</u> "is constructed from buttery lambskin leather, not vinyl" (Cox).

"A real Chanel Ligne Cambon multipocket bag, for example, is constructed from buttery lambskin leather, not vinyl," <u>observes one celebrity fashion columnist</u> (Cox).

FYI

Identifying Sources

Instead of repeating the word *says*, you can use one of the words or phrases below to identify the source of a quotation, paraphrase, or summary.

admits	concludes	points out
believes	explains	remarks
claims	notes	states
comments	observes	suggests

Synthesizing

When you **synthesize**, you combine ideas from two or more sources with your own ideas. The goal of a synthesis is to use sources to develop your own point about a topic. In a synthesis, then, your own ideas, not those of your sources, should dominate the discussion. In a sense, every time you weave together paraphrase, summary, and quotation to support a point, you are writing a synthesis.

Writing a Synthesis

1. Decide on the point you want to develop.

2. Select at least two or three sources to support your point.

3. Read each source carefully, taking note of how they are alike, how they are different, and how they relate to your point.

4. Begin your synthesis by clearly stating the point you are going to develop.

5. Use specific examples (paraphrases, summaries, and quotations) from your sources to support your point.

6. When you revise, make sure that you have used appropriate transitions to indicate the movement from one source to another. Also be sure that you have clearly identified each source that you discuss.

7. Document all words and ideas that you take from your sources.

Here is a paragraph from May Compton's research paper on pages 348–351 in which she incorporates material from three different sources. Notice how she uses source material (underlined) to develop her point that buying counterfeit items is really stealing.

What most people choose to ignore is that buying counterfeit items is really stealing. <u>Between 2002 and 2012, 325 percent more counterfeit goods were seized than in the previous decade</u> (O'Donnell 03b). <u>The FBI estimates that in the United States alone, companies lose about $250 billion as a result of counterfeits</u> (Wallace). In addition, buyers of counterfeit items avoid the state and local sales taxes that legitimate companies pay. <u>Thus, New York City alone loses about a billion dollars every year as a result of the sale of counterfeit merchandise</u> ("Counterfeit Goods"). When this happens, everyone loses. After all, a billion dollars would pay for a lot of police officers and teachers, would fill a lot of potholes, and would pave a lot of streets. Buyers of counterfeit designer goods do not think of themselves as thieves, but that is exactly what they are.

take notes

Review the information you gathered for your research paper. Then, take notes, making sure that you fairly and accurately paraphrase, summarize, quote, and synthesize your sources. Keep your notes either in computer files or on index cards. (Don't forget to include full source information, including page numbers, with these notes.)

17d   Watching Out for Plagiarism

As a rule, you must **document** (give source information for) all words, ideas, or statistics from an outside source. You must also document all visuals—tables, graphs, photographs, and so on—that you do not create yourself. (It is not necessary, however, to document **common knowledge**, factual information widely available in various reference works.)

When you present information from another source as if it is your own (whether you do it intentionally or unintentionally), you commit **plagiarism**—and plagiarism is theft. Although most plagiarism is accidental, the penalties can still be severe. You can avoid plagiarism by understanding what you must document and what you do not have to document.

FYI

What to Document

You should document

- All quotations from a source
- All summaries and paraphrases of source material
- All ideas—opinions, judgments, and insights—of others
- All tables, graphs, charts, and statistics from a source

You do not need to document

- Your own ideas
- Common knowledge
- Familiar quotations

Read the following paragraph from "The Facts on Fakes!,"an article by Adele R. Meyer, and the four rules that follow it. This matcrial will help you understand the most common causes of plagiarism and show you how to avoid it.

ORIGINAL

Is imitation really the sincerest form of flattery? Counterfeiting deceives the consumer and tarnishes the reputation of the genuine manufacturer. Brand value can be destroyed when a trademark is imposed on counterfeit products of inferior quality—hardly a form of flattery! Therefore, prestigious companies who are the targets of counterfeiters have begun to battle an industry that copies and sells their merchandise. They have filed lawsuits and in some cases have employed private investigators across the nation to combat the counterfeit trade. A quick search of the Internet brings up dozens of press releases from newspapers throughout the country, all reporting instances of law enforcement cracking down on sellers of counterfeit goods by confiscating bogus merchandise and imposing fines.

Rule 1. Document Ideas from Your Sources

PLAGIARISM

When counterfeits are sold, the original manufacturer does not take it as a compliment.

Even though the student writer does not quote her source directly, she must identify the article as the source of this material because it expresses the article's ideas, not her own.

CORRECT

When counterfeits are sold, the original manufacturer does not take it as a compliment (Meyer).

Rule 2. Place Borrowed Words in Quotation Marks

PLAGIARISM

It is possible to ruin the worth of a brand by selling counterfeit products of inferior quality—hardly a form of flattery (Meyer).

Although the student writer cites the source, the passage incorrectly uses the source's exact words without quoting them. She must quote the borrowed words.

CORRECT (BORROWED WORDS IN QUOTATION MARKS)

It is possible to ruin the worth of a brand by selling "counterfeit products of inferior quality—hardly a form of flattery" (Meyer).

Rule 3. Use Your Own Phrasing

PLAGIARISM

Is copying a design a compliment? Not at all. The fake design not only tries to fool the buyer but also harms the original company. It can ruin the worth of a brand. Because counterfeits are usually of poor quality, they pay the original no compliment. As a result, companies whose products are often copied have started to fight back. They have sued the counterfeiters and have even used private detectives to identify phony goods. Throughout the United States, police have fined people who sell counterfeits and have seized their products (Meyer).

Even though the student writer acknowledges Meyer as her source, and even though she does not use the source's exact words, her passage closely follows the order, emphasis, sentence structure, and phrasing of the original.

In the following passage, the student writer uses her own wording, quoting one distinctive phrase from the source.

CORRECT

According to "The Facts on Fakes!" it is not a compliment when an original design is copied by a counterfeiter. The poor quality of most fakes is "hardly a form of flattery." The harm to the image of the original manufacturers has caused them to fight back against the counterfeiters, sometimes using their own detectives. As a result, lawsuits and criminal charges have led to fines and confiscated merchandise (Meyer).

Note: The quotation does not require separate documentation because the identifying tag According to "The Facts on Fakes!" makes it clear that all the borrowed material in the passage is from the same source.

Rule 4. Distinguish Your Ideas from the Source's Ideas

PLAGIARISM

Counterfeit goods are not harmless. Counterfeiting not only fools the consumer, but it also destroys confidence in the quality of the real thing. Manufacturers know this and have begun to fight back. A number have begun to sue "and in some cases have employed private investigators across the nation to combat the counterfeit trade" (Meyer).

In the passage above, it appears that only the quotation in the last sentence is borrowed from the article by Meyer. In fact, however, the ideas in the second sentence also come from Meyer's article.

In the following passage, the student writer uses an identifying tag to acknowledge the borrowed material in the second sentence.

CORRECT

Counterfeit goods are not harmless. According to the article "The Facts on Fakes!," counterfeiting not only fools the consumer, but it also destroys confidence in the quality of the real thing. Manufacturers know this and have begun to fight back. A number have begun to sue "and in some cases have employed private investigators across the nation to combat the counterfeit trade" (Meyer).

watch out for plagiarism

Look back at the notes you took for your research paper. First, make sure that you have included documentation for all information that came from a source. Then, check your notes against the examples in 17d to make sure that you have avoided the most common types of accidental plagiarism.

17e   Developing a Thesis

After you have taken notes, review the information you have gathered, and develop a thesis statement. Your **thesis statement** is a single sentence that states the main idea of your paper and tells readers what to expect.

After reviewing her notes, May Compton came up with the following thesis statement for her paper on counterfeit designer goods.

THESIS STATEMENT

People should not buy counterfeit designer merchandise, no matter how tempted they are to do so.

develop a thesis

Review your notes again, and then draft a thesis statement for your research paper.

17f Making an Outline

Once you have a thesis statement, you are ready to make an outline. Your outline, which covers just the body paragraphs of your paper, can be either a **topic outline** (in which each idea is expressed in a word or a short phrase) or a **sentence outline** (in which each idea is expressed in a complete sentence).

After reviewing her notes, May Compton wrote the following sentence outline for her paper:

I. Many people consider real designer goods too expensive.
   A. Genuine designer merchandise costs ten times more than it costs to make it.
   B. Even people who can afford it buy fakes.
II. Buying designer knockoffs is a form of stealing.
   A. The buyer is stealing the work of the original designer.
   B. Counterfeiting operations take jobs away from legitimate workers.
   C. The buyer is stealing the sales taxes that would be paid by the original designer.
III. Buying designer knockoffs supports organized crime.
   A. The production of designer knockoffs requires money and organization, which often come from organized crime.

B. Buying knockoffs supports other illegal activities.
   1. The profits of selling knockoffs support murder, prostitution, and drug rings.
   2. Knockoffs are made in shops that violate labor and other laws.
IV. There is evidence that designer knockoffs support terrorism.
   A. The 1993 World Trade Center bombing has been connected to a counterfeit operation.
   B. The 2001 World Trade Center bombing has been connected to counterfeiting.
   C. The 2004 Madrid train bombing has been connected to counterfeiting.

---

make an outline

Review all your notes as well as your thesis statement. Then, make an outline of the body paragraphs of your paper.

17g Writing Your Paper

Once you have decided on a thesis and written an outline, you are ready to write a draft of your essay. When you are finished, you will **TEST**, revise, and edit your paper.

Remember, you will probably write several drafts of your essay before you hand it in. As you draft your essay, be sure to include parenthetical citations so that you do not lose track of your sources and accidentally commit plagiarism. After you revise and edit, you can check to make sure your documentation formats are correct. (See 17h for information on documentation.)

May Compton's completed essay on counterfeit designer goods begins on page 348.

---

write your paper

Using your thesis statement and your outline to guide you, write a draft of your research paper.

TEST · Revise · Edit

TEST the draft of your paper by referring to the TEST checklist on page 240. Then, use the Self-Assessment checklists in 13i and 13j to help you revise and edit your paper.

17h   Documenting Your Sources

When you **document** your sources, you tell readers where you found the information you used in your essay. The Modern Language Association (MLA) recommends the following documentation style for essays that use sources. This format consists of *parenthetical references* in the body of the paper that refer to a *works-cited list* at the end of the paper.

Parenthetical References in the Text

A parenthetical reference should include enough information to lead readers to a specific entry in your works-cited list. A typical parenthetical reference consists of the author's last name and the page number (Brown 2). Notice that there is no comma and no *p* or *p.* before the page number.

Whenever possible, introduce information from a source with a phrase that includes the author's name. (If you do this, include only the page number in parentheses.) Place documentation so that it does not interrupt the flow of your ideas, preferably at the end of a sentence.

> As Jonathan Brown observes in "Demand for Fake Designer Goods Is Soaring," as many as 70 percent of buyers of luxury goods are willing to wear designer brands alongside of fakes (2).

In the four special situations listed below, the format for parenthetical references departs from these guidelines.

1. WHEN YOU ARE CITING A WORK BY TWO AUTHORS

   Instead of buying nonbranded items of similar quality, many customers are willing to pay extra for the counterfeit designer label (Grossman and Shapiro 79).

2. WHEN YOU ARE CITING A WORK WITHOUT PAGE NUMBERS

   A seller of counterfeited goods in California "now faces 10 years in prison and $20,000 in fines" (Cox).

3. WHEN YOU ARE CITING A WORK WITHOUT A LISTED AUTHOR OR PAGE NUMBERS

More counterfeit goods come from China than from any other country ("Counterfeit Goods").

Note: Material from the Internet frequently lacks some publication information—for example, page or paragraph numbers. For this reason, the parenthetical references that cite it may contain just the author's name (as in example 2 above) or just a shortened title (as in example 3) if the article appears without an author.

4. WHEN YOU ARE CITING A STATEMENT BY ONE AUTHOR THAT IS QUOTED IN A WORK BY ANOTHER AUTHOR

Speaking of consumers' buying habits, designer Miuccia Prada says, "There is a kind of an obsession with bags" (qtd. in Thomas A23).

FYI

Formatting Quotations

1. **Short quotations** Quotations of no more than four typed lines share the same margins as the rest of your paper. End punctuation comes after the parenthetical reference (which follows the quotation marks).

   According to Dana Thomas, customers often "pick up knockoffs for one-tenth the legitimate bag's retail cost, then pass them off as real" (A23).

2. **Long quotations** Quotations of more than four lines are set off from the text of your paper. Begin a long quotation one inch from the left-hand margin, and do not enclose it in quotation marks. Do not indent the first line of a single paragraph. If a quoted passage has more than one paragraph, indent the first line of each paragraph (including the first) an extra one-quarter inch. Introduce a long quotation with a complete sentence followed by a colon, and place the parenthetical reference one space *after* the end punctuation.

   The editorial "Terror's Purse Strings" describes a surprise visit to a factory that makes counterfeit purses:

   > On a warm winter afternoon in Guangzhao, I accompanied Chinese police officers on a raid in a decrepit tenement. We found two dozen children, ages 8 to 13, gluing and sewing together fake luxury-brand handbags. The police confiscated everything, arrested the owner and sent the children out. Some punched their timecards, hoping to still get paid. (Thomas A23)

The Works-Cited List

The works-cited list includes all the works you **cite** (refer to) in your essay. Use the guidelines in the FYI box on page 347 to help you prepare your list.

The following sample works-cited entries cover the situations you will encounter most often.

Periodicals

JOURNALS

A **journal** is a periodical aimed at readers who know a lot about a particular subject—literature or history, for example.

When citing an article from a journal, include the volume number of the journal, followed by a period and the issue number. Leave no space after the period. Include page numbers, if there are any, and the medium of publication, such as *Print* or *Web*. Add the name of the online database (such as Academic Search Premier) if you used one to find the source. For all Web sources, add the date you accessed the source.

Article in a Print Journal

Kessler-Harris, Alice. "Why Biography?" *American Historical Review* 114.3 (2009): 625–30. Print.

Article in a Journal Accessed through a Library Database

Favret, Mary A. "Jane Austen at 25: A Life in Numbers." *English Language Notes* 46.1 (2008): 9–20. *Expanded Academic ASAP*. Web. 9 Mar. 2013.

MAGAZINES

A **magazine** is a periodical aimed at general readers, rather than people who already know a lot about a subject. Frequently, an article in a magazine is not printed on consecutive pages. For example, it may begin on page 40, skip to page 47, and continue on page 49. If this is the case, your citation should include only the first page, followed by a plus sign. Include the medium of publication.

Article in a Print Magazine

Weisberg, Jacob. "All Lobbyists Are Not Created Equal." *Newsweek* 27 Apr. 2009: 35. Print.

Article in a Magazine Accessed through a Library Database

Larmer, Brook. "The Real Price of Gold." *National Geographic* Jan. 2009: 34+. *Academic Search Premier*. Web. 23 Feb. 2013.

NEWSPAPERS

List page numbers, section numbers, and any special edition information (such as "late ed.") as provided by the source. If the article falls into a special category, such as an editorial, letter to the editor, or review, add this label to your entry, after the title.

Article in a Print Newspaper

> Campoy, Ana. "'Water Hog' Label Haunts Dallas." *Wall Street Journal*
>   15 July 2009, late ed.: A4. Print.

Article from a Newspaper Accessed through a Library Database

> Marklein, Mary Beth. "Virtually Eliminating Snow Days." *USA Today* 8 Feb.
>   2011, sec. A: 01. *National Newspaper Index*. Web. 9 Mar. 2013.

Books

Books by One Author

List the author with last name first. Italicize the title. Include the city of publication and a shortened form of the publisher's name—for example, *Bedford* for *Bedford/St. Martin's*. Use the abbreviation *UP* for *University Press*, as in *Princeton UP* and *U of Chicago P*. Include the date of publication. End with the medium of publication.

> Russo, Richard. *Bridge of Sighs*. New York: Knopf, 2007. Print.

Books by Two or More Authors

For books with more than one author, list second and subsequent authors with first name first, in the order in which they are listed on the book's title page.

> Mooney, Chris, and Sheril Kirshenbaum. *Unscientific America: How*
>   *Scientific Illiteracy Threatens Our Future*. New York: Basic, 2009. Print.

For books with more than three authors, you may list only the first author, followed by the abbreviation *et al.* ("and others").

> Beer, Andrew, et al. *Consuming Housing? Transitions through the Housing*
>   *Market in the 21st Century*. Bristol: Policy Press, 2010. Print.

You may also list all the authors in the order in which they appear on the book's title page: Beer, Andrew, Debbie Faulkner, Chris Paris, and Terry Clower.

Two or More Books by the Same Author

List two or more books by the same author in alphabetical order according to title. In each entry after the first, use three unspaced hyphens (followed by a period) instead of the author's name.

> Alda, Alan. *Never Have Your Dog Stuffed*. New York: Arrow, 2007. Print.
> ---. *Things I Overheard While Talking to Myself*. New York: Random, 2007.
>   Print.

Edited Book

Thompson, Hunter S. *Gonzo*. Ed. Steve Crist. Los Angeles: AMMO Books, 2007. Print.

Anthology

Adler, Frances P., Debra Busman, and Diana Garcia, eds. *Fire and Ink: An Anthology of Social Action Writing*. Tucson: U of Arizona P, 2009. Print.

Essay in an Anthology or Chapter of a Book

Welty, Eudora. "Writing and Analyzing a Story." *Signet Book of American Essays*. Ed. M. Terry Weiss and Helen Weiss. New York: Signet, 2006. 21–30. Print.

Internet Sources

Full source information is not always available for Internet sources. When citing Internet sources, include whatever information you can find—ideally, the name of the author (or authors), the title of the article or other document (in quotation marks), the title of the site (italicized), the sponsor or publisher, the date of publication or last update, and the date on which you accessed the source. Include the medium of publication (Web) between the publication date and the access date.

It is not necessary to include a Web address (URL) when citing an electronic source. However, you should include a URL (in angle brackets) if your instructor requires that you do so or if you think readers might not be able to locate the source without it (see the "Personal Site" entry below).

Document within a Web Site

Baker, Fred W. "Army Lab Works to Improve Soldier Health, Performance." *DefenseLINK*. U.S. Department of Defense, 25 June 2009. Web. 15 Aug. 2013.

Personal Site

Bricklin, Dan. Home page. Dan Bricklin, 23 Apr. 2012. Web. 15 July 2013. <www.bricklin.com>.

Article in an Online Reference Book or Encyclopedia

"Sudan." *Infoplease World Atlas and Map Library*. Pearson Education, 2009. Web. 29 Apr. 2013.

Article in an Online Newspaper

Wilbon, Michael. "The 'One and Done' Song and Dance." *Washington Post*. The Washington Post Company, 25 June 2009. Web. 1 Sept. 2013.

FYI

Preparing the Works-Cited List

- Begin the works-cited list on a new page after the last page of your paper.
- Number the works-cited page as the next page of your paper.
- Center the heading Works Cited one inch from the top of the page; do not italicize the heading or place it in quotation marks.
- Double-space the list.
- List entries alphabetically according to the author's last name.
- Alphabetize unsigned articles according to the first major word of the title.
- Begin typing each entry at the left-hand margin.
- Indent second and subsequent lines of each entry one-half inch.
- Separate major divisions of each entry—author, title, and publication information—by a period and one space.

document your sources

Check to make sure that you have included correct parenthetical citations in the body of your paper for all information that requires documentation. Then, consulting the guidelines above, prepare your works-cited list.

Sample MLA-Style Paper

On the pages that follow is May Compton's completed essay on the topic of counterfeit designer goods. The paper uses MLA documentation style and includes a works-cited page.

May Compton

Professor DiSalvo

English 100

29 Apr. 2013

Include your last name and the page number in the upper-right-hand corner of every page.

Center your title; do not italicize or underline.

Include your name, instructor's name, course title, and date on first page.

Introduction

Thesis statement

Paragraph combines paraphrase, quotation, and May's own ideas.

The True Price of Counterfeit Goods

At purse parties in city apartments and suburban homes, customers can buy "designer" handbags at impossibly low prices. On street corners, sidewalk vendors sell name-brand perfumes and sunglasses for much less than their list prices. On the Internet, buyers can buy fine watches for a fraction of the prices charged by manufacturers. Is this too good to be true? Of course it is. All of these "bargains" are knockoffs—counterfeit copies of the real thing. What the people who buy these items do not know (or prefer not to think about) is that the money they are spending supports organized crime—and, sometimes, terrorism. For this reason, people should not buy counterfeit designer merchandise, no matter how tempted they are to do so.

People who buy counterfeit designer merchandise defend their actions by saying that designer products are very expensive. This is certainly true. According to Dana Thomas, the manufacturers of genuine designer merchandise charge more than ten times what it costs to make it (A23). A visitor from Britain, who bought an imitation Gucci purse in New York City for fifty dollars, said, "The real thing is so overpriced. To buy a genuine Gucci purse, I would have to pay over a thousand dollars" (qtd. in "Counterfeit Goods"). Even people who can easily afford to pay the full amount buy fakes. For example, movie stars like Jennifer Lopez openly wear counterfeit goods, and many customers think that if it is all right for celebrities like Lopez to buy fakes, it must also be all right for them too (Malone). However, as the well-known designer Giorgio Armani points out, counterfeiters create a number of problems for legitimate companies because they use the brand name but do not maintain quality control.

What most people choose to ignore is that buying counterfeit items is really stealing. Between 2002 and 2012, 325 percent more counterfeit

Compton 2

goods were seized than in the previous decade (O'Donnell 03b). The FBI estimates that in the United States alone, companies lose about $250 billion as a result of counterfeits (Wallace). In addition, buyers of counterfeit items avoid the state and local sales taxes that legitimate companies pay. Thus, New York City alone loses about a billion dollars every year as a result of the sale of counterfeit merchandise ("Counterfeit Goods"). When this happens, everyone loses. After all, a billion dollars would pay for a lot of police officers and teachers, would fill a lot of potholes, and would pave a lot of streets. Buyers of counterfeit designer goods do not think of themselves as thieves, but that is exactly what they are.

> Paragraph contains May's own ideas combined with paraphrases of material from three articles.

Buyers of counterfeit merchandise also do not realize that the sale of knockoffs is a criminal activity. Most of the profits go to the criminal organization that either makes or imports the counterfeit goods—not to the person who sells the items. In fact, the biggest manufacturer and distributor of counterfeit items is organized crime (Nellis). Michael Kessler, who heads a company that investigates corporate crime, makes this connection clear when he describes the complicated organization that is needed to make counterfeit perfume:

> They need a place that makes bottles, a factory with pumps to fill the bottles, a printer to make the labels, and a box manufacturer to fake the packaging. Then, they need a sophisticated distribution network, as well as all the cash to set everything up. (qtd. in Malone)

> Long quotation is set off one inch from the left-hand margin. No quotation marks are used.

Kessler concludes that only an organized crime syndicate—not an individual—has the money to support this illegal activity. For this reason, anyone who buys counterfeits may also be supporting activities such as prostitution, drug distribution, smuggling of illegal immigrants, gang warfare, extortion, and murder (Nellis). In addition, the people who make counterfeits often work in sweatshops where labor and environmental laws are ignored. As Dana Thomas points out, a worker in China who makes counterfeits earns only a fraction of the salary of a worker who makes the real thing (A23).

Compton 3

Paragraph contains May's own ideas as well as a paraphrase and a quotation.

Finally, and perhaps most shocking, is the fact that some of the money earned from the sale of counterfeit designer goods also supports international terrorism. For example, Kim Wallace reports in her *Times Daily* article that during Al-Qaeda training, terrorists are advised to sell fakes to get money for their operations. According to Interpol, an international police organization, the bombing of the World Trade Center in 1993 was paid for in part by the sale of counterfeit T-shirts. Also, evidence suggests that associates of the 2001 World Trade Center terrorists may have been involved with the production of imitation designer goods (Malone). Finally, the 2004 bombing of commuter trains in Madrid was financed in part by the sale of counterfeits. In fact, an intelligence source states, "It would be more shocking if Al-Qaeda *wasn't* involved in counterfeiting. The sums involved are staggering—it would be inconceivable if money were not being raised for their terrorist activities" (qtd. in Malone).

Conclusion contains May's original ideas, so no documentation is necessary.

Consumers should realize that when they buy counterfeits, they are actually breaking the law. By doing so, they are making it possible for organized crime syndicates and terrorists to earn money for their illegal activities. Although buyers of counterfeit merchandise justify their actions by saying that the low prices are impossible to resist, they might reconsider if they knew the uses to which their money was going. The truth of the matter is that counterfeit designer products, such as handbags, sunglasses, jewelry, and T-shirts, are luxuries, not necessities. By resisting the temptation to buy knockoffs, consumers could help to eliminate the companies that hurt legitimate manufacturers, exploit workers, and even finance international terrorism.

Compton 4

Works Cited

Armani, Giorgio. "10 Questions for Giorgio Armani." *Time*. Time, 12 Feb. 2009.
    Web. 24 Mar. 2013.

"Counterfeit Goods Are Linked to Terror Groups." *International Herald Tribune*.
    International Herald Tribune, 12 Feb. 2007. Web. 24 Mar. 2013.

Malone, Andrew. "Revealed: The True Cost of Buying Cheap Fake Goods."
    Mail Online. Daily Mail, 29 July 2007. Web. 25 Mar. 2013.

Nellis, Cynthia. "Faking It: Counterfeit Fashion." *About.com: Women's Fashion*.
    About.com, 2009. Web. 24 Mar. 2013.

O'Donnell, Jayne. "Counterfeits Are a Growing—and Dangerous—Problem."
    USA Today 6 June 2012, sec. Money: 03b. Print.

Thomas, Dana. "Terror's Purse Strings." Editorial. *New York Times* 30 Aug. 2007,
    late ed.: A23. *Academic One File*. Web. 25 Mar. 2013.

Wallace, Kim. "A Counter-Productive Trade." *TimesDaily.com*. Times Daily,
    28 July 2007. Web. 31 Mar. 2013.

> Works-cited list starts a new page.

> This Internet source has no listed author.

> First lines of entries are set flush left; subsequent lines are indented one-half inch.

EDITING PRACTICE: AVOIDING PLAGIARISM

Read the paragraph below, from the *New York Times* online article "The New Math on Campus," by Alex Williams. Then, read the three student paragraphs that use this article as a source. In each of these paragraphs, student writers have accidentally committed plagiarism. On the line below each student paragraph, explain the problem. Then, edit the paragraph so that it correctly documents the source and avoids plagiarism.

> North Carolina, with a student body that is nearly 60 percent female, is just one of many large universities that at times feel eerily like women's colleges. Women have represented about 57 percent of enrollments at American colleges since at least 2000, according to a recent report by the American Council on Education. Researchers there cite several reasons: women tend to have higher grades; men tend to drop out in disproportionate numbers; and female enrollment skews higher among older students, low-income students, and black and Hispanic students.

About 60% female, the University of North Carolina is an example of large universities with many more women than men. According to a report from the American Council on Education, one reason is that "female enrollment skews higher among older students, low-income students, and black and Hispanic students" (Williams). If this is true, what will this mean for the black and Hispanic communities?

_____

_____

In recent years, colleges and universities have taken on a very different atmosphere. The reason is clear to anyone who takes a casual look around at just about any college campus. Women now outnumber men, so much so that some colleges at times feel eerily like women's colleges (Williams). This situation seems likely to continue in the years to come.

_____

Why do women outnumber men in today's colleges? Researchers at the American Council on Education mention a few reasons: women often have higher grades, men tend to drop out in larger numbers, and female enrollment is especially high for some groups such as older students, low-income students, and black and Hispanic students (Williams). These reasons may all be true at our school, which certainly has more women than men.

COLLABORATIVE ACTIVITY: CREATING A WORKS-CITED LIST

Working in a group of three or four students, create a works-cited list for a paper that uses the following three sources. Make sure that you arrange the entries in alphabetical order and that you use the correct format for each type of source.

Article in a Journal Accessed through a Library Database

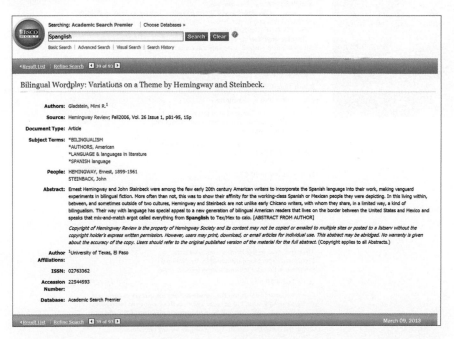

Book (Print)

Library of Congress Cataloging-in-Publication Data

Spanglish / edited by Ilan Stavans.
    p. cm. — (The Ilan Stavans library of Latino civilization, ISSN 1938–615X)
  Includes bibliographical references and index.
  ISBN 978–0–313–34804–4 (alk. paper)
 1. Spanish language—Foreign elements—English. 2. English language—
Influence on Spanish. 3. Languages in contact—America. I. Stavans,
Ilan.
  PC4582.E6S63   2008
  460'.4221—dc22   2008014855

British Library Cataloguing in Publication Data is available.

Copyright © 2008 by Ilan Stavans

All rights reserved. No portion of this book may be
reproduced, by any process or technique, without the
express written consent of the publisher.

Library of Congress Catalog Card Number: 2008014855
ISBN: 978–0–313–34804–4
ISSN: 1938–615X

First published in 2008

Greenwood Press, 88 Post Road West, Westport, CT 06881
An imprint of Greenwood Publishing Group, Inc.
www.greenwood.com

Printed in the United States of America

The paper used in this book complies with the
Permanent Paper Standard issued by the National
Information Standards Organization (Z39.48–1984).

10 9 8 7 6 5 4 3 2 1

Every reasonable effort has been made to trace the owners of copyright
materials in this book, but in some instances this has proven impossible.
The editor and publisher will be glad to receive information leading to
a more complete acknowledgments in subsequent printings of the book
and in the meantime extend their apologies for any omissions.

iv

Document within a Web Site

Works Cited

_____

_____

_____

_____

_____

_____

_____

18 Writing Simple Sentences

focus on writing

Many baseball fans wish they could trade places with someone like Chase Utley, a second baseman for the Philadelphia Phillies with a storybook career. Think for a bit about someone with whom you would like to trade places, and then write a paragraph about why you'd like to trade. What appeals to you about this person's life?

In this chapter, you will learn to
- identify a sentence's subject (18a)
- identify prepositions and prepositional phrases (18b)
- distinguish a prepositional phrase from a subject (18b)
- identify a sentence's verb (18c)

A **sentence** is a group of words that expresses a complete thought. Every sentence includes both a subject and a verb. A **simple sentence** consists of a single **independent clause**: one <u>subject</u> and one <u>verb</u>.

Chase Utley <u>plays</u> baseball.

18a Subjects

Every sentence includes a subject. The **subject** of a sentence tells who or what is being talked about in the sentence. Without a subject, a sentence is not complete. In the following three sentences, the subject is underlined.

<u>Derek Walcott</u> won the Nobel Prize in Literature.

<u>He</u> was born in St. Lucia.

<u>St. Lucia</u> is an island in the Caribbean.

The subject of a sentence can be a noun or a pronoun. A **noun** names a person, place, or thing—*Derek Walcott, St. Lucia*. A **pronoun** takes the place of a noun—*I, you, he, she, it, we, they,* and so on.

The subject of a sentence can be *singular or plural*. A **singular subject** is one person, place, or thing (*Derek Walcott, St. Lucia, he*).

A **plural subject** is more than one person, place, or thing (*poets, people, they*).

<u>Readers</u> admire Walcott's poems.

A plural subject that joins two subjects with *and* is called a **compound subject**.

<u>St. Lucia and Trinidad</u> are Caribbean islands.

PRACTICE

18-1 In the following paragraph, underline the subject of each sentence.

Example: <u>Amazon.com</u> is named after the Amazon River.

(1) In just 20 years, Amazon.com has become an extremely successful business. (2) Jeff Bezos founded the company in 1994. (3) In 1995, the business made its first sale. (4) Originally, Amazon.com sold only books. (5) In 1998, music and videos became available as well. (6) Since then, the company has expanded greatly. (7) Amazon owns many other businesses. (8) It also produces its own consumer electronics. (9) The Kindle is just one example. (10) Bezos is known for his patience as well as for his smart management. (11) Amazon.com did not earn a profit until 2001. (12) Now, Bezos's company is the biggest online retailer in the world.

PRACTICE

18-2

Underline the subject in each sentence. Then, write *S* above singular subjects and *P* above plural subjects. Remember, compound subjects are plural.

S

Example: <u>Agritainment</u> introduces tourists to agriculture and entertainment at the same time.

1. Today, tourists can have fun on working farms.

2. In the past, visitors came to farms just to pick fruits and vegetables.

3. Now, some farms have mazes and petting zoos.

4. One farm has a corn maze every year.

5. Sometimes the maze is in the shape of a train.

6. Visitors can also enjoy giant hay-chute slides, pedal go-carts, and hayrides.

7. Working farms start agritainment businesses to make money.

8. However, insurance companies and lawyers worry about the dangers of agritainment.

9. Tourists have gotten animal bites, fallen from rides and machinery, and suffered from food poisoning.

10. Agritainment, like other businesses, has advantages and disadvantages.

LearningCurve
Prepositions and
Conjunctions
bedfordstmartins.com
/focusonwriting

18b Prepositional Phrases

A **prepositional phrase** consists of a **preposition** (a word such as *on*, *to*, *in*, or *with*) and its **object** (the noun or pronoun it introduces).

PREPOSITION	+	OBJECT	=	PREPOSITIONAL PHRASE
on		the stage		on the stage
to		Nia's house		to Nia's house
in		my new car		in my new car
with		them		with them

Because the object of a preposition is a noun or a pronoun, it may seem to be the subject of a sentence. However, the object of a preposition can never be the subject of a sentence. To identify a sentence's true subject, cross out each prepositional phrase. (Remember, every prepositional phrase is introduced by a preposition.)

SUBJECT　PREP PHRASE
The cost ~~of the repairs~~ was astronomical.

PREP PHRASE　　　　　PREP PHRASE　　　　　SUBJECT
~~At the end of the novel~~, ~~after an exciting chase~~, the lovers flee

PREP PHRASE
~~to Mexico~~.

Frequently Used Prepositions

about	before	except	on	underneath
above	behind	for	onto	until
across	below	from	out	up
after	beneath	in	outside	upon
against	beside	inside	over	with
along	between	into	through	within
among	beyond	like	throughout	without
around	by	near	to	
as	despite	of	toward	
at	during	off	under	

PRACTICE

18-3　Each of the following sentences includes at least one prepositional phrase. To identify each sentence's subject, begin by crossing out each prepositional phrase. Then, underline the subject of the sentence.

Example: Bicycling ~~on busy city streets~~ can be dangerous.

(1) In many American cities, cyclists are concerned about sharing the road with cars. (2) For this reason, people are becoming more interested in "green" lanes. (3) These bike lanes are different from traditional bike lanes in one important way. (4) Green lanes are separated from the road by curbs, planters, or parked cars. (5) For years, people in Europe have been creating and using these protected bike lanes. (6) Until recently, however, few green lanes were created in the United States. (7) Now, with the help of the Bikes Belong Foundation and the Federal Highway Administration, several U.S. cities are installing green lanes. (8) For their supporters, these bike lanes are a positive step toward healthier, safer cities. (9) However, some critics worry about reduced space for traffic lanes and parking. (10) Still, despite the criticism, green lanes are increasing the number of bike riders and reducing the number of bike accidents.

18c Verbs

In addition to its subject, every sentence also includes a verb. This **verb** (also called a **predicate**) tells what the subject does or connects the subject to words that describe or rename it. Without a verb, a sentence is not complete.

☑ **LearningCurve**
Verbs, Adjectives, and Adverbs
bedfordstmartins.com /focusonwriting

Action Verbs

An **action verb** tells what the subject does, did, or will do.

David Beckham <u>plays</u> soccer.
Amelia Earhart <u>flew</u> across the Atlantic.
Renee <u>will drive</u> to Tampa on Friday.

Action verbs can also show mental and emotional actions.

Travis always <u>worries</u> about his job.

Sometimes the subject of a sentence performs more than one action. In this case, the sentence includes two or more action verbs that form a **compound predicate**.

He <u><u>hit</u></u> the ball, <u><u>threw</u></u> down his bat, and <u><u>ran</u></u> toward first base.

PRACTICE

18-4   In the following sentences, underline each action verb twice. Some sentences contain more than one action verb.

Example: Some new reality shows <u>introduce</u> viewers to people with disabilities.

1. The reality show *Push Girls* explores the lives of five beautiful disabled women.

2. All the women live in Los Angeles and travel in wheelchairs.

3. These women push many boundaries.

4. They drive their own cars and pursue ambitious careers.

5. Attractive and talented, they reject other people's assumptions about disability.

6. One woman works as a model and an actress.

7. Another dances for a living.

8. Like other reality shows, *Push Girls* shows us people's private lives.

9. However, this reality series also challenges stereotypes.

10. Ultimately, viewers admire these capable women and envy their fulfilling lives.

Linking Verbs

A **linking verb** does not show action. Instead, it connects the subject to a word or words that describe or rename it. The linking verb tells what the subject is (or what it was, will be, or seems to be).

A googolplex <u><u>is</u></u> an extremely large number.

Many linking verbs, like *is*, are forms of the verb *be*. Other linking verbs refer to the senses (*look, feel,* and so on).

The photocopy <u>looks</u> blurry.

Some students <u>feel</u> anxious about the future.

Frequently Used Linking Verbs

act	feel	seem
appear	get	smell
be (am, is, are,	grow	sound
was, were)	look	taste
become	remain	turn

PRACTICE
18-5

In the following sentences, underline each linking verb twice.

Example: Many urban legends <u>seem</u> true.

1. Urban legends are folktales created to teach a lesson.

2. One familiar urban legend is the story of Hookman.

3. According to this story, a young man and woman are alone in Lovers' Lane.

4. They are in a car, listening to a radio announcement.

5. An escaped murderer is nearby.

6. The murderer's left hand is a hook.

7. The young woman becomes hysterical.

8. Suddenly, Lovers' Lane seems very dangerous.

9. Later, they are shocked to see a hook hanging from the passenger-door handle.

10. The purpose of this legend is to convince young people to avoid dangerous places.

PRACTICE
18-6

In each of the following sentences, underline every verb twice. Remember that a verb can be an action verb or a linking verb.

Example: Airplane pilots and investment bankers <u>use</u> checklists.

(1) In *The Checklist Manifesto*, surgeon Atul Gawande argues for using checklists in operating rooms. (2) Gawande reminds readers of the complexity of modern medicine. (3) Currently, there are 6,000 drugs and 4,000 medical and surgical procedures. (4) Each year, the number of drugs and procedures increases. (5) As a result, even knowledgeable and highly trained surgeons make mistakes. (6) For some types of patients, the error rate is very high. (7) For example, doctors deliver inappropriate care to 40 percent of patients with coronary artery disease. (8) Luckily, checklists make a big difference for these and other patients. (9) In fact, checklists reduce complications by more than one-third. (10) It is hard to imagine an argument against such a simple and effective tool.

Helping Verbs

Many verbs consist of more than one word. For example, the verb in the following sentence consists of two words.

Minh <u>must make</u> a decision about his future.

In this sentence, *make* is the **main verb**, and *must* is a **helping verb**.

Frequently Used Helping Verbs			
does	was	must	should
did	were	can	would
do		could	will
is	have	may	
are	has	might	
am	had		

A sentence's **complete verb** is made up of a main verb plus any helping verbs that accompany it. In the following sentences, the complete verb is underlined twice, and the helping verbs are checkmarked.

      ✓   ✓
Minh should have gone earlier.

     ✓
Did Minh ask the right questions?

       ✓
Minh will work hard.

      ✓
Minh can really succeed.

FYI

Helping Verbs with Participles

Participles, such as *going* and *gone*, cannot stand alone as main verbs in a sentence. They need a helping verb to make them complete.

INCORRECT	Minh going to the library.
CORRECT	Minh is going to the library.
INCORRECT	Minh gone to the library.
CORRECT	Minh has gone to the library.

PRACTICE

18-7 The verbs in the sentences that follow consist of a main verb and one or more helping verbs. In each sentence, underline the complete verb twice, and put a check mark above each helping verb.

                                     ✓
Example: In 1954, the Salk polio vaccine was given to more than a million schoolchildren.

(1) By the 1950s, polio had become a serious problem throughout the United States. (2) For years, it had puzzled doctors and researchers. (3) Thousands had become ill each year in the United States alone. (4) Children should have been playing happily. (5) Instead, they would get very sick. (6) Polio was sometimes called infantile paralysis. (7) In fact, it did cause paralysis in children and in adults as well. (8) Some patients could breathe only with the help of machines called iron lungs.

(9) Others would remain in wheelchairs for life. (10) By 1960, Jonas Salk's vaccine had reduced the incidence of polio in the United States by more than 90 percent.

TEST · Revise · Edit

Look back at your response to the Focus on Writing prompt on page 359. Circle every subject and every action verb. Then, try to replace some of them with more descriptive subjects (such as *linebacker* instead of *athlete*) and more specific action verbs (for example, *shouted* or *whispered* instead of *said*). When you have finished, TEST your paragraph. Then, revise and edit your work.

EDITING PRACTICE

Read the following student essay. Underline the subject of each sentence once, and underline the complete verb of each sentence twice. If you have trouble locating the subject, try crossing out the prepositional phrases. The first sentence has been done for you.

A New Way to Learn

Salman Khan founded the nonprofit online Khan Academy in 2009. Khan Academy promises "a free world-class education for anyone anywhere." With the help of short videos, people can learn a subject like physics or economics at their own pace. According to some, Khan Academy is in the process of revolutionizing education.

Salman Khan was born in New Orleans in 1976. His parents had moved to Louisiana from Bangladesh. During his childhood, Khan attended public schools in New Orleans. After high school, he earned three degrees from MIT and one degree from Harvard. His degrees are in math, engineering, computer science, and business. He had never considered a career in education. However, in 2004, Khan's cousin asked him for help with algebra. He made some short YouTube videos for her. To his surprise, the lessons became extremely popular. He had a talent for teaching. In 2009, with a small donation from an investor, Salman Khan started Khan Academy.

Khan Academy has succeeded well beyond Khan's expectations. Now, the organization receives millions of dollars in donations. The Khan Academy Web site has more than 3,200 videos. Every video is available for free to anyone. Khan teaches many of the lessons himself. He researches his subjects. Then, without a script, he records each video in one take. These videos are not traditional lectures. The audience never sees Khan's face. Throughout each lesson,

Khan's writing appears on the screen. Related images appear as well. For viewers, each lesson feels like a one-on-one tutoring session.

The site also offers exercises for students and tools for teachers. Students can practice subjects by themselves. They can progress at their own speed. Some schools are even using Khan Academy lessons in their classrooms. With the help of Khan's videos, teachers can create a "flipped" classroom. Students learn basic concepts at night on their computers. Then, during the day, students work on problems with the teacher's help. This means more time for questions. For some students, this method has been extremely effective.

Without any training in education, Salman Khan has changed people's ideas about learning. Around the world, people are using his Web site. They are learning new ideas. Khan is happy about this. In his view, education should be accessible for all.

COLLABORATIVE ACTIVITY

Fold a sheet of paper in half vertically. Working in a group of three or four students, spend two minutes listing as many nouns as you can in the column to the left of the fold. When your time is up, exchange papers with another group of students, and write an appropriate action verb beside each noun. (Each noun will now be the subject of a short sentence.)

Then, choose five of your sentences, and collaborate with the other students in your group to create more fully developed sentences. First, expand each subject by adding words or prepositional phrases that give more information about the subject. (For example, you could expand *boat* to *the small, leaky boat with the red sail*.) Then, expand each sentence further, adding ideas after the verb. (For example, the sentence *The boat bounced* could become *The small, leaky boat with the red sail bounced helplessly on the water*.)

review checklist

Writing Simple Sentences

☐ A sentence expresses a complete thought. The subject tells who or what is being talked about in the sentence. (See 18a.)

☐ A prepositional phrase consists of a preposition and its object (the noun or pronoun it introduces). (See 18b.)

☐ The object of a preposition cannot be the subject of a sentence. (See 18b.)

☐ An action verb tells what the subject does, did, or will do. (See 18c.)

☐ A linking verb connects the subject to a word or words that describe or rename it. (See 18c.)

☐ Many verbs are made up of more than one word. The complete verb in a sentence includes the main verb plus any helping verbs. (See 18c.)

19 Writing Compound Sentences

focus on writing

Some teenage students are parents, like those pictured here at their high school graduation with their children. Think about how their responsibilities as parents might affect such students' future studies; then, write a one-paragraph email to the president of your college explaining why your campus needs a day-care center. (If your school already has a day-care center, explain why it deserves continued—or increased—funding.)

In this chapter, you will learn to

- form compound sentences with coordinating conjunctions (19a)
- form compound sentences with semicolons (19b)
- form compound sentences with transitional words and phrases (19c)

The most basic kind of sentence, a **simple sentence**, consists of a single **independent clause**: one <u>subject</u> and one <u>verb</u>.

> European <u>immigrants</u> <u>arrived</u> at Ellis Island.

A **compound sentence** is made up of two or more simple sentences (independent clauses).

19a Using Coordinating Conjunctions

One way to form a compound sentence is by joining two independent clauses with a **coordinating conjunction** preceded by a comma.

> Many European immigrants arrived at Ellis Island, <u>but</u> many Asian immigrants arrived at Angel Island.

Coordinating Conjunctions

and	for	or	yet
but	nor	so	

LearningCurve
Prepositions and Conjunctions
bedfordstmartins.com /focusonwriting

WORD POWER

coordinate (verb) to link two or more things that are equal in importance, rank, or degree

FYI

Use the letters that spell *FANBOYS* to help you remember the coordinating conjunctions.

F	for
A	and
N	nor
B	but
O	or
Y	yet
S	so

Coordinating conjunctions join two ideas of equal importance. They describe the relationship between two ideas, showing how and why the ideas are related. Different coordinating conjunctions have different meanings.

- To indicate addition, use *and*.

     He acts like a child, <u>and</u> people think he is cute.

- To indicate contrast or contradiction, use *but* or *yet*.

     He acts like a child, <u>but</u> he is an adult.

     He acts like a child, <u>yet</u> he wants to be taken seriously.

- To indicate a cause-and-effect relationship, use *so* or *for*.

     He acts like a child, <u>so</u> we treat him like one.

     He acts like a child, <u>for</u> he needs attention.

- To present alternatives, use *or*.

     He acts like a child, <u>or</u> he is ignored.

- To eliminate alternatives, use *nor*.

     He does not act like a child, <u>nor</u> does he look like one.

FYI

Commas with Coordinating Conjunctions

When you use a coordinating conjunction to join two independent clauses into a single compound sentence, always put a comma before the coordinating conjunction.

   We can stand in line all night, or we can go home now.

PRACTICE

19-1   Fill in the coordinating conjunction—*and, but, for, nor, or, so,* or *yet*—that most logically links the two parts of each compound sentence. Remember to insert a comma before each coordinating conjunction.

Example: Fairy tales have been told by many people around the world, ___*but*___ the stories by two German brothers may be the most famous.

(1) Jakob and Wilhelm Grimm lived in the nineteenth century _____ they wrote many well-known fairy tales. (2) Most people think fondly of fairy tales _____ the Brothers Grimm wrote many unpleasant and violent stories. (3) In their best-known works, children are abused _____ endings are not always happy. (4) Either innocent children are brutally punished for no reason _____ they are neglected. (5) For example, in "Hansel and Gretel," the stepmother mistreats the children _____ their father abandons them in the woods. (6) In this story, the events are horrifying _____ the ending is still happy. (7) The children outwit the evil adults _____ they escape unharmed. (8) Apparently, they are not injured physically _____ are they harmed emotionally. (9) Nevertheless, their story can hardly be called pleasant _____ it remains a story of child abuse and neglect.

PRACTICE

19-2   Join each of the following pairs of independent clauses with a coordinating conjunction. Be sure to place a comma before the coordinating conjunction.

Example: A computer makes drafting essays easier/ ~~It~~ also makes *, and it* revision easier.

1. Training a dog to heel is difficult. Dogs naturally resist strict control from their owners.

2. A bodhran is an Irish drum. It is played with a wooden stick.

3. Students should spend two hours studying for each hour in class. They may not do well in the course.

4. Years ago, students wrote their lessons on slates. The teacher was able to correct each student's work individually.

5. Each state in the United States has two senators. The number of representatives in Congress depends on a state's population.

6. In 1973, only 2.5 percent of those in the U.S. military were women. Today, that percentage has increased to about 20 percent.

7. A small craft advisory warns boaters of bad weather conditions. These conditions can be dangerous to small boats.

8. A DVD looks just like a CD. It can hold fifteen times as much information.

9. Hip-hop fashions include sneakers and baggy pants. These styles are very popular among young men.

10. Multiple births have become more and more common. Even some septuplets and octuplets now survive.

PRACTICE

19-3 Add coordinating conjunctions to combine some of the simple sentences in the following paragraph. Remember to put a comma before each coordinating conjunction you add.

Example: Years ago, few Americans lived to be one hundred. ~~Today,~~ , but today, there are over 70,000 centenarians.

(1) Diet, exercise, and family history may explain centenarians' long lives. (2) This is not the whole story. (3) A recent study showed surprising similarities among centenarians. (4) They did not all avoid tobacco and alcohol. (5) They did not have low-fat diets. (6) In fact, they ate relatively large amounts of fat, cholesterol, and sugar. (7) Diet could not explain their long lives. (8) They did, however, share four key traits. (9) First, all the centenarians were optimistic about life. (10) All were positive thinkers. (11) They also had deep religious faith. (12) In addition, they had all continued to lead physically active lives. (13) They remained mobile even as

elderly people. (14) Finally, all were able to adapt to loss. (15) They had all lost friends, spouses, or children. (16) They were able to get on with their lives.

PRACTICE

19-4   Write another simple sentence to follow each of the sentences below. Then, connect the sentences with a coordinating conjunction and the correct punctuation.

Example: Many patients need organ transplants/ *, but there is a serious shortage of organ donors.*

1. Secondhand smoke is dangerous. _____

_____

2. Many cars are now equipped with GPS systems. _____

_____

3. Diamonds are very expensive. _____

_____

4. Kangaroos carry their young in pouches. _____

_____

5. Dancing is good exercise. _____

_____

6. Motorcycle helmet laws have been dropped in some states. _____

_____

7. Some businesses sponsor bowling leagues for their employees. _____

_____

8. Pretzels are a healthier snack than potato chips. _____

_____

9. Many juice drinks actually contain very little real fruit juice. _____

_____

10. People tend to resist change. _____

_____

19b   Using Semicolons

Another way to create a compound sentence is by joining two simple sentences (independent clauses) with a **semicolon**. A semicolon connects clauses whose ideas are closely related.

> The AIDS Memorial Quilt contains thousands of panels; each panel represents a life lost to AIDS.

Also use a semicolon to show a strong contrast between two ideas.

> With new drugs, people can live with AIDS for years; many people, however, cannot get these drugs.

FYI

Avoiding Fragments

A semicolon can only join two complete sentences (independent clauses). A semicolon cannot join a sentence and a fragment.

	─────── FRAGMENT ───────
INCORRECT	Because millions worldwide are still dying of AIDS; more research is needed.

	─────── SENTENCE ───────
CORRECT	Millions worldwide are still dying of AIDS; more research is needed.

PRACTICE

19-5   Each of the following items consists of one simple sentence. Create a compound sentence for each item by changing the period to a semicolon and then adding another simple sentence.

Example: My brother is addicted to fast food; *he eats it every day.*

1. Fast-food restaurants are an American institution. _____

   _____

2. Families often eat at these restaurants. _____

   _____

3. Many teenagers work there. _____

_____

4. McDonald's is known for its hamburgers. _____

_____

5. KFC is famous for its fried chicken. _____

_____

6. Taco Bell serves Mexican-style food. _____

_____

7. Pizza Hut specializes in pizza. _____

_____

8. Many fast-food restaurants offer some low-fat menu items. _____

_____

9. Some offer recyclable packaging. _____

_____

10. Some even have playgrounds. _____

_____

19c Using Transitional Words and Phrases

Another way to create a compound sentence is by combining two simple sentences (independent clauses) with a **transitional word or phrase**. When you use a transitional word or phrase to join two sentences, always place a semicolon *before* the transitional word or phrase and a comma *after* it.

Some college students receive grants; in addition, they often have to take out loans.

He had a miserable time at the party; besides, he lost his wallet.

Frequently Used Transitional Words

also	instead	still
besides	later	subsequently
consequently	meanwhile	then
eventually	moreover	therefore
finally	nevertheless	thus
furthermore	now	
however	otherwise	

Frequently Used Transitional Phrases

after all	in comparison
as a result	in contrast
at the same time	in fact
for example	in other words
for instance	of course
in addition	on the contrary

Adding a transitional word or phrase makes the connection between ideas in a sentence clearer and more precise than it would be if the ideas were linked with just a semicolon. Different transitional words and phrases convey different meanings.

■ Some signal addition (*also, besides, furthermore, in addition, moreover,* and so on).

I have a lot on my mind; <u>also</u>, I have a lot of things to do.

■ Some make causal connections (*therefore, as a result, consequently, thus,* and so on).

I have a lot on my mind; <u>therefore</u>, it is hard to concentrate.

■ Some indicate contradiction or contrast (*nevertheless, however, in contrast, still,* and so on).

I have a lot on my mind; <u>still</u>, I must try to relax.

■ Some present alternatives (*instead, on the contrary, otherwise,* and so on).

I have a lot on my mind; <u>otherwise</u>, I could relax.

I will try not to think; <u>instead</u>, I will relax.

■ Some indicate time sequence (*eventually*, *finally*, *at the same time*, *later*, *meanwhile*, *now*, *subsequently*, *then*, and so on).

I have a lot on my mind; <u>meanwhile</u>, I still have work to do.

PRACTICE
19-6
Add semicolons and commas where required to set off transitional words and phrases that join two independent clauses.

Example: Ketchup is a popular condiment ; therefore , it is available in almost every restaurant.

> **WORD POWER**
> **condiment** a prepared sauce or pickle used to add flavor to food

(1) Andrew F. Smith, a food historian, wrote a book about the tomato later he wrote a book about ketchup. (2) This book, *Pure Ketchup*, was a big project in fact Smith worked on it for five years. (3) The word *ketchup* may have come from a Chinese word however Smith is not certain of the word's origins. (4) Ketchup has existed since ancient times in other words it is a very old product. (5) Ketchup has changed a lot over the years for example special dyes were developed in the nineteenth century to make it red. (6) Smith discusses many other changes for instance preservative-free ketchup was invented in 1907. (7) Ketchup is now used by people in many cultures still salsa is more popular than ketchup in the United States. (8) Today, designer ketchups are being developed meanwhile Heinz has introduced green and purple ketchup in squeeze bottles. (9) Some of today's ketchups are chunky in addition some ketchups are spicy. (10) Ketchup continues to evolve meanwhile Smith has written a book about hamburgers.

PRACTICE
19-7
Consulting the lists of transitional words and phrases on page 380, choose a word or phrase that logically connects each pair of simple sentences in the following paragraph into one compound sentence. Be sure to punctuate appropriately.

Example: *Time's* Man of the Year is often a prominent politician ;
however, sometimes
~~Sometimes~~ it is not.

(1) Every year since 1927, *Time* has designated a Man of the Year. The Man of the Year has almost never been an average man—or even a "man" at all. (2) In the 1920s and 1930s, world leaders were often chosen. Franklin Delano Roosevelt was chosen twice. (3) During World War II, Hitler, Stalin, Churchill, and Roosevelt were all chosen. Stalin was featured twice. (4) Occasionally, the Man of the Year was not an individual. In 1950, it was The American Fighting Man. (5) In 1956, The Hungarian Freedom Fighter was Man of the Year. In 1966, *Time* editors chose The Young Generation. (6) A few women have been selected. Queen Elizabeth II of England was featured in 1952. (7) In 1975, American Women were honored as a group. The Man of the Year has nearly always been male. (8) Very few people of color have been designated Man of the Year. Martin Luther King Jr. was honored in 1963. (9) The Man of the Year has almost always been one or more human beings. The Computer was selected in 1982 and Endangered Earth in 1988. (10) In 2003, *Time* did not choose a politician. It honored The American Soldier. (11) In 2005, *Time* wanted to honor the contributions of philanthropists. The magazine named Bill Gates, Melinda Gates, and Bono its Persons of the Year. (12) For 2010 and 2012, *Time* chose Facebook founder Mark Zuckerberg and President Barack Obama, respectively. In 2011, it chose The Protester, recognizing dissidents in the Middle East and North Africa.

WORD POWER

philanthropist
someone who tries to improve human lives through charitable aid

PRACTICE

19-8   Add the suggested transitional word or phrase to each of the following simple sentences. Then, add a new independent clause after it. Be sure to punctuate correctly.

Example: Commuting students do not really experience campus life.
(however)

Commuting students do not really experience campus life; however, there are some

benefits to being a commuter.

1. Campus residents may have a better college experience. (still)

   _____

   _____

2. Living at home gives students access to home-cooked meals. (in contrast)

   _____

   _____

3. Commuters have a wide choice of jobs in the community. (on the
   other hand)

   _____

   _____

4. Commuters get to see their families every day. (however)

   _____

   _____

5. There are also some disadvantages to being a commuter. (for example)

   _____

   _____

6. Unlike dorm students, many commuters have family responsibilities.
   (in fact)

   _____

   _____

7. Commuters might have to help take care of their parents or grandparents. (in addition)

   _____

   _____

8. Commuters might need a car to get to school. (consequently)

_____

_____

9. Younger commuters may have to follow their parents' rules. (of course)

_____

_____

10. Commuting to college has pros and cons. (therefore)

_____

_____

PRACTICE

19-9 Using both the specified topics and transitional words and phrases, create five compound sentences. Be sure to punctuate appropriately.

Example
Topic: fad diets
Transitional phrase: for example

People are always falling for fad diets; for example, some people eat only

pineapple to lose weight.

1. *Topic:* laws to protect people with disabilities
   Transitional phrase: in addition

_____

_____

2. *Topic:* single men and women as adoptive parents
   Transitional word: however

_____

_____

3. *Topic:* prayer in public schools
   Transitional word: therefore

_____

_____

4. *Topic:* high school proms
   Transitional word: also

   _____

   _____

5. *Topic:* course requirements at your school
   Transitional word: instead

   _____

   _____

TEST · Revise · Edit

Look back at your response to the Focus on Writing prompt on page 372. TEST what you have written. Then, revise and edit your work, checking each compound sentence to make sure you have used the coordinating conjunction or transitional word or phrase that best conveys your meaning and that you have punctuated these sentences correctly.

EDITING PRACTICE

Read the following student essay. Then, create compound sentences by linking pairs of simple sentences where appropriate, joining them with a coordinating conjunction, a semicolon, or a transitional word or phrase. Remember to put commas before coordinating conjunctions and to use semicolons and commas correctly with transitional words and phrases. The first two sentences have been combined for you.

My Grandfather's Life

My great-grandparents were born in Ukraine, *but they* ~~They~~ raised my grandfather in western Pennsylvania. The ninth of their ten children, he had a life I cannot begin to imagine. To me, he was my big, strong, powerful grandfather. He was also a child of poverty.

My great-grandfather worked for the American Car Foundry. The family lived in a company house. They shopped at the company store. In 1934, my great-grandfather was laid off. He went to work digging sewer lines for the government. At that time, the family was on welfare. Every week, they were entitled to get food rations. My grandfather would go to pick up the food. The family desperately needed the prunes, beans, flour, margarine, and other things.

For years, my grandfather wore his brothers' hand-me-down clothes. He wore thrift-shop shoes with cardboard over the holes in the soles. He was often hungry. He would sometimes sit by the side of the railroad tracks, waiting for the engineer to throw him an orange. My grandfather would do any job to earn a quarter. Once, he weeded a mile-long row of tomato plants. For this work, he was paid twenty-five cents and a pack of NECCO wafers.

My grandfather saved his pennies. Eventually, he was able to buy a used bicycle for two dollars. He dropped out of school at fourteen and got a job. The family badly needed his income. He woke up every day at 4 a.m. He rode his bike to his job at a meatpacking plant. He worked for fifty cents a day.

In 1943, at the age of seventeen, my grandfather joined the U.S. Navy. He discovered a new world. For the first time in his life, he had enough to eat. He was always first in line at the mess hall. He went back for seconds and thirds before anyone else. After the war ended in 1945, he was discharged from the Navy. He went to work in a meat market in New York City. The only trade he knew was the meat business. Three years later, when he had saved enough to open his own store, Pete's Quality Meats, he knew his life of poverty was finally over.

COLLABORATIVE ACTIVITY

Working in a small group, pair each of the simple sentences in the left-hand column below with a sentence in the right-hand column to create ten compound sentences. Use as many different coordinating conjunctions as you can to connect the independent clauses. Be sure each coordinating conjunction you choose conveys a logical relationship between ideas, and remember to put a comma before each one. You may use some of the listed sentences more than once. *Note:* Many different combinations— some serious and factually accurate, some humorous—are possible.

Some dogs wear little sweaters.	Many are named Hamlet.
Pit bulls are raised to fight.	They live in groups.
Bonobos are pygmy chimpanzees.	One even sings Christmas carols.
Many people fear Dobermans.	They can wear bandanas.
Leopards have spots.	They can play Frisbee.
Dalmatians can live in firehouses.	Many live in equatorial Zaire.
Horses can wear blankets.	Some people think they are gentle.
All mules are sterile.	They don't get cold in winter.
Great Danes are huge dogs.	They are half horse and half donkey.
Parrots can often speak.	They can be unpredictable.

review checklist

Writing Compound Sentences

☐ A compound sentence is made up of two simple sentences (independent clauses).

☐ A coordinating conjunction—*and, but, for, nor, or, so,* or *yet*—can join two independent clauses into one compound sentence. A comma always comes before the coordinating conjunction. (See 19a.)

☐ A semicolon can join two independent clauses into one compound sentence. (See 19b.)

☐ A transitional word or phrase can also join two independent clauses into one compound sentence. When it joins two independent clauses, a transitional word or phrase is always preceded by a semicolon and followed by a comma. (See 19c.)

20 Writing Complex Sentences

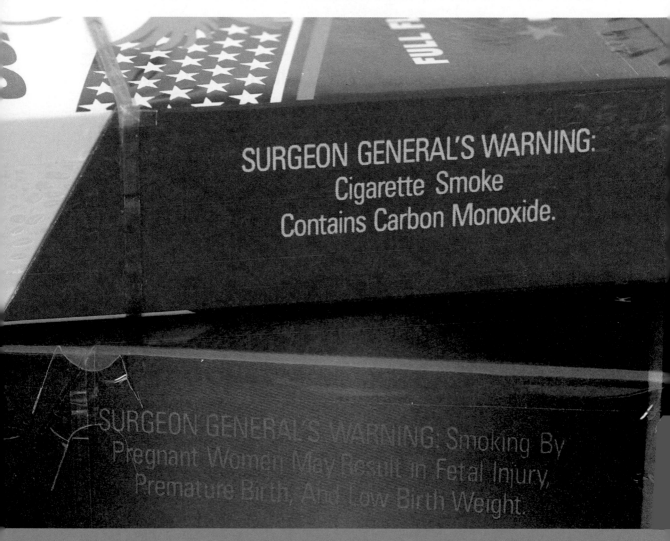

SURGEON GENERAL'S WARNING:
Cigarette Smoke
Contains Carbon Monoxide.

SURGEON GENERAL'S WARNING: Smoking By
Pregnant Women May Result in Fetal Injury,
Premature Birth, And Low Birth Weight.

focus on writing

In 1963, the U.S. government began requiring that all cigarette packages
include a warning label, two versions of which appear on this page.
Think about why this law might have passed. Then, write a paragraph
about a different law that you think should be passed, and explain why
you think this law is necessary.

In this chapter, you will learn to

- identify complex sentences (20a)
- use subordinating conjunctions to form complex sentences (20b)
- use relative pronouns to form complex sentences (20c)

20a Identifying Complex Sentences

As you learned in Chapter 19, an **independent clause** can stand alone as a sentence.

INDEPENDENT
CLAUSE   The exhibit was controversial.

However, a **dependent clause** cannot stand alone as a sentence.

DEPENDENT   Because the exhibit was controversial
CLAUSE

What happened because the exhibit was controversial? To answer this question, you need to add an independent clause that completes the idea begun in the dependent clause. The result is a **complex sentence**— a sentence that consists of one independent clause and one or more dependent clauses.

                  ┌───────── DEPENDENT CLAUSE ─────────┐ ┌ INDEPENDENT CLAUSE ┐
COMPLEX   Because the exhibit was controversial, many people
SENTENCE   ─────────────────────
           came to see it.

PRACTICE

20-1 In the blank after each of the following items, indicate whether the group of words is an independent clause (*IC*) or a dependent clause (*DC*).

Example: When novelist Toni Morrison was born in Ohio in 1931.

_DC_

1. As a young reader, Toni Morrison liked the classic Russian novelists.

_____

2. After she graduated from Howard University with a bachelor's degree in English. ⎯⎯⎯⎯⎯

3. Morrison based her novel *The Bluest Eye* on a childhood friend's prayers to God for blue eyes. ⎯⎯⎯⎯⎯

4. While she raised two sons as a single mother and worked as an editor at Random House. ⎯⎯⎯⎯⎯

5. As her reputation as a novelist grew with the publication of *Song of Solomon* and *Tar Baby*. ⎯⎯⎯⎯⎯

6. Her picture appeared on the cover of *Newsweek* in 1981. ⎯⎯⎯⎯⎯

7. Before her novel *Beloved* won the 1988 Pulitzer Prize for fiction.

⎯⎯⎯⎯⎯

8. *Beloved* was made into a film starring Oprah Winfrey. ⎯⎯⎯⎯⎯

9. In 1993, Morrison became the first African American woman to win the Nobel Prize in Literature. ⎯⎯⎯⎯⎯

10. Who published the novel *A Mercy* in 2008 to favorable reviews.

⎯⎯⎯⎯⎯

20b Using Subordinating Conjunctions

One way to form a complex sentence is to use a **subordinating conjunction**—a word such as *although* or *because*—to join two simple sentences (independent clauses). When the subordinating conjunction is added to the beginning of the simple sentence, the sentence becomes dependent for its meaning on the other simple sentence.

✓ LearningCurve
Prepositions and Conjunctions
bedfordstmartins.com
/focusonwriting

WORD POWER

subordinate (adj) lower in rank or position; secondary in importance

TWO SIMPLE SENTENCES	Muhammad Ali was stripped of his heavyweight title for refusing to go into the army. Many people admired his antiwar position.
COMPLEX SENTENCE	⎯⎯⎯⎯⎯⎯ DEPENDENT CLAUSE ⎯⎯⎯⎯⎯⎯ Although Muhammad Ali was stripped of his heavy- weight title for refusing to go into the army, many people admired his antiwar position.

Frequently Used Subordinating Conjunctions

after	even though	since	whenever
although	if	so that	where
as	if only	than	whereas
as if	in order that	that	wherever
as though	now that	though	whether
because	once	unless	while
before	provided that	until	
even if	rather than	when	

As the chart below shows, different subordinating conjunctions express different relationships between dependent and independent clauses.

Relationship between Clauses	Subordinating Conjunction	Example
Time	after, before, since, until, when, whenever, while	When the whale surfaced, Ahab threw his harpoon.
Reason or cause	as, because	Scientists scaled back the project because the government cut funds.
Result or effect	in order that, so that	So that students' math scores will improve, many schools have begun special programs.
Condition	even if, if, unless	The rain forest may disappear unless steps are taken immediately.
Contrast	although, even though, though	Although Thomas Edison had almost no formal education, he was a successful inventor.
Location	where, wherever	Pittsburgh was built where the Allegheny and Monongahela Rivers meet.

FYI

Punctuating with Subordinating Conjunctions

In a complex sentence, use a comma after the dependent clause.

┌─────────── DEPENDENT CLAUSE ───────────┐ ┌── INDEPENDENT CLAUSE ──┐
Although she wore the scarlet letter, Hester carried herself
proudly.

Do not use a comma after the independent clause.

┌──── INDEPENDENT CLAUSE ────┐ ┌────────── DEPENDENT CLAUSE ──────────┐
Hester carried herself proudly although she wore the scarlet letter.

PRACTICE

20-2 In the blank in each of the sentences below, write an appropriate subordinating conjunction. Look at the lists of subordinating conjunctions on page 392 to help you choose a conjunction that expresses the logical relationship between the two clauses it links. (The required punctuation has been provided.)

Example: Movie cowboys are usually portrayed as white _*although*_ many were African American.

(1) Few people today know about black cowboys _____ they were once common. (2) _____ the transcontinental railroad was built, cowboys were in high demand. (3) The ranchers hired cowboys to drive their cattle to the Midwest, _____ the cows were loaded on trains headed to eastern cities. (4) Many former slaves became cowboys _____ they wanted a new start. (5) Many African Americans also became cowboys _____ they had experience working with horses and cattle on Southern plantations or farms. (6) However, black cowboys faced difficulties _____ they arrived in the West. (7) African American cowboys often had to work much harder than whites _____ earn the same pay and respect. (8) _____ almost one-fourth of cowboys were black, few writers wrote about them.

(9) The myth of the white-only cowboy was spread in novels, films, and television shows _____ black cowboys never existed. (10) Black cowboys did appear in some films of the 1970s _____ by this time Westerns were no longer popular. (11) Things started to change in the 1970s _____ several museums honored black, Indian, and Mexican cowboys. (12) _____ African American cowboys have finally received some recognition, their history can now be more fully understood.

PRACTICE

20-3   Combine each of the following pairs of sentences to create one complex sentence. Use a subordinating conjunction from the list on page 392 to indicate the relationship between the dependent and independent clauses in each sentence. Make sure you include a comma where one is required.

> **Example:**   Orville and Wilbur Wright built the first powered plane/
> *although they*
> ~~They~~ had no formal training as engineers.
> ^

1. Professional midwives are used widely in Europe. In the United States, they usually practice only in areas with few doctors.

2. John Deere constructed his first steel plow in 1837. A new era began in farming.

3. Stephen Crane describes battles in *The Red Badge of Courage.* He never saw a war.

4. Elvis Presley died in 1977. Thousands of his fans gathered in front of his mansion.

5. Jonas Salk developed the first polio vaccine in the 1950s. The number of polio cases in the United States declined.

6. The salaries of baseball players rose in the 1980s. Some sportswriters predicted a drop in attendance at games.

7. The Du Ponts arrived from France in 1800. American gunpowder was not as good as French gunpowder.

8. Margaret Sanger opened her first birth-control clinic in America in 1916. She was arrested and put in jail.

9. Thaddeus Stevens thought plantation land should be given to freed slaves. He disagreed with Lincoln's peace terms for the South.

10. Steven Spielberg directed some very popular movies. He did not win an Academy Award until *Schindler's List* in 1993.

20c Using Relative Pronouns

Another way to form a complex sentence is to use **relative pronouns** (*who, that, which,* and so on) to join two simple sentences (independent clauses).

✔ LearningCurve
Nouns and Pronouns
bedfordstmartins.com
/focusonwriting

TWO SIMPLE SENTENCES	Harry Potter is an adolescent wizard. He attends Hogwarts School of Witchcraft and Wizardry.
COMPLEX SENTENCE	┌───── DEPENDENT CLAUSE ─────┐ Harry Potter, who attends Hogwarts School of Witchcraft and Wizardry, is an adolescent wizard.

Note: The relative pronoun always refers to a word or words in the independent clause. (In the complex sentence above, *who* refers to *Harry Potter.*)

Relative Pronouns

that	which	whoever	whomever
what	who	whom	whose

Relative pronouns indicate the relationships between the ideas in the independent and dependent clauses they link.

TWO SIMPLE SENTENCES	Nadine Gordimer lived in South Africa. She won the Nobel Prize in Literature in 1991.

COMPLEX SENTENCE	Nadine Gordimer, who won the Nobel Prize in Literature in 1991, lived in South Africa.
TWO SIMPLE SENTENCES	Last week I had a job interview. It went very well.
COMPLEX SENTENCE	Last week I had a job interview that went very well.
TWO SIMPLE SENTENCES	Transistors have replaced vacuum tubes in radios and televisions. They were invented in 1948.
COMPLEX SENTENCE	Transistors, which were invented in 1948, have replaced vacuum tubes in radios and televisions.

PRACTICE

20-4 In each of the following complex sentences, underline the dependent clause once, and underline the relative pronoun twice. Then, draw an arrow from the relative pronoun to the word or words to which it refers.

> **Example:** MTV, which was the first television network devoted to popular music videos, began in 1981.

1. MTV's very first music video, which was performed by a group called the Buggles, contained the lyric "Video killed the radio star."

2. The earliest videos on MTV were simple productions that recorded live studio performances.

3. Music videos eventually became complicated productions that featured special effects and large casts of dancers.

4. Music video directors gained recognition at MTV's Video Music Awards presentation, which first aired in September 1984.

5. *The Real World*, a reality series that featured a group of young people living together in New York City, was introduced by MTV in 1992.

6. MTV's later reality shows featured celebrities such as Jessica Simpson, who starred in *Newlyweds: Nick and Jessica* in 2003.

7. Today, MTV, which devotes less and less time to music videos, produces many hours of original programming.

8. One of MTV's most popular recent reality shows, which featured cast members at the beach, was *Jersey Shore*.

9. Another popular but controversial show is *16 and Pregnant*, which presents the stories of pregnant high school girls.

10. Needless to say, these shows have their critics, who claim that the shows undermine society's most basic values.

PRACTICE

20-5   Combine each of the following pairs of simple sentences into one complex sentence. Use the relative pronoun that follows each pair.

Example: Elias Howe invented an early type of zipper. He was too busy with his other invention—the sewing machine—to work on it. (who)

Elias Howe, who invented an early type of zipper, was too busy with his other

invention—the sewing machine—to work on it.

1. Early zippers were just hooks and eyes. These hooks and eyes were fastened to a cloth tape. (that)

2. Gideon Sundback invented the first useful zipper. He worked endless hours to help him stop grieving for his wife. (who)

3. Their "high" price kept early zippers from becoming popular. It was about eighteen cents. (which)

4. The word *zipper* began as a brand name. It was coined by a company executive. (which)

_____

_____

5. At first, zipper manufacturers could not convince people to use zippers in clothing. They sold many zippers for boots. (who)

_____

_____

TEST · Revise · Edit

Look back at your response to the Focus on Writing prompt on page 389. TEST what you have written. Then, revise and edit your paragraph, checking carefully to make sure that you have used subordinating conjunctions and relative pronouns correctly and that your complex sentences are punctuated correctly.

EDITING PRACTICE

Read the following student essay. Then, revise it by combining pairs of simple sentences with subordinating conjunctions or relative pronouns that indicate the relationship between them. Be sure to punctuate correctly. The first two sentences have been combined for you.

Community Art

When a   *, the*
A city has a crime problem, The police and the courts try to solve it. Some cities have come up with creative ways to help young people stay out of trouble. One example is the Philadelphia Mural Arts Program. It offers free art education for high school students.

In the 1960s, Philadelphia had a serious problem. The problem was graffiti. Graffiti artists had painted on buildings all over the city. A solution to the problem was the Philadelphia Anti-Graffiti Network. This offered graffiti artists an alternative. The artists would give up graffiti. They would not be prosecuted. The artists enjoyed painting. They could paint murals on public buildings instead. They could create beautiful landscapes, portraits of local heroes, and abstract designs. The graffiti artists had once been lawbreakers. They could now help beautify the city.

The Mural Arts Program began in 1984 as a part of the Philadelphia Anti-Graffiti Network. By 1996, the Philadelphia Anti-Graffiti Network was focusing on eliminating graffiti, and its Mural Arts Program was working to improve the community. It no longer worked with graffiti offenders. It ran after-school and summer programs for students. The Mural Arts Program got national recognition in 1997. That is when President Bill Clinton helped paint a mural. So far, the Mural Arts Program has completed more than 2,800 murals. This is more than any other public art program in the country.

Over 20,000 students have taken part in the Mural Arts Program. The students come from all parts of the city. In one part of the program, students work alongside professional artists. The students get to paint parts of the artists' murals themselves. The artwork is on public buildings. The artwork can be seen by everyone.

The Mural Arts Program continues to build a brighter future for students and their communities. It is now over a quarter of a century old. Students help bring people together to create a mural. They feel a stronger connection to their community and more confidence in themselves. They leave the program. They are equipped to make a positive difference in their communities and in their own lives.

COLLABORATIVE ACTIVITY

Working in a group of four students, make a list of three or four of your favorite television shows. Then, divide into pairs, and with your partner, write two simple sentences describing each show. Next, use subordinating conjunctions or relative pronouns to combine each pair of sentences into one complex sentence. With your group, discuss how the ideas in each complex sentence are related, and make sure you have used the subordinating conjunction or relative pronoun that best conveys this relationship.

> **Example:** *Mad Men* is a period drama set in the 1960s. It appeals to many of today's viewers.
>
> Although *Mad Men* is a period drama set in the 1960s, it appeals to many of today's viewers.

review checklist

Writing Complex Sentences

☐ A complex sentence consists of one independent clause (simple sentence) combined with one or more dependent clauses. (See 20a.)

☐ Subordinating conjunctions—dependent words such as *although, after, when, while,* and *because*—can join two independent clauses into one complex sentence. (See 20b.)

☐ Relative pronouns—dependent words such as *who, which,* and *that*—can also join two independent clauses into one complex sentence. The relative pronoun shows the relationship between the ideas in the two independent clauses that it links. (See 20c.)

21 Writing Varied Sentences

focus on writing

This picture shows items about to be preserved in a time capsule at the History Center in Pittsburgh. Write a paragraph about a time capsule you might construct for your children to open when they are adults. What items would you include? How would you expect each item to communicate to your children what you and your world were like? Be sure to include explanations for your decisions.

In this chapter, you will learn to
- vary sentence types (21a)
- vary sentence openings (21b)
- combine sentences (21c)
- mix long and short sentences (21d)

Sentence variety is important because a paragraph of varied sentences flows more smoothly, is easier to read and understand, and is more interesting than one in which all the sentences are structured in the same way.

21a Varying Sentence Types

Most English sentences are **statements**. Others are **questions** or **exclamations**. One way to vary your sentences is to use an occasional question or exclamation where it is appropriate.

In the following paragraph, a question and an exclamation add variety.

> Jacqueline Cochran, the first woman pilot to break the sound barrier, was one of the most important figures in aviation history. In 1996, the United States Postal Service issued a stamp honoring Cochran; the words "Pioneer Pilot" appear under her name. <u>What did she do to earn this title and this tribute?</u> Cochran broke more flight records than anyone else in her lifetime and won many awards, including the United States Distinguished Service Medal in 1945 and the United States Air Force Distinguished Flying Cross in 1969. During World War II, she helped form the WASPs, the Women's Air Force Service Pilots program, so that women could fly military planes to their bases (even though they were not allowed to go into combat). Remarkably, she accomplished all this with only three weeks of flying instruction. She only got her pilot's license in the first place because she wanted to start her own cosmetics business and flying would enable her to travel quickly around the country. Although she never planned to be a pilot, once she discovered flying she quickly became the best. <u>Not surprisingly, when the Postal Service honored Jacqueline Cochran, it was with an airmail stamp!</u>

Question

Exclamation

PRACTICE

21-1 Revise the following paragraph by changing one of the statements into a question and one of the statements into an exclamation.

Example: The cell phone may be making the wristwatch obsolete. (statement)

Is the cell phone making the wristwatch obsolete? (question)

(1) As cell phones and other small electronic devices become more common, fewer people are wearing watches. (2) Most cell phones, iPads, and MP3 players display the time. (3) Moreover, cell-phone clocks give very accurate time. (4) This is because they set themselves with satellite signals. (5) They also adjust automatically to time-zone changes. (6) Typical wristwatches cannot compete with these convenient features. (7) After all, unlike the newer devices, watches are not computers. (8) However, watches do remain appealing for other reasons. (9) For many people, they are fashion accessories or status symbols. (10) For some, watches are still essential for telling time.

21b   Varying Sentence Openings

When all the sentences in a paragraph begin the same way, your writing is likely to seem dull and repetitive. In the following paragraph, for example, every sentence begins with the subject.

> Scientists have been observing a disturbing phenomenon. The population of frogs, toads, and salamanders has been declining. This decline was first noticed in the mid-1980s. Some reports blamed chemical pollution. Some biologists began to suspect that a fungal disease was killing these amphibians. The most reasonable explanation seems to be that the amphibians' eggs are threatened by solar radiation. This radiation penetrates the thinned ozone layer, which used to shield them from the sun's rays.

WORD POWER

amphibians cold-blooded vertebrates, such as frogs, that live both in the water and on land

Beginning with Adverbs

Instead of opening every sentence in a paragraph with the subject, you can try beginning some sentences with one or more **adverbs**.

> Scientists have been observing a disturbing phenomenon. <u>Gradually but steadily</u>, the population of frogs, toads, and salamanders has been declining. This decline was first noticed in the mid-1980s. Some

reports blamed chemical pollution. Some biologists began to suspect that a fungal disease was killing these amphibians. However, the most reasonable explanation seems to be that the amphibians' eggs are threatened by solar radiation. This radiation penetrates the thinned ozone layer, which used to shield them from the sun's rays.

PRACTICE

21-2 Underline the adverb in each of the following sentences, and then rewrite the sentence so that the adverb appears at the beginning. Be sure to punctuate correctly.

Example: An internship is <u>usually</u> a one-time work or service experience related to a student's career plans.

Usually, an internship is a one-time work or service experience related to a student's

career plans.

1. Internships are sometimes paid or counted for academic credit.

   _____

2. A prospective student intern should first talk to an academic adviser.

   _____

3. The student should next write a résumé listing job experience, education, and interests.

   _____

4. The student can then send the résumé to organizations that are looking for interns.

   _____

5. Going to job fairs and networking are often good ways to find internships.

   _____

PRACTICE

21-3 In each of the following sentences, fill in the blank with an appropriate adverb. Be sure to punctuate correctly.

Example: ___*Slowly,*___ the sun crept over the horizon.

1. _____ the speeding car appeared from out of nowhere.

2. _____ it crashed into the guardrail.

3. _____ the car jackknifed across the highway.

4. _____ drivers behind the car slammed on their brakes.

5. _____ someone called 911.

6. _____ a wailing siren could be heard.

7. _____ the ambulance arrived.

8. _____ emergency medical technicians went to work.

9. _____ a police officer was on hand to direct traffic.

10. _____ no one was badly hurt in the accident.

Beginning with Prepositional Phrases

Another way to create sentence variety is to begin some sentences with prepositional phrases. A **prepositional phrase** (such as *along the river* or *near the diner*) is made up of a preposition and its object.

> In recent years, scientists have observed a disturbing phenomenon. Gradually but steadily, the population of frogs, toads, and salamanders has been declining. This was first noticed in the mid-1980s. At first, some reports blamed chemical pollution. After a while, some biologists began to suspect that a fungal disease was killing them. However, the most reasonable explanation seems to be that the amphibians' eggs are threatened by solar radiation. This radiation penetrates the thinned ozone layer, which used to shield them from the sun's rays.

PRACTICE

21-4 Underline the prepositional phrase in each of the following sentences, and then rewrite the sentence so that the prepositional phrase appears at the beginning. Be sure to punctuate correctly.

Example: Very few American women did factory work before the 1940s.

Before the 1940s, very few American women did factory work.

1. Many male factory workers became soldiers during World War II.

_____

2. The U.S. government encouraged women to take factory jobs in the war's early years.

_____

_____

3. Over six million women took factory jobs between 1942 and 1945.

_____

4. A new female image emerged with this greater responsibility and independence.

_____

_____

5. Many women wore pants for the first time.

_____

6. Most women lost their factory jobs after the war and returned to "women's work."

_____

PRACTICE

21-5   In each of the following sentences, fill in the blank with an appropriate prepositional phrase. Be sure to punctuate correctly.

Example: _At the start of the New York Marathon,_   Justin felt as if he could run forever.

1. _____ he warmed up by stretching and bending.

2. _____ all the runners were crowded together.

3. _____ they crossed a bridge over the Hudson River.

4. _____ the route became more and more challenging.

5. _____ Justin grabbed some water from a helpful onlooker.

6. _____ he staggered across the finish line.

PRACTICE

21-6   Every sentence in the following paragraph begins with the subject, but several contain prepositional phrases or adverbs that could be moved to the beginning. To vary the sentence openings, move prepositional phrases to the beginnings of four sentences, and move adverbs to the beginnings of two other sentences. Be sure to place a comma after these introductory phrases.

Example: *By the end of the 1800s,* Spain ~~by the end of the 1800s~~ had lost most of its colonies.

(1) People in the Cuban American community often mention José Julián Martí as one of their heroes. (2) José Martí was born in Havana in 1853, at a time when Cuba was a colony of Spain. (3) He had started a newspaper demanding Cuban freedom by the time he was sixteen years old. (4) The Spanish authorities forced him to leave Cuba and go to Spain in 1870. (5) He published his first pamphlet calling for Cuban independence while in Spain, openly continuing his fight. (6) He then lived for fourteen years in New York City. (7) He started the journal of the Cuban Revolutionary Party during his time in New York. (8) Martí's essays and poems argued for Cuba's freedom and for the individual freedom of Cubans. (9) He died in battle against Spanish soldiers in Cuba, passionately following up his words with actions.

21c Combining Sentences

You can also create sentence variety by experimenting with different ways of combining sentences.

Using *-ing* Modifiers

A **modifier** identifies or describes other words in a sentence. You can use an *-ing* modifier to combine two sentences.

TWO SENTENCES	Duke Ellington composed more than a thousand songs. He worked hard to establish his reputation.
COMBINED WITH -*ING* MODIFIER	Composing more than a thousand songs, Duke Ellington worked hard to establish his reputation.

When the two sentences above are combined, the *-ing* modifier (*composing more than a thousand songs*) describes the new sentence's subject (*Duke Ellington*).

PRACTICE

21-7 Use an *-ing* modifier to combine each of the following pairs of sentences into a single sentence. Eliminate any unnecessary words, and place a comma after each *-ing* modifier.

Example: Many American colleges are setting an example for the rest of the country. They are going green.

Setting an example for the rest of the country, many American colleges are going green.

1. Special lamps in the dorms of one Ohio college change from green to red. They warn of rising energy use.

   _____

   _____

2. A Vermont college captures methane from dairy cows. It now needs less energy from other sources.

   _____

   _____

3. Student gardeners at a North Carolina college tend a campus vegetable plot. They supply the cafeteria with organic produce.

   _____

   _____

4. A building on a California campus proves that recycled materials can be beautiful. It is built from redwood wine casks.

   _____

   _____

5. Some colleges offer courses in sustainability. They are preparing students to take the green revolution beyond campus.

   _____

   _____

Using *-ed* Modifiers

You can also use an *-ed* modifier to combine two sentences.

TWO SENTENCES Nogales is located on the border between Arizona and Mexico. It is a bilingual city.

COMBINED WITH Located on the border between Arizona and Mexico,
-ED MODIFIER Nogales is a bilingual city.

When the two sentences above are combined, the *-ed* modifier (*located on the border between Arizona and Mexico*) describes the new sentence's subject (*Nogales*).

PRACTICE

21-8 Use an *-ed* modifier to combine each of the following pairs of sentences into a single sentence. Eliminate any unnecessary words, and use a comma to set off each *-ed* modifier. When you are finished, underline the *-ed* modifier in each sentence.

> **Example:** Potato chips and cornflakes were invented purely by accident. They are two of America's most popular foods.
>
> <u>Invented purely by accident,</u> potato chips and cornflakes are two of America's most
>
> popular foods.

1. George Crum was employed as a chef in a fancy restaurant. He was famous for his french fries.

   _____

2. A customer was dissatisfied with the fries. He complained and asked for thinner fries.

   _____

3. The customer was served thinner fries. He was still not satisfied and complained again.

   _____

4. Crum was now very annoyed. He decided to make the fries too thin and crisp to eat with a fork.

   _____

5. The customer was thrilled with the extra-thin and crisp potatoes. He ate them all.

   _____

6. Potato chips were invented to get even with a customer. They are the most popular snack food in America today.

   _____

   _____

7. Dr. John Kellogg was concerned about the diet of patients at his hospital. He and his brother set out to make healthy foods.

      _____

      _____

8. The brothers were called away on an urgent matter. They left a pot of boiled wheat on the stove.

      _____

9. The wheat had hardened by the time they returned. It broke into flakes when they rolled it.

      _____

10. The brothers were delighted with the results. They came up with a new flake made of corn.

      _____

Using a Series of Words

Another way to vary your sentences is to combine a group of sentences into one sentence that includes a **series** of words (nouns, verbs, or adjectives). Combining sentences in this way eliminates a boring string of similar sentences and repetitive phrases and also makes your writing more concise.

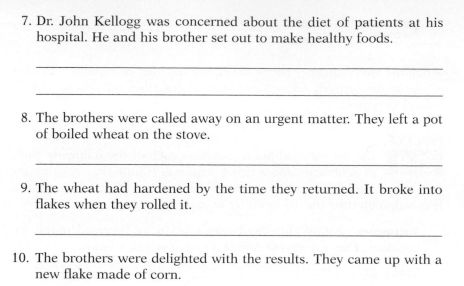

GROUP OF SENTENCES	College presidents want to improve athletes' academic performance. Coaches too want to improve athletes' academic performance. The players themselves also want to improve their academic performance.
COMBINED (SERIES OF NOUNS)	College <u>presidents</u>, <u>coaches</u>, and the <u>players</u> themselves want to improve athletes' academic performance.
GROUP OF SENTENCES	In 1997, Arundhati Roy published her first novel, *The God of Small Things*. She won the Pulitzer Prize. She became a literary sensation.
COMBINED (SERIES OF VERBS)	In 1997, Arundhati Roy <u>published</u> her first novel, *The God of Small Things*, <u>won</u> the Pulitzer Prize, and <u>became</u> a literary sensation.
GROUP OF SENTENCES	As the tornado approached, the sky grew dark. The sky grew quiet. The sky grew threatening.

COMBINED
(SERIES OF
ADJECTIVES)

As the tornado approached, the sky grew <u>dark</u>, <u>quiet</u>, and <u>threatening</u>.

PRACTICE
21-9

Combine each of the following groups of sentences into one sentence that includes a series of nouns, verbs, or adjectives.

Example: Many years ago, Pacific Islanders from Samoa settled in Hawaii. Pacific Islanders from Fiji also settled in Hawaii. Pacific Islanders from Tahiti settled in Hawaii, too.

Many years ago, Pacific Islanders from Samoa, Fiji, and Tahiti settled

in Hawaii.

1. In the eighteenth century, the British explorer Captain Cook came to Hawaii. Other explorers also came to Hawaii. European travelers came to Hawaii, too.

2. Explorers and traders brought commerce to Hawaii. They brought new ideas. They brought new cultures.

3. Missionaries introduced the Christian religion. They introduced a Hawaiian-language bible. Also, they introduced a Hawaiian alphabet.

4. In the mid-nineteenth century, pineapple plantations were established in Hawaii. Sugar plantations were established there as well. Other industries were also established.

5. By 1900, Japanese people were working on the plantations. Chinese people were also working on the plantations. In addition, native Hawaiians were working there.

6. People of many different races and religions now live in Hawaii. People of many different races and religions now go to school in Hawaii. People of many different races and religions now work in Hawaii.

_____

_____

7. Schoolchildren still study the Hawaiian language. They learn about the Hawaiian kings and queens. They read about ancient traditions.

_____

_____

8. Today, Hawaii is well known for its tourism. It is well known too for its weather. It is especially well known for its natural beauty.

_____

_____

9. Tourists can swim. They can surf. They can play golf. They can ride in outrigger canoes.

_____

_____

10. Today, the state of Hawaii remains lively. It remains culturally diverse. It remains very beautiful.

_____

_____

Using Appositives

WORD POWER

adjacent next to

An **appositive** is a word or word group that identifies, renames, or describes an adjacent noun or pronoun. Creating an appositive is often a good way to combine two sentences about the same subject.

TWO SENTENCES   C. J. Walker was the first American woman to be-come a self-made millionaire. She marketed a line of hair-care products for black women.

COMBINED WITH   C. J. Walker, the first American woman to become
APPOSITIVE   a self-made millionaire, marketed a line of
                hair-care products for black women.

In the example on page 412, the appositive appears in the middle of a sentence. However, an appositive can also come at the beginning or at the end of a sentence.

> The first American woman to become a self-made millionaire, C. J. Walker marketed a line of hair-care products for black women. (appositive at the beginning)
>
> Several books have been written about C. J. Walker, the first American woman to become a self-made millionaire. (appositive at the end)

PRACTICE

21-10 Combine each of the following pairs of sentences into one sentence by creating an appositive. Note that the appositive may appear at the beginning, in the middle, or at the end of the sentence. Be sure to use commas appropriately.

Example: *Wikipedia* is a popular online information source, It is available in more than two hundred languages.

(1) *Wikipedia* is one of the largest reference sites on the Web. It is different from other encyclopedias in many ways. (2) This site is a constant work-in-progress. It allows anyone to add, change, or correct information in its articles. (3) For this reason, researchers have to be careful when using information from *Wikipedia*. *Wikipedia* is a source that may contain factual errors. (4) The older articles are the ones that have been edited and corrected the most. These often contain the most trustworthy information. (5) Despite some drawbacks, *Wikipedia* has many notable advantages. These advantages include free and easy access, up-to-date information, and protection from author bias.

21d Mixing Long and Short Sentences

A paragraph of short, choppy sentences—or a paragraph of long, rambling sentences—can be monotonous. By mixing long and short sentences, perhaps combining some simple sentences to create **compound** and **complex** sentences, you can create a more interesting paragraph.

In the following paragraph, the sentences are all short, and the result is boring and hard to follow.

> The world's first drive-in movie theater opened on June 6, 1933. This drive-in was in Camden, New Jersey. Automobiles became more popular. Drive-ins did, too. By the 1950s, there were more than four thousand drive-ins in the United States. Over the years, the high cost of land led to a decline in the number of drive-ins. So did the rising popularity of television. Soon, the drive-in movie theater had almost disappeared. It was replaced by the multiplex. In 1967, there were forty-six drive-ins in New Jersey. Today, only one is still open. That one is the Delsea Drive-in in Vineland, New Jersey.

The revised paragraph that follows is more interesting and easier to read. (Note that the final short sentence is retained for emphasis.)

> The world's first drive-in movie theater opened on June 6, 1933, in Camden, New Jersey. As automobiles became more popular, drive-ins did, too, and by the 1950s, there were more than four thousand drive-ins in the United States. Over the years, the high cost of land and the rising popularity of television led to a decline in the number of drive-ins. Soon, the drive-in movie theater had almost disappeared, replaced by the multiplex. In 1967, there were forty-six drive-ins in New Jersey, but today, only one is still open. That one is the Delsea Drive-in in Vineland, New Jersey.

PRACTICE

21-11 The following paragraph contains a series of short, choppy sentences that can be combined. Revise the paragraph so that it mixes long and short sentences. Be sure to use commas and other punctuation appropriately.

Example: Kente cloth has special significance for many African
Americans./ ~~Some~~ *, but some* other people do not understand this significance.

(1) Kente cloth is made in western Africa. (2) It is produced primarily by the Ashanti people. (3) It has been worn for hundreds of years by African royalty. (4) They consider it a sign of power and status. (5) Many African Americans wear kente cloth. (6) They see it as a link to their heritage. (7) Each pattern on the cloth has a name. (8) Each color has a special significance. (9) For example, red and yellow suggest a

long and healthy life. (10) Green and white suggest a good harvest.
(11) African women may wear kente cloth as a dress or head wrap.
(12) African American women, like men, usually wear strips of cloth
around their shoulders. (13) Men and women of African descent wear
kente cloth as a sign of racial pride. (14) It often decorates college students'
gowns at graduation.

TEST · Revise · Edit

Look back at your response to the Focus on Writing prompt on
page 401. TEST what you have written. Then, using the strategies
discussed in this chapter that seem appropriate, revise your writing
so that your sentences are varied, interesting, and smoothly connected.
Finally, edit your work.

EDITING PRACTICE

The following student essay lacks sentence variety. All of its sentences begin with the subject, and the essay includes a number of short, choppy sentences. Using the strategies discussed in this chapter as well as strategies for creating compound and complex sentences, revise the essay to achieve greater sentence variety. The first sentence has been edited for you.

Toys by Accident

Many popular toys and games are the result of accidents. *when people* ~~People~~ try to invent one thing but discover something else instead. Sometimes they are not trying to invent anything at all. They are completely surprised to find a new product.

Play-Doh is one example of an accidental discovery. Play-Doh is a popular preschool toy. Play-Doh first appeared in Cincinnati. A company made a compound to clean wallpaper. They sold it as a cleaning product. The company then realized that this compound could be a toy. Children could mold it like clay. They could use it again and again. The new toy was an immediate hit. Play-Doh was first sold in 1956. Since then, more than two billion cans of Play-Doh have been sold.

The Slinky was discovered by Richard James. He was an engineer. At the time, he was trying to invent a spring to keep ships' instruments steady at sea. He tested hundreds of springs of varying sizes, metals, and tensions. None of them worked. One spring fell off the desk and "walked" down a pile of books. It went end over end onto the floor. He thought his children might enjoy playing with it. James took the spring home. They loved it. Every child in the neighborhood wanted one. The first Slinky was demonstrated at Gimbel's Department Store in Philadelphia in 1945. All four hundred Slinkys were sold within ninety minutes. The Slinky is simple and inexpensive. The Slinky is still popular with children today.

The Frisbee was also discovered by accident. According to one story, a group of Yale University students were eating pies from a local bakery. The bakery was called Frisbies. They finished eating the pies. They started throwing the empty pie tins around. A carpenter in California made a plastic version. He called it the Pluto Platter. The Wham-O company bought the patent on the product. Wham-O renamed it the Frisbee after the bakery. This is how the Frisbee came to be.

Some new toys are not developed by toy companies. Play-Doh, the Frisbee, and the Slinky are examples of very popular toys that were discovered by accident. Play-Doh started as a cleaning product. The Slinky was discovered by an engineer who was trying to invent something else. The Frisbee was invented by students having fun. The toys were discovered unexpectedly. All three toys have become classics.

COLLABORATIVE ACTIVITY

Read the following list of sentences. Working in a small group, change one sentence to a question and one to an exclamation. Then, add adverbs or prepositional phrases at the beginning of several of the sentences in the list.

Many well-known African American writers left the United States in the
   years following World War II.
Many went to Paris.
Richard Wright was a novelist.
He wrote *Native Son* and *Black Boy.*
He wrote *Uncle Tom's Children.*
He left the United States for Paris in 1947.
James Baldwin wrote *Another Country, The Fire Next Time,* and *Giovanni's
   Room.*
He also wrote essays.
He came to Paris in 1948.
Chester Himes was a detective story writer.
He arrived in Paris in 1953.
William Gardner Smith was a novelist and journalist.
He also left the United States for Paris.
These expatriates found Paris more hospitable than America.
They also found it less racist.

Finally, use the strategies discussed and illustrated in 21c and 21d to help you combine the sentences listed on the previous page into a paragraph. (You may keep the sentences in the order in which they appear.)

review checklist

Writing Varied Sentences

☐ Vary sentence types. (See 21a.)

☐ Vary sentence openings. (See 21b.)

☐ Combine sentences. (See 21c.)

☐ Mix long and short sentences. (See 21d.)

22 Using Parallelism

focus on writing

This picture shows a green market in an urban neighborhood, part of a growing trend that many people think is making U.S. cities more livable. Write a paragraph discussing three positive things about your own neighborhood, school, or workplace. Support your statements with specific examples.

In this chapter, you will learn to

- recognize parallel structure (22a)
- use parallel structure (22b)

22a Recognizing Parallel Structure

Parallelism is the use of matching words, phrases, clauses, and sentence structure to highlight similar ideas in a sentence. When you use parallelism, you are telling readers that certain ideas are related and have the same level of importance. By repeating similar grammatical patterns to express similar ideas, you create sentences that are clearer, more concise, and easier to read.

In the following examples, the parallel sentences highlight similar ideas; the other sentences do not.

PARALLEL	NOT PARALLEL
Please leave your name, your number, and your message.	Please leave your name, your number, and you should also leave a message.
I plan to graduate from high school and become a nurse.	I plan to graduate from high school, and then becoming a nurse would be a good idea.
The grass was soft, green, and sweet smelling.	The grass was soft, green, and the smell was sweet.
Making the team was one thing; staying on it was another.	Making the team was one thing, but it was very difficult to stay on it.
We can register for classes in person, or we can register by email.	We can register for classes in person, or registering by email is another option.

PRACTICE
22-1

In the following sentences, decide whether the underlined words and phrases are parallel. If so, write *P* in the blank. If not, rewrite the sentences so that the underlined ideas are presented in parallel terms.

Examples: The missing dog had brown fur, a red collar, and a long

tail. _____*P*_____

Signs of drug abuse in teenagers include <u>falling grades</u>, <u>mood swings</u>,

and ~~they lose~~ <u>weight</u>./ *loss.* _____
                              ^

1. The food in the cafeteria is <u>varied</u>, <u>tasty</u>, and <u>it is healthy</u>. _____

2. Do you want the job done <u>quickly</u>, or do you want it done <u>well</u>?

   _____

3. Last summer <u>I worked at the library</u>, <u>babysat for my neighbor's</u>

   <u>daughter</u>, and <u>there was a soup kitchen where I volunteered</u>.

   _____

4. <u>Pandas eat bamboo leaves</u>, and <u>eucalyptus leaves are eaten by</u>

   <u>koalas</u>. _____

5. Skydiving is <u>frightening</u> but <u>fun</u>. _____

6. A number of interesting people work at the co-op with me, including

   <u>an elderly German man</u>, <u>there is a middle-aged Chinese woman</u>, and

   <u>a teenaged Mexican boy</u>. _____

7. <u>The bell rang</u>, and <u>the students stood up</u>. _____

8. To conserve energy while I was away, I <u>unplugged the television</u>, <u>closed</u>

   <u>the curtains</u>, and <u>the thermostat was set at 65 degrees</u>. _____

9. I <u>put away the dishes</u>; will you <u>put away the laundry</u>? _____

10. For several weeks after the storm, the supermarkets had <u>no eggs</u>,

    <u>they were out of milk</u>, and <u>they did not have any bread</u>. _____

22b Using Parallel Structure

Parallel structure is especially important in *paired items*, *items in a series*, and *items in a list or in an outline*.

Paired Items

Use parallel structure when you connect ideas with a **coordinating conjunction**—*and*, *but*, *for*, *nor*, *or*, *so*, and *yet*.

George believes in <u>doing a good job</u> and <u>minding his own business</u>.

You can <u>pay me now</u> or <u>pay me later</u>.

You should also use parallel structure for paired items joined by *both . . . and, not only . . . but also, either . . . or, neither . . . nor,* and *rather . . . than.*

Jan is both <u>skilled in writing</u> and <u>fluent in French</u>.

The group's new recording not only <u>has a dance beat</u> but also <u>has thought-provoking lyrics</u>.

I'd rather <u>eat one worm by itself</u> than <u>eat five worms with ice cream</u>.

Items in a Series

Use parallel structure for items in a series—words, phrases, or clauses. (Be sure to use commas to separate three or more items in a series. Never put a comma after the final item.)

Every Wednesday I have <u>English</u>, <u>math</u>, and <u>psychology</u>. (three words)

<u>Increased demand</u>, <u>high factory output</u>, and <u>a strong dollar</u> will help the economy. (three phrases)

She is a champion because she <u>stays in excellent physical condition</u>, <u>puts in long hours of practice</u>, and <u>has an intense desire to win</u>. (three clauses)

Items in a List or in an Outline

Use parallel structure for items in a numbered or bulleted list.

There are three reasons to open an Individual Retirement Account (IRA):
1. To save money
2. To reduce taxes
3. To be able to retire

Use parallel structure for the elements in an outline.

  A. Types of rocks
    1. Igneous
    2. Sedimentary
    3. Metamorphic

PRACTICE

22-2   Fill in the blanks in the following sentences with parallel words, phrases, or clauses of your own that make sense in context.

Example: At the lake, we can ___*go for a swim*___, ___*paddle a canoe*___, and ___*play volleyball*___.

1. When I get too little sleep, I am _____, _____, and _____.

2. I am good at _____ but not at _____.

3. My ideal mate is _____ and _____.

4. I personally define success not only as _____ but also as _____.

5. I use my computer for both _____ and _____.

6. I like _____ and _____.

7. You need three qualities to succeed in college: _____, _____, and _____.

8. I enjoy not only _____ but also _____.

9. I would rather _____ than _____.

10. Football _____, but baseball _____.

PRACTICE

22-3   Rewrite the following sentences so that matching ideas are presented in parallel terms. Add punctuation as needed.

Example: Some experts believe homework is harmful to learning, and also it is harmful to children's health and to family life.

Some experts believe homework is harmful to learning, to children's health,

and to family life.

1. Experts who object to homework include Dorothy Rich and Harris Cooper, and another expert, Alfie Kohn, also objects to homework.

_____

_____

2. Harris Cooper of Duke University says that middle school students do not benefit from more than one and a half hours of homework, and more than two hours of homework does not benefit high school students.

_____

_____

_____

_____

3. In his book *The Homework Myth*, Alfie Kohn says that homework creates family conflict, and stress is also created in children.

_____

_____

4. Kohn suggests that children could do other things after school to develop their bodies and minds, and they could also do some things to develop their family relationships.

_____

_____

_____

5. Kohn believes that instead of doing homework, children could interview parents about family history and also chemistry could be learned through cooking.

_____

_____

_____

6. Harris Cooper advises that homework should take a short amount of time and should advance learning and also reading skills should be promoted.

_____

_____

_____

7. There seems to be no relationship between the amount of homework assigned and students are getting lower test scores.

_____

_____

8. For example, students in countries that assign less homework, such as Japan and Denmark, score higher on achievement tests than American students, and the Czech Republic does, too.

_____

_____

_____

9. Students in countries that assign more homework, such as Greece and Thailand, score lower on achievement tests than American students; in Iran, they also assign more homework.

_____

_____

_____

10. All critics of homework agree that elementary school students receive too much homework, middle school students receive too much homework, and too much homework is done by high school students.

_____

_____

_____

TEST · Revise · Edit

Look back at your response to the Focus on Writing prompt on page 419. **TEST** what you have written. Then, revise and edit your paragraph, checking carefully to make sure you used parallel structure to highlight similar ideas or items in your sentences. If you used parallel structure to present three or more items in a series, make sure you used commas to separate the items.

EDITING PRACTICE

Read the following student essay, which contains examples of faulty parallelism. Identify the sentences you think need to be corrected, and make the changes required to achieve parallelism. Be sure to supply all words necessary for clarity, grammar, and sense. Add punctuation as needed. The first error has been edited for you.

Self-Made Men and Women Helping Others

Many self-made people go from poverty to ~~achieving~~ success. Quite a few of them not only achieve such success but also they help others. Three of these people are Oprah Winfrey, Alfredo Quiñones-Hinojosa, and Geoffrey Canada. Their lives are very different, but all possess great strength, being determined, and concern for others.

Oprah is one of the most influential people in the world, and she has more money than almost anyone in the world. She came from a very poor family. First, she lived with her grandmother on a Mississippi farm, and then her mother in Milwaukee. During this time, she was abused by several relatives. When she was thirteen, she was sent to Nashville to live with her father. He used strict discipline, and she was taught by him to value education. Through her own determination and because she was ambitious, Winfrey got a job at a local broadcasting company. This started her career. However, Oprah was not satisfied with being successful. Through Oprah's Angel Network and the Oprah Winfrey Leadership Academy, she helps others and making the world a better place.

Today, Alfredo Quiñones-Hinojosa is a top brain surgeon and conducting research on new ways to treat brain cancer. At age nineteen, he was an illegal immigrant from Mexico, worked in the fields, and without any English. When he told his cousin he wanted to learn English and get a better job, his cousin told him he was crazy. Then, while a welder on a railroad crew, he fell into an empty petroleum tank and was almost dying from the fumes. However, Alfredo overcame these hardships. He enrolled in a community college, and with determination and by working hard, he began to change his life. He won a scholarship to Berkeley, went on to medical school at Harvard, and eventually winding up as director of the brain tumor program at Johns Hopkins University. In 1997, he became a citizen of the United States. At each step of the way, he has made a special effort to reach out to students from low-income backgrounds and to inspire others.

Geoffrey Canada grew up in a New York City neighborhood that was poor, dangerous, and where violence was not uncommon. His mother was a single parent who struggled to support Geoffrey and his three brothers. Geoffrey learned to survive on the streets, but he also studied a lot in school. Thanks to this hard work, he won a scholarship to college in Maine and went on to a career in education. Deciding to leave his neighborhood in New York wasn't hard, but to decide to come back wasn't hard either. He wanted to help children in poor families to succeed in school and so they could have better lives. With this in mind, he started the Harlem Children's Zone (HCZ). HCZ includes (1) workshops for parents, (2) a preschool and three charter schools, and (3) running health programs for children and families. President Obama has said he would like to see more programs like HCZ.

Oprah Winfrey, Alfredo Quiñones-Hinojosa, and Geoffrey Canada have very different careers—in entertainment, in medicine, and educating children. However, all three overcame great adversity, all three have achieved enormous success, and they have helped others. They have helped their communities, their country, and have contributed to the world.

COLLABORATIVE ACTIVITY

Working in a group, list three or four qualities that you associate with each word in the following pairs.

Brothers/sisters
Teachers/students
Parents/children

City/country
Fast food/organic food
Movies/TV shows
Work/play

Then, write a compound sentence comparing the two words in each pair. Use a coordinating conjunction to join the clauses, and make sure each sentence uses clear parallel structure, mentions both words, and includes the qualities you listed for the word pairs.

_____

_____

review checklist

☑ LearningCurve
Parallelism
**bedfordstmartins.com
/focusonwriting**

Using Parallelism

☐ Use matching words, phrases, clauses, and sentence structure to highlight similar items or ideas. (See 22a.)

☐ Use parallel structure with paired items. (See 22b.)

☐ Use parallel structure for items in a series. (See 22b.)

☐ Use parallel structure for items in a list or in an outline. (See 22b.)

23 Using Words Effectively

focus on writing

This picture shows a house on the island of Bermuda. Look the house over carefully, and then write a paragraph in which you describe *your* dream house. Would it resemble the house in the picture, or would it be different? How? What would be inside the house? Be as specific as possible.

In this chapter, you will learn to

- use specific words (23a)
- use concise language (23b)
- avoid slang (23c)
- avoid clichés (23d)
- use similes and metaphors (23e)
- avoid sexist language (23f)
- avoid commonly confused words (23g)

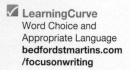

LearningCurve
Word Choice and
Appropriate Language
bedfordstmartins.com
/focusonwriting

23a Using Specific Words

Specific words refer to particular people, places, things, ideas, or qualities. **General words** refer to entire classes or groups. Sentences that contain specific words are more precise and vivid than those that contain only general words.

SENTENCES WITH GENERAL WORDS	SENTENCES WITH SPECIFIC WORDS
While walking in the woods, I saw an <u>animal</u>.	While walking in the woods, I saw a <u>baby skunk</u>.
<u>Someone</u> decided to run for Congress.	<u>Rebecca</u> decided to run for Congress.
<u>Weapons</u> are responsible for many murders.	<u>Unregistered handguns</u> are responsible for many murders.
Denise bought new <u>clothes</u>.	Denise bought a new <u>blue dress</u>.
I really enjoyed my <u>meal</u>.	I really enjoyed my <u>pepperoni pizza with extra cheese</u>.
Darrell had always wanted a <u>classic car</u>.	Darrell had always wanted a <u>black 1969 Chevrolet Camaro</u>.

FYI

Using Specific Words

One way to strengthen your writing is to avoid general words like *good*, *nice*, or *great*. Take the time to think of more specific words. For example, when you say the ocean looked *pretty*, do you really mean that it *sparkled*, *glistened*, *rippled*, *foamed*, *surged*, or *billowed*?

PRACTICE

23-1   In the following passage, underline the specific words that help you imagine the scene the writer describes. The first sentence has been done for you.

Last summer, I spent three weeks backpacking through <u>the remote rural province of Yunnan in China</u>. One day, I came across four farm women playing a game of mahjong on a patch of muddy ground. Squatting on rough wooden stools around a faded green folding table, the women picked up and discarded the smooth ivory mahjong tiles as if they were playing cards. In the grassy field around them, their chestnut-colored horses grazed with heavy red and black market bags tied to their backs. A veil of shimmering white fog hung over a nearby hill, and one woman sat under a black umbrella to shelter herself from the sun. A fifth woman watched, with her wrinkled hands on her hips and a frown on her face. The only sound was the sharp click of the tiles and the soft musical talk of the women as they played.

PRACTICE

23-2   In the blank beside each of the five general words below, write a more specific word. Then, use the more specific word in an original sentence.

Example: child _____*six-year-old*_____

All through dinner, my six-year-old chattered excitedly about his first

day of school.

1. emotion _____

_____

_____

2. building _____

_____

_____

3. said _____

_____

_____

4. animal _____

_____

_____

5. went _____

_____

_____

PRACTICE

23-3 The following one-paragraph job-application letter uses many general words. Rewrite the paragraph, substituting specific words and adding details where necessary. Start by making the first sentence, which identifies the job, more specific: for example, "I would like to apply for the <u>dental technician</u> position you advertised on <u>March 15</u> in the <u>*Post*</u>." Then, add information about your background and qualifications. Expand the original paragraph into a three-paragraph letter.

I would like to apply for the position you advertised in today's paper. I graduated from high school and am currently attending college. I have taken several courses that have prepared me for the duties the position requires. I also have several personal qualities that I think you would find useful in a person holding this position. In addition, I have had certain experiences that qualify me for such a job. I would appreciate the opportunity to meet with you to discuss your needs as an employer. Thank you.

23b Using Concise Language

Concise language says what it has to say in as few words as possible. Too often, writers use words and phrases that add nothing to a sentence's meaning. A good way to test a sentence for these words is to see if crossing them out changes the sentence's meaning. If the sentence's meaning does not change, you can assume that the words you crossed out are unnecessary.

The
~~It is clear that the~~ United States was not ready to fight World War II.
To ^
~~In order to~~ follow the plot, you must make an outline.
^

Sometimes you can replace several unnecessary words with a single word.

Because
~~Due to the fact that~~ I was tired, I missed my first class.
    ^

FYI

Using Concise Language

The following wordy phrases add nothing to a sentence. You can usually delete or condense them with no loss of meaning.

WORDY	CONCISE
It is clear that	(delete)
It is a fact that	(delete)
The reason is because	Because
The reason is that	Because
It is my opinion that	I think/I believe
Due to the fact that	Because
Despite the fact that	Although
At the present time	Today/Now
At that time	Then
In most cases	Usually
In order to	To
In the final analysis	Finally
Subsequent to	After

Unnecessary repetition—saying the same thing twice for no reason—can also make your writing wordy. When you revise, delete repeated words and phrases that add nothing to your sentences.

My instructor told me the book was ~~old-fashioned and~~ outdated. (An old-fashioned book *is* outdated.)

The ~~terrible~~ tragedy of the fire could have been avoided. (A tragedy is *always* terrible.)

PRACTICE

23-4 To make the following sentences more concise, eliminate any unnecessary repetition, and delete or condense wordy expressions.

Each
Example: ~~It is a fact that each individual~~ production of *Sesame*
                                              ^

Street around the world is geared toward the local children ~~in that~~
                                                                ^

~~region.~~

(1) In order to meet the needs of international children all over the world, Sesame Workshop helps produce versions of its popular show *Sesame Street* in other countries outside the United States. (2) Due to the fact that each country has different issues and concerns, the content of these shows varies. (3) In most cases, the producers focus on and concentrate on the cultural diversity in their country. (4) In order to develop the most appropriate material for their shows, producers also consult with and talk to local educators and child development experts, people who are experts in the field. (5) At the present time, versions of *Sesame Street* exist in a wide variety of places and countries. They include Mexico, Russia, South Africa, Bangladesh, and Egypt. (6) Created in 1972, Mexico's *Plaza Sésamo* is one of the oldest international versions, having been around longer than versions in other countries. (7) This Spanish-language show includes and brings in familiar and well-known characters like Elmo and Cookie Monster as well as unique and original characters like Abelardo and Pancho. (8) Like all versions of *Sesame Street*, *Plaza Sésamo*'s main and most important focus is on educating and teaching children about letters, numbers, and the diverse world around them.

23c Avoiding Slang

Slang is nonstandard language that calls attention to itself. It is usually associated with a particular social group—instant-message users or skateboarders, for example. Some slang eventually spreads beyond its original context and becomes widely used. Often, it is used for emphasis or to produce a surprising or original effect. In any case, because it is very informal, slang is not acceptable in your college writing.

My psychology exam was really ~~sweet.~~ *easy.*

On the weekends, I like to ~~chill~~ *relax* and watch movies on my laptop.

If you have any question about whether a term is slang or not, look it up in a dictionary. If the term is identified as *slang* or *informal*, find a more suitable term.

FYI

Avoiding Abbreviations and Shorthand

While abbreviations and shorthand such as *LOL*, *BTW*, *IMO*, and *2day* are acceptable in informal electronic communication, they are not acceptable in your college writing, in emails to your instructors, or in online class discussions.

In my opinion,
~~IMO~~ your essay needs a strong thesis statement.
^

                     you   *today.*
I would like to meet with ~~u~~ for a conference ~~2day~~.
                       ^   ^

PRACTICE
23-5

Edit the following sentences, replacing the slang expressions with clearer, more precise words and phrases.

               yelled at me
Example: My father ~~lost it~~ when I told him I crashed the car.
              ^

1. Whenever I get bummed, I go outside and jog.

2. Tonight I'll have to leave by 11 because I'm wiped out.

3. I'm not into movies or television.

4. Whenever we argue, my boyfriend knows how to push my buttons.

5. I really lucked out when I got this job.

23d Avoiding Clichés

Clichés are expressions—such as "easier said than done" and "last but not least"—that have been used so often that they have lost their meaning. These worn-out expressions get in the way of clear communication.

    When you identify a cliché in your writing, replace it with a direct statement—or, if possible, with a fresher expression.

CLICHÉ   When school was over, she felt free ~~as a bird~~.

CLICHÉ   These days, you have to be *seriously ill* ~~sick as a dog~~ before

you are admitted to a hospital.

FYI

Avoiding Clichés

Here are examples of some clichés you should avoid in your writing.

back in the day	play God
better late than never	pushing the envelope
beyond a shadow of a doubt	raining cats and dogs
break the ice	selling like hotcakes
cutting edge	the bottom line
face the music	think outside the box
give 110 percent	touched base
hard as a rock	tried and true
it goes without saying	water under the bridge
keep your eye on the ball	what goes around comes around

PRACTICE

23-6   Cross out any clichés in the following sentences. Then, either substitute a fresher expression or restate the idea more directly.

Example: Lottery winners often think they will be *free of financial worries* ~~on easy street~~ for

the rest of their lives.

(1) Many people think that a million-dollar lottery jackpot allows the winner to stop working like a dog and start living high on the hog. (2) All things considered, however, the reality for lottery winners is quite different. (3) For one thing, lottery winners who hit the jackpot do not always receive their winnings all at once; instead, yearly payments—for example, $50,000—can be paid out over twenty years. (4) Of that $50,000

a year, close to $20,000 goes to taxes and anything else the lucky stiff already owes the government, such as student loans. (5) Next come relatives and friends with their hands out, leaving winners between a rock and a hard place. (6) They can either cough up gifts and loans or wave bye-bye to many of their loved ones. (7) Adding insult to injury, many lottery winners lose their jobs because employers think that, now that they are "millionaires," they no longer need to draw a salary. (8) Many lottery winners wind up way over their heads in debt within a few years. (9) In their hour of need, many might like to sell their future payments to companies that offer lump-sum payments of forty to forty-five cents on the dollar. (10) This is easier said than done, however, because most state lotteries do not allow winners to sell their winnings.

23e Using Similes and Metaphors

A **simile** is a comparison of two unlike things that uses *like* or *as*.

> His arm hung at his side <u>like</u> a broken branch.
> He was <u>as</u> content <u>as</u> a cat napping on a windowsill.

A **metaphor** is a comparison of two unlike things that does not use *like* or *as*.

> Invaders from another world, the dandelions conquered my garden.
> He was a beast of burden, hauling cement from the mixer to the building site.

The impact of similes and metaphors comes from the surprise of seeing two seemingly unlike things being compared. Used in moderation, similes and metaphors can make your writing more lively and more interesting.

PRACTICE
23-7   Use your imagination to complete each of the following items by creating three original similes.

Example: A boring class is like _____ *toast without jam.* _____

_____ *a four-hour movie.* _____

_____ *a bedtime story.* _____

1. A good friend is like _____

_____

_____

2. A thunderstorm is like _____

_____

_____

3. A workout at the gym is like _____

_____

_____

PRACTICE
23-8   Think of a person you know well. Using that person as your subject, fill in each of the following blanks to create metaphors. Try to complete each metaphor with more than a single word, as in the example.

Example: If _____ *my baby sister* _____ were an animal, _____ *she* _____ would

be _____ *a curious little kitten.* _____

1. If _____ were a musical instrument, _____ would be _____

_____

2. If _____ were a food, _____ would be _____

_____

3. If _____ were a means of transportation, _____ would be

_____

_____

4. If _____ were a natural phenomenon, _____ would be

_____

5. If _____ were a toy, _____ would be _____

_____

23f Avoiding Sexist Language

Sexist language refers to men and women in insulting terms. Sexist language is not just words such as *stud* or *babe*, which people may find objectionable. It can also be words or phrases that unnecessarily call attention to gender or that suggest a job or profession is held only by a man (or only by a woman) when it actually is not.

You can avoid sexist language by using a little common sense. There is always an acceptable nonsexist alternative for a sexist term.

SEXIST	NONSEXIST
man, mankind	humanity, humankind, the human race
businessman	executive, businessperson
fireman, policeman, mailman	firefighter, police officer, letter carrier
male nurse, woman engineer	nurse, engineer
congressman	member of Congress, representative
stewardess, steward	flight attendant
man and wife	man and woman, husband and wife
manmade	synthetic
chairman	chair, chairperson
anchorwoman, anchorman	anchor
actor, actress	actor

FYI

Avoiding Sexist Language

Do not use *he* when your subject could be either male or female.

> **SEXIST**   Everyone should complete his assignment by next week.

You can correct this problem in three ways.

- *Use* he or she *or* his or her.

    Everyone should complete his or her assignment by next week.

- *Use plural forms.*

    Students should complete their assignments by next week.

- *Eliminate the pronoun.*

    Everyone should complete the assignment by next week.

PRACTICE

23-9   Edit the following sentences to eliminate sexist language.

or her (or omit "his")

Example: A doctor should be honest with his patients.

1. Many people today would like to see more policemen patrolling the streets.

2. The attorneys representing the plaintiff are Geraldo Diaz and Mrs. Barbara Wilkerson.

3. Every soldier picked up his weapons.

4. Christine Fox is the female mayor of Port London, Maine.

5. Travel to other planets will be a significant step for man.

23g   Commonly Confused Words

Accept/Except   *Accept* means "to receive something." *Except* means "with the exception of" or "to leave out or exclude."

> "I <u>accept</u> your challenge," said Alexander Hamilton to Aaron Burr.
> Everyone <u>except</u> Darryl visited the museum.

Affect/Effect   *Affect* is a verb meaning "to influence." *Effect* is a noun meaning "result."

> Carmen's job could <u>affect</u> her grades.
> Overexposure to sun can have a long-term <u>effect</u> on skin.

All ready/Already   *All ready* means "completely prepared." *Already* means "previously, before."

> Serge was <u>all ready</u> to take the history test.
> Gina had <u>already</u> been to Italy.

Brake/Break   *Brake* is a noun that means "a device to slow or stop a vehicle." *Break* is a verb meaning "to smash" or "to detach" and sometimes a noun meaning either "a gap" or "an interruption" or "a stroke of luck."

> Peter got into an accident because his foot slipped off the <u>brake</u>.
> Babe Ruth thought no one would ever <u>break</u> his home run record.
> The baseball game was postponed until there was a <u>break</u> in the bad weather.

Buy/By   *Buy* means "to purchase." *By* is a preposition meaning "close to," "next to," or "by means of."

> The Stamp Act forced colonists to <u>buy</u> stamps for many public documents.
> He drove <u>by</u> but did not stop.
> He stayed <u>by</u> her side all the way to the hospital.
> Malcolm X wanted "freedom <u>by</u> any means necessary."

Conscience/Conscious   *Conscience* is a noun that refers to the part of the mind that urges a person to choose right over wrong. *Conscious* is an adjective that means "aware" or "deliberate."

After he cheated at cards, his <u>conscience</u> started to bother him.

As she walked through the woods, she became <u>conscious</u> of the hum of insects.

Elliott made a <u>conscious</u> decision to stop smoking.

Everyday/Every day   *Everyday* is a single word that means "ordinary" or "common." *Every day* is two words that mean "occurring daily."

Friends was a successful comedy show because it appealed to <u>everyday</u> people.

<u>Every day</u>, the six friends met at the Central Perk café.

Fine/Find   *Fine* means "superior quality" or "a sum of money paid as a penalty." *Find* means "to locate."

He sang a <u>fine</u> solo at church last Sunday.

Demi had to pay a <u>fine</u> for speeding.

Some people still use a willow rod to <u>find</u> water.

Hear/Here   *Hear* means "to perceive sound by ear." *Here* means "at or in this place."

I moved to the front so I could <u>hear</u> the speaker.

My great-grandfather came <u>here</u> in 1883.

Its/It's   *Its* is the possessive form of *it*. *It's* is the contraction of *it is* or *it has*.

The airline canceled <u>its</u> flights because of the snow.

<u>It's</u> twelve o'clock, and we are late.

Ever since <u>it's</u> been in the accident, the car has rattled.

Know/No/Knew/New   *Know* means "to have an understanding of" or "to have fixed in the mind." *No* means "not any," "not at all," or "not one." *Knew* is the past tense form of the verb *know*. *New* means "recent or never used."

I <u>know</u> there will be a lunar eclipse tonight.

You have <u>no</u> right to say that.

He <u>knew</u> how to install a <u>new</u> light switch.

Lie/Lay   *Lie* means "to rest or recline." The past tense of *lie* is *lay*. *Lay* means "to put or place something down." The past tense of *lay* is *laid*.

Every Sunday, I <u>lie</u> in bed until noon.

They <u>lay</u> on the grass until it began to rain, and then they went home.

Tammy told Carl to <u>lay</u> his cards on the table.

Brooke and Cassia finally <u>laid</u> down their hockey sticks.

Loose/Lose   *Loose* means "not fixed or rigid" or "not attached securely." *Lose* means "to mislay" or "to misplace."

In the 1940s, many women wore <u>loose</u>-fitting pants.

I never gamble because I hate to <u>lose</u>.

Passed/Past   *Passed* is the past tense of the verb *pass*. It means "moved by" or "succeeded in." *Past* is a noun or an adjective meaning "earlier than the present time."

The car that <u>passed</u> me was doing more than eighty miles an hour.

David finally <u>passed</u> his driving test.

The novel was set in the <u>past</u>.

The statement said that the bill was <u>past</u> due.

Peace/Piece   *Peace* means "the absence of war" or "calm." *Piece* means "a part of something."

The British prime minister tried to achieve <u>peace</u> with honor.

My <u>peace</u> of mind was destroyed when the flying saucer landed.

"Have a <u>piece</u> of cake," said Marie.

Principal/Principle   *Principal* means "first" or "highest" or "the head of a school." *Principle* means "a law or basic assumption."

She had the <u>principal</u> role in the movie.

I'll never forget the day the <u>principal</u> called me into his office.

It was against his <u>principles</u> to lie.

Quiet/Quit/Quite   *Quiet* means "free of noise" or "still." *Quit* means "to leave a job" or "to give up." *Quite* means "actually" or "very."

Jane looked forward to the <u>quiet</u> evenings at the lake.

Sammy <u>quit</u> his job and followed the girls into the parking lot.

"You haven't <u>quite</u> got the hang of it yet," she said.

After practicing all summer, Tamika got <u>quite</u> good at tennis.

Raise/Rise   *Raise* means "to elevate" or "to increase in size, quantity, or worth." The past tense of *raise* is *raised*. *Rise* means "to stand up" or "to move from a lower position to a higher position." The past tense of *rise* is *rose*.

Carlos <u>raises</u> his hand whenever the teacher asks for volunteers.

They finally <u>raised</u> the money for the down payment.

The crowd <u>rises</u> every time their team scores a touchdown.

Kim <u>rose</u> before dawn so she could see the eclipse.

Sit/Set   *Sit* means "to assume a sitting position." The past tense of *sit* is *sat*. *Set* means "to put down or place" or "to adjust something to a desired position." The past tense of *set* is *set*.

I usually <u>sit</u> in the front row at the movies.

They <u>sat</u> at the clinic waiting for their names to be called.

Elizabeth <u>set</u> the mail on the kitchen table and left for work.

Every semester I <u>set</u> goals for myself.

Suppose/Supposed   *Suppose* means "to consider" or "to assume." *Supposed* is both the past tense and the past participle of *suppose*. *Supposed* also means "expected" or "required." (Note that when *supposed* has this meaning, it is always followed by *to*.)

<u>Suppose</u> researchers were to find a cure for cancer.

We <u>supposed</u> the movie would be over by ten o'clock.

You were <u>supposed</u> to finish a draft of the report by today.

Their/There/They're   *Their* is the possessive form of the pronoun *they*. *There* means "at or in that place." *There* is also used in the phrases *there is* and *there are*. *They're* is the contraction of *they are*.

They wanted poor people to improve <u>their</u> living conditions.

I put the book over <u>there</u>.

<u>There</u> are three reasons I will not eat meat.

<u>They're</u> the best volunteer firefighters I've ever seen.

Then/Than   *Then* means "at that time" or "next in time." *Than* is used in comparisons.

He was young and naive <u>then</u>.

I went to the job interview and <u>then</u> stopped off for coffee.

My dog is smarter <u>than</u> your dog.

Threw/Through   *Threw* is the past tense of *throw*. *Through* means "in one side and out the opposite side" or "finished."

> Satchel Paige <u>threw</u> a baseball more than ninety-five miles an hour.
>
> It takes almost thirty minutes to go <u>through</u> the tunnel.
>
> "I'm <u>through</u>," said Clark Kent, storming out of Perry White's office.

To/Too/Two   *To* means "in the direction of." *Too* means "also" or "more than enough." *Two* denotes the numeral 2.

> During spring break, I am going <u>to</u> Disney World.
>
> My roommates are coming <u>too</u>.
>
> The microwave popcorn is <u>too</u> hot to eat.
>
> "If we get rid of the Tin Man and the Cowardly Lion, the <u>two</u> of us can go to Oz," said the Scarecrow to Dorothy.

Use/Used   *Use* means "to put into service" or "to consume." *Used* is both the past tense and the past participle of *use*. *Used* also means "accustomed." (Note that when *used* has this meaning, it is followed by *to*.)

> I <u>use</u> a soft cloth to clean my glasses.
>
> "Hey! Who <u>used</u> all the hot water?" he yelled from the shower.
>
> Marisol had <u>used</u> all the firewood during the storm.
>
> After two years in Alaska, they got <u>used</u> to the short winter days.

Weather/Whether   *Weather* refers to temperature, humidity, precipitation, and so on. *Whether* is used to introduce alternative possibilities.

> The *Farmer's Almanac* says that the <u>weather</u> this winter will be severe.
>
> <u>Whether</u> or not this prediction will be correct is anyone's guess.

Where/Were/We're   *Where* means "at or in what place." *Were* is the past tense of *are*. *We're* is the contraction of *we are*.

> <u>Where</u> are you going, and <u>where</u> have you been?
>
> Charlie Chaplin and Mary Pickford <u>were</u> popular stars of silent movies.
>
> <u>We're</u> doing our back-to-school shopping early this year.

Whose/Who's   *Whose* is the possessive form of *who*. *Who's* is the contraction of either *who is* or *who has*.

My roommate asked, "<u>Whose</u> book is this?"

"<u>Who's</u> there?" squealed the second little pig as he leaned against the door.

<u>Who's</u> been blocking the driveway?

Your/You're *Your* is the possessive form of *you*. *You're* is the contraction of *you are*.

"You should have worn <u>your</u> running shoes," said the hare as he passed the tortoise.

"<u>You're</u> too kind," said the tortoise sarcastically.

TEST · Revise · Edit

Look back at your response to the Focus on Writing prompt on page 429. **TEST** what you have written. Then, revise and edit your paragraph, making sure that your language is specific as well as concise; that you have avoided slang, clichés, and sexist language; and that you have not made any errors in word usage. Finally, add a simile or metaphor to add interest to your writing.

EDITING PRACTICE

Read the following student essay carefully, and then revise it. Make sure that your revision is concise, uses specific words, and includes no slang, sexist language, clichés, or confused words. Add an occasional simile or metaphor if you like. The first sentence has been edited for you.

Unexpected Discoveries

When we ~~here~~ *hear* the word "accident," we think of bad things/ But accidents *, like dented fenders and broken glass.* can be good, too. Modern science has made advances as a result of accidents. It is a fact that a scientist sometimes works like a dog for years in his laboratory, only to make a weird discovery because of a mistake.

The most famous example of a good, beneficial accident is the discovery of penicillin. A scientist, Alexander Fleming, had seen many soldiers die of infections after they were wounded in World War I. All things considered, many more soldiers died due to the fact that infections occurred than from wounds. Fleming wanted to find a drug that could put an end to these terrible, fatal infections. One day in 1928, Fleming went on vacation, leaving a pile of dishes in the lab sink. As luck would have it, he had been growing bacteria in those dishes. When he came back, he noticed that one of the dishes looked moldy. What was strange was that near the mold, the bacteria were dead as a doornail. It was crystal clear to Fleming that the mold had killed the bacteria. He had discovered penicillin, the first antibiotic.

Everyone has heard the name "Goodyear." It was Charles Goodyear who made a discovery that changed and revolutionized the rubber industry. In the early nineteenth century, rubber products became thin and runny in hot weather and cracked in cold weather. One day in 1839, Goodyear accidentally dropped some rubber mixed with sulfur on a hot stove. It changed color and turned black. After being cooled, it could be stretched, and it would return to its original size and shape. This kind of rubber is now used in tires and in many other products.

Another thing was also discovered because of a lab accident involving rubber. In 1953, Patsy Sherman, a female chemist for the 3M company, was trying to find a new type of rubber. She created a batch of man-made liquid rubber. Some of the liquid accidentally spilled onto a lab assistant's new white canvas sneaker. Her assistant used everything but the kitchen sink to clean the shoe, but nothing worked. Over time, the rest of the shoe became dirty, but the part where the spill had hit was still clean as a whistle. Sherman new that she had found something that could actually keep fabrics clean by doing a number on dirt. The 3M Corporation named it's brand new product Scotchgard.

A scientist can be clumsy and careless, but sometimes his mistakes lead to great and important discoveries. Penicillin, better tires, and Scotchgard are examples of products that were the result of scientific accidents.

COLLABORATIVE ACTIVITY

Photocopy two or three paragraphs of description from a romance novel, a western novel, or a mystery novel, and bring your paragraphs to class. Working in a group, choose one paragraph that seems to need clearer, more specific language. As a group, revise the paragraph you chose, making it as specific as possible and eliminating any clichés or sexist language. Then, exchange your revised paragraph with the paragraph revised by another group, and check the other group's work. Make any additional changes you think the paragraph needs.

review checklist

Using Words Effectively

☐ Use specific words that convey your ideas clearly and precisely. (See 23a.)

☐ Use concise language that says what it has to say in the fewest possible words. (See 23b.)

☐ Avoid slang. (See 23c.)

☐ Avoid clichés. (See 23d.)

☐ When appropriate, use similes and metaphors to make your writing more lively and more interesting. (See 23e.)

☐ Avoid sexist language. (See 23f.)

☐ Avoid commonly confused words. (See 23g.)

✓ LearningCurve
Word Choice and
Appropriate Language
**bedfordstmartins.com
/focusonwriting**

Read the following student essay. Then, edit it by creating more effective sentences and correcting any misspelled words. Combine simple sentences into compound or complex sentences, use parallelism, create varied sentences, and use words that are concise, specific, and original. The first editing change has been made for you.

Eating Street Food

Street food, food cooked and served at a portable stand, is extremely popular in the United States. ~~Street~~-food customers *Usually, street* usually get ~~there~~ *their* food quickly, *and* ~~They~~ do not pay much. Some regional or ethnic foods are sold as street food. Then, they become popular There are concerns about the cleanliness and freshness of street food. These problems can be avoided. It is a fact that street food has many advantages.

Street food is the original fast food. Street food is both fast and cheap. Customers usually do not have much time to wait for it to be cooked. Vendors have to offer food that can be made beforehand or prepared quickly. The original U.S. street food is the hot dog. It can be steamed ahead of time and quickly be put into a bun. Some customers want things like relish, onions, and chili. They can be added. Street food does not cost as much as restaurant food. Vendors usually have to by a license in order to sell food at a particular location. They do not have to rent a store, pay waiters and waitresses, and supply tablecloths and dishes therefore they can charge much less then a restaurant. Street-food customers do not have to make the commitment of time and money required at a sit-down restaurant. They do not have to tip the server. Customers cannot sit at tables, however. There are no tables. They have to eat while standing or walking. Customers often do not have much time. This situation suits them. Students need fast and cheap food, especially on college campuses. Food carts make them happy as a clam.

Street food is often regional or ethnic. Vendors sell cheese steaks and soft pretzels in Philadelphia. They sell reindeer sausages in Alaska. They sell tacos and tamales in Mexican neighborhoods. In Chicago, customers can buy kielbasa sandwiches and pierogies. Often, food carts offer ethnic foods to customers who are tasting them for the first time. A person can see if he likes Indian curry, Israeli falafel, Italian panini, or a gyro from Greece. Because of the success of street vendors, many ethnic foods have gone mainstream and are now widely offered in sit-down restaurants.

There is some concern about the safety of street food. Refrigeration may be limited or nonexistent. Cleanliness sometimes can be a problem. Food from a street-corner cart may be safer than food cooked in a restaurant kitchen. In the restaurant, it may sit for a long time. Also, due to the fact that food carts may lack refrigeration, very fresh ingredients are often used. Still, customers should follow some tips for buying street food. The food should be kept covered until it is cooked. The money and food should not be touched by the same individual. Local customers are a good guide to the best street food. They know where the food is freshest. A long line usually indicates a good and safe source of street food.

In the United States, street food is especially varied. In the United States, there are many immigrants. Food is an important part of culture. The popularity of ethnic street food can be a sign that the immigrants' culture has been accepted.

unit

6

Solving Common Sentence Problems

REVISING
AND EDITING
YOUR
WRITING

24 Run-Ons

focus on writing

Why do you think so many American children are physically out of shape? What do you think can be done about this problem? Write a paragraph that answers these questions.

In this chapter, you will learn to

- recognize run-ons (24a)
- correct run-ons in five different ways (24b)

☑ LearningCurve
Run-Ons
**bedfordstmartins.com
/focusonwriting**

24a Recognizing Run-Ons

A **sentence** consists of at least one independent clause—one subject and one verb.

College costs are rising.

A **run-on** is an error that occurs when two sentences are joined incorrectly. There are two kinds of run-ons: *fused sentences* and *comma splices*.

■ A **fused sentence** occurs when two sentences are joined without any punctuation.

> FUSED SENTENCE [College costs are rising] [many students are worried.]

■ A **comma splice** occurs when two sentences are joined with just a comma.

> COMMA SPLICE [College costs are rising], [many students are worried.]

WORD POWER

fused joined together

splice (verb) to join together at the ends

PRACTICE

24-1 Some of the sentences in the following paragraph are correct, but others are run-ons. In the answer space after each sentence, write *C* if the sentence is correct, *FS* if it is a fused sentence, and *CS* if it is a comma splice.

Example: Using a screen reader is one way for blind people to access the Web, two popular programs are JAWS for Windows and Window-Eyes. ____*CS*____

(1) The Internet should be accessible to everyone, this is not always the case. _____ (2) Many blind computer users have trouble finding information on the Web. _____ (3) Often, this is the result of poor Web design it is the designer's job to make the site accessible. _____

(4) Most blind people use special software called screen readers, this

technology translates text into speech or Braille. _____ (5) However, screen readers do not always work well the information is sometimes hard to access. _____ (6) Web sites need to be understandable to all Internet users. _____ (7) The rights of blind Internet users may be protected by the Americans with Disabilities Act (ADA). _____ (8) We will have to wait for more cases to come to trial then we will know more. _____ (9) Meanwhile, we have to rely on software companies to make the necessary changes, this will take some time. _____ (10) However, there are incentives for these companies, the 1.5 million blind computer users are all potential customers. _____

24b Correcting Run-Ons

FYI

Correcting Run-Ons

You can correct run-ons in five ways:

1. *Use a period to create two separate sentences.*

   College costs are rising. Many students are worried.

2. *Use a coordinating conjunction (**and, but, or, nor, for, so,** or **yet**) to connect ideas.*

   College costs are rising, and many students are worried.

3. *Use a semicolon to connect ideas.*

   College costs are rising; many students are worried.

4. *Use a semicolon followed by a transitional word or phrase to connect ideas.*

   College costs are rising; as a result, many students are worried.

5. *Use a dependent word (**although, because, when,** and so on) to connect ideas.*

   Because college costs are rising, many students are worried.

The pages that follow explain and illustrate the five different ways to correct run-ons.

1. **Use a period to create two separate sentences.** Be sure each sentence begins with a capital letter and ends with a period.

INCORRECT (FUSED SENTENCE)	Gas prices are very high some people are buying hybrid cars.
INCORRECT (COMMA SPLICE)	Gas prices are very high, some people are buying hybrid cars.
CORRECT	Gas prices are very high. Some people are buying hybrid cars. (two separate sentences)

PRACTICE

24-2 Correct each of the following run-ons by using a period to create two separate sentences. Be sure both of your new sentences begin with a capital letter and end with a period.

Example: Stephen Colbert used to appear on *The Daily Show with Jon Stewart,* ~~now,~~ . Now, he has his own show called *The Colbert Report.*

1. In 2010, David Cameron became prime minister of the United Kingdom, he replaced Gordon Brown.

2. New York–style pizza usually has a thin crust Chicago-style "deep-dish pizza" has a thick crust.

3. Last week, Soraya won a text-messaging contest the prize for texting the fastest was five hundred dollars.

4. In some parts of Canada's Northwest Territory, the only way to transport supplies is over frozen lakes, being an ice road trucker is one of the most dangerous jobs in the world.

5. In 1961, the first Six Flags opened in Arlington, Texas, the six flags represent the six governments that have ruled the area that is now Texas.

2. **Use a coordinating conjunction to connect ideas.** If you want to indicate a particular relationship between ideas—for example, cause and effect or contrast—you can connect two independent clauses with a coordinating conjunction that makes this relationship clear. Always place a comma before the coordinating conjunction.

Coordinating Conjunctions			
and	for	or	yet
but	nor	so	

INCORRECT **(FUSED SENTENCE)**	Some schools require students to wear uni- forms other schools do not.
INCORRECT **(COMMA SPLICE)**	Some schools require students to wear uni- forms, other schools do not.
CORRECT	Some schools require students to wear uni- forms, but other schools do not. (clauses con- nected with the coordinating conjunction *but*, preceded by a comma)

PRACTICE

24-3   Correct each of the following run-ons by using a coordinating conjunction (*and, but, or, nor, for, so,* or *yet*) to connect
ideas. Be sure to put a comma before each coordinating conjunction.

Example: Many college students use Facebook to keep up with old

friends they also use the site to find new friends.
  , and

1. A car with soft tires gets poor gas mileage, keeping tires inflated is

   a good way to save money on gas.

2. It used to be difficult for football fans to see the first-down line

   on television, the computer-generated yellow line makes it much

   easier.

3. Indonesia has more volcanoes than any other country in the world

   the United States has the biggest volcano in the world, Hawaii's

   Mauna Loa.

4. Chefs can become famous for cooking at popular restaurants they

   can gain fame by hosting television shows.

5. Overcrowded schools often have to purchase portable classrooms or

   trailers this is only a temporary solution.

3. **Use a semicolon to connect ideas.** If you want to indicate a particularly close connection—or a strong contrast—between two ideas, use a semicolon.

> **INCORRECT**
> **(FUSED SENTENCE)**   Most professional basketball players go to college most professional baseball players do not.

> **INCORRECT**
> **(COMMA SPLICE)**   Most professional basketball players go to college, most professional baseball players do not.

> **CORRECT**   Most professional basketball players go to college; most professional baseball players do not. (clauses connected with a semicolon)

PRACTICE

24-4   Correct each of the following run-ons by using a semicolon to connect ideas. Do not use a capital letter after the semicolon unless the word that follows it is a proper noun.

Example: From 1930 until 2006, Pluto was known as a planet$\overset{;}{\underset{\wedge}{}}$ it is now known as a "dwarf planet."

1. Of all the states, Alaska has the highest percentage of Native American residents 16 percent of Alaskans are of Native American descent.

2. Satellites and global positioning systems (GPS) can help farmers to better understand the needs of their crops, these new tools are part of a trend called "precision agriculture."

3. Enforcing traffic laws can be difficult some cities use cameras to photograph cars that run red lights.

4. Old landfills can sometimes be made into parks, Cesar Chavez Park in Berkeley, California, is one example.

5. Freestyle motocross riders compete by doing jumps and stunts some famous FMX riders are Carey Hart, Nate Adams, and Travis Pastrana.

4. **Use a semicolon followed by a transitional word or phrase to connect ideas.** To show how two closely linked ideas are related, add a transitional word or phrase after the semicolon. The transition will indicate the specific relationship between the two clauses.

INCORRECT **(FUSED SENTENCE)**	Finding a part-time job can be challenging sometimes it is even hard to find an unpaid internship.
INCORRECT **(COMMA SPLICE)**	Finding a part-time job can be challenging, sometimes it is even hard to find an unpaid internship.
CORRECT	Finding a part-time job can be challenging; in fact, sometimes it is even hard to find an unpaid internship. (clauses connected with a semicolon followed by the transitional phrase *in fact*)

Some Frequently Used Transitional Words and Phrases

after all	for this reason	now
also	however	still
as a result	in addition	then
eventually	in fact	therefore
finally	instead	thus
for example	moreover	unfortunately
for instance	nevertheless	

For more complete lists of transitional words and phrases, see 19c.

PRACTICE

24-5 Correct each of the following run-ons by using a semicolon, followed by the transitional word or phrase in parentheses, to connect ideas. Be sure to put a comma after the transitional word or phrase.

Example: When babies are first born, they can only see black and
                   ; still,
white most baby clothes and blankets are made in pastel colors. (still)
      ^

1. Restaurant goers can expect to see different condiments in different regions of the country, few tables in the Southwest are without a bottle of hot sauce. (for example)

2. Every April, millions of people participate in TV-Turnoff Week by not watching television they read, spend time with family and friends, and generally enjoy their free time. (instead)

3. Today, few people can count on company pension plans, thirty years ago, most people could. (however)

4. Many people see bottled water as a waste of money tap water is free. (after all)

5. Dog breeders who run "puppy mills" are only concerned with making money they are not particularly concerned with their dogs' well-being. (unfortunately)

FYI

Connecting Ideas with Semicolons

Run-ons often occur when you use a transitional word or phrase to join two independent clauses *without also using a semicolon.*

INCORRECT (FUSED SENTENCE)	It is easy to download information from the Internet however it is not always easy to evaluate the information.
INCORRECT (COMMA SPLICE)	It is easy to download information from the Internet, however it is not always easy to evaluate the information.

To avoid this kind of run-on, always put a semicolon before the transitional word or phrase and a comma after it.

CORRECT	It is easy to download information from the Internet; however, it is not always easy to evaluate the information.

5. **Use a dependent word to connect ideas.** When one idea is dependent on another, you can connect the two ideas by adding a dependent word, such as *when, who, although,* or *because.*

INCORRECT (FUSED SENTENCE)	American union membership was high in the mid-twentieth century it has declined in recent years.

INCORRECT (COMMA SPLICE)	American union membership was high in the mid-twentieth century, it has declined in recent years.
CORRECT	Although American union membership was high in the mid-twentieth century, it has declined in recent years. (clauses connected with the dependent word *although*)
CORRECT	American union membership, which was high in the mid-twentieth century, has declined in recent years. (clauses connected with the dependent word *which*)

Some Frequently Used Dependent Words

after	even though	until
although	if	when
as	since	which
because	that	who
before	unless	

For complete lists of dependent words, including subordinating conjunctions and relative pronouns, see 20b and 20c.

PRACTICE

24-6 Correct each run-on in the following paragraph by adding a dependent word. Consult the list above to help you choose a logical dependent word. Be sure to add correct punctuation where necessary.

Example: Harlem was a rural area *until* improved transportation linked it to lower Manhattan.

(1) Contemporary historians have written about the Harlem Renaissance, its influence is still not widely known. (2) Harlem was populated mostly by European immigrants at the turn of the last century, it saw an influx of African Americans beginning in 1910. (3) This migration from the South continued Harlem became one of the largest African American

communities in the United States. (4) Many black artists and writers settled in Harlem during the 1920s. African American art flourished. (5) This "Harlem Renaissance" was an important era in American literary history it is not even mentioned in some textbooks. (6) Scholars recognize the great works of the Harlem Renaissance, they point to the writers Langston Hughes and Countee Cullen and the artists Henry Tanner and Sargent Johnson. (7) Zora Neale Hurston moved to Harlem from her native Florida in 1925, she began a book of African American folklore. (8) Harlem was an exciting place in the 1920s people from all over the city went there to listen to jazz and to dance. (9) The white playwright Eugene O'Neill went to Harlem to audition actors for his play *The Emperor Jones*, he made an international star of the great Paul Robeson. (10) The Great Depression occurred in the 1930s it led to the end of the Harlem Renaissance.

PRACTICE

24-7   Correct each of the following run-ons in one of these four ways: by creating two separate sentences, by using a coordinating conjunction, by using a semicolon, or by using a semicolon followed by a transitional word or phrase. Remember to put a semicolon before, and a comma after, each transitional word or phrase.

> **Example:**   Some fish-and-chip shops in Scotland sell deep-fried
>   *. Children*
> MARS bars ~~children~~ are the biggest consumers of these calorie-rich
>   ^
> bars.

1. Twenty-five percent of Americans under the age of fifty have one or more tattoos 50 percent of Americans under the age of twenty-five have one or more tattoos.

2. The ancient Greeks built their homes facing south this practice took advantage of light and heat from the winter sun.

3. In 1985, a team of musical artists recorded "We Are the World" in support of African famine relief in 2010, artists recorded the same song in support of Haitian earthquake relief.

4. The comic-strip cat Garfield is not cuddly Garzooka, a superhero cat who spits up radiated hairballs, is even less cuddly.

5. Horse-racing fans love jockey Calvin Borel for his enthusiasm during postrace interviews fellow jockeys respect him for his work ethic.

6. The average Swiss eats twenty-three pounds of chocolate each year the average American eats less than half that amount.

7. Flamenco—a Spanish style of dancing, singing, and clapping—was traditionally informal and unplanned it has been compared to improvisational American jazz.

8. Seattle is considered to have the most-educated population of any major city the medium-sized city of Arlington, Virginia, has a higher percentage of college graduates.

9. In Acadia National Park in Maine, large stones line the edges of steep trails the stones are called "Rockefeller's teeth" in honor of the trails' patron.

10. Allen Ginsberg was charged with obscenity for his book *Howl* the charges were dismissed.

PRACTICE

24-8   Correct each run-on in the following paragraph in the way that best indicates the relationship between ideas. Be sure to use appropriate punctuation.

Example: E. L. Doctorow's *Homer and Langley* tells the story of two
eccentric brothers it shows that truth can be stranger than fiction.
, and
^

(1) The Collyer brothers were wealthy and educated they lived and died alone in a filthy apartment. (2) Langley and Homer Collyer were

the sons of a doctor and an opera singer the brothers seemed to be as talented and motivated as their parents. (3) Langley played piano and studied engineering Homer had a law degree. (4) However, in their twenties and thirties, the brothers did not have jobs they lived with their parents in a Manhattan apartment. (5) Their parents died Langley and Homer inherited the apartment. (6) Gradually, they became frightened of outsiders they boarded up the windows and set traps for burglars. (7) They stopped paying their bills their heat, water, and electricity were shut off. (8) They also became compulsive hoarders, they could not throw anything away. (9) They accumulated thousands and thousands of books, numerous bundles of old newspapers, and fourteen pianos, they saved tons of garbage. (10) They got their water from a public park they collected discarded food from grocery stores and butcher shops. (11) Eventually, Langley was caught in one of his own burglar traps, the trap sent three bundles of newspapers and a suitcase tumbling on top of him. (12) Langley died of his injuries Homer died by his side, surrounded by mountains of trash.

TEST · Revise · Edit

Look back at your response to the Focus on Writing prompt on page 455. TEST what you have written. Then, revise and edit your work, making sure you identify and correct any run-ons.

EDITING PRACTICE: PARAGRAPH

Read the following student paragraph, and revise it to eliminate run-ons. Correct each run-on in the way that best indicates the relationship between ideas. Be sure to use appropriate punctuation. The first error has been corrected for you.

Cold Cases

 Cold cases are criminal investigations that have not been solved, they are not

officially closed. New evidence is found, cold cases may be reexamined. DNA tests

might provide new clues, a witness may come forward with new testimony. The

new evidence might lead to new suspects it might change the nature of the

crime. In some cases, an accident might be reclassified a homicide, in other cases

a murder might be ruled a suicide. Sometimes a person who was convicted of a

crime is found to be innocent. Cold cases usually involve violent crimes, rape and

murder are two examples. Investigators sometimes reopen very old cold cases, they

usually focus on more recent cases with living suspects. For serious crimes, there

is no limit on how much time may pass before a suspect is brought to justice, a

criminal may be convicted many years after the crime was committed. When cold

cases are solved, the crime is not undone, nevertheless victims' families finally

feel that justice has been served.

EDITING PRACTICE: ESSAY

Read the following student essay, and revise it to eliminate run-ons. Correct each run-on in the way that best indicates the relationship between ideas, and be sure to punctuate correctly. The first error has been corrected for you.

Comic-Book Heroes

Comic-book heroes have a long history, ~~they~~ *. They* originated in comic strips and radio shows. In the "Golden Age" of comic books, individual superheroes were the most popular characters, then teams and groups of superheroes were introduced. Today, some of these superheroes can be found in movies and in longer works of graphic fiction. Over the years, superheroes have remained very popular.

One of the first comic-book heroes was Popeye. Popeye had no supernatural powers, he battled his enemy, Bluto, with strength supplied by spinach. Another early comic-book hero was The Shadow he fought crime while wearing a cape and mask. The Shadow first appeared in comic books in 1930 later the character had his own radio show.

The late 1930s and 1940s are considered the Golden Age of comic books, many famous comic-book heroes were introduced at that time. The first Superman comic appeared in 1939. Superman came out from behind his secret identity as Clark Kent, he could fly "faster than a speeding bullet." Superman was the first comic-book hero who clearly had a superhuman ability to fight evil. Batman was different from Superman he had no real superpowers. Also, Superman was decent and moral, Batman was willing to break the rules. Wonder Woman appeared in 1941, she truly had superhuman qualities. For example, she could catch a bullet in one hand. She could also regrow a limb, she could tell when someone was not telling the truth.

Superheroes sometimes had help. Batman had Robin, Wonder Woman had her sister, Wonder Girl. Sometimes there were superhero teams, these were groups of superheroes who helped each other fight evil. The first team was the Justice League of America it included Superman, Batman, and Wonder Woman. Eventually, the Justice League fought against threats to the existence of the earth these threats even included alien invasions. Another superhero team was the X-Men they were mutants with supernatural abilities.

Now, comic books are not as popular as they used to be, however, superheroes can still be found in popular movies. Superman has been the main character in many movies there have also been several successful Batman, Spider-Man, Iron Man, and Fantastic Four movies. In longer works of graphic fiction, Superman, Batman, and the Fantastic Four are still heroes, recent works of graphic fiction feature Captain America and the Runaways. Apparently, people still want to see superheroes fight evil and win.

COLLABORATIVE ACTIVITY

Find an interesting paragraph in a newspaper or magazine article or on the Web. Working in a small group, recopy the paragraph onto a separate sheet of paper, creating run-ons. Exchange exercises with another group. Then, work in your own group to correct each fused sentence and comma splice in an exercise prepared by another group of students. When you have finished, return the exercise to the group that created it. Finally, continuing to work with members of your group, evaluate the other group's work on your exercise, comparing it to the original newspaper, magazine, or online paragraph.

review checklist

Run-Ons

☐ A run-on is an error that occurs when two sentences are joined incorrectly. There are two kinds of run-ons: fused sentences and comma splices. (See 24a.)

☐ A fused sentence occurs when two sentences are incorrectly joined without any punctuation. (See 24a.)

☐ A comma splice occurs when two sentences are joined with just a comma. (See 24a.)

☐ Correct a run-on in one of the following ways:

1. by creating two separate sentences

_____ . _____ .

(continued)

☑ LearningCurve
Run-Ons
bedfordstmartins.com
/focusonwriting

(continued from previous page)

2. by using a coordinating conjunction

_____, [coordinating conjunction] _____.

3. by using a semicolon

_____; _____.

4. by using a semicolon followed by a transitional word or phrase

_____; [transitional word or phrase], _____.

5. by using a dependent word

[Dependent word] _____, _____.

_____ [dependent word] _____. (See 24b.)

25 Fragments

focus on writing

Imagine you are writing a magazine ad for your favorite beverage, footwear, or health or beauty product. Write a paragraph that describes the product as persuasively as possible. Try to include a few memorable advertising slogans.

In this chapter, you will learn to
- recognize fragments (25a)
- correct missing-subject fragments (25b)
- correct phrase fragments (25c)
- correct -*ing* fragments (25d)
- correct dependent-clause fragments (25e)

25a   Recognizing Fragments

☑ LearningCurve
Fragments
**bedfordstmartins.com
/focusonwriting**

A **fragment** is an incomplete sentence. Every sentence must include at least one subject and one verb, and every sentence must express a complete thought. If a group of words does not do *both* these things, it is a fragment and not a sentence—even if it begins with a capital letter and ends with a period.

The following is a complete sentence.

S   V

SENTENCE   The <u>actors</u> in the play <u>were</u> very talented. (The sentence includes both a subject and a verb and expresses a complete thought.)

Because a sentence must have both a subject and a verb and express a complete thought, the following groups of words are not complete sentences; they are fragments.

FRAGMENT (NO VERB)   The actors in the play. (What point is being made about the actors?)

FRAGMENT (NO SUBJECT)   Were very talented. (Who were very talented?)

FRAGMENT (NO SUBJECT OR VERB)   Very talented. (Who was very talented?)

FRAGMENT (DOES NOT EXPRESS COMPLETE THOUGHT)   Because the actors in the play were very talented. (What happened because they were very talented?)

FYI

Spotting Fragments

Fragments almost always appear next to complete sentences.

┌──── COMPLETE SENTENCE ────┐┌───────── FRAGMENT ─────────┐
Celia took two electives. Physics 320 and Spanish 101.

The fragment above does not have a subject or a verb. The complete sentence that comes before it, however, has both a subject (*Celia*) and a verb (*took*).

Often, you can correct a fragment by attaching it to an adjacent sentence that supplies the missing words. (This sentence will usually appear right before the fragment.)

Celia took two electives, Physics 320 and Spanish 101.

WORD POWER

adjacent next to

PRACTICE

25-1 Some of the following items are fragments, and others are complete sentences. On the line following each item, write *F* if it is a fragment and *S* if it is a complete sentence.

Example: Star formations in the night sky. ____*F*____

1. To save as much as possible for college. _____

2. The judge gave her a two-year sentence. _____

3. A birthday on Christmas Day. _____

4. Because he lost ten pounds on his new diet. _____

5. Working in the garden and fixing the roof. _____

6. Sonya flew to Mexico. _____

7. Starts in August in many parts of the country. _____

8. And slept in his own bed last night. _____

9. Famous for her movie roles. _____

10. A phone that also plays music and takes photos. _____

PRACTICE

25-2   In the following paragraph, some of the numbered groups of words are missing a subject, a verb, or both. First, underline each fragment. Then, decide how each fragment could be attached to a nearby word group to create a complete new sentence. Finally, rewrite the entire paragraph, using complete sentences, on the lines provided.

Example: Gatorade was invented at the University of Florida. <u>To help the Florida Gators fight dehydration.</u>

Rewrite: *Gatorade was invented at the University of Florida to help the Florida Gators fight dehydration.*

(1) Doctors discovered that football players were losing electrolytes and carbohydrates. (2) Through their sweat. (3) They invented a drink. (4) That replaced these important elements. (5) Gatorade tasted terrible. (6) But did its job. (7) The Florida Gators survived a very hot season. (8) And won most of their games. (9) Now, Gatorade is used by many college and professional football teams. (10) As well as baseball, basketball, tennis, and soccer teams.

Rewrite:

_____

_____

_____

_____

_____

25b Missing-Subject Fragments

Every sentence must include both a subject and a verb. If the subject is left out, the sentence is incomplete. In the following example, the first word group is a sentence. It includes both a subject (*He*) and a verb (*packed*). However, the second word group is a fragment. It includes a verb (*took*), but it does not include a subject.

┌──────── SENTENCE ────────┐ ┌──────── FRAGMENT ────────┐
He packed his books and papers. And also took an umbrella.

The best way to correct this kind of fragment is to attach it to the sentence that comes right before it. This sentence will usually contain the missing subject.

> **CORRECT**   He packed his books and papers and also took an umbrella.

Another way to correct this kind of fragment is to add the missing subject.

> **CORRECT**   He packed his books and papers. He also took an umbrella.

PRACTICE

25-3   Each of the following items includes a missing-subject fragment. Using one of the two methods explained above, correct each fragment.

Example: Back-to-school sales are popular with students. And with their parents.

Back-to-school sales are popular with students and with their parents.   or

Back-to-school sales are popular with students. The sales are also popular

with their parents.

1. Quitting smoking is difficult. But is really worth the effort.

   _____

2. Some retailers give a lot of money to charity. And even donate part of their profits.

   _____

   _____

3. Geography bees resemble spelling bees. But instead test the contestants' knowledge of countries around the world.

   _____

   _____

4. School uniforms are often preferred by parents. And also favored by many school principals.

_____

_____

5. During the Cold War, the Soviet Union and the United States were rivals. But never actually fought a war with each other.

_____

_____

6. Scooters have been around for many years. And have recently become popular again.

_____

_____

7. After cosmetic surgery, one can look younger. And feel younger, too.

_____

_____

8. Online shopping sites sometimes offer free shipping. Or have lower prices than local stores.

_____

_____

9. Pro-football linemen can weigh more than 300 pounds. But are still able to run fast.

_____

_____

10. Using an electric toothbrush can be good for the teeth. And promotes healthy gums.

_____

_____

25c   Phrase Fragments

Every sentence must include a subject and a verb. A **phrase** is a group of words that is missing a subject or a verb or both. When you punctuate a phrase as if it is a sentence, you create a fragment.

If you spot a phrase fragment in your writing, you can often correct it by attaching it to the sentence that comes directly before it.

Appositive Fragments

An **appositive** identifies, renames, or describes an adjacent noun or pronoun. An appositive cannot stand alone as a sentence.

To correct an appositive fragment, attach it to the sentence that comes right before it. (This sentence will contain the noun or pronoun that the appositive describes.)

┌─ FRAGMENT ─

INCORRECT   He decorated the room in his favorite colors. Brown and

black.

CORRECT   He decorated the room in his favorite colors, brown and

black.

Sometimes a word or expression like *especially, except, including, such as, for example,* or *for instance* introduces an appositive. Even if an appositive is introduced by one of these expressions, it is still a fragment.

┌FRAGMENT┐

INCORRECT   A balanced diet should include high-fiber foods. Such as

leafy vegetables, fruits, beans, and whole-grain bread.

CORRECT   A balanced diet should include high-fiber foods, such as

leafy vegetables, fruits, beans, and whole-grain bread.

Prepositional Phrase Fragments

A **prepositional phrase** consists of a preposition and its object. A prepositional phrase cannot stand alone as a sentence. To correct a prepositional phrase fragment, attach it to the sentence that comes immediately before it.

	┌────── FRAGMENT ──────┐
INCORRECT	She promised to stand by him. In sickness and in health.
CORRECT	She promised to stand by him in sickness and in health.

Infinitive Fragments

An **infinitive** consists of *to* plus the base form of the verb (*to be, to go, to write*). An infinitive phrase (*to be free, to go home, to write a novel*) cannot stand alone as a sentence. You can usually correct an infinitive fragment by attaching it to the sentence that comes directly before it.

	┌───── FRAGMENT ─────┐
INCORRECT	Eric considered dropping out of school. To start his own business.
CORRECT	Eric considered dropping out of school to start his own business.

You can also add the words needed to complete the sentence.

CORRECT	Eric considered dropping out of school. He wanted to start his own business.

PRACTICE

25-4 In the following paragraph, some of the numbered groups of words are phrase fragments. First, identify each fragment by labeling it *F.* Then, decide how each fragment could be attached to an adjacent sentence to create a complete new sentence. Finally, rewrite the entire paragraph, using complete sentences, on the lines provided.

Example: Mazes have been popular among puzzle solvers. _____
For years. _____*F*_____

Rewrite: *Mazes have been popular among puzzle solvers for years.*

(1) Mazes challenge people to find their way. _____ (2) Through a complicated route. _____ (3) Mazes have been constructed out of paving stones, cornfields, and rooms. _____ (4) Connected by doors. _____ (5) Printed mazes can be solved with a pen or

pencil. _____ (6) During the 1970s, many books and magazines published printed mazes. _____ (7) For children and adults. _____ (8) There is no foolproof way to escape. _____ (9) From a maze. _____ (10) One strategy is to keep turning to either the right or the left. _____ (11) To keep from getting lost. _____ (12) Mazes can be fun to explore. _____ (13) On foot or on paper. _____

Rewrite:

_____

_____

_____

_____

_____

_____

_____

PRACTICE
25-5

In the following paragraph, some of the numbered groups of words are phrase fragments. First, underline each fragment. Then, decide how each fragment could be attached to an adjacent sentence to create a complete new sentence. Finally, rewrite the entire paragraph, using complete sentences, on the lines provided.

Example: Florence Nightingale worked as a nurse. <u>During the Crimean War.</u>

Rewrite: *Florence Nightingale worked as a nurse during the Crimean War.*

(1) Nurses' uniforms have changed a lot. (2) Over the years. (3) Originally, nurses' uniforms looked like nuns' habits because nuns used to provide care. (4) To sick people. (5) In the late 1800s, a student of Florence Nightingale created a brown uniform. (6) With a white apron and cap.

(7) This uniform was worn by student nurses at her school. (8) The Florence Nightingale School of Nursing and Midwifery. (9) Eventually, nurses began to wear white uniforms, white stockings, white shoes, and starched white caps. (10) To stress the importance of cleanliness. (11) Many older people remember these uniforms. (12) With affection. (13) Today, most nurses wear bright, comfortable scrubs. (14) To help patients (especially children) feel more at ease.

Rewrite:

_____

_____

_____

_____

_____

_____

_____

_____

_____

PRACTICE

25-6 Each of the following items is a phrase fragment, not a sentence. Correct each fragment by adding any words needed to turn the fragment into a complete sentence. (You may add words before or after the fragment.)

Example: During World War I. _A flu epidemic killed millions of people during_

World War I. or _During World War I, a flu epidemic killed millions of people._

1. To be the best player on the team. _____

_____

2. From a developing nation in Africa. _____

_____

3. Such as tulips or roses. _____

_____

4. Behind door number 3. _____

_____

5. Including my parents and grandparents. _____

_____

6. With a new car in the driveway. _____

_____

7. To make a difficult career decision. _____

_____

8. For a long time. _____

_____

9. Turkey, stuffing, mashed potatoes, and cranberry sauce. _____

_____

10. In less than a year. _____

_____

25d   *-ing* Fragments

Every sentence must include a subject and a verb. If the verb is incomplete, a word group is a fragment, not a sentence.

An *-ing* verb cannot be a complete verb. It needs a **helping verb** to complete it. An *-ing* verb, such as **looking**, cannot stand alone in a sentence without a helping verb (*is looking, was looking, were looking,* and so on). When you use an *-ing* verb without a helping verb, you create a fragment.

FRAGMENT

INCORRECT   The twins are full of mischief. Always looking for trouble.

The best way to correct an *-ing* fragment is to attach it to the sentence that comes right before it.

CORRECT   The twins are full of mischief, always looking for trouble.

Another way to correct an *-ing* fragment is to add a subject and a helping verb.

CORRECT   The twins are full of mischief. They are always looking for trouble.

FYI

Being

As you write, be careful not to use the *-ing* verb *being* as if it were a complete verb.

INCORRECT   I decided to take a nap. The outcome being that I slept through calculus class.

To correct this kind of fragment, substitute a form of the verb *be* that can serve as the main verb in a sentence—for example, *is*, *was*, *are*, or *were*.

CORRECT   I decided to take a nap. The outcome was that I slept through calculus class.

PRACTICE

25-7   Each of the following items includes an *-ing* fragment. In each case, correct the fragment by attaching it to the sentence before it.

Example: Certain tips can help grocery shoppers. Saving them a lot of money.

Certain tips can help grocery shoppers, saving them a lot of money.

1. Always try to find a store brand. Costing less than the well-known and widely advertised brands.

   _____

   _____

2. Look for a product's cost per pound. Comparing it to the cost per pound of similar products.

   _____

   _____

3. Examine sale-priced fruits and vegetables. Checking carefully for damage or spoilage.

_____

_____

4. Buy different brands of the same product. Trying each one to see which brand you like best.

_____

_____

5. Use coupons whenever possible. Keeping them handy for future shopping trips.

_____

_____

PRACTICE

25-8   Each of the following items is an *-ing* fragment. Turn each fragment into a complete sentence by adding a subject and a helping verb. Write your revised sentence on the line below each fragment.

Example: Running up and down the stairs.

Revised: *Jane and her dog are always running up and down the stairs.*

1. Trying to decide where to live.

   Revised:_____

   _____

2. Really feeling optimistic about the future.

   Revised:_____

   _____

3. Always complaining about the lab manual.

   Revised:_____

   _____

4. Deciding whether or not to get a new cell phone.

Revised: _____

_____

5. Minding their own business.

Revised: _____

_____

25e Dependent-Clause Fragments

Every sentence must include a subject and a verb. Every sentence must also express a complete thought.

A **dependent clause** is a group of words that is introduced by a dependent word, such as *although, because, that,* or *after.* A dependent clause includes a subject and a verb, but it does not express a complete thought. Therefore, it cannot stand alone as a sentence. To correct a dependent-clause fragment, you must complete the thought.

The following dependent clause is incorrectly punctuated as if it were a sentence.

> **FRAGMENT**   After Simon won the lottery.

This fragment includes both a subject (*Simon*) and a complete verb (*won*), but it does not express a complete thought. What happened after Simon won the lottery? To turn this fragment into a sentence, you need to complete the thought.

> **SENTENCE**   After Simon won the lottery, he quit his night job.

Some dependent clauses are introduced by dependent words called **subordinating conjunctions**.

> **FRAGMENT**   Although Marisol had always dreamed of visiting America.

This fragment includes a subject (*Marisol*) and a complete verb (*had dreamed*), but it is not a sentence; it is a dependent clause introduced by the subordinating conjunction *although*.

To correct this kind of fragment, attach it to an **independent clause** (a simple sentence) to complete the idea. (You can often find the independent clause you need right before or right after the fragment.)

SENTENCE Although Marisol had always dreamed of visiting America, <u>she did not have enough money for the trip</u> until 1985.

Subordinating Conjunctions

after	even though	since	whenever
although	if	so that	where
as	if only	than	whereas
as if	in order that	that	wherever
as though	now that	though	whether
because	once	unless	while
before	provided that	until	
even if	rather than	when	

For information on how to use subordinating conjunctions, see 20b.

FYI

Correcting Dependent-Clause Fragments

The simplest way to correct a dependent-clause fragment is to cross out the dependent word that makes the idea incomplete.

~~Although~~ Marisol had always dreamed of visiting America.

However, when you delete the dependent word, readers may have trouble seeing the connection between the new sentence and the one before or after it. A better way to revise is to attach the dependent-clause fragment to an adjacent independent clause, as illustrated in the example at the top of this page.

Some dependent clauses are introduced by dependent words called **relative pronouns**.

FRAGMENT Novelist Richard Wright, <u>who</u> came to Paris in 1947.

FRAGMENT A quinceañera, <u>which</u> celebrates a Latina's fifteenth birthday.

FRAGMENT A key World War II battle <u>that</u> was fought on the Pacific island of Guadalcanal.

Each of the above sentence fragments includes a subject (*Richard Wright, quinceañera, battle*) and a complete verb (*came, celebrates, was fought*). However, they are not sentences because they do not express complete thoughts. In each case, a relative pronoun creates a dependent clause.

To correct each of these fragments, add the words needed to complete the thought.

> **SENTENCE** Novelist Richard Wright, who came to Paris in 1947, <u>spent the rest of his life there.</u>

> **SENTENCE** A quinceañera, which celebrates a Latina's fifteenth birthday, <u>signifies her entrance into womanhood.</u>

> **SENTENCE** A key World War II battle that was fought on the Pacific island of Guadalcanal <u>took place in 1943.</u>

Relative Pronouns

that	who	whomever
what	whoever	whose
which	whom	

For information on how to use relative pronouns, see 20c.

PRACTICE

25-9 Correct each of the following dependent-clause fragments by attaching it to the sentence before or after it. If the dependent clause comes at the beginning of a sentence, place a comma after it.

> **Example:** Before it became a state. West Virginia was part of Virginia.
>
> *Before it became a state, West Virginia was part of Virginia.*
> _____

1. Because many homeless people are mentally ill. It is hard to find places for them to live. _____

   _____

2. People do not realize how dangerous raccoons can be. Even though they can be found in many parts of the United States. _____

   _____

   _____

3. I make plans to be a better student. Whenever a new semester begins.

   _____

4. Until something changes. We will just have to accept the situation.

_____

5. Because it is a very controversial issue. My parents and I have agreed

not to discuss it. _____

_____

PRACTICE
25-10   Correct each of these dependent-clause fragments by adding the words needed to complete the idea.

Example: Many minor species of animals, which are rapidly disappearing.

Many minor species of animals, which are rapidly disappearing, need to be

protected.

1. The film that frightened me. _____

_____

2. People who drink and drive. _____

_____

3. Some parents who are very strict with their children. _____

_____

4. The Vietnam War, which many Americans did not support. _____

_____

5. Animals that are used in medical research. _____

_____

PRACTICE
25-11   Each of the following is a fragment. Some are missing a subject, some are phrases incorrectly punctuated as sentences, others do not have a complete verb, and still others are dependent clauses punctuated as sentences. Turn each fragment into a complete sentence, writing the revised sentence on the line below the fragment. Whenever possible, try creating two different revisions.

Example: Waiting in the dugout.

Revised: *Waiting in the dugout, the players chewed tobacco.*

Revised: *The players were waiting in the dugout.*

1. Although three-year-olds are still very attached to their parents.

Revised: _____

_____

Revised: _____

_____

2. Going around in circles.

Revised: _____

_____

Revised: _____

_____

3. To win the prize for the most unusual costume.

Revised: _____

_____

Revised: _____

_____

4. Students who thought they could afford to go to college.

Revised: _____

_____

Revised: _____

_____

5. On an important secret mission.

Revised: _____

_____

Revised: _____

_____

6. Because many instructors see cheating as a serious problem.

Revised: _____

_____

Revised: _____

_____

7. Hoping to get another helping of chocolate fudge cake.

Revised: _____

_____

Revised: _____

_____

8. The rule that I always felt was the most unfair.

Revised: _____

_____

Revised: _____

_____

9. A really exceptional worker.

Revised: _____

_____

Revised: _____

_____

10. Finished in record time.

Revised: _____

_____

Revised: _____

_____

TEST · Revise · Edit

Look back at your response to the Focus on Writing prompt on page 471. Reread each word group you have punctuated as a sentence, starting with the last one and working your way back; make sure that each one contains a subject and a verb. Then, underline any words ending in -*ing*; any subordinating conjunctions; and the words *which*, *that*, and *who*, making sure that the word groups they appear in are complete sentences. When you have finished, **TEST** the entire paragraph. Then, revise and edit your work.

EDITING PRACTICE: PARAGRAPH

Read the following student paragraph, which includes incomplete sentences. Underline each fragment. Then, correct the fragment by attaching it to a nearby sentence that completes the thought. The first fragment has been underlined and corrected for you.

Committed to Education

Teach for America is a nonprofit organization/ ~~That~~ *that* aims to improve education in poor communities. Teach for America hires recent college graduates and professionals. To teach in underserved schools. These teachers are not officially certified. But do receive intensive training. Working in these schools can be very challenging. It can also be very rewarding. For both the teachers and the students. Admission into the Teach for America program is very competitive. Even for graduates of Ivy League schools. Only 11 percent of applicants are accepted. These talented people become members of the teaching corps. Bringing with them a variety of experiences and backgrounds. Corps members commit to teach for two years. Although many choose to stay longer.

EDITING PRACTICE: ESSAY

Read the following student essay, which includes incomplete sentences. Underline each fragment. Then, correct the fragment by attaching it to an adjacent sentence that completes the idea. Be sure to punctuate correctly. The first fragment has been underlined and corrected for you.

Bad Behavior at the Movies

Some people have completely stopped/ ~~Going~~ *going* to the movies. They have

not stopped because they dislike the movies but because they dislike the

rude moviegoers. Who ruin their experience. One big problem is irritating cell-

phone use. There are also problems with noise. And with sharing the theater

space with strangers. All these issues can make going to the movies seem like

more trouble than it is worth.

Cell phones cause all sorts of problems. In movie theaters. People are told

to turn off their phones. But do not always do so. Loud cell-phone conversations

can be infuriating. To people who want to hear the movie. When a phone rings

during an important scene in the movie. It is especially annoying. Some

moviegoers even complain that bright text-message screens distract them. From

the movie. Of course, theaters could use jammers. To block all cell-phone signals.

Unfortunately, they would also block incoming emergency calls.

Noise in the movies also comes from other sources. Such as crying babies.

People pay money to watch a movie. Not to listen to a baby screaming. Crinkling

candy wrappers are also annoying. In addition, some moviegoers insist on talking

to each other. During the movie. In fact, they may make watching a movie an

interactive event. Talking to the actors and telling them what they should do

next. If they have seen the movie before, they may recite lines of dialogue

before the actors do. Spoiling the suspense for everyone else. Sometimes people

even talk loudly about subjects. That have nothing to do with the movie. In all

these cases, the noise is a problem. For anyone who wants to watch the movie

and hear the actors on the screen.

Finally, going to the movies requires sharing the theater with other people.

Who are neither relatives nor friends. Unfortunately, many people behave in

movie theaters the same way they behave at home. When they are watching television. They may put their feet up on the seats in front of them. Making it impossible for others to sit there. Moviegoers become very annoyed if someone sits right in front of them. And blocks their view of the screen. Of course, these issues do not come up at home. Where friends and relatives can easily work out any problems.

Irritating movie behavior has driven many people to stop going to movie theaters. To end this rude behavior, moviegoers need to become aware of the needs of others. And make a real effort to change their behavior. Selfishness is the problem; thinking about other people is the solution.

COLLABORATIVE ACTIVITY

Working in a group of three or four students, build as many sentences as you can from the fragments listed below. Use your imagination to create as many creative sentences as you can.

Example

FRAGMENT   Knowing he has an incredible memory

SENTENCES   Zack, knowing he has an incredible memory, wonders how he managed to forget everything he learned about chemistry.

Knowing he has an incredible memory, Monty the Magnificent is confident that he can amaze his audience.

FRAGMENTS

1. Wandering in the desert
2. Never worrying about anything
3. Looking for his ideal mate
4. Always using as much ketchup as possible
5. Starting a new job

review checklist

Fragments

☐ A fragment is an incomplete sentence. Every sentence must include a subject and a verb and express a complete thought. (See 25a.)

☐ Every sentence must include a subject. (See 25b.)

☐ Phrases cannot stand alone as sentences. (See 25c.)

☐ Every sentence must include a complete verb. (See 25d.)

☐ Dependent clauses cannot stand alone as sentences. (See 25e.)

26 Subject-Verb Agreement

focus on writing

This painting by Ralph Fasanella is called *Baseball Panorama*. In a paragraph, describe what is happening on the field and in the stands. (Use present tense verbs.)

In this chapter, you will learn to avoid agreement problems

- with compound subjects (26b)
- with *be*, *have*, and *do* (26c)
- when words come between the subject and the verb (26d)
- with collective noun subjects (26e)
- with indefinite pronoun subjects (26f)
- when verbs come before subjects (26g)

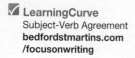

LearningCurve
Subject-Verb Agreement
**bedfordstmartins.com
/focusonwriting**

26a Understanding Subject-Verb Agreement

A sentence's subject (a noun or a pronoun) and its verb must **agree**: singular subjects take singular verbs, and plural subjects take plural verbs.

> The museum opens at ten o'clock. (singular noun subject *museum* takes singular verb *opens*)
>
> Both museums open at ten o'clock. (plural noun subject *museums* takes plural verb *open*)
>
> She always watches the eleven o'clock news. (singular pronoun subject *she* takes singular verb *watches*)
>
> They always watch the eleven o'clock news. (plural pronoun subject *they* takes plural verb *watch*)

Subject-Verb Agreement with Regular Verbs

	SINGULAR	PLURAL
First person	I play	Molly and I/we play
Second person	you play	you play
Third person	he/she/it plays	they play
	the man plays	the men play
	Molly plays	Molly and Sam play

**PRACTICE
26-1**

Underline the correct form of the verb in each of the following sentences. Make sure the verb agrees with its subject.

Example: Sometimes local farmers (<u>grow</u>/grows) unusual vegetables.

(1) Locavores (<u>choose</u>/chooses) to eat locally grown food for a number of reasons. (2) Some locavores (eat/eats) local food simply because they (like/likes) the taste. (3) When food (travel/travels) a long distance, it (lose/loses) some of its flavor and freshness. (4) By eating locally grown food, locavores also (hope/hopes) to decrease the use of fossil fuels. (5) After all, food transportation (require/requires) a lot of energy. (6) In addition, locavores (visit/visits) farmers' markets to support local producers. (7) Local farmers (need/needs) their community's support to survive. (8) In some cases, local food supporters (buy/buys) only food produced within 50 or 100 miles. (9) In colder or drier regions, however, the climate (make/makes) such a strict policy difficult. (10) More often, a locavore diet (contain/contains) a mix of food from local and faraway places.

> **WORD POWER**
>
> **locavore** a person who eats only locally produced foods

PRACTICE
26-2
Fill in the blank with the correct present tense form of the verb.

Example: Americans ___*commute*___ an average of 25 minutes to work each day. (commute)

(1) "Extreme commuters" _____ at least 90 minutes getting to work. (spend) (2) Their commutes _____ much longer than the average American's trip to work. (take) (3) Sometimes an extreme commuter even _____ state lines to get to work. (cross) (4) Often, a person _____ an extra-long commute for housing reasons. (choose) (5) Far outside the city, the "exurbs" _____ more affordable houses. (offer) (6) A more rural area usually _____ more peaceful surroundings as well. (provide) (7) Many extreme commuters _____ the time they spend commuting. (hate) (8) Others _____ the time they get

to think, talk to other commuters, or listen to music. (enjoy) (9) In any case, extreme commuters usually _____ a long way to work because they have to. (travel) (10) For better or worse, more and more people _____ extreme commuters every year. (become)

26b Compound Subjects

The subject of a sentence is not always a single word. It can also be a **compound subject**, made up of two or more subjects joined by *and* or *or*. To avoid subject-verb agreement problems with compound subjects, follow these rules.

1. When the parts of a compound subject are connected by *and*, the compound subject takes a plural verb.

   John and Marsha share an office.

2. When the parts of a compound subject are connected by *or*, the verb agrees with the part of the subject that is closer to it.

   The mayor or the council members meet with community groups.

   The council members or the mayor meets with community groups.

PRACTICE
26-3 Underline the correct form of the verb in each of the following sentences. Make sure that the verb agrees with its compound subject.

Example: Every summer, wind and rain (<u>pound</u>/pounds) the small shack on the beach.

1. Trophies and medals (fill/fills) my sister's bedroom.

2. Mashed potatoes and gravy (come/comes) with all our chicken dinners.

3. The instructor or his graduate students (grade/grades) the final exams.

4. A voice coach and a piano instructor (teach/teaches) each of the gifted students.

5. Pollen or cat hair (trigger/triggers) allergies in many people.

6. Psychologists or social workers (provide/provides) crisis counseling.

7. Exercise and healthy eating habits (lead/leads) to longer lives.

8. Both parents or only the father (walk/walks) the bride down the aisle at a wedding.

9. The restaurant owner and his daughters (greet/greets) customers as they enter.

10. Flowers or a get-well balloon (cheer/cheers) people up when they are ill.

26c   *Be, Have,* and *Do*

The verbs *be, have,* and *do* are irregular in the present tense. For this reason, they can present problems with subject-verb agreement. Memorizing their forms is the only sure way to avoid such problems.

Subject-Verb Agreement with *Be*

	SINGULAR	PLURAL
First person	I am	we are
Second person	you are	you are
Third person	he/she/it is	they are
	Tran is	Tran and Ryan are
	the boy is	the boys are

Subject-Verb Agreement with *Have*

	SINGULAR	PLURAL
First person	I have	we have
Second person	you have	you have
Third person	he/she/it has	they have
	Shana has	Shana and Robert have
	the student has	the students have

> ### Subject-Verb Agreement with *Do*
>
> | | SINGULAR | PLURAL |
> |--------------|----------------|----------------|
> | First person | I do | we do |
> | Second person | you do | you do |
> | Third person | he/she/it does | they do |
> | | Ken does | Ken and Mia do |
> | | the book does | the books do |

PRACTICE

26-4   Fill in the blank with the correct present tense form of the verb *be*, *have*, or *do*.

Example: Sometimes people ____*do*____ damage without really meaning to. (do)

(1) Biologists _____ serious worries about the damage that invading species of animals can cause. (have) (2) The English sparrow _____ one example. (be) (3) It _____ a role in the decline in the number of bluebirds. (have) (4) On the Galapagos Islands, cats _____ another example. (be) (5) Introduced by early explorers, they currently _____ much damage to the eggs of the giant tortoises that live on the islands. (do) (6) Scientists today _____ worried now about a new problem. (be) (7) This _____ a situation caused by wildlife agencies that put exotic fish into lakes and streams. (be) (8) They _____ this to please those who enjoy fishing. (do) (9) Although popular with people who fish, this policy _____ major drawbacks. (have) (10) It _____ one drawback in particular: many native species of fish have been pushed close to extinction. (have)

26d   Words between Subject and Verb

Keep in mind that a verb must always agree with its subject. Don't be confused when a group of words (for example, a prepositional phrase) comes between the subject and the verb. These words do not affect subject-verb agreement.

	s	v
CORRECT	High <u>levels</u> of mercury <u>occur</u> in some fish.	
	s	v
CORRECT	<u>Water</u> in the fuel lines <u>causes</u> an engine to stall.	
	s	v
CORRECT	<u>Food</u> between the teeth <u>leads</u> to decay.	

An easy way to identify the subject of the sentence is to cross out the words that come between the subject and the verb.

High levels ~~of mercury~~ occur in some fish.

Water ~~in the fuel lines~~ causes an engine to stall.

Food ~~between the teeth~~ leads to decay.

FYI

Words between Subject and Verb

Look out for words such as *in addition to, along with, together with, as well as, except,* and *including*. Phrases introduced by these words do not affect subject-verb agreement.

s   v

St. <u>Thomas</u>, ~~along with St. Croix and St. John~~, <u>is</u> part of the

United States Virgin Islands.

PRACTICE

26-5 In each of the following sentences, cross out the words that separate the subject and the verb. Then, underline the subject of the sentence once and the verb that agrees with the subject twice.

Example: The <u>messages</u> ~~on the phone~~ (say/<u><u>says</u></u>) that Carol is out

of town.

1. Each summer, fires from lightning (cause/causes) great damage.

2. Books downloaded onto an eReader usually (cost/costs) less than

 print books.

3. One out of ten men (gets/get) prostate cancer.

4. The woodstove in the living room (heat/heats) the entire house.

5. Trans fat in a variety of foods (lead/leads) to increased rates of heart disease.

6. A good set of mechanic's tools (costs/cost) a lot of money.

7. New Orleans, along with other Gulf Coast cities, (suffers/suffer) from severe flooding.

8. The United States as well as Germany and Japan (produces/produce) the world's best cars.

9. Fans at a concert (gets/get) angry if the band is late.

10. The book on the table (look/looks) interesting.

26e   Collective Noun Subjects

Collective nouns are words (such as *family* and *audience*) that name a group of people or things but are singular. Because they are singular, they always take singular verbs.

>   s   v
> The <u>team</u> <u>practices</u> five days a week in the gym.

Frequently Used Collective Nouns

army	club	family	jury
association	committee	gang	mob
band	company	government	team
class	corporation	group	union

PRACTICE
26-6   Fill in the blank with the correct present tense form of the verb.

Example: Our government ____*is*____ democratically elected by the people. (be)

1. The Caribbean Culture Club _____ on the first Thursday of every month. (meet)

2. The company no longer _____ health insurance for part-time employees. (provide)

3. The basketball team _____ competing in the division finals next week. (be)

4. After two days, the jury _____ been unable to reach a verdict. (have)

5. The union _____ guaranteed raises for its members. (want)

26f   Indefinite Pronoun Subjects

Indefinite pronouns—*anybody, everyone,* and so on—do not refer to a particular person, place, or idea.

Most indefinite pronouns are singular and take singular verbs.

    s   v
No one likes getting up early.
    s   v
Everyone likes to sleep late.
    s   v
Somebody likes beets.

Singular Indefinite Pronouns

another	either	neither	somebody
anybody	everybody	nobody	someone
anyone	everyone	no one	something
anything	everything	nothing	
each	much	one	

A few indefinite pronouns (*both, many, several, few, others*) are plural and take plural verbs.

    s   v
Many were left homeless by the flood.

FYI

Indefinite Pronouns as Subjects

If a prepositional phrase comes between the indefinite pronoun and the verb, cross out the prepositional phrase to help you identify the sentence's subject.

s   v

Each ~~of the boys~~ has a bike.

s   v

Many ~~of the boys~~ have bikes.

PRACTICE

26-7   Underline the correct verb in each sentence.

Example: As my friends and I know, anything (<u>helps</u>/help) when it comes to paying for college.

1. One of my friends (has/have) an academic scholarship.

2. Another (relies/rely) entirely on loans.

3. Several of us (works/work) on weekends.

4. Everybody (says/say) that work-study jobs are best.

5. Many of the most interesting work-study jobs (is/are) located on campus.

6. Others (places/place) students off campus with nonprofits or government agencies.

7. Some of the work-study jobs (tends/tend) to be better than a regular job.

8. Not everyone (understands/understand) the demands of school, but work-study employers do.

9. Nobody (says/say) juggling work and school is simple, but work-study makes it easier.

10. Each of my work-study friends (is/are) glad to have this option.

26g   Verbs before Subjects

A verb always agrees with its subject—even if the verb comes *before* the subject. In questions, for example, word order is reversed, with the verb coming before the subject or with the subject coming between two parts of the verb.

> V   S
> Where is the bank?
>
> V   S   V
> Are you going to the party?

If you have trouble identifying the subject of a question, answer the question with a statement. (In the statement, the subject will come before the verb.)

> V   S   S   V
> Where is the bank? The bank is on Walnut Street.

FYI

There Is and There Are

When a sentence begins with *there is* or *there are*, the word *there* is not the subject of the sentence. The subject comes after the form of the verb *be*.

> V   S
> There is one chief justice on the Supreme Court.
>
> V   S
> There are nine justices on the Supreme Court.

PRACTICE
26-8

Underline the subject of each sentence, and circle the correct form of the verb.

Example: Who (is/are) the baseball player who broke Hank Aaron's home-run record?

1. Where (do/does) snakes go in the winter?

2. Why (do/does) people who cannot afford them buy lottery tickets?

3. (Is/Are) there any states that do not follow Daylight Savings Time?

4. How (do/does) an immigrant become a citizen?

5. There (is/are) three branches of government in the United States.

6. There (is/are) one way to improve vocabulary—read often.

7. There (is/are) some money available for financial aid.

8. There (is/are) four steps involved in changing the oil in a car.

9. What (is/are) the country with the highest literacy rate?

10. Where (do/does) the football team practice in the off-season?

TEST · Revise · Edit

Look back at your response to the Focus on Writing prompt on page 495. **TEST** what you have written. Then, revise and edit your work, making sure that all your verbs agree with their subjects. Pay particular attention to agreement problems when sentences contain the following elements:

- Compound subjects
- The verbs *be*, *have*, and *do*
- Words between the subject and the verb
- Collective noun subjects
- Indefinite pronoun subjects
- Verbs before subjects

EDITING PRACTICE: PARAGRAPH

Read the following student paragraph, which includes errors in subject-verb agreement. Decide whether each of the underlined verbs agrees with its subject. If it does not, cross out the verb, and write in the correct form. If it does, write *C* above the verb. The first sentence has been done for you.

Conflict Diamonds

Today, many people <u>know</u> about conflict diamonds, and most ~~wants~~ *want* this violent trade to end. These illegal diamonds <u>comes</u> from countries where there <u>are</u> civil war. Most often, the origin of these stones <u>is</u> an unstable central or west African nation. Rebel groups in these countries <u>mines</u> the diamonds and <u>sells</u> them to raise money for weapons. In the process, local people, who <u>does</u> not benefit from the sale of the diamonds, often <u>gets</u> hurt or killed. How <u>does</u> a person who wants to buy a diamond avoid buying a conflict diamond? Once a diamond <u>reach</u> a store, neither a customer nor a gem expert <u>have</u> the ability to determine its history just by looking at it. However, a consumer can ask for proof that the diamond <u>is</u> "conflict-free." Each of the diamonds in a store <u>are</u> supposed to have an official certificate to prove that it <u>is</u> legal.

EDITING PRACTICE: ESSAY

Read the following student essay, which includes errors in subject-verb agreement. Decide whether each of the underlined verbs agrees with its subject. If it does not, cross out the verb, and write in the correct form. If it does, write *C* above the verb. The first sentence has been done for you.

Party in the Parking Lot

Fun at football games ~~are~~ *is* not limited to cheering for the home team. Many people <u>arrives</u> four or five hours early, <u>sets</u> up grills in the parking lot, and <u>start</u> cooking. Typically, fans <u>drives</u> to the stadium in a pickup truck, a station wagon,

507

or an SUV. They <u>open</u> up the tailgate, <u>puts</u> out the food, and <u>enjoys</u> the fun with their friends. In fact, tailgating <u>is</u> so popular that, for some fans, it is more important than the game itself.

What <u>do</u> it take to tailgate? First, most tailgaters <u>plan</u> their menus in advance. To avoid forgetting anything, they <u>makes</u> lists of what to bring. Paper plates, along with a set of plastic cups, <u>make</u> it unnecessary to bring home dirty dishes. Jugs of water <u>is</u> essential, and damp towels <u>helps</u> clean up hands and faces. Also, lightweight chairs or another type of seating <u>is</u> important.

At the game, parking near a grassy area or at the end of a parking row <u>are</u> best. This location <u>give</u> tailgaters more space to cook and eat. If the food <u>are</u> ready two hours before the game <u>start</u>, there <u>is</u> plenty of time to eat and to clean up.

Some tailgaters <u>buys</u> expensive equipment. The simple charcoal grill <u>have</u> turned into a combination grill, cooler, and foldout table with a portable awning. There <u>is</u> grills with their own storage space. Other grills <u>swings</u> out from the tailgate to provide easy access to the vehicle's storage area. Some deluxe grills even <u>has</u> their own beer taps, stereo systems, and sinks.

Whatever equipment tailgaters <u>brings</u> to the game, the most important factors <u>is</u> food and companionship. There <u>is</u> a tradition of sharing food and swapping recipes with other tailgaters. Most tailgaters <u>loves</u> to meet and to compare recipes. For many, the tailgating experience <u>is</u> more fun than the game itself.

COLLABORATIVE ACTIVITY

Working in a group of four students, list ten nouns (five singular and five plural)—people, places, or things—along the left-hand side of a sheet of paper. Beside each noun, write the present tense form of a verb that could logically be used with the noun. Then, expand each noun-and-verb combination you listed into a complete sentence. Next, write a sentence that could logically follow each of these sentences, using a pronoun as the subject of the new sentence. Make sure the pronoun you choose refers to the noun in the previous sentence, as in this example: *Alan watches three movies a week. He is addicted to films.* Check to be certain the subjects in your sentences agree with the verbs.

review checklist

Subject-Verb Agreement

- Singular subjects (nouns and pronouns) take singular verbs, and plural subjects take plural verbs. (See 26a.)

- Special rules govern subject-verb agreement with compound subjects. (See 26b.)

- The irregular verbs *be*, *have*, and *do* often present problems with subject-verb agreement in the present tense. (See 26c.)

- Words that come between the subject and the verb do not affect subject-verb agreement. (See 26d.)

- Collective nouns are singular and take singular verbs. (See 26e.)

- Most indefinite pronouns, such as *no one* and *everyone*, are singular and take a singular verb when they serve as the subject of a sentence. A few are plural and take plural verbs. (See 26f.)

- A sentence's subject and verb must always agree, even if the verb comes before the subject. (See 26g.)

LearningCurve
Subject-Verb Agreement
bedfordstmartins.com /focusonwriting

27 Illogical Shifts

focus on writing

This picture shows a mother and daughter on Take Your Daughters and Sons to Work Day. Do you think programs like this help children succeed? Think for a bit about how parents can motivate their children to set appropriate goals and work to achieve them. Then, write a paragraph expressing your ideas.

In this chapter, you will learn to avoid illogical shifts in

- tense (27a)
- person (27b)
- voice (27c)

A **shift** occurs whenever a writer changes **tense**, **person**, or **voice**. As you write and revise, be sure that any shifts you make are **logical**—that is, that they occur for a reason.

27a Shifts in Tense

Tense is the form a verb takes to show when an action takes place or when a situation occurs. Some shifts in tense are necessary—for example, to indicate a change from past time to present time.

☑ LearningCurve
Verbs
bedfordstmartins.com
/focusonwriting

> LOGICAL SHIFT   When they first came out, cell phones were large and bulky, but now they are small and compact.

An **illogical shift in tense** occurs when a writer shifts from one tense to another for no apparent reason.

> ILLOGICAL SHIFT IN TENSE   The dog walked to the fireplace. Then, he circles twice and lies down in front of the fire. (shift from past tense to present tense)

> REVISED   The dog walked to the fireplace. Then, he circled twice and lay down in front of the fire. (consistent use of past tense)

> REVISED   The dog walks to the fireplace. Then, he circles twice and lies down in front of the fire. (consistent use of present tense)

PRACTICE

27-1 Edit the sentences in the following paragraph to correct illogical shifts in tense. If a sentence is correct, write *C* in the blank.

Example: The 100th Battalion of the 442nd Infantry is the only remaining United States Army Reserve ground combat unit that fought in World War II. _____*C*_____

(1) During World War II, the 100th Battalion of the 442nd Combat Infantry Regiment was made up of young Japanese Americans who are eager to serve in the U.S. Army. _____ (2) At the start of World War II, 120,000 Japanese Americans were sent to relocation camps because the government feared that they might be disloyal to the United States. _____ (3) However, in 1943, the United States needed more soldiers, so it sends recruiters to the camps to ask for volunteers. _____ (4) The Japanese American volunteers are organized into the 442nd Combat Infantry Regiment. _____ (5) The soldiers of the 442nd Infantry fought in some of the bloodiest battles of the war, including the invasion of Italy at Anzio and a battle in Bruyeres, France, where they capture over two hundred enemy soldiers. _____ (6) When other U.S. troops are cut off by the enemy, the 442nd Infantry soldiers were sent to rescue them. _____ (7) The Japanese American soldiers suffered the highest casualty rate of any U.S. unit and receive over eighteen thousand individual decorations. _____ (8) Former senator Daniel Inouye of Hawaii, a Japanese American, was awarded the Distinguished Service Cross for his bravery in Italy and has to have his arm amputated. _____ (9) The 442nd Infantry was awarded more decorations than any other combat unit of its size and earns eight Presidential Unit citations. _____ (10) Today, the dedication and sacrifice of the 442nd Infantry is seen as evidence that Japanese Americans were patriotic and committed to freedom and democracy. _____

27b Shifts in Person

✓ **LearningCurve**
Pronoun Agreement and
Pronoun Reference
**bedfordstmartins.com
/focusonwriting**

Person is the form a pronoun takes to show who is speaking, spoken about, or spoken to.

Person

	SINGULAR	PLURAL
First person	I	we
Second person	you	you
Third person	he, she, it	they

An **illogical shift in person** occurs when a writer shifts from one person to another for no apparent reason.

ILLOGICAL SHIFT IN PERSON	The hikers were told that you had to stay on the trail. (shift from third person to second person)
REVISED	The hikers were told that they had to stay on the trail. (consistent use of third person)

ILLOGICAL SHIFT IN PERSON	Anyone can learn to cook if you practice. (shift from third person to second person)
REVISED	You can learn to cook if you practice. (consistent use of second person)
REVISED	Anyone can learn to cook if he or she practices. (consistent use of third person)

PRACTICE

27-2   The sentences in the following paragraph contain illogical shifts in person. Edit each sentence so that it uses pronouns consistently. Be sure to change any verbs that do not agree with the new subjects.

Example: Before a person finds a job in the fashion industry,
~~you have~~ *he or she has* to have some experience.

(1) Young people who want careers in the fashion industry do not always realize how hard you will have to work. (2) They think that working in the world of fashion will be glamorous and that you will make a lot of money. (3) In reality, no matter how talented you are, a recent college graduate entering the industry is paid only about $22,000 a year. (4) The manufacturers who employ new graduates expect you to work at least three years at this salary before you are promoted.

(5) A young designer may get a big raise if you are very talented, but this is unusual. (6) New employees have to pay their dues, and you soon realize that most of your duties are boring. (7) An employee may land a job as an assistant designer but then find that you have to color in designs that have already been drawn. (8) Other beginners discover that you spend most of your time typing up orders. (9) If a person is serious about working in the fashion industry, you have to be realistic. (10) For most newcomers to the industry, the ability to do what you are told to do is more important than your talent.

27c Shifts in Voice

Voice is the form a verb takes to indicate whether the subject is acting or is acted upon. When the subject is acting, the sentence is in the **active voice**. When the subject is acted upon, the sentence is in the **passive voice**.

> **ACTIVE VOICE** Nat Turner organized a slave rebellion in August 1831. (Subject *Nat Turner* is acting.)

> **PASSIVE VOICE** A slave rebellion was organized by Nat Turner in 1831. (Subject *rebellion* is acted upon.)

An **illogical shift in voice** occurs when a writer shifts from active to passive voice or from passive to active voice for no apparent reason.

> **ILLOGICAL SHIFT IN VOICE** J. D. Salinger wrote *The Catcher in the Rye*, and *Franny and Zooey* was also written by him. (active to passive)

> **REVISED** J. D. Salinger wrote *The Catcher in the Rye*, and he also wrote *Franny and Zooey*. (consistent use of active voice)

> **ILLOGICAL SHIFT IN VOICE** Radium was discovered by Marie Curie in 1910, and she won a Nobel Prize in chemistry in 1911. (passive to active)

> **REVISED** Marie Curie discovered radium in 1910, and she won a Nobel Prize in chemistry in 1911. (consistent use of active voice)

FYI

Correcting Illogical Shifts in Voice

You should usually use the active voice in your college writing because it is stronger and more direct than the passive voice.

To change a sentence from the passive to the active voice, determine who or what is acting, and make this noun the subject of a new active voice sentence.

PASSIVE VOICE   The campus escort service is used by my friends. (*My friends* are acting.)

ACTIVE VOICE   My friends use the campus escort service.

PRACTICE

27-3   The following sentences contain illogical shifts in voice. Revise each sentence by changing the underlined passive voice verb to the active voice.

Example:

Two teachers believed they could help struggling students in New York City schools, so "Chess in the Schools" was founded by them.

Two teachers believed they could help struggling students in New York City

schools, so they founded "Chess in the Schools."

1. Chess develops critical-thinking skills, and self-discipline and self-esteem are developed by players, too.

_____

_____

2. Because players face complicated chess problems, good problem-solving skills are developed by them.

_____

_____

3. Student chess players improve their concentration, and reading and math skills <u>can be improved</u> through this better concentration.

_____

_____

4. Chess teaches students how to lose as well as win, and that ability <u>will be needed</u> by students throughout their lives.

_____

_____

5. "Chess in the Schools" also helps keep students out of trouble because of the conflict-resolution skills <u>developed</u> by them.

_____

_____

TEST · Revise · Edit

Look back at your response to the Focus on Writing prompt on page 510. **TEST** what you have written. Then, revise and edit your work, paying particular attention to illogical shifts in tense, person, or voice.

EDITING PRACTICE: PARAGRAPH

Read the following student paragraph, which includes illogical shifts in tense, person, and voice. Edit the passage to eliminate the unnecessary shifts, making sure subjects and verbs agree. The first error has been corrected for you.

The Origin of Baseball Cards

The first baseball cards appeared in the late 1800s. These cardboard pictures

were

~~are~~ inserted in packs of cigarettes. Some people collected the cards, and the

cigarette companies use the cards to encourage people to buy their products.

By the early twentieth century, it was found by candy makers that one could use

baseball cards to sell candy to children, so they developed new marketing plans.

For example, each Cracker Jack box contains a baseball card. In 1933, gum

manufacturers packaged bubble gum with baseball cards to make "bubble gum

cards." Children could trade these cards. Sometimes children would put cards

in the spokes of their bike wheels. The cards made noise when the wheels turns.

Eventually, the bubble gum is dropped by the card manufacturers, and people

just bought the cards. Still, collecting baseball cards was seen as a hobby for

children until the 1970s, when dealers began to sell their rarest cards at high

prices. Today, baseball-card collectors were mainly adults who are interested in

investment, not baseball. For example, in 2007, a rare Honus Wagner baseball

card sells for a record $2.8 million.

EDITING PRACTICE: ESSAY

Read the following essay, which includes illogical shifts in tense, person, and voice. Edit the passage to eliminate the illogical shifts, making sure subjects and verbs agree. The first sentence has been edited for you.

A Different Kind of Vacation

During our upcoming winter break, my sister and I ~~were~~ ^{are} going to Belize to help build a school. Like many people, we want to travel and see new places, but we did not want to be tourists who only see what is in a guidebook. We also want to help people who are less fortunate than we were. Volunteering gives us the opportunity to combine travel with community service and to get to know a different culture at the same time.

These days, many people are using his or her vacation time to do volunteer work. Lots of charitable organizations offer short-term projects during school or holiday breaks. For most projects, no experience was necessary. All people need is his or her interest in other people and a desire to help.

For example, last year my aunt goes to Tanzania to work in a health clinic. She loved her experience volunteering in a poor rural community where you help local doctors. She also loved the host family who shared their modest house with her. Before she left Tanzania, she and some of the other volunteers climb Mount Kilimanjaro. She said it was the best vacation she had ever had.

Although many volunteer vacations focus on improving schools or health care, a wide range of projects was available. Everyone can find work that suits their interests. For instance, people can volunteer to help preserve the environment, or you can work to protect women's rights. Countries all over the world welcome volunteers because help is needed by a lot of people.

My sister and I decided to help with the school in Belize because we believe a clean and safe place to learn is deserved by everyone. We are also eager to do some construction, get to know the local people, and enjoy the warm weather. If we have enough time, we hoped to visit some Mayan ruins as well. All in all, we are looking forward to a rewarding and unforgettable experience.

COLLABORATIVE ACTIVITY

Working in a group of three or four students, make up a test with five sentences containing illogical shifts in tense, person, and voice. Exchange tests with another group in the class. After you have taken their test, compare your answers with theirs.

review checklist

Illogical Shifts

- [ ] An illogical shift in tense occurs when a writer shifts from one tense to another for no apparent reason. (See 27a.)

- [ ] An illogical shift in person occurs when a writer shifts from one person to another for no apparent reason. (See 27b.)

- [ ] An illogical shift in voice occurs when a writer shifts from active to passive voice or from passive to active voice for no apparent reason. (See 27c.)

28 Misplaced and Dangling Modifiers

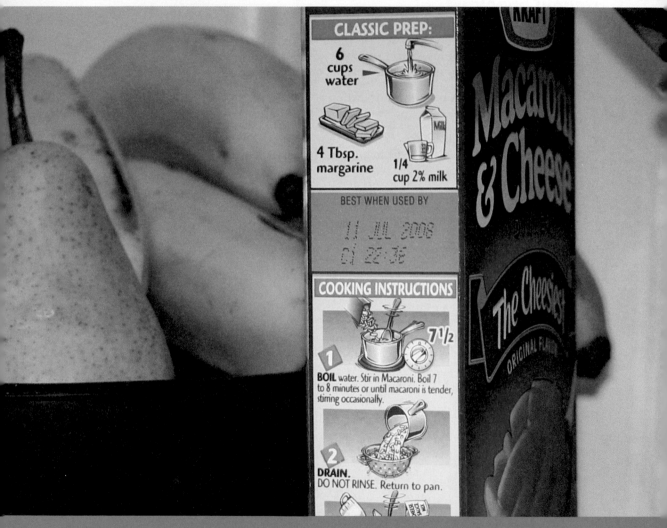

focus on writing

Think about your favorite food. Then—whether you've actually ever prepared it or not—try to write a one-paragraph recipe for it. Begin by describing the food; then, list the ingredients, and explain how to make it ready for the table.

In this chapter, you will learn to recognize and correct

- misplaced modifiers (28a)
- dangling modifiers (28b)

A **modifier** is a word or word group that identifies or describes another word in a sentence. Many word groups that act as modifiers are introduced by *-ing* (present participle) or *-ed* (past participle) modifiers. To avoid confusion, a modifier should be placed as close as possible to the word it modifies—ideally, directly before or directly after it.

Working in his garage, Steve Jobs invented the personal computer.

Rejected by Hamlet, Ophelia goes mad and drowns herself.

Used correctly, *-ing* and *-ed* modifiers provide useful information. Used incorrectly, however, these types of modifiers can be very confusing.

The two most common problems with modification are *misplaced modifiers* and *dangling modifiers*.

28a Correcting Misplaced Modifiers

A **misplaced modifier** appears to modify the wrong word because it is placed incorrectly in the sentence. To correct this problem, move the modifier so it is as close as possible to the word it is supposed to modify (usually directly before or after it).

INCORRECT Sarah fed the dog wearing her pajamas. (Was the dog wearing Sarah's pajamas?)

CORRECT Wearing her pajamas, Sarah fed the dog.

INCORRECT Dressed in a raincoat and boots, I thought my son was prepared for the storm. (Who was dressed in a raincoat and boots?)

CORRECT I thought my son, dressed in a raincoat and boots, was prepared for the storm.

PRACTICE

28-1 Underline the modifier in each of the following sentences. Then, draw an arrow to the word it modifies.

Example: Helping people worldwide, Doctors Without Borders is a group of volunteer medical professionals.

1. Suffering from famine and other disasters, some people are unable to help themselves.

2. Feeding and healing them, Doctors Without Borders improves their lives.

3. Responding to a recent earthquake, doctors arrived within three days to help with the relief effort.

4. Setting up refugee camps in Thailand, the group quickly helped its first survivors.

5. Some doctors, chartering a ship called *The Island of Light*, once provided medical aid to people escaping Vietnam by boat.

PRACTICE

28-2 Rewrite the following sentences, which contain misplaced modifiers, so that each modifier clearly refers to the word it logically modifies.

Example: Mark ate a pizza standing in front of the refrigerator.

Standing in front of the refrigerator, Mark ate a pizza.

1. The cat broke the vase frightened by a noise.

_____

_____

2. Running across my bathroom ceiling, I saw two large, hairy bugs.

_____

_____

3. Lori looked at the man sitting in the chair with red hair.

_____

_____

4. *ET* is a film about an alien directed by Steven Spielberg.

_____

_____

5. Covered with chocolate sauce, Fred loves ice cream sundaes.

_____

_____

6. After reading the poem, the meaning became clear to me.

_____

_____

7. The deer was hit by a car running across the street.

_____

_____

8. Dressed in a beautiful wedding gown, the groom watched the bride walk down the aisle.

_____

_____

9. The exterminator sprayed the insect wearing a mask.

_____

_____

10. With a mysterious smile, Leonardo da Vinci painted the *Mona Lisa*.

_____

_____

28b Correcting Dangling Modifiers

A **dangling modifier** "dangles" because the word it modifies does not appear in the sentence. Often, a dangling modifier comes at the beginning of a sentence and appears to modify the noun or pronoun that follows it.

Using my computer, the report was finished in two days.

In the sentence above, the modifier *Using my computer* seems to be modifying *the report*. But this makes no sense. (How can the report use a computer?) The word the modifier should logically refer to is missing. To correct this sentence, you need to supply this missing word.

Using my computer, I finished the report in two days.

To correct a dangling modifier, supply a word to which the modifier can logically refer.

INCORRECT Moving the microscope's mirror, the light can be directed onto the slide. (Can the light move the mirror?)

CORRECT Moving the microscope's mirror, you can direct the light onto the slide.

INCORRECT Paid in advance, the furniture was delivered. (Was the furniture paid in advance?)

CORRECT Paid in advance, the movers delivered the furniture.

PRACTICE

28-3 Each of the following sentences contains a dangling modifier. To correct each sentence, add a word to which the modifier can logically refer.

Example: Waiting inside, my bus passed by.

Waiting inside, I missed my bus.

1. Ordered by the school, the librarians sorted the books.

   _____

   _____

2. Pushing on the brakes, my car would not stop for the red light.

   _____

   _____

3. Short of money, the trip was canceled.

   _____

   _____

4. Working overtime, his salary almost doubled.

   _____

   _____

5. Angered by the noise, the concert was called off.

   _____

   _____

6. Using the correct formula, the problem was easily solved.

   _____

   _____

7. Tired and hungry, the assignment was finished by midnight.

   _____

   _____

8. Sitting on a park bench, the pigeons were fed.

   _____

   _____

9. Staying in bed on Sunday, the newspaper was read from beginning
   to end.

   _____

   _____

10. Driving for a long time, my leg began to hurt.

_____

_____

PRACTICE

28-4 Complete the following sentences, making sure to include a word to which each modifier can logically refer.

Example: Dancing with the man of her dreams, _she decided it was_

time to wake up.

1. Blocked by the clouds, _____

_____

2. Applying for financial aid, _____

_____

3. Settled into his recliner chair, _____

_____

4. Fearing that they might catch a cold, _____

_____

5. Hearing strange noises through the wall, _____

_____

6. Soaked by the rain, _____

_____

7. Looking at Facebook until after midnight, _____

_____

8. Lighting the candles, _____

_____

9. Donated by disaster aid groups, _____

_____

10. Wearing their best clothes, ——————————————————

——————————————————————————

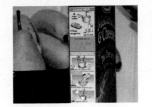

TEST · Revise · Edit

Look back at your response to the Focus on Writing prompt on page 520. TEST what you have written. Then, revise and edit your work, paying particular attention to *-ing* and *-ed* modifiers. Check your work to make sure that you do not have any misplaced or dangling modifiers.

EDITING PRACTICE: PARAGRAPH

Read the following student paragraph, which includes modification errors. Rewrite sentences where necessary to correct misplaced and dangling modifiers. In some cases, you may have to supply a word to which the modifier can logically refer. The first incorrect sentence has been corrected for you.

Beyond Mickey Mouse

For more than twenty years, Pixar computer animation studios have produced movies. Sketched by hand before Pixar, ~~artists provided thousands~~ *thousands of pictures were provided by artists* ~~of pictures~~ for traditional animated films. Led by Steve Jobs, animation was revolutionized by Pixar. Using computers, special software was used by animators to create speech and movement. Invented by Pixar, animators were able to achieve startling lifelike effects. The typical Pixar plot shows characters growing as they move into the world. Encouraging this growth, the characters' friends offer advice and guidance. The first commercially successful Pixar film was *Toy Story*. Completed in 1995, the use of computer animation made *Toy Story* a success. *Toy Story* was followed by *A Bug's Life*, *Finding Nemo*, and *The Incredibles*. Bringing in more than $525 million, audiences made these movies very successful. In 2006, Disney bought Pixar for $7.4 billion. Now, the company that pioneered traditional animation eighty years ago owns Pixar.

EDITING PRACTICE: ESSAY

Read the following student essay, which includes modification errors. Rewrite sentences to correct dangling and misplaced modifiers. In some cases, you will have to supply a word to which the modifier can logically refer. The first sentence has been corrected for you.

Eating as a Sport

After eating a big meal, ~~the food often makes~~ you *often* feel stuffed. Imagine how

someone participating in competitive eating feels. To win, you have to eat more

food faster than anyone else. Training for days, many different kinds of food

are eaten in these contests. For example, contestants eat chicken wings, pizza,

ribs, hot dogs, and even matzo balls. Training for events, competitive eating is

considered a sport by participants. By winning, a good living can be made by a

competitive eater. Considered dangerous by some, competitive eaters and their

fans nevertheless continue to grow.

The way it works is that each competitor eats the same weight or portion

of food. Giving the signal, the competitors begin eating. Breaking the food

in pieces or just eating the food whole, any technique can be used. The

competitors, soaked in water, can make the food softer. They can even eat hot

dogs separately from their buns. Good competitors are usually not overweight.

In fact, some are quite thin. Keeping the stomach from expanding, competitors

are hurt by extra fat. By drinking large amounts of water, their stomachs stretch

and increase their chances of winning. This is one technique many competitors

use when they train.

The International Federation of Competitive Eating watches over the

contests to make sure they are fair and safe. Providing the dates and locations,

contests are listed on its Web site. Often, contests are held at state fairs. Also

listing participants, prizes, and rankings of winners, new participants are

invited. Before entering the contests, their eating specialty and personal profile

must be indicated by new participants. Competitors must also be at least eigh-

teen years old.

Many competitive eaters participate in lots of contests. For example, weigh-

ing only 100 pounds, 8.1 pounds of sausage was eaten in only 10 minutes by

Sonya Thomas. At another contest, she ate 46 crab cakes in 10 minutes. Held in the United States, some participants come from other countries. For instance, Takeru Kobayashi, who comes from Japan, once ate 18 pounds of cow brains in 15 minutes. Winners usually get cash prizes. The largest prize, $20,000, was awarded in a hot dog–eating contest at Coney Island, which was televised by ESPN. By eating 66 hot dogs and their buns in 12 minutes, the contest was won by Joey Chestnut, a professional speed eater. Almost 50,000 people attended the contest in person, and millions watched on television.

There is some concern about competitive eating. By stretching the stomach, a person's health may be affected. There is also concern about obesity and overeating. Worried about choking, events should have doctors present some people argue. Still, many people like to watch these contests, and they seem to be getting more popular each year.

COLLABORATIVE ACTIVITY

Working in a group of five or six students, make a list of five modifiers that end in -*ing* and five modifiers that end in -*ed*. Exchange your list with another group, and complete each other's sentences.

Examples

<u>Typing</u> as fast as he could, *John could not wait to finish his screenplay.*

<u>Frightened</u> by a snake, *the horse ran away.*

review checklist

Misplaced and Dangling Modifiers

- [ ] Correct a misplaced modifier by placing the modifier as close as possible to the word it modifies. (See 28a.)

- [ ] Correct a dangling modifier by supplying a word to which the modifier can logically refer. (See 28b.)

Read the following student essay, which contains run-ons, sentence fragments, errors with subject-verb agreement, illogical shifts, and dangling and misplaced modifiers. Edit the essay to correct the errors. The first error has been corrected for you.

Not In My Back Yard

NIMBY, a term that was coined in 1980, stands for "Not In My Back Yard." "NIMBYs" are people who are against certain changes in their communities, *even* Even though these changes will benefit the general population. For example, NIMBYs may oppose new public housing, "big box" stores, prisons, airports, or highways. Because may harm the community. These people also fear the presence in their neighborhoods of certain groups. Such as people with certain disabilities. They did not want these people. To live anywhere near them. NIMBYs have raised important issues. About the conflict between the rights of the individual and the rights of the population as a whole.

NIMBYs are suspicious of the government, they worry that the government will ignore their community's needs. For example, the government may say new jobs will be available, however, what if the jobs pay low wages? What if the new employers force locally owned small stores out of business? Low-income housing may be badly needed, but what if one of the results are a reduction in the value of nearby property? What if the strains on schools and traffic is unacceptable? NIMBYs always worry about these questions.

NIMBYs understand that certain facilities must be built or improved nevertheless, they worry that each change may have their own negative effects. For example, needing new airport runways in order to reduce delays, NIMBYs object to the increased noise it causes. Although new sources of energy is badly needed, NIMBYs oppose the noise pollution. That windmills would bring to their community. New sites may be needed to dispose of hazardous waste, but

NIMBYs are afraid of leaking waste containers. That may contaminate homes and neighborhoods.

Finally, there is always going to be fears. Of the unknown. Group homes for people with physical disabilities and mental illness is often a problem for NIMBYs. They are also opposed to having sex offenders living in their community. Of course, no one wants a dangerous criminal living in their neighborhood. However, if someone has completed the required prison sentence, they have to live somewhere. Some of these negative attitudes is a result of lack of information others are based on a parent's real concerns about the safety of their children. Parents did not quarrel with the right of sex offenders to find a place to live they just do not want them to live anywhere near their children. NIMBYs feel that they have to protect themselves and their families.

The conflicts of NIMBY involve a real moral dilemma. On the one hand, belief in the importance of individuals mean that people should rely on themselves, not on government. On the other hand, belief in social responsibility means that people should think about the well-being of others. The conflict between these two positions may be very difficult to resolve. Because sometimes the needs of the individual is in conflict with the needs of the general community.

unit
7 Understanding Basic Grammar

29 Verbs: Past Tense

focus on writing

The obituary on the following page provides a short recap of the life of Apple cofounder Steve Jobs. Read the obituary, and then write one for yourself. (Refer to yourself by name or by *he* or *she*.) As you write, assume that you have led a long life and have achieved everything you hoped you would. Be sure to include the accomplishments for which you would most like to be remembered. Don't forget to use transitional words and phrases that clearly show how one event in your life relates to another.

In this chapter, you will learn to

- understand regular verbs in the past tense (29a)
- understand irregular verbs in the past tense (29b)
- deal with problem verbs in the past tense (29c and 29d)

Apple's Visionary Redefined Digital Age

New York Times
October 5, 2011

Steven P. Jobs, the visionary co-founder of Apple who helped usher in the era of personal computers and then led a cultural transformation in the way music, movies and mobile communications were experienced in the digital age, died Wednesday. He was 56.

The death was announced by Apple, the company Mr. Jobs and his high school friend Stephen Wozniak started in 1976 in a suburban California garage. A friend of the family said the cause was complications of pancreatic cancer. . . .

Mr. Jobs had largely come to define the personal computer industry and an array of digital consumer and entertainment businesses centered on the Internet. He had also become a very rich man, worth an estimated $8.3 billion.

Mr. Jobs was neither a hardware engineer nor a software programmer, nor did he think of himself as a manager. He considered himself a technology leader, choosing the best people possible, encouraging and prodding them, and making the final call on product design. . . .

He put much stock in the notion of "taste," a word he used frequently. It was a sensibility that shone in products that looked like works of art and delighted users. Great products, he said, were a triumph of taste, of "trying to expose yourself to the best things humans have done and then trying to bring those things into what you are doing."

Tense is the form a verb takes to show when an action or situation takes place. The **past tense** indicates that an action occurred in the past.

29a Regular Verbs

☑ LearningCurve
Verbs
bedfordstmartins.com
/focusonwriting

Regular verbs form the past tense by adding either *-ed* or *-d* to the **base form** of the verb (the present tense form of the verb that is used with *I*).

We register**ed** for classes yesterday.

Walt Disney produc**ed** short cartoons in 1928.

Regular verbs that end in *-y* form the past tense by changing the *y* to *i* and adding *-ed*.

tr**y**	tr**ied**
appl**y**	appl**ied**

PRACTICE

29-1   Change the regular verbs below to the past tense.

visited

Example: Every year, my mother ~~visits~~ her family in Bombay.
                                          ^

(1) My mother always returns from India with henna designs on her hands and feet. (2) In India, henna artists create these patterns. (3) Henna originates in a plant found in the Middle East, India, Indonesia, and northern Africa. (4) Many women in these areas use henna to color their hands, nails, and parts of their feet. (5) Men dye their beards as well as the manes and hooves of their horses. (6) They also color animal skins with henna. (7) In India, my mother always celebrates the end of the Ramadan religious fast by going to a "henna party." (8) A professional henna artist attends the party to apply new henna decorations to the women. (9) After a few weeks, the henna designs wash off. (10) In the United States, my mother's henna designs attract the attention of many people.

29b Irregular Verbs

Unlike regular verbs, whose past tense forms end in *-ed* or *-d*, **irregular verbs** have irregular forms in the past tense. In fact, their past tense forms may look very different from their present tense forms.

The following chart lists the base form and past tense form of many of the most commonly used irregular verbs.

Irregular Verbs in the Past Tense

BASE FORM	PAST	BASE FORM	PAST
awake	awoke	keep	kept
be	was, were	know	knew
beat	beat	lay (to place)	laid
become	became	lead	led
begin	began	leave	left
bet	bet	let	let
bite	bit	lie (to recline)	lay
blow	blew	light	lit
break	broke	lose	lost
bring	brought	make	made
build	built	meet	met
buy	bought	pay	paid
catch	caught	quit	quit
choose	chose	read	read
come	came	ride	rode
cost	cost	ring	rang
cut	cut	rise	rose
dive	dove (dived)	run	ran
do	did	say	said
draw	drew	see	saw
drink	drank	sell	sold
drive	drove	send	sent
eat	ate	set	set
fall	fell	shake	shook
feed	fed	shine	shone (shined)
feel	felt	sing	sang
fight	fought	sit	sat
find	found	sleep	slept
fly	flew	speak	spoke
forgive	forgave	spend	spent
freeze	froze	spring	sprang
get	got	stand	stood
give	gave	steal	stole
go (goes)	went	stick	stuck
grow	grew	sting	stung
have	had	swear	swore
hear	heard	swim	swam
hide	hid	take	took
hold	held	teach	taught
hurt	hurt	tear	tore

BASE FORM	PAST	BASE FORM	PAST
tell	told	wake	woke
think	thought	wear	wore
throw	threw	win	won
understand	understood	write	wrote

PRACTICE

29-2   Fill in the correct past tense form of each irregular verb in parentheses, using the chart above to help you. If you cannot find a particular verb on the chart, look it up in a dictionary.

Example: Security on Campus ____*was*____ (be) founded in 1987.

(1) After their daughter, Jeanne, _____ (be) murdered at Lehigh University, Connie and Howard Cleary _____ (begin) a movement to improve safety on college campuses. (2) Jeanne _____ (think) she was safe. (3) However, her attacker _____ (get) into her dorm room through three different doors that had all been left unlocked. (4) Shockingly, Jeanne's attacker actually _____ (go) to Lehigh. (5) Shattered by the loss of their daughter, her parents _____ (do) not withdraw into their pain. (6) Instead, they _____ (feel) that the best memorial to their daughter would be the prevention of similar crimes, so they founded Security on Campus, Inc. (7) SOC _____ (make) legal information available to victims of crimes on college campuses. (8) Because of the efforts of SOC, Congress _____ (write) a law that forced colleges to disclose their crime statistics. (9) Colleges also _____ (have) to explain the steps they _____ (take) to protect their students. (10) Because of this law, the number of campus crimes _____ (fall).

29c   Problem Verbs: *Be*

The irregular verb *be* causes problems because it has two different past tense forms—*was* for singular subjects and *were* for second-person singular subjects as well as for plural subjects. (All other English verbs have just one past tense form.)

> Carlo <u>was</u> interested in becoming a city planner. (singular)
> They <u>were</u> happy to help out at the school. (plural)

Past Tense Forms of the Verb *Be*

	Singular	Plural
First person	I <u>was</u> tired.	We <u>were</u> tired.
Second person	You <u>were</u> tired.	You <u>were</u> tired.
Third person	He <u>was</u> tired.	
	She <u>was</u> tired.	They <u>were</u> tired.
	It <u>was</u> tired.	
	The man <u>was</u> tired.	Frank and Billy <u>were</u> tired.

PRACTICE

29-3   Edit the following passage for errors in the use of the verb *be*. Cross out any underlined verbs that are incorrect, and write the correct forms above them. If a verb form is correct, label it *C*.

Example: Before 1990, there ~~was~~ *were* no female Hispanic astronauts in the NASA program.

(1) Although there had never been a Hispanic woman astronaut, it <u>was</u> impossible for NASA to ignore Ellen Ochoa's long career in physics and engineering. (2) When Ochoa <u>was</u> young, her main interests <u>was</u> music, math, and physics. (3) After getting a degree in physics at San Diego State University, she <u>were</u> considering a career in music or business. (4) However, she <u>was</u> convinced by her mother to continue her education. (5) In 1983, Ochoa <u>was</u> studying for a doctorate in electrical engineering at Stanford University when the first female astronaut, Sally Ride, flew

on the space shuttle. (6) Ochoa <u>were</u> inspired by Sally Ride to become an astronaut. (7) More than 2,000 people <u>was</u> also inspired to apply for the astronaut program. (8) In 1990, Ochoa <u>was</u> picked to fly into space. (9) On one of her flights, she <u>was</u> a mission specialist and used a remote-controlled robotic arm to catch a satellite. (10) After four space flights, Ochoa <u>were</u> made Director of Flight Crew Operations.

29d Problem Verbs: Can/Could and Will/Would

The helping verbs *can/could* and *will/would* present problems because their past tense forms are sometimes confused with their present tense forms.

Can/Could

Can, a present tense verb, means "is able to" or "are able to."

First-year students <u>can</u> apply for financial aid.

Could, the past tense of *can*, means "was able to" or "were able to."

Escape artist Harry Houdini claimed that he <u>could</u> escape from any prison.

Will/Would

Will, a present tense verb, talks about the future from a point in the present.

A solar eclipse <u>will</u> occur in ten months.

Would, the past tense of *will*, talks about the future from a point in the past.

I told him yesterday that I <u>would</u> think about it.

Would is also used to express a possibility or wish.

> If we stuck to our budget, we <u>would</u> be better off.
>
> Laurie <u>would</u> like a new stuffed animal.

FYI

Will and *Would*

Note that *will* is used with *can* and that *would* is used with *could*.

> I will feed the cats if I can find their food.
>
> I would feed the cats if I could find their food.

PRACTICE
29-4

Circle the appropriate helping verb from the choices in parentheses.

Example: People who don't want to throw things away ((can), could) rent a self-storage unit.

(1) In the past, warehouse storage (will, would) provide a place to store excess items. (2) However, people (will, would) have to hire moving vans and (can, could) hardly ever have access to their stored items. (3) They (will, would) have to sign an expensive long-term contract. (4) Now, however, they (can, could) take advantage of another option. (5) They (can, could) store possessions in a space as small as a closet or as large as a house. (6) With self-storage, people (can, could) easily move their belongings in and out of the storage unit. (7) When they need more space, they (will, would) be able to get it. (8) In fact, the managers of self-storage facilities (can, could) suggest how much space owners (will, would) need. (9) The only person who (can, could) get into the self-storage unit is the person who has rented it. (10) If people need a

hand truck to move their belongings, they (can, could) usually borrow one. (11) All in all, using self-storage (can, could) solve a lot of problems for people with too many possessions.

TEST · **Revise** · **Edit**

Look back at your response to the Focus on Writing prompt on page 535. **TEST** what you have written. Then, revise and edit your work, making sure that you have used the correct past tense form for each of your verbs.

EDITING PRACTICE

Read the following student essay, which includes errors in past tense verb forms. Decide whether each of the underlined past tense verbs is correct. If the verb is correct, write *C* above it. If it is not, cross out the verb, and write in the correct past tense form. The first sentence has been corrected for you. (If necessary, consult the list of irregular verbs on pages 538–539.)

Healing

The window seat were *was* our favorite place to sit. I piled pillows on the ledge and <u>spended</u> several minutes rearranging them. Then, my friend and I <u>lied</u> on our backs and propped our feet on the wall. We <u>sat</u> with our arms around our legs and <u>thinked</u> about the mysteries of life.

We stared at the people on the street below and <u>wonder</u> who they <u>was</u> and where they <u>was</u> going. We imagined that they <u>can</u> be millionaires, foreign spies, or drug smugglers. We believed that everyone except us <u>leaded</u> wonderful and exciting lives.

I <u>heard</u> a voice call my name. Reluctantly, I <u>standed</u> up, tearing myself away from my imaginary world. My dearest and oldest friend—my teddy bear—and I came back to the real world. I grabbed Teddy and <u>brung</u> him close to my chest. Together, we <u>go</u> into the cold dining room, where twelve other girls <u>sit</u> around a table eating breakfast. None of them looked happy.

In the unit for eating disorders, meals <u>was</u> always tense. Nobody <u>wants</u> to eat, but the nurses watched us until we <u>eated</u> every crumb. I <u>set</u> Teddy on the chair beside me and stared gloomily at the food on our plate. I closed my eyes and <u>taked</u> the first bite. I <u>feeled</u> the calories adding inches of ugly fat. Each swallow <u>were</u> like a nail being ripped from my finger. At last, it <u>was</u> over. I had survived breakfast.

Days passed slowly. Each passing minute <u>was</u> a victory. After a while, I learned how to eat properly. I learned about other people's problems. I also learned that people loved me. Eventually, even Teddy stopped feeling sorry for me. I <u>begun</u> to smile—and laugh. Sometimes I even considered myself happy. My doctors challenged me—and, surprisingly, I <u>rised</u> to the occasion.

COLLABORATIVE ACTIVITY

Form a group with three other students. What national or world events do you remember most clearly? Take ten minutes to list news events that you think have defined the last five years. On your own, write a few paragraphs in which you discuss the significance of the three or four events that the members of your group agree were the most important.

review checklist

Verbs: Past Tense

- The past tense is the form a verb takes to show that an action occurred in the past.

- Regular verbs form the past tense by adding either *-ed* or *-d* to the base form of the verb. (See 29a.)

- Irregular verbs have irregular forms in the past tense. (See 29b.)

- *Be* has two different past tense forms—*was* for singular subjects and *were* for second-person singular subjects as well as for plural subjects. (See 29c.)

- *Could* is the past tense of *can*. *Would* is the past tense of *will*. (See 29d.)

LearningCurve
Verbs
bedfordstmartins.com
/focusonwriting

30 Verbs: Past Participles

focus on writing

This still from the 2005 film *Mad Hot Ballroom* shows children practicing ballroom dancing. Write a paragraph about an activity—a hobby or a sport, for example—that you have been involved in for a relatively long time. Begin by identifying the activity and stating why it has been important to you. Then, describe the activity, paying particular attention to what you have gained from it over the years.

In this chapter, you will learn to

- identify regular past participles (30a)
- identify irregular past participles (30b)
- use the present perfect tense (30c)
- use the past perfect tense (30d)
- use past participles as adjectives (30e)

30a Regular Past Participles

Every verb has a past participle form. The **past participle** form of a regular verb is identical to its past tense form. Both are formed by adding either *-ed* or *-d* to the **base form** of the verb (the present tense form of the verb that is used with the pronoun *I*).

PAST TENSE	PAST PARTICIPLE
He earned a fortune.	He has earned a fortune.

PAST TENSE	PAST PARTICIPLE
He created a work of art.	He has created a work of art.

PRACTICE

30-1 Fill in the correct past participle form of each regular verb in parentheses.

Example: For years, volunteer vacationers have ___visited___ (visit) remote areas to build footpaths, cabins, and shelters.

(1) Recently, vacationers have _____ (discover) some new opportunities to get away from it all and to do good at the same time. (2) Groups such as Habitat for Humanity, for example, have _____ (offer) volunteers a chance to build homes in low-income areas. (3) Habitat's Global Village trips have _____ (raise) awareness about the lack of affordable housing in many countries. (4) Participants in Sierra Club programs have _____ (donate) thousands of work hours all over the United States. (5) Sometimes these volunteers have _____ (join) forest service workers to help restore wilderness

areas. (6) They have _____ (clean) up trash at campsites. (7) They have also _____ (remove) nonnative plants. (8) Some volunteer vacationers have _____ (travel) to countries such as Costa Rica, Russia, and Thailand to help with local projects. (9) Other vacationers have _____ (serve) as English teachers. (10) Volunteering vacations have _____ (help) to strengthen cross-cultural understanding.

30b Irregular Past Participles

Irregular verbs nearly always have irregular past participles. Irregular verbs do not form the past participle by adding -ed or -d to the base form of the verb.

The following chart lists the base form, the past tense form, and the past participle of the most commonly used irregular verbs.

Irregular Past Participles

BASE FORM	PAST TENSE	PAST PARTICIPLE
awake	awoke	awoken
be (am, are)	was (were)	been
beat	beat	beaten
become	became	become
begin	began	begun
bet	bet	bet
bite	bit	bitten
blow	blew	blown
break	broke	broken
bring	brought	brought
build	built	built
buy	bought	bought
catch	caught	caught
choose	chose	chosen
come	came	come
cost	cost	cost
cut	cut	cut
dive	dove, dived	dived
do	did	done

BASE FORM	PAST TENSE	PAST PARTICIPLE
draw	drew	drawn
drink	drank	drunk
drive	drove	driven
eat	ate	eaten
fall	fell	fallen
feed	fed	fed
feel	felt	felt
fight	fought	fought
find	found	found
fly	flew	flown
forgive	forgave	forgiven
freeze	froze	frozen
get	got	got, gotten
give	gave	given
go	went	gone
grow	grew	grown
have	had	had
hear	heard	heard
hide	hid	hidden
hold	held	held
hurt	hurt	hurt
keep	kept	kept
know	knew	known
lay (to place)	laid	laid
lead	led	led
leave	left	left
let	let	let
lie (to recline)	lay	lain
light	lit	lit
lose	lost	lost
make	made	made
meet	met	met
pay	paid	paid
quit	quit	quit
read	read	read
ride	rode	ridden
ring	rang	rung
rise	rose	risen
run	ran	run
say	said	said
see	saw	seen
sell	sold	sold

(continued)

(continued from previous page)

BASE FORM	PAST TENSE	PAST PARTICIPLE
send	sent	sent
set	set	set
shake	shook	shaken
shine	shone, shined	shone, shined
sing	sang	sung
sit	sat	sat
sleep	slept	slept
speak	spoke	spoken
spend	spent	spent
spring	sprang	sprung
stand	stood	stood
steal	stole	stolen
stick	stuck	stuck
sting	stung	stung
swear	swore	sworn
swim	swam	swum
take	took	taken
teach	taught	taught
tear	tore	torn
tell	told	told
think	thought	thought
throw	threw	thrown
understand	understood	understood
wake	woke, waked	woken, waked
wear	wore	worn
win	won	won
write	wrote	written

PRACTICE

30-2   Fill in the correct past participle of each irregular verb in parentheses. Refer to the chart on pages 548–550 as needed. If you cannot find a particular verb on the chart, look it up in a dictionary.

Example: Occasionally, a wildfire has _____*caught*_____ (catch) firefighters unprepared.

(1) Wildfires have always _____ (be) a part of nature. (2) In some cases, fires have _____ (come) and _____ (go) without causing much destruction. (3) In other cases, fires have _____ (cost) people a lot of time, money, and pain. (4) All of us have _____ (have) to accept

the fact that healthy forests occasionally burn. (5) However, according to some people, wildfires have _____ (become) more dangerous and more common in recent years. (6) One reason is that more people have _____ (build) houses close to wooded areas. (7) In addition, many areas of the United States have _____ (see) unusually hot and dry weather. (8) Occasionally, fires have _____ (sweep) through acres of forest before firefighters could set up firebreaks. (9) However, firefighters have _____ (do) their best to stop fires that threaten people's property. (10) In all cases, firefighting agencies have _____ (make) protection of human life their first priority.

PRACTICE

30-3   Edit the following paragraph for errors in irregular past participles. Cross out any underlined past participles that are incorrect, and write in the correct form above them. If the verb form is correct, label it *C*.

> *stood*
> **Example:**   In recent years, some people have ~~standed~~ up against
>   ^
> overseas sweatshops.

(1) Buying products from overseas sweatshops has became controversial over the last few decades. (2) American manufacturers have sended their materials to developing countries where employees work under terrible conditions for very low wages. (3) Violations of basic U.S. labor laws—such as getting extra pay for overtime and being paid on time—have lead to protests. (4) Low-wage workers in developing countries have finded themselves facing dangerous working conditions as well as verbal and sexual abuse. (5) Even well-known retailers—such as Walmart, Nike, Reebok, Tommy Hilfiger, and Target—have gotten in trouble for selling items made in sweatshops. (6) Recently, colleges have be criticized for using overseas sweatshops to make clothing featuring school names.

(7) Students have <u>spoke</u> out against such practices, and schools have <u>had</u> to respond. (8) While some manufacturers may have <u>losed</u> money by increasing wages for overseas workers, they have <u>understanded</u> that this is the right thing to do. (9) They have <u>made</u> a promise to their customers that they will not employ sweatshop labor. (10) Critics have <u>argue</u>, however, that in developing countries sweatshop jobs are often an improvement over other types of employment.

30c   The Present Perfect Tense

The past participle can be combined with the present tense forms of *have* to form the **present perfect tense**.

The Present Perfect Tense

(*have* or *has* + past participle)

SINGULAR	PLURAL
I <u>have gained</u>.	We <u>have gained</u>.
You <u>have gained</u>.	You <u>have gained</u>.
He <u>has gained</u>.	They <u>have gained</u>.
She <u>has gained</u>.	
It <u>has gained</u>.	

- Use the present perfect tense to indicate an action that began in the past and continues into the present.

  PRESENT PERFECT   The nurse <u>has worked</u> at the Welsh Mountain clinic for two years. (The working began in the past and continues into the present.)

- Use the present perfect tense to indicate that an action has just occurred.

  PRESENT PERFECT   I <u>have</u> just <u>eaten</u>. (The eating has just occurred.)

PRACTICE
30-4   Circle the appropriate verb tense (past tense or present perfect) from the choices in parentheses.

Example: When I was in Montreal, I (heard, have heard) both English and French.

(1) When I (visited, have visited) Montreal, I was surprised to find a truly bilingual city. (2) Montreal (kept, has kept) two languages as a result of its history. (3) Until 1763, Montreal (belonged, has belonged) to France. (4) Then, when France (lost, has lost) the Seven Years' War, the city (became, has become) part of England. (5) When I was there last year, most people (spoke, have spoken) both French and English. (6) Although I (knew, have known) no French, I (found, have found) that I was able to get along quite well. (7) For example, all the museums (made, have made) their guided tours available in English. (8) Most restaurants (offered, have offered) bilingual menus. (9) There (were, have been) even English radio and television stations and English newspapers. (10) In Montreal, I (felt, have felt) both at home and in a foreign country.

PRACTICE
30-5   Fill in the appropriate tense (past tense or present perfect) of the verb in parentheses.

Example: Now, cell phones fit easily into a pocket, but the first mobile-phone users _____*carried*_____ (carry) devices that were more than a foot long.

(1) In recent years, the size of many everyday items _____ (change) considerably. (2) Cell phones and computers _____ (undergo) the biggest changes. (3) There was a time, not long ago, when a single computer _____ (fill) an entire room and a cell phone weighed as much as two pounds. (4) Since then, we

_____ (invent) smaller and smaller devices. (5) Now, we _____ (become) accustomed to tiny devices that act as both phone and computer yet weigh only a few ounces. (6) However, while these items have shrunk, other things _____ (get) bigger. (7) For example, flat-screen TVs now come in sizes up to 100 inches. (8) Moreover, as Americans _____ (grow) heavier, hospital equipment has had to get sturdier. (9) Ten years ago, manufacturers _____ (build) operating tables that supported a maximum of 700 pounds. (10) Now, medical supply companies _____ (develop) a standard table that supports up to 1,200 pounds. (11) To accommodate the growing number of overweight people, movie theater seats and caskets _____ (increase) in size as well. (12) While moviegoers in the 1980s _____ (sit) in 20-inch seats, today's viewers sit in 26-inch seats. (13) Similarly, standard-size caskets have expanded in width from 24 to 28 inches, and some companies _____ (start) making plus-size caskets as large as 52 inches across. (14) Clearly, consumers prefer some items to be smaller even as they themselves _____ (get) bigger.

30d The Past Perfect Tense

The past participle can also be used to form the **past perfect tense**, which consists of the past tense of *have* plus the past participle.

The Past Perfect Tense

(*had* + past participle)

SINGULAR	PLURAL
I had returned.	We had returned.
You had returned.	You had returned.

SINGULAR	PLURAL
He <u>had returned</u>.	They <u>had returned</u>.
She <u>had returned</u>.	
It had returned.	

Use the past perfect tense to show that an action occurred before another past action.

PAST PERFECT TENSE   PAST TENSE

Chief Sitting Bull <u>had fought</u> many battles before <u>he</u> <u>defeated</u> General Custer. (The fighting was done before Sitting Bull defeated Custer.)

PRACTICE

30-6   Underline the appropriate verb tense (present perfect or past perfect) from the choices in parentheses.

Example: Although he (has missed/<u>had missed</u>) his second free throw, the crowd cheered for him anyway.

1. Meera returned to Bangladesh with the money she (has raised/had raised).

2. Her contributors believe that she (has shown/had shown) the ability to spend money wisely.

3. The planner told the commission that she (has found/had found) a solution to the city's traffic problem.

4. It seems clear that traffic cameras (have proven/had proven) successful in towns with similar congestion problems.

5. Emily says she (has saved/had saved) a lot of money by driving a motor scooter instead of a car.

6. She sold the car she (has bought/had bought) three years before.

7. Because they are huge fans, Esteban and Tina (have camped/had camped) out in front of the theater to buy tickets.

8. The people who (have waited/had waited) all night were the first to get tickets.

9. Sam and Ryan volunteer at Habitat for Humanity, where they (have learned/had learned) many useful skills.

10. After they (have completed/had completed) 500 hours of work, they were eligible to get their own house.

30e   Past Participles as Adjectives

In addition to functioning as verbs, past participles can function as adjectives modifying nouns that follow them.

I cleaned up the broken glass.

The exhausted runner finally crossed the finish line.

Past participles are also used as adjectives after **linking verbs**, such as *seemed* or *looked*.

Jason seemed surprised.

He looked shocked.

PRACTICE
30-7   Edit the following passage for errors in past participle forms used as adjectives. Cross out any underlined participles that are incorrect, and write the correct form above them. If the participle form is correct, label it *C*.

Example: College students are often worried about money.

(1) College students are surprise when they get preapprove applications for credit cards in their mail. (2) Credit-card companies also recruit targeted students through booths that are locate on or near college campuses. (3) The booths are design to attract new customers with offers of gifts. (4) Why have companies gone to all this trouble to attract

qualified students? (5) Most older Americans already have at least five credit cards that are <u>stuff</u> in their wallets. (6) Banks and credit-card companies see younger college students as a major <u>untapped</u> market. (7) According to experts, students are a good credit risk because <u>concern</u> parents usually bail them out when they cannot pay a bill. (8) Finally, people tend to feel emotionally <u>tie</u> to their first credit card. (9) Companies want to be the first card that is <u>acquire</u> by a customer. (10) For this reason, credit-card companies target <u>uninform</u> college students.

TEST · Revise · Edit

Look back at your response to the Focus on Writing prompt on page 546. **TEST** what you have written. Then, revise and edit your work, paying particular attention to present perfect and past perfect verb forms and to past participles used as adjectives.

EDITING PRACTICE

Read the following student essay, which includes errors in the use of past participles and perfect tenses. Decide whether each of the underlined verbs or participles is correct. If it is correct, write *C* above it. If it is not, write in the correct verb form. The first error has been corrected for you.

The Flash Mob Phenomenon

The first flash mob ~~had take~~ *took* place in 2003 when two hundred people assembled in a New York City Macy's store. Since then, these strange spontaneous gatherings had popped up in cities around the world and have involve all kinds of unusual behaviors. Occasionally, a group has organized a flash mob for criminal purposes, but in most cases, flash mobs had been harmless acts of group expression.

Organizer Bill Wasik had actually intend the first flash mob to be a social commentary. Wasik has wanted to make fun of "hipster" New Yorkers who showed up at events simply because other people did. However, almost no one had saw the first flash mob that way. In fact, people mostly have thought it was cool. As a result, admirers started organizing their own flash mobs.

So far, few of the subsequent flash mobs had have a political or social purpose. Typically, people had participate simply because these gatherings are fun. For example, over the years, people have gathered in cities around the world to dance to Michael Jackson's "Thriller." People had also enjoyed getting together in public spaces for massive pillow fights. In addition, several groups have coordinated group "freeze frames," in which participants all "freeze" at the same moment. Organized quietly by text messages or social media, most flash mobs have not publicize their plans in traditional media. Consequently, passers-by have enjoyed the feeling that the group had gathered spontaneously.

Although the majority of flash mob organizers have create these brief performances to entertain, people have occasionally use flash mobs to commit crimes. Over the last few years, several groups <u>have robbed</u> stores by entering in large numbers, stealing merchandise, and then separating quickly. Worse, several groups <u>have came</u> together to commit violent acts or destroy property. Most of today's flash mobs, however, are peaceful.

Over the last decade, flash mobs <u>have became</u> more popular than anyone could have imagined. Although they have not had the impact that creator Bill Wasik <u>had hoped</u> for, they <u>given</u> a lot of people a lot of enjoyment. Flash mobs allow people to be creative, to work together, and to have fun. Although a few flash mobs <u>have done</u> harm, most <u>have offer</u> people a way to be a part of something memorable.

COLLABORATIVE ACTIVITY

Assume that you are a restaurant employee who has been nominated for the Employee-of-the-Year Award. To win this award (along with a thousand-dollar prize), you have to explain in writing what you have done during the past year to deserve this honor. Write a letter to your supervisor and the awards committee. When you have finished, trade papers with another student and edit his or her letter. Read all the letters to the class, and have the class decide which is the most convincing.

review checklist

Verts: Past Participles

☐ The past participle of regular verbs is formed by adding *-ed* or *-d* to the base form. (See 30a.)

☐ Irregular verbs usually have irregular past participles. (See 30b.)

☐ The past participle is combined with the present tense forms of *have* to form the present perfect tense. (See 30c.)

☐ The past participle is used to form the past perfect tense, which consists of the past tense of *have* plus the past participle. (See 30d.)

☐ The past participle can function as an adjective. (See 30e.)

☑ LearningCurve
Verbs
bedfordstmartins.com /focusonwriting

31 Nouns and Pronouns

MATT GROENING

focus on writing

The TV show *The Simpsons* first aired in 1989 and continues to entertain viewers today. Write a paragraph about a particular TV show, musical group, or movie you like, and explain why you like it. Assume your readers are not familiar with the subject you are writing about.

In this chapter, you will learn to

- identify nouns (31a) and pronouns (31c)
- form plural nouns (31b)
- understand (31d) and solve special problems with (31e) pronoun-antecedent agreement
- avoid vague and unnecessary pronouns (31f)
- understand (31g) and solve special problems with (31h) pronoun case
- identify reflexive and intensive pronouns (31i)

31a Identifying Nouns

A **noun** is a word that names a person (*singer, Jay-Z*), an animal (*dolphin, Flipper*), a place (*downtown, Houston*), an object (*game, Scrabble*), or an idea (*happiness, Darwinism*).

A **singular noun** names one thing. A **plural noun** names more than one thing.

☑ **LearningCurve**
Nouns and Pronouns
bedfordstmartins.com
/focusonwriting

FYI

When to Capitalize Nouns

Most nouns, called **common nouns**, begin with lowercase letters.

character   holiday

Some nouns, called **proper nouns**, name particular people, animals, places, objects, or events. A proper noun always begins with a capital letter.

Homer Simpson   Labor Day

31b Forming Plural Nouns

Most nouns that end in consonants add *-s* to form plurals. Other nouns add *-es* to form plurals. For example, most nouns that end in *-o* add *-es* to form plurals. Other nouns, whose singular forms end in *-s, -ss, -sh, -ch, -x,* or *-z,* also add *-es* to form plurals. (Some nouns that end in *-s* or *-z* double the *s* or *z* before adding *-es*.)

SINGULAR	PLURAL
street	streets
tomato	tomatoes
gas	gases
class	classes
bush	bushes
church	churches
fox	foxes
quiz	quizzes

Irregular Noun Plurals

Some nouns form plurals in unusual ways.

- Nouns whose plural forms are the same as their singular forms

SINGULAR	PLURAL
a deer	a few deer
this species	these species
a television series	two television series

- Nouns ending in *-f* or *-fe*

SINGULAR	PLURAL
each half	both halves
my life	our lives
a lone thief	a gang of thieves
one loaf	two loaves
the third shelf	several shelves

Exceptions: *roof* (plural *roofs*), *proof* (plural *proofs*), *belief* (plural *beliefs*)

- Nouns ending in *-y*

SINGULAR	PLURAL
another baby	more babies
every worry	many worries

Note that when a vowel (*a, e, i, o, u*) comes before the *y*, the noun has a regular plural form: *monkey* (plural *monkeys*), *day* (plural *days*).

■ Hyphenated compound nouns

SINGULAR	PLURAL
Lucia's sister-in-law	Lucia's two favorite sisters-in-law
a mother-to-be	twin mothers-to-be
the first runner-up	all the runners-up

Note that the plural ending is attached to the compound's first word: *sister, mother, runner.*

■ Miscellaneous irregular plurals

SINGULAR	PLURAL
that child	all children
a good man	a few good men
the woman	lots of women
my left foot	both feet
a wisdom tooth	my two front teeth
this bacterium	some bacteria

PRACTICE

31-1

Next to each of the following singular nouns, write the plural form of the noun. Then, circle the irregular noun plurals.

Examples: bottle __*bottles*__   child __(*children*)__

1. headache _____

2. life _____

3. foot _____

4. chain _____

5. deer _____

6. honey _____

7. bride-to-be _____

8. woman _____

9. loaf _____

10. kiss _____

11. beach _____

12. duty _____

13. son-in-law _____

14. species _____

15. wife _____

16. city _____

17. elf _____

18. tooth _____

19. catalog _____

20. patty _____

PRACTICE

31-2   Proofread the underlined nouns in the following paragraph, checking to make sure singular and plural forms are correct. If a correction needs to be made, cross out the noun, and write the correct form above it. If the noun is correct, write *C* above it.

Example: Austin's Museum of the Weird displays many delightful
oddities
~~odditys~~.
^

(1) If America had a contest for the weirdest museum, there would be plenty of interesting <u>contestantes</u>. (2) The United States is full of strange <u>establishments</u> although many are hidden in small <u>townnes</u> or down back <u>streets</u>. (3) Most are dedicated to untold <u>historys</u>, unusual <u>heros</u>, or bizarre <u>collections</u> of items. (4) Philadelphia's Mutter Museum offers medical <u>specimen</u>, like <u>skullz</u>, <u>brains</u>, <u>bonz</u>, and <u>organs</u> of people who suffered from strange <u>illnessess</u>. (5) The Mutter could definitely win the prize for the weirdest museum, but other <u>places</u> could easily be <u>runner-ups</u>. (6) At the Kansas Barbed Wire Museum, <u>visitors</u> can see over 2,400 <u>varietees</u> of barbed wire. (7) The National Mustard Museum in Middleton, Wisconsin, has <u>thousandes</u> of <u>jarrs</u> of mustard from <u>countrys</u> all over the world. (8) Leila's Hair Museum in Independence, Missouri, has hundreds of <u>wreaths</u>, <u>necklaces</u>, and <u>broochs</u> made from human hair. (9) All of these weird museums welcome <u>sightseers</u>. (10) However, <u>touristes</u> should know that many of these places do not have fixed hours and are closed on <u>holidaies</u>.

31c Identifying Pronouns

A **pronoun** is a word that refers to and takes the place of a noun or another pronoun. In the following sentence, the pronouns *she* and *her* take the place of the noun *Michelle*.

Michelle was really excited because <u>she</u> had finally found a job that made <u>her</u> happy. (*She* refers to *Michelle*; *her* refers to *she*.)

Pronouns, like nouns, can be singular or plural.

- Singular pronouns (*I*, *he*, *she*, *it*, *him*, *her*, and so on) always take the place of singular nouns or pronouns.

    Geoff left his jacket at work, so <u>he</u> went back to get <u>it</u> before <u>it</u> could be stolen. (*He* refers to *Geoff*; *it* refers to *jacket*.)

- Plural pronouns (*we*, *they*, *our*, *their*, and so on) always take the place of plural nouns or pronouns.

    Jessie and Dan got up early, but <u>they</u> still missed <u>their</u> train. (*They* refers to *Jessie and Dan*; *their* refers to *they*.)

- The pronoun *you* can be either singular or plural.

    When the volunteers met the mayor, they said, "We really admire <u>you</u>." The mayor replied, "I admire <u>you</u>, too." (In the first sentence, *you* refers to *the mayor*; in the second sentence, *you* refers to *the volunteers*.)

FYI

Demonstrative Pronouns

Demonstrative pronouns—*this*, *that*, *these*, and *those*—point to one or more items.

- *This* and *that* point to one item: <u>This</u> is a work of fiction, and <u>that</u> is a nonfiction book.

- *These* and *those* point to more than one item: <u>These</u> are fruits, but <u>those</u> are vegetables.

PRACTICE

31-3   In the following sentences, fill in each blank with an appropriate pronoun.

Example: Ever since ____*I*____ had my first scuba-diving experience, ____*I*____ have wanted to search for sunken treasure.

(1) Three friends and _____ decided to explore an area off the Florida coast where a shipwreck had occurred almost three hundred years ago. (2) The first step was to buy a boat; _____ all

agreed on a used rubber boat with a fifteen-horsepower engine. (3) _____ had hardly been used and was in very good condition. (4) _____ also needed some equipment, including an anchor and metal detectors. (5) If there was treasure on the bottom of the ocean, _____ would find it. (6) _____ stayed in the boat while my friends made the first dive. (7) At first, _____ found only fish and sea worms, but _____ didn't give up. (8) Finally, one of the metal detectors started beeping because _____ had located a cannon and two cannonballs. (9) Then, it started beeping again; this time, _____ had found some pieces of pottery and an old pistol. (10) Although our group didn't find any coins, _____ all enjoyed our search for sunken treasure.

31d Pronoun-Antecedent Agreement

The word that a pronoun refers to is called the pronoun's **antecedent**. In the following sentence, the noun *leaf* is the antecedent of the pronoun *it*.

The leaf turned yellow, but it did not fall.

A pronoun must always agree with its antecedent. If an antecedent is singular, as it is in the sentence above, the pronoun must be singular. If the antecedent is plural, as it is in the sentence below, the pronoun must also be plural.

The leaves turned yellow, but they did not fall.

If an antecedent is feminine, the pronoun that refers to it must also be feminine.

Melissa passed her driver's exam with flying colors.

If an antecedent is masculine, the pronoun that refers to it must also be masculine.

Matt wondered what courses he should take.

If an antecedent is **neuter** (neither masculine nor feminine), the pronoun that refers to it must also be neuter.

The car broke down, but they refused to fix it again.

PRACTICE
31-4
In the following sentences, circle the antecedent of each underlined pronoun. Then, draw an arrow from the pronoun to the antecedent it refers to.

Example: College students today often fear they will be the victims of crime on campus.

(1) Few campuses are as safe as they should be, experts say. (2) However, crime on most campuses is probably no worse than it is in any other community. (3) Still, students have a right to know how safe their campuses are. (4) My friend Joyce never walks on campus without her can of Mace. (5) Joyce believes she must be prepared for the worst. (6) Her boyfriend took a self-defense course that he said was very helpful. (7) My friends do not let fear of crime keep them from enjoying the college experience. (8) We know that our school is doing all it can to make the campus safe.

PRACTICE
31-5
Fill in each blank in the following passage with an appropriate pronoun.

Example: Americans celebrate July 4 because _____it_____ is Independence Day.

(1) For some Germans, November 9 is a day to celebrate positive change; for others, _____ recalls the human potential for violence and destruction. (2) November 9, designated "World Freedom Day," is important because _____ is the day the Berlin Wall fell. (3) On that day in 1989, residents of East and West Germany were allowed to cross the barrier that had separated _____ since the end of World War II.

(4) However, Germans have mixed feelings about this date because November 9 also reminds ———————— of a dark moment in their history. (5) On the night of November 9, 1938, Nazis took sledgehammers and axes to as many Jewish businesses, synagogues, and homes as ———————— could find. (6) In German, this violent event is called *Kristallnacht*; in English, ———————— is known as "the Night of Broken Glass." (7) Because November 9 has been so important in German history, journalists sometimes refer to ———————— as Germany's "day of fate." (8) Coincidentally, Albert Einstein, a German Jew, received the Nobel Prize on November 9, 1921; the theories ———————— described have changed how scientists think. (9) Thus, November 9 in Germany is a day of opposites; like so many dates in human history, ———————— marks both triumph and tragedy.

31e Special Problems with Agreement

Certain kinds of antecedents can cause problems for writers because they cannot easily be identified as singular or plural.

Compound Antecedents

A **compound antecedent** consists of two or more words connected by *and* or *or*.

- Compound antecedents connected by *and* are plural, and they are used with plural pronouns.

  During World War II, Belgium and France tried to protect their borders.

- Compound antecedents connected by *or* may take a singular or a plural pronoun. The pronoun always agrees with the word that is closer to it.

  Is it possible that European nations or Russia may send its [not *their*] troops?

  Is it possible that Russia or European nations may send their [not *its*] troops?

PRACTICE

31-6   In each of the following sentences, underline the compound antecedent, and circle the connecting word (*and* or *or*). Then, circle the appropriate pronoun in parentheses.

Example: Marge (and) Homer Simpson love (his or her/(their)) children very much in spite of the problems they cause.

1. Either *24* or *Lost* had the highest ratings for any television show in (its/their) final episode.

2. In *South Park*, Geek 1 and Geek 2 help create a time machine out of (his/their) friend Timmy's wheelchair.

3. Both Netflix and Blockbuster offer (its/their) movie rentals online.

4. Either cable stations or the networks hire the most attractive anchors to host (its/their) prime-time shows.

5. Recent movies and documentaries about penguins have delighted (its/their) audiences.

6. In baseball, pitchers and catchers communicate (his or her/their) plays with hand signals.

7. Either Playstation3 or Xbox gives (its/their) players many hours of gaming fun.

8. In summer, many parents and children enjoy spending (his or her/their) time at water parks.

9. Hurricanes or tornadoes can be frightening to (its/their) victims.

Indefinite Pronoun Antecedents

Most pronouns refer to a specific person or thing. However, **indefinite pronouns** do not refer to any particular person or thing.

Most indefinite pronouns are singular.

Singular Indefinite Pronouns

another	everybody	no one
anybody	everyone	nothing
anyone	everything	one
anything	much	somebody
each	neither	someone
either	nobody	something

When an indefinite pronoun antecedent is singular, use a singular pronoun to refer to it.

> Everything was in its place. (*Everything* is singular, so it is used with the singular pronoun *its*.)

FYI

Indefinite Pronouns with *Of*

The singular indefinite pronouns *each*, *either*, *neither*, and *one* are often used in phrases with *of*—*each of*, *either of*, *neither of*, or *one of*—followed by a plural noun. Even in such phrases, these indefinite pronoun antecedents are always singular and take singular pronouns.

> Each of the routes has its [not *their*] own special challenges.

A few indefinite pronouns are plural.

Plural Indefinite Pronouns

both
few
many
others
several

When an indefinite pronoun antecedent is plural, use a plural pronoun to refer to it.

> They all wanted to graduate early, but few received their diplomas in January. (*Few* is plural, so it is used with the plural pronoun *their*.)

FYI

Using *His* or *Her* with Indefinite Pronouns

Even though the indefinite pronouns *anybody, anyone, everybody, everyone, somebody, someone,* and so on are singular, many people use plural pronouns to refer to them.

Everyone must hand in their completed work before 2 p.m.

This usage is widely accepted in spoken English. Nevertheless, indefinite pronouns like *everyone* are singular, and written English requires a singular pronoun.

However, using the singular pronoun *his* to refer to *everyone* suggests that *everyone* refers to a male. Using *his or her* is more accurate because the indefinite pronoun can refer to either a male or a female.

Everyone must hand in his or her completed work before 2 p.m.

When used over and over again, *he or she, him or her,* and *his or her* can create wordy or awkward sentences. Whenever possible, use plural forms.

All students must hand in their completed work before 2 p.m.

PRACTICE

31-7 In each of the following sentences, first circle the indefinite pronoun. Then, circle the pronoun in parentheses that refers to the indefinite pronoun antecedent.

Example: (Each) of the lacrosse players will have (his or her)/their) own locker at training camp.

1. Everyone likes to choose (his or her/their) own class schedule.

2. Somebody left (his or her/their) iPod on the bus.

3. Most of the *American Idol* contestants did (his or her/their) best for the judges.

4. Someone in the audience forgot to turn off (his or her/their) cell phone before the performance.

5. Neither of the dogs wanted to have (its/their) coat brushed.

6. Coach Reilly personally gave each of the players (his or her/their) trophy.

7. Both of the soldiers donated (his or her/their) cars to Purple Heart, an organization that helps veterans.

8. No one should ever give (his or her/their) Social Security number to a telephone solicitor.

9. Anyone who works hard in college can usually receive (his or her/their) degree.

10. Everyone loves receiving presents on (his or her/their) birthday.

PRACTICE
31-8 Edit the following sentences for errors in pronoun-antecedent agreement. When you edit, you have two options: either substitute *its* or *his or her* for *their* to refer to the singular antecedent, or replace the singular antecedent with a plural word.

Examples: Everyone is responsible for ~~their~~ *his or her* own passport.
All
~~Each~~ of the children took their books out of their backpacks.

1. Either of the hybrid cars comes with their own tax rebate.

2. Anyone who loses their locker key must pay $5.00 for a new one.

3. Everyone loves seeing their home team win.

4. Somebody left their scarf and gloves on the subway.

5. Almost everyone waits until the last minute to file their tax returns.

6. Each student returned their library books on time.

7. Everything we need to build the model airplane comes in their kit.

8. Anyone who wants to succeed needs to develop their public-speaking skills.

9. One of the hockey teams just won their first Olympic medal.

10. No one leaving the show early will get their money back.

Collective Noun Antecedents

Collective nouns are words (such as *band* and *team*) that name a group of people or things but are singular. Because they are singular, collective noun antecedents are used with singular pronouns.

The band played on, but it never played our song.

Frequently Used Collective Nouns			
army	club	gang	mob
association	committee	government	posse
band	company	group	team
class	family	jury	union

PRACTICE

31-9 Circle the collective noun antecedent in each of the following sentences. Then, circle the correct pronoun in parentheses.

Example: The jury returned with (its / their) verdict.

1. The company offers good benefits to (its / their) employees.

2. All five study groups must hand in (its / their) projects by Tuesday.

3. Any government should be concerned about the welfare of (its / their) citizens.

4. The Asian Students Union is sponsoring a party to celebrate (its / their) twentieth anniversary.

5. Every family has (its / their) share of problems.

6. To join the electricians' union, applicants had to pass (its / their) test.

7. Even the best teams have (its / their) bad days.

8. The orchestra has just signed a contract to make (its / their) first recording.

9. The math class did very well with (its / their) new teacher.

10. The club voted to expand (its / their) membership.

PRACTICE

31-10   Edit the following passage for correct pronoun-antecedent agreement. First, circle the antecedent of each underlined pronoun. Then, cross out any pronoun that does not agree with its antecedent, and write the correct form above it. If the pronoun is correct, write *C* above it.

Example: Many Americans believe that the (country) is ready for its first female president.

(1) The history of woman suffrage in the United States shows that women were determined to achieve her equal rights. (2) Before 1920, most American women were not allowed to vote for the candidates they preferred. (3) Men ran the government, and a woman could not express their views at the ballot box. (4) However, in the mid-1800s, women began to demand her right to vote—or "woman suffrage." (5) Supporters of woman suffrage believed everyone, regardless of their gender, should be able to vote. (6) At the first woman suffrage convention, Elizabeth Cady Stanton and Lucretia Mott gave speeches explaining his or her views. (7) Susan B. Anthony started the National Woman Suffrage Association, which opposed the Fifteenth Amendment to the Constitution because it gave the vote to black men but not to women. (8) The first state to permit women to vote was Wyoming, and soon other states became more friendly to her cause. (9) Many women participated in marches where he or she carried banners and posters for their cause. (10) During World War I, the U.S. government found that the cooperation of women was essential to their military success. (11) Finally, in 1919, the House of Representatives and the states gave its approval to the Nineteenth Amendment, which gave American women the right to vote.

31f Vague and Unnecessary Pronouns

Vague and unnecessary pronouns clutter up your writing and make it hard to understand. Eliminating them will make your writing clearer and easier for readers to follow.

Vague Pronouns

A pronoun should always refer to a specific antecedent. When a pronoun—such as *they* or *it*—has no antecedent, readers will be confused.

> **VAGUE PRONOUN** On the news, <u>they</u> said baseball players would strike. (Who said baseball players would strike?)

> **VAGUE PRONOUN** <u>It</u> says in today's paper that our schools are overcrowded. (Who says schools are overcrowded?)

If a pronoun does not refer to a specific word in the sentence, replace the pronoun with a noun.

> **REVISED** On the news, the <u>sportscaster</u> said baseball players would strike.

> **REVISED** An <u>editorial</u> in today's paper says that our schools are overcrowded.

Unnecessary Pronouns

When a pronoun comes directly after its antecedent, it is unnecessary.

> **UNNECESSARY PRONOUN** The librarian, <u>he</u> told me I should check the database.

In the sentence above, the pronoun *he* serves no purpose. Readers do not need to be directed back to the pronoun's antecedent (the noun *librarian*) because it appears right before the pronoun. The pronoun should therefore be deleted.

> **REVISED** The librarian told me I should check the database.

PRACTICE
31-11   The following sentences contain vague or unnecessary pronouns. Revise each sentence on the line below it.

Example: On their Web site, they advertised a special offer.

On its Web site, the Gap advertised a special offer.

1. In Jamaica, they love their spectacular green mountains.

_____

2. My hamster, he loves his exercise wheel.

_____

3. On *Jeopardy!* they have to give the answers in the form of questions.

_____

4. On televisions all over the world, they watched the moon landing.

_____

5. In Sociology 320, they do not use a textbook.

_____

31g Pronoun Case

A **personal pronoun** refers to a particular person or thing. Personal pronouns change form according to their function in a sentence. Personal pronouns can be *subjective*, *objective*, or *possessive*.

Personal Pronouns

SUBJECTIVE	OBJECTIVE	POSSESSIVE
I	me	my, mine
he	him	his
she	her	her, hers
it	it	its
we	us	our, ours
you	you	your, yours
they	them	their, theirs
who	whom	whose
whoever	whomever	

Subjective Case

When a pronoun is a subject, it is in the **subjective case**.

Finally, <u>she</u> realized that dreams could come true.

Objective Case

When a pronoun is an object, it is in the **objective case**.

If Joanna hurries, she can stop <u>him</u>. (The pronoun *him* is the object of the verb *can stop*.)

Professor Miller sent <u>us</u> information about his research. (The pronoun *us* is the object of the verb *sent*.)

Marc threw the ball to <u>them</u>. (The pronoun *them* is the object of the preposition *to*.)

Possessive Case

When a pronoun shows ownership, it is in the **possessive case**.

Hieu took <u>his</u> lunch to the meeting. (The pronoun *his* indicates that the lunch belongs to Hieu.)

Debbie and Kim decided to take <u>their</u> lunches, too. (The pronoun *their* indicates that the lunches belong to Debbie and Kim.)

PRACTICE

31-12 In the following passage, fill in the blank after each pronoun to indicate whether the pronoun is subjective (*S*), objective (*O*), or possessive (*P*).

Example: Famous criminals Bonnie and Clyde committed their

_____*P*_____ crimes in broad daylight.

(1) Bonnie Parker and Clyde Barrow are remembered today because they _____ were the first celebrity criminals. (2) With their _____ gang, Bonnie and Clyde robbed a dozen banks as well as many stores and gas stations. (3) In small towns, they _____ terrorized the police. (4) Capturing them _____ seemed impossible. (5) To many Americans, however, their _____ crimes seemed exciting. (6) Because Bonnie was

a woman, she _____ was especially fascinating to them _____.
(7) During their _____ crimes, Bonnie and Clyde would often carry a camera, take photographs of themselves, and then send them _____ to the newspapers, which were happy to publish them _____.
(8) By the time they _____ were killed in an ambush by Texas and Louisiana law officers, Bonnie and Clyde were famous all over the United States.

31h   Special Problems with Pronoun Case

When you are trying to determine which pronoun case to use in a sentence, three kinds of pronouns can cause problems: pronouns in compounds, pronouns in comparisons, and the pronouns *who* and *whom* (or *whoever* and *whomever*).

Pronouns in Compounds

Sometimes a pronoun is linked to a noun or to another pronoun with *and* or *or* to form a **compound**.

> The teacher and I met for an hour.
>
> He or she can pick up Jenny at school.

To determine whether to use the subjective or objective case for a pronoun in the second part of a compound, follow the same rules that apply for a pronoun that is not part of a compound.

- If the compound is a subject, use the subjective case.

  > Toby and I [not *me*] like jazz.
  >
  > He and I [not *me*] went to the movies.

- If the compound is an object, use the objective case.

  > The school sent my father and me [not *I*] the financial-aid forms.
  >
  > This argument is between Kate and me [not *I*].

FYI

Choosing Pronouns in Compounds

To determine which pronoun case to use in a compound that joins a noun and a pronoun, rewrite the sentence with just the pronoun.

Toby and [*I* or *me*?] like jazz.

I like jazz. (not *Me like jazz*)

Toby and I like jazz.

PRACTICE
31-13
In the following sentences, the underlined pronouns are parts of compounds. Check them for correct subjective or objective case. If the pronoun is incorrect, cross it out, and write the correct form above it. If the pronoun is correct, write *C* above it.

C

Example: My classmates and I were surprised by the results of a study on listening.

(1) According to a recent study, the average listener remembers only 50 percent of what him or her hears. (2) Two days later, he or she can correctly recall only 25 percent of the total message. (3) My friend Alyssa and me decided to ask our school to sponsor a presentation about listening in the classroom. (4) One point the speaker made was especially helpful to Alyssa and I. (5) We now know that us and the other students in our class each have four times more mental "room" than we need for listening. (6) The presenter taught the other workshop participants and we how to use this extra space. (7) Now, whenever one of our professors pauses to write on the board or take a sip of water, Alyssa and I remember to silently summarize the last point he or she made. (8) Throughout the lecture, we pay attention to the big ideas and overall structure that the professor wants the other students and us to take away. (9) Also, to keep ourselves actively thinking about the topic, we try to predict where the professor will lead our peers and us next. (10) Above all, we do not waste

our mental energy on distractions that other students and <u>us</u> ourselves create, such as dropped books or our own worries. (11) Comedian Lily Tomlin's advice to "listen with an intensity most people save for talking" now makes a lot of sense to Alyssa and <u>me</u>.

Pronouns in Comparisons

Sometimes a pronoun appears after the word *than* or *as* in the second part of a **comparison**.

> John is luckier <u>than I</u>.
> The inheritance changed Raymond as much <u>as her</u>.

■ If the pronoun is a subject, use the subjective case.

> John is luckier <u>than I</u> [am].

■ If the pronoun is an object, use the objective case.

> The inheritance changed Raymond as much <u>as</u> [it changed] <u>her</u>.

FYI

Choosing Pronouns in Comparisons

Sometimes the pronoun you use can change your sentence's meaning. For example, if you say, "I like Cheerios more than *he*," you mean that you like Cheerios more than the other person likes them.

> I like Cheerios more than he [does].

If, however, you say, "I like Cheerios more than *him*," you mean that you like Cheerios more than you like the other person.

> I like Cheerios more than [I like] him.

PRACTICE

31-14 Each of the following sentences includes a comparison with a pronoun following the word *than* or *as*. Write in each blank the correct form (subjective or objective) of the pronoun in parentheses. In brackets, add the word or words needed to complete the comparison.

Example: Many people are better poker players than ___*I [am]*___ (I/me).

1. The survey showed that most people like the candidate's wife as much as _____ (he/him).

2. No one enjoys shopping more than _____ (she/her).

3. My brother and Aunt Cecile were very close, so her death affected him more than _____ (I/me).

4. No two people could have a closer relationship than _____ (they/them).

5. My neighbor drives better than _____ (I/me).

6. He may be as old as _____ (I/me), but he does not have as much work experience.

7. That jacket fits you better than _____ (I/me).

8. The other company had a lower bid than _____ (we/us), but we were awarded the contract.

Who and *Whom*, *Whoever* and *Whomever*

To determine whether to use *who* or *whom* (or *whoever* or *whomever*), you need to know how the pronoun functions within the clause in which it appears.

- When the pronoun is the subject of the clause, use *who* or *whoever*.

  I wonder <u>who</u> wrote that song. (*Who* is the subject of the clause *who wrote that song*.)

  I will vote for <u>whoever</u> supports the youth center. (*Whoever* is the subject of the clause *whoever supports the youth center*.)

- When the pronoun is the object, use *whom* or *whomever*.

  <u>Whom</u> do the police suspect? (*Whom* is the direct object of the verb *suspect*.)

  I wonder <u>whom</u> the song is about. (*Whom* is the object of the preposition *about* in the clause *whom the song is about*.)

  Vote for <u>whomever</u> you prefer. (*Whomever* is the object of the verb *prefer* in the clause *whomever you prefer*.)

FYI

Who and **Whom**

To determine whether to use *who* or *whom*, try substituting another pronoun for *who* or *whom* in the clause. If you can substitute *he* or *she*, use *who*; if you can substitute *him* or *her*, use *whom*.

[Who/Whom] wrote a love song? He wrote a love song.

[Who/Whom] was the song about? The song was about her.

The same test will work for *whoever* and *whomever*.

PRACTICE

31-15 Circle the correct form—*who* or *whom* (or *whoever* or *whomever*)—in parentheses in each sentence.

Example: With (who/whom) did Rob collaborate?

1. The defense team learned (who/whom) was going to testify for the prosecution.

2. (Who/Whom) does she think she can find to be a witness?

3. The runner (who/whom) crosses the finish line first will be the winner.

4. They will argue their case to (whoever/whomever) will listen.

5. It will take time to decide (who/whom) is the record holder.

6. Take these forms to the clerk (who/whom) is at the front desk.

7. We will have to penalize (whoever/whomever) misses the first training session.

8. (Who/Whom) did Kobe take to the prom?

9. We saw the man (who/whom) fired the shots.

10. To (who/whom) am I speaking?

31i Reflexive and Intensive Pronouns

Two special kinds of pronouns, *reflexive pronouns* and *intensive pronouns*, end in *-self* (singular) or *-selves* (plural). Although the functions of the two kinds of pronouns are different, their forms are identical.

Reflexive and Intensive Pronouns	
Singular Forms	
ANTECEDENT	REFLEXIVE OR INTENSIVE PRONOUN
I	myself
you	yourself
he	himself
she	herself
it	itself
Plural Forms	
ANTECEDENT	REFLEXIVE OR INTENSIVE PRONOUN
we	ourselves
you	yourselves
they	themselves

Reflexive Pronouns

Reflexive pronouns indicate that people or things did something to themselves or for themselves.

Rosanna lost herself in the novel.

You need to watch yourself when you mix those solutions.

Mehul and Paul made themselves cold drinks.

Intensive Pronouns

Intensive pronouns always appear directly after their antecedents, and they are used for emphasis.

I myself have had some experience in sales and marketing.

The victim himself collected the reward.

They themselves were uncertain of the significance of their findings.

PRACTICE

31-16 Fill in the correct reflexive or intensive pronoun in each of the following sentences.

Example: The opening act was exciting, but the main attraction ___*itself*___ was boring.

1. My aunt welcomed her visitors and told them to make _____ at home.

2. Migrating birds can direct _____ through clouds, storms, and moonless nights.

3. The First Lady _____ gave a speech at the rally.

4. We all finished the marathon without injuring _____.

5. Even though the government offered help to flood victims, the residents _____ did most of the rebuilding.

6. Sometimes he finds _____ daydreaming in class.

7. The guide warned us to watch _____ on the slippery path.

8. The senators were not happy about committing _____ to vote for lower taxes.

9. She gave _____ a manicure.

10. Although everyone else in my family can sing or play a musical instrument, I _____ am tone-deaf.

TEST · Revise · Edit

Look back at your response to the Focus on Writing prompt on page 560. **TEST** what you have written. Then, revise and edit your work, paying special attention to your use of nouns and pronouns.

EDITING PRACTICE

Read the following student essay, which includes noun and pronoun errors. Check for errors in plural noun forms, pronoun case, and pronoun-antecedent agreement. Then, make any editing changes you think are necessary. The first sentence has been edited for you.

Cell-Phone Misbehavior

Good ~~manneres~~ *manners* used to mean using the right fork and holding the door open for others. Today, however, people may find that good manners are more complicated than it used to be. New inventions have led to new challenges. Cell phones, in particular, have created some problems.

One problem is the "cell yell," which is the tendency of a person to shout while they are using their cell phones. Why do they do this? Maybe they do not realize how loudly they are talking. Maybe they yell out of frustration. Anyone can become angry when they lose a call. Dead batterys can be infuriating. Unfortunately, the yeller annoys everyone around them.

Even if cell-phone users theirselves speak normally, other people can hear them. My friends and me are always calling each other, and we do not always pay attention to whom can hear us. The result is that other people are victims of "secondhand conversations." These conversations are not as bad for people's health as secondhand smoke, but it is just as annoying. Whom really wants to hear about the private lifes of strangers? Restrooms used to be private; now, whomever is in the next stall can overhear someone's private cell-phone conversation and learn their secrets.

Also, some cell-phone user seem to think that getting his calls is more important than anything else that might be going on. Phones ring, chirp, or play silly tunes at concertes, in classrooms, at weddings, in churchs, and even at funerals. Can you picture a grieving family at a cemetery having their service interrupted by a ringing phone? People should have enough sense to turn off his or her cell phones at times like these.

In the United States, there are more than 150 million cell phones. Some people hate being tied to cell phones, but they do not think they can live without it. The problem is that cell phones became popular before there were any rules for its use. However, even if the government passed laws about cell-phone behavior, they would have a tough time enforcing it. In any case, cell-phone users should not need laws to make them behave theirself.

COLLABORATIVE ACTIVITY

Working in a group, fill in the following chart, writing one noun on each line. If the noun is a proper noun, be sure to capitalize it.

CARS	TREES	FOODS	FAMOUS COUPLES	CITIES
_____	_____	_____	_____	_____
_____	_____	_____	_____	_____
_____	_____	_____	_____	_____
_____	_____	_____	_____	_____
_____	_____	_____	_____	_____
_____	_____	_____	_____	_____
_____	_____	_____	_____	_____

Now, using as many of the nouns listed above as you can, write a one-paragraph news article that describes an imaginary event. Exchange your work with another group, and check the other group's article to be sure the correct pronoun refers to each noun. Return the articles to their original groups for editing.

review checklist

Nouns and Pronouns

- [ ] A noun is a word that names something. A singular noun names one thing; a plural noun names more than one thing. (See 31a.)

- [ ] Most nouns add *-s* or *-es* to form plurals. Some nouns have irregular plural forms. (See 31b.)

- [ ] A pronoun is a word that refers to and takes the place of a noun or another pronoun. (See 31c.)

- [ ] The word a pronoun refers to is called the pronoun's antecedent. A pronoun and its antecedent must always agree. (See 31d.)

- [ ] Compound antecedents connected by *and* are plural and are used with plural pronouns. Compound antecedents connected by *or* may take singular or plural pronouns. (See 31e.)

- [ ] Most indefinite pronoun antecedents are singular and are used with singular pronouns; some are plural and are used with plural pronouns. (See 31e.)

- [ ] Collective noun antecedents are singular and are used with singular pronouns. (See 31e.)

- [ ] A pronoun should always refer to a specific antecedent. (See 31f.)

- [ ] Personal pronouns can be in the subjective, objective, or possessive case. (See 31g.)

- [ ] Pronouns present special problems when they are used in compounds and comparisons. The pronouns *who* and *whom* and *whoever* and *whomever* can also cause problems. (See 31h.)

- [ ] Reflexive and intensive pronouns must agree with their antecedents. (See 31i.)

✔ **LearningCurve**
Nouns and Pronouns
bedfordstmartins.com
/focusonwriting

32 Adjectives and Adverbs

focus on writing

This picture shows children being homeschooled by their mother. Write a paragraph about the advantages and disadvantages of being educated at home by parents instead of at school by professional teachers.

In this chapter, you will learn to

- understand the difference between adjectives and adverbs (32a)
- identify demonstrative adjectives (32a)
- form comparatives and superlatives of adjectives and adverbs (32b)

32a Identifying Adjectives and Adverbs

Adjectives and adverbs are words that modify (identify or describe) other words. They help make sentences more specific and more interesting.

An **adjective** answers the question *What kind? Which one?* or *How many?* Adjectives modify nouns or pronouns.

> The Turkish city of Istanbul spans two continents. (*Turkish* modifies the noun *city*, and *two* modifies the noun *continents*.)
>
> It is fascinating because of its location and history. (*Fascinating* modifies the pronoun *it*.)

✅ **LearningCurve**
Verbs, Adjectives, and Adverbs
**bedfordstmartins.com
/focusonwriting**

FYI

Demonstrative Adjectives

Demonstrative adjectives—*this*, *that*, *these*, and *those*—do not describe other words. They simply identify particular nouns.

This and *that* identify singular nouns and pronouns.

> This Web site is much more up-to-date than that one.

These and *those* identify plural nouns.

> These words and phrases are French, but those expressions are Creole.

An **adverb** answers the question *How? Why? When? Where?* or *To what extent?* Adverbs modify verbs, adjectives, or other adverbs.

> Traffic moved steadily. (*Steadily* modifies the verb *moved*.)
>
> Still, we were quite impatient. (*Quite* modifies the adjective *impatient*.)
>
> Very slowly, we moved into the center lane. (*Very* modifies the adverb *slowly*.)

FYI

Distinguishing Adjectives from Adverbs

Many adverbs are formed when -*ly* is added to an adjective form.

ADJECTIVE	ADVERB
slow	slowly
nice	nicely
quick	quickly
real	really

ADJECTIVE Let me give you one quick reminder. (*Quick* modifies the noun *reminder*.)

ADVERB He quickly changed the subject. (*Quickly* modifies the verb *changed*.)

PRACTICE

32-1 In the following sentences, circle the correct form (adjective or adverb) from the choices in parentheses.

Example: Beatles enthusiasts all over the world have formed tribute bands devoted to the (famous/famously) group's music.

(1) To show appreciation for their favorite musicians, tribute bands go to (great/greatly) lengths. (2) Fans who have a (real/really) strong affection for a particular band may decide to play its music and copy its style. (3) Sometimes they form their own groups and have successful careers (simple/simply) performing that band's music. (4) These groups are (usual/usually) called "tribute bands." (5) Most tribute bands are (passionate/passionately) dedicated to reproducing the original group's work. (6) They not only play the group's songs but (careful/carefully) imitate the group's look. (7) They study the band members' facial expressions and body movements and create (exact/exactly) copies of the band's costumes and instruments. (8) Some more (inventive/inventively) tribute bands take the original band's songs and interpret them (different/differently).

(9) For example, by performing Beatles songs in the style of Metallica, the tribute band Beatallica has created a (unique/uniquely) sound. (10) Some people believe such tributes are the (ultimate/ultimately) compliment to the original band; others feel (sure/surely) that tribute groups are just copycats who (serious/seriously) lack imagination.

FYI

Good and *Well*

Be careful not to confuse *good* and *well*. Unlike regular adjectives, whose adverb forms add *-ly*, the adjective *good* is irregular. Its adverb form is *well*.

ADJECTIVE Fred Astaire was a good dancer. (*Good* modifies the noun *dancer*.)

ADVERB He danced especially well with Ginger Rogers. (*Well* modifies the verb *danced*.)

Always use *well* when you are describing a person's health.

He really didn't feel well [not *good*] after eating the entire pizza.

PRACTICE

32-2 Circle the correct form (*good* or *well*) in the sentences below.

Example: It can be hard for some people to find a (good/well) job that they really like.

(1) Some people may not do (good/well) sitting in an office. (2) Instead, they may prefer to find jobs that take advantage of their (good/well) physical condition. (3) Such people might consider becoming smoke jumpers—firefighters who are (good/well) at parachuting from small planes into remote areas to battle forest fires. (4) Smoke jumpers must be able to work (good/well) even without much sleep. (5) They must also handle danger (good/well). (6) They look forward to the (good/well) feeling of saving a forest or someone's home. (7) As they battle fires, surrounded

by smoke and fumes, smoke jumpers may not feel very (good/well). (8) Sometimes things go wrong; for example, when their parachutes fail to work (good/well), jumpers may be injured or even killed. (9) Smoke jumpers do not get paid particularly (good/well). (10) However, they are proud of their strength and endurance and feel (good/well) about their work.

32b Comparatives and Superlatives

The **comparative** form of an adjective or adverb compares two people or things. Adjectives and adverbs form the comparative with -*er* or *more*. The **superlative** form of an adjective or adverb compares more than two things. Adjectives and adverbs form the superlative with -*est* or *most*.

ADJECTIVES	This film is <u>dull</u> and <u>predictable</u>.
COMPARATIVE	The film I saw last week was even <u>duller</u> and <u>more predictable</u> than this one.
SUPERLATIVE	The film I saw last night was the <u>dullest</u> and <u>most predictable</u> one I've ever seen.
ADVERBS	For a beginner, Jane did needlepoint <u>skillfully</u>.
COMPARATIVE	After she had watched the demonstration, Jane did needlepoint <u>more skillfully</u> than Rosie.
SUPERLATIVE	Of the twelve beginners, Jane did needlepoint the <u>most skillfully</u>.

Forming Comparatives and Superlatives

Adjectives

■ One-syllable adjectives generally form the comparative with -*er* and the superlative with -*est*.

great	greater	greatest

■ Adjectives with two or more syllables form the comparative with *more* and the superlative with *most*.

wonderful	more wonderful	most wonderful

Exception: Two-syllable adjectives ending in *-y* add *-er* or *-est* after changing the *y* to an *i*.

funny	funnier	funniest

Adverbs

■ All adverbs ending in *-ly* form the comparative with *more* and the superlative with *most*.

efficiently	more efficiently	most efficiently

■ Some other adverbs form the comparative with *-er* and the superlative with *-est*.

soon	sooner	soonest

Solving Special Problems with Comparatives and Superlatives

The following rules will help you avoid errors with comparatives and superlatives.

■ Never use both *-er* and *more* to form the comparative or both *-est* and *most* to form the superlative.

> Nothing could have been <u>more awful</u>. (not *more awfuller*)
>
> Space Mountain is the <u>most frightening</u> (not *most frighteningest*) ride at Disney World.

■ Never use the superlative when you are comparing only two things.

> This is the <u>more serious</u> (not *most serious*) of the two problems.

■ Never use the comparative when you are comparing more than two things.

> This is the <u>worst</u> (not *worse*) day of my life.

PRACTICE

32-3 Fill in the correct comparative form of the word supplied in parentheses.

Example: Children tend to be ____*noisier*____ (noisy) than adults.

1. Traffic always moves _____ (slow) during rush hour than

late at night.

2. The weather report says temperatures will be _____ (cold) tomorrow.

3. Some elderly people are _____ (healthy) than younger people.

4. It has been proven that pigs are _____ (intelligent) than dogs.

5. When someone asks you to repeat yourself, you usually answer _____ (loud).

6. The _____ (tall) of the two buildings was damaged by the earthquake.

7. They want to teach their son to be _____ (respectful) of women than many young men are.

8. Las Vegas is _____ (famous) for its casinos than for its natural resources.

9. The WaterDrop is _____ (wild) than any other ride in the amusement park.

10. You must move _____ (quick) if you expect to catch the ball.

PRACTICE

32-4   Fill in the correct superlative form of the word supplied in parentheses.

Example: The first remote controls came with only the __most expensive__ (expensive) televisions.

(1) The invention of the remote control in the 1950s was one of the _____ (important) moments in television history. (2) The remote was especially welcomed by lazy viewers, who were the _____ (empowered) by the new device. (3) Even the _____ (lazy) people could now change channels without getting off the couch. (4) However, as remote controls developed, even the _____ (simple) devices could sometimes confuse the _____ (skilled) users. (5) The

large number of buttons became one of the _____ (irritating) features. (6) Even today, remotes remain one of the _____ (unnecessarily) complicated electronic devices. (7) According to one critic, the TV remote is one of the _____ (poorly) designed inventions of all time. (8) Improving the remote is one of the _____ (challenging) projects for inventors. (9) Already, the _____ (innovative) companies are adding voice and motion control to the _____ (late) remotes. (10) One of the _____ (astonishing) possible new developments may be a remote control operated entirely by the viewer's mind.

FYI

Good/Well and Bad/Badly

Most adjectives and adverbs form the comparative with -er or more and the superlative with -est or most. The adjectives good and bad and their adverb forms well and badly are exceptions.

ADJECTIVE	COMPARATIVE FORM	SUPERLATIVE FORM
good	better	best
bad	worse	worst

ADVERB	COMPARATIVE FORM	SUPERLATIVE FORM
well	better	best
badly	worse	worst

PRACTICE

32-5 Fill in the correct comparative or superlative form of *good*, *well*, *bad*, or *badly*.

Example: My sister is a ___*better*___ (good) runner than I am.

1. Neela was certain she was the _____ (good) chef in the competition.

2. Because he studied more, Helio earned _____ (good) grades than his sister.

3. An optimist, Mara always thinks she will do _____ (well) next time.

4. Many people drive the _____ (badly) when they are in a hurry.

5. Of all the mortgage companies Ramon researched, Plains Bank had the _____ (good) interest rate.

6. I feel bad when I get rejected, but I feel _____ (bad) when I do not try.

7. For nontraditional students, access to education is _____ (good) than it used to be.

8. Jamie sings badly, but Simon sings _____ (badly).

9. I learn the _____ (well) when I am not distracted.

10. After looking at every painting in the gallery, they decided that the landscapes were definitely the _____ (bad) paintings there.

TEST · Revise · Edit

Look back at your response to the Focus on Writing prompt on page 588. **TEST** what you have written. Then, revise and edit your work, paying special attention to your use of adjectives and adverbs.

EDITING PRACTICE

Read the following student essay, which includes errors in the use of adjectives and adverbs. Make any changes necessary to correct adjectives incorrectly used for adverbs and adverbs incorrectly used for adjectives. Also, correct any errors in the use of comparatives and superlatives and in the use of demonstrative adjectives. Finally, try to add some adjectives and adverbs that you feel would make the writer's ideas clearer or more specific. The first sentence has been edited for you.

Starting Over

most joyful

A wedding can be the ~~joyfullest~~ occasion in two people's lives, the

beginning of a couple's most happiest years. For some unlucky women, however,

a wedding can be the worse thing that ever happens; it is the beginning not of

their happiness but of their battered lives. As I went through the joyful day

of my wedding, I wanted bad to find happiness for the rest of my life, but what

I hoped and wished for did not come true.

I was married in the savannah belt of the Sudan in the eastern part of

Africa, where I grew up. I was barely twenty-two years old. The first two years

of my marriage progressed peaceful, but problems started as soon as our first

child was born.

Many American women say, "If my husband hit me just once, that would be

it. I'd leave." But those attitude does not work in cultures where tradition has

overshadowed women's rights and divorce is not accepted. All women can do

is accept their sadly fate. Battered women give many reasons for staying in their

marriages, but fear is the commonest. Fear immobilizes these women, ruling

their decisions, their actions, and their very lives. This is how it was for me.

Of course, I was real afraid whenever my husband hit me. I would run to

my mother's house and cry, but she would always talk me into going back and

being more patiently with my husband. Our tradition discourages divorce, and wife-beating is taken for granted. The situation is really quite ironic: the religion I practice sets harsh punishments for abusive husbands, but tradition has so overpowered religion that the laws do not really work very good.

One night, I asked myself whether life had treated me fair. True, I had a high school diploma and two of the beautifullest children in the world, but all this was not enough. I realized that to stand up to the husband who treated me so bad, I would have to achieve a more better education than he had. That night, I decided to get a college education in the United States. My husband opposed my decision, but with the support of my father and mother, I was able to begin to change my life. My years as a student and single parent in the United States have been real difficult for me, but I know I made the right choice.

COLLABORATIVE ACTIVITY

Working in a small group, write a plot summary for an imaginary film. Begin with one of the following three sentences.

- Dirk and Clive were sworn enemies, but that night on Boulder Ridge they vowed to work together just this once, for the good of their country.
- Genevieve entered the room in a cloud of perfume, and when she spoke, her voice was like velvet.
- The desert sun beat down on her head, but Susanna was determined to protect what was hers, no matter what the cost.

Now, exchange summaries with another group, and add as many adjectives and adverbs as you can to the other group's summary. Finally, reread your own group's plot summary, and edit it carefully, paying special attention to the way adjectives and adverbs are used.

review checklist

Adjectives and Adverbs

- [ ] Adjectives modify nouns or pronouns. (See 32a.)

- [ ] Demonstrative adjectives—*this, that, these,* and *those*—identify particular nouns. (See 32a.)

- [ ] Adverbs modify verbs, adjectives, or other adverbs. (See 32a.)

- [ ] To compare two people or things, use the comparative form of an adjective or adverb. To compare more than two people or things, use the superlative form of an adjective or adverb. (See 32b.)

- [ ] The adjectives *good* and *bad* and their adverb forms *well* and *badly* have irregular comparative and superlative forms. (See 32b.)

LearningCurve
Verbs, Adjectives, and
Adverbs
**bedfordstmartins.com
/focusonwriting**

33 Grammar and Usage for ESL Writers

focus on writing

This painting by Frederick Childe Hassam shows American flags displayed on the Fourth of July, Independence Day. Using the present tense, write a paragraph explaining how you and your family celebrate a holiday that is important to you.

In this chapter, you will learn to

- understand how subjects are used in sentences (33a)
- identify plural nouns (33b)
- understand and use determiners with count and noncount nouns (33c and 33d)
- understand articles (33e)
- form negative statements and questions (33f)
- indicate verb tense (33g)
- recognize stative verbs (33h)
- use modal auxiliaries (33i)
- understand gerunds (33j)
- place modifiers in order (33k)
- choose correct prepositions (33l) and use them in familiar expressions (33m)
- use prepositions in phrasal verbs (33n)

Learning English as a second language involves more than just learning grammar. In fact, if you have been studying English as a second language, you may know more about English grammar than many native speakers do. However, you will still need to learn the conventions and rules that most native speakers already know.

LearningCurve
Sentence Structure for
Multilingual Writers
**bedfordstmartins.com
/focusonwriting**

33a   Subjects in Sentences

English requires that every sentence state its subject. Every independent clause and every dependent clause must also have a subject.

INCORRECT   Elvis Presley was only forty-two years old when died. (When who died?)

CORRECT   Elvis Presley was only forty-two years old when he died.

When the real subject follows the verb and the normal subject position before the verb is empty, it must be filled by a "dummy" subject, such as *it* or *there*.

INCORRECT   Is hot in this room.

CORRECT   It is hot in this room.

INCORRECT   Are many rivers in my country.

CORRECT   There are many rivers in my country.

601

Standard English also does not permit a two-part subject in which the second part of the subject is a pronoun referring to the same person or thing as the first part.

INCORRECT The Caspian Sea it is the largest lake in the world.

CORRECT The Caspian Sea is the largest lake in the world.

PRACTICE

33-1 Each of the following sentences is missing the subject of a dependent or an independent clause. On the lines provided, rewrite each sentence, adding an appropriate subject. Then, underline the subject you have added.

Example: Because college students often have very little money, are always looking for inexpensive meals.

Because college students often have very little money, <u>they</u> are always looking

for inexpensive meals.

1. Ramen noodles are a popular choice for students because are cheap, tasty, and easy to prepare.

   _____

   _____

2. In minutes, a student can enjoy hot noodles flavored with chicken, shrimp, or beef, and sell vegetarian versions, too.

   _____

   _____

3. Although high in carbohydrates (a good source of energy), also contain saturated and trans fats and few vitamins or minerals.

   _____

   _____

4. Cookbooks provide special recipes for preparing ramen noodles; include "Ramen Shrimp Soup" and "Ramen Beef and Broccoli."

   _____

   _____

5. Ramen noodles are not just popular with American college students; are also popular in many other countries around the world.

_____

_____

6. The noodles have even found their way to the International Space Station, where enjoy them in space.

_____

_____

7. The noodles originated in China many years ago, where were deep fried so that they could be stored for a long time without spoiling.

_____

_____

8. For today's college students, however, spoilage is not a problem because are usually eaten long before their expiration date.

_____

_____

PRACTICE

33-2 The following sentences contain unnecessary two-part subjects. Cross out the unnecessary pronoun. Then, rewrite each sentence correctly on the lines provided.

Example: Travelers to China ~~they~~ often visit the Great Wall.

Travelers to China often visit the Great Wall.

1. The first parts of the Great Wall they were built around 200 AD.

_____

_____

2. The Great Wall it was built to keep out invading armies.

_____

_____

3. The sides of the Great Wall they are made of stone, brick, and earth.

_____

_____

4. The top of the Great Wall it is paved with bricks, forming a roadway for horses.

_____

_____

5. The Great Wall it is so huge that it can be seen by astronauts in space.

_____

_____

 **LearningCurve**
Multilingual Writers:
Articles and Nouns
bedfordstmartins.com
/focusonwriting

33b Plural Nouns

In English, most nouns add -s to form plurals. Every time you use a noun, ask yourself whether you are talking about one item or more than one, and choose a singular or plural form accordingly. Consider the following sentence.

CORRECT   The <u>books</u> in both <u>branches</u> of the <u>library</u> are deteriorating.

The three nouns in this sentence are underlined: one is singular (*library*), and the other two are plural (*books, branches*). The word *both* is not enough to indicate that *branch* is plural. Even if a sentence includes information that tells you that a noun is plural, you must always use a form of the noun that indicates that it is plural.

PRACTICE
33-3   Underline the plural nouns in the following sentences. (Not all of the sentences contain plural nouns.)

Example: Mass immigration and lack of employment created unexpected social <u>problems</u> in the United States in the nineteenth century.

1. In 1850, New York City estimated that about thirty thousand homeless children lived on its streets.

2. The children were considered "orphans" because their parents had died, lost jobs, or were ill.

3. A social service agency in New York City suggested a solution to this problem.

4. The solution was to send these children to America's heartland—to states like Iowa, Kansas, and Arkansas.

5. There, the children could be accepted into families and help with farming and other chores.

6. In 1854, the first "orphan train" headed to western cities and towns.

7. The children were lined up in a local hall, looked over, and selected by interested families.

8. Then, the remaining children got back on the train and went on to the next town to go through the process again.

9. Most of the children found happy homes and loving parents, but others were treated like servants by their new families.

10. By 1930, social service agencies had begun to reconsider the plan and stopped the orphan trains.

33c   Count and Noncount Nouns

☑ **LearningCurve**
Multilingual Writers:
Articles and Nouns
**bedfordstmartins.com
/focusonwriting**

A **count noun** names one particular thing or a group of particular things that can be counted: *a teacher, a panther, a bed, an ocean, a cloud, an ice cube; two teachers, many panthers, three beds, two oceans, several clouds, some ice cubes.* A **noncount noun** names things that cannot be counted: *gold, cream, sand, blood, smoke, water.*

Count nouns usually have a singular form and a plural form: *cube, cubes.* Noncount nouns usually have only a singular form: *water.* Note how the nouns *cube* and *water* differ in the way they are used in sentences.

> CORRECT   The glass is full of ice cubes.
>
> CORRECT   The glass is full of water.
>
> INCORRECT   The glass is full of waters.

CORRECT   The glass contains five ice cubes.

CORRECT   The glass contains some water.

INCORRECT   The glass contains five waters.

Often, the same idea can be expressed with either a count noun or a noncount noun.

COUNT	NONCOUNT
people (plural of *person*)	humanity [*not* humanities]
tables, chairs, beds	furniture [*not* furnitures]
letters	mail [*not* mails]
supplies	equipment [*not* equipments]
facts	information [*not* informations]
guns	ammunition [*not* ammunitions]

Some words can be either count or noncount, depending on the meaning intended.

COUNT   He had many interesting underline{experiences} at his first job.

NONCOUNT   It is often difficult to get a job if you do not have underline{experience}.

Here are some guidelines for using count and noncount nouns:

■ Use a count noun to refer to a living animal, but use a noncount noun to refer to the food that comes from that animal.

COUNT   There are three live lobsters in the tank.

NONCOUNT   This restaurant specializes in lobster.

■ If you use a noncount noun for a substance or class of things that can come in different varieties, you can often make that noun plural if you want to talk about those varieties.

NONCOUNT   Cheese is a rich source of calcium.

COUNT   Many different cheeses come from Italy.

■ If you want to shift attention from a concept in general to specific examples of it, you can often use a noncount noun as a count noun.

NONCOUNT   You have a great deal of talent.

COUNT   My talents do not include singing.

PRACTICE

33-4   In each of the following sentences, decide if the underlined word is being used as a count or a noncount noun. If it is being used as a noncount noun, circle the *N* following the sentence. If it is being used as a count noun, circle the *C*.

Examples: As a Peace Corps <u>volunteer</u> in Ecuador, Dave Schwei-denback realized how important bicycles could be.   N   Ⓒ

Using his <u>imagination</u>, Dave figured out an effective way to recycle America's unwanted bicycles.   Ⓝ   C

1. Pedals for Progress is an American nonprofit <u>organization</u>.   N   C

2. Founded in 1991 by Dave Schweidenback, the <u>group</u> collects and repairs old bicycles and sends them to countries where they are needed.   N   C

3. Pedals for Progress aims to reduce the amount of bicycle <u>waste</u> that ends up in American landfills.   N   C

4. People in the United States throw away millions of bikes and bike parts every <u>year</u>.   N   C

5. At the same time, lack of <u>transportation</u> is a serious problem for many people in developing countries.   N   C

6. Without an efficient and affordable way to get to work, a person cannot hold a <u>job</u>.   N   C

7. A working bicycle provides an easy and environmentally friendly <u>way</u> to get around.   N   C

8. Bicycles from Pedals for Progress only cost the user a small amount of <u>money</u>.   N   C

9. To help maintain these recycled bikes, the organization also helps to establish local repair <u>shops</u>.   N   C

10. By making it easier for people to work, Pedals for Progress hopes to reduce <u>poverty</u>.   N   C

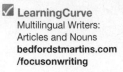

LearningCurve
Multilingual Writers:
Articles and Nouns
bedfordstmartins.com
/focusonwriting

33d Determiners with Count and Noncount Nouns

Determiners are adjectives that *identify* rather than describe the nouns they modify. Determiners may also *quantify* nouns (that is, indicate an amount or a number).

Determiners include the following words.

- Articles: *a, an, the*
- Demonstrative pronouns: *this, these, that, those*
- Possessive pronouns: *my, our, your, his, her, its, their*
- Possessive nouns: *Sheila's, my friend's,* and so on
- *Whose, which, what*
- *All, both, each, every, some, any, either, no, neither, many, most, much, a few, a little, few, little, several, enough*
- All numerals: *one, two,* and so on

When a determiner is accompanied by one or more other adjectives, the determiner always comes first. For example, in the phrase *my expensive new digital watch, my* is a determiner; you cannot put *expensive, new, digital,* or any other adjective before *my.*

A singular count noun must always be accompanied by a determiner—for example, *my watch* or *the new digital watch,* not just *watch* or *new digital watch.* However, noncount nouns and plural count nouns sometimes have determiners but sometimes do not. *This honey is sweet* and *Honey is sweet* are both acceptable, as are *These berries are juicy* and *Berries are juicy.* (In each case, the meaning is different.) You cannot say, *Berry is juicy,* however; say instead, *This berry is juicy, Every berry is juicy,* or *A berry is juicy.*

FYI

Determiners

Some determiners can be used only with certain types of nouns.

- *This* and *that* can be used only with singular nouns (count or noncount): *this berry, that honey.*
- *These, those, a few, few, many, both,* and *several* can be used only with plural count nouns: *these berries, those apples, a few ideas, few people, many students, both sides, several directions.*

- *Much, little,* and *a little* can be used only with noncount nouns: *much affection, little time, a little honey.*
- *Some, enough, all,* and *most* can be used only with noncount or plural count nouns: *some honey, some berries; enough trouble, enough problems; all traffic, all roads; most money, most coins.*
- *A, an, every, each, either,* and *neither* can be used only with singular count nouns: *a berry, an elephant, every possibility, each citizen, either option, neither candidate.*

PRACTICE
33-5
In each of the following sentences, circle the more appropriate choice from each pair of words or phrases in parentheses.

Examples: Volcanoes are among the most destructive of (all/every) natural forces on earth.

People have always been fascinated and terrified by (this/these) force of nature.

1. Not (all/every) volcano is considered a danger.

2. In (major some/some major) volcanic eruptions, huge clouds rise over the mountain.

3. In 2010, ash from a volcano in Iceland caused (many/much) disruption for airline passengers throughout Europe.

4. (A few violent/Violent a few) eruptions are so dramatic that they blow the mountain apart.

5. (Most/Much) volcanic eruptions cannot be predicted.

6. Since the 1400s, (many/much) people—almost 200,000—have lost their lives in volcanic eruptions.

7. When a volcano erupts, (little/a little) can be done to prevent property damage.

8. By the time people realize an eruption is about to take place, there is rarely (many/enough) time to escape.

9. Volcanoes can be dangerous, but they also produce (a little/some) benefits.

10. For example, (a few/a little) countries use energy from underground steam in volcanic areas to produce electric power.

✅ **LearningCurve**
Multilingual Writers:
Articles and Nouns
**bedfordstmartins.com
/focusonwriting**

33e   Articles

The **definite article** *the* and the **indefinite articles** *a* and *an* are determiners that tell readers whether the noun that follows is one they can identify (*the book*) or one they cannot yet identify (*a book*).

The Definite Article

When the definite article *the* is used with a noun, the writer is saying to readers, "You can identify which particular thing or things I have in mind. The information you need to make that identification is available to you. Either you have it already, or I am about to give it to you."

Readers can find the necessary information in the following ways.

- By looking at other information in the sentence

    Meet me at the corner of Main Street and Lafayette Road.

    In this example, *the* is used with the noun *corner* because other words in the sentence tell readers which particular corner the writer has in mind: the one located at Main and Lafayette.

- By looking at information in other sentences

    Aisha ordered a slice of pie and a cup of coffee. The pie was delicious. She asked for a second slice.

    Here, *the* is used before the word *pie* in the second sentence to indicate that it is the same pie identified in the first sentence. Notice, however, that the noun *slice* in the third sentence is preceded by an indefinite article (*a*) because it is not the same slice referred to in the first sentence.

■ By drawing on general knowledge

> The earth revolves around the sun.

Here, *the* is used with the nouns *earth* and *sun* because readers are expected to know which particular things the writer is referring to.

FYI

The Definite Article

Always use *the* (rather than *a* or *an*) in the following situations:

■ Before the word *same*: *the same day*
■ Before the superlative form of an adjective: *the youngest son*
■ Before a number indicating order or sequence: *the third time*

Indefinite Articles

When an indefinite article is used with a noun, the writer is saying to readers, "I don't expect you to have enough information right now to identify a particular thing that I have in mind. I do, however, expect you to recognize that I'm referring to only one item."

Consider the following sentences.

> We need a table for our computer.

> I have a folding table; maybe you can use that.

In the first sentence, the writer is referring to a hypothetical table, not an actual one. Because the table is indefinite to the writer, it is clearly indefinite to the reader, so *a* is used, not *the*. The second sentence refers to an actual table, but because the writer does not expect the reader to be able to identify the table specifically, it is also used with *a* rather than *the*.

WORD POWER

hypothetical
assumed or supposed; not supported by evidence

FYI

Indefinite Articles

Unlike the definite article (*the*), the indefinite articles *a* and *an* occur only with singular count nouns. *A* is used when the next sound is a consonant, and *an* is used when the next sound is a vowel. In choosing *a* or *an*, pay attention to sound rather than to spelling: *a house, a year, a union,* but *an hour, an uncle.*

No Article

Only noncount and plural count nouns can stand without articles: *butter*, *chocolate*, *cookies*, *strawberries* (but *a cookie* or *the strawberry*).

Nouns without articles can be used to make generalizations.

<u>Infants</u> need <u>affection</u> as well as <u>food</u>.

Here, the absence of articles before the nouns *infants*, *affection*, and *food* indicates that the statement is not about particular infants, affection, or food but about infants, affection, and food in general. Remember not to use *the* in such sentences; in English, a sentence like *The infants need affection as well as food* can only refer to particular, identifiable infants, not to infants in general.

Articles with Proper Nouns

Proper nouns can be divided into two classes: names that take *the* and names that take no article.

- Names of people usually take no article unless they are used in the plural to refer to members of a family, in which case they take *the*: *Napoleon*, *Mahatma Gandhi* (but *the Parkers*).

- Names of places that are plural in form usually take *the*: *the Andes*, *the United States*.

- The names of most places on land (cities, states, provinces, and countries) take no article: *Salt Lake City*, *Mississippi*, *Alberta*, *Japan*. The names of most bodies of water (rivers, seas, and oceans, although not lakes or bays) take *the*: *the Mississippi*, *the Mediterranean*, *the Pacific* (but *Lake Erie*, *San Francisco Bay*).

- Names of streets take no article: *Main Street*. Names of unnumbered highways take *the*: *the Belt Parkway*.

PRACTICE

33-6 In the following passage, decide whether each blank needs a definite article (*the*), an indefinite article (*a* or *an*), or no article. If a definite or an indefinite article is needed, write it in the space provided. If no article is needed, leave the space blank.

Example: A sundial can be _____*an*_____ attractive addition to _____

backyard gardens.

(1) Sundials take many forms, and they have come _____ _____ long way from their origins. (2) Today's backyard sundials usually feature _____ small, circular table where _____ triangular fin casts _____ shadow. (3) Two hundred years ago, however, _____ most popular sundials were small enough to be carried in _____ pocket. (4) Pocket sundials were used instead of _____ watches until _____ 1800s even though _____ first watch was made in 1504. (5) It took watchmakers centuries to get _____ tiny parts inside _____ watch to run smoothly. (6) For this reason, _____ rich European during _____ Renaissance might have bought _____ watch as _____ fancy toy but used _____ pocket sundial to tell time. (7) Pocket sundials are certainly _____ thing of _____ past, but larger sundials continue to be built for _____ variety of purposes. (8) _____ large sundial is often much more than _____ attractive decoration for _____ garden. (9) It might be _____ sophisticated timekeeper, _____ architectural wonder, or _____ symbol. (10) For example, at _____ Jantar Mantar observatory in Jaipur, India, _____ three-hundred-year-old disk dial tells time as accurately as _____ cell phone equipped with GPS. (11) At _____ university in Hong Kong, _____ red, flame-shaped sundial is a startling sculpture for _____ main entrance to its campus. (12) And in California, _____ bridge that spans _____ Sacramento River is held up by _____ enormous sundial. (13) This "Sundial Bridge" was built to represent _____ relationship between _____ humans and _____ nature. (14) As these examples show, we remain fascinated by _____ precision, simplicity, and beauty of sundials even though we no longer need _____ sun to help us tell time.

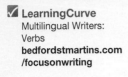
LearningCurve
Multilingual Writers:
Verbs
bedfordstmartins.com
/focusonwriting

33f Negative Statements and Questions

Negative Statements

To form a negative statement, add the word *not* directly after the first helping verb of the complete verb.

> Global warming has been getting worse.

> Global warming has <u>not</u> been getting worse.

When there is no helping verb, a form of the verb *do* must be inserted before *not*.

> Automobile traffic contributes to pollution.

> Automobile traffic <u>does not</u> contribute to pollution.

However, if the main verb is *am, is, are, was,* or *were,* do not insert a form of *do* before *not*: *Harry was late. Harry was <u>not</u> late.*

Remember that when *do* is used as a helping verb, the form of *do* used must match the tense and number of the original main verb. Note that in the negative statement above, the main verb loses its tense and appears in the base form (*contribute,* not *contributes*).

Questions

To form a question, move the helping verb that follows the subject to the position directly before the subject.

> The governor <u>is</u> trying to compromise.
> <u>Is</u> the governor trying to compromise?

> The governor <u>is</u> working on the budget.
> <u>Is</u> the governor working on the budget?

The same rule applies even when the verb is in the past or future tense.

> The governor <u>was</u> trying to lower state taxes.
> <u>Was</u> the governor trying to lower state taxes?

> The governor <u>will</u> try to get reelected.
> <u>Will</u> the governor try to get reelected?

As with negatives, when the verb does not include a helping verb, you must supply a form of *do*. To form a question, put the correct form of *do* directly before the subject.

The governor <u>works</u> hard.

<u>Does</u> the governor <u>work</u> hard?

The governor <u>improved</u> life in his state.

<u>Did</u> the governor <u>improve</u> life in his state?

However, if the main verb is *am, is, are, was,* or *were,* do not insert a form of *do* before the verb. Instead, move the main verb to before the subject: *Harry was late. <u>Was</u> Harry late?*

Note: The helping verb never comes before the subject if the subject is a question word, such as *who* or *which.*

<u>Who</u> is talking to the governor?

<u>Which</u> bills have been vetoed by the governor?

PRACTICE

33-7   Rewrite each of the following sentences in two ways: first, turn the sentence into a question; then, rewrite the original sentence as a negative statement.

Example: Her newest album is selling as well as her first one.

Question: _Is her newest album selling as well as her first one?_

Negative statement: _Her newest album is not selling as well as her first one._

1. Converting metric measurements to the system used in the United States is difficult.

   Question: _____

   _____

   Negative statement: _____

   _____

2. The early frost damaged some crops.

   Question: _____

   _____

   Negative statement: _____

   _____

3. That family was very influential in the early 1900s.

    Question: _____

    _____

    Negative statement: _____

    _____

4. Most stores in malls are open on Sundays.

    Question: _____

    _____

    Negative statement: _____

    _____

5. Choosing the right gift is a difficult task.

    Question: _____

    _____

    Negative statement: _____

    _____

6. Most great artists are successful during their lifetimes.

    Question: _____

    _____

    Negative statement: _____

    _____

7. The lawyer can verify the witness's story.

    Question: _____

    _____

    Negative statement: _____

    _____

8. American cities are as dangerous as they were thirty years ago.

    Question: _____

    _____

Negative statement: _____

_____

9. The British royal family is loved by most of the British people.

   Question: _____

   _____

   Negative statement: _____

   _____

10. Segregation in the American South ended with the Civil War.

    Question: _____

    _____

    Negative statement: _____

    _____

33g   Verb Tense

In English, a verb's form must indicate when an action took place (for instance, in the past or in the present). Always use the appropriate tense of the verb even if the time is obvious or if the sentence includes other indications of time (such as *two years ago* or *at present*).

> **INCORRECT**   Albert Einstein emigrate from Germany in 1933.

> **CORRECT**   Albert Einstein emigrated from Germany in 1933.

33h   Stative Verbs

Stative verbs usually tell that someone or something is in a state that will not change, at least for a while.

> Hiro <u>knows</u> American history very well.

Most English verbs show action, and these action verbs can be used in the progressive tenses. The **present progressive** tense consists of the present tense of *be* plus the present participle (*I am going*). The **past**

☑ **LearningCurve**
Multilingual Writers:
Verbs
**bedfordstmartins.com
/focusonwriting**

progressive tense consists of the past tense of *be* plus the present participle (*I was going*). Unlike most verbs, however, stative verbs are rarely used in the progressive tenses.

> **INCORRECT**   Hiro is knowing American history very well.

> **CORRECT**   Hiro knows American history very well.

FYI

Stative Verbs

Verbs that are stative—such as *know, understand, think, believe, want, like, love,* and *hate*—often refer to mental states. Other stative verbs include *be, have, need, own, belong, weigh, cost,* and *mean.* Certain verbs of sense perception, like *see* and *hear,* are also stative even though they can refer to momentary events as well as to unchanging states.

Many verbs have more than one meaning, and some of these verbs are active with one meaning but stative with another. An example is the verb *weigh.*

> **ACTIVE**   The butcher <u>weighs</u> the meat.

> **STATIVE**   The meat <u>weighs</u> three pounds.

In the first sentence above, the verb *weigh* means "to put on a scale"; it is active, not stative. In the second sentence, however, the same verb means "to have weight," so it is stative, not active. It would be unacceptable to say "The meat is weighing three pounds," but "The butcher is weighing the meat" would be correct.

PRACTICE

33-8   In each of the following sentences, circle the verb or verbs. Then, correct any problems with stative verbs by crossing out the incorrect verb tense and writing the correct verb tense above the line. If the verb is correct, write *C* above it.

> *know*
> **Example:**   Police officers ~~are knowing~~ that fingerprint identification
> *C*
> is one of the best ways to catch criminals.

1. As early as 1750 BC, ancient Babylonians were signing their identi-

   ties with fingerprints on clay tablets.

2. By 220 AD, the Chinese were becoming aware that ink fingerprints could identify people.

3. However, it was not until the late 1800s that anyone was believing that criminal identification was possible with fingerprints.

4. Today, we know that each person is having unique patterns on the tips of his or her fingers.

5. When police study a crime scene, they want to see whether the criminals have left any fingerprint evidence.

6. There is always a layer of oil on the skin, and police are liking to use it to get fingerprints.

7. Crime scene experts are often seeing cases where the criminals are touching their hair and pick up enough oil to leave a good fingerprint.

8. The police are needing to judge whether the fingerprint evidence has been damaged by sunlight, rain, or heat.

9. In the courtroom, juries often weigh fingerprint evidence before they are deciding on their verdict.

10. The FBI is collecting millions of fingerprints, which police departments can compare with the fingerprints they find at crime scenes.

33i Modal Auxiliaries

A **modal auxiliary** (such as *can*, *may*, *might*, or *must*) is a helping verb that is used with another verb to express ability, possibility, necessity, intent, obligation, and so on. In the following sentence, *can* is the modal auxiliary, and *imagine* is the main verb.

> I <u>can</u> imagine myself in Hawaii.

Modal auxiliaries usually intensify the dominant verb's meaning:

> I <u>must</u> run as fast as I can.
> You <u>ought to</u> lose some weight.

✓ **LearningCurve**
Multilingual Writers:
Verbs
bedfordstmartins.com
/focusonwriting

> ### Modal Auxiliaries
>
> | | |
> |---|---|
> | can | ought to |
> | could | shall |
> | may | should |
> | might | will |
> | must | would |

Modal auxiliaries are used in the following situations:

- To express physical ability

  I can walk faster than my brother.

- To express the possibility of something occurring

  He might get the job if his interview goes well.

- To express or request permission

  May I use the restroom in the hallway?

- To express necessity

  I must get to the train station on time.

- To express a suggestion or advice

  To be healthy, you should [or ought to] exercise and eat balanced meals.

- To express intent

  I will try to study harder next time.

- To express a desire

  Would you please answer the telephone?

PRACTICE
33-9

In the exercise below, circle the correct modal auxiliary for each sentence.

Example: (May/Would) you help me complete the assignment?

1. It doesn't rain very often in Arizona, but today it looks like it (can/ might).

2. I know I (will/ought to) call my aunt on her birthday, but I always find an excuse.

3. Sarah (should/must) study for her English exam, but she prefers to spend time with her friends.

4. John (can/would) be the best person to represent our class.

5. Many people believe they (could/should) vote in every election.

6. All students (will/must) bring two pencils, a notebook, and a dictionary to class every day.

7. (Would/May) you show me the way to the post office?

8. I (could/should) not ask for more than my health, my family, and my job.

9. Do you think they (could/can) come back tomorrow to finish the painting job?

10. A dog (should/might) be a helpful companion for your disabled father.

33j Gerunds

A **gerund** is a verb form ending in *-ing* that acts as a noun.

<u>Reading</u> the newspaper is one of my favorite things to do on Sundays.

Just like a noun, a gerund can be used as a subject, a direct object, a subject complement, or the object of a preposition:

- A gerund can be a subject.

  Playing tennis is one of my hobbies.

- A gerund can be a direct object.

  My brother influenced my racing.

- A gerund can be a subject complement.

  The most important thing is winning.

- A gerund can be the object of a preposition.

  The teacher rewarded him for passing.

LearningCurve
Multilingual Writers:
Verbs
**bedfordstmartins.com
/focusonwriting**

PRACTICE

33-10 To complete the sentences below, fill in the blanks with the gerund form of the verb provided in parentheses.

Example: ___*Typing*___ (type) is a skill that used to be taught in high school.

1. _____ (eat) five or six smaller meals throughout the day is healthier than eating two or three big meals.

2. In the winter, there is nothing better than _____ (skate) outdoors on a frozen pond.

3. The household task I dread the most is _____ (clean).

4. The fish avoided the net by _____ (swim) faster.

5. _____ (quit) is easier than accomplishing a goal.

6. Her parents praised her for _____ (remember) their anniversary.

7. Her favorite job is _____ (organize) her files.

8. I did not like his _____ (sing).

9. For me, _____ (cook) is relaxing.

10. The best way to prepare for the concert is by _____ (practice).

33k Placing Modifiers in Order

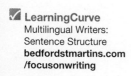

LearningCurve
Multilingual Writers:
Sentence Structure
**bedfordstmartins.com
/focusonwriting**

Adjectives and other modifiers that come before a noun usually follow a set order.

Required Order

- Determiners always come first in a series of modifiers: *these fragile glasses*. The determiners *all* or *both* always precede any other determiners: *all these glasses*.
- If one of the modifiers is a noun, it must come directly before the noun it modifies: *these wine glasses*.

- Descriptive adjectives are placed between the determiners and the noun modifiers: *these fragile wine glasses*. If there are two or more descriptive adjectives, the following order is preferred.

Preferred Order

- Adjectives that show the writer's attitude generally precede adjectives that merely describe: *these lovely fragile wine glasses*.
- Adjectives that indicate size generally come early: *these lovely large fragile wine glasses*.

PRACTICE

33-11 Arrange each group of modifiers in the correct order, and rewrite the complete phrase in the blank.

Example: (powerful, a, twenty-first-century) businesswoman

a powerful twenty-first-century businesswoman

1. (voter, an, impressive) turnout

_____

2. (new, their, taco, orange) truck

_____

3. (neighborhood's, numerous, the, vegetable) gardens

_____

4. (pilot, well-funded, brilliant, a) project

_____

5. (the, city's, African American, brand-new) mayor

_____

6. (those, all, chocolate, delicious) desserts

_____

7. (twenty, these, young, brave) soldiers

_____

8. (the, hard-earned, workers') money

_____

9. (extraordinary, the, group's, two) leaders

_____

10. (postcollege, teaching, a, promising) career

_____

33l Choosing Prepositions

A **preposition** introduces a noun or pronoun and links it to other words in the sentence. The word the preposition introduces is called the **object** of the preposition.

A preposition and its object combine to form a **prepositional phrase**: _on the table, near the table, under the table._

> I thought I had left the book on the table or somewhere near the table, but I found it under the table.

The prepositions _at, in,_ and _on_ sometimes cause problems for non-native speakers of English. For example, to identify the location of a place or an event, you can use _at, in,_ or _on._

- The preposition _at_ specifies an exact point in space or time.

  > The museum is at 1000 Fifth Avenue. Let's meet there at 10:00 tomorrow morning.

- Expanses of space or time are treated as containers and therefore require _in._

  > Women used to wear long skirts in the early 1900s.

- _On_ must be used in two cases: with names of streets (but not with exact addresses) and with days of the week or month.

  > We will move into our new office on 18th Street either on Monday or on March 12.

33m Prepositions in Familiar Expressions

Many familiar expressions end with prepositions. Learning to write clearly and **idiomatically**—following the conventions of written English—means learning which preposition is used in such expressions. Even native speakers of English sometimes have trouble choosing the correct preposition.

The sentences that follow illustrate idiomatic use of prepositions in various expressions. Note that sometimes different prepositions are used with the same word. For example, both *on* and *for* can be used with *wait* to form two different expressions with two different meanings (*He waited on their table*; *She waited for the bus*). Which preposition you choose depends on your meaning. (In the list that follows, pairs of similar expressions that end with different prepositions are bracketed.)

EXPRESSION WITH PREPOSITION	SAMPLE SENTENCE
acquainted with	During orientation, the university offers workshops to make sure that students are <u>acquainted with</u> its rules and regulations.
addicted to	I think Abby is becoming <u>addicted to</u> pretzels.
agree on (a plan or objective)	It is vital that all members of the school board <u>agree on</u> goals for the coming year.
agree to (a proposal)	Striking workers finally <u>agreed to</u> the terms of management's offer.
angry about or at (a situation)	Taxpayers are understandably <u>angry about</u> (or at) the deterioration of city recreation facilities.
angry with (a person)	When the mayor refused to hire more police officers, his constituents became <u>angry with</u> him.
approve of	Amy's adviser <u>approved of</u> her decision to study in Guatemala.
bored with	Salah got <u>bored with</u> economics, so he changed his major to psychology.
capable of	Hannah is a good talker, but she is not <u>capable of</u> acting as her own lawyer.
consist of	The deluxe fruit basket <u>consisted of</u> five pathetic pears, two tiny apples, a few limp bunches of grapes, and one lonely kiwi.
contrast with	Coach Headley's relaxed style <u>contrasts with</u> Coach Pauley's more formal approach.
convenient for	The proposed location of the new day-care center is <u>convenient for</u> many families.
deal with	Many parents and educators believe it is possible to <u>deal with</u> the special needs of autistic children in a regular classroom.
depend on	Children <u>depend on</u> their parents for emotional as well as financial support.

differ from (something else)	A capitalist system <u>differs from</u> a socialist system in its view of private ownership.
differ with (someone else)	When Miles realized that he <u>differed with</u> his boss on most important issues, he handed in his resignation.
emigrate from	My grandfather and his brother <u>emigrated from</u> the part of Russia that is now Ukraine.
grateful for (a favor)	If you can arrange an interview next week, I will be very <u>grateful for</u> your time and trouble.
grateful to (someone)	Jerry Garcia was always <u>grateful to</u> his loyal fans.
immigrate to	Many Cubans want to leave their country and <u>immigrate to</u> the United States.
impatient with	Keshia often gets <u>impatient with</u> her four younger brothers.
interested in	Tomiko had always been <u>interested in</u> computers, so no one was surprised when she became a Web designer.
interfere with	College athletes often find that their dedication to sports <u>interferes with</u> their schoolwork.
meet with	I hope I can <u>meet with</u> you soon to discuss my research project.
object to	The defense attorney <u>objected to</u> the prosecutor's treatment of the witness.
pleased with	Most of the residents are <u>pleased with</u> the mayor's crackdown on crime.
protect against	Nobel Prize winner Linus Pauling believed that large doses of vitamin C could <u>protect</u> people <u>against</u> the common cold.
reason with	When two-year-olds have tantrums, it is nearly impossible to <u>reason with</u> them.
reply to	If no one <u>replies to</u> our ad within two weeks, we will advertise again.
responsible for	Should teachers be held <u>responsible for</u> their students' low test scores?
similar to	The blood sample found at the crime scene was remarkably <u>similar to</u> one found in the suspect's residence.

specialize in	Dr. Casullo is a dentist who <u>specializes in</u> periodontal surgery.
succeed in	Lisa hoped her MBA would help her <u>succeed in</u> a business career.
take advantage of	Some consumer laws are designed to prevent door-to-door salespeople from <u>taking advantage of</u> buyers.
wait for (something to happen)	Many parents of teenagers experience tremendous anxiety while <u>waiting for</u> their children to come home at night.
wait on (in a restaurant)	We sat at the table for twenty minutes before someone <u>waited on</u> us.
worry about	Why <u>worry about</u> things you cannot change?

FYI

Using Prepositions in Familiar Expressions

Below is a list of familiar expressions that have similar meanings. They are often used in the same contexts.

acquainted with, familiar with
addicted to, hooked on
angry with (a person), upset with
bored with, tired of
capable of, able to
consist of, have, contain, include
deal with, address (a problem)
depend on, rely on
differ from (something else), be different from
differ with (someone else), disagree
emigrate from, move from (another country)
grateful for (a favor), thankful for
immigrate to, move to (another country)

interested in, fascinated by
interfere with, disrupt
meet with, get together with
object to, oppose
pleased with, happy with
protect against, guard against
reply to, answer
responsible for, accountable for
similar to, almost the same as
succeed in, attain success in
take advantage of, use an opportunity to
wait for (something to happen), expect
wait on (in a restaurant), serve

PRACTICE

33-12 In the following passage, fill in each blank with the correct preposition.

Example: Like other struggling artists, writers often make a living working ____*in*____ restaurants and waiting ____*on*____ customers.

(1) Most writers, even those who succeed _____ the literary world, need day jobs to help pay _____ food and rent. (2) Many _____ them work _____ related fields—for example, _____ bookstores, _____ publishing houses, or _____ newspapers. (3) Some take advantage _____ their talents and devote themselves _____ teaching others _____ language and literature. (4) For example, _____ the 1990s, *Harry Potter* author J. K. Rowling worked as a teacher _____ Portugal and _____ Britain. (5) _____ the 1960s and '70s, students _____ Howard University _____ Washington, D.C., could enroll _____ classes taught _____ Nobel Prize winner Toni Morrison. (6) Other writers work _____ fields unrelated _____ writing. (7) For instance, poet William Carlos Williams was a medical doctor who wrote poetry only _____ the evenings. (8) Science fiction writer Isaac Asimov worked _____ Boston University _____ the department _____ biochemistry. (9) Occasionally, an aspiring writer has friends and family who approve _____ his or her goals, and he or she can depend _____ them _____ financial help. (10) However, many family members, wanting to protect young writers _____ poverty, try to encourage them to focus _____ other goals.

33n   Prepositions in Phrasal Verbs

A **phrasal verb** consists of two words, a verb and a preposition, that are joined to form an idiomatic expression. Many phrasal verbs are **separable**. This means that a direct object can come between the verb and the preposition. However, some phrasal verbs are **inseparable**; that is, the preposition must always come immediately after the verb.

Separable Phrasal Verbs

In many cases, phrasal verbs may be split, with the direct object coming between the two parts of the verb. When the direct object is a noun, the second word of the phrasal verb can come either before or after the object.

In the sentences below, *fill out* is a phrasal verb. Because the object of the verb *fill out* is a noun (*form*), the second word of the verb can come either before or after the verb's object.

> **CORRECT**   Please fill out the form.

> **CORRECT**   Please fill the form out.

When the object is a pronoun, however, these phrasal verbs must be split, and the pronoun must come between the two parts of the verb.

> **INCORRECT**   Please fill out it.

> **CORRECT**   Please fill it out.

Some Common Separable Phrasal Verbs

ask out	give away	put back	throw away
bring up	hang up	put on	try out
call up	leave out	set aside	turn down
carry out	let out	shut off	turn off
drop off	make up	take down	wake up
fill out	put away	think over	

Remember, when the object of the verb is a pronoun, these phrasal verbs must be split, and the pronoun must come between the two parts (for example, *take it down, put it on, let it out,* and *make it up*).

Inseparable Phrasal Verbs

Some phrasal verbs, however, cannot be separated; that is, the preposition cannot be separated from the verb. This means that a direct object cannot come between the verb and the preposition.

> **INCORRECT**   Please go the manual over carefully.

> **CORRECT**   Please go over the manual carefully.

Notice that in the correct sentence above, the direct object (*manual*) comes right after the preposition (*over*).

Some Common Inseparable Phrasal Verbs

come across	run across	show up
get along	run into	stand by
go over	see to	

PRACTICE

33-13   In each of the following sentences, look closely at the phrasal verb, and decide whether the preposition is placed correctly in the sentence. If it is, write *C* in the blank after the sentence. If the preposition needs to be moved, edit the sentence.

> **Example:**   People who live in American suburbs are often surprised to come across wild animals in their neighborhoods. ____*C*____

1. In one case, a New Jersey woman was startled when a hungry bear woke up her from a nap one afternoon. _____

2. She called the police, hung up the phone, and ran for her life. _____

3. Actually, although it is a good idea to stay from bears away, most wild bears are timid. _____

4. When there is a drought, people are more likely to run into bears and other wild animals. _____

5. The amount of blueberries and other wild fruit that bears eat usually drops in dry weather off. _____

6. Bears need to put on weight before the winter, so they may have to find food in suburban garbage cans. _____

7. It is a good idea for families to go their plans over to safeguard their property against bears. _____

8. People should not leave pet food out overnight, or else their dog may find that a hungry bear has eaten its dinner. _____

9. If people have a bird feeder in the yard, they should put away it during the autumn. _____

10. As the human population grows, more and more houses are built in formerly wild areas, so bears and people have to learn to get along with each other. _____

TEST · Revise · Edit

Look back at your response to the Focus on Writing prompt on page 600. TEST what you have written. Then, revise and edit your work, paying special attention to the grammar and usage issues discussed in this chapter.

EDITING PRACTICE

Read the following student essay, which includes errors in the use of subjects, nouns, articles and determiners, and stative verbs, as well as errors with prepositions in idiomatic expressions. Check each underlined word or phrase. If it is not used correctly, write in any necessary changes. If the underlined word or phrase is correct, write *C* above it. The title of the essay has been edited for you.

in
How to Succeed ~~on~~ Multinational Business

Success in multinational business often <u>depends in</u> the ability to understand other countries' cultures. Understanding how cultures <u>differ to</u> our own, however, is only one key to <u>these</u> success. Also, <u>is</u> crucial that businesses learn to adapt to different cultures. <u>The ethnocentrism</u> is the belief that one's own culture has <u>a</u> best way of doing things. In international business, <u>is</u> necessary to <u>set aside</u> this belief. A company cannot <u>be using</u> the same methods or sell the same products overseas as it does at home. Though making these changes requires a lot of work, companies that choose to adjust to new <u>market</u> are usually <u>happy with</u> their decision.

<u>It is</u> many aspects of a country that must be understood before <u>successful international business</u> can be <u>carried out</u>. To protect itself <u>from</u> legal errors, a company needs to understand the country's legal system, which may be very different from its home country's legal system. <u>May be</u> necessary to get licenses to export products <u>onto</u> other countries. The role of <u>women</u> is also likely to be different; without knowing this, businesspeople might unintentionally offend people. Also, <u>much</u> personal interactions in other countries may give the wrong impression to someone who is inexperienced. For example, in Latin American countries, people <u>are often standing</u> close together and touch each other when they are talking. Americans may feel uncomfortable in such a situation <u>unless understand</u> it.

To <u>succeed in</u> international business, companies <u>are also needing</u> to understand what people buy and why. To avoid problems, a company that wants to sell its product internationally it should do a few market research. For example, when McDonald's opened restaurants on India, realized that beef burgers would not work in a country where many people believe that cows are sacred. Instead, burgers were made from ground chickens. For India's many vegetarians, McDonald's created several different vegetable patty. McDonald's understood that both the religious and cultural characteristic of India had to be considered if its new restaurants were going to succeed.

Looking to attract new customer in today's international market, companies they are noticing a growing demand for *halal* goods and services. The word *halal* indicates an object or action that is permissible by Islamic law. Businesses are realizing that world's Muslims depend in companies to provide acceptable *halal* foods, banks, hotels, magazines, and other services. Nestlé, Kentucky Fried Chicken, Subway, LG, and Nokia are just a few of the well-known companies that have been successfully remaking their products to appeal in Muslim consumers. Because these high-quality items also appeal to non-Muslims, many of this companies are discovering that meeting cultural needs and desires are simply good business.

Over time, the marketplace is becoming more global. In those setting, individuals from numerous cultures come together. To take advantage from opportunities and perform effectively, an international company must hire people with the right experiences. To deal with other cultures, multinational companies inside today's global market must have good informations and show other cultures the highest respects.

COLLABORATIVE ACTIVITY

Working in a small group, make a list of ten prepositional phrases that include the prepositions *above, around, at, between, from, in, on, over, under,* and *with.* Use appropriate nouns as objects of these prepositions, and use as many modifying words as you wish. (Try, for example, to write something like *above their hideous wedding portrait,* not just *above the picture.*) Now, work together to compose a list of ten sentences, each including one of your ten prepositional phrases.

review checklist

Grammar and Usage for ESL Writers

☐ English sentences must state their subjects. (See 33a.)

☐ In English, most nouns add -*s* to form plurals. Always use a form that indicates that a noun is plural. (See 33b.)

☐ English nouns may be count nouns or noncount nouns. A count noun names one particular thing or a group of particular things (*a teacher*, *oceans*). A noncount noun names something that cannot be counted (*gold*, *sand*). (See 33c.)

☐ Determiners are adjectives that identify rather than describe the nouns they modify. Determiners may also indicate amount or number. (See 33d.)

☐ The definite article *the* and the indefinite articles *a* and *an* are determiners that indicate whether the noun that follows is one readers can identify (*the book*) or one they cannot yet identify (*a book*). (See 33e.)

☐ To form a negative statement, add the word *not* directly after the first helping verb of the complete verb. To form a question, move the helping verb that follows the subject to the position directly before the subject. (See 33f.)

☐ A verb's form must indicate when an action took place. (See 33g.)

☐ Stative verbs indicate that someone or something is in a state that will not change, at least for a while. Stative verbs are rarely used in the progressive tenses. (See 33h.)

☐ A modal auxiliary is a helping verb that expresses ability, possibility, necessity, intent, obligation, and so on. (See 33i.)

☐ A gerund is a verb form ending in -*ing* that is always used as a noun. (See 33j.)

☐ Adjectives and other modifiers that come before a noun usually follow a set order. (See 33k.)

☐ The prepositions *at*, *in*, and *on* sometimes cause problems for nonnative speakers of English. (See 33l.)

☐ Many familiar expressions end with prepositions. (See 33m.)

☐ A phrasal verb consists of two words, a verb and a preposition, that are joined to form an idiomatic expression. (See 33n.)

Read the following student essay, which includes errors in the use of verbs, nouns, pronouns, adjectives, and adverbs, as well as ESL errors. Make any changes necessary to correct the basic grammar of the sentences. The first sentence has been edited for you.

The Mystery of the Bermuda Triangle

The Bermuda Triangle is an area in the Atlantic Ocean also ~~know~~ *known* as the Devil's Triangle. Its size, between 500,000 and 1.5 million square miles, depends on who you are believing. Strange events happen there.

During the past century, more than fifty ships and twenty airplanes have disappeared to these area. According to some people, a mysterious force causes ships and planes to vanish in the Bermuda Triangle. Everyone who hears about the mystery has to decide for themselves what to believe. However, according to the U.S. Coast Guard, the explanations are not mysterious.

The stories about odd these occurrences they may have started as early as 1492. When Columbus sailed through the area, him and his crew seen unusual lights in the sky. In addition, his compass reacted strangely. Now is believed that the lights came from a meteor that crashed into the ocean. The peculiar compass readings were probably cause from the fact that in this area, magnetic compasses point toward true north rather than magnetic north. These variation can cause navigators to sail off course.

The modern Bermuda Triangle legend started in 1945, when Flight 19, compose of five U.S. Navy Avenger torpedo bombers, disappeared while on a routine training mission. Rescue plane that has been sent to search for them also disappeared. Six aircraft and twenty-seven man vanished. Not only were their lifes lost, but no bodies were ever found. Were a mysterious force responsible? Although the events themselves seem strange, there are several good explanation. First, all the crew members except his leader were trainees.

It is quite possibly that they flied through a magnetic storm or that the leader's compass was not working. If so, they would have become confused of their location. Radio transmissions were unreliable because of a bad weather and a broken receiver in one of the planes. The crew leader was not functioning very good. The leader told his pilots to head east; he thought that they were over the Gulf of Mexico. However, they were flying up the Atlantic coastline, so his instructions sent him further out to sea. If the planes crashed into the ocean at night, it is not likely there would have been any survivors. No wreckage was ever recover.

After Flight 19 disappeared, storys start to appear about the events that have occurred. The odd compass readings, the problems with radio transmissions, and the missing wreckage lead to strange tales. Some people believed that the missing ships and planes were taken by UFOs (unidentified flying objects) to a different dimension. Others thought that those whom disappeared were kidnapped from aliens from other planets. However, there are most logical explanations. The fact that magnetic compasses point toward true north in this area is now well known. It is also well known that the weather patterns in the southern Atlantic and Caribbean is unpredictable. In addition, human error may have been involved. For these reason, the tales of the Bermuda Triangle are clearly science fiction, not fact.

34 Using Commas

focus on writing

One of these pictures shows public housing in disrepair; one shows new affordable housing units. Write a paragraph that explains your idea of ideal affordable housing. Where should complexes for low-income families be located? What kinds of buildings should they consist of? What facilities and services should be offered to residents?

PREVIEW

In this chapter, you will learn to

- use commas in a series (34a)
- use commas to set off introductory phrases and transitional words and phrases (34b)
- use commas with appositives (34c)
- use commas to set off nonrestrictive clauses (34d)
- use commas in dates and addresses (34e)
- avoid unnecessary commas (34f)

A **comma** is a punctuation mark that separates words or groups of words within sentences. In this way, commas keep ideas distinct from one another.

In earlier chapters, you learned to use a comma between two simple sentences (independent clauses) linked by a coordinating conjunction to form a compound sentence.

> Some people are concerned about climate change, but others are not.

You also learned to use a comma after a dependent clause that comes before an independent clause in a complex sentence.

> Although bears in the wild can be dangerous, hikers can take steps to protect themselves.

In addition, commas are used to set off directly quoted speech or writing from the rest of the sentence.

> John F. Kennedy said, "Ask not what your country can do for you; ask what you can do for your country."

As you will learn in this chapter, commas have several other uses as well.

34a Commas in a Series

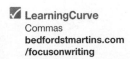

LearningCurve
Commas
bedfordstmartins.com
/focusonwriting

Use commas to separate all elements in a **series** of three or more words, phrases, or clauses.

> <u>Leyla</u>, <u>Zack</u>, and <u>Kathleen</u> campaigned for Representative Lewis.
>
> <u>Leyla</u>, <u>Zack</u>, or <u>Kathleen</u> will be elected president of Students for Lewis.

Leyla <u>made phone calls</u>, <u>licked envelopes</u>, and <u>ran errands</u> for the campaign.

Leyla <u>is president</u>, <u>Zack is vice president</u>, and <u>Kathleen is treasurer</u>.

FYI

Using Commas in a Series

Newspapers and magazines usually omit the comma before the coordinating conjunction in a series. However, in college writing, you should always use a comma before the coordinating conjunction.

Leyla, Zack, and Kathleen worked on the campaign.

Exception: Do not use *any* commas if all the items in a series are separated by coordinating conjunctions.

Leyla or Zack or Kathleen will be elected president of Students for Lewis.

PRACTICE

34-1 Edit the following sentences for the use of commas in a series. If the sentence is correct, write *C* in the blank.

Examples

Costa Rica produces bananas, cocoa, and sugarcane. _____*C*_____

The pool rules state that there is no running/ or jumping/ or diving.

_____

1. The musician plays guitar bass and drums. _____

2. The organization's goals are feeding the hungry, housing the homeless and helping the unemployed find work. _____

3. *The Price Is Right*, *Let's Make a Deal*, and *Jeopardy!* are three of the longest-running game shows in television history. _____

4. In native Hawaiian culture, yellow was worn by the royalty red was worn by priests and a mixture of the two colors was worn by others of high rank. _____

5. The diary Anne Frank kept while her family hid from the Nazis is insightful, touching and sometimes humorous. _____

6. A standard bookcase is sixty inches tall forty-eight inches wide and twelve inches deep. _____

7. Most coffins manufactured in the United States are lined with bronze, or copper, or lead. _____

8. Young handsome and sensitive, Leonardo DiCaprio was the 1990s answer to the 1950s actor James Dean. _____

9. California's capital is Sacramento, its largest city is Los Angeles and its oldest settlement is San Diego. _____

10. Watching television, playing video games, and riding a bicycle are some of the average ten-year-old boy's favorite pastimes. _____

34b   Commas with Introductory Phrases and Transitional Words and Phrases

Introductory Phrases

Use a comma to set off an **introductory phrase** from the rest of the sentence.

> In the event of a fire, proceed to the nearest exit.
> Walking home, Nelida decided to change her major.
> To keep fit, people should try to exercise regularly.

**PRACTICE
34-2**   Edit the following sentences for the use of commas with introductory phrases. If the sentence is correct, write *C* in the blank.

Examples

For some medical conditions, effective treatments are hard to find.

_____

After taking placebos, some depressed patients experience relief from their symptoms. _____C_____

(1) Also known as sugar pills placebos contain no actual medicine. _____ (2) Despite this fact, placebos sometimes have positive effects on patients who take them. _____ (3) For years researchers have used placebos in experiments. _____ (4) To evaluate the effectiveness of a medication scientists test the drug on volunteers. _____ (5) To ensure that the experiment's results are reliable, researchers always have a control group. _____ (6) Instead of taking the drug the control group takes a placebo. _____ (7) Thinking they are taking an actual medicine patients in the control group may experience the "placebo effect." _____ (8) After receiving treatment with a placebo, they feel better. _____ (9) In some cases patients feel better even when they know they have taken a placebo. _____ (10) Puzzling to researchers, this "honest placebo effect" is the subject of several new scientific studies. _____

Transitional Words and Phrases

Also use commas to set off **transitional words or phrases**, whether they appear at the beginning, in the middle, or at the end of a sentence.

In fact, Thoreau spent only one night in jail.
He was, of course, bailed out by a friend.
He did spend more than two years at Walden Pond, however.

FYI

Using Commas in Direct Address

Always use commas to set off the name of someone whom you are addressing (speaking to) directly, whether the name appears at the beginning, in the middle, or at the end of a sentence.

Molly, come here and look at this.
Come here, Molly, and look at this.
Come here and look at this, Molly.

PRACTICE

34-3 Edit the following sentences for the use of commas with transitional words and phrases. If the sentence is correct, write *C* in the blank.

Example: Eventually, most people build a personal credit history.

(1) Often establishing credit can be difficult. _____ (2) College students for example often have no credit history of their own, especially if their parents pay their bills. _____ (3) Similarly some married women have no personal credit history. _____ (4) In fact their credit cards may be in their husbands' names. _____ (5) As a result, they may be unable to get their own loans. _____ (6) Of course one way to establish credit is to apply for a credit card at a local department store. _____ (7) Also, it is relatively easy to get a gas credit card. _____ (8) It is important to pay these credit-card bills promptly however. _____ (9) In addition having checking and savings accounts can help to establish financial reliability. _____ (10) Finally, people who want to establish a credit history can sign an apartment lease and pay the rent regularly to show that they are good credit risks. _____

34c Commas with Appositives

Use commas to set off an **appositive**—a word or word group that identifies, renames, or describes a noun or a pronoun.

I have visited only one country, <u>Canada</u>, outside the United States. (*Canada* is an appositive that identifies the noun *country*.)

Carlos Santana, <u>leader of the group Santana</u>, played at Woodstock in 1969. (*Leader of the group Santana* is an appositive that identifies *Carlos Santana*.)

<u>A really gifted artist</u>, he is also a wonderful father. (*A really gifted artist* is an appositive that describes the pronoun *he*.)

FYI

Using Commas with Appositives

Most appositives are set off by commas, whether they fall at the beginning, in the middle, or at the end of a sentence.

> A dreamer, he spent his life thinking about what he could not have.

> He always wanted to build a house, a big white one, overlooking the ocean.

> He finally built his dream house, a log cabin.

PRACTICE

34-4   Underline the appositive in each of the following sentences. Then, check each sentence for the correct use of commas to set off appositives, and add any missing commas. If the sentence is correct, write *C* in the blank.

> **Example:**   Wendy Kopp, a college student, developed the Teach For America program to help minority students get a better education.
>
> _____

1. Guglielmo Marconi a young Italian inventor, sent the first wireless message across the Atlantic Ocean in 1901. _____

2. A member of the boy band 'N Sync Justin Timberlake went on to establish a successful career as a solo musician and an actor. _____

3. HTML hypertext markup language, is the set of codes used to create Web documents. _____

4. William Filene, founder of Filene's Department Store, invented the "bargain basement." _____

5. Known as NPR National Public Radio presents a wide variety of programs. _____

6. On the southwest coast of Nigeria lies Lagos a major port. _____

7. Home of the 2008 Olympics, Beijing continues to have serious problems with its air quality. _____

8. Lightning a strong electrical charge can be both beautiful and dangerous. _____

9. A plant that grows on mountains and in deserts, the fern is surprisingly adaptable. _____

10. Golf a game developed in Scotland, is very popular in the United States. _____

34d   Commas with Nonrestrictive Clauses

Clauses are often used to add information within a sentence. In some cases, you need to add commas to set off these clauses; in other cases, commas are not required.

Use commas to set off **nonrestrictive clauses**, clauses that are not essential to a sentence's meaning. Do not use commas to set off **restrictive clauses**.

- A **nonrestrictive clause** does *not* contain essential information. Nonrestrictive clauses are set off from the rest of the sentence by commas.

   Telephone calling-card fraud, <u>which cost consumers and phone companies four billion dollars last year</u>, is increasing.

  Here, the clause between the commas (underlined) provides extra information to help readers understand the sentence, but the sentence would still communicate the same idea without this information.

   Telephone calling-card fraud is increasing.

- A **restrictive clause** contains information that is essential to a sentence's meaning. Restrictive clauses are *not* set off from the rest of the sentence by commas.

   Many rock stars <u>who recorded hits in the 1950s</u> made little money from their songs.

  In the sentence above, the clause *who recorded hits in the 1950s* supplies specific information that is essential to the idea the sentence is communicating: it tells readers which group of rock stars made little money. Without the clause, the sentence does not communicate the same idea because it does not tell which rock stars made little money.

   Many rock stars made little money from their songs.

Compare the meanings of the following pairs of sentences with non-restrictive and restrictive clauses.

NONRESTRICTIVE Young adults, <u>who text while driving</u>, put themselves and others in danger. (This sentence says that all young adults text while driving and all pose a danger.)

RESTRICTIVE Young adults <u>who text while driving</u> put themselves and others in danger. (This sentence says that only those young adults who text and drive pose a danger.)

NONRESTRICTIVE Student loans, <u>which are based on need</u>, may not be fair to middle-class students. (This sentence says that all student loans are based on need and all may be unfair to middle-class students.)

RESTRICTIVE Student loans <u>that are based on need</u> may not be fair to middle-class students. (This sentence says that only those student loans that are based on need may be unfair to middle-class students.)

FYI

Which, That, and *Who*

- *Which* always introduces a nonrestrictive clause.

     The job, <u>which had excellent benefits</u>, did not pay well. (clause set off by commas)

- *That* always introduces a restrictive clause.

     He accepted the job <u>that had the best benefits</u>. (no commas)

- *Who* can introduce either a restrictive or a nonrestrictive clause.

     RESTRICTIVE Many parents <u>who work</u> feel a lot of stress. (no commas)

     NONRESTRICTIVE Both of my parents, <u>who have always wanted the best for their children</u>, have worked two jobs for years. (clause set off by commas)

PRACTICE

34-5   Edit the following sentences so that commas set off all nonrestrictive clauses. (Remember, commas are *not* used to set off restrictive clauses.) If a sentence is correct, write *C* in the blank.

Example: A museum exhibition that celebrates the Alaska highway tells the story of its construction. _____*C*_____

(1) During the 1940s, a group of African American soldiers who defied the forces of nature and human prejudice were shipped to Alaska. _____ (2) They built the Alaska highway which stretches twelve hundred miles across Alaska. _____ (3) The troops who worked on the highway have received little attention in most historical accounts. _____ (4) The highway which cut through some of the roughest terrain in the world was begun in 1942. _____ (5) The Japanese had just landed in the Aleutian Islands which lie west of the tip of the Alaska Peninsula. _____ (6) Military officials, who oversaw the project, doubted the ability of the African American troops. _____ (7) As a result, they made them work under conditions, that made construction difficult. _____ (8) The troops who worked on the road proved their commanders wrong by finishing the highway months ahead of schedule. _____ (9) In one case, white engineers, who surveyed a river, said it would take two weeks to bridge. _____ (10) To the engineers' surprise, the soldiers who worked on the project beat the estimate. _____ (11) A military report that was issued in 1945 praised them. _____ (12) It said the goals that the African American soldiers achieved would be remembered through the ages. _____

34e   Commas in Dates and Addresses

Dates

Use commas in dates to separate the day of the week from the month and the day of the month from the year.

> The first Cinco de Mayo we celebrated in the United States was Tuesday, May 5, 1998.

When a date that includes commas does not fall at the end of a sentence, place a comma after the year.

> Tuesday, May 5, 1998, was the first Cinco de Mayo we celebrated in the United States.

Addresses

Use commas in addresses to separate the street address from the city and the city from the state or country.

> The office of the famous fictional detective Sherlock Holmes was located at 221b Baker Street, London, England.

When an address that includes commas falls in the middle of a sentence, place a comma after the state or country.

> The office at 221b Baker Street, London, England, belonged to the famous fictional detective Sherlock Holmes.

PRACTICE
34-6

Edit the following sentences for the correct use of commas in dates and addresses. Add any missing commas, and cross out any unnecessary commas. If the sentence is correct, write *C* in the blank.

Examples

Usher's album *Looking 4 Myself* was released on June 8, 2012.

_____

The entertainer grew up in Chattanooga, Tennessee. _____

1. On Tuesday June 5, 2012, people around the world witnessed the rare astronomical phenomenon known as the transit of Venus. _____

2. For traditional Venezuelan food, locals go to Café Casa Veroes on Avenida Norte in Caracas Venezuela. _____

3. Stefani Joanne Angelina Germanotta, more commonly known as Lady Gaga, was born on March 28 1986 in New York New York. _____

4. Mets pitcher Johan Santana threw the team's first no-hitter on June 1, 2012. _____

5. Donations can be sent to the American Red Cross at P. O. Box 4002018 in Des Moines, Iowa. _____

6. To visit the New York Transit Museum, visitors must travel to 130 Livingston Street in Brooklyn New York. _____

7. The Anne Frank House in Amsterdam the Netherlands became a museum on May 3 1960. _____

8. First released on November 1 1997, *Titanic* remains one of the highest-grossing movies of all time. _____

9. Fans from around the world travel to visit Ernest Hemingway's houses in Key West Florida and San Francisco de Paula, Cuba. _____

10. Oprah addressed the graduating class at Spelman College on Sunday May 20, 2012 in College Park Georgia. _____

34f Unnecessary Commas

In addition to knowing where commas are required, it is also important to know when *not* to use commas.

■ Do not use a comma before the first item in a series.

INCORRECT   *Duck Soup* starred, Groucho, Chico, and Harpo Marx.

CORRECT   *Duck Soup* starred Groucho, Chico, and Harpo Marx.

- Do not use a comma after the last item in a series.

INCORRECT   Groucho, Chico, and Harpo Marx, starred in *Duck Soup*.

CORRECT   Groucho, Chico, and Harpo Marx starred in *Duck Soup*.

- Do not use a comma between a subject and a verb.

INCORRECT   Students and their teachers, should try to respect one another.

CORRECT   Students and their teachers should try to respect one another.

- Do not use a comma before the coordinating conjunction that separates the two parts of a compound predicate.

INCORRECT   The transit workers voted to strike, and walked off the job.

CORRECT   The transit workers voted to strike and walked off the job.

- Do not use a comma before the coordinating conjunction that separates the two parts of a compound subject.

INCORRECT   The transit workers, and the sanitation workers voted to strike.

CORRECT   The transit workers and the sanitation workers voted to strike.

- Do not use a comma to set off a restrictive clause.

INCORRECT   People, who live in glass houses, should not throw stones.

CORRECT   People who live in glass houses should not throw stones.

■ Finally, do not use a comma before a dependent clause that follows an independent clause.

INCORRECT He was exhausted, because he had driven all night.

CORRECT He was exhausted because he had driven all night.

PRACTICE

34-7 Some of the following sentences contain unnecessary commas. Edit to eliminate unnecessary commas. If the sentence is correct, write *C* in the blank following it.

Example: Both the Dominican Republic, and the republic of Haiti occupy the West Indian island of Hispaniola. _____

1. The capital of the Dominican Republic, is Santo Domingo. _____

2. The country's tropical climate, generous rainfall, and fertile soil, make the Dominican Republic suitable for many kinds of crops. _____

3. Some of the most important crops are, sugarcane, coffee, cocoa, and rice. _____

4. Mining is also important to the country's economy, because the land is rich in many ores. _____

5. Spanish is the official language of the Dominican Republic, and Roman Catholicism is the state religion. _____

6. In recent years, resort areas have opened, and brought many tourists to the country. _____

7. Tourists who visit the Dominican Republic, remark on its tropical beauty. _____

8. Military attacks, and political unrest have marked much of the Dominican Republic's history. _____

9. Because the republic's economy has not always been strong, many Dominicans have immigrated to the United States. _____

10. However, many Dominican immigrants maintain close ties to their

home country, and return often to visit. _____

TEST · Revise · Edit

Look back at your response to the Focus on Writing prompt on page 639. **TEST** what you have written. Then, make the following additions.

1. Add a sentence that includes a series of three or more words or word groups.
2. Add introductory phrases to two of your sentences.
3. Add an appositive to one of your sentences.
4. Add a transitional word or phrase to one of your sentences (at the beginning, in the middle, or at the end).
5. Add a nonrestrictive clause to one of your sentences.

When you have made all the additions, revise and edit your work, carefully checking your use of commas.

EDITING PRACTICE

Read the following student essay, which includes errors in comma use. Add commas where necessary between items in a series and with introductory phrases, transitional words and phrases, appositives, and nonrestrictive clauses. Cross out any unnecessary commas. The first sentence has been edited for you.

Brave Orchid

One of the most important characters in *The Woman Warrior*, Maxine Hong Kingston's autobiographical work, is Brave Orchid, Kingston's mother. Brave Orchid was a strong woman, but not a happy one. Through Kingston's stories about her mother, readers learn a lot about Kingston herself.

Readers are introduced to Brave Orchid, a complex character as an imaginative storyteller, who tells her daughter vivid tales of China. As a young woman she impresses her classmates with her intelligence. She is a traditional woman. However she is determined to make her life exactly what she wants it to be. Brave Orchid strongly believes in herself; still, she considers herself a failure.

In her native China Brave Orchid trains to be a midwife. The other women in her class envy her independence brilliance and courage. One day Brave Orchid bravely confronts the Fox Spirit, and tells him he will not win. First of all, she tells him she can endure any pain that he inflicts on her. Next she gathers together the women in the dormitory to burn the ghost away. After this event the other women admire her even more.

Working hard Brave Orchid becomes a midwife in China. After coming to America however she cannot work as a midwife. Instead she works in a Chinese laundry, and picks tomatoes. None of her classmates in China would have imagined this outcome. During her later years in America Brave Orchid becomes a woman, who is overbearing and domineering. She bosses her children around, she tries to ruin her sister's life and she criticizes everyone and everything around her. Her daughter, a straight-A student is the object of her worst criticism.

Brave Orchid's intentions are good. Nevertheless she devotes her energy to the wrong things. She expects the people around her to be as strong as she is. Because she bullies them however she eventually loses them. In addition she is too busy criticizing her daughter's faults to see all her accomplishments. Brave Orchid an independent woman and a brilliant student never achieves her goals. She is hard on the people around her, because she is disappointed in herself.

COLLABORATIVE ACTIVITY

Bring a homemaking, sports, or fashion magazine to class. Working in a small group, look at the people pictured in the ads. In what roles are men most often depicted? In what roles are women presented? Identify the three or four most common roles for each sex, and give each kind of character a descriptive name—*athlete* or *mother*, for example.

Working on your own, choose one type of character, and write a paragraph in which you describe his or her typical appearance and habits. Then, circle every comma in your paragraph, and work with your group to explain why each comma is used. If no one in your group can explain why a particular comma is used, cross it out.

review checklist

Using Commas

☐ Use commas to separate all elements in a series of three or more words or word groups. (See 34a.)

☐ Use commas to set off introductory phrases and transitional words and phrases from the rest of the sentence. (See 34b.)

☐ Use commas to set off appositives from the rest of the sentence. (See 34c.)

☐ Use commas to set off nonrestrictive clauses. (See 34d.)

☐ Use commas to separate parts of dates and addresses. (See 34e.)

☐ Avoid unnecessary commas. (See 34f.)

✔ LearningCurve
Commas
**bedfordstmartins.com
/focusonwriting**

35 Using Apostrophes

focus on writing

Certain jobs have traditionally been considered "men's work," and others have been viewed as "women's work." Although the workplace has changed considerably in recent years, some things have remained the same. Write a paragraph about the tasks that are considered "men's work" and "women's work" at your job or in your current household. Be sure to give examples of the responsibilities you discuss. (*Note:* Contractions, such as *isn't* or *don't*, are acceptable in this informal response.)

In this chapter, you will learn to
- use apostrophes to form contractions (35a)
- use apostrophes to form possessives (35b)
- revise incorrect use of apostrophes (35c)

An **apostrophe** is a punctuation mark that is used in two situations: to form a contraction and to form the possessive of a noun or an indefinite pronoun.

35a Apostrophes in Contractions

A **contraction** is a word that uses an apostrophe to combine two words. The apostrophe takes the place of omitted letters.

> I didn't (*did not*) realize how late it was.
>
> It's (*it is*) not right for cheaters to go unpunished.

Frequently Used Contractions

I + am = I'm	are + not = aren't
we + are = we're	can + not = can't
you + are = you're	do + not = don't
it + is = it's	will + not = won't
I + have = I've	should + not = shouldn't
I + will = I'll	let + us = let's
there + is = there's	that + is = that's
is + not = isn't	who + is = who's

PRACTICE
35-1

In the following sentences, add apostrophes to contractions if needed. If the sentence is correct, write *C* in the blank.

Example: ~~Whats~~ *What's* the deadliest creature on earth? _____

(1) Bacteria and viruses, which we cant see without a microscope, kill many people every year. _____ (2) When we speak about the deadliest creatures, however, usually were talking about creatures that cause

illness or death from their poison, which is called venom. _____
(3) After your bitten, stung, or stuck, how long does it take to die?
_____ (4) The fastest killer is a creature called the sea wasp, but it
isn't a wasp at all. _____ (5) The sea wasp is actually a fifteen-foot-
long jellyfish, and although its not aggressive, it can be deadly. _____
(6) People who've gone swimming off the coast of Australia have encountered this creature. _____ (7) While jellyfish found off the Atlantic
coast of the United States can sting, they arent as dangerous as the sea
wasp, whose venom is deadly enough to kill sixty adults. _____ (8) A
person whos been stung by a sea wasp has anywhere from thirty seconds
to four minutes to get help or die. _____ (9) Oddly, it's been found
that something as thin as pantyhose worn over the skin will prevent these
stings. _____ (10) Also, theres an antidote to the poison that can
save victims. _____

35b Apostrophes in Possessives

Possessive forms of nouns and pronouns show ownership. Nouns and
indefinite pronouns do not have special possessive forms. Instead, they
use apostrophes to indicate ownership.

Singular Nouns and Indefinite Pronouns

To form the possessive of **singular nouns** (including names) and
indefinite pronouns, add an apostrophe plus an *s*.

> <u>Cesar Chavez's</u> goal (*the goal of Cesar Chavez*) was justice for
> American farmworkers.
> The <u>strike's</u> outcome (*the outcome of the strike*) was uncertain.
> Whether it would succeed was <u>anyone's</u> guess (*the guess of anyone*).

FYI

Singular Nouns Ending in -s

Even if a singular noun already ends in -s, add an apostrophe plus an s to form the possessive.

The class's next assignment was a research paper.

Dr. Ramos's patients are participating in a clinical trial.

Plural Nouns

Most plural nouns end in -s. To form the possessive of **plural nouns ending in -s** (including names), add just an apostrophe (not an apostrophe plus an s).

The two drugs' side effects (*the side effects of the two drugs*) were quite different.

The Johnsons' front door (*the front door of the Johnsons*) is red.

Some irregular noun plurals do not end in -s. If a plural noun does not end in -s, add an apostrophe plus an s to form the possessive.

The men's room is right next to the women's room.

PRACTICE

35-2   Rewrite the following phrases, changing the noun or indefinite pronoun that follows *of* to the possessive form. Be sure to distinguish between singular and plural nouns.

Examples

the mayor of the city   *the city's mayor*

the uniforms of the players   *the players' uniforms*

1. the video of the singer _____

2. the scores of the students _____

3. the favorite band of everybody _____

4. the office of the boss _____

5. the union of the players _____

6. the specialty of the restaurant _____

7. the bedroom of the children _____

8. the high cost of the tickets _____

9. the dreams of everyone _____

10. the owner of the dogs _____

35c Incorrect Use of Apostrophes

Be careful not to confuse a plural noun (*boys*) with the singular posses-sive form of the noun (*boy's*). Never use an apostrophe with a plural noun unless the noun is possessive.

Termites can be dangerous <u>pests</u> [not *pest's*].

The <u>Velezes</u> [not *Velez's*] live on Maple Drive, right next door to the <u>Browns</u> [not *Brown's*].

Also remember not to use apostrophes with possessive pronouns that end in *-s*: *theirs* (not *their's*), *hers* (not *her's*), *its* (not *it's*), *ours* (not *our's*), and *yours* (not *your's*).

Be especially careful not to confuse possessive pronouns with sound-alike contractions. Possessive pronouns never include apostrophes.

POSSESSIVE PRONOUN	CONTRACTION
The dog bit its master.	It's (*it is*) time for breakfast.
The choice is theirs.	There's (*there is*) no place like home.
Whose house is this?	Who's (*who is*) on first base?
Is this your house?	You're (*you are*) late again.

PRACTICE

35-3 Check the underlined words in the following sentences for correct use of apostrophes. If a correction needs to be made, cross out the word and write the correct version above it. If the noun or pronoun is correct, write *C* above it.

Example: The <u>president's</u> views were presented after several other
C

speakers *theirs.*
<u>speaker's</u> first presented <u>their's.</u>
^ ^

1. Parent's should realize that when it comes to disciplining children, the responsibility is <u>there's</u>.

2. <u>It's</u> also important that parents offer praise for a <u>child's</u> good behavior.

3. In <u>it's</u> first few <u>week's</u> of life, a dog is already developing a personality.

4. His and <u>her's</u> towels used to be popular with <u>couple's,</u> but <u>it's</u> not so common to see them today.

5. All the <u>Ryan's</u> spent four <u>year's</u> in college and then got good jobs.

6. From the radio came the lyrics "<u>You're</u> the one <u>who's</u> love I've been waiting for."

7. If you expect to miss any <u>class's,</u> you will have to make arrangements with someone <u>who's</u> willing to tell you <u>you're</u> assignment.

8. No other <u>school's</u> cheerleading squad tried as many stunts as <u>our's</u> did.

9. Surprise <u>test's</u> are common in my economics <u>teacher's</u> class.

10. <u>Jazz's</u> influence on many mainstream <u>musician's</u> is one of the <u>book's</u> main <u>subject's</u>.

TEST · **Revise** · **Edit**

Look back at your response to the Focus on Writing prompt on page 656. **TEST** what you have written. Then, revise and edit your work, checking to make sure you have used apostrophes correctly in possessive forms and contractions. (Remember, because this is an informal exercise, contractions are acceptable.)

EDITING PRACTICE

Read the following student essay, which includes errors in the use of apostrophes. Edit it to eliminate errors by crossing out incorrect words and writing corrections above them. (Note that this is an informal response paper, so contractions are acceptable.) The first sentence has been edited for you.

The Women of Messina

In William ~~Shakespeares'~~ *Shakespeare's* play *Much Ado about Nothing*, the women of Messina, whether they are seen as love objects or as ~~shrew's,~~ *shrews,* have very few options. A womans role is to please a man. She can try to resist, but she will probably wind up giving in.

The plays two women, Hero and Beatrice, are very different. Hero is the obedient one. Heroes cousin, Beatrice, tries to challenge the rules of the mans world in which she lives. However, in a place like Messina, even women like Beatrice find it hard to get the respect that should be their's.

Right from the start, we are drawn to Beatrice. Shes funny, she has a clever comment for most situation's, and she always speaks her mind about other peoples behavior. Unlike Hero, she tries to stand up to the men in her life, as we see in her and Benedicks conversations. But even though Beatrice's intelligence is obvious, she often mocks herself. Its clear that she doesn't have much self-esteem. In fact, Beatrice is'nt the strong woman she seems to be.

Ultimately, Beatrice does get her man, and she will be happy—but at what cost? Benedicks' last word's to her are "Peace! I will stop your mouth." Then, he kisses her. The kiss is a symbolic end to their bickering. It is also the mark of Beatrices defeat. She has lost. Benedick has silenced her. Now, she will be Benedick's wife and do what he wants her to do. Granted, she will have more say in her marriage than Hero will have in her's, but she is still defeated.

Shakespeares audience might have seen the plays ending as a happy one. For contemporary audience's, however, the ending is disappointing. Even Beatrice, the most rebellious of Messinas women, finds it impossible to achieve anything of importance in this male-dominated society.

COLLABORATIVE ACTIVITY

Bring to class a book, magazine, or newspaper whose style is informal—for example, a romance novel, *People*, your school newspaper, or even a comic book. Working in a group, circle every contraction you can find on one page of each publication, and substitute for each contraction the words it combines. Are your substitutions an improvement? (You may want to read a few paragraphs aloud before you reach a conclusion.)

review checklist

Using Apostrophes

- [ ] Use apostrophes to form contractions. (See 35a.)

- [ ] Use an apostrophe plus an *s* to form the possessive of singular nouns and indefinite pronouns, even when a noun ends in *-s*. (See 35b.)

- [ ] Use an apostrophe alone to form the possessive of plural nouns ending in *-s*, including names. If a plural noun does not end in *-s*, add an apostrophe plus an *s*. (See 35b.)

- [ ] Do not use apostrophes with plural nouns unless they are possessive. Do not use apostrophes with possessive pronouns. (See 35c.)

✔ LearningCurve
Apostrophes
**bedfordstmartins.com
/focusonwriting**

36 Understanding Mechanics

focus on writing

This picture shows a familiar scene from the classic 1939 film *The Wizard of Oz*. Write a paragraph describing a memorable scene from your favorite movie. Begin by giving the film's title and listing the names of the major stars and the characters they play. Then, tell what happens in the scene, quoting a few words of dialogue, if possible.

In this chapter, you will learn to

- capitalize proper nouns (36a)
- punctuate direct quotations (36b)
- set off titles (36c)
- use hyphens correctly (36d)
- abbreviate words correctly (36e)
- use numerals and spelled-out numbers (36f)
- use minor punctuation marks correctly (36g)

36a Capitalizing Proper Nouns

A **proper noun** names a particular person, animal, place, object, or idea. Proper nouns are always capitalized. The list that follows explains and illustrates specific rules for capitalizing proper nouns.

☑ LearningCurve
Capitalization
bedfordstmartins.com
/focusonwriting

■ Always capitalize names of **races, ethnic groups, tribes, nationalities, languages, and religions**.

> The census data revealed a diverse community of Caucasians, African Americans, and Asian Americans, with a few Latino and Navajo residents. Native languages included English, Korean, and Spanish. Most people identified themselves as Catholic, Protestant, or Muslim.

■ Capitalize names of **specific people and the titles that accompany them**. In general, do not capitalize titles used without a name.

> In 1994, President Nelson Mandela was elected to lead South Africa.
>
> The newly elected fraternity president addressed the crowd.

■ Capitalize names of **specific family members and their titles**. Do not capitalize words that identify family relationships, including those introduced by possessive pronouns.

> The twins, Aunt Edna and Aunt Evelyn, are Dad's sisters.
>
> My aunts, my father's sisters, are twins.

■ Capitalize names of **specific countries, cities, towns, bodies of water, streets, and so on**. Do not capitalize words that do not name specific places.

> The Seine runs through Paris, France.
>
> The river runs through the city.

■ Capitalize names of **specific geographical regions**. Do not capitalize such words when they specify direction.

> William Faulkner's novels are set in the South.

> Turn right at the golf course, and go south for about a mile.

■ Capitalize names of **specific buildings and monuments**. Do not capitalize general references to buildings and monuments.

> He drove past the Liberty Bell and looked for parking near City Hall.

> He drove past the monument and looked for a parking space near the building.

■ Capitalize names of **specific groups, clubs, teams, and associations**. Do not capitalize general references to such groups.

> The Teamsters Union represents workers who were at the stadium for the Republican Party convention, the Rolling Stones concert, and the Phillies-Astros game.

> The union represents workers who were at the stadium for the political party's convention, the rock group's concert, and the baseball teams' game.

■ Capitalize names of **specific historical periods, events, and documents**. Do not capitalize nonspecific references to periods, events, or documents.

> The Emancipation Proclamation was signed during the Civil War, not during Reconstruction.

> The document was signed during the war, not during the postwar period.

■ Capitalize **names of businesses, government agencies, schools, and other institutions**. Do not capitalize nonspecific references to such institutions.

> The Department of Education and Apple Computer have launched a partnership project with Central High School.

> A government agency and a computer company have launched a partnership project with a high school.

■ Capitalize **brand names**. Do not capitalize general references to kinds of products.

> While Jeff waited for his turn at the Xerox machine, he drank a can of Coke.

> While Jeff waited for his turn at the copier, he drank a can of soda.

■ Capitalize **titles of specific academic courses**. Do not capitalize names of general academic subject areas, except for proper nouns—for example, a language or a country.

> Are Introduction to American Government and Biology 200 closed yet?

> Are the introductory American government course and the biology course closed yet?

■ Capitalize **days of the week, months of the year, and holidays**. Do not capitalize the names of seasons.

> The Jewish holiday of Passover usually falls in April.

> The Jewish holiday of Passover falls in the spring.

PRACTICE

36-1 Edit the following sentences, capitalizing letters or changing capitals to lowercase where necessary.

Example: The third-largest City in the united states is chicago, illinois.

(1) Located in the midwest on lake Michigan, chicago is an important port city, a rail and highway hub, and the site of o'hare international airport, one of the Nation's busiest. (2) The financial center of the city is Lasalle street, and the lakefront is home to Grant park, where there are many Museums and monuments. (3) To the North of the city, soldier field is home to the chicago bears, the city's football team, and wrigley field is home to the chicago cubs, a national league Baseball Team. (4) In the mid-1600s, the site of what is now Chicago was visited by father jacques marquette, a catholic missionary to the ottawa and huron tribes, who were native to the area. (5) By the 1700s, the city was a trading post run by john kinzie. (6) The city grew rapidly in the 1800s, and immigrants included germans, irish, italians, poles, greeks, and chinese, along with african americans who migrated from the south. (7) In 1871, much of the city was destroyed in one of the worst fires

in united states history; according to legend, the fire started when mrs. O'Leary's Cow kicked over a burning lantern. (8) Today, Chicago's skyline has many Skyscrapers, built by businesses like the john hancock company, sears, and amoco. (9) I know Chicago well because my Mother grew up there and my aunt jean and uncle amos still live there. (10) I also got information from the Chicago Chamber of Commerce when I wrote a paper for introductory research writing, a course I took at Graystone high school.

36b Punctuating Direct Quotations

A **direct quotation** shows the *exact* words of a speaker or writer. Direct quotations are always placed in quotation marks.

A direct quotation is usually accompanied by an **identifying tag**, a phrase (such as "she said") that names the person being quoted. In the following sentences, the identifying tag is underlined.

> <u>Lauren said</u>, "My brother and Tina have gotten engaged."
> A <u>famous advertising executive wrote</u>, "Don't sell the steak; sell the sizzle."

When a quotation is a complete sentence, it begins with a capital letter and ends with a period (or a question mark or exclamation point). When a quotation falls at the end of a sentence (as in the two examples above) the period is placed *before* the quotation marks.

If the quotation is a question or an exclamation, the question mark or exclamation point is also placed *before* the closing quotation mark.

> The instructor asked, "Has anyone read *Sula*?"
> Officer Warren shouted, "Hold it right there!"

If the quotation itself is not a question or an exclamation, the question mark or exclamation point is placed *after* the closing quotation mark.

> Did Joe really say, "I quit"?
> I can't believe he really said, "I quit"!

FYI

Indirect Quotations

A direct quotation shows someone's *exact* words, but an **indirect quotation** simply summarizes what was said or written.
Do not use quotation marks with indirect quotations.

DIRECT QUOTATION	Martin Luther King Jr. said, "I have a dream."
INDIRECT QUOTATION	Martin Luther King Jr. said that he had a dream.

The rules for punctuating direct quotations with identifying tags are summarized below.

Identifying Tag at the Beginning

When the identifying tag comes *before* the quotation, it is followed by a comma.

Alexandre Dumas wrote, "Nothing succeeds like success."

Identifying Tag at the End

When the identifying tag comes at the *end* of a quoted sentence, it is followed by a period. A comma (or, sometimes, a question mark or an exclamation point) inside the closing quotation mark separates the quotation from the identifying tag.

"Life is like a box of chocolates," stated Forrest Gump.
"Is that so?" his friends wondered.
"That's amazing!" he cried.

Identifying Tag in the Middle

When the identifying tag comes in the *middle* of the quoted sentence, it is followed by a comma. The first part of the quotation is also followed by a comma, placed inside the closing quotation mark. Because the part of the quotation that follows the identifying tag is not a new sentence, it does not begin with a capital letter.

"This is my life," Bette insisted, "and I'll live it as I please."

Identifying Tag between Two Sentences

When the identifying tag comes *between two* quoted sentences, it is preceded by a comma and followed by a period. (The second quoted sentence begins with a capital letter.)

> "Producer Berry Gordy is an important figure in the history of music," Tony explained. "He was the creative force behind Motown records."

PRACTICE

36-2   The following sentences contain direct quotations. First, underline the identifying tag. Then, punctuate the quotation correctly, adding capital letters as necessary.

Example: Why Darryl asked are teachers so strict about deadlines?

1. We who are about to die salute you said the gladiators to the emperor.

2. When we turned on the television, the newscaster was saying ladies and gentlemen, we have a new president-elect.

3. The bigger they are said boxer John L. Sullivan the harder they fall.

4. Do you take Michael to be your lawfully wedded husband asked the minister.

5. Lisa Marie replied I do.

6. If you believe the *National Enquirer* my friend always says then you'll believe anything.

7. When asked for the jury's verdict, the foreperson replied we find the defendant not guilty.

8. I had felt for a long time that if I was ever told to get up so a white person could sit Rosa Parks recalled I would refuse to do so.

9. Yabba dabba doo Fred exclaimed this brontoburger looks great.

10. Where's my money Addie Pray asked you give me my money!

36c   Setting Off Titles

Some titles are typed in *italics*. Others are enclosed in quotation marks. The following box shows how to set off different kinds of titles.

Italics or Quotation Marks?

ITALICIZED TITLES

Books: *How the García Girls Lost Their Accents*
Newspapers: *Miami Herald*
Magazines: *People*
Long poems: *John Brown's Body*
Plays: *Death of a Salesman*
Films: *The Rocky Horror Picture Show*
Television or radio series: *Battlestar Galactica*

TITLES IN QUOTATION MARKS

Book chapters: "Understanding Mechanics"
Short stories: "The Tell-Tale Heart"
Essays and articles: "The Suspected Shopper"
Short poems: "Richard Cory"
Songs and speeches: "America the Beautiful"; "The Gettysburg Address"
Individual episodes of television or radio series: "The Montgomery Bus Boycott" (an episode of the PBS series *Eyes on the Prize*)

FYI

Capital Letters in Titles

Capitalize the first letters of all important words in a title. Do not capitalize an **article** (*a, an, the*), a **preposition** (*to, of, around*, and so on), the *to* in an infinitive, or a **coordinating conjunction** (*and, but*, and so on)—unless it is the first or last word of the title or subtitle (*On the Road*; "To an Athlete Dying Young"; *No Way Out*; *And Quiet Flows the Don*).

PRACTICE
36-3   Edit the following sentences, capitalizing letters as necessary in titles.

Example: *New York Times* best-seller *Three Cups of Tea* is about

Greg Mortenson's work building schools in Pakistan and Afghanistan.

1. When fans of the television show *lost* voted for their favorite episodes, "through the looking glass," "the shape of things to come," and "the incident" were in the top ten.

2. In 1948, Eleanor Roosevelt delivered her famous speech "the struggle for human rights" and published an article titled "toward human rights throughout the world."

3. Before being elected president, Barack Obama wrote and published two books: *dreams from my father* and *the audacity of hope*.

4. English actor Daniel Craig plays secret agent James Bond in the films *casino royale* and *quantum of solace*.

5. *janis joplin's greatest hits* includes songs written by other people, such as "piece of my heart," as well as songs she wrote herself, such as "mercedes benz."

PRACTICE

36-4 In the following sentences, underline titles to indicate italics or place them in quotation marks. (Remember that titles of books and other long works are italicized, and titles of stories, essays, and other shorter works are enclosed in quotation marks.)

Example: An article in the <u>New York Times</u> called "Whoopi Goldberg Joins <u>The View</u>" talks about a television talk show hosted by women.

1. Oprah Winfrey publishes a magazine called O.

2. At the beginning of most major American sporting events, the crowd stands for The Star Spangled Banner.

3. People who want to purchase new cars often compare the different models in Consumer Reports magazine.

4. U2's song Pride (in the Name of Love) is about Martin Luther King Jr.

5. Edgar Allan Poe wrote several mysterious short stories, two of which are called The Tell-Tale Heart and The Black Cat.

6. The popular Broadway show Fela! was based on the life of the Nigerian musician Fela Kuti.

7. Tina Fey, who has won two Golden Globes for her role in the hit TV show 30 Rock, wrote a bestselling autobiography called Bossypants.

8. In a college textbook called Sociology: A Brief Introduction, the first chapter is titled The Essence of Sociology.

36d Hyphens

A hyphen has two uses: to divide a word at the end of a line and to join words in compounds.

■ Use a **hyphen** to divide a word at the end of a line. If you need to divide a word, divide it between syllables. (Check your dictionary to see how a word is divided into syllables.) Never break a one-syllable word, no matter how long it is.

> When the speaker began his talk, the people seated in the <u>audi-torium</u> grew very quiet.

■ Use a hyphen in a **compound**—a word that is made up of two or more words.

> This theater shows <u>first-run</u> movies.

PRACTICE

36-5 Add hyphens to join words in compounds in the following sentences.

Example: The course focused on nineteenth-century American literature.

1. The ice skating rink finally froze over.

2. We should be kind to our four legged friends.

3. The first year students raised money for charity.

4. The well liked professor gave a speech to new students during orientation.

5. The hand carved sculpture looked like a pair of doves.

36e   Abbreviations

An **abbreviation** is a shortened form of a word. Although abbreviations are generally not used in college writing, it is acceptable to abbreviate the following.

- Titles—such as Mr., Ms., Dr., and Jr.—that are used along with names
- a.m. and p.m.
- BC and AD (in dates such as 43 BC)
- Names of organizations (NRA, CIA) and technical terms (DNA). Note that some abbreviations, called **acronyms**, are pronounced as words: AIDS, FEMA.

Keep in mind that it is *not* acceptable to abbreviate days of the week, months, names of streets and places, names of academic subjects, or titles that are not used along with names.

PRACTICE
36-6   Edit the incorrect use of abbreviations in the following sentences.

                                    February

Example: In leap years, ~~Feb.~~ has twenty-nine days.

1. The dr. diagnosed a case of hypertension.

2. Nov. 11 is a federal holiday.

3. Derek registered for Eng. literature and a psych elective.

4. The museum was located at the corner of Laurel Ave. and Neptune St.

5. The clinic is only open Tues. through Thurs. and every other Sat.

36f   Numbers

In college writing, most numbers are spelled out (*forty-five*) rather than written as numerals (*45*). However, numbers more than two words long are always written as **numerals** (*4,530,* not *four thousand five hundred thirty*).

In addition, you should use numerals in the following situations.

DATES   January 20, 1976

ADDRESSES   5023 Schuyler Street

EXACT TIMES	10:00 (If you use *o'clock*, spell out the number: *ten o'clock*)
PERCENTAGES AND DECIMALS	80% 8.2
DIVISIONS OF BOOKS	Chapter 3 Act 4 Page 102

Note: Never begin a sentence with a numeral. Use a spelled-out number, or reword the sentence so the numeral does not come at the beginning.

PRACTICE

36-7 Edit the incorrect use of numbers in the following sentences.

Example: The population of the United States is over ~~three hundred~~ ³⁰⁰ million.

1. Only 2 students in the 8 o'clock lecture were late.

2. More than seventy-five percent of the class passed the exit exam.

3. Chapter six begins on page 873.

4. The wedding took place on October twelfth at 7:30.

5. Meet me at Sixty-five Cadman Place.

36g Using Minor Punctuation Marks

The Semicolon

Use a **semicolon** to join independent clauses in a compound sentence.

Twenty years ago, smartphones did not exist; today, many people cannot imagine life without them.

The Colon

- Use a **colon** to introduce a quotation.

 Our family motto is a simple one: "Accept no substitutes."

- Use a colon to introduce an explanation, a clarification, or an example.

 Only one thing kept him from climbing Mt. Everest: fear of heights.

■ Use a colon to introduce a list.

> I left my job for four reasons: boring work, poor working conditions, low pay, and a terrible supervisor.

The Dash

Use **dashes** to set off important information.

> She parked her car—a red Firebird—in a towaway zone.

Parentheses

Use **parentheses** to enclose material that is relatively unimportant.

> The weather in Portland (a city in Oregon) was overcast.

PRACTICE

36-8 Add semicolons, colons, dashes, and parentheses to the following sentences where necessary.

Example: Megachurches (those with more than two thousand worshippers at a typical service) have grown in popularity since the 1950s.

1. Megachurches though they are Protestant are not always affiliated with the main Protestant denominations.

2. Services in megachurches are creative preaching is sometimes accompanied by contemporary music and video presentations.

3. Although many of these churches are evangelical actively recruiting new members, people often join because of friends and neighbors.

4. Megachurches tend to keep their members because they encourage a variety of activities for example, hospitality committees and study groups.

5. Worshippers say that their services are upbeat they are full of joy and spirituality.

6. Megachurches in nearly all cases use technology to organize and communicate with their members.

7. The largest of these churches with ten thousand members would be unable to function without telecommunications.

8. Some even offer services in a format familiar to their younger members the podcast.

9. Critics of megachurches and there are some believe they take up too much tax-exempt land.

10. Other critics fear that smaller churches already struggling to keep members will lose worshippers to these huge congregations and eventually have to close.

TEST · Revise · Edit

Look back at your response to the Focus on Writing prompt on page 664. TEST what you have written.

   If you have quoted any dialogue from the film you wrote about, try varying the placement of the identifying tags you have used. If you did not include any lines of dialogue, try adding one or two. Then, add an example or list to your writing, introducing this new material with a colon. Make sure that a complete sentence comes before the colon.

   Finally, revise and edit your work, paying special attention to the issues covered in this chapter.

EDITING PRACTICE

Read the following student essay, which includes errors in capitalization and punctuation and in the use of direct quotations and titles. Correct any errors you find. The first sentence has been edited for you.

A Threat to Health

Pandemics are like Ĕpidemics, only more widespread, perhaps even spreading throughout the World. In a pandemic, a serious Disease spreads very easily. In the past, there have been many pandemics. In the future, in spite of advances in Medicine, there will still be pandemics. In fact, scientists agree that not every pandemic can be prevented, so pandemics will continue to be a threat.

Probably the best-known pandemic is the bubonic plague. It killed about one-third of the Population of europe during the middle ages. Some areas suffered more than others. According to Philip ziegler's book the black Death, at least half the people in florence, Italy, died in one year. Many years later, in 1918, a flu pandemic killed more than 50 million people worldwide, including hundreds of thousands in the United states.

Unfortunately, pandemics have not disappeared. AIDS, for example, is a current pandemic. Philadelphia the 1993 movie starring denzel washington and tom hanks is still one of the most moving depictions of the heartbreak of AIDS. The rate of AIDS infection is over 30% in parts of africa, the disease continues to spread on other Continents as well. So far, efforts to find an AIDS vaccine have failed. Dr. anthony s. Fauci discussed recent AIDS research on NPR's series All things considered in a program called Search for an HIV vaccine expands.

Although some pandemic diseases, such as Smallpox, have been wiped out by Vaccination, new pandemics remain a threat. Many viruses and Bacteria change in response to treatment, so they may become resistant to Vaccination and Antibiotics. Also, with modern transportation, a disease can move quickly from Country to Country. For example, the disease known as severe acute respiratory syndrome (SARS) began in china but was spread to other countries by travelers. Hundreds died as a result of the SARS pandemic between November 2002 and july 2003. Birds also remain a threat because they can transmit disease. It is obviously impossible to prevent birds from flying from one country to another. Markos kyprianou, health commissioner of the European union, has said that I am concerned that birds in Turkey have been found with the bird flu Virus. He said, There is a direct relationship with viruses found in Russia, Mongolia and china. If this Virus changes so that it can move easily from birds to Humans, bird flu could become the next pandemic.

Public Health Officials are always on the lookout for diseases with three characteristics they are new, they are dangerous, and they are very contagious. Doctors try to prevent them from becoming Pandemics. However, they continue to warn that some Pandemics cannot be prevented.

COLLABORATIVE ACTIVITY

Working in pairs, write a conversation between two characters, real or fictional, who have very different positions on a particular issue. Place all direct quotations within quotation marks, and include identifying tags that clearly indicate which character is speaking. (Begin a new paragraph each time a new person speaks.)

Exchange your conversation with another pair, and check their work to see that directly quoted speech is set within quotation marks and that capital letters and other punctuation are used correctly.

review checklist

Understanding Mechanics

- Capitalize proper nouns. (See 36a.)

- Always place direct quotations within quotation marks. (See 36b.)

- In titles, capitalize all important words. Use italics or quotation marks to set off titles. (See 36c.)

- Use a hyphen to divide a word at the end of a line or to join words in compounds. (See 36d.)

- Abbreviate titles used with names, a.m. and p.m., BC and AD, names of organizations, and technical terms. (See 36e.)

- Use numerals for numbers more than two words long and in certain other situations. (See 36f.)

- Use semicolons to join independent clauses in a compound sentence. (See 36g.)

- Use colons, dashes, and parentheses to set off material from the rest of the sentence. (See 36g.)

Read the following student essay, which contains errors in the use of punctuation and mechanics. Identify the sentences that need to be corrected, and edit the faulty sentences. (Underline to indicate italics where necessary.) The first sentence has been edited for you.

Telenovelas

What is the most-watched kind of television program in Spanish-speaking countries/ It's the telenovela, a Spanish language soap opera. Televised on Weeknights in the prime evening hour's; telenovelas started in the early nineteen fifties and are still popular today. In fact more telenovelas are shown in central America and South america than any other type of tv drama. In a 1998 study more than half the population of Latin American countries said "that they watch these shows." Telenovelas are different from american soap operas in the way they are planned and scheduled. Also they dont have the same kind of plots. Telenovela's popularity can be seen in their Web sites, and by their growth in countries that dont speak spanish.

Telenovelas are quite different from. American Soap Operas. In the United States, there have been some evening soap opera dramas (dallas and dynasty are good examples but they have usually been televised only once-a-week, however telenovelas usually appear Mon. through Fri. In the United States soap operas generally continue for mos. and yrs. until viewers stop watching, and ratings fall. The writers of an american soap opera, do not know how the plot will develop; or when it will end. In contrast telenovela's are usually completely mapped out at the beginning. In general a telenovela continues for about 8 months and then the short lived drama is over. A new telenovela takes it's place.

The plots may seem strange to american viewers. In a typical telenovela the beautiful Heroine is a girl—who has no money, but has a good heart. The hero—a rich, handsome man, rejects his rich but evil girlfriend in favor of the heroine. Eventually the heroine may turn out to be the secret child of a wealthy family. The unhappy villain's may wind up in the cemetery and the heroine and her hero will live "happily ever after." Other telenovelas occur in the past, or may deal with modern social problems such as drug abuse, or prejudice. Some telenovelas are really serial comedies and are more, like American sitcoms.

Telenovelas are becoming more and more popular. There are even Web sites dedicated to: popular telenovelas and their actors. For example viewers can go to the Web site called topnovelas to access: plot summaries lists of the most popular shows and downloads of episodes'. Although telenovelas started in Spanish-speaking countries they have spread to other countries. The 1st telenovela to be translated into another language was "The Rich Cry too" (Los Ricos También Lloran) which was first produced in Mexico in nineteen seventy-nine and was brought to, China, the Soviet Union and the United States. Other places where telenovelas are popular include the following countries; france israel japan, malaysia Singapore and indonesia.

The popularity of the telenovela in the United states is only partly a reflection of its' millions of spanish speaking viewers. While it is true that Networks want to attract hispanic viewers it is also true that the format, and subject matter interest English-Speaking viewers. Its quite possible that one day, telenovelas in English will appear every night?

37 Reading Critically

In this chapter, you will learn to

- preview (37a), highlight (37b), annotate (37c), outline (37d), and summarize (37e) a reading assignment
- write a response paragraph (37f)
- use active reading skills in the classroom, in the community, and in the workplace (37g)

Reading is essential in all your college courses. To get the most out of your reading, you should approach the books, articles, and Web pages you read in a practical way, always asking yourself what information they can offer you. You should also approach assigned readings critically, just as you approach your own writing when you revise.

Reading critically does not mean challenging or arguing with every idea, but it does mean wondering, commenting, questioning, and assessing. Most of all, it means being an active rather than a passive reader. Being an **active reader** means participating in the reading process: approaching a reading assignment with a clear understanding of your purpose, previewing a selection, highlighting and annotating it, and perhaps outlining it—all *before* you begin to respond in writing to what you have read.

To gain an understanding of your **purpose**—your reason for reading—you should start by answering some questions.

QUESTIONS ABOUT YOUR PURPOSE

- Why are you reading?
- Will you be expected to discuss what you are reading? If so, will you discuss it in class or in a conference with your instructor?
- Will you have to write about what you are reading? If so, will you be expected to write an informal response (for example, a journal entry) or a more formal one (for example, an essay)?
- Will you be tested on the material?

Once you understand your purpose, you are ready to begin reading.

37a Previewing

Your first step is to *preview* the material you have been assigned to read. When you **preview**, you try to get a sense of the writer's main idea and key supporting points as well as the general emphasis of the passage. You can begin by focusing on the title, the first paragraph (which often contains a thesis statement or overview), and the last paragraph (which often contains a summary of the writer's key points). You should also look for clues to content and emphasis in other **visual signals** (headings, boxes, and so on) as well as in **verbal signals** (the words and phrases the writer uses to indicate which points are stressed and how ideas are arranged).

Previewing: Visual Signals

- Look at the title.
- Look at the opening and closing paragraphs.
- Look at each paragraph's first sentence.
- Look at headings.
- Look at *italicized* and **boldfaced** words.
- Look at numbered lists.
- Look at bulleted lists (like this one).
- Look at graphs, charts, tables, photographs, and so on.
- Look at any information that is boxed.
- Look at any information that is in color.

Previewing: Verbal Signals

- Look for phrases that signal emphasis ("The *primary* reason"; "The *most important* idea").
- Look for repeated words and phrases.
- Look for words that signal addition (*also, in addition, furthermore*).
- Look for words that signal time sequence (*first, after, then, next, finally*).
- Look for words that identify causes and effects (*because, as a result, for this reason*).
- Look for words that introduce examples (*for example, for instance*).
- Look for words that signal comparison (*likewise, similarly*).
- Look for words that signal contrast (*unlike, although, in contrast*).
- Look for words that signal contradiction (*however, on the contrary*).
- Look for words that signal a narrowing of the writer's focus (*in fact, specifically, in other words*).
- Look for words that signal summaries or conclusions (*to sum up, in conclusion*).

When you have finished previewing, you should have a general sense of what the writer wants to communicate.

PRACTICE
37-1

"No Comprendo" ("I Don't Understand") is a newspaper opinion article by Barbara Mujica, a professor of Spanish at Georgetown University in Washington, D.C. In this article, which was published in the *New York Times*, Mujica argues against bilingual education (teaching students in their native language as well as in English).

In preparation for class discussion and for other activities that will be assigned later in this chapter, preview the article. As you read, try to identify the writer's main idea and key supporting points. Then, write them on the lines that follow the article.

NO COMPRENDO

Barbara Mujica

Last spring, my niece phoned me in tears. She was graduating from high school and had to make a decision. An outstanding soccer player, she was offered athletic scholarships by several colleges. So why was she crying?

My niece came to the United States from South America as a child. Although she had received good grades in her schools in Miami, she spoke English with a heavy accent, and her comprehension and writing skills were deficient. She was afraid that once she left the Miami environment, she would feel uncomfortable and, worse still, have difficulty keeping up with class work.

Programs that keep foreign-born children in Spanish-language classrooms for years are only part of the problem. During a visit to my niece's former school, I observed that all business, not just teaching, was conducted in Spanish. In the office, secretaries spoke to the administrators and the children in Spanish. Announcements over the public-address system were made in an English so fractured that it was almost incomprehensible.

I asked my niece's mother why, after years in public schools, her daughter had poor English skills. "It's the whole environment," she replied. "All kinds of services are available in Spanish or Spanglish. Sports and after-school activities are conducted in Spanglish. That's what the kids hear on the radio and in the street."

WORD POWER

Spanglish A mixture of Spanish and English

Until recently, immigrants made learning English a priority. But 5
even when they didn't learn English themselves, their children grew up
speaking it. Thousands of first-generation Americans still strive to learn
English, but others face reduced educational and career opportunities
because they have not mastered this basic skill they need to get ahead.

According to the 1990 census, 40 percent of the Hispanics born in 6
the United States do not graduate from high school, and the Department
of Education says that a lack of proficiency in English is an important
factor in the drop-out rate.

People and agencies that favor providing services only in foreign 7
languages want to help people who do not speak English, but they may
be doing these people a disservice by condemning them to a linguistic
ghetto from which they cannot easily escape.

And my niece? She turned down all of her scholarship opportuni- 8
ties, deciding instead to attend a small college in Miami, where she will
never have to put her English to the test.

Writer's main idea

_____

_____

Key supporting points

1. _____

2. _____

3. _____

4. _____

37b Highlighting

After previewing the assigned material, read through it carefully, *highlighting* as you read. **Highlighting** means using underlining and symbols to identify key ideas. This active reading strategy will help you understand the writer's ideas and make connections among them when you reread.

Be selective; don't highlight too much. Remember, you will eventually be rereading every highlighted word, phrase, and sentence—so highlight only the most important, most useful information.

Using Highlighting Symbols

- Underline key ideas—for example, topic sentences.
- Box or circle words or phrases you want to remember.
- Place a check mark (✓) or star (✲) next to an important idea.
- Place a double check mark (✓✓) or double star (✲✲) next to an especially significant idea.
- Draw lines or arrows to connect related ideas.
- Put a question mark (?) beside a word or idea that you need to look up.
- Number the writer's key supporting points or examples.

FYI

Knowing What to Highlight

You want to highlight what's important—but how do you *know* what's important? As a general rule, you should look for the same **visual signals** you looked for when you did your previewing. Many of the ideas you will need to highlight will probably be found in material that is visually set off from the rest of the text—opening and closing paragraphs, lists, and so on.

Also, continue to look for **verbal signals**—words and phrases like *however, therefore, another reason, the most important point*, and so on—that often introduce key points. Together, these visual and verbal signals will give you clues to the writer's meaning and emphasis.

Here is how one student highlighted an excerpt from a newspaper column, "Barbie at Thirty-Five" by Anna Quindlen.

✲ But consider the recent study at the University of Arizona investigating the attitudes of white and black teenage girls toward body image. The attitudes of the white girls were a nightmare. Ninety percent expressed

✓ dissatisfaction with their own bodies, and many said they saw dieting as a kind of all-purpose panacea. "I think the reason I would diet would be to gain self-confidence," said one. "I'd feel like it was a way of getting control," said another. And they were curiously united in their description of the perfect girl. She's 5 feet 7 inches, weighs just over 100 pounds, has long legs and flowing hair. The researchers concluded, "The ideal girl was a living manifestation of the Barbie doll."

While white girls described an impossible ideal, black teenagers talked about appearance in terms of style, attitude, pride, and personality. White respondents talked "thin," black ones "shapely." Seventy percent of the black teenagers said they were <u>satisfied with their weight</u>, and ✓ there was little emphasis on dieting. "We're all brought up and taught to be realistic about life," said one, "and we don't look at things the way you want them to be. You look at them the way they are."

The student who highlighted the passage above was preparing to write an essay about eating disorders. Because the passage included no visual signals apart from the paragraph divisions, she looked carefully for verbal signals.

The student began her highlighting by underlining and starring the writer's main idea. She then boxed the names of the two key groups the passage compares—*white girls* and *black teenagers*—and underlined two phrases that illustrate how the attitudes of the two groups differ (*dissatisfaction with their own bodies* and *satisfied with their weight*). Check marks in the margin remind the student of the importance of these two phrases, and arrows connect each phrase to the appropriate group of girls.

The student also circled three related terms that characterize white girls' attitudes—*perfect girl*, *Barbie doll*, and *impossible ideal*—drawing lines to connect them. Finally, she circled the unfamiliar word *panacea* and put a question mark above it to remind herself to look up the word's meaning.

PRACTICE

37-2 Review the highlighted passage above. How would your own highlighting of this passage be similar to or different from the sample student highlighting?

PRACTICE

37-3 Reread "No Comprendo" (p. 688). As you reread, highlight the article by underlining and starring main ideas, boxing and circling key words, checkmarking important points, and drawing lines and arrows to connect related ideas. Be sure to circle each unfamiliar word and to put a question mark above it.

37c Annotating

As you highlight, you should also *annotate* what you are reading. **Annotating** a passage means reading critically and making notes—of questions, reactions, reminders, and ideas for writing or discussion—in the margins or between the lines. (If you run out of room on the page, you can use sticky notes.) Keeping an informal record of ideas as they occur to you will prepare you for class discussion and for writing.

As you read, asking the following questions will help you make useful annotations.

Questions for Critical Reading

- What is the writer saying? What do you think the writer is suggesting or implying? What makes you think so?
- What is the writer's purpose (his or her reason for writing)?
- What kind of audience is the writer addressing?
- Is the writer responding to another writer's ideas?
- What is the writer's main idea?
- How does the writer support his or her points? Does the writer use facts? Opinions? Both?
- What kind of supporting details and examples does the writer use?
- Does the writer include enough supporting details and examples?
- What pattern of development does the writer use to arrange his or her ideas? Is this pattern the best choice?
- Does the writer seem well informed? Reasonable? Fair?
- Do you understand the writer's vocabulary?
- Do you understand the writer's ideas?
- Do you agree with the points the writer is making?
- How are the ideas presented in this reading selection like (or unlike) those presented in other selections you have read?

The following passage, which reproduces the student's highlighting from pages 690–691, also illustrates her annotations.

But consider the recent study at the University of Arizona investigating

✱ the attitudes of white and black teenage girls toward body image. The attitudes of the white girls were a nightmare. Ninety percent expressed

✓ dissatisfaction with their own bodies, and many said they saw dieting

as a kind of all-purpose panacea. "I think the reason I would diet would   = cure-all

be to gain self-confidence," said one. "I'd feel like it was a way of getting

control," said another. And they were curiously united in their descrip-   Need for control,
                                                                              perfection. Why?
tion of the perfect girl. She's 5 feet 7 inches, weighs just over 100 pounds, Media? Parents?

has long legs and flowing hair. The researchers concluded, "The ideal girl

was a living manifestation of the Barbie doll."   Barbie doll
                                                                              = plastic, unreal

   While white girls described an impossible ideal, black teenagers

talked about appearance in terms of style, attitude, pride, and personality.

White respondents talked "thin," black ones "shapely." Seventy percent   "Thin" vs. "shapely"

✓ of the black teenagers said they were satisfied with their weight, and   Only 30% dissatisfied—
                                                                              but 90% of white girls
there was little emphasis on dieting. "We're all brought up and taught to

be realistic about life," said one, "and we don't look at things the way you

want them to be. You look at them the way they are."

                                    overgeneralization?

          vs. Barbie doll (= unrealistic)

   In her annotations, this student wrote down the meaning of the word *panacea*, put the study's conclusions and the contrasting statistics into her own words, and recorded questions she intended to explore further.

**PRACTICE
37-4**   Reread "No Comprendo" (p. 688). As you reread, refer to the Questions for Critical Reading (p. 692), and use them to guide you as you write down your own thoughts and questions in the margins of the article. Note where you agree or disagree with the writer, and briefly explain why. Quickly summarize any points you think are particularly important. Take time to look up any unfamiliar words you have circled and to write brief definitions. Think of these annotations as your preparation for discussing the article in class and eventually writing about it.

37d Outlining

Outlining is another technique you can use to help you understand a reading assignment. Unlike a **formal outline**, which follows strict conventions, an **informal outline** enables you to record a passage's ideas in the order in which they are presented. After you have made an informal outline of a passage, you should be able to see the writer's emphasis (which ideas are more important than others) as well as how the ideas are related.

FYI

Constructing an Informal Outline

To construct an informal outline, follow these guidelines:

1. Write or type the passage's main idea at the top of a sheet of paper. (This will remind you of the writer's focus and help keep your outline on track.)

2. At the left margin, write down the most important idea of the first body paragraph or first part of the passage.

3. Indent the next line a few spaces, and list the examples or details that support this idea. (You can use your computer's Tab key to help you set up your outline.)

4. As ideas become more specific, indent further. (Ideas that have the same degree of importance are indented the same distance from the left margin.)

5. Repeat the process with each body paragraph or part of the passage.

The student who highlighted and annotated the excerpt from Anna Quindlen's "Barbie at Thirty-Five" (pp. 690–691 and 692–693) made the following informal outline to help her understand the writer's ideas.

Main idea: Black and white teenage girls have very different attitudes about their body images.

White girls dissatisfied
    90% dissatisfied with appearance
    Dieting = cure-all
      –self-confidence
      –control
    Ideal = unrealistic
      –tall and thin
      –Barbie doll

Black girls satisfied
    70% satisfied with weight
    Dieting not important
    Ideal = realistic
      –shapely
      –not thin

PRACTICE

37-5 Working on your own or in a small group, make an informal outline of "No Comprendo" (p. 688). Refer to your highlighting and annotations as you construct your outline. When you have finished, check to make certain your outline accurately represents the writer's emphasis and the relationships among her ideas.

37e Summarizing

Once you have highlighted, annotated, and outlined a passage, you may want to *summarize* it to help you understand it better. A **summary** retells, *in your own words*, what a passage is about. A summary condenses a passage, so it leaves out all but the main idea and perhaps the key supporting points. A summary omits supporting examples and details, and it does *not* include your own ideas or opinions.

To summarize a reading assignment, follow these guidelines:

1. Review your outline.
2. Consulting your outline, restate the passage's main idea *in your own words*.
3. Consulting your outline, restate the passage's key supporting points. Add transitional words and phrases between sentences where necessary.
4. Reread the original passage to make sure you have not left out anything significant.

FYI

To avoid accidentally using the exact language of the original, do not look at the passage while you are writing your summary. If you want to use a distinctive word or phrase from the original passage, put it in quotation marks.

The student who highlighted, annotated, and outlined the excerpt from "Barbie at Thirty-Five" (pp. 690–695) wrote the following summary.

> As Anna Quindlen reports in "Barbie at Thirty-Five," a University of Arizona study found that black and white teenage girls have very different attitudes about their body images. Almost all white girls said they were dissatisfied with their appearance. To them, the "perfect girl" would look like a Barbie doll (tall and very thin). Quindlen sees this attitude as unrealistic. Black girls in the study, however, were generally happy with their weight. They did not say they wanted to be thin; they said they wanted to be "shapely."

PRACTICE

37-6   Write a brief summary of "No Comprendo" (p. 688). Use your outline to guide you, and keep your summary short and to the point. Your summary should be about one-quarter to one-third the length of the original article.

37f Writing a Response Paragraph

Once you have highlighted and annotated a reading selection, you are ready to write about it—perhaps in a **response paragraph** in which you record your informal reactions to the writer's ideas.

Because a response paragraph is informal, no special guidelines or rules govern its format or structure. As in any paragraph, however, you should include a topic sentence and supporting evidence, use complete sentences, and link sentences with appropriate transitions. In a response paragraph, informal style and personal opinions are acceptable.

The student who highlighted, annotated, outlined, and summarized "Barbie at Thirty-Five" wrote the following response paragraph.

> Why are white and black girls' body images so different? Why do black girls think it's okay to be "shapely" while white girls want to be thin? Maybe it's because music videos and movies and fashion magazines show so many more white models, all half-starved, with perfect hair and legs. Or maybe white girls get different messages from their parents or from the people they date. Do white and black girls' attitudes about their bodies stay the same when they get older? And what about <u>male</u> teenagers' self-images? Do white and black <u>guys</u> have different body images, too?

The process of writing this paragraph was very helpful to the student. The questions she asked suggested some interesting ideas that she could explore in class discussion or in a more fully developed piece of writing.

PRACTICE

37-7 Write a response paragraph expressing your reactions to "No Comprendo" (p. 688) and to the issue of bilingual education.

37g Reading in the Classroom, in the Community, and in the Workplace

In college, in your life as a citizen of your community, and in the workplace, you will read material in a variety of different formats—for example, textbooks, newspapers, Web pages, and job-related documents.

Although the active reading process you have just reviewed can be applied to all kinds of material, various kinds of reading require slightly different strategies during the previewing stage. One reason for this is that different kinds of reading may have different purposes (for example, to present information or to persuade). Another reason is that the various documents you read are aimed at different audiences, and different readers require different signals about content and emphasis. For these reasons, you need to look for different kinds of verbal and visual signals when you preview different kinds of reading material.

Reading Textbooks

Much of the reading you do in college is in textbooks (like this one). The purpose of a textbook is to present information, and when you read a textbook, your goal is to understand that information. To do this, you need to figure out which ideas are most important as well as which points support those ideas and which examples illustrate them.

checklist

Reading Textbooks

Look for the following features as you preview:

- [ ] **Boldfaced** and *italicized* words, which can indicate terms to be defined

- [ ] Boxed checklists or summaries, which may appear at the ends of sections or chapters

- [ ] Bulleted or numbered lists, which may list key reasons or examples or summarize important material

- [ ] Diagrams, charts, tables, graphs, photographs, and other visuals that illustrate the writer's points

- [ ] Marginal quotations and definitions

- [ ] Marginal cross-references

- [ ] Web links

PRACTICE

37-8   Using the checklist above as a guide, preview the page from the textbook *Psychology*, Sixth Edition (2013), by Don H. Hockenbury and Sandra E. Hockenbury, on page 699. When you have finished, highlight and annotate it.

Reading News Articles

As a student, as an employee, and as a citizen, you read school, community, local, and national newspapers in print and online. Like textbooks, news articles communicate information. In addition, newspapers also publish editorials (which aim to persuade) as well as feature articles (which may be designed to entertain as well as to inform).

Many people read news articles online rather than in print form. If this is what you usually do, keep in mind that newspaper Web pages tend to be very busy and crowded, so you may have to work hard to distinguish important information from not-so-important material. For example, a news article that you read online may be surrounded by advertising and include links to irrelevant (and potentially distracting) material. For this reason, it is very important to read online material with care.

Hearing
From Vibration to Sound

▰▰▰ **KEY THEME**

› Auditory sensation, or hearing, results when sound waves are collected in the outer ear, amplified in the middle ear, and converted to neural messages in the inner ear.

▰▰▰ **KEY QUESTIONS**

› How do sound waves produce different auditory sensations?

› What are the key structures of the ear and their functions?

› How do place theory and frequency theory explain pitch perception?

We have hiked in a desert area that was so quiet we could hear the whir of a single grasshopper's wings in the distance. And we have waited on a subway platform where the screech of metal wheels against metal rails forced us to cover our ears.

The sense of hearing, or **audition,** is capable of responding to a wide range of sounds, from faint to blaring, simple to complex, harmonious to discordant. The ability to sense and perceive very subtle differences in sound is important to physical survival, social interactions, and language development. Most of the time, all of us are bathed in sound—so much so that moments of near-silence, like our experience in the desert, can seem almost eerie.

What We Hear
The Nature of Sound

Whether it's the ear-splitting screech of metal on metal or the subtle whir of a grass-hopper's wings, *sound waves* are the physical stimuli that produce our sensory experience of sound. Usually, sound waves are produced by the rhythmic vibration of air molecules, but sound waves can be transmitted through other media, such as water, too. Our perception of sound is directly related to the physical properties of sound waves (see Figure 3.7).

One of the first things that we notice about a sound is how loud it is. **Loudness** is determined by the intensity, or **amplitude,** of a sound wave and is measured in units called **decibels.** Zero decibels represents the loudness of the softest sound that humans can hear, or the absolute threshold for hearing. As decibels increase, perceived loudness increases.

Pitch refers to the relative "highness" or "lowness" of a sound. Pitch is determined by the frequency of a sound wave. **Frequency** refers to the rate of vibration, or number of waves per second, and is measured in units called *hertz*. Hertz simply refers to the number of wave peaks per second. The faster the vibration, the higher the frequency, the closer together the waves are—and the higher the tone produced. If you pluck the high E and the low E strings on a guitar, you'll notice that the low E vibrates far fewer times per second than does the high E.

Most of the sounds we experience do not consist of a single frequency but are *complex*, consisting of several sound-wave frequencies. This combination of frequencies produces the distinctive quality, or **timbre,** of a sound, which enables us to distinguish easily between the same note played on a saxophone and on a piano. Every human voice has its own distinctive timbre, which is why you can immediately identify a friend's voice on the telephone from just a few words, even if you haven't talked to each other for years.

▰ **audition** The technical term for the sense of hearing.

▰ **loudness** The intensity (or amplitude) of a sound wave, measured in decibels.

▰ **amplitude** The intensity or amount of energy of a wave, reflected in the height of the wave; the amplitude of a sound wave determines a sound's loudness.

▰ **decibel** (DESS-uh-bell) The unit of measurement for loudness.

▰ **pitch** The relative highness or lowness of a sound, determined by the frequency of a sound wave.

▰ **frequency** The rate of vibration, or the number of sound waves per second.

▰ **timbre** (TAM-ber) The distinctive quality of a sound, determined by the complexity of the sound wave.

FIGURE 3.7 Characteristics of Sound Waves The length of a wave, its height, and its complexity determine the loudness, pitch, and timbre that we hear. The sound produced by **(a)** would be high-pitched and loud. The sound produced by **(b)** would be soft and low. The sound in **(c)** is complex, like the sounds we usually experience in the natural world.

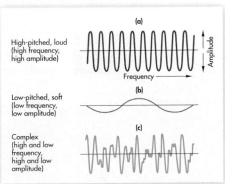

High-pitched, loud (high frequency, high amplitude)

Low-pitched, soft (low frequency, low amplitude)

Complex (high and low frequency, high and low amplitude)

checklist

Reading News Articles

Look for the following features as you preview:

- Headlines

- **Boldfaced** headings within articles

- Labels like *editorial, commentary,* or *opinion,* which indicate that an article communicates the writer's own views

- Brief biographical information at the end of an opinion piece

- Phrases or sentences in **boldface** (to emphasize key points)

- The article's first sentence, which often answers the questions *who, what, why, where, when,* and *how*

- The **dateline**, which tells you the date and the city the writer is reporting from

- Photographs, charts, graphs, and other visuals

- In *print news articles,* related articles that appear on the same page—for example, boxed information and **sidebars,** short related articles that provide additional background on people and places mentioned in the article

- In *online news articles,* links to related articles, reader comments, and other useful material

PRACTICE

37-9   Using the checklist above as a guide, preview the online news article on pages 701–702. Then, highlight and annotate it.

School is too easy, students report

By Greg Toppo, USA TODAY   Updated 7/9/2012 11:43 PM

Comment   Recommend 2   Tweet 766   +1 6   ✉ 🖨 ➕

Reprints & Permissions

Millions of kids simply don't find school very challenging, a new analysis of federal survey data suggests. The report could spark a debate about whether new academic standards being piloted nationwide might make a difference.

By Gerry Broome, AP

Students return for their first day of classes at Barwell Road Elementary School in Raleigh, N.C., on Monday.

The findings, out today from the Center for American Progress, a Washington think tank that champions "progressive ideas," analyze three years of questionnaires from the Department of Education's National Assessment of Educational Progress, a national test given each year.

Among the findings:

•37% of fourth-graders say their math work is "often" or "always" too easy;

•57% of eighth-graders say their history work is "often" or "always" too easy;

•39% of 12th-graders say they rarely write about what they read in class.

Ulrich Boser, a senior fellow at the center who co-wrote the report, said the data challenge the "school-as-pressure-cooker" image found in recent movies such as *Race to Nowhere*. Although those kids certainly exist at one end of the academic spectrum, Boser said, "the broad swath of American students are not as engaged as much in their schoolwork."

Robert Pondiscio of the Core Knowledge Foundation, a Virginia non-profit that pushes for more rigorous academics, says the pressure-cooker environment applies only to a "small, rarefied set" of high school students. The notion that "every American kid is going home with a backpack loaded with 70 pounds of books — that's not happening."

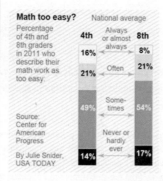

Math too easy?

National average

Percentage of 4th and 8th graders in 2011 who describe their math work as too easy:

	4th		8th
Always or almost always	16%		8%
Often	21%		21%
Sometimes	49%		54%
Never or hardly ever	14%		17%

Source: Center for American Progress

By Julie Snider, USA TODAY

The data suggest that many kids simply aren't pushed academically: Only one in five eighth-graders read more than 20 pages a day, either in school or for homework. Most report that they read far less.

"It's fairly safe to say that potentially high-achieving kids are probably not as challenged as they could be or ought to be," Boser said.

The center supports new Common Core standards that are to be implemented nationwide in the 2014-15 school year. The standards, adopted by 45 states, are meant to be "robust and relevant to the real world," giving schools "a consistent, clear understanding of what students are expected to learn," according to the initiative.

Gladis Kersaint, a math education professor at the University of South Florida and a board member of the National Council of Teachers of Mathematics, said she's not surprised by the findings. "I think we underestimate students," she said.

The push for higher standards — and students' willingness to meet those standards — "suggests that they're ready to be more challenged in math classes," she said. "Hopefully this can be a motivator for teachers to say, 'Yes, we're moving in the right direction.' "

Florida State University English education professor Shelbie Witte, a former classroom teacher, said standardized tests limit material teachers can cover. "The curriculum is just void of critical thinking, creative thinking," she said. As a result, students are "probably bored, and when they're bored, they think the classes are easy."

Witte, who trains teachers, said both their conception and their students' conception of school have been heavily influenced by testing. "That's what they think school is, and that's really a shame," she said.

Reading on the Job

In your workplace, you may be called on to read email messages, memos, letters, and reports. These documents, which may be designed to convey information or to persuade, are often addressed to a group rather than to a single person. (Note that the most important information is often presented *first*—in a subject line or in the first paragraph.)

checklist

Reading on the Job

Look for the following features as you preview:

- ☐ Numbered or bulleted lists of tasks or problems (numbers indicate the order of the items' importance)

- ☐ The first and last paragraphs and the first sentence of each body paragraph, which often contain key information

- ☐ **Boldfaced**, <u>underlined</u>, or *italicized* words

- ☐ In a report, visuals that illustrate key concepts

- ☐ In electronic communications, the person(s) addressed, the subject line, and links to the Web

- ☐ In a memo or a report, headings that highlight key topics or points

PRACTICE

37-10

Using the checklist above as a guide, preview the email message on page 704. What is the writer's purpose? What is the most important piece of information she wants to communicate? Highlight and annotate the memo, and then write a two-sentence summary of it.

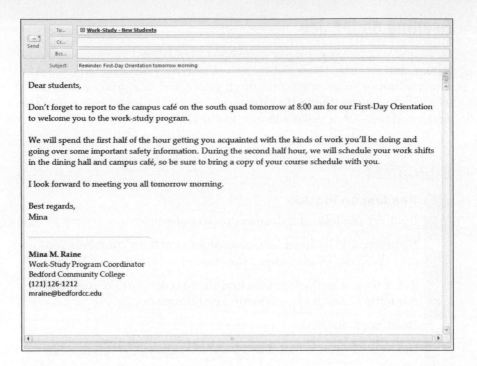

review checklist

Reading Critically

- [ ] Preview the material. (See 37a.)

- [ ] Highlight the material. (See 37b.)

- [ ] Annotate the material. (See 37c.)

- [ ] Outline the material. (See 37d.)

- [ ] Summarize the material. (See 37e.)

- [ ] Write a response paragraph. (See 37f.)

- [ ] Use active reading strategies when reading textbooks, news articles, and workplace communications. (See 37g.)

38 Readings for Writers

The following nineteen essays by professional writers offer interesting material to read, react to, think critically about, discuss, and write about. In addition, these essays illustrate some of the ways you can organize ideas in your own writing.

The essays in this chapter use the nine patterns of development you learned about in Units 1 through 3 of this book: exemplification, narration, description, process, cause and effect, comparison and contrast, classification, definition, and argument. Of course, these patterns are not your only options for arranging ideas in essays; in fact, many essays combine several patterns of development. Still, understanding how each of these nine patterns works will help you choose the most effective organization strategy when you are writing for a particular purpose and audience.

In this chapter, two essays by professional writers illustrate each pattern of development. (For argument, three model essays are included.) Each essay is preceded by a short **headnote**, an introduction that tells you something about the writer and suggests what to look for as you read. Following each selection are five sets of questions.

- **Focus on Meaning** questions help you to assess your understanding of the basic ideas the essay communicates.

- **Focus on Strategy** questions ask you to consider the writer's purpose and intended audience, the essay's opening and closing strategies, and the thesis statement.

- **Focus on Language and Style** questions ask you to think about the writer's stylistic decisions and word choice as well as the **connotations** (meanings associated with the word) and **denotations** (dictionary definitions).

- **Focus on the Pattern** questions help you to see how the writer's ideas are arranged within the essay.

- **Focus on Critical Thinking** questions encourage you to make judgments about the writer's rhetorical choices. Sometimes these questions ask you to move beyond what is on the page to consider the essay's wider implications or how the writer's ideas intersect with your own life.

Two or three **Writing Practice** prompts also follow each essay.

As you read each of these essays, you should **preview**, **highlight**, and **annotate** it to help you understand what you are reading. (Previewing, highlighting, and annotating are explained and illustrated in Chapter 37.) Then, you should reread each essay more carefully in preparation for class discussion and writing.

ARGUMENT

38a   Exemplification

An **exemplification** essay uses specific examples to support a thesis statement. The two selections that follow, "The Case for Short Words" by Richard Lederer and "Around the World, Women Are on the Move" by Richard Rodriguez, are exemplification essays.

THE CASE FOR SHORT WORDS
Richard Lederer

Known for his love of words and wordplay, Richard Lederer began his career teaching English and media at St. Paul's School in New Hampshire. After twenty-seven years, he left teaching and went on to write over thirty popular books on language and trivia, beginning with the humorous *Anguished English* (1989). In "The Case for Short Words," Lederer uses examples ranging from famous literary works to high school students' essays to illustrate the power of short words.

When you speak and write, there is no law that says you have to use big words. Short words are as good as long ones, and short, old words—like *sun* and *grass* and *home*—are best of all. A lot of small words, more than you might think, can meet your needs with a strength, grace, and charm that large words do not have.   1

Big words can make the way dark for those who read what you write and hear what you say. Small words cast their clear light on big things—night and day, love and hate, war and peace, and life and death. Big words at times seem strange to the eye and the ear and the mind and the heart. Small words are the ones we seem to have known from the time we were born, like the hearth fire that warms the home.   2

Short words are bright like sparks that glow in the night, prompt like the dawn that greets the day, sharp like the blade of a knife, hot like salt tears that scald the cheek, quick like moths that flit from flame to flame, and terse like the dart and sting of a bee.   3

Here is a sound rule: Use small, old words where you can. If a long word says just what you want to say, do not fear to use it. But know that our tongue is rich in crisp, brisk, swift, short words. Make them the spine and the heart of what you speak and write. Short words are like fast friends. They will not let you down.   4

WORD POWER

wrought crafted

The title of this chapter and the four paragraphs that you have just 5 read are wrought entirely of words of one syllable. In setting myself this task, I did not feel especially cabined, cribbed, or confined. In fact, the structure helped me to focus on the power of the message I was trying to put across.

One study shows that twenty words account for twenty-five percent 6 of all spoken English words, and all twenty are monosyllabic. In order of frequency they are: *I, you, the, a, to, is, it, that, of, and, in, what, he, this, have, do, she, not, on,* and *they.* Other studies indicate that the fifty most common words in written English are each made of a single syllable.

For centuries our finest poets and orators have recognized and 7 employed the power of small words to make a straight point between two minds. A great many of our proverbs punch home their points with pithy monosyllables: "Where there's a will, there's a way," "A stitch in time saves nine," "Spare the rod and spoil the child," "A bird in the hand is worth two in the bush."

WORD POWER

pithy brief but meaningful

Nobody used the short word more skillfully than William Shakespeare, 8 whose dying King Lear laments:

> And my poor fool is hang'd! No, no, no life!
> Why should a dog, a horse, a rat have life,
> And thou no breath at all? . . .
> Do you see this? Look on her; look, her lips.
> Look there, look there!

Shakespeare's contemporaries made the King James Bible a center- 9 piece of short words—"And God said, Let there be light: and there was light. And God saw the light, that it was good." The descendants of such mighty lines live on in the twentieth century. When asked to explain his policy to Parliament, Winston Churchill responded with these ringing monosyllables: "I will say: It is to wage war, by sea, land, and air, with all our might and with all the strength that God can give us." In his "Death of the Hired Man" Robert Frost observes that "Home is the place where, when you have to go there, / They have to take you in." And William H. Johnson uses ten two-letter words to explain his secret of success: "If it is to be, / It is up to me."

WORD POWER

obligatory required

You don't have to be a great author, statesman, or philosopher to tap 10 the energy and eloquence of small words. Each winter I ask my ninth graders at St. Paul's School to write a composition composed entirely of one-syllable words. My students greet my request with obligatory moans and groans, but, when they return to class with their essays, most feel that, with the pressure to produce high-sounding polysyllables relieved, they have created some of their most powerful and luminous prose. Here are submissions from two of my ninth graders:

What can you say to a boy who has left home? You can say that he has done wrong, but he does not care. He has left home so that he will not have to deal with what you say. He wants to go as far as he can. He will do what he wants to do.

This boy does not want to be forced to go to church, to comb his hair, or to be on time. A good time for this boy does not lie in your reach, for what you have he does not want. He dreams of ripped jeans, shorts with no starch, and old socks.

So now this boy is on a bus to a place he dreams of, a place with no rules. This boy now walks a strange street, his long hair blown back by the wind. He wears no coat or tie, just jeans and an old shirt. He hates your world, and he has left it.

—Charles Shaffer

For a long time we cruised by the coast and at last came to a wide bay past the curve of a hill, at the end of which lay a small town. Our long boat ride at an end, we all stretched and stood up to watch as the boat nosed its way in.

The town climbed up the hill that rose from the shore, a space in front of it left bare for the port. Each house was a clean white with sky blue or grey trim; in front of each one was a small yard, edged by a white stone wall strewn with green vines.

As the town basked in the heat of noon, not a thing stirred in the streets or by the shore. The sun beat down on the sea, the land, and the back of our necks, so that, in spite of the breeze that made the vines sway, we all wished we could hide from the glare in a cool, white house. But, as there was no one to help dock the boat, we had to stand and wait.

At last the head of the crew leaped from the side and strode to a large house on the right. He shoved the door wide, poked his head through the gloom, and roared with a fierce voice. Five or six men came out, and soon the port was loud with the clank of chains and creak of planks as the men caught ropes thrown by the crew, pulled them taut, and tied them to posts. Then they set up a rough plank so we could cross from the deck to the shore. We all made for the large house while the crew watched, glad to be rid of us.

—Celia Wren

You, too, can tap into the vitality and vigor of compact expression. 11 Take a suggestion from the highway department. At the boundaries of your speech and prose place a sign that reads "Caution: Small Words at Work."

Focus on Meaning

1. What "case for short words" is Lederer making in this essay?

2. In paragraph 6, Lederer discusses two studies. What information is given in these studies? Do you think he needs this information to make his point?

Focus on Strategy

1. Do you think Lederer is writing for a general audience? For students? For teachers? How can you tell?

2. Evaluate Lederer's concluding paragraph. Is his use of "You, too" effective here? Is the closing quotation appropriate for his audience and purpose? Explain.

Focus on Language and Style

1. As Lederer points out in paragraph 5, his essay's title and first four paragraphs are composed entirely of one-syllable words. Why does he decide to write this way? Is this an effective stylistic choice?

2. In paragraph 7, Lederer says, "For centuries our finest poets have recognized and employed the power of small words to make a straight point between two minds." What does he mean by "a straight point between two minds"? How else could he have expressed this idea?

Focus on the Pattern

1. In addition to his many short examples, Lederer uses longer examples from the Bible, literature, and politics as well as passages from two student writers. How do these examples support his thesis?

2. In paragraphs 2–4, Lederer uses comparison and contrast to point out the differences between long and short words. What key difference does he identify?

Focus on Critical Thinking

1. Which of Lederer's many examples do you find most convincing? Why?

2. Choose a sentence from the essay that is *not* composed entirely of one-syllable words, and rewrite it using words of only one syllable. Is your sentence as clear and effective as Lederer's original? If not, does this undercut his essay's thesis?

3. Evaluate the "sound rule" Lederer presents in paragraph 4. Is it useful? Practical? Logical?

Writing Practice

1. In paragraph 10, Lederer reproduces two short student essays that use only one-syllable words. Write a short essay of your own composed entirely of one-syllable words. Use a series of examples to support your thesis.

2. Write an exemplification essay focusing on three or four stylistic choices you habitually make when you write. For example, do you prefer to begin or end your essays with a particular strategy? Do you like to use quotations or anecdotes for support? In your thesis, state the advantages (or disadvantages) of these writing choices.

AROUND THE WORLD, WOMEN ARE ON THE MOVE

Richard Rodriguez

Richard Rodriguez, a Mexican-American writer whose work explores the issues of class, race, and ethnicity, is best known for his autobiographical trilogy, which includes *Hunger of Memory* (1982), *Days of Obligation: An Argument with My Mexican Father* (1992), and *Brown: The Last Discovery of America* (2002). In 1997, Rodriguez won a Peabody Award, one of television's highest honors, for the essays on American life that he contributes regularly to PBS's *NewsHour*, where "Around the World, Women Are on the Move" first aired in 2009. As you read, consider how Rodriguez moves from examples of the gender revolution in America to examples from around the world.

1 In 1996, President Bill Clinton appointed Madeleine Albright as Secretary of State. Because of Madeleine Albright, because of Condoleezza Rice who came soon after, because of Hillary Clinton, we scarcely mark the gender revolution that has taken place in just over a decade. Today, the diplomatic face of America is a woman's face.

2 All over the world, women and girls are on the move. In Pakistani and Afghan villages, girls make their way to school, sometimes furtively, wary of boys or men who might splash them with acid for daring to learn to read and to write. In the last half-century, hundreds of thousands of Mexican women have left their villages to find jobs in America or to work in Mexican border town assembly plants. In Ciudad Juárez, hundreds of women who ventured into the world alone have been murdered. The world remains a dangerous place for women.

> **WORD POWER**
>
> **furtively** cautiously and secretly

3 Even so, at U.S. colleges, female students are signing up for study-abroad programs by a 2-to-1 ratio over males. Indeed, female students, many the daughters and granddaughters of women who did not assume college in their lives, now outnumber male students on American campuses.

4 In American legend, as in so many of the world's myths, it is the young man who leaves home to find gold or slay the dragon. Lewis and Clark are paradigmatic American explorers, blazing a trail from St. Louis to the Pacific Coast. But as it happened, they were led up the Missouri River and across the Rockies by a Shoshone Indian. Her name was Sacagawea.

> **WORD POWER**
>
> **paradigmatic** typical; serving as a model

5 In the Americas, there were other stories like hers, native women who became go-betweens, translators, even lovers of the foreign. In colonial Virginia, Pocahontas left her tribe to marry an Englishman, and she traveled with him to London to become a figure in history. In Mexico, male history still reviles Doña Marina, La Malinche, as a sexual traitor. She was an Indian woman who became the lover of the Spaniard Cortés. Marina conspired with Cortés against the Aztecs who had imprisoned her own tribe.

What are we to make of these stories of women moving among cultures and conflict? Today we have the story of Kansas-born Ann Dunham, an anthropologist, whose son is now president of the United States. In interviews, Barack Obama describes his mother as searching but also reckless. Her life was a series of journeys. In Hawaii, white Ann Dunham married a black Kenyan. When their marriage failed, he returned to Africa, which for him was the known world. She ventured outward to Muslim Indonesia. 6

In American homes when marriages fail, it is usually the husband who disappears. Women become the head of the family, responsible for instilling in sons as well as daughters the meaning of adulthood. Professional athletes, movie stars, convicts, presidents all testify to the importance of single mothers. At last summer's Olympics, the world saw Michael Phelps emerge from the pool after each event to search the crowd for his mother. 7

The news this evening is of failing male oligarchies on Wall Street. The news this evening is of tribal chieftains at war with modernity. The news is of religious leaders who forbid the ordination of women, even as they stumble from one diplomatic gaffe to another. 8

Throughout history, the world has been largely governed by men. When the male order falters and fails—as it seems now—we would make a mistake if we assumed the world was collapsing. All over the world, millions of women are valiantly venturing far from custom, little girls are walking across the desert to school. 9

WORD POWER

oligarchies organizations led by small groups of people

ordination the giving of ministerial or priestly authority

gaffe a noticeable mistake

Focus on Meaning

1. What failures does Rodriguez suggest men have been responsible for? What specific criticisms does he have of male world leaders, financiers, and religious leaders? Do you agree with these criticisms?

2. How does Rodriguez expect women to solve the problems men have created? Do you think he is right to expect this?

Focus on Strategy

1. At the end of paragraph 1, Rodriguez says, "Today, the diplomatic face of America is a woman's face." Is this sentence his essay's thesis? Explain.

2. In paragraph 6, Rodriguez notes that Barack Obama "describes his mother as searching but also reckless." What does he mean? How does this paragraph support Rodriguez's thesis?

Focus on Language and Style

1. What different meanings could the expression "on the move" have? Which meaning do you think Rodriguez has in mind?

2. What positive adjectives and adverbs does Rodriguez use to describe the women he discusses? Can you suggest places where he might have used additional descriptive words?

3. What words are repeated in the three sentences in paragraph 8? Why?

Focus on the Pattern

1. In paragraph 2, Rodriguez says that despite their advances, the "world remains a dangerous place for women." What examples does he give to support this statement? Can you give additional examples?

2. How are the examples that Rodriguez gives in paragraph 2, paragraph 3, and paragraphs 4–5 different? Why are these different kinds of examples grouped as they are?

Focus on Critical Thinking

1. Do you think Rodriguez was right to include the material about single mothers in paragraph 7? Does this paragraph support his thesis? Why or why not?

2. Do you agree with Rodriguez that the world is still a "dangerous place for women" (2)? Do you agree with him that women are "on the move"? Explain.

Writing Practice

1. Write an exemplification essay called "In My Family, Women Are on the Move." Support your thesis with specific examples of achievements by the women in your family. You may focus on one example in each body paragraph, or you can combine several related examples in some of your paragraphs.

2. In paragraph 3, Rodriguez presents some information about the progress made by college women. Write an exemplification essay in which you develop this idea further, illustrating the advances and achievements of female students at your school.

38b Narration

A **narrative** essay tells a story by presenting a series of events in chronological order. In the first of the two essays that follow, "The Sanctuary of School," Lynda Barry tells a story about home and family. In the second essay, "My Half-Baked Bubble," Joshuah Bearman recounts an experience from his elementary school days.

THE SANCTUARY OF SCHOOL

Lynda Barry

In her many illustrated works—including graphic novels, comic books, and a weekly cartoon strip, *Ernie Pook's Comeek*, which appears in a number of newspapers and magazines—Lynda Barry looks at the world through the eyes of children. Her characters remind adult readers of the complicated world of young people and of the clarity with which they see social situations. In "The Sanctuary of School," first published in the *Baltimore Sun* in 1992, Barry tells a story from her own childhood. As you read this essay, note how Barry relates her personal experience to a broader issue.

1   I was 7 years old the first time I snuck out of the house in the dark. It was winter and my parents had been fighting all night. They were short on money and long on relatives who kept "temporarily" moving into our house because they had nowhere else to go.

2   My brother and I were used to giving up our bedroom. We slept on the couch, something we actually liked because it put us that much closer to the light of our lives, our television.

3   At night when everyone was asleep, we lay on our pillows watching it with the sound off. We watched Steve Allen's mouth moving. We watched Johnny Carson's mouth moving.[1] We watched movies filled with gangsters shooting machine guns into packed rooms, dying soldiers hurling a last grenade and beautiful women crying at windows. Then the sign-off finally came and we tried to sleep.

4   The morning I snuck out, I woke up filled with a panic about needing to get to school. The sun wasn't quite up yet but my anxiety was so fierce that I just got dressed, walked quietly across the kitchen and let myself out the back door.

5   It was quiet outside. Stars were still out. Nothing moved and no one was in the street. It was as if someone had turned the sound off on the world.

6   I walked the alley, breaking thin ice over the puddles with my shoes. I didn't know why I was walking to school in the dark. I didn't think about it. All I knew was a feeling of panic, like the panic that strikes kids when they realize they are lost.

7   That feeling eased the moment I turned the corner and saw the dark outline of my school at the top of the hill. My school was made up of about 15 nondescript portable classrooms set down on a fenced concrete lot in a rundown Seattle neighborhood, but it had the most beautiful view of the Cascade Mountains. You could see them from

---

1. Steve Allen and Johnny Carson were late-night television hosts.

anywhere on the playfield and you could see them from the windows of my classroom—Room 2.

I walked over to the monkey bars and hooked my arms around the cold metal. I stood for a long time just looking across Rainier Valley. The sky was beginning to whiten and I could hear a few birds. 8

In a perfect world my absence at home would not have gone unnoticed. I would have had two parents in a panic to locate me, instead of two parents in a panic to locate an answer to the hard question of survival during a deep financial and emotional crisis. 9

But in an overcrowded and unhappy home, it's incredibly easy for any child to slip away. The high levels of frustration, depression and anger in my house made my brother and me invisible. We were children with the sound turned off. And for us, as for the steadily increasing number of neglected children in this country, the only place where we could count on being noticed was at school. 10

"Hey there, young lady. Did you forget to go home last night?" It was Mr. Gunderson, our janitor, whom we all loved. He was nice and he was funny and he was old with white hair, thick glasses and an unbelievable number of keys. I could hear them jingling as he walked across the playfield. I felt incredibly happy to see him. 11

He let me push his wheeled garbage can between the different portables as he unlocked each room. He let me turn on the lights and raise the window shades and I saw my school slowly come to life. I saw Mrs. Holman, our school secretary, walk into the office without her orange lipstick on yet. She waved. 12

I saw the fifth-grade teacher Mr. Cunningham, walking under the breezeway eating a hard roll. He waved. 13

And I saw my teacher, Mrs. Claire LeSane, walking toward us in a red coat and calling my name in a very happy and surprised way, and suddenly my throat got tight and my eyes stung and I ran toward her crying. It was something that surprised us both. 14

It's only thinking about it now, 28 years later, that I realize I was crying from relief. I was with my teacher, and in a while I was going to sit at my desk, with my crayons and pencils and books and classmates all around me, and for the next six hours I was going to enjoy a thoroughly secure, warm and stable world. It was a world I absolutely relied on. Without it, I don't know where I would have gone that morning. 15

Mrs. LeSane asked me what was wrong and when I said "Nothing," she seemingly left it at that. But she asked me if I would carry her purse for her, an honor above all honors, and she asked if I wanted to come into Room 2 early and paint. 16

She believed in the natural healing power of painting and drawing for troubled children. In the back of her room there was always a drawing table and an easel with plenty of supplies, and sometimes during the day she would come up to you for what seemed like no good reason and quietly ask if you wanted to go to the back table and "make some 17 pictures for Mrs. LeSane." We all had a chance at it—to sit apart from the class for a while to paint, draw and silently work out impossible problems on 11 × 17 sheets of newsprint.

Drawing came to mean everything to me. At the back table in 18 Room 2, I learned to build myself a life preserver that I could carry into my home.

We all know that a good education system saves lives, but the people 19 of this country are still told that cutting the budget for public schools is necessary, that poor salaries for teachers are all we can manage and that art, music and all creative activities must be the first to go when times are lean.

Before- and after-school programs are cut and we are told that pub- 20 lic schools are not made for baby-sitting children. If parents are neglectful temporarily or permanently, for whatever reason, it's certainly sad, but their unlucky children must fend for themselves. Or slip through the cracks. Or wander in a dark night alone.

We are told in a thousand ways that not only are public schools not 21 important, but that the children who attend them, the children who need them most, are not important either. We leave them to learn from the blind eye of a television, or to the mercy of "a thousand points of light"[2] that can be as far away as stars.

I was lucky. I had Mrs. LeSane. I had Mr. Gunderson. I had an abun- 22 dance of art supplies. And I had a particular brand of neglect in my home that allowed me to slip away and get to them. But what about the rest of the kids who weren't as lucky? What happened to them?

By the time the bell rang that morning I had finished my drawing 23 and Mrs. LeSane pinned it up on the special bulletin board she reserved for drawings from the back table. It was the same picture I always drew—a sun in the corner of a blue sky over a nice house with flowers all around it.

Mrs. LeSane asked us to please stand, face the flag, place our right 24 hands over our hearts and say the Pledge of Allegiance. Children across the country do it faithfully. I wonder now when the country will face its children and say a pledge right back.

Focus on Meaning

1. In paragraph 10, Barry characterizes herself and her brother as "children with the sound turned off." What do you think she means?

2. How are Barry's home and school worlds different? Identify specific negative features of her home life and specific positive features of her school life.

3. A number of adults came to Barry's rescue during her childhood. Who were these adults? What did each one contribute?

---

2. Phrase used by former president George Herbert Walker Bush to promote volunteerism.

WORD POWER

fend to manage

Focus on Strategy

1. What point is Barry making in paragraph 10? In paragraphs 20–21? In her conclusion? To whom does she seem to be addressing her comments? Explain.

2. What is the main idea of Barry's essay—the idea she wants to convince readers to accept? Is this idea actually stated in her essay? If so, where? If not, do you think it should be?

Focus on Language and Style

1. Look up the word *sanctuary* in several different dictionaries. Which of the definitions do you think comes closest to Barry's meaning? Why?

2. Now, look up the word *sanctuary* in a thesaurus. What synonyms are listed? Would any other word be a better choice in Barry's title? Explain.

Focus on the Pattern

1. Paragraphs 9–10 and 19–22 interrupt Barry's narrative. What purpose do these paragraphs serve? Do you think the essay would be more effective if paragraphs 9 and 10 came earlier? If paragraphs 19–22 came after paragraph 24? Explain.

2. What transitional words and phrases does Barry use in her narrative to move readers from one event to the next? Do you think her essay needs more transitions? If so, where should they be added?

Focus on Critical Thinking

1. Do you see Barry's narrative as primarily a story of her childhood or as a persuasive essay with a message about needed social change? Why? Specifically, what do you think she expected her essay to accomplish?

2. This essay was first published in the *Baltimore Sun*, a newspaper with a wide general audience. Which sections of the essay do you think would have the strongest impact on this audience? What different reactions would you expect readers to have? Why?

Writing Practice

1. Did you see elementary school as a "sanctuary" or as something quite different? Write a narrative essay that conveys to readers what school meant to you when you were a child.

2. In addition to school, television was a sanctuary for Barry and her brother. Did television watching (or some other activity) serve this function for you when you were younger? Is there some activity that fills this role now? In a narrative essay, write about your own "sanctuary."

MY HALF-BAKED BUBBLE

Joshuah Bearman

Joshuah Bearman is a writer and editor whose work has appeared in *LA Weekly*, *Rolling Stone*, *Harper's*, *Wired*, the *New York Times Magazine*, the *Believer*, and *McSweeney's*. He also contributes frequently to Chicago Public Radio's *This American Life*. In "My Half-Baked Bubble," an op-ed article that appeared in the *New York Times* in 2009, Bearman writes about a fondly remembered childhood experience. As you read, note that he begins and ends his article with quotations, and uses a humorous tone to engage readers in his story.

1 "Sardines are better than candy," my father said. "They're oily, but nutritious!" Easy for him to say. I was 8 and had just moved to a new, fancier school. The socioeconomic shift was most apparent to me in the cafeteria, where there was a wide disparity between my lunch and everyone else's. Ours was a Spartan household: no chocolate, cookies or extraneous sugar. For us, Rice Krispies cereal was supposed to be some kind of special indulgence.

2 My childhood happened to coincide with that historic moment in the early '80s when the full ingenuity of modern science was brought to bear on lunch snacks. Fruit roll-ups had just hit the scene. Capri Sun was like quicksilver-cocooned astronaut juice with a cool dagger straw. Chocolate pudding came in palm-sized cups!

3 My dad was a physicist, so I thought he should know the formula for turning our flavorless Rice Krispies into Rice Krispie treats. And yet he packed me the same lunch day after day: one peanut butter and jelly sandwich, one apple, one box of raisins. When I complained, he solved the problem (and taught me a lesson) by giving me sardines instead. As if that was an upgrade.

4 So I became the weird kid in the corner, opening a tin of sardines, like a hobo—when I managed not to lose the key, that is. "Stick with sardines," my dad said. "Cheap sweets are empty promises."

5 But they didn't seem so empty to me. Every day at lunchtime the cafeteria turned into an informal marketplace. My classmates laid out their wares on one of the big tables, displaying a panoply of forbidden processed delights. While I was busy trying to open my indestructible sardine can with a sharp rock, a brisk trading economy was under way.

6 "I am so bored with my Chunky," a luckier boy would say, considering the options before him. "Maybe I'll give Mr. E. L. Fudge a try!" And with a quick swap, the deal was done.

7 I must admit, it was a fairly efficient market. Everyone got what he wanted. Except for me. My sardines had zero value as trading currency. With no way into this economy, I had to watch from the sidelines.

WORD POWER

disparity lack of similarity or equality

Spartan simple, frugal; marked by avoidance of luxury

WORD POWER

panoply a wide-ranging and impressive array

Until one day, out of the depths of my isolation, I developed what 8
you might call a creative business prospectus.

I'm not sure how I came up with this idea, but what I told my class- 9
mates was this: my mom is an expert baker, and at the end of the year
she always bakes this incredible cake, the best cake ever, for me and my
best friends at school. It's coming, this wonderful cake. Can you picture
it in your mind? It will be a great day. But in the meantime, I said, I will
let you in on this special opportunity! If you give me, say, your Cheetos
now, you can stake a claim on this fantastic pending cake. Like a de-
posit. One Hostess cupcake equals one share.

Just like that, I became a market maker, peddling delicious cake 10
futures.

And people were buying! First came a round of vanguard investors. 11
Then others followed, figuring they had to get in on the ground floor
with this cake deal. From there it went wide. My table in the lunchroom
became the hot new trading floor. The bell would ring and my classmates would line up with their items, eager to buy in.

At the beginning, of course, I figured I could really persuade my 12
mom to bake such a cake, and so I'd dutifully record all the trading
"transactions" in my Trapper Keeper. Twinkie = one piece of cake.
Chunky = half-a-piece. Fruit roll-up = two pieces. Watermelon-flavored
Jolly Rancher?! I don't even want that. Zero pieces! I was setting the
terms! It was like a dream come true.

Soon enough, however, the market was spiraling out of control. 13
I started allowing customized cake shares. My Trapper Keeper ledger
kept growing, and getting more complicated. The records described a
wildly fantastic cake: hundreds of layers, rising to the heavens in all
different flavors—chocolate mousse on top of meringue on top of half
angel food and half red velvet. I was drunk with power, the creator of a
bizarre lunchroom derivatives bubble.

Had anyone thought about it, it would have been clear that my 14
mother, no matter how skilled a baker, could not fulfill my debts. But
no one thought about it. We were all in too deep. I had to let the ledger
keep growing.

The thing was, we all wanted to believe in this cake. For my investors, 15
it was pragmatic: people were already into this cake for, like, 14 bags of
Doritos, and they couldn't just walk away from the whole idea. So they kept
pouring more Doritos in and hoping for the best. Even I sort of believed in
it—and I could see the numbers. I too was deluded, imagining the hero's
welcome I would receive when my mom and I eventually wheeled this
amalgamated baked colossus into the schoolyard. I couldn't face the truth.

This was the mutually reinforcing psychology that allowed the cake 16
futures market to continue. Just like the Dutch tulip mania.[1] Or the

---

1. Seventeenth-century economic crash associated with sudden collapse (after wildly
   inflated prices) of the tulip-bulb market.

South Sea Bubble.[2] Or the American housing market. We were trafficking in dreams. Is there anything wrong with that?

The answer, as we all know, is yes—there is something wrong with 17 that. Like all bubbles, mine couldn't last forever. Eventually, someone was going to blow the whistle.

Spencer. Spencer was both good at math and jealous; he'd always 18 done well by the original cafeteria economy. Since everyone had been lured over to the fancy new derivatives guy, the old trading table had sat empty, and it was Spencer, Mr. Fundamentals, who did a back-of-the-napkin calculation to demonstrate how irrational our exuberance was. If you look at the numbers, he pointed out, my cake would defy the laws of physics.

At first no one wanted to believe him. If Spencer wants to be left 19 out of the glorious new cake era, everyone thought, then, hey, fine by us. But then Spencer won a few people over with his sober analysis. And then a few more. And just as quickly as confidence in the cake was built, it eroded. We crossed the crash threshold and, overnight, belief in the cake evaporated. My classmates knew that the ledger was a sham, and they were not getting their investments back. The Fritos, Nutter Butters, Hostess pies—they were all gone, good snacks after bad.

The bigger the bubble, the harder the fall. I was an outsider before, 20 but now I was a pariah. The old snack economy quietly rebuilt itself, and I was back to knocking my sardine can against the monkey bars out in the playground.

When my dad found out about my mischief, I got a lecture. It was 21 one big "I told you so," because, well, he had told me so. "Stick with the sardines," he'd said. "Cheap sweets are empty promises."

> **WORD POWER**
>
> **pariah** someone who is despised or rejected; an outcast

Focus on Meaning

1. How is Bearman's lunch different from his friends' lunches? Why is this difference so important to him?
2. Why did Bearman first decide to develop his "creative business prospectus" (paragraph 8)? Explain how his plan worked.
3. Why did Bearman's idea get out of hand?

Focus on Strategy

1. In paragraphs 4 and 21, Bearman quotes his father, who says, "Cheap sweets are empty promises." Do you think this sentence is the essay's thesis? If not, what thesis statement would you suggest? Is there any other sentence in the essay that might serve as a thesis statement?

---

2. Eighteenth-century economic disaster caused by stock speculation.

2. Bearman's essay begins and ends with quotations from his father. Why? Is this an appropriate strategy for this essay? Explain.

Focus on Language and Style

1. What does the expression *half-baked* mean? What two meanings does it have in the title of this essay?

2. Bearman compares his experiences in his school cafeteria to stock-market speculation, using words like "transactions" (12) and "derivatives" (13). List other words and phrases used here that suggest financial activity. What are the advantages and disadvantages of using this kind of vocabulary here?

Focus on the Pattern

1. Although this essay is a narrative, Bearman also uses other patterns to develop his ideas. Where does he use description? Where does he use exemplification?

2. In paragraph 8, with the phrase "Until one day, . . ." Bearman begins his story. What transitional words and phrases does he use to move readers from one event to the next? List as many as you can.

Focus on Critical Thinking

1. Unlike the childhood experiences described by Lynda Barry (p. 714), Bearman's memories of his childhood are very positive. How are his impressions of school—and of his family different from Barry's? For example, is school a sanctuary for him? Who is more important to him, his teachers or his parents?

2. What responsibility, if any, do you think schools have to ensure that children are happy and well adjusted (in addition to educated)? Did the schools you attended when you were a child serve your emotional as well as your intellectual needs?

Writing Practice

1. In paragraph 4, Bearman describes himself as "the weird kid in the corner." Write a narrative essay about a time in your childhood when you were an outsider. What did you do to try to fit in?

2. Retell Bearman's narrative as a fairy tale directed at elementary school children. Begin with "Once upon a time, . . ." use third-person (*Joshuah, he, the boy*), and use the sentence "Cheap sweets are empty promises" as the tale's moral.

38c Description

A **descriptive** essay tells what something looks, sounds, smells, tastes, or feels like. It uses details to give readers a clear, vivid picture of a person, place, or object. In "Fish Cheeks," Amy Tan describes a family meal. In "A Fable for Tomorrow," Rachel Carson describes an environmental disaster.

FISH CHEEKS

Amy Tan

Born in California shortly after her parents immigrated there from China, Amy Tan started writing at an early age. Author of the best-selling novel *The Joy Luck Club* (1989) and the more recent *Saving Fish from Drowning* (2006) and *The Hundred Secret Senses* (2010), Tan is known for exploring Chinese-American mother-daughter relationships. In "Fish Cheeks," originally published in 1987 in *Seventeen* magazine, Tan describes her family's Christmas dinner and the lessons she learns about sharing and appreciating her Chinese heritage. As you read, note how her descriptions reflect her mixed feelings about the dinner.

1   I fell in love with the minister's son the winter I turned fourteen. He was not Chinese, but as white as Mary in the manger. For Christmas I prayed for this blond-haired boy, Robert, and a slim new American nose.

2   When I found out that my parents had invited the minister's family over for Christmas Eve dinner, I cried. What would Robert think of our shabby *Chinese* Christmas? What would he think of our noisy *Chinese* relatives who lacked proper American manners? What terrible disappointment would he feel upon seeing not a roasted turkey and sweet potatoes but *Chinese* food?

3   On Christmas Eve I saw that my mother had outdone herself in creating a strange menu. She was pulling black veins out of the backs of fleshy prawns. The kitchen was littered with appalling mounds of raw food: a slimy rock cod with bulging fish eyes that pleaded not to be thrown into a pan of hot oil. Tofu, which looked like stacked wedges of rubbery white sponges. A bowl soaking dried fungus back to life. A plate of squid, their backs crisscrossed with knife markings so they resembled bicycle tires.

4   And then they arrived—the minister's family and all my relatives in a clamor of doorbells and rumpled Christmas packages. Robert grunted hello, and I pretended he was not worthy of existence.

5   Dinner threw me deeper into despair. My relatives licked the ends of their chopsticks and reached across the table, dipping them into the dozen

or so plates of food. Robert and his family waited patiently for platters to be passed to them. My relatives murmured with pleasure when my mother brought out the whole steamed fish. Robert grimaced. Then my father poked his chopsticks just below the fish eye and plucked out the soft meat. "Amy, your favorite," he said, offering me the tender fish cheek. I wanted to disappear.

At the end of the meal my father leaned back and belched loudly, 6 thanking my mother for her fine cooking. "It's a polite Chinese custom to show you are satisfied," explained my father to our astonished guests. The minister managed to muster up a quiet burp. I was stunned into silence the rest of the night.

After everyone had gone, my mother said to me, "You want to be 7 the same as American girls on the outside." She handed me an early gift. It was a miniskirt in beige tweed. "But inside you must always be Chinese. You must be proud you are different. Your only shame is to have shame."

And even though I didn't agree with her then, I knew that she 8 understood how much I had suffered during the evening's dinner. It wasn't until many years later—long after I had gotten over my crush on Robert—that I was able to fully appreciate her lesson and the true purpose behind our particular menu. For Christmas Eve that year, she had chosen all my favorite meals.

Focus on Meaning

1. How did Tan feel at the time about the meal her mother prepares for Christmas Eve? How did her feelings change later in life?

2. How is the Tan family's Christmas Eve dinner different from the traditional American Christmas Eve dinner the minister's family was expecting?

Focus on Strategy

1. Tan is of Chinese heritage. Do you think she is writing here for an audience of Chinese, Chinese Americans, or Americans of various ethnic backgrounds? What makes you think so?

2. Does this essay have a thesis statement? If so, where? If not, suggest a possible thesis statement. Where would you place this new sentence?

Focus on Language and Style

1. Look carefully at each use of the word *Chinese* in this essay. What does the word suggest in each case? Does it suggest something positive, negative, or neutral?

2. Locate all the adjectives in this essay that convey a negative impression—for example, *shabby* and *terrible* in paragraph 2. Then, explain what you think these negative words contribute to the essay.

Focus on the Pattern

1. In paragraph 2, Tan asks, "What would Robert think of our shabby *Chinese* Christmas?" How does this question help to establish the dominant impression Tan wants to convey to readers?

2. In paragraph 3, Tan describes the food that was served; in paragraphs 5 and 6, she describes the people. How do the descriptive details she chooses support her essay's dominant impression?

3. Is this essay primarily a subjective or an objective description? Explain.

Focus on Critical Thinking

1. Tan is very nervous about the encounter between her family and Robert's. What do you think she is really afraid of?

2. What does Tan's mother mean by "Your only shame is to have shame" (paragraph 7)?

Writing Practice

1. Describe a family meal of your own—either a typical breakfast, lunch, or dinner or a "company" or holiday meal.

2. Describe the Tan family's meal from Robert's point of view. What does he see? How do the scene and the food look to him?

A FABLE FOR TOMORROW

Rachel Carson

Rachel Carson (1907–1964) is often credited with starting the modern-day environmental movement. Her book *Silent Spring* (1962) exposed the devastating effects of pesticides on the environment. In the excerpt that follows, part of the introduction to that book, Carson uses specific details to create a powerful picture of the place she describes. As you read, consider how today's readers might react to this essay.

There was once a town in the heart of America where all life seemed to live 1
in harmony with its surroundings. The town lay in the midst of a check-erboard of prosperous farms, with fields of grain and hillsides of orchards where, in spring, white clouds of bloom drifted above the green fields. In autumn, oak and maple and birch set up a blaze of color that flamed and flickered across a backdrop of pines. Then foxes barked in the hills and deer silently crossed the fields, half hidden in the mists of the fall mornings.

Along the roads, laurel, viburnum and alder, great ferns and wild- 2
flowers delighted the traveler's eye through much of the year. Even in winter the roadsides were places of beauty, where countless birds came to feed on the berries and on the seed heads of the dried weeds rising

WORD POWER

viburnum a type of shrub with large, bright flower clusters

above the snow. The countryside was, in fact, famous for the abundance and variety of its bird life, and when the flood of migrants was pouring through in spring and fall people traveled from great distances to observe them. Others came to fish the streams, which flowed clear and cold out of the hills and contained shady pools where trout lay. So it had been from the days many years ago when the first settlers raised their houses, sank their wells, and built their barns.

Then a strange blight crept over the area and everything began to 3 change. Some evil spell had settled on the community: mysterious maladies swept the flocks of chickens; the cattle and sheep sickened and died. Everywhere was a shadow of death. The farmers spoke of much illness among their families. In the town the doctors had become more and more puzzled by new kinds of sickness appearing among their patients. There had been several sudden and unexplained deaths, not only among adults but even among children, who would be stricken suddenly while at play and die within a few hours.

There was a strange stillness. The birds, for example—where had 4 they gone? Many people spoke of them, puzzled and disturbed. The feeding stations in the backyards were deserted. The few birds seen anywhere were moribund; they trembled violently and could not fly. It was a spring without voices. On the mornings that had once throbbed with the dawn chorus of robins, catbirds, doves, jays, wrens, and scores of other bird voices there was now no sound; only silence lay over the fields and woods and marsh.

On the farms the hens brooded, but no chicks hatched. The farmers 5 complained that they were unable to raise any pigs—the litters were small and the young survived only a few days. The apple trees were coming into bloom but no bees droned among the blossoms, so there was no pollination and there would be no fruit.

The roadsides, once so attractive, were now lined with browned and 6 withered vegetation as though swept by fire. These, too, were silent, deserted by all living things. Even the streams were now lifeless. Anglers no longer visited them, for all the fish had died.

In the gutters under the eaves and between the shingles of the roofs, 7 a white granular powder still showed a few patches; some weeks before it had fallen like snow upon the roofs and the lawns, the fields and streams.

No witchcraft, no enemy action had silenced the rebirth of new life 8 in this stricken world. The people had done it themselves.

This town does not actually exist, but it might easily have a thou- 9 sand counterparts in America or elsewhere in the world. I know of no community that has experienced all the misfortunes I describe. Yet every one of these disasters has actually happened somewhere, and many real communities have already suffered a substantial number of them. A grim specter has crept upon us almost unnoticed, and this imagined tragedy may easily become a stark reality we all shall know. . . .

WORD POWER
moribund dying

Focus on Meaning

1. What is a fable? In what sense was this essay—written for the introduction to Carson's 1962 book *Silent Spring*, which exposed the dangerous effects of pesticides on the environment—a "fable for tomorrow"?

2. What is the "strange blight" (paragraph 3) that comes to the town? What signs are there that the town has changed? How do the townspeople react to the changes?

3. What does Carson mean when she says, "The people had done it themselves" (8)?

4. What "stark reality" (9) is Carson warning against in this essay?

Focus on Strategy

1. Why do you suppose Carson opened *Silent Spring* with this story? How do you think she expected readers to react? Do you think today's readers would be likely to react differently from those reading in 1962? If so, how? If not, why not?

2. Do you think Carson expected her story to enlighten readers? To entertain them? To frighten them? To persuade them? Explain.

3. In paragraph 9, Carson admits that the town she has been describing does not exist. Do you think this admission weakens her essay? Why or why not?

Focus on Language and Style

1. This essay is called "A Fable for Tomorrow," but, except for the last paragraph, it is written in past tense. Why do you think Carson uses past tense?

2. Throughout this essay, Carson uses strong language, such as "evil spell" (3) and "grim specter" (9), to get her point across. Identify other examples of such language. Do you think these expressions are effective, or do you think Carson goes too far?

Focus on the Pattern

1. Where does Carson describe the town in positive terms, and what positive features does she identify? Where does she describe the town in negative terms, and what negative features does she identify?

2. How does Carson indicate to readers that she is moving from positive to negative description?

3. Is this a subjective or an objective description? How can you tell?

Focus on Critical Thinking

1. Where is the town "in the heart of America" (1) actually located? Why do you think the author doesn't give more identifying information about this town?

2. Do you think Carson's predictions have come true?

3. Is there a situation affecting our environment that you see as just as alarming as the one Carson writes about? In what sense do you see this situation as a threat?

Writing Practice

1. Write your own "fable for tomorrow" describing the likely effects on our environment of the unchecked piling up of nonbiodegradable trash in our landfills. In the thesis statement of your descriptive essay, encourage readers to recycle to avoid the outcome you describe.

2. Many people see climate change as a destructive environmental problem of epic proportions—as an even greater problem than the pesticides whose use Carson warned against. Write a "fable for tomorrow" in which you describe an extreme scenario that could possibly result from increased global warming.

38d Process

A **process** essay explains the steps in a procedure, telling how something is (or was) done. In "How to Mummify a Pharaoh," Adam Goodheart presents a set of instructions for mummifying a body. In "My Grandmother's Dumpling," Amy Ma explains the stages in the process of making dumplings with her family.

HOW TO MUMMIFY A PHARAOH

Adam Goodheart

Adam Goodheart is a writer, editor, and historian. One of the founders of *Civilization* magazine, where this piece originally appeared, he has published widely on subjects including travel, anthropology, science, and history. His book *1861: The Civil War Awakening* (2011) was a *New York Times* best-seller. In this essay, Goodheart explains the steps required for making a mummy. As you read, try to picture the process Goodheart describes.

Old pharaohs never died—they just took long vacations. Ancient Egyptians believed that at death a person's spirit, or *ka*, was forcibly

WORD POWER

pharaoh ancient Egyptian ruler

separated from the body. But it returned now and then for a visit, to snack on the food that had been left in the tomb. It was crucial that the body stay as lifelike as possible for eternity—that way, the *ka* (whose life was hard enough already) would avoid reanimating the wrong corpse. These days, dead pharaohs are admittedly a bit hard to come by. If you decide to practice mummification on a friend or relative, please make sure that the loved one in question is fully deceased before you begin.

1. Evisceration Made Easy. The early stages of the process can be 2 a bit malodorous, so it's recommended that you follow the ancient custom of relocating to a well-ventilated tent. (You'll have trouble breathing anyway, since tradition also prescribes that you wear a jackal-head mask in honor of Anubis, god of the dead.) After cleansing the body, break the nose by pushing a long iron hook up the nostrils. Then use the hook to remove the contents of the skull. You can discard the brain (the ancient Egyptians attributed no special significance to it).

Next, take a flint knife and make a long incision down the left side 3 of the abdomen. Actually, it's best to have a friend do this, since the person who cuts open the body must be pelted with stones to atone for the profanation. After you've stoned your friend, use a bronze knife to remove the internal organs through the incision. Wash them in palm wine as a disinfectant and set them aside to inter later in separate alabaster jars. Leave the heart in place (Egyptians believed it was the seat of consciousness).

2. Salting and Stuffing. Once the abdominal cavity is empty, fill 4 it with natron, a natural salt found at the Wadi Natrun in the western Nile delta. Heap more natron on top of the body until it is completely covered. According to a papyrus in the Louvre, it should then be left for 42 days, after which it will be almost totally desiccated. Having removed the natron, anoint the head with frankincense and the body with sacred oil. Pack the skull and abdomen with myrrh and other spices, and cover the incision with a sheet of gold.

For an extra-lifelike effect, you can stuff the corpse's skin with a 5 compound of sawdust, butter, and mud. Don't overdo it, though. Queen Henettowey, wife of Pinedjem I, was so overstuffed that when archaeologists found her, her face had split open like an old sofa.

3. Wrapping Up. If you thought mummies wrapped in bedsheets 6 were the stuff of B movies, think again: Even pharaohs were usually wound in strips cut from household linens. Pour molten pine resin over the body; in the course of centuries this will turn the flesh black, glassy, and rock-hard. While the resin's still tacky, bandage each of the extremities separately, including fingers and toes. Then brush on another coat and repeat. (Go easy on the resin—Tutankhamen stuck to his coffin and had to be chipped out piece by piece.) Amulets can be placed between the layers of bandages; a scarab over the heart is the minimum. The last layers should secure the arms and legs to the body. Your mummy is now ready to be entombed in grand style.

WORD POWER

evisceration removal of organs

WORD POWER

profanation disrespectful act

WORD POWER

papyrus an ancient paper or document made from a tall, grasslike plant

desiccated dry

WORD POWER

amulet a charm worn around the neck to ward off evil

scarab a decorative item in the shape of the scarab beetle

A note on sarcophagi: Careful labeling will prevent embarrassing   7
mix-ups later on. A mummy long thought to be Princess Mutemhet of
the 21st dynasty was recently x-rayed and found to be a pet baboon.

Focus on Meaning

1. Why did the ancient Egyptians practice mummification?
2. What equipment is needed for the process Goodheart describes?

Focus on Strategy

1. Goodheart knows that his readers will never be called upon to mummify their friends or relatives. Why, then, does he use commands
   and "you," telling readers how to perform this process?
2. What do you think is this essay's primary purpose? Is the essay
   meant to be a serious treatment of the subject it discusses? How
   can you tell?
3. This essay does not include a thesis statement. Write one that would
   be suitable. Where should this new sentence be located?
4. Do you think the essay's last paragraph is necessary, or should the
   essay have ended with the last sentence of paragraph 6? Explain.

Focus on Language and Style

1. Goodheart's style and tone are light and irreverent. For example, he
   observes, "These days, dead pharaohs are admittedly a bit hard to
   come by" (paragraph 1), and he notes that, when overstuffed, Queen
   Henettowey's face "split open like an old sofa" (5). Identify some
   other examples of this kind of language.
2. Do you think Goodheart's style and tone are appropriate for his subject? Why or why not?

Focus on the Pattern

1. Goodheart numbers and names three key stages of the process. Do
   you think the names he chooses are appropriate? If not, what names
   would you use instead?
2. List the individual steps in the process. Are they all presented in
   chronological order?
3. What transitional words and phrases does Goodheart use to link the
   steps in the process? Does he need any additional transitions?

Focus on Critical Thinking

1. Many of the details in this essay are extremely graphic. Why do you
   think Goodheart chose to include such harsh—even disgusting—

details? Do you think these details add to the essay's appeal, or do you think they do just the opposite?

2. What factual information did you learn from this essay? Do you think you would have learned more if the information on mummification had been presented in a more serious, straightforward way? Explain.

Writing Practice

1. Write a straightforward description of the process of mummifying a body for an audience of middle school students. Your purpose is to educate these readers about the process, making it sound as interesting as possible.

2. Think of a process you practice yourself—for example, creating a perfect party playlist or using computer software to edit your photos. Write a set of instructions for this process.

MY GRANDMOTHER'S DUMPLING

Amy Ma

Amy Ma is a writer who trained as a pastry chef in New York City and now lives in Hong Kong. This article, which first appeared in the *Wall Street Journal*, provides both information about how to make dumplings and the story of several generations of Ma's family. As you read, think about how cooking and family intersect in your own life.

There was no denying a dumpling error. If the meat tumbled out of a poorly made one as it cooked, Grandmother could always tell who made it because she had personally assigned each of us a specific folding style at the onset of our dumpling-making education. In our house, a woman's folding style identified her as surely as her fingerprints.   1

"From now on, you and only you will fold it in this way," she instructed me in our Taipei kitchen in 1994, the year I turned 13. That is when I had reached a skill level worthy of joining the rest of the women—10 in all, from my 80-year-old grandmother, Lu Xiao-fang, to my two middle-aged aunts, my mother and the six children of my generation—in the folding of *jiao zi*, or dumplings, for Chinese New Year. Before then I had been relegated to prep work: mixing the meat filling or cutting the dough and flattening it.   2

Cousin Mao Mao, the eldest daughter of my grandmother's first son, had been away for four years at college in the U.S. But with casual ease, she fashioned her dumplings in the style of the rat, tucking in the creases and leaving a small tail that pinched together at one end. Two distinct pleats in a fan-shaped dumpling marked the work of Aunt Yee, Mao Mao's mother, who had just become a grandmother herself with the birth   3

WORD POWER

relegated assigned [to a lower position]

of a grandson. A smaller purse-like dumpling with eight folds toward the center was my mother's. Grandmother's dumplings were the simplest of the bunch—flat, crescent-shaped with no creases and a smooth edge. And as I was the youngest in my generation, she'd thought it appropriate to make my signature design a quirky variation of her own, with an added crimping to create a rippling *hua bian*, or flower edge.

"A pretty little edge, for a pretty little girl," she said.

While dumplings graced our tables year-round, they were a requisite dish during the Lunar New Year holidays. The Spring Festival, as it is known in China—*chun jie*—is arguably the most important celebration of the year: It is a time to be with family, to visit friends and start life anew—and eat dumplings.

The length of observance varies. Today in Taiwan, the national holiday stretches to nine days—including two weekends—with all businesses and government offices closed. In mainland China, officials rearrange the working calendar to give the public seven consecutive days off, while in Hong Kong there are three public holidays and in Singapore, two. Unofficially, many Chinese people consider the traditional period of the first 15 days appropriate to welcome the new year.

My family celebrated the first three days of the Spring Festival in a traditional way: Everyone came "home," which meant to my grandfather's house. We were already home—my father, mother, brother and I lived in Taipei with my father's parents, who had moved from China in the late 1940s. Most of my father's family lived nearby. On *chu yi*, the first day of the new year, friends came to our house to extend greetings. For *chu er*, the second day, married women returned to their parents' house. The third day, *chu san*, was always celebrated united, as a family. And on each of those days, dumplings were the main food served during lunch and dinner. There might be other side dishes—leftovers from New Year's Eve—but no other food was prepared from scratch during the holiday. It was considered bad luck to do any work during this time; to ensure a peaceful year ahead, you had to rest and that meant no cooking.

Though it isn't known exactly when dumplings came into being, author and Chinese food expert Fuchsia Dunlop says *jiao zi* date as far back as 1,100 years ago. "In the city of Turpan, a tomb was uncovered that had boiled dumplings from the Tang dynasty (618–907) preserved in much the same shape with similar fillings as they are today," says Ms. Dunlop.

Many people believe the practice of eating these dumplings on Chinese New Year became popular in the Yuan and Ming dynasties, which stretched from 1271 to 1644, when *yuan bao*—gold and silver ingots—began to take hold as currency in China; the dumplings take the shape of those coins. During new year celebrations, filling your stomach with edible replicas of ingots was thought to ensure a year of prosperity ahead. The packaged bites also celebrated a letting go of the past, since the word *"jiao"* also means "the end of something."

WORD POWER

4
5 **requisite** necessary

6

7

8

9

WORD POWER

ingots solid metal bars

Traditions have relaxed: Not every family eats only dumplings for 10 three days. They also vary regionally: In the south of China, *nian gao,* or rice cakes, are often served instead of these dough-swaddled morsels at Chinese New Year. Still, hefty portions of dumplings undoubtedly remain a big attraction this time of year in many Chinese households.

Even now, that initial bite of any dumpling transports me back to 11 our Taipei kitchen: the women packed like sardines working on their craft with a Zen-like rhythm, the flour-dusted countertops, the air redolent with the scent of dough, and the faded brown ceramic tiles on the floor polished smooth by countless footsteps over the years.

WORD POWER

redolent fragrant

The great dumpling cook-off commenced each year following 12 Lunar New Year's Eve dinner, a family meal of Grandmother's best dishes—sweet soy-braised pork, *ru yi cai* (10 vegetables tossed together with a soy-sauce vinaigrette), and always steamed fish since its term in Mandarin, *"yu,"* is a homonym for "plenty." By 9 p.m., the plates were cleared and washed, and the women were clustered in the kitchen.

The men, forbidden to enter the cooking area, dispersed to their 13 separate corners to talk politics and play dice or mahjong while awaiting the countdown to midnight. Every room of the house swelled with festivity as the whole family of more than 30 members—four generations —gathered for this night in my grandparents' house.

Amid the bustle, the kitchen alone had an air of serenity and purpose as the women worked through the night. Before dawn of the next 14 morning, there would be enough dumplings to cover two large dining room tables and every kitchen countertop.

To start, Grandmother unloaded from the refrigerator the large ball 15 of dough made from flour, cold water and a dash of egg white (her secret ingredient) that she had prepared the day before. Setting it onto the butcher block with her plump and sturdy hands, she ripped off two large balls and rolled each into a log, starting her gentle kneading from the center and stretching out to both sides. The remaining dough she kept covered under a damp towel.

Meanwhile, the rest of the women—my mother and two aunts and 16 my cousins and me—picked over bunches of coriander and peeled off the wilted layers of scallions and cabbages. A liberal douse of salt sprinkled over the cabbage drew out the excess water, and the chopped confetti-like bits were hand-squeezed to prevent a watery dumpling filling. The butcher knife rocked repeatedly back and forth on the ginger and garlic until it was almost a paste. Likewise, the vegetables had to be diced as finely as possible so they would be evenly spread through every bite of the final product.

Ignoring the slew of innovative options for fillings popular in con- 17 temporary restaurants—shrimp and chives, shark's fin and vermicelli —we filled our no-frills dumplings with minced pork. Into the pink ground meat went the chopped speckles of vegetables and herbs along with sesame oil, Shaoxin wine, salt, soy sauce, a pinch of sugar, white pepper, five-spice powder and an egg. Nothing was measured, yet it always tasted the same.

18   "That's enough mixing," Grandmother cautioned. My mother was using a pair of wooden chopsticks to combine the ingredients in large circular motions. Grandmother insisted on only combing through the filling in one direction—clockwise—so as to not over-mix, which would make it tough.

19   Then like a carefully orchestrated master plan, a natural assembly line formed. First, Grandmother cut off equal-size segments of her log of dough and then passed them to my mother, who used a wooden roller to flatten them into circles, a process called *gan mien*. Two aunts continued to fashion new dough into logs on one end of the kitchen counter, and three cousins lined up on the other end to begin filling and folding dumplings. The positions would alternate periodically, and makers would move up the line over the years as their skills improved. At 5 years old, my job had been the menial task of pressing the just-cut dough segments into flat disks so they would be easier to roll out, but I had since graduated to a dumpling folder. All together, we women stood, each ready to play her part in this culinary theater.

20   "Every step requires its own *kung fu*," Grandmother instructed in Mandarin. She was short, but her chubby silhouette held the solid stance of a symphony conductor. The process was tedious, but a mere mention of serving a frozen dumpling from a supermarket would be confronted with a gaze that screamed: uncultured, unbelievable, un-*Chinese*. The matriarch in her kitchen was doing more than just cooking; she was training the next generation of wives, daughters and mothers as her mother-in-law had taught her.

21   "Use your palm to control the roller, not your fingertips," she barked. "Keep a steady rhythm, consistent like your pulse." The dumpling skins weren't flattened in one fell swoop like a pie crust. Each one had to be rolled just around the rim and rotated so that the resulting circle was thinner on the edges than in the center. When folded in half the two sides met; the dumpling skin was uniform in thickness. It was a painstaking task when repeated over the span of many hours, and my mother once showed me her swollen palms after a night of *gan mien*.

22   The amount of meat filling had to be just right. Not too much—"too greedy!"—and not too little: "too stingy!"

23   And dumplings had to be folded with both hands. "It's a superstition," Grandmother told us. "Women who fold dumplings with one hand won't have children. Your right and left hand have to work together to be a good mother." Grandmother demonstrated how she used the fleshy part of the index finger and thumb to press together the dough. Fresh dough, unlike frozen dough, didn't need water to seal the seams. Only a firm pinch.

24   "Beautifully folded," Grandmother commented on the dumpling of the newest granddaughter-in-law, Mei Fang. "But it took you too long to make. What good is a wife who makes lovely dumplings if there's not enough to feed everyone?" Grandmother asked.

WORD POWER

acrid sharp

crucible severe test

The women smirked at the acrid words—she had been equally harsh 25 to all of them when they first joined the family. Grandmother had taken her lumps, too: After she married grandfather, her mother-in-law had harassed her on the ways of making a proper dumpling. Now, Grandmother reigned over her kitchen; it was a classroom and crucible we all endured.

"It's better that I am more strict on you girls now," she sighed. "Lest 26 you get criticized by someone else even worse than me." My mother looked over her shoulder to check on me, her only daughter, and smiled when I gave her an assuring nod.

When no one was looking, Grandmother washed a small coin and 27 hid it in one of the dumplings to be discovered by a lucky winner, who was said to be blessed with extra good fortune for the new year. Despite my best efforts, I never chanced upon it.

Working until the early hours of the next morning in the kitchen 28 brought out the juicier stories, ones laced with family secrets, scandals, gossips and tall tales, all soaked up by my youthful ears.

"Did you hear? Second uncle's daughter got a tattoo." 29

"So-and-so's sister is really her daughter." 30

By the time the echoes of popping firecrackers filled the streets signaling 31 the stroke of midnight, hundreds of dumplings, ready for boiling, were lined up on the kitchen sheet pans like tiny soldiers pending a final command.

With only the boiling of the dumplings left to do, the women then 32 took turns cleaning up and bathing, all the while trailing after their children and lulling them to bed. But the majority of the family didn't sleep. The custom of *shou sui*, or staying up all night to symbolize having unlimited energy for the upcoming year, was usually followed.

Around 5 a.m., the tables were set in preparation for the midmorn- 33 ing dumpling brunch. But there was no counting of bowls or chopsticks. "You're not allowed to count anything during the first day of the year," reminded Grandmother. "If you don't count anything today, then the amount of possessions you have will be countless for next year." So we grabbed chopsticks by the handfuls—some wooden, some metal, all mixed in a pile—and laid them on the table alongside stacks of blue and white porcelain bowls and plates.

Before long, the first doorbell rang, and along with it came the bois- 34 terous greetings from guests, friends and neighbors. The words *gong xi fa cai* ("congratulations and be prosperous") were audible even from inside the kitchen, and they drew out the younger girls, who were eager for their *hong bao*, or red packets. These waxy packets stuffed with money were given by elders to children as a gift, and the youngest in the house could often rack up what seemed to them a small fortune. Their flour-covered fingerprints dotted the envelopes as they calculated the year's gains.

At 9 a.m. or when the guest count reached 10—enough to fill a 35 table—we slid the dumplings into the stainless steel pot, careful not to let the boiling water splatter onto our bare toes, peeking out from house slippers. Grandmother insisted on never stirring the pot, and to ensure the dumplings wouldn't stick together, she slid a spatula through the bubbling broth just once in a pushing motion. Thrice the water came to a boil and each time we added more water. By the fourth time, the dumplings bobbed merrily on the surface. They were done.

Grandmother fished out the broken dumplings before turning to 36 Cousin Jia Yin, often the culprit, in half jest. "Ah . . . thanks to you, the dumpling soup will be especially tasty this year since you've flavored it with all the filling that busted out." The casualties were fished out and quickly disposed of; broken dumplings are considered bad luck if served. To save Jia Yin's face, her father, grandmother's second son, often said at the table, "Dumplings are great, but my favorite is still the dumpling soup," ladling up another bowl.

Guests and grandparents ate first and the two large tables in the din- 37 ing room were seated by gender. My grandfather took the head seat at one table with his friends, and my grandmother with hers at the other. After they ate, the tables were reset and the second generation took its turn, with my father and uncles at one table, my mother and aunts at the other. The third and fourth generations had less strict table assignments and took whatever empty chairs opened up—it could be two or three hours before it was our turn to eat.

Steaming plates were heaped high with dumplings still glistening 38 from their hot-water bath. Diners readied themselves with their own taste-tinkering rituals in concocting the perfect dipping sauce—a combination of soy sauce, vinegar, minced garlic and sometimes sesame oil or chili paste. Grandmother's special *la ba* vinegar, marinated with whole garlic cloves, was the most coveted condiment.

Before the first bite, everyone gathered around Grandfather, who 39 made a toast—usually with tea though sometimes he would sneak in some Chinese wine—to ring in the new year. Then, he took the first pick of the dumplings—something of an honor among the women, who held their breath in hopes that his choice of the perfect dumpling would be their own. It would have to have the ideal skin-to-filling ratio, every bite an equal portion of meat and dough, and expert craftsmanship—a balanced and symmetrical shape with firmly sealed seams.

"This one looks good to me," my grandfather decided, gently lifting the 40 plump parcel with the tips of his chopsticks. It was Grandmother's dumpling, and she stood poker-faced next to him, not revealing her triumph.

She remembered a time when her dumplings were the only ones on 41 the platter. As her family grew, so too did the styles of dumplings until the plate resembled an eclectic family tree, and each doughy pouch carried within it the cross-generational memoirs of its maker. The dumpling ritual slowly faded after Grandmother's passing in 1999; Grandfather died soon after and the family scattered. But every Chinese New Year, I still make dumplings in Grandmother's way, repeating her lessons in my head.

"Eat more! Eat more! There's magic in these dumplings," Grand- 42 mother would say. And she meant it truly.

Focus on Meaning

1. What different kinds of dumpling "folding style" do the various women have? Why are these differences important?

2. What significance do dumplings have in Chinese culture? What significance do dumplings (and the dumpling-making process) have to Ma?

3. In paragraph 20, Ma says that her grandmother is "training the next generation of wives, daughters and mothers as her mother-in-law had taught her." What, besides dumpling making, does this "training" involve?

4. Reread this essay's conclusion. In what sense does Ma herself see "magic in these dumplings"?

Focus on Strategy

1. What kind of information does Ma provide in paragraphs 1–11 (before she focuses on the process)? Why do you think she provides all this information?

2. Whom do you think Ma expected to read her essay? For example, do you see her target audience as largely male or female? Chinese or American? Her age or her grandmother's age? Explain.

3. What do paragraphs 5–10 tell you about Ma's purpose in writing this essay? About her intended audience?

Focus on Language and Style

1. At various points, Ma quotes her grandmother. What do these quotations tell you about Ma's grandmother? About Ma herself?

2. In paragraph 19, Ma describes the process of making dumplings as "a carefully orchestrated master plan"; in paragraph 20, she calls the process "tedious." Identify other descriptions of the process in this essay, and then write a single sentence that characterizes the process.

Focus on the Pattern

1. How can you tell this is an explanation of a process rather than a set of instructions?

2. Why do you think Ma did not write this essay as a set of instructions? If it were written as instructions, what cautions or reminders might she have had to add?

3. What are the main steps in the process Ma explains? If you can, group the steps in this long process into stages.

4. What transitional words and phrases does Ma use to move readers from one step to the next?

Focus on Critical Thinking

1. This essay's title is "My Grandmother's Dumpling," but it also discusses other people (and other people's dumplings). Who, or what, do you think is the essay's central focus? What makes you think so? Do you think the essay should have a different title? Explain.

2. In paragraph 41, Ma refers to the dumplings on the plate as "an eclectic family tree" and says that "each doughy pouch carried within it the cross-generational memoirs of its maker." What does she mean? Do you think she is making too much of the significance of the ritual she describes? Why or why not?

Writing Practice

1. Explain the process of preparing a meal or dish that is traditional in your culture or in your family. Begin with several paragraphs of background to help readers to understand what the preparation process means to you.

2. Rewrite Ma's process explanation as a set of instructions to be followed by her daughters. Remember to include any necessary cautions and reminders.

38e Cause and Effect

A **cause-and-effect** essay identifies causes or predicts effects; sometimes, it does both. In "How Facebook Is Making Friending Obsolete," Julia Angwin considers how Facebook has changed the nature of friendship. In "The Seat Not Taken," John Edgar Wideman considers the possible motives of train passengers who choose not to sit beside him.

HOW FACEBOOK IS MAKING FRIENDING OBSOLETE

Julia Angwin

Before taking up her current post at the *Wall Street Journal* as a technology editor and columnist, Julia Angwin covered technology at the *San Francisco Chronicle*. In 2009, she published the book *Stealing MySpace*, which examines the cultural phenomenon of MySpace and other social-networking sites. In "How Facebook Is Making Friending Obsolete," first published in the *Wall Street Journal*, Angwin comments on the potential consequences of Facebook's efforts to make it harder to keep profiles private. As you read, consider your own feelings about Facebook and privacy.

WORD POWER

void empty space; emptiness

"Friending" wasn't used as a verb until about five years ago, when social networks such as Friendster, MySpace and Facebook burst onto the scene. ¹

Suddenly, our friends were something even better—an audience. If blogging felt like shouting into the void, posting updates on a social network felt more like an intimate conversation among friends at a pub. ²

Inevitably, as our list of friends grew to encompass acquaintances, friends of friends and the girl who sat behind us in seventh-grade homeroom, online friendships became devalued. ³

Suddenly, we knew as much about the lives of our distant acquaintances as we did about the lives of our intimates—what they'd had for dinner, how they felt about Tiger Woods and so on. ⁴

Enter Twitter with a solution: no friends, just followers. These one-way relationships were easier to manage—no more annoying decisions about whether to give your ex-boyfriend access to your photos, no more fussing over who could see your employment and contact information. ⁵

WORD POWER

prowess ability; skill

Twitter's updates were also easily searchable on the Web, forcing users to be somewhat thoughtful about their posts. The intimate conversation became a talent show, a challenge to prove your intellectual prowess in 140 characters or less. ⁶

This fall, Twitter turned its popularity into dollars, inking lucrative deals to allow its users' tweets to be broadcast via search algorithms on Google and Bing. ⁷

Soon, Facebook followed suit with deals to distribute certain real-time data to Google and Bing. (Recall that despite being the fifth-most-popular Web site in the world, Facebook is barely profitable.) Facebook spokesman Barry Schnitt says no money changed hands in the deals but says there was "probably an exchange of value." ⁸

Just one catch: Facebook had just "exchanged" to Google and Microsoft something that didn't exist. ⁹

The vast majority of Facebook users restrict updates to their friends, and do not expect those updates to appear in public search results. (In fact, many people restrict their Facebook profile from appearing at all in search results.) ¹⁰

So Facebook had little content to provide to Google's and Bing's real-time search results. When Google's real-time search launched earlier this month, its results were primarily filled with Twitter updates. ¹¹

Coincidentally, Facebook presented its 350 million members with a new default privacy setting last week. For most people, the new suggested settings would open their Facebook updates and information to the entire world. Mr. Schnitt says the new privacy suggestions are an acknowledgement of "the way we think the world is going." ¹²

Facebook Chief Executive Mark Zuckerberg led by example, opening up his previously closed profile, including goofy photos of himself curled up with a teddy bear. ¹³

Facebook also made public formerly private info such as profile pic- 14
tures, gender, current city and the friends list. (Mr. Schnitt suggests that
users are free to lie about their hometown or take down their profile
picture to protect their privacy; in response to users' complaints, the
friends list can now be restricted to be viewed only by friends.)

Of course, many people will reject the default settings on Facebook 15
and keep on chatting with only their Facebook friends. (Mr. Schnitt said
more than 50% of its users had rejected the defaults at last tally.)

But those who want a private experience on Facebook will have 16
to work harder at it: if you inadvertently post a comment on a friend's
profile page that has been opened to the public, your comment will be
public too.

Just as Facebook turned friends into a commodity, it has likewise 17
gathered our personal data—our updates, our baby photos, our endless
chirping birthday notes—and readied it to be bundled and sold.

So I give up. Rather than fighting to keep my Facebook profile pri- 18
vate, I plan to open it up to the public—removing the fiction of intimacy
and friendship.

But I will also remove the vestiges of my private life from Facebook 19
and make sure I never post anything that I wouldn't want my parents,
employer, next-door neighbor or future employer to see. You'd be smart
to do the same.

We'll need to treat this increasingly public version of Facebook with 20
the same hard-headedness that we treat Twitter: as a place to broadcast,
but not a place for vulnerability. A place to carefully calibrate, sanitize
and bowdlerize our words for every possible audience, now and forever.
Not a place for intimacy with friends.

> **WORD POWER**
>
> **calibrate** to adjust
> precisely for a
> particular function
>
> **bowdlerize** edit by
> removing or changing
> parts that might be
> considered offensive

Focus on Meaning

1. Angwin claims that online friendships have been "devalued" (paragraph 3). What does she mean? Do you agree with her? Why or
   why not?

2. According to Angwin, how is Facebook different from Twitter? How
   does Twitter offer a solution to Facebook's problems?

3. How, according to Angwin, is Facebook "making friending obsolete"?

Focus on Strategy

1. In paragraph 19, Angwin explains that she is removing private information from her Facebook page and advises, "You'd be smart to do
   the same." What kind of audience does she seem to be addressing
   here—and in her essay as a whole? How can you tell?

2. Angwin is critical of Facebook and its effect on friendship, but she
   does not call for users to abandon it. What is she actually recommend-
   ing? Summarize her position in a one-sentence thesis statement.

Focus on Language and Style

1. Write a one-sentence definition of the verb *to friend*.

2. In paragraph 18, Angwin says, "Rather than fighting to keep my Facebook profile private, I plan to open it up to the public. . . ." What do the words *private* and *public* mean in this context?

Focus on the Pattern

1. As Angwin points out, Facebook has taken a number of steps to make its information more public. What does she say caused these actions? What has been the result of these actions?

2. Is this essay's emphasis on causes, on effects, or on both causes and effects? Explain.

Focus on Critical Thinking

1. In paragraph 4, Angwin mentions a few things people can learn about their "distant acquaintances" on social-networking sites. Generally speaking, do you think this kind of knowledge is a good thing or a bad thing? Explain.

2. What do you see as the primary differences between your friends and your Facebook friends? Do both kinds of friends play essential roles in your life?

3. Angwin believes Facebook has "turned friends into a commodity" (17) and reduced them to "an audience" (2). Do you agree that Facebook has changed the nature of friendship? If so, how? If not, why not?

Writing Practice

1. Angwin plans to open her Facebook profile to the public. Would you do—or have you already done—the same? Why or why not? Write a cause-and-effect essay in which you give your reasons for making your profile public—or your reasons for keeping it private.

2. How would your life change if you lost access to social networking? Write an essay explaining the possible results of this loss of access.

THE SEAT NOT TAKEN

John Edgar Wideman

John Edgar Wideman has published numerous books, both fiction and nonfiction, as well as articles in publications such as the *New York Times*, *The New Yorker*, *Vogue*, *Emerge*, and *Esquire*. Wideman has received the O. Henry Award, the American Book Award for Fiction, the Lannan Literary Fellowship for Fiction, the PEN/Faulkner Award for Fiction (twice—the first person so honored), and a MacArthur Fellowship. He is currently professor of Africana Studies and Literary Arts at Brown University. In "The Seat Not Taken," an op-ed article first published in the *New York Times*, Wideman reflects on his weekly train commute and raises questions about the motives his fellow commuters have for not sitting in the empty seat beside him. As you read, think about how you would react in Wideman's situation.

1   At least twice a week I ride Amtrak's high-speed Acela train from my home in New York City to my teaching job in Providence, R.I. The route passes through a region of the country populated by, statistics tell us, a significant segment of its most educated, affluent, sophisticated and enlightened citizens.

2   Over the last four years, excluding summers, I have conducted a casual sociological experiment in which I am both participant and observer. It's a survey I began not because I had some specific point to prove by gathering data to support it, but because I couldn't avoid becoming aware of an obvious, disquieting truth.

WORD POWER
disquieting upsetting

3   Almost invariably, after I have hustled aboard early and occupied one half of a vacant double seat in the usually crowded quiet car, the empty place next to me will remain empty for the entire trip.

4   I'm a man of color, one of the few on the train and often the only one in the quiet car, and I've concluded that color explains a lot about my experience. Unless the car is nearly full, color will determine, even if it doesn't exactly clarify, why 9 times out of 10 people will shun a free seat if it means sitting beside me.

WORD POWER
shun to avoid

5   Giving them and myself the benefit of the doubt, I can rule out excessive body odor or bad breath; a hateful, intimidating scowl; hip-hop clothing; or a hideous deformity as possible objections to my person. Considering also the cost of an Acela ticket, the fact that I display no visible indications of religious preference and, finally, the numerous external signs of middle-class membership I share with the majority of the passengers, color appears to be a sufficient reason for the behavior I have recorded.

6   Of course, I'm not registering a complaint about the privilege, conferred upon me by color, to enjoy the luxury of an extra seat to myself. I relish the opportunity to spread out, savor the privacy and quiet and work or gaze at the scenic New England woods and coast. It's a particularly appealing perk if I compare the train to air travel or any other mode of transportation, besides walking or bicycling, for negotiating the mercilessly congested Northeast Corridor. Still, in the year 2010, with an African-descended, brown president in the White House and a nation confidently asserting its passage into a postracial era, it strikes me as odd to ride beside a vacant seat, just about every time I embark on a three-hour journey each way, from home to work and back.

7   I admit I look forward to the moment when other passengers, searching for a good seat, or any seat at all on the busiest days, stop anxiously prowling the quiet-car aisle, the moment when they have all settled

elsewhere, including the ones who willfully blinded themselves to the open seat beside me or were unconvinced of its availability when they passed by. I savor that precise moment when the train sighs and begins to glide away from Penn or Providence Station, and I'm able to say to myself, with relative assurance, that the vacant place beside me is free, free at last, or at least free until the next station. I can relax, prop open my briefcase or rest papers, snacks or my arm in the unoccupied seat.

But the very pleasing moment of anticipation casts a shadow, be- 8 cause I can't accept the bounty of an extra seat without remembering why it's empty, without wondering if its emptiness isn't something quite sad. And quite dangerous, also, if left unexamined. Posters in the train, the station, the subway warn: if you see something, say something.

WORD POWER

bounty generous gift

Focus on Meaning

1. What "casual sociological experiment" (paragraph 2) does Wideman conduct? What are the results of this experiment? How does he interpret these results?

2. Why does Wideman see the empty seat beside him as not simply sad but also dangerous? Do you think he is right to see it this way, or do you think he is overreacting? Why?

Focus on Strategy

1. What do you think Wideman hoped to accomplish in this essay? For example, do you think he was trying to change readers' minds—or their behavior? To issue a warning? To suggest a change in Amtrak policy? Do you think this essay accomplishes his goal?

2. Why does Wideman end his essay with the words "if you see something, say something" (8)? In what context does this sentence usually appear? What is the "something" he wants people to say in this case?

Focus on Language and Style

1. Which words in this essay refer specifically to race? Do you think Wideman should have included more references to his own race (and to the races of his fellow passengers)? Why or why not?

2. In paragraph 1, Wideman suggests that his fellow passengers are some of the United States's "most educated, affluent, sophisticated and enlightened citizens." What point is he trying to make by using these adjectives to characterize the other passengers?

Focus on the Pattern

1. This essay focuses on examining causes. What do you think might be the *effects* (on Wideman and on society in general) of the behavior Wideman describes?

2. Write a one-sentence thesis statement for this essay, including at least one word or phrase (for example, *because, for this reason*, or *as a result*) that indicates it is a cause-and-effect essay.

Focus on Critical Thinking

1. Consider all the reasons you might have (apart from the reasons Wideman lists in paragraph 5) for choosing not to sit next to a particular person on a train, bus, or plane. Might any of these reasons explain why the seat beside Wideman so often remains empty?

2. In paragraph 5, Wideman mentions the "numerous external signs of middle-class membership" that he, like the other passengers, exhibits. What do you think these "external signs" are? Why do you think he mentions them?

Writing Practice

1. How do you account for the empty seat beside Wideman on so many train trips? Do you agree with his analysis of the situation, or can you think of other explanations that he has not considered? Write a cause-and-effect essay responding to Wideman's article and its reflections on race.

2. What kinds of people would you try to avoid sitting next to on a train? Why? Do you see your objections as reasonable, or do you think some of your objections might be considered prejudice? Write an essay in which you explain your objections as clearly and thoughtfully as possible.

38f   Comparison and Contrast

A **comparison-and-contrast** essay explains how two things are alike or how they are different; sometimes, it discusses both similarities and differences. In "The Twin Revolutions of Lincoln and Darwin," Steven Conn compares two important historical figures. In "Men Are from Mars, Women Are from Venus," John Gray compares men and women.

THE TWIN REVOLUTIONS OF LINCOLN AND DARWIN

Steven Conn

Steven Conn is a professor of American cultural and intellectual history and director of the Public History Program at Ohio State University. He is the author of five books, most recently *Do Museums Still Need*

Objects? (2009). In "The Twin Revolutions of Lincoln and Darwin," which first appeared in the *Philadelphia Inquirer* in 2009, Conn compares the lives of two seemingly unrelated historical figures—Abraham Lincoln and Charles Darwin. As you read, note any points of comparison that you find surprising.

Abraham Lincoln, the Great Emancipator, has been much on our minds recently. Today, exactly 200 years after Lincoln's birth, Barack Obama's presidency is one fulfillment of the work Lincoln started.   1

Lincoln shares his birthday with Charles Darwin, the other Great Emancipator of the 19th century. In different ways, each liberated us from tradition.   2

Charles Darwin and Abraham Lincoln were exact contemporaries. Both were born on Feb. 12, 1809—Darwin into a comfortable family in Shropshire, England; Lincoln into humble circumstances on the American frontier.   3

They also came to international attention at virtually the same moment. Darwin published his epochal book, *On the Origin of Species*, in 1859. The following year, Lincoln became the 16th president of the United States. Also in 1860, Harvard botanist Asa Gray wrote the first review of Darwin's book to appear in this country.   4

Lincoln and Darwin initiated twin revolutions. One brought the Civil War and the emancipation of roughly four million slaves; the other, a new explanation of the natural world. Lincoln's war transformed the social, political and racial landscape in ways that continue to play out. Darwin transformed our understanding of biology, paving the way for countless advances in science, especially medicine.   5

With his powerful scientific explanation of the origins of species, Darwin dispensed with the pseudoscientific assertions of African American inferiority. In this way, Darwin provided the scientific legitimacy for Lincoln's political and moral actions.   6

The two revolutions shared a commitment to one proposition: that all human beings are fundamentally equal. In this sense, both Lincoln and Darwin deserve credit for emancipating us from the political and intellectual rationales for slavery.   7

For Lincoln, this was a political principle and a moral imperative. He was deeply ambivalent about the institution of slavery. As the war began, he believed that saving the Union, not abolishing slavery, was the cause worth fighting for. But as the war ground gruesomely on, he began to see that ending slavery was the only way to save the Union without making a mockery of the nation's founding ideals.   8

This is what Lincoln meant when he promised, in the 1863 Gettysburg Address, that the war would bring "a new birth of freedom." He was even more emphatic about it in his second inaugural address, in 1865. Slavery could not be permitted to exist in a nation founded on the belief that we are all created equal.   9

WORD POWER

epochal extremely important, significant, or influential

WORD POWER

imperative an obligation or duty

ambivalent having mixed feelings

WORD POWER

emphatic forceful and insistent

Darwin, for his part, was a deeply committed abolitionist from a family of deeply committed abolitionists. Exposed to slavery during his travels in South America, Darwin wrote, "It makes one's blood boil." He called abolishing slavery his "sacred cause." In some of his first notes about evolution, he railed against the idea that slaves were somehow less than human. 10

For Darwin, our shared humanity was a simple biological fact. Whatever variations exist among the human species—what we call *races*—are simply the natural variations that occur within all species. Like it or not, in a Darwinian world we are all members of one human family. This truth lay at the center of Darwin's science and his abolitionism. 11

That understanding of human equality—arrived at from different directions and for different reasons—helps explain the opposition to the revolutions unleashed by Lincoln and Darwin. It's also why many Americans—virtually alone in the developed world—continue to deny Darwinian science. 12

Many white Southerners never accepted Lincoln's basic proposition about the political equality of black Americans. In the years after the Civil War and Reconstruction, they set up the brutal structures and rituals of segregation. All of the elaborate laws, customs and violence of the segregated South served to deny the basic truth that all Americans are created equal. Most Northerners, meanwhile, didn't care much about the "Southern problem." 13

No wonder, then, that many Americans simply rejected Darwin's insights out of hand. Slavery and segregation rested on the assumption that black Americans were not fully human. Darwinian science put the lie to all that. 14

Lincoln insisted on equality as a political fact. Darwin demonstrated it as a biological fact. In their shared commitment to human equality, each in his own realm, these two Great Emancipators helped us break free from the shackles of the past. 15

Focus on Meaning

1. How are Lincoln and Darwin alike? What are their "twin revolutions"? How are these revolutions similar?

2. How are Lincoln and Darwin different? In Conn's view, is it their similarities or their differences that are most significant?

3. Why, according to Conn, were so many people opposed to both Lincoln's and Darwin's ideas?

Focus on Strategy

1. What is Conn's thesis? Where does he state it? Write a sentence that paraphrases this thesis statement.

2. What is Conn's rationale for comparing Lincoln and Darwin?

Focus on Language and Style

1. What does the word *emancipator* mean? What associations does this word have for you?

2. What exactly does Conn mean when he calls Lincoln and Darwin "these two Great Emancipators" (paragraph 15)?

3. What does Conn mean by "the shackles of the past" (15)? What connotations does the word *shackles* have for you?

Focus on the Pattern

1. Which paragraphs focus on Lincoln? Which focus on Darwin? Which discuss both men?

2. Is this a point-by-point or a subject-by-subject comparison? How can you tell?

3. Does Conn make the same points about the two men he focuses on, or does he discuss some points for one man and not for the other? If the points he presents do not match exactly, does this weaken the effect of his comparison? Why or why not?

4. What specific words and phrases does Conn use to introduce similarities and differences? (For example, in paragraph 7, he uses the word *both*.) Do you think he needs more such words and phrases to make his points of comparison or contrast clear? If so, where?

5. Create an outline for this essay. Based on your outline, do you think any information should be relocated?

Focus on Critical Thinking

1. Do you think it makes sense to compare Lincoln and Darwin, or do you think this comparison diminishes the achievements of either (or both) of these two men? Explain.

2. Whom do you see as the more important historical figure, Lincoln or Darwin? Whose legacy do you think is more important? Why?

Writing Practice

1. Write a comparison-and-contrast essay in which you compare and/or contrast two historical figures or fictional characters. In your thesis statement, be sure to communicate the significance of the central parallel or contrast you identify.

2. Write a comparison-and-contrast essay in which you compare and/or contrast your life before and after an important personal or historical event. What changed for you, and what remained the same?

MEN ARE FROM MARS, WOMEN ARE FROM VENUS

John Gray

Marriage counselor, seminar leader, and author John Gray has written a number of books that examine relationships between men and women. His best-known book, *Men Are from Mars, Women Are from Venus* (1992), suggests that men and women are at times so different that they might as well come from different planets. In the following excerpt from this book, Gray contrasts the different communication styles that he believes are characteristic of men and women. As you read, consider whether Gray's comparison oversimplifies the gender differences he discusses.

The most frequently expressed complaint women have about men is that men don't listen. Either a man completely ignores [a woman] when she speaks to him, or he listens for a few beats, assesses what is bothering her, and then proudly puts on his Mr. Fix-It cap and offers her a solution to make her feel better. He is confused when she doesn't appreciate this gesture of love. No matter how many times she tells him that he's not listening, he doesn't get it and keeps doing the same thing. She wants empathy, but he thinks she wants solutions. 1

> **WORD POWER**
> **empathy** identification with another person's situation and feelings

The most frequently expressed complaint men have about women is that women are always trying to change them. When a woman loves a man she feels responsible to assist him in growing and tries to help him improve the way he does things. She forms a home-improvement committee, and he becomes her primary focus. No matter how much he resists her help, she persists—waiting for any opportunity to help him or tell him what to do. She thinks she's nurturing him, while he feels he's being controlled. Instead, he wants her acceptance. 2

> **WORD POWER**
> **nurturing** supporting and encouraging

These two problems can finally be solved by first understanding why men offer solutions and why women seek to improve. Let's pretend to go back in time, where by observing life on Mars and Venus—before the planets discovered one another or came to Earth—we can gain some insights into men and women. 3

Martians value power, competency, efficiency, and achievement. They are always doing things to prove themselves and develop their power and skills. Their sense of self is defined through their ability to achieve results. They experience fulfillment primarily through success and accomplishment. 4

Everything on Mars is a reflection of these values. Even their dress is designed to reflect their skills and competence. Police officers, soldiers, businessmen, scientists, cab drivers, technicians, and chefs all wear uniforms or at least hats to reflect their competence and power. 5

They don't read magazines like *Psychology Today*, *Self*, or *People*. 6
They are more concerned with outdoor activities, like hunting, fishing,
and racing cars. They are interested in the news, weather, and sports
and couldn't care less about romance novels and self-help books.

They are more interested in "objects" and "things" rather than peo- 7
ple and feelings. Even today on Earth, while women fantasize about
romance, men fantasize about powerful cars, faster computers, gadgets,
gizmos, and new more powerful technology. Men are preoccupied with
the "things" that can help them express power by creating results and
achieving their goals.

Achieving goals is very important to a Martian because it is a way for 8
him to prove his competence and thus feel good about himself. And for
him to feel good about himself he must achieve these goals by himself.
Someone else can't achieve them for him. Martians pride themselves
in doing things all by themselves. Autonomy is a symbol of efficiency,
power, and competence.

Understanding this Martian characteristic can help women un- 9
derstand why men resist so much being corrected or being told what
to do. To offer a man unsolicited advice is to presume that he doesn't
know what to do or that he can't do it on his own. Men are very touchy
about this, because the issue of competence is so very important to
them.

Because he is handling his problems on his own, a Martian rarely 10
talks about his problems unless he needs expert advice. He reasons:
"Why involve someone else when I can do it by myself?" He keeps his
problems to himself unless he requires help from another to find a solution. Asking for help when you can do it yourself is perceived as a sign
of weakness.

However, if he truly does need help, then it is a sign of wisdom to 11
get it. In this case, he will find someone he respects and then talk about
his problem. Talking about a problem on Mars is an invitation for advice. Another Martian feels honored by the opportunity. Automatically
he puts on his Mr. Fix-It hat, listens for a while, and then offers some
jewels of advice.

This Martian custom is one of the reasons men instinctively offer 12
solutions when women talk about problems. When a woman innocently
shares upset feelings or explores out loud the problems of her day, a
man mistakenly assumes she is looking for some expert advice. He puts
on his Mr. Fix-It hat and begins giving advice; this is his way of showing
love and of trying to help.

He wants to help her feel better by solving her problems. He wants 13
to be useful to her. He feels he can be valued and thus worthy of her love
when his abilities are used to solve her problems.

Once he has offered a solution, however, and she continues to be 14
upset it becomes increasingly difficult for him to listen because his solution is being rejected and he feels increasingly useless.

WORD POWER

autonomy
independence or
freedom

unsolicited not
asked for

He has no idea that by just listening with empathy and interest he can be supportive. He does not know that on Venus talking about problems is not an invitation to offer a solution. 15

Venusians have different values. They value love, communication, beauty, and relationships. They spend a lot of time supporting, helping, and nurturing one another. Their sense of self is defined through their feelings and the quality of their relationships. They experience fulfillment through sharing and relating. 16

Everything on Venus reflects these values. Rather than building highways and tall buildings, the Venusians are more concerned with living together in harmony, community, and loving cooperation. Relationships are more important than work and technology. In most ways their world is the opposite of Mars. 17

They do not wear uniforms like the Martians (to reveal their competence). On the contrary, they enjoy wearing a different outfit every day, according to how they are feeling. Personal expression, especially of their feelings, is very important. They may even change outfits several times a day as their mood changes. 18

Communication is of primary importance. To share their personal feelings is much more important than achieving goals and success. Talking and relating to one another is a source of tremendous fulfillment. 19

This is hard for a man to comprehend. He can come close to understanding a woman's experience of sharing and relating by comparing it to the satisfaction he feels when he wins a race, achieves a goal, or solves a problem. 20

Instead of being goal oriented, women are relationship oriented; they are more concerned with expressing their goodness, love, and caring. Two Martians go to lunch to discuss a project or business goal; they have a problem to solve. In addition, Martians view going to a restaurant as an efficient way to approach food: no shopping, no cooking, and no washing dishes. For Venusians, going to lunch is an opportunity to nurture a relationship, for both giving support to and receiving support from a friend. Women's restaurant talk can be very open and intimate, almost like the dialogue that occurs between therapist and patient. 21

On Venus, everyone studies psychology and has at least a master's degree in counseling. They are very involved in personal growth, spirituality, and everything that can nurture life, healing, and growth. Venus is covered with parks, organic gardens, shopping centers, and restaurants. 22

Venusians are very intuitive. They have developed this ability through centuries of anticipating the needs of others. They pride themselves in being considerate of the needs and feelings of others. A sign of great love is to offer help and assistance to another Venusian without being asked. 23

Because proving one's competence is not as important to a Venusian, offering help is not offensive, and needing help is not a sign of weakness. A man, however, may feel offended because when a woman offers advice he doesn't feel she trusts his ability to do it himself. 24

A woman has no conception of this male sensitivity because for her 25 it is another feather in her hat if someone offers to help her. It makes her feel loved and cherished. But offering help to a man can make him feel incompetent, weak, and even unloved.

On Venus it is a sign of caring to give advice and suggestions. 26 Venusians firmly believe that when something is working it can always work better. Their nature is to want to improve things. When they care about someone, they freely point out what can be improved and suggest how to do it. Offering advice and constructive criticism is an act of love.

Mars is very different. Martians are more solution oriented. If some- 27 thing is working, their motto is don't change it. Their instinct is to leave it alone if it is working. "Don't fix it unless it is broken" is a common expression.

When a woman tries to improve a man, he feels she is trying to fix 28 him. He receives the message that he is broken. She doesn't realize her caring attempts to help him may humiliate him. She mistakenly thinks she is just helping him to grow.

Focus on Meaning

1. What specific character traits and habits does Gray associate with men?
2. What character traits and habits does he associate with women?
3. Does Gray see one set of characteristics as superior to the other, or does he consider them to be comparable?

Focus on Strategy

1. What serious point is Gray making by characterizing men as Martians and women as Venusians?
2. If you were going to add a more fully developed conclusion to sum up Gray's point about the differences between men and women, what kind of closing strategy would you use? Do you think the essay needs such a conclusion?

Focus on Language and Style

1. Do you think Gray's choice of the labels *Martians* and *Venusians* is appropriate? Explain.
2. What other labels could Gray have used to contrast men and women?

Focus on the Pattern

1. This essay is a subject-by-subject comparison. How does Gray signal the movement from the first subject to the second? Why do you suppose he chose to write a subject-by-subject rather than a point-by-point comparison?

2. Create an outline that arranges Gray's points as a point-by-point comparison. What advantages and disadvantages does this organization have?

Focus on Critical Thinking

1. Do you think Gray is stereotyping men and women? Explain.

2. Regardless of how you answered the previous question, do you agree with Gray that men and women seem to be from two different planets? Why or why not?

Writing Practice

1. Are young boys and girls also from two different planets? Take a position on this issue, and support it in a subject-by-subject comparison. In your thesis statement, try to account for the differences you identify between boys and girls.

2. Identify one general area in which you believe men's and women's attitudes, behavior, or expectations are very different—for example, dating, careers, eating habits, sports, housekeeping, or driving. Write a comparison-and-contrast essay (serious or humorous) that explores the differences you identify.

38g Classification

A **classification** essay divides a whole into parts and sorts various items into categories. In "The Men We Carry in Our Minds," Scott Russell Sanders classifies the working men he has known. On a lighter note, Carolyn Foster Segal's "The Dog Ate My Flash Drive, and Other Tales of Woe" classifies students' excuses.

THE MEN WE CARRY IN OUR MINDS

Scott Russell Sanders

Scott Russell Sanders is a Distinguished Professor Emeritus at Indiana University, a children's book author, and an essayist. His essays are often personal reflections that include social and philosophical commentary. In the classic essay "The Men We Carry in Our Minds," first published in the *Milkweed Chronicle* in 1984, Sanders reflects on the working lives of the men he knew as a boy and classifies them according to the kind of work they do. His essay discusses not only his boyhood impressions of the men's jobs but also the direction his own professional life has taken. As you read, notice how Sanders moves from classifying men's work to comparing men's lives to women's lives.

The first men, besides my father, I remember seeing were black convicts and white guards, in the cottonfield across the road from our farm on the outskirts of Memphis. I must have been three or four. The prisoners wore dingy gray-and-black zebra suits, heavy as canvas, sodden with sweat. Hatless, stooped, they chopped weeds in the fierce heat, row after row, breathing the acrid dust of boll-weevil poison. The overseers wore dazzling white shirts and broad shadowy hats. The oiled barrels of their shotguns flashed in the sunlight. Their faces in memory are utterly blank. Of course those men, white and black, have become for me an emblem of racial hatred. But they have also come to stand for the twin poles of my early vision of manhood—the brute toiling animal and the boss. 1

When I was a boy, the men I knew labored with their bodies. They were marginal farmers, just scraping by, or welders, steelworkers, carpenters; they swept floors, dug ditches, mined coal, or drove trucks, their forearms ropy with muscle; they trained horses, stoked furnaces, built tires, stood on assembly lines wrestling parts onto cars and refrigerators. They got up before light, worked all day long whatever the weather, and when they came home at night they looked as though somebody had been whipping them. In the evenings and on weekends they worked on their own places, tilling gardens that were lumpy with clay, fixing broken-down cars, hammering on houses that were always too drafty, too leaky, too small. 2

The bodies of the men I knew were twisted and maimed in ways visible and invisible. The nails of their hands were black and split, the hands tattooed with scars. Some had lost fingers. Heavy lifting had given many of them finicky backs and guts weak from hernias. Racing against conveyor belts had given them ulcers. Their ankles and knees ached from years of standing on concrete. Anyone who had worked for long around machines was hard of hearing. They squinted, and the skin of their faces was creased like the leather of old work gloves. There were times, studying them, when I dreaded growing up. Most of them coughed, from dust or cigarettes, and most of them drank cheap wine or whiskey, so their eyes looked bloodshot and bruised. The fathers of my friends always seemed older than the mothers. Men wore out sooner. Only women lived into old age. 3

As a boy I also knew another sort of men, who did not sweat and break down like mules. They were soldiers, and so far as I could tell they scarcely worked at all. During my early school years we lived on a military base, an arsenal in Ohio, and every day I saw GIs in the guard-shacks, on the stoops of barracks, at the wheels of olive drab Chevrolets. The chief fact of their lives was boredom. Long after I left the Arsenal I came to recognize the sour smell the soldiers gave off as that of souls in limbo. They were all waiting—for wars, for transfers, for leaves, for promotions, for the end of their hitch—like so many braves waiting for the hunt to begin. Unlike the warriors of older tribes, however, they would have no say about when the battle would start or how it would be 4 waged. Their waiting was broken only when they practiced for war. They fired guns at targets, drove tanks across the churned-up fields of the military reservation, set off bombs in the wrecks of old fighter planes. I knew this was all play. But I also felt certain that when the hour for killing arrived, they would kill. When the real shooting started, many of them would die. This was what soldiers were *for*, just as a hammer was for driving nails.

Warriors and toilers: those seemed, in my boyhood vision, to be the 5 chief destinies for men. They weren't the only destinies, as I learned from having a few male teachers, from reading books, and from watching television. But the men on television—the politicians, the astronauts, the generals, the savvy lawyers, the philosophical doctors, the bosses who gave orders to both soldiers and laborers—seemed as removed and unreal to me as the figures in tapestries. I could no more imagine growing up to become one of these cool, potent creatures than I could imagine becoming a prince.

A nearer and more hopeful example was that of my father, who had 6 escaped from a red-dirt farm to a tire factory, and from the assembly line to the front office. Eventually he dressed in a white shirt and tie. He carried himself as if he had been born to work with his mind. But his body, remembering the earlier years of slogging work, began to give out on him in his fifties, and it quit on him entirely before he turned sixty-five. Even such a partial escape from man's fate as he had accomplished did not seem possible for most of the boys I knew. They joined the Army, stood in line for jobs in the smoky plants, helped build highways. They were bound to work as their fathers had worked, killing themselves or preparing to kill others.

A scholarship enabled me not only to attend college, a rare enough 7 feat in my circle, but even to study in a university meant for the children of the rich. Here I met for the first time young men who had assumed from birth that they would lead lives of comfort and power. And for the first time I met women who told me that men were guilty of having kept all the joys and privileges of the earth for themselves. I was baffled. What privileges? What joys? I thought about the maimed, dismal lives of most of the men back home. What had they stolen from their wives and daughters? The right to go five days a week, twelve months a year, for thirty or forty years to a steel mill or a coal mine? The right to drop bombs and die in war? The right to feel every leak in the roof, every gap in the fence, every cough in the engine, as a wound they must mend? The right to feel, when the layoff comes or the plant shuts down, not only afraid but ashamed?

I was slow to understand the deep grievances of women. This was 8 because, as a boy, I had envied them. Before college, the only people I had ever known who were interested in art or music or literature, the only ones who read books, the only ones who ever seemed to enjoy a sense of ease and grace were the mothers and daughters. Like the menfolk, they fretted about money, they scrimped and made-do. But, when the pay stopped coming in, they were not the ones who had failed. Nor did they have to go to war, and that seemed to me a blessed fact. By comparison with the narrow, ironclad days of fathers, there was an expansiveness, I thought, in the days of mothers. They went to see neighbors, to shop in town, to run errands at school, at the library, at church. No doubt, had I looked harder at their lives, I would have envied them less. It was not my fate to become a woman, so it was easier for me to see the graces. Few of them held jobs outside the home, and those who did filled thankless roles as clerks and waitresses. I didn't see, then, what a prison a house could be, since houses seemed to me brighter, handsomer places than any factory. I did not realize—because such things were never spoken of—how often women suffered from men's bullying. I did learn about the wretchedness of abandoned wives, single mothers, widows; but I also learned about the wretchedness of lone men. Even then I could see how exhausting it was for a mother to cater all day to the needs of young children. But if I had been asked, as a boy, to choose between tending a baby and tending a machine, I think I would have chosen the baby. (Having now tended both, I know I would choose the baby.)

So I was baffled when the women at college accused me and my sex 9 of having cornered the world's pleasures. I think something like my bafflement has been felt by other boys (and by girls as well) who grew up in dirt-poor farm country, in mining country, in black ghettos, in Hispanic barrios, in the shadows of factories, in Third World nations—any place where the fate of men is as grim and bleak as the fate of women. Toilers and warriors. I realize now how ancient these identities are, how deep the tug they exert on men, the undertow of a thousand generations. The miseries I saw, as a boy, in the lives of nearly all men I continue to see in the lives of many—the body-breaking toil, the tedium, the call to be tough, the humiliating powerlessness, the battle for a living and for territory.

When the women I met at college thought about the joys and privi- 10 leges of men, they did not carry in their minds the sort of men I had known in my childhood. They thought of their fathers, who were bankers, physicians, architects, stockbrokers, the big wheels of the big cities. These fathers rode the train to work or drove cars that cost more than any of my childhood houses. They were attended from morning to night by female helpers, wives and nurses and secretaries. They were never laid off, never short of cash at month's end, never lined up for welfare. These fathers made decisions that mattered. They ran the world.

The daughters of such men wanted to share in this power, this glory. 11 So did I. They yearned for a say over their future, for jobs worthy of their abilities, for the right to live at peace, unmolested, whole. Yes, I thought, yes yes. The difference between me and these daughters was that they saw me, because of my sex, as destined from birth to become like their fathers, and therefore as an enemy to their desires. But I knew better. I wasn't an enemy, in fact or in feeling. I was an ally. If I had known, then, how to tell them so, would they have believed me? Would they now?

WORD POWER

undertow an underlying force or pull

Focus on Meaning

1. What two types of men did Sanders know when he was young? How were they different? What did they have in common?
2. When Sanders was growing up, what did he see as his destiny? Why? How did he escape his fate?
3. What were the grievances of the women Sanders met at college? Why did he have trouble understanding these grievances?

Focus on Strategy

1. Sanders opens his essay with a description of "black convicts and white guards." Why?
2. This essay closes with two questions. Is this an effective closing strategy? Explain.

Focus on Language and Style

1. What connotations do the words *warriors* and *toilers* have?
2. Suggest two or three alternative pairs of names for the categories *warriors* and *toilers*. Do you think your suggestions are better than Sanders's choices? If so, why?

Focus on the Pattern

1. What kinds of men mentioned in this essay do not fit into either of the two categories Sanders identifies in paragraphs 2–4? Why don't they fit?
2. Sanders does not categorize the women he discusses. Can you think of a few categories into which these women could fit?

Focus on Critical Thinking

1. Who do you believe has an easier life, men or women? Why?

Writing Practice

1. Write a classification essay in which you identify and discuss three or four categories of workers (females as well as males) you observed in your community when you were growing up. In your thesis statement, draw a conclusion about the relative status and rewards of these workers' jobs.
2. Consider your own work history as well as your future career. Write a classification essay in which you discuss your experience in several different categories of employment in the past, present, and future. Give each category a descriptive title, and include a thesis statement that sums up your progress.
3. Write an essay in which you categorize the workers in your current place of employment or on your college campus.

THE DOG ATE MY FLASH DRIVE, AND OTHER TALES OF WOE

Carolyn Foster Segal

Carolyn Foster Segal, Professor Emerita of English at Cedar Crest College in Pennsylvania and a lecturer at Muhlenberg College, has heard practically every student excuse for handing in late papers. In this humorous essay, she divides student excuses into categories. This article originally appeared, under the title "The Dog Ate My Disk, and Other Tales of Woe," in the *Chronicle of Higher Education*, a periodical for college teachers and administrators. As you read, think about the kinds of excuses you have given to instructors for late work.

Taped to the door of my office is a cartoon that features a cat explaining to his feline teacher, "The dog ate my homework." It is intended as a gently humorous reminder to my students that I will not accept excuses for late work, and it, like the lengthy warning on my syllabus, has had absolutely no effect. With a show of energy and creativity that would be admirable if applied to the (missing) assignments in question, my students persist, week after week, semester after semester, year after year, in offering excuses about why their work is not ready. Those reasons fall into several broad categories: the family, the best friend, the evils of dorm life, the evils of technology, and the totally bizarre.

The Family The death of the grandfather/grandmother is, of course, the grandmother of all excuses. What heartless teacher would dare to question a student's grief or veracity? What heartless student would lie, wishing death on a revered family member, just to avoid a deadline? Creative students may win extra extensions (and days off) with a little careful planning and fuller plot development, as in the sequence of "My grandfather/grandmother is sick"; "Now my grandfather/grandmother is in the hospital"; and finally, "We could all see it coming—my grandfather/grandmother is dead."

Another favorite excuse is "the family emergency," which (always) goes like this: "There was an emergency at home, and I had to help my family." It's a lovely sentiment, one that conjures up images of Louisa May Alcott's little women rushing off with baskets of food and copies of *Pilgrim's Progress,* but I do not understand why anyone would turn to my most irresponsible students in times of trouble.

The Best Friend This heartwarming concern for others extends beyond the family to friends, as in, "My best friend was up all night and I had to (a) stay up with her in the dorm, (b) drive her to the hospital, or (c) drive to her college because (1) her boyfriend broke up with her, (2) she was throwing up blood [no one catches a cold anymore; everyone throws up blood], or (3) her grandfather/grandmother died."

1

2

3

4

At one private university where I worked as an adjunct, I heard an   5
interesting spin that incorporated the motifs of both best friend and
dead relative: "My best friend's mother killed herself." One has to admire
the cleverness here: A mysterious woman in the prime of her life has al-
legedly committed suicide, and no professor can prove otherwise! And
I admit I was moved, until finally I had to point out to my students that
it was amazing how the simple act of my assigning a topic for a paper
seemed to drive large numbers of otherwise happy and healthy middle-
aged women to their deaths. I was careful to make that point during an
off week, during which no deaths were reported.

The Evils of Dorm Life   These stories are usually fairly predict-   6
able; they almost always feature the evil roommate or hallmate, with my
student in the role of the innocent victim; and can be summed up as follows: My roommate, who is a horrible person, likes to party, and I, who
am a good person, cannot concentrate on my work when he or she is
partying. Variations include stories about the two people next door who
were running around and crying loudly last night because (a) one of
them had boyfriend/girlfriend problems; (b) one of them was throwing
up blood; or (c) someone, somewhere, died. A friend of mine in graduate
school had a student who claimed that his roommate attacked him with
a hammer. That, in fact, was a true story; it came out in court when the
bad roommate was tried for killing his grandfather.

The Evils of Technology   The computer age has revolutionized the   7
student story, inspiring almost as many new excuses as it has Internet
businesses. Here are just a few electronically enhanced explanations.

- The computer wouldn't let me save my work.
- The printer wouldn't print.
- The printer wouldn't print this file.
- The printer wouldn't give me time to proofread.
- The printer made a black line run through all my words, and I know
  you can't read this, but do you still want it, or wait, here, take my
  flash drive. File name? I don't know what you mean.
- I swear I attached it.
- It's my roommate's computer, and she usually helps me, but she had
  to go to the hospital because she was throwing up blood.
- I did write to the listserv, but all my messages came back to me.
- I just found out that all my other listserv messages came up under
  a different name. I just want you to know that its really me who
  wrote all those messages, you can tel which ones our mine because
  I didnt use the spelcheck! But it was yours truely :) Anyway, just in
  case you missed those messages or dont belief its my writting. I'll
  repeat what I sad: I thought the last movie we watched in clas was
  borring.

The Totally Bizarre   I call the first story "The Pennsylvania Chain   8
Saw Episode." A commuter student called to explain why she had
missed my morning class. She had gotten up early so that she would be
wide awake for class. Having a bit of extra time, she walked outside to
see her neighbor, who was cutting some wood. She called out to him,
and he waved back to her with the saw. Wouldn't you know it, the safety
catch wasn't on or was broken, and the blade flew right out of the saw
and across his lawn and over her fence and across her yard and severed
a tendon in her right hand. So she was calling me from the hospital,
where she was waiting for surgery. Luckily, she reassured me, she had
remembered to bring her paper and a stamped envelope (in a plastic
bag, to avoid bloodstains) along with her in the ambulance, and a nurse
was mailing everything to me even as we spoke.

That wasn't her first absence. In fact, this student had missed most   9
of the class meetings, and I had already recommended that she withdraw
from the course. Now I suggested again that it might be best if she dropped
the class. I didn't harp on the absences (what if even some of this story
were true?). I did mention that she would need time to recuperate and that
making up so much missed work might be difficult. "Oh, no," she said,
"I can't drop this course. I had been planning to go on to medical school
and become a surgeon, but since I won't be able to operate because of my
accident, I'll have to major in English, and this course is more important
than ever to me." She did come to the next class, wearing—as evidence of
her recent trauma—a bedraggled Ace bandage on her left hand.

You may be thinking that nothing could top that excuse, but in fact I   10
have one more story, provided by the same student, who sent me a letter
to explain why her final assignment would be late. While recuperating
from her surgery, she had begun corresponding on the Internet with a
man who lived in Germany. After a one-week, whirlwind Web romance,
they had agreed to meet in Rome, to rendezvous (her phrase) at the
papal Easter Mass. Regrettably, the time of her flight made it impossible
for her to attend class, but she trusted that I—just this once—would
accept late work if the pope wrote a note.

Focus on Meaning

1. Why does Segal see a grandparent's death as "the grandmother of all
   excuses" (paragraph 2)?
2. What problems do students' friends always seem to have?
3. What are some of "the evils of dorm life"(6)?
4. What problems do computers cause for students?
5. What are some of the "totally bizarre" (8) excuses students come up with?

Focus on Strategy

1. Who is the intended audience for this essay? How can you tell?

2. Why does Segal begin her essay by describing a cartoon? Is this an effective opening strategy? Why or why not?

3. In her first paragraph, Segal includes a sentence that lists the five categories she will discuss. Do you think she needs this sentence?

4. Do you think this essay needs a formal conclusion, or is the story in its last paragraph an appropriate ending? Explain.

Focus on Language and Style

1. Segal uses boldface headings (**The Family**, for example) to identify her categories. Does she need these headings, or do her topic sentences clearly identify all the categories she discusses? Which sentences, if any, would need to be rewritten if the headings were not included?

2. **Sarcastic** remarks, which mean the opposite of what they say, are usually meant to make fun of something or someone. Where does Segal use sarcasm? Considering her audience, do you think this language is appropriate? Why or why not?

Focus on the Pattern

1. What categories of excuses does Segal identify?

2. Are Segal's categories arranged in random order? If not, what determines the order in which she presents them?

3. The "totally bizarre" category is broader than the others. Do you think it needs to be divided into smaller categories? If so, what would you call these new subcategories?

Focus on Critical Thinking

1. In addition to the excuses Segal discusses for handing in late assignments, what other excuses can you think of? Do they fit into the categories Segal has established? If not, what new category (or categories) would you add to Segal's?

2. Do you see all the excuses Segal lists as valid reasons for handing in a late paper or asking for more time to complete an assignment? Why or why not?

3. Do you think this essay is funny? Do you find it offensive in any way? How do you suppose your instructors would react to Segal's ideas?

4. What would Segal have to change if she were to rewrite this essay for her school's student newspaper? Why?

Writing Practice

1. Write about the strangest excuse you have ever been given by someone for not doing something he or she was supposed to do. Explain the circumstances of this excuse in a humorous manner.

2. Write a letter to Carolyn Foster Segal explaining why your English paper will be late. Explain that you have read her essay about various categories of student excuses but that *your* excuse is valid.

38h Definition

A **definition** essay presents an extended definition, using other patterns of development to move beyond a simple dictionary definition. In "Quinceañera," Julia Alvarez defines a coming-of-age ritual for Latinas. In "I Want a Wife," Judy Brady defines a family role.

QUINCEAÑERA

Julia Alvarez

Born in New York City to Dominican parents, Julia Alvarez has published numerous works of fiction and nonfiction, including poetry, children's stories, novels, and essays. One of her most famous books, *In the Time of the Butterflies* (1994), offers a fictionalized account of the tragic story of three sisters who became revolutionary leaders in the Dominican Republic under the dictatorship of Rafael Trujillo. (Alvarez's own family fled this regime in 1960.) As you read this excerpt from the nonfiction work *Once Upon a Quinceañera: Coming of Age in the USA* (2007), note how Alvarez uses her own childhood experiences to help her define a *quinceañera*.

WORD POWER

rhetorical used simply for style or effect

What exactly is a *quinceañera*? 1

The question might soon be rhetorical in our quickly Latinoizing 2 American culture. Already, there is a *Quinceañera* Barbie; *quinceañera* packages at Disney World and Las Vegas; an award-winning movie, *Quinceañera*; and for tots, *Dora the Explorer* has an episode about her cousin Daisy's *quinceañera*.

A *quinceañera* (the term is used interchangeably for the girl and her 3 party) celebrates a girl's passage into womanhood with an elaborate, ritualized *fiesta* on her fifteenth birthday. (*Quince años*, thus *quinceañera*, pronounced: keen-seah-gnéer-ah.) In the old countries, this was a marker birthday: after she turned fifteen, a girl could attend adult parties; she was allowed to tweeze her eyebrows, use makeup, shave her legs, wear jewelry and heels. In short, she was ready for marriage. (Legal age for marriage in many Caribbean and Latin and Central American countries is, or until recently was, fifteen or younger for females, sixteen or older for males.) Even humble families marked a girl's fifteenth birthday as special, perhaps with a cake, certainly with a gathering of family and friends at which the *quinceañera* could now socialize and dance with young men. Upper-class families, of course, threw more elaborate parties at which girls dressed up in long, formal gowns and danced waltzes with their fathers.

Somewhere along the way these fancier parties became highly ritualized. In one or another of our Latin American countries, the *quinceañera* was crowned with a tiara; her flat shoes were changed by her father to heels; she was accompanied by a court of fourteen *damas* escorted by fourteen *chambelanes*, who represented her first fourteen years; she received a last doll, marking both the end of childhood and her symbolic readiness to bear her own child. And because our countries were at least nominally Catholic, the actual party was often preceded by a Mass or a blessing in church or, at the very least, a priest was invited to give spiritual heft to the *fiesta*. These celebrations were covered in newspapers, lavish spreads of photos I remember poring over as a little girl in the Dominican Republic, reassured by this proof that the desire to be a princess did not have to be shed at the beginning of adulthood, but could in fact be played out happily to the tune of hundreds upon thousands of Papi's *pesos*.

In the late sixties, when many of our poor headed to *el Norte*'s land of opportunity, they brought this tradition along, and with growing economic power, the no-longer-so-poor could emulate the rich back home. The spin-offs grew (*quinceañera* cruises, *quinceañera* resort packages, *quinceañera* videos and photo shoots); stories of where this *quinceañera* custom had come from proliferated (an ancient Aztec tradition, an import from European courts); further elaborations were added (Disney themes, special entrances, staged dance routines à la Broadway musicals); and in our Pan-Hispanic mixing stateside, the U.S. *quinceañera* adopted all the little touches of specific countries to become a much more elaborate (and expensive) ceremony, exported back to our home countries. But rock-bottom, the U.S. *quinceañera* is powered by that age-old immigrant dream of giving the children what their parents had never been able to afford back where they came from.

In fact, the *quince* expression notwithstanding, many of us older first-generation Latinas never had a *quinceañera*. There was no money back when we were fifteen, or we had recently arrived in the United States and didn't want anything that would make us stand out as other than all-American. Or we looked down our noses at such girly-girl fuss and said we didn't want a *quince* because we didn't understand that this was not just about us.

These cultural celebrations are also about building community in a new land. Lifted out of the context of our home cultures, traditions like the *quinceañera* become malleable; they mix with the traditions of other cultures that we encounter here; they become exquisite performances of our ethnicities within the larger host culture while at the same time

4

5

6

7

WORD POWER

nominally in name only

heft significance or importance

WORD POWER

emulate try to be like or better than

proliferate to quickly increase in number or amount

reaffirming that we are not "them" by connecting us if only in spirit to our root cultures. In other words, this tradition tells a larger story of our transformation into Latinos, a Pan-Hispanic group made in the USA, now being touted as the "new Americans."

WORD POWER

touted promoted

Focus on Meaning

1. In paragraph 5, Alvarez explains how the *quinceañera* grew and changed as Latino families settled in the United States. What is her attitude toward these changes? For example, does she seem to suggest that they have somehow lessened the meaning of the ritual?

2. According to Alvarez, what is the value of the *quinceañera* for Latinas? For the culture of which they are a part?

Focus on Strategy

1. Alvarez opens her essay with a one-sentence paragraph that asks the question, "What exactly is a *quinceañera*?" What are the advantages and disadvantages of this opening strategy?

2. Do you think Alvarez expects her readers to be familiar with the term she is defining? How can you tell? What does your answer tell you about her intended audience and purpose?

Focus on Language and Style

1. Alvarez uses a number of Spanish words other than *quinceañera* in this essay, but she does not define them. Do you think she should have? Why or why not?

2. In paragraph 4, Alvarez observes that the *quinceañera* has become "highly ritualized." What does the word *ritualized* mean in this context? Is it a positive, negative, or neutral term?

Focus on the Pattern

1. Where does Alvarez give information about the origin of the term *quinceañera*?

2. Where does Alvarez develop her definition with examples? Where does she use description? Does she use any other patterns of development?

Focus on Critical Thinking

1. At different points in her essay, Alvarez sees the *quinceañera* as a "passage into womanhood" (paragraph 3), a traditional religious celebration (4), a way of "building community in a new land" (7), and the realization of an "age-old immigrant dream" (5). Which of these different impressions does her definition communicate most strongly? Explain.

Writing Practice

1. Write a definition essay about a coming-of-age ritual that is significant in your own community, culture, or religion. Assume that your readers are not familiar with the ritual you are discussing, and develop your definition with exemplification and description. (You can also use comparison and contrast if you think explaining your ritual by showing how it is like a more familiar practice will be helpful to your readers.)

2. Write a definition essay about a coming-of-age ritual with which you are familiar. Develop your definition primarily through narration—by telling the story of your own introduction to this ritual.

I WANT A WIFE

Judy Brady

Writer and activist Judy Brady helped found the Toxic Links Coalition, an organization dedicated to exposing the dangers of environmental toxins and their impact on public health. She was also active in the women's movement, and her classic essay "I Want a Wife" was published in the first issue of *Ms.* magazine (1971). As you read, think about how relevant this essay is to today's relationships.

I belong to that classification of people known as wives. I am A Wife. 1
And, not altogether incidentally, I am a mother.

Not too long ago a male friend of mine appeared on the scene fresh 2
from a recent divorce. He had one child, who is, of course, with his ex-
wife. He is looking for another wife. As I thought about him while I was
ironing one evening, it suddenly occurred to me that I, too, would like
to have a wife. Why do I want a wife?

I would like to go back to school so that I can become economically 3
independent, support myself, and, if need be, support those dependent
upon me. I want a wife who will work and send me to school. And while
I am going to school I want a wife to take care of my children. I want
a wife to keep track of the children's doctor and dentist appointments.
And to keep track of mine, too. I want a wife to make sure my children eat properly and are kept clean. I want a wife who will wash the
children's clothes and keep them mended. I want a wife who is a good
nurturant attendant to my children, who arranges for their schooling,
makes sure that they have an adequate social life with their peers, takes
them to the park, the zoo, etc. I want a wife who takes care of the children when they are sick, a wife who arranges to be around when the
children need special care, because, of course, I cannot miss classes at
school. My wife must arrange to lose time at work and not lose the job.

> **WORD POWER**
>
> **nurturant** providing physical and emotional care

It may mean a small cut in my wife's income from time to time, but I guess I can tolerate that. Needless to say, my wife will arrange and pay for the care of the children while my wife is working.

I want a wife who will take care of *my* physical needs. I want a wife who will keep my house clean. A wife who will pick up after my children, a wife who will pick up after me. I want a wife who will keep my clothes clean, ironed, mended, replaced when need be, and who will see to it that my personal things are kept in their proper place so that I can find what I need the minute I need it. I want a wife who cooks the meals, a wife who is a *good* cook. I want a wife who will plan the menus, do the necessary grocery shopping, prepare the meals, serve them pleasantly, and then do the cleaning up while I do my studying. I want a wife who will care for me when I am sick and sympathize with my pain and loss of time from school. I want a wife to go along when our family takes a vacation so that someone can continue to care for me and my children when I need a rest and change of scene.

I want a wife who will not bother me with rambling complaints about a wife's duties. But I want a wife who will listen to me when I feel the need to explain a rather difficult point I have come across in my course of studies. And I want a wife who will type my papers for me when I have written them.

I want a wife who will take care of the details of my social life. When my wife and I are invited out by my friends, I want a wife who will take care of the babysitting arrangements. When I meet people at school that I like and want to entertain, I want a wife who will have the house clean, will prepare a special meal, serve it to me and my friends, and not interrupt when I talk about things that interest me and my friends. I want a wife who will have arranged that the children are fed and ready for bed before my guests arrive so that the children do not bother us. I want a wife who takes care of the needs of my guests so that they feel comfortable, who makes sure that they have an ashtray, that they are passed the hors d'oeuvres, that they are offered a second helping of the food, that their wine glasses are replenished when necessary, that their coffee is served to them as they like it. And I want a wife who knows that sometimes I need a night out by myself.

I want a wife who is sensitive to my sexual needs, a wife who makes love passionately and eagerly when I feel like it, a wife who makes sure that I am satisfied. And, of course, I want a wife who will not demand sexual attention when I am not in the mood for it. I want a wife who assumes the complete responsibility for birth control, because I do not want more children. I want a wife who will remain sexually faithful to me so that I do not have to clutter up my intellectual life with jealousies. And I want a wife who understands that *my* sexual needs may entail more than strict adherence to monogamy. I must, after all, be able to relate to people as fully as possible.

4

5

6

7

WORD POWER

replenished made full or complete again

WORD POWER

adherence steady or faithful attachment

monogamy having one spouse or sexual partner at a time

If, by chance, I find another person more suitable as a wife than the   8
wife I already have, I want the liberty to replace my present wife with
another one. Naturally, I will expect a fresh new life; my wife will take
the children and be solely responsible for them so that I am left free.

When I am through with school and have a job, I want my wife to   9
quit working and remain at home so that my wife can more fully and
completely take care of a wife's duties.

My God, who *wouldn't* want a wife?   10

Focus on Meaning

1. In one sentence, summarize Brady's definition of *wife*. How is her definition like and unlike your own?

2. What central point or idea do you think Brady wants to communicate to her readers? Does she ever actually state this idea? If not, do you think she should?

Focus on Strategy

1. Write a thesis statement for this essay.

2. Brady ends her essay with a **rhetorical question**, a question readers are not expected to answer. Is this an effective concluding strategy? Why or why not?

Focus on Language and Style

1. Brady repeats the word *wife* over and over again. Why? Does this repetition strengthen or weaken her essay?

2. Can you think of other words Brady could have used instead of *wife*? How might using these alternative words change her essay?

Focus on the Pattern

1. Does Brady include a formal definition of *wife* anywhere in her essay? If so, where? If not, do you think she should?

2. Brady develops her definition with examples. What are some of her most important examples?

3. Besides exemplification, what other patterns of development does Brady use to develop her definition?

Focus on Critical Thinking

1. Brady's essay was written in 1971. Does her definition of *wife* seem dated, or does it still seem accurate (at least in some respects) to you?

2. Answer the question Brady asks in paragraph 10: Would you like to have the kind of wife she defines? Why or why not?

Writing Practice

1. Assume you are Brady's husband and feel unjustly attacked by her essay. Write her a letter in which you define *husband*, using as many examples as you can to show how overworked and underappreciated you are.

2. Write an essay in which you define your ideal teacher, parent, spouse, or boss.

38i　Argument

An **argument** essay takes a stand on one side of a debatable issue, using facts, examples, and expert opinion to persuade readers to accept a position. The writers of the three essays that follow—Mary Sherry in "In Praise of the F Word," Oprah Winfrey in "Dnt Txt N Drv," and Adam Winkler in "The Guns of Academe"—try to convince readers to accept their positions or at least to acknowledge that they are reasonable.

IN PRAISE OF THE F WORD

Mary Sherry

Mary Sherry is a writer and an adult literacy educator. "In Praise of the F Word," which was first published in the "My Turn" column of *Newsweek* in 1991, argues that it is good for students to fail once in a while because it motivates them to continue to do their best work. As you read Sherry's essay, think about how persuasive her argument is, noting the facts and examples she uses to support her claims.

WORD POWER

semiliterate barely able to read or write

Tens of thousands of 18-year-olds will graduate this year and be handed meaningless diplomas. These diplomas won't look any different from those awarded their luckier classmates. Their validity will be questioned only when their employers discover that these graduates are semiliterate.

Eventually a fortunate few will find their way into educational-repair shops—adult-literacy programs, such as the one where I teach basic grammar and writing. There, high-school graduates and high-school dropouts pursuing graduate-equivalency certificates will learn the skills they should have learned in school. They will also discover they have been cheated by our educational system.

As I teach, I learn a lot about our schools. Early in each session I ask my students to write about an unpleasant experience they had in school. No writers' block here! "I wish someone would have had made me stop doing drugs and made me study." "I liked to party and no one seemed to care." "I was a good kid and didn't cause any trouble, so they just passed me along even though I didn't read and couldn't write." And so on.

I am your basic do-gooder, and prior to teaching this class I blamed the poor academic skills our kids have today on drugs, divorce and other impediments to concentration necessary for doing well in school. But, as I rediscover each time I walk into the classroom, before a teacher can expect students to concentrate, he has to get their attention, no matter what distractions may be at hand. There are many ways to do this, and they have much to do with teaching style. However, if style alone won't do it, there is another way to show who holds the winning hand in the classroom. That is to reveal the trump card of failure. 4

WORD POWER

trump card a key resource to be used at the right moment

I will never forget a teacher who played that card to get the attention of one of my children. Our youngest, a world-class charmer, did little to develop his intellectual talents but always got by. Until Mrs. Stifter. 5

Our son was a high-school senior when he had her for English. "He sits in the back of the room talking to his friends," she told me. "Why don't you move him to the front row?" I urged, believing the embarrassment would get him to settle down. Mrs. Stifter looked at me steely-eyed over her glasses. "I don't move seniors," she said. "I flunk them." I was flustered. Our son's academic life flashed before my eyes. No teacher had ever threatened him with that before. I regained my composure and managed to say that I thought she was right. By the time I got home I was feeling pretty good about this. It was a radical approach for these times, but, well, why not? "She's going to flunk you," I told my son. I did not discuss it any further. Suddenly English became a priority in his life. He finished out the semester with an A. 6

WORD POWER

flustered in a state of worry or confusion

composure calmness

I know one example doesn't make a case, but at night I see a parade of students who are angry and resentful for having been passed along until they could no longer even pretend to keep up. Of average intelligence or better, they eventually quit school, concluding they were too dumb to finish. "I should have been held back," is a comment I hear frequently. Even sadder are those students who are high-school graduates who say to me after a few weeks of class, "I don't know how I ever got a high-school diploma." 7

Passing students who have not mastered the work cheats them and the employers who expect graduates to have basic skills. We excuse this dishonest behavior by saying kids can't learn if they come from terrible environments. No one seems to stop to think that—no matter what environments they come from—most kids don't put school first on their list unless they perceive something is at stake. They'd rather be sailing. 8

Many students I see at night could give expert testimony on unemployment, chemical dependency, abusive relationships. In spite of these difficulties, they have decided to make education a priority. They are motivated by the desire for a better job or the need to hang on to the one they've got. They have a healthy fear of failure. 9

WORD POWER

merit value or worth

conspiracy a joining or acting together

People of all ages can rise above their problems, but they need to have a reason to do so. Young people generally don't have the maturity to value education in the same way my adult students value it. But fear of failure, whether economic or academic, can motivate both. Flunking as a regular policy has just as much merit today as it did two generations ago. We must review the threat of flunking and see it as it really is—a positive teaching tool. It is an expression of confidence by both teachers and parents that the students have the ability to learn the material presented to them. However, making it work again would take a dedicated, caring conspiracy between teachers and parents. It would mean facing the tough reality that passing kids who haven't learned the material—while it might save them grief for the short term—dooms them to long-term illiteracy. It would mean that teachers would have to follow through on their threats, and parents would have to stand behind them, knowing their children's best interests are indeed at stake. This means no more doing Scott's assignments for him because he might fail. No more passing Jodi because she's such a nice kid.

This is a policy that worked in the past and can work today. A wise teacher, with the support of his parents, gave our son the opportunity to succeed—or fail. It's time we return this choice to all students.

Focus on Meaning

1. Who or what does Sherry blame for the "meaningless diplomas" (paragraph 1) that are issued each year? What other reasons for this situation can you think of?

2. What does Sherry mean in paragraph 10 when she says, "Flunking as a regular policy has just as much merit today as it did two generations ago"?

3. How does the experience Sherry's son had in high school convince her that the threat of failure is a "positive teaching tool" (10)?

Focus on Strategy

1. Where does Sherry state her thesis? Where else could she have stated it? Would it have been more or less effective there? Why?

2. What reaction does Sherry assume her readers will have to her argument? Does she think they will be surprised? Shocked? Angry? Motivated? Something else? How do you know?

3. Throughout her essay, Sherry establishes her credentials as a teacher. Why? If she weren't a teacher, would her argument be as convincing?

Focus on Language and Style

1. In her title, Sherry refers to flunking as the "F Word." What point is she making by doing this?

2. In paragraph 4, Sherry calls herself a "do-gooder." What does this term mean? How does Sherry use it in her essay? What other term could she have used instead?

Focus on the Pattern

1. Sherry organizes her argument inductively. List the evidence that she uses to reach her conclusion. Has she provided enough evidence? Explain. (For a discussion of inductive reasoning, see page 312.)

2. In paragraph 7, Sherry says, "I know one example doesn't make a case. . . ." What does she mean? How does she overcome this problem?

3. Does Sherry address arguments against her position? If so, where? What other opposing arguments can you think of? How would you refute them?

Focus on Critical Thinking

1. In paragraphs 9 and 10, Sherry argues that if students do not have a "healthy fear of failure" (9), they will not be motivated to work. What does she mean? Do you have a "healthy fear of failure"? If so does it motivate you, or does it get in your way? Explain.

Writing Practice

1. Write an argument essay that supports or opposes the idea of using failure as a teaching tool. Do you, like Sherry, believe that flunking is a policy that "can work today" (11)? Or, do you think that there are other, better ways to motivate students? In your essay, address at least two arguments against your thesis.

2. Write a letter to a teacher who threatened you with failure. Make the case that his or her methods either motivated you or did more harm than good. Support your points with specific examples.

3. Do you in any way feel "cheated by our educational system" (2)? Write an argument essay in which you answer this question. Use examples from your own experience as well as from Sherry's essay as evidence.

DNT TXT N DRV

Oprah Winfrey

One of the most famous and successful women in the world today, Oprah Winfrey has made her mark as a television host, actress, producer, and philanthropist. She began her career in radio and television broadcasting, and in 1985, her role in the film *The Color Purple* earned her an Academy Award nomination for Best Supporting Actress. The following year, Winfrey began her twenty-five-year run as host of *The Oprah Winfrey Show*, eventually building a media empire that included the magazine *O: The Oprah Magazine* and OWN, the Oprah Winfrey television network. In "Dnt Txt N Drv," first published as an opinion column in the *New York Times* in 2010, Winfrey makes the argument that texting while driving is an unfortunate but avoidable cause of many fatal car accidents. As you read, try to determine Winfrey's primary purpose in writing the article. Consider, too, the effect of her powerful final sentence.

WORD POWER

stakes something to be won or lost in a game or contest

1   When I started out as a TV reporter in Nashville in 1973, a death from drunken driving was big news. One person killed by a drunken driver would lead our local broadcast. Then, as the number of drunken driving deaths across the country continued to rise, the stakes for coverage got even higher. One death wasn't good enough anymore. Two deaths—that would warrant a report. Then a whole family had to die before the news would merit mention at the top of the broadcast. The country, all of us, had gotten used to the idea of drunken driving. I just kept thinking: How many people have to die before we "get it"?

2   Fortunately, we did get it, and since 1980, the number of annual traffic fatalities due to drunken driving has decreased to under 15,500 from more than 30,000. But in recent years, another kind of tragic story has begun to emerge with ever greater frequency. This time, we are mourning the deaths of those killed by people talking or sending text messages on their cellphones while they drive.

3   Earlier this month, I visited Shelley and Daren Forney, a couple in Fort Collins, Colo., whose 9-year-old daughter, Erica, was on her bicycle, just 15 pedals from her front door, when she was struck and killed by a driver who was distracted by a cellphone. I think about Erica's death and how senseless and stupid it was—caused by a driver distracted by a phone call that just couldn't wait.

4   Sadly, there are far too many stories like hers. At least 6,000 people were killed by distracted drivers in 2008, according to the National Highway Traffic Safety Administration, and the number is rising. A lot of good work already is happening to try to change this. President Obama signed an executive order banning texting while driving on federal business. Transportation Secretary Ray LaHood is pushing for tougher laws and more enforcement. States are passing laws, too. Local groups are gaining strength, spurred by too many deaths close to home.

WORD POWER

executive order an order issued by the executive branch of the U.S. government that has the force of law

spurred inspired to act; motivated

5   But we are hesitant to change. I saw this firsthand when I instituted a policy at my company that forbids employees from using their phones for company business while driving. I heard countless stories about how hard it was for people to stop talking and texting while driving. Everyone is busy. Everyone feels she needs to use time in the car to get things done. But what happened to just driving?

It was difficult for my employees to adjust, but they have. Life is 6 more precious than taking a call or answering an e-mail message. Because even though we think we can handle using our cellphone in the car, the loss of thousands of lives has shown we can't.

So many issues that we have to deal with seem beyond our control: 7 natural disasters, child predators, traffic jams. Over the years, I've done shows on just about all of them. But this is a real problem we can do something about and get immediate results. All we have to do is hang up or switch off. It really is that simple. Once we do that, not another son or daughter will have to die because someone was on the phone and behind the wheel—and just not paying attention.

So starting from the moment you finish this article, and in the days, 8 weeks and years that follow, give it up. Please. And to those who feel like this is asking too much, think about your own child just 15 pedals from your front door. Struck down.

> **WORD POWER**
>
> **predators** people who victimize others

Focus on Meaning

1. According to Winfrey, how is texting while driving similar to driving while drunk? How is it different?

2. What is being done at a national level to address the problem of distracted drivers? Do you see this as primarily a national or a local problem? Explain.

3. Why is it so difficult for people to stop texting while driving? Do you think that Winfrey's policy had much of an effect on her employees? Explain.

Focus on Strategy

1. Rewrite Winfrey's thesis statement in your own words.

2. Winfrey begins her essay with an anecdote about her time as a TV reporter in Nashville. Why? Would another introductory strategy have been more effective? Explain.

3. In her conclusion, Winfrey begs people to stop texting as they drive. Do you think this highly emotional appeal is appropriate? Is it effective?

Focus on Language and Style

1. Evaluate the essay's title.

2. Winfrey uses first-person pronouns, such as *we*, *us*, and *our*, throughout her essay, characterizing herself as part of the general public about whom she is writing. How might this strategy affect her readers' reactions to the argument she is making? Would changing *we* and *us* to *they* and *people*, respectively, alter the tone of the essay? Explain.

Focus on the Pattern

1. Where in her essay does Winfrey introduce opposing arguments? Do you think she addresses them in enough detail? Explain.

2. Winfrey relies primarily on examples from her own experience. In selecting evidence, what are the advantages and disadvantages of this strategy? What other kinds of evidence does she use?

3. Does Winfrey organize her argument inductively or deductively? What is the primary advantage of the method of organization she uses? (For a discussion of these two types of argument, see pages 312–313.)

Focus on Critical Thinking

1. Think of some other potentially distracting activities that people routinely engage in as they drive. Do you think texting is more or less dangerous than these other activities? Explain.

Writing Practice

1. Nearly all states prohibit texting while driving. Write a letter to the National Highway Traffic Safety Administration arguing for or against this policy. Like Winfrey, use examples from your own experience to support your thesis.

2. Assume that you are an employee at Winfrey's company, Harpo Productions, and that you have been told that you cannot use your cell phone for company business while you drive. Write an email to Winfrey telling her why you disagree or agree with this decision.

3. Many high schools do not allow students to carry cell phones anywhere on school property. Assume that you are the parent of a high school student who is not permitted to carry a cell phone. Write a letter either to your child or to his or her principal in which you argue for or against this rule. (Be sure to refute the main arguments against your thesis.)

THE GUNS OF ACADEME

Adam Winkler

Adam Winkler is a professor of law at the University of California, Los Angeles, and his work has been used in important Supreme Court cases. A contributor to CNN, the *New York Times*, the *Los Angeles Times*, the *Wall Street Journal*, the *Daily Beast*, and the *Huffington Post*, he has authored the book *Gunfight: The Battle over the Right to Bear Arms in America* (2011). Winkler specializes in American constitutional law, including the right to bear arms, which serves as the topic of this essay. As you read "The Guns of Academe," notice how Winkler carefully considers arguments on both sides of the issue.

By Monday, Gov. Jan Brewer of Arizona must decide whether to sign a 1 bill partly lifting her state's ban on guns on college and university campuses. Gun advocates insist that will make campuses safer by discouraging mass killers and giving students the ability to fight back. Gun control proponents warn the law will lead to more lethal violence.

Both sides are probably wrong. Gun violence at colleges and 2 universities—there are fewer than 20 homicides on campus per year—will probably not be affected much, one way or another. What is really at stake is America's gun culture.

Colleges and universities have long been gun-free zones. In 1745, 3 Yale adopted a policy punishing any student who "shall keep a gun or pistol, or fire one in the college-yard or college." Today, most universities, public and private, prohibit anyone but authorized security and law enforcement officers from bringing guns onto campuses. Arizona would join Utah as the only states to require public colleges to permit guns on campus, but Texas and eight other states are considering similar laws.

Many find the idea of students with guns shocking. They fear that 4 undergraduates are too young to handle firearms responsibly and that the presence of guns will lead to the deadly escalation of minor disagreements. Others worry about the volatile mix of guns and alcohol. Glocks don't belong at a frat party.

Even if the bans are lifted, however, few students will tote guns 5 around the quad. Under federal law, those under 21 cannot buy guns from a dealer. And most states require a permit to carry a concealed weapon. (Arizona only requires such a permit for persons under 21.)

As a professor, I'd feel safer if guns were not permitted on campus. 6 I worry more about being the target of a student upset about failing grades than about a mass killer roaming the hallways.

But there is little evidence to support my gut feeling. Utah, for ex- 7 ample, has not seen an increase in campus gun violence since it changed its law in 2006. And a disturbed student can simply sneak a gun on campus in his backpack, as the Virginia Tech killer did in 2007. Indeed, lost in the debate is the fact that guns, being easy to conceal, are almost certainly on campus already.

On the other hand, gun rights advocates are too quick to assume 8 that laws allowing guns on campus will discourage mass murderers. Arizona has among the most liberal gun-carrying laws in the nation, but that didn't prevent Jared L. Loughner from shooting Representative Gabrielle Giffords and killing six other people in Tucson in January. Nor did permissive carry laws lead to people defending themselves by shooting back. (Mr. Loughner was tackled and brought to the ground by unarmed bystanders.)

WORD POWER

advocates people who defend or maintain a cause

proponents supporters

WORD POWER

volatile likely to lead to sudden change or violence

tote to carry

Even if a student with a gun can use it to defend against a mass   9
murderer, it's hardly clear that anyone, including the armed student, is
made safer. Policemen or other students with guns might not be able
to differentiate among gunmen, putting the person defending herself
at risk of being shot by mistake. Even well-trained gun owners suffer
enormous mental stress in a shootout, making hitting a target extremely
difficult.

Gun control groups are fighting to retain the bans. This is one of the   10
few areas in which they've had success in recent years. There have been
more than 40 attempts to lift the bans in 24 states, and nearly all have
failed. Even the proposed Arizona law was a victory of sorts, as the final
bill omitted provisions allowing guns in classrooms; it would permit
guns only on campus streets and sidewalks.

Yet gun rights proponents are redoubling their repeal efforts. They   11
aren't reacting to a wave of violence on campus. The true motivation is
to remove the stigma attached to guns. Many in the gun rights movement believe there should be no gun-free zones and seek to make the
public possession of firearms a matter of course. The protesters who
last year carried guns into Starbucks shops and Tea Party rallies had
the same goal. They weren't expecting to defend themselves; they were
aiming to build broader public acceptance of guns.

Exposure can breed tolerance. Arguably, that is exactly what's be-   12
hind the growing acceptance of gays and lesbians. The visibility of gay
couples in society and popular culture has led many Americans to realize that homosexuality is not wrong. Gun advocates are betting the same
can happen with firearms.

The strategy, however, is risky. Teenagers might begin to see carrying   13
a gun as a mark of adulthood, like smoking and drinking. Without the
maturity of age, they might turn to violence too quickly.

Gun rights advocates are willing to take these risks because colleges   14
are where the next generation of America's leaders will be produced.
What better place to affect people's attitudes about guns than the very
institutions responsible for teaching our most cherished values and
ideals?

> **WORD POWER**
>
> **motivation** driving force; goal
>
> **stigma** a mark of disgrace or infamy

> **WORD POWER**
>
> **cherished** treasured, precious

Focus on Meaning

1. Proponents of lifting the ban on guns from Arizona's college campuses maintain that it will make campuses safer. Gun control advocates claim that lifting the ban will lead to increased violence. Why
   does Winkler think both sides in this debate are wrong?

2. In paragraph 5, Winkler says that if the bans against guns were
   lifted, few students would carry them. According to him, why is this
   so? Do you think he is right?

3. According to Winkler, what really motivates people who want to
   allow guns on campus?

Focus on Strategy

1. Where does Winkler state his thesis? How does paragraph 1 set the stage for his thesis?

2. Do you think Winkler expects readers to be for or against allowing guns on college campuses? How can you tell?

3. What point does Winkler emphasize in his conclusion? Why? How else could he have ended his essay?

Focus on Language and Style

1. What does *academe* mean in the essay's title? What are the strengths and weaknesses of this title? What other titles could Winkler have used?

2. In paragraphs 5 and 6, Winkler shifts from third person (*he, she*) to first person (*I*). Why?

3. In paragraph 12, Winkler compares the acceptance of gays and lesbians to the acceptance of guns. How effective is this comparison? What does the writer mean when he says that exposure to guns "can breed tolerance"? Do you agree?

Focus on the Pattern

1. In paragraph 3, Winkler discusses how colleges traditionally have banned firearms from campuses. What does this paragraph add to his argument?

2. Winkler relies on evidence from his own experience to support his points. Should he have also included statistics and expert opinion? Why or why not?

3. What arguments against his thesis does Winkler discuss? How successful is he in refuting each of these arguments?

Focus on Critical Thinking

1. Would you feel safer if you (or someone you knew) were permitted to carry a gun on campus? What are the advantages of such a policy? What are its disadvantages?

2. This essay was written before the 2012 Connecticut school shooting in which twenty-six people, including twenty very young children, were killed by a gunman. Has the nature of the gun debate (or your opinion about what, if anything, should be done to address this issue) changed since the shooting? Do you believe, as some have suggested, that school principals should be armed?

Writing Practice

1. In paragraph 9, Winkler says, "Even if a student with a gun can use it to defend against a mass murderer, it's hardly clear that anyone,

including the armed student, is made safer." Winkler then mentions two reasons why he thinks this is so. Read the paragraph, and then write an essay in which you agree or disagree with Winkler's points. Make sure that your essay has a clear thesis and that you address each of his points individually.

2. Gun violence is a fact of life in many American cities—for example, Philadelphia, Chicago, and Detroit. Assume that you have been asked to write a blog for a Web site aimed specifically at teenagers. As your thesis, use Winkler's point that contrary to what young people might think, carrying a gun is not a sign of adulthood or maturity. Be specific, and support your thesis with your own ideas and experiences.

Acknowledgments

Picture Acknowledgments

1 iStockphoto; **25T** Rene Sheret; **25B** Bill Aron/PhotoEdit, Inc.; **54** Photography: Lara Schneider; **77** iStockphoto; **87** Courtesy of The Advertising Council; **88** From *One! Hundred! Demons!* by Lynda Barry. Copyright © 2002 by Lynda Barry. Published by Sasquatch Books and used courtesy of Darhansoff & Verrill; **97** JupiterImages/Getty Images; **98** iStockphoto; **108** Shutterstock; **109** iStockphoto; **120** Photofest; **121** iStockphoto; **132** iStockphoto; **133L** James Devaney/Getty Images; **133R** John Shearer/Getty Images; **147** Dennis Macdonald/Getty Images; **148** Richard Pasley/Stock Boston; **149** AP Photo/Kathy Willens; **159** U.S. Department of Agriculture; **160** Photo by Emily Behrendt; **172TL** JupiterImages/Alamy; **172R** Jose Luis Pelaez, Inc./Getty Images; **172BL** Rachel Epstein/The Image Works; **172BR** Michael Newman/PhotoEdit, Inc.; **173** Will McNamee/Getty Images; **187** Giannina Amato, Creative Director and Copywriter; **191** David Sinyakov/Reuters; **230** OKCupid.com; **241** Photofest; **253** David Young-Wolff/PhotoEdit, Inc.; **325** © 2012 About.com. All rights reserved; **353** © EBSCO Publishing, Inc. 2012. All rights reserved; **354** *Spanglish* by Ilan Stavans. Copyright © 2008 by Ilan Stavans. Reproduced with permission of ABC-CLIO, LLC; **355** © Latism 2012; **359** AP Photo/Kathy Willens; **372** Stephen Ferry/Redux Pictures; **389** Eric Fowke/PhotoEdit, Inc.; **401** Senator John Heinz History Center; **419** iStockphoto; **429** Photodisc/Getty Images; **455** David Young-Wolff/PhotoEdit, Inc.; **471** Erick W. Rasco/Getty Images; **495** Image courtesy of Andrew Edlin Gallery; **510** Michael Newman/PhotoEdit, Inc.; **535** AP Photo/Jeff Chiu; **546** Paramount Classics/Everett Collection; **560** Photofest; **588** Amy Etra/PhotoEdit, Inc.; **600** Christie's Images Ltd./SuperStock; **639T** Mario Tama/Getty Images; **639B** Joshua Lutz/Redux Pictures; **656** Tony Freeman/PhotoEdit, Inc.; **664** Photofest; **701–702** From *USA Today* (Academic Permission), 7/9/2012 © 2012 Gannett. All rights reserved. Used by permission and protected by the Copyright Laws of the United States. The printing, copying, redistribution, or retransmission of this Content without express written permission is prohibited; **701** AP Photo/Gerry Broome

Text Acknowledgments

Julia Alvarez. "Quinceañera." From *Once Upon a Quinceañera: Coming of Age in the USA,* by Julia Alvarez. Copyright © 2007 by Julia Alvarez. Published by Plume, an imprint of the Penguin Group (USA), Inc., and in hardcover by Viking. By permission of Susan Bergholz Literary Services, New York, NY, and Lamy, NM. All rights reserved.

Julia Angwin. "How Facebook Is Making Friending Obsolete." December 15, 2009. From *The Wall Street Journal* by News Corporation; Dow Jones & Company. Copyright © 2009. Reproduced with permission of Dow Jones & Company, Inc., in the format Republish in a textbook and "other" book via Copyright Clearance Center.

Lynda Barry. "The Sanctuary of School." From *The New York Times*, January 5, 1992. Copyright © 1992. Reprinted by permission of Darhansoff & Verrill Literary Agents.

Joshuah Bearman. "My Half-Baked Bubble." From *The New York Times*, December 20, 2009. Copyright © 2009 by The New York Times. All rights reserved. Used by permission and protected by the Copyright Laws of the United States. The printing, copying, redistribution, or retransmission of the Material without express written permission is prohibited.

Judy Brady. "I Want a Wife." Originally published in the first edition of *Ms.* magazine, 1971. Copyright © 1970 by Judy Brady. Used by permission of the author.

Rachel Carson. "A Fable for Tomorrow." From *Silent Spring*, by Rachel Carson. Copyright © 1962 by Rachel L. Carson, renewed 1990 by Roger Christie. Reprinted by permission of Houghton Mifflin Harcourt Publishing Company and Frances Collin, Trustee. All rights reserved. All copying, including electronic, or redistribution of this text, is expressly forbidden.

Steven Conn. "The Twin Revolutions of Lincoln and Darwin." From *Philadelphia Inquirer*, February 12, 2009. Reprinted by permission of the author.

Index

Note: Page numbers in **bold** type indicate pages on which terms are defined.

Bailey

The English language has eight basic parts of speech: nouns, pronouns, verbs, adjectives, adverbs, prepositions, conjunctions, and interjections.

Nouns A noun names a person, an animal, a place, an object, or an idea.

Christine brought her dog Bailey to obedience school in Lawndale.
 noun　　　　　 *noun noun*　　　　　　　 *noun*　　　 *noun*

Pronouns A pronoun refers to and takes the place of a noun or another pronoun.

Bailey did very well in her lessons and seemed to enjoy them.
 noun　　　　　 *pronoun noun*　　　　　　　　　 *pronoun*

Verbs A verb tells what someone or something does, did, or will do.

Sometimes Bailey rolls over, but earlier today she refused.
　　　　　 verb　　　　　　　　　　 *verb*

Maybe she will change someday.
　　　　 verb

Adjectives An adjective identifies or describes a noun or a pronoun.

This dog is a small Beagle with a brown and white coat and long ears.
adj noun　　 *adj noun*　　　 *adj*　　 *adj noun*　　 *adj noun*

Adverbs An adverb identifies or describes a verb, an adjective, or another adverb.

Bailey is old now, so she moves very slowly and seldom barks.
　　　　　　　　　　　 verb adverb adverb　　 *adverb verb*

Prepositions A preposition is a word—such as *to*, *on*, or *with*—that introduces a noun or pronoun and connects it to other words in a sentence.

Bailey likes sitting quietly in her box at the foot of the stairs.

Conjunctions A conjunction is a word that connects parts of a sentence.

People say you can't teach an old dog new tricks, but Bailey might be an exception.

Interjections An interjection is a word—such as *Oh!* or *Hey!*—that is used to express emotion.

Wow! Bailey finally rolled over!

The eight basic parts of speech can be combined to form sentences, which always include at least one subject and one verb. The subject tells who or what is being talked about, and the verb tells what the subject does, did, or will do.

Bailey graduated from obedience school at the head of her class.
　 s　　 *v*